SWEETENING 'BITTER SUGAR'

SWEETENING 'BITTER SUGAR'

✳✳✳✳✳✳✳✳✳✳✳✳✳✳✳

JOCK CAMPBELL
THE BOOKER REFORMER
IN BRITISH GUIANA 1934 - 1966

CLEM SEECHARAN

Ian Randle Publishers
Kingston • Miami

First published in Jamaica, 2005 by
Ian Randle Publishers
11 Cunningham Avenue
Box 686
Kingston 6
www.ianrandlepublishers.com

© Clem Seecharan

National Library of Jamaica Cataloguing in Publication Data

Seecharan, Clem
    Sweetening "bitter sugar" : Jock Campbell, the Booker reformer in British
Guiana, 1934 – 1966 / Clem Seecharan.

        p. : ill. ;   cm

    Bibliography : p.   .– Includes index

    ISBN   976-637-193-8   (pbk)
    ISBN   976-637-199-7   (hbk)

    1. Campbell, Jock , 1912 – 1994   2. Sugar – Guyana – History
    3. Sugar trade – Guyana   4. Sugarcane industry – Guyana
    5. Sugar workers – Guyana – Labour unions

    I. Title

    338.1763109881   dc 21

Cover design by Karen Resnick West
Book design by Shelly-Gail Cooper
Printed in the United States of America

To Ian McDonald

Table of Contents

PART 4:
REVOLUTION OR REFORM?:
JAGAN'S MARXISM v. CAMPBELL'S REFORMISM

PART 5:
SWEETENING 'BITTER SUGAR' I:
SHAPING THE INSTRUMENTS FOR REFORM

PART 6:
SWEETENING 'BITTER SUGAR' II:
MODERNISING BOOKER, 1950-1951

PART 7:
SWEETENING 'BITTER SUGAR' III:
REFORMS ON THE PLANTATIONS, 1934-1964

PART 8:
JAGAN, CAMPBELL AND THE POLITICS
OF SUGAR IN THE CONTEXT OF THE COLD WAR, 1960-1964

CONCLUSION

List of Illustrations

Abbreviations

AFL-CIO	American Federation of Labor and Congress of Industrial Organizations
AIFLD	American Institute for Free Labour Development
BG	British Guiana
BGWL	British Guiana Workers' League
BSE	Booker Sugar Estates Ltd
CAB	Cabinet
Cmd.	Paper Presented to Parliament by Command
CO	Colonial Office
CSA	Commonwealth Sugar Agreement
Encl.	Enclosure
FO	Foreign Office
GAWU	Guyana Agricultural Workers' Union
GIWU	Guiana Industrial Workers' Union
HMG	His/Her Majesty's Government
ICFTU	International Confederation of Free Trade Unions
ICTA	Imperial College of Tropical Agriculture
MPCA	Manpower Citizens' Association
NPQ	National Price Quota
PAC	Political Affairs Committee
PNC	People's National Congress
PPP	People's Progressive Party
PR	Proportional Representation
PREM	Prime Minister
PSF	Price Stabilisation Fund
SILWF	Sugar Industry Labour Welfare Fund
SIRF	Sugar Industry Rehabilitation Fund
SPA	Sugar Producers' Association
UCWI	University College of the West Indies
UF	United Force
USG	United States Government
WFTU	World Federation of Trade Unions

Preface

This work has been in the making for over ten years. It was intercepted, though never eclipsed, by several other projects. It is, primarily, a study of one of the great men in twentieth century British West Indian affairs. Jock Campbell was not just a businessman with a strong sense of responsibility towards British Guiana (Guyana), where his company, Booker, was 'a state within a state', as he so often put it; he was a man of daunting intellect, charm, wit and powers of persuasion, but relentless and selfish, too, in getting what he wanted. I grew up knowing seven names of people — good or bad — who I knew were important to us in an Indian village in British Guiana, on the edge of a Booker plantation: Jawaharlal Nehru, Cheddi Jagan, Forbes Burnham, Rohan Kanhai, Duncan Sandys, John Kennedy and Jock Campbell — Sir Jock, at all times, to my father and grandfather. That was in the late 1950s and early 1960s. Most of them are encountered in this book. I met Jagan, Burnham and Campbell on several occasions and got to know them. But I did not meet Campbell until April 1990, when he was nearly 78 years old and in poor health. However, there was nothing wrong with his mind. It was an education for me to interview him, to chat with him intermittently, over the next four and a half years. He died on December 26, 1994. I did my last interview with him four days before he died. His intellect, wit and charm had not deserted him.

Jock had asked me on that occasion how the writing was coming along. I responded: 'Getting there. Slowly.' I had not written a word at this point and did not write the first sentence until the summer of 1996. It was the eternal project and Jock suspected it. He retorted: 'Slowly! Get to it, Clem, before they plant me!'

It was Ian McDonald who had given me the idea that a book on Campbell was a worthy undertaking. This was in 1986, in Georgetown. He never lost interest in the project. I dedicate this book to him, belatedly, on his 70th birthday.

It required a Herculean effort to persist with this work at a time when I had virtually no earnings. Therefore, I am deeply indebted to the following for providing me with grants at the early stage of my research: the British Academy; the Nuffield Foundation; and the late Anthony Rampton and the Hilden Charitable Fund. Barry Newton (of Booker/Tate) and Ian McDonald secured for me access to the Booker documents in London and Guyana, and made my many visits to the plantations in Guyana productive and pleasurable. The study could not have been completed without two sabbaticals and travel grants provided by the Research Committee at the University of North London (now London Metropolitan University); Lyn Thomas's support has been important.

It is impossible for me to thank the hundreds of people in the UK, the US, Canada, Trinidad and Guyana, who have helped in diverse ways in the making of this book. I have acknowledged, in the bibliography, the contribution of those whom I interviewed, but I wish to express my gratitude to several old Booker hands and a number of people in Guyana: John Bart, the late George Bishop and Una Bishop, the late Sir Michael Caine, Colin and Molly Campbell, Antony Haynes, Ian McDonald, Barry Newton, J.B. Raghurai; and the late Dr Cheddi Jagan, Eusi Kwayana, Dr Fenton Ramsahoye, the late Jainarine Singh, Premchand Das, Lloyd Searwar, Yesu Persaud, Joe Solomon and the late 'Uncle' Joe Dhanna.

Many of my colleagues, former students and friends have been a source of encouragement, inspiration and intellectual challenge and some have shared with me periodic 'recreation': Kamal Amin, Mazrul Bacchus, Peter Bacchus, Kassem Baksh, Frank Birbalsingh, Andrew Bishop, Bridget Brereton, Helen Camplin, Kathy Castle, Sui-Mee Chan, David Dabydeen, Evi Fishburn, Peter Fraser, John Hardial, Alistair Hennessy, Gad Heuman, Farouk Jahoor, Ruby Joseph, Denis Judd, Kampta Karran, Brij Lal, Robert Lalljie, Basdeo Mangru, Jonathan Moore, Kimani Nehusi, Bishnodat Persaud, Harold Persaud (1922–1992), Baytoram Ramharack, Roopram Ramharack, Veeram Ramharack, Brinsley Samaroo, Roy Sawh, Maurice St. Pierre, Leila Stewart, Jean Stubbs, Mary Turner, Inge Weber-Newth, Donald Wood (1923–2002) and Andrew Wright. I am deeply indebted to my friend and colleague, Rita Christian, who stoically performed many tasks during several sabbaticals. Kusha Haraksingh and Alvin Thompson of the University of the West Indies, the official readers, made valuable criticisms of the manuscript; I have tried to address most of these.

My family's support never faltered, even during periods of intellectual slumber when it appeared as if the project were 'planted' with its principal subject. I am, as always, grateful to Chris for her love and support and for making me rethink. I wish to thank Saba for her generosity over many decades, and Roy, Soan, Simone and Seeta for the good times — away from the project — and for believing in me. Jack Balder, Esna Balder and Sarran Jagmohan are always interested in my work; that is important to the effort.

The staff at several libraries and archives were very helpful. I wish to acknowledge the support of those at the Public Record Office, The British Library (Newspaper Library, Colindale), The University of Warwick Library, The University of the West Indies Library (St. Augustine, Trinidad), The National Library, Guyana, The National Archives, Georgetown, Guyana (especially Cecil Eversley), The Cheddi Jagan Research Centre, Georgetown, Guyana (Dudley Kissore) and the London Metropolitan University Library (especially Denise Amalemba and Crispin Partridge).

I am grateful to Jock Campbell for allowing me to disrupt many hours of his last years as he spoke into 'Clem's infernal machine'; Beth Hall, a New Zealander, who was his housekeeper during those years and considered it a privilege; and Colin Campbell, Lara Agnew and Rosalind Campbell who provided me with many of the pictures in the book. I must thank Mazrul Bacchus for the last picture taken of Jock, and Barry Newton for the pictures of Ayube Edun and Sir Gordon Lethem, as well as the maps. Finally, I am grateful to Ian Randle for his fortitude in publishing this book, and Kim Hoo Fatt for her sterling work in getting it ready for publication.

Clem Seecharan
Professor of Caribbean History
London Metropolitan University

Part 1

Forces That Shaped
A Radical Temperament

PROLOGUE — FROM CHEDDI JAGAN'S *BITTER SUGAR* (1953)

Sugar has indeed played a major role in the agricultural economy of British Guiana, so much so that the history of B.G. can truly be said to be a history of sugar. This history abounds with many instances of looting, bloodshed and murder. As late as 1948, at Plantation Enmore, five workers were killed and several others severely injured …. Agricultural policy has always been determined not so much 'in conjunction with' sugar but 'after' sugar. Sugar has indeed been 'king'. This has been possible because the sugar plantation owners are mostly absentee British Imperialists.

Booker is the Symbol of British Imperialism in B.G…. It is represented in all phases of the economic life, so much so that B.G. is sometimes colloquially referred to as Booker's Guiana. It controls a greater part of the sugar estates, and has a dominant position in commerce….The workers are sweated, and millions of dollars produced by them find their way into the pockets of sugar 'gods' in England…As a socialist party [Jagan's PPP], nationalisation of the sugar industry, and indeed all major industries is our objective. In the interim, while we are still tied to British imperialism with limited constitutional powers certain reforms have to be undertaken to break the back of imperialism….Join the fight against sugar imperialism. Make B.G. British Guiana and not Booker's Guiana.

Chapter One

SUGAR IN MY BLOOD

Our most personal attitudes are deeply affected by elements in the environment which seem to have no connection with them at all.
Walter E. Houghton (1957)

Like Jock Campbell [John Middleton Campbell, later Lord Campbell of Eskan] (1912–94), the radical Chairman of Booker Bros, McConnell and Co [Booker] in British Guiana [Guyana] between 1952 and 1967, I have sugar in my blood; but we got it through different veins. For six generations, as he would often say, his family had grown rich on the labour of African slaves and indentured Indian 'coolies' in British Guiana. I am the great-grandson of indentured coolies brought from the United Provinces of India, between 1875 and 1909, to labour on the sugar plantations, some on Plantation Albion, one of the Campbell estates, on the Corentyne Coast, in the county of Berbice.

Jock spent 18 months at Albion during his first sojourn in the colony, between 1934 and 1937. On his first tour of that plantation, escorted by the manager, James Bee, an autocratic, humourless Scot, he encountered the hovels of the resident Indian workers, the infamous 'logies' or ranges with roots in African slavery. Neighbouring these was a more pretentious building — clean, painted, obtrusive. Jock enquired who lived in the hovels: 'Our coolies', replied Bee. He then asked of the residents of the trimmed building; Bee said: 'Oh! We keep our mules there.' A naïve 22-year-old Jock asked flippantly: 'Why don't you move your coolies to the mules' palace and put the mules in the hovels?' A stunned Bee exclaimed cryptically: 'Mules cost money, sir!'[1]

My father's maternal grandfather, Sewnath (1881–1956), was an indentured child-labourer on this Campbell estate. He was taken from Kharaura village, Ghazipur District, eastern United Provinces [Uttar Pradesh]. He embarked at Calcutta, bound for British Guiana, on October 8, 1892, aged 11. Nothing is known of his parents other than that they were of Ahir caste, the traditional cattle-rearers of Uttar Pradesh and Bihar, the Hindu heartland in the Gangetic plain of North India. Sewnath was accompanied by his older sister, Sonbersi, aged 22, and her husband, Raghu, aged 30. They were all indentured to Albion. So those ghastly logies — 'pig sties', as Jock saw them — would have been the home of my great-grandfather, this child-labourer, many years before Jock discovered them.[2]

By the time Campbell got to Albion in 1934–35, Sewnath had long left the plantation: sometime before the First World War. Frugal to the bone, he had saved enough from his puny wages to buy a property at Palmyra Village, seven miles from Albion, on the north–western perimeter of Rose Hall estate, a Booker sugar plantation. He left behind those derelict ranges that, more than two decades later, were to make an enduring impression on young Jock Campbell. They helped to reshape his romantic boyhood vision of Demerara. As he would relate time and again, and as he did to me four days before he died on December 26, 1994, the guilt festered. It became the principal prompting of his life, a reflex — the notion of debts unpaid, of wealth extracted by sordid means, the taint of slavery and indentureship — and a compunction to compensate, belatedly, for ancient wrongs. Over and over, in numerous speeches and interviews, in casual conversation, he would repeat the following almost verbatim — a mantra of his Guyana awakening:

> The conditions in which past members of my family had ... made considerable fortunes came as a great shock to me. Conditions of employment were disgraceful; wages were abysmally low; housing was unspeakable; workers were treated with contempt — as chattels. Animals and machinery were, in fact, cared for better than the workers because they cost money to buy and replace ... the sugar industry had been founded on slavery, continued on indentureship and maintained by exploitation.[3]

For me this was no abstraction. It was etched on the weary bodies of my great-grandparents, whose aching bones I was often bribed to massage, a task I played at purely for the reward. Sewnath and his wife, Etwaria, my father's maternal grandmother, had an amazing consistency of purpose — as labourers in the cane-fields as well as in their own rice-field and provision ground, as cattle-rearers, too. My mother's paternal grandfather, Sohan, was indentured to Plantation Rose Hall in 1875, but he, also, had bought a small property and was rearing cattle at Palmyra: this eased his dependence on the sugar estate but it never eliminated it. My mother's maternal grandfather and grandmother were 'bound' to Rose Hall in 1908 and 1909 respectively. Unremitting toil on the estate, coupled with extraordinary thrift bordering on miserliness, enabled them, too, to buy land at Palmyra. Although they continued to live in the logies, the old barracks, at Rose Hall, they had moved their cattle to Palmyra where my maternal grandmother, their only child, married Sohan's youngest son in 1930. She was 14 years old. My people were mainly Ahir, from eastern Uttar Pradesh, whose frugality enabled them to squeeze savings to sustain their ancestral caste-calling — the cow had made the crossing.[4]

So, by the time Jock Campbell was serving his apprenticeship in sugar, at Albion, in the mid-1930s, most of them were settled away from the plantation, at Palmyra village. As he drove his two-seater Ford V8, fast, to New Amsterdam, the county town, he would have passed them grazing their cattle along the edge of the road or planting or reaping rice and vegetables. They had become masters at exploiting every village niche, but proximity to the estate and access to the joint family as a unit of production, allowed them to tap into niches on the estate also, often surreptitiously, with practised ease. They stole grass, wild vegetables and wood from the cane-fields and canals, or garnered a rich harvest from the flood-fallowed cane-fields teeming with fish; they stole water, too, during the dry season (there was no artesian well in the village until the late 1940s). Jock was familiar with the rhythm of Indian village life, its work-cycles and consuming rituals, festivals and weddings, which shaped a sense of community in the new land.[5]

These were hard times, the 1930s: poor sugar prices ate into the meagre wages of the sugar workers, the first victims of austerity during the Depression. Meanwhile, the absence of a recognised trade union until 1939, impeded their ventilation of grievances as it stifled concession of basic rights by the plantocracy. An impotent rage festered, enriching the folklore — a story which spoke vaguely, yearningly, of a mythical, idyllic India (from the *Ramayana*), juxtaposed with vivid, poignantly fresh tales of oppression on the estates.[6] The latter were replenished by the perceptibly supercilious manner of most white managers and overseers in our midst: remote, incomprehensible Scottish men, invariably in cork hats and short khaki pants, exaggeratedly whiskered and stockinged, on horseback — awe-inspiring colossuses, evocative of older oppressions.

The great divide between coolies and 'backra', the white elite on the estate, had no more enduring symbol than the impressive colonial bungalows of the latter, with their white picket-fences protecting cultured lawns, verdant fruit-trees and gardens ablaze with flowers, separated by a canal from patched-up ranges, 'barracks', reeking in a sea of slush and refuse during the heavy rains — order and power on one hand, decay and subservience on the other. This, too, lodged in Jock Campbell's memory.

I was born in 1950. Jock's family firm, Curtis Campbell and Co, had been acquired by the giant sugar company, Booker Bros, McConnell and Co, in 1939; so had he. His rise in Booker was astounding: in 1943 he became a director; managing director in 1945; in 1947, aged 35, he was made vice-chairman. In 1952 Jock, aged 40, was made Chairman of Booker. My memories of sugar culture in British Guiana and Plantation Rose Hall in particular, one of Booker's best estates in the late 1950s–60s, are still fresh. I grew up on its periphery, at Palmyra, amidst a large, extended family, many of whom continued to work some of the time on the sugar estate. But my memories of sugar, one generation away from the Great Depression, though mildly tainted by the remorseless tales of suffering and deprivation, are essentially happy ones: not images of the bitterness of 'King Sugar' but of hope, of possibilities as capacious as the Corentyne sky which Jock Campbell adored: 'the great big skies; those marvellous skies, immensely unclaustrophobic', he would recall. My vision, too, was as expansive as the sugar-cane fields of Rose Hall that met those of Albion, touching those skies, in my boyhood imagination.

The smells, the tastes, the spirit of the plantation cling to me; they are inseparable from my conception of self — the construct I am. My oldest recollections are from around 1955, the year I started school. The cane-fields of Jock Campbell's Rose Hall began across the main road from our house at Palmyra. This road was separated from our yard by a narrow ditch where I learnt to fish with hook and ink earthworm for lure. We *kept* our catch; we ate it, except for *yarrow*, a pariah snake-like, flat-head fish, which we relished slaughtering. Behind our house the rice-fields began a two-mile journey to the foreshore, where the mighty Berbice River, belatedly, only just before it entered the Atlantic, made room for its tributary, the Canje. This little river watered the big Corentyne plantations: Albion, Port Mourant, Skeldon and our own Rose Hall. The latter's cane-fields, to our eternal dismay, were protected from us by a broad, deep canal, which spoke of King Sugar's power to define.

From our veranda I would survey the sea of cane. The smoke belching into the sky from the factories at Rose Hall and Albion spoke of the annual cycle. By the age of five or six, I could read the rhythm of the sugar culture: flood-fallowing; the release of the water after nine months and the fishing carnival in the muddy fields; planting, manuring, weeding; the prolific cane-arrows, on the eve of the harvest; the burning of the cane and its evocatively syrupy rich smell; the amazingly quick reaping by raucously loud cutters and loaders who never ceased to enthral us, as acres of cane disappeared to reveal a daunting, bewitching man-made landscape of drains, ditches, canals, dams — Holland in the Tropics, I call it elsewhere.[7] I was already conscious of the order, the higher skills of sugar, on one hand, and the chaotic, eclectic character of our rice and vegetable plots on the other. But rice culture, too, had its own rhythm with its peculiar evocation of smells and images, its own rich tapestry of tasks, feverish activity and accompanying Hindu rituals for a good harvest, to placate our gods.

In August, during our school-holidays, the cane-fields in our village were harvested. A consuming expectancy claimed us all as, impatiently, we awaited the burning of the cane to remove the thick undergrowth, the impenetrable thrash which colonised the ground as the cane reached 12 feet or more. The aroma of burnt cane and scalded cane-juice was seductive. It was a signal for *our* harvest to begin. The night before the cane was cut, in darkness or in moonlight, our reaping of choice, juicy stalks, provided sheer bliss through many spacious hours of cane-sucking, heightening the peculiar freedom stolen by boys in the night. The navigation canal between the road and the fields quickly exuded a cocktail of foetid odour of decaying cane-tops, muddy water churned up by the iron cane-punts, and decomposing crocodiles crushed by colliding punts. It was most satisfying to steal cane from the punts as they were tugged to the factory — at one time, lazily, by mules; later, swiftly, by tractors, 'Farmall', a skeletal tractor, almost a toy.[8]

The lush contact of machete on juice-saturated cane began before dawn. Soon cutters, blackened by ash, would harangue each other. Invariably this had nothing to do with work; the source of the animation was more elevated — sex, whore-houses, rum and cricket. Subtlety would have been out-of-place. The raucousness and crudity of the exchange must have helped to lighten the hard tasks, made more burdensome by bodies smeared with the sticky cane juice, ash and sweat in the remorseless heat.[9] It always astounded me how fast the forest of cane would disappear, yielding its daunting secret: a complex hydraulic system of canals, drains, ditches, dams, *kokers* — geometric precision, symmetry, etchings on the heavy clay, as if to ease the monotony of this flat land.

At the time I could not have made the connection between this complexity and the use of the land. I could not have grasped how tenuous was our grip on the Guyana coastland; but something lodged in me in those innocent, spacious days. For, over and over, I would sketch, badly but avidly, scenes from the cane-fields: men cutting; women manuring; boys leading mules tugging punts to the factory belching smoke; men manoeuvring big machines like toys, to the edge of the water. But always, the crudity of execution was marred further by the canals and trenches, which I hated to sketch, but somehow could not leave out: it would not have been real.

It was many years later, into my young adulthood, that I learnt to read this landscape, to begin to conjure up the monumental feats of the imagination, skill and brawn-power expended in its original construction.[10] This suggested the scale of discipline and will — consistency of effort — central to the maintenance of the drainage and irrigation system. Even now I can see half-clad men, specks in the huge fields, clearing a drain, adding earth to a weak dam, adroitly locating, under water, a potentially serious leak. These seemingly trivial acts of little men, many of whom I knew, were crucial in the minding of the larger plantation order. I took it for granted then, so did most Guyanese, in the Campbell years, in the late 1950s and early 1960s.

Soon after the harvest, the trash, the stripped leaves, were burnt; then young men and women would spread manure on the new shoots, the ratoons. Replanting was only done every five or six years. As the canes sprouted, water was pumped into the fields to speed up the process. Quickly, this astounding, man-made landscape was reclaimed by the lushness. Women would then begin weeding the grasses and parasitic plants that retarded sugar-cane growth. Periodically, invisible but vocal men ensconced in the big cane, could be heard as they checked on water-levels in fields and canals, or mended a leaking *koker* or piled dirt on weak side-line embankments. The days when a small plane visited, spraying chemicals on the growing cane, in what seemed like touching distance, were magical. A supposed nod from the pilot made our day.

A sample of the complex hydraulic system on the plantations: drains, cross canal, middle-walk dam, cane-punts

The flood-fallowing years were especially trying for our parents: numerous domestic routines were evaded or done in a fashion. We were enthralled by the mechanical wonder in the fields: we, therefore, had to 'supervise' the ploughing and the carving out of the drains and ditches. By the mid-1950s 'TD18' Caterpillar tractors and draglines gave these tasks a magical dimension, but we felt an intimacy with them for many of the operators of these machines were known to us. It was exhilarating to watch men whom we knew one day as inept cricketers or 'rum-suckers' (boozers), who cursed and stumbled and went to 'hutel' (whore houses) on Saturday nights, manipulate these stupendous machines to the edge of canals, five or six feet deep. We were entranced by these feats of supreme control and timing, although we felt they were exaggerated specially for the young women, drawn to men and machine.

We had sugar in our blood. At play we mimicked all these fascinating facets of the sugar culture. We were also drawn to what seemed like roles of power on the plantation: playing at being managers and overseers, affecting what we thought was the white man's accent, as incomprehensible to us as the Scottish brogue was to the workers. We pretended to be stockinged white men, smoking pipes: a thick cake of dried white mud up to our knees, fitted us for the former role.

We had no idea that every square mile of cane on our flat alluvial coast, several feet below sea-level and vulnerable to flooding and periodic drought, required 49 miles of drainage ditches and 16 miles of high-level waterways.[11] Even older people appeared to take this for granted. Although the workers seemed to be on strike often in the 1960s, cane-cutting, a job saddled with associations of slavery and indentureship and with failure in school — the end of the road — had acquired a sudden gloss. From the 1950s many young Indian men saw it as a remunerative job, however demanding. One could earn enough to buy a piece of land, build a little wooden house and paint it. Indeed a job on the plantation acquired a new meaning: generally, it no longer spoke of subjugation or failure; it now carried suggestions of mobility, even ambition.

By the late 1950s we knew people who worked in the estate's office as clerks or typists, or were skilled workers in the factory or 'tractor field', servicing those giant machines which mesmerised us. Some were supervisors in field and factory: one woman from our village, Iris Ramjeet (Auntie Baba), a distant relative, represented women workers as a trade unionist, at home and abroad — she was sent to Brazil, 'on union business', the papers told us. By the early 1960s many cane-cutters owned brand new 'Triumph' bicycles, shining machines with yellow dusters dangling ostentatiously from the stems of the saddles. Another relative of mine, a cane-cutter at Rose Hall (we called him Bullet), told me in 1960 that Booker made them an irresistible offer, enabling them to become bicycle owners: they could make a deposit of $1 and pay instalments, only during the grinding season, of a $1 per week. He showed up with a 'Triumph' a few days later, yellow duster knotted inside of his shirt collar in the triumphal manner of our great cricketer, Rohan Kanhai, from Plantation Port Mourant. Bullet quickly added a contraption that emitted an annoying melody from a Hindi movie, in order to impress a girl whom he fancied. He inscribed, in red paint, on the fender by the rear light: 'My Desia'. The bike brought the cane-cutter much pride: Jock Campbell was good at seeing 'the importance of small causes'.

I shared in Bullet's romance with his bike. I had the rare privilege, in March 1960, of being towed on his cross-bar to the new, impressive cricket ground and community centre, at Rose Hall, to watch our county, Berbice, play England — it was fantastic to read 'Berbice v. England' on the giant, freshly-painted scoreboard. We were proud of the fact that our team had three West Indian Test batsmen — Basil Butcher, Rohan Kanhai and Joe Solomon, all of whom came from Port Mourant, one of Jock Campbell's estates.[12] It seemed as if our whole village was there, including some of the older boys who were studying at the Booker Training School for Apprentices at Port Mourant.

Sugar was in our blood. But growing up in an Indian village at the edge of a thriving sugar estate, when the stature of our charismatic Indian leader, Cheddi Jagan, also from Port Mourant, seemed unassailable, around 1959–60, with three of our cricketers in the West Indies team, and a battery of lawyers and doctors returning from England, it was easy to take sugar for granted, to assume that its profits were limitless; paradoxically, to absorb Jagan's messianic doctrine that the 'sugar gods' were preventing us from reaching the stars.

There was, however, perceptible improvement in the sugar worker's condition; but that simply reinforced what Jagan taught us, that the profits accruing to sugar were huge; that we were given the crumbs, to placate us. Only nationalisation of the 'commanding heights of the economy', starting with sugar, could get us to the promised land. Of course, we all knew of Sir Jock Campbell. We heard that he was a better man than anybody hitherto involved with sugar; that he was more responsive to our people's needs than his predecessors. But immersed in the anti-colonial euphoria, after the freedom of 'Mother India', and dazed by the millennial message of Cheddi Jagan — a simple, credible tale of King Sugar's insatiable greed — we could see nothing redeeming in Campbell's reforms. To have attempted to give any credence to his programme for change, was to let the side down, to be seen as a stooge of the 'imperialists', a traitor. Jock understood this perfectly:

> It is easier for a Campbell to pass through the eye of a needle than for Booker to be loved; we wish to be understood and respected and worthy of respect.[13]

A plantation people, many of us still barely a generation away from the logies — coolies — our world was dramatised and made intelligible for us by Cheddi. His utopian vision told us that Booker kept us back, that our universe was perfectible if only we would expel the 'sugar gods'. His message spoke to us the way the great Hindu classic did, promising a kind of *Rama Rajya*, the rule of Lord Rama in the *Ramayana*, a golden age. We could muster no patience for reason, for notions of gradualism, incremental change. We were nurtured on El Dorado, visions of illimitable possibilities: we could not be delayed by submissions about the hazards of the Guyanese environment, about the minutiae of sugar agronomy or the monumental organisational effort required to sustain large-scale production on this harsh land.[14]

In May 1967, one year after the British gave independence to the African Guyanese leader, L.F.S. Burnham, a man for whom Campbell often expressed private contempt, he resigned as the Chairman of Booker. The inflexibility of Jagan's Marxist illumination and racial violence between 1962 and 1964 had taken its toll. By the early 1970s virtually every local politician was supporting nationalisation of Booker, the panacea of all our ills. It was a quick fix. It made hard thinking unnecessary. With the support of Jagan, Burnham nationalised the sugar industry in 1976 — hailed by most as the greatest step in the reclamation of the nation's dignity.

In 1982 I returned to Guyana for four months and stayed for four years: I experienced the most repellent phase of Burnham's dictatorial rule. I quickly realised that the nationalisation of sugar was a massive, backward step. This was an empty harvest, engendered by the sterile dogmas about sugar's perennially bounteous returns, on one hand, and the El Dorado syndrome, the millennial reflex bred into the Guyanese psyche, on the other.[15] Production had slumped to less than half its level at nationalisation: from 330,000 tons to 129,000 tons. The delicate, complex hydraulic system had been gravely undermined on most estates. Most of the technical people, trained since Campbell's time at Booker, had fled to America and Canada, while Burnham's incompetent hacks tried to explain away the failure and Jagan's people, asserting a monopoly on communist infallibility, called for authentic 'workers' control', as in their utopia, the Soviet Union, and more nationalisation — 80 per cent of the fragile economy was already state-controlled.

I despaired. It was then that I started to appreciate the pernicious effect of dogmas and the centrality of good management; slowly, reluctantly, I recognised some of the merits of the culture of reform of Campbell's Booker in the 1950s–60s — a change of perspective that evoked opprobrium from many of my compatriots. I was beginning to grow wings, to escape the limitations of my Marxist theology that had imprisoned my thoughts for years. My reassessment led me to the work of Jock Campbell in British Guiana, for which many expressed private respect but were afraid to say so in public: it was the time of the zealots.

In June 1985, Ian McDonald, who had worked with Booker and Campbell since 1955, sent me a copy of a book on Guyanese sugar by M. Shahabuddeen, Burnham's attorney-general.[16]I had come to respect this author's intellectual vigour. Now, however, it pained me to discover that he had no backbone: he was unable to transcend his master's frame of reference. He did not have a word to say of Campbell's obvious contribution to the advancement of the sugar industry and his role in post-war change in Guyana. In a footnote at the end of his book of more than 400 pages, Shahabuddeen belatedly assembled a few quotes — prompted and provided by McDonald — reflecting the progressive temper of Campbell, and he concluded, rightly but limply, that a biography of the man 'should form a good part' of any history of British Guiana. [17]

This book is not a biography. I could not write this, as Jock kept very few private papers. Such a work requires greater intimacy, a feel for the inner promptings. I could not reach that. This study is an attempt to comprehend the work of a complex, progressive, contradictory, compassionate man, and its effect on British Guiana, in the exciting period between the mid-1930s and the mid-1960s: the time of nationalist stirrings, mobilisation for decolonisation, the fragmenting of the nationalist coalition and the descent into racial hatred and violence. It is about hope, passion and the death of a dream to forge a nation. Jock Campbell's work was essentially an exercise in exorcising the ghosts of what Jagan called 'bitter sugar'. Campbell realised that he could not erase the sordid legacy of King Sugar and he felt guilty about this; but he had a passion to ameliorate it, to sweeten it at least, in a radical independent Guyana.

Three days after Campbell died in December 1994, my father wrote to me from Palmyra: 'I am sorry to hear of Sir Jock Campbell's death. He was a giant of a man. He came here to shape the destiny of East Indians.'[18] Whether one agrees or not with this sentiment, the man deserves a place in Guyanese history. This is a book about Campbell and his times in British Guiana.

Endnotes

1. Jock Campbell, interview by the author, Nettlebed, Oxfordshire, May 9, 1990, Tape 1.
2. See my 'Tiger in the Stars': The Anatomy of Indian Achievement in British Guiana', 1919-29 (London: Macmillan, 1997), xx-xxii.

3. See, for example, 'Sixth Generation Reformer', *The Times Review of Industry and Technology'* (September 1964): [Appendix 1]; 'Men of Note: Lord Campbell of Eskan', *Jamaican and West Indian Review,* (June 1966): 23; Lord Campbell of Eskan, 'Private Enterprise and Public Morality', *New Statesman,* May 27, 1966; Lord Campbell of Eskan, speech to the Fabian Society, October 22, 1969, (mimeo.), pp. 18-20.

4. See note 1.

5. Interviews with the following relatives, Palmyra, East Canje, Berbice, Guyana: Ramdularie (1916–85), May 1982; Latchman Sohan (1908–89), December 1985; Sarran Jagmohan (1920–), April 1986.

6. For an assessment of the *Ramayana* as a text of exile in British Guiana, see my *'Tiger in the Stars',* 44-53.

7. See my 'The Shaping of the Indo-Caribbean People: Guyana and Trinidad to the 1940s', *Journal of Caribbean Studies* 14, nos. 1&2 (1999–2000): 61-92.

8. Although my recollections are based on Rose Hall, knowledge of other plantations in Berbice and Demerara acquired in the late 1960s confirmed that these images were representative of all estates.

9. See David Dabydeen, *Slave Song* (1984) for a poetic evocation of the power of this crude estate 'coolie' idiom.

10. I started to explore this hard land and its impact on the Guyanese psyche after I had read, in 1971, the introductory chapter to Donald Wood's book, *Trinidad in Transition* (London: OUP, 1968).

11. This is a classic quote that the Venn Commission of 1949 had used to dramatise the hazards of the coastal environment; see *Report of a Commission of Inquiry into the Sugar Industry of British Guiana,* Col. No. 249 (London: HMSO, 1949), 9. See also A.C. Barnes, *The Sugar Cane* (Aylesbury, Bucks.: Leonard Hill Books, 1974 [1964]), 119-21, 161-2.

12. See my essay, 'The Tiger of Port Mourant — R.B. Kanhai: Fact and Fantasy in the Making of an Indo-Guyanese Legend', in *Indo-West Indian Cricket,* Frank Birbalsingh and Clem Seecharan (London: Hansib, 1988), 41-77.

13. Quoted from a mimeographed biographical sketch Campbell drafted some years after he had left Booker. It was among the papers he gave me in 1992.

14. These hazards had been articulated by Jock Campbell in a letter to the *New Statesman and Nation* (October 24, 1953), after the suspension of the constitution.

15. See note 7.

16. M. Shahabuddeen, *From Plantocracy to Nationalisation: A Profile of Sugar in Guyana* (Georgetown: University of Guyana, 1983).

17. Ibid., 410 [footnote 120a].

18. Personal correspondence from Sydney Seecharan, Palmyra, Guyana, December 29, 1994.

Chapter Two

SUGAR IN HIS BLOOD: JOCK CAMPBELL'S ANTECEDENTS

It is impossible to ascertain precisely what of a man's family history shapes him; what, ineluctably and decisively, lodges in his consciousness. How much, for instance, did the mind of Campbell owe to his diverse ancestral roots? The best the historian can do is to try to reconstruct some of those antecedents, to stimulate empathy for them — the people, the places, the times, the discernible cardinal events, which facilitate an intellectual scrutiny of the man in the Guyanese context between 1934 and 1966. One hopes that the narrative coheres sufficiently to give an appreciation of the deeper prompting, the forces that shaped a reformer and the context and consequences of the reforms.

Jock would speak often of a perennial split between the taciturnity of his head and the spontaneity of his heart: the attitudes inspired by his paternal Scottish ancestors, on one hand, and those fed by his maternal ancestors, Irish Protestants, on the other. It is noteworthy that he named his last home, in Nettlebed, Oxfordshire, 'Lawers', after his first known Scottish ancestor, Sir John Campbell of Lawers, who was killed at the Battle of Flodden Field in 1513. Another forebear, John Campbell of Kinleh (Perth), died around 1671. It was his great grandson, John Campbell (senior), ship-owner and merchant of Glasgow, who established the fortunes of the Campbells through the West Indies trade, during slavery, in the last quarter of the eighteenth century.[1]

The American War of Independence precipitated a significant diversion of Scottish trade to the West Indies. Imports from the latter rose from £164,848 in 1783 to £288,121 in 1785; by 1790 it was £371,656; in these years Scottish exports to the slave plantations of the West Indies reached £198,976, £124,016 and £318,805 respectively. In 1790 exports to the area constituted 26 per cent of all exports from Scotland.[2] Richard Sheridan has sketched this remarkable trade from the 1780s:

> After the collapse of the Virginian [linen] market at the outbreak of the American Revolution, Jamaica alone took off 40% of all Scottish linen exports to be made up into clothing for the planters and their slaves. Other exports consisted of haberdashery, goods of leather, iron, copper, tin, hats, ropes, delft and stoneware, herrings and conches. From the Caribbean, Scots vessels returned with sugar, rum, coffee, raw cotton, indigo, nutmeg, cochineal, tobacco, hides, logwood, fustic and other dyewoods.... Trade with the West Indies was a stepping stone to the acquisition of plantations. This was especially the case after the shipping and trade of Glasgow and Edinburgh were established on a regular basis, for it was customary for merchants to then employ their countrymen as resident agents or factors, who were in a favourable situation to commute mercantile capital into planter capital.[3]

Glasgow trading houses in particular, with long experience of servicing the needs of North American slave plantations, were ideally placed to capitalise on the new opportunities in the West Indies. Already, by the early eighteenth century, some Scottish merchants were more enamoured of the West Indies sugar trade than they were of Virginia tobacco. Therefore, by the 1780s they could easily supply 'the two most important British exports to the West Indies, herring and coarse linen goods'.[4]

Among the principal beneficiaries of the West Indian bonanza were John Campbell (Senior) and Co of Glasgow. By the 1760s they were already suppliers of merchandise to the slave plantations on the coast of Guyana, then under Dutch control. This was the context in which they acquired plantations on the Essequibo Coast — from planters who were facing bankruptcy in the 1780s. These were later amalgamated as Plantation Anna Regina, after the British conquest of 1803.[5] T.M. Devine observes of the late eighteenth century West Indies: '...plantation ownership was ... one consequence of planter indebtedness to merchant houses, since loans were often secured on the plantations and failure to liquidate debts within specified periods could result in foreclosure'.[6] Jock remarked, often, that in acquiring estates in Guyana through foreclosure, his ancestors had become slave-owners. He told me that he was once shown an inventory of the Campbell slaves in Essequibo. It had been retained in the Curtis Campbell archives in Liverpool.[7]

John Campbell (Senior) and Co were clearly buoyed by their slave plantations. Profits from this source were an established mechanism for mercantile and industrial expansion in Glasgow. Between 1790 and 1814 the book capital of the firm rose from £40,000 to £179,000. Indeed, by 1800, they had become one of the top three Scottish companies trading with the West Indies — not an ordinary feat for a man whose father, Alexander Campbell, was a captain in the Black Watch regiment. Commercial success lifted the Campbells to the stature of landowners in Scotland, as it did in the West Indies. In 1796 John Campbell (senior) bought Morriston Estate in Lanarkshire; his brother, Mungo Nutter Campbell (1785–1862), a shareholder in the company, bought Belvedere Estate in Scotland (a section of Albion Estate in Guyana was given the same name). Mungo also acquired Baltimore Estate in Argyllshire and became a planter and slaveholder in Grenada.[8]

Colin Campbell of Colgrain (1782–1863), third son of Colin Campbell (senior), Jock's great-great-grandfather, who held shares in his father's company, acquired Park Estate in Renfrewshire. He was also a partner of the great social reformer and socialist thinker, Robert Owen, between 1810 and 1812, in the New Lanark Cotton Co.[9] But as Jock remarked to the Fabian Society on October 22, 1969 and to the House of Lords on May 5, 1971, on the occasion of the bi-centenary of Owen's birth, his great-great-grandfather shared none of Owen's idealism, his conviction of broader responsibilities of business to the community. For Colin Campbell, business was important only as a source of profits; he was intolerant of Owen's lofty business ethic. On both occasions Jock quoted Owen's indictment of Colin Campbell and his ilk, to underline his own reformist philosophy in business:

I was completely tired of partners who were merely trained to buy cheap and sell dear. This occupation deteriorates, and often destroys, the finest and best faculties of our nature. From an experience of a long life, in which I passed through all the gradations of trade, manufactures and commerce, I am thoroughly convinced that there can be no superior character formed under this thoroughly selfish system.... Under this system there can be no true civilisation.... It is a low, vulgar, ignorant, and inferior way of conducting the affairs of society.[10]

On May 5, 1971, in the House of Lords, Jock had dissociated himself from those Campbells who had proved such unworthy partners of Robert Owen, arguing that 'maximising profits cannot and should not be the sole purpose, or even the primary purpose, of business .... Robert Owen was right in his vision, and... we [still] have a great deal to learn from him today'.[11]

This narrow, selfish outlook characterised the Campbells' treatment of their African slaves and, later, their Indian indentured labourers in British Guiana well into the twentieth century. It is interesting that the Campbells' family home in Georgetown was called 'Colgrain House', after Owen's partner, Colin Campbell of Colgrain, who owned several slave plantations in Guyana, among his many business ventures. His brother, James Campbell, apart from being a shareholder in John Campbell Senior and Co, owned one-third of the capital in the Newark Sugar Refining Co, Greenock.[12] There was a lot of sugar in Jock's blood; and in his picturesque, self-deprecating way, he often sought to explain away his own achievements by alluding to his family's West Indies connection: 'I was born with a sugar spoon in my mouth'.

Colin Campbell's second son, also called Colin Campbell of Colgrain (1819–86), Jock's great-grandfather was married to Jessie Middleton, the source of his grandfather's and his middle name, Middleton. Under Colin Campbell, in the 1860s–70s, the family consolidated their sugar plantations in British Guiana. They had expanded beyond the damp, malarial Essequibo Coast to the East Coast Demerara and the substantially more salubrious Corentyne Coast, in Berbice, Jock's favourite part of Guyana. Abundant indentured Indian coolies and good prices for sugar in the 1870s, boosted the family's wealth consistently. When Jock's great-grandfather died in 1886, he left more than £1 million, a substantial sum at the time.[13]

Dire sugar prices in the 1880s forced the family into an amalgamation with Hogg, Curtis, Campbell and Co. Quintin Hogg (1845–1903), a robust, autocratic, frontier-type of a Scottish capitalist, became the senior partner. He was a hard driver of men. As his daughter recalled in 1904, the year after he died, his regular visits to Demerara (British Guiana) struck fear in all his employees:

> [H]is visits to the estates were not always eagerly looked for. Nothing escaped his keen eye. Ready to acknowledge and encourage industry and alertness, he was equally quick to detect and punish any whom he thought had failed in his duty towards the firm. His indomitable will and untiring perseverance often led him to undertake work that proved too severe a trial to stronger but less enthusiastic men than himself.[14]

Quintin Hogg's hard attitudes did not alleviate established local perceptions of his partners, the Campbells. This was exacerbated, in October 1896, by the shooting of five Indian indentured labourers and the wounding of 59 at Non Pareil, one of the Hogg, Curtis, and Campbell estates in Demerara. The deputy manager's sexual relations with one of the married Indian women on the plantation had precipitated the tragedy; but it was the perceived inflexibility of management and the unilateral slashing of wages during the prolonged depression of the 1890s that had fed a smouldering discontent.[15]

In 1898, amidst the severe depression in the sugar industry and with his own health deteriorating, Quintin Hogg resigned from the firm. But, as *The Times* (January 19, 1903) remarked when he died in 1903, it was with cash earned from the plantations in British Guiana, during good times, that he had founded the Regent St. Polytechnic:

> Mr. Hogg at one time had large estates in the West Indies, and while he prospered in the West Indies trade he was able to save the large sum of money which he afterwards devoted to the Polytechnic. Later on, however, the sugar bounties seriously

affected his revenue; and, in fact, so much curtailed his income that he was compelled, in 1888, to transfer to public hands the institution he had called into existence.... Nobody can say how much the Polytechnic cost him in actual money, but it is believed that £6,000 a year is a moderate estimate.

In June 1898 Quintin Hogg's son, Douglas M. Hogg, also, had resigned from the firm of Hogg, Curtis, Campbell and Co. Thus Jock's grandfather, William Middleton Campbell (1849–1919), became the senior partner while his father, Colin Algernon Campbell (1874–1957), became a partner, as did his brother, Henry Campbell. With the departure of the Hoggs, it quickly reverted to being a family firm. On July 1, 1899 the name was changed to Curtis, Campbell and Co.[16]

What Robert Owen had said about Colin Campbell, early in the nineteenth century, apparently, needed no revision at the end of the century. In October 1897 even the staunchly pro-planter paper in British Guiana, *The Argosy,* had expressed disgust at the conduct of William Middleton Campbell towards his workers at Plantation Anna Regina and Reliance, on the Essequibo Coast. He had, a few months before, initiated a scheme by which, from January 1898, small farmers would grow most of the cane to be ground on the estate; they would lease the land from the company. Then came news that the plantation was to be cropped — usually 'the first step in the abandonment' of an estate. The paper was appalled:

[T]he change has been brought about at the instance of Mr.[W.M.] Campbell, one of the owners, a very rich man, whose richness, however, has not prevented him from adopting a course which even a poor proprietor who had due respect for the farmers with whom negotiations had been concluded, would have hesitated to adopt.... The contracts were printed, and the representative had taken them to be signed when the retreat was sounded. The gentleman in question has done the colony much harm by his action, and he has broken faith with a class of people to whom men of his standing should be always the embodiment of rectitude. He may, of course, be under the conviction that the colony is heavily water-logged and rather dangerous, although fortunately, we do not think alike; but all things considered, his wealth amongst them, he need not have

seized for himself the ignoble distinction of being the pioneer rat
to leave the ship.[17]

Stunned by the vitriolic response of a traditional ally, Curtis,
Campbell and Co claimed that they were misunderstood on the cane-
farming issue at Anna Regina and that they wished to 'resume
negotiations with the farmers and carry them through to completion'.
The Argosy welcomed this because they felt that the measure offered
small farmers a 'real stake in the colony', and consequently
possibilities for removing 'the stigma from the name of a powerful
and influential firm'. [18] In fact, nothing came of it. By early 1898 H.K.
Davson, a friend of the Campbells and proprietor of Plantation
Blairmont, in Berbice, had expressed need for more indentured
coolies, which he deemed more important to the resuscitation of the
sugar industry than grants-in-aid, bounties or countervailing duties.
He submitted that 'the withdrawal of coolies from the estate for rice
cultivation, railway works, huckstering, shopkeeping, cattle farming
.... etc., had diminished the supply of coolies to the estates, and since
commencement of the first named [rice], the price of labour had
risen 20%'.[19]

The gloom of the sugar depression of the 1890s was lifting. That
was why W.M. Campbell was no longer interested in promoting small
farming, now seen as diverting coolie labour from its more lucrative
plantation mould. Meanwhile, the end of the reign of the authoritarian
Quintin Hogg seemed to have given the Campbells a kind of liberation.
In July 1898 it was announced that W.M. Campbell, the owner of Non
Pareil (of 1896 infamy) and Anna Regina, was negotiating to acquire
Plantation Ogle, contiguous with Goedverwagting which they already
owned. Ogle was bought.[20] The Campbells were expanding: there
could be no space for independent farmers in this scheme.

In August 1898 W.M. Campbell wrote to Joseph Chamberlain,
Secretary of State for the Colonies, with regard to the resuscitation
of sugar cultivation at Anna Regina — the proposal for peasant cane-
farming was scrapped. Campbell remarked that there was hope for
the estate if the drainage were rehabilitated. Moreover, if planters
were guaranteed coolies, indentured Indians, the whole colony would
benefit: this would 'obviate the abandonment of valuable estates with

all the accompanying deterioration of the labourers, and evils resulting from the removal of the European staff'. Campbell elaborated: 'The past has shown that when the white man leaves, the natives sink back into barbarism'.[21]

Plantocratic wisdom decreed that initiatives to develop an independent peasantry were conducive to the propagation of 'barbarism'. *The Daily Chronicle* reported in December 1898 that 500 to 600 shovelmen were engaged in the resuscitation of the drainage at Anna Regina. Big canals were being dug, linking several estates that had been amalgamated with Anna Regina: Mainstay, Land-of Plenty, Reliance, Bush Lot, Henrietta, Richmond, La Belle Alliance. They added that the peasant cane-farming scheme had been shelved because the people could not agree to the proposed terms of cultivation. But the paper suggested an alternative cause, something sinister — W.M. Campbell's strategy for stemming the potential for 'barbarism' among his coolies on the estate:

> The estate's authorities have notified a large number of coolie rice farmers to quit the lands occupied by them within a limited period of time. A large area of land connected with the estates enumerated above has been in rice cultivation for some time. There is much dissatisfaction amongst the rice farmers. Plantation Golden Fleece is also rapidly improving its cultivation, which certainly shows that the planters in this part of the world are sanguine as to the future of the staple industry, 'King Sugar'.... One of the principal activities that the authorities have in view, in dispossessing the free coolie immigrants of their rice farms on the estate, is to secure an adequate supply of labour, the coolies having devoted their whole time and attention to the cultivation of their farms. [22]

The plantocracy defined the national interest as coterminous with theirs: no coolies, no sugar; no sugar, no colony (barbarism). In February 1900 the Executive Council rejected the planters' requisition of 4,240 indentured labourers for the 1900–01 season, contending that the 'precarious financial condition of the colony does not justify the charge on public revenue which the introduction of that number would entail'. They argued for a reduction to 2,500 and the Governor, Sir Walter Sendall, concurred.[23] On March 9, 1900 William Middleton Campbell wrote to the Colonial Office, countering the government's argument. He submitted that every man, woman and child imported into the colony was a benefit to every other interest, not merely sugar. He then exposed the roots of his conduct at Anna Regina in 1897:

> [I]t is the wish of the Colonial Government as well as the proprietors that everything should be done to encourage free coolies being located either on the Estates on which they have worked or in the neighbourhood, and thus lead to their spending the rest of their lives in the Colony rather than go back to India entailing as it does considerable expenditure to the colony. Now how can you expect the proprietors to encourage this settlement of coolies on their own allotments if they find they cannot get new immigrants to take their place?[24]

Campbell concluded with a request that the Secretary of State for the Colonies 'instruct' the Government of British Guiana to accede to the planters' requisition of 4,240 coolies. On March 13, 1900 his friend and fellow planter, H.K. Davson, made the same request of the Colonial Office: 'I am very much troubled about the financial position of the colony but it is the Sugar industry that keeps it going and it is Coolie immigration that enables it to do so'.[25] Two days later, on March 15, 1900, a week after Campbell's letter to the Colonial Office, Governor Sendall informed the Secretary of State that a revised vote in favour of 4,000 indentured labourers — only 240 below the planters' order — was passed 'by a large majority' in the legislature. Writing exactly one month after he had cited financial constraints in recommending the reduced figure of 2,500 labourers, he argued, strangely, that the revised higher vote was arrived at 'having regard to the improved financial outlook and the estimated revenue for the coming financial year...'!26

In June 1901 Sendall made another revealing volte-face to the Secretary of State: he could see no way of recommending a remunerative scheme for the drainage and irrigation (empoldering) of the comparatively healthy, potentially rich Corentyne Coast. The people, he argued, could not afford the costs and were not willing to embrace any scheme at the present time. Nothing should be done.[27] This was congruent with the sugar planters' argument that the empoldering of the coastland was potentially subversive of their captive work-force. The state concurred: it could not use public funds to develop private property. This was a ruse: one-third of the cost of importing indentured labourers from India came from general revenue; in fact, between 1894 and 1897, during the sugar depression, two-thirds came from this source. The state was, in fact, subsidising the sugar industry; it was deemed inviolable, the fount of civilisation. The Campbells were among the minority who benefited from this policy.

The venerable Sir George William Des Voeux, who had challenged the plantocracy in 1869 on behalf of Indians and paid severely for it, made a poignant comment on the colonial condition in November 1894, a quarter of a century after he left British Guiana. Writing to the Colonial Office, he observed: '[T]he Government of British Guiana instead of being as described by Anthony Trollope as a "despotism tempered by sugar" is, in the hands of any other than a strong Governor, apt to become a despotism controlled by sugar.' It was easier, indeed, for a Campbell to go through a needle's eye than for a Governor in British Guiana to control the plantocracy. The Colonial Office had resigned itself to that, as an official minuted in 1894: 'I rather concur with Sir Geo Des Voeux's views...'[28]

On February 28, 1901 *The Daily Chronicle* reported that Mr Henry Campbell, the brother of Jock's grandfather, William Middleton Campbell, and one of the proprietors of Plantation Anna Regina and the owner of Plantation De Kinderen, had arrived in the colony the previous day, in his yacht. The paper elaborated on Henry Campbell's voyage to British Guiana:

> The yacht 'Cuhona' arrived in port yesterday morning, from England, on a cruise by way of Gibraltar, the Canary Islands and St.Vincent, with Mr. H[enry] Campbell on board.... He will probably stay in the colony for a week and will then continue his cruise by way of the United States. The 'Cuhona' is an auxiliary screw schooner, built of iron and has three masts. Her tonnage is 498 yacht measurement, and she is 163.5 feet long with 26.1

feet beam, and a depth of 14.15 feet. She was built by the Earles Co. Ltd., Hull, in 1882, and is classed 100A1 at Lloyd's.

The vicissitudes of the market notwithstanding, sugar did pay. Jock, as noted earlier, said that when his great-grandfather, Colin Campbell of Colgrain, died in 1886 he left £1 million. When his grandfather, William Middleton Campbell, died in 1919, he left £1.5 million — virtually all of it made from sugar in British Guiana. This was the source of Jock Campbell's guilt, the making of the reformer: 'I was born with a sugar spoon in my mouth.'

Endnotes

1. Jock Campbell, interview by the author, Nettlebed, Oxfordshire, May 9, 1990, Tape 1.
2. T.M. Devine, 'An Eighteenth-Century Business Elite: Glasgow-West India Merchants', *Scottish Historical Review* 57 (1978): 40.
3. Richard Sheridan, 'The Role of Scots in the Economy and Society of the West Indies', *Annals of the New York Academy of Sciences* 292 (1977): 95.
4. See note 2 [pp. 40-1].
5. See note 1.
6. See note 2 [p. 43].
7. See note 1.
8. See note 2 [pp. 47, 50, 56, 57].
9. Ibid., 56.
10. 'Speech by Lord Campbell of Eskan to the Fabian Society', October 22, 1969.
11. *Parliamentary Debates (Hansard), House of Lords Official Report*, Vol. 318, No. 95, May 5, 1971.
12. See note 2 [p. 57].
13. See note 1.
14. Ethel M. Hogg, *Quintin Hogg* (London: Constable, 1904), 326.
15. See my *Bechu: 'Bound Coolie' Radical in British Guiana, 1894-1901* (Mona, Jamaica: University of the West Indies Press, 1999).
16. *The Argosy*, June 18, 1898; July 1, 1899.
17. Leader, *The Argosy*, October 23, 1897.
18. *The Argosy*, November 27, 1897.
19. CO [Colonial Office]111/509, (Individuals), [Henry K. Davson to Secretary of State for the Colonies], February 15, 1898.
20. *The Argosy*, July 9, 1898.
21. CO111/509, (Individuals), [W.M. Campbell], August 6, 1898.

22. *The Daily Chronicle,* December 13, 1898.

23. CO111/517, Sendall to Chamberlain, no.53, February 15, 1900.

24. CO111/525, (Individuals), [W.M. Campbell], March 9, 1900.

25. CO111/525, (Individuals), [H. K. Davson], March 13, 1900.

26. CO111/518, Sendall to Chamberlain, no. 71, March 15, 1900.

27. CO111/527, Sendall to Chamberlain, no. 203, June 6, 1901.

28. CO111/474, (Individuals), [Sir G.W. DesVoeux], November 2, 1894.

Chapter Three

CAMPBELL'S BOYHOOD: THE IMPACT OF THE 'OTHER'

It was a privileged boyhood. His grandfather, William Middleton Campbell (1849–1919), was very Scottish: upright, very Presbyterian, self-assured. Apart from his sugar interests in Guyana, he had prestige in British society. He was governor of the Bank of England between 1907 and 1909. He was obsessively ambitious and, as seen above, tenacious of opinion and resolved to get his own way. He was never taciturn or indecisive. He was also capable of great rudeness.

Jock told me a story of his grandfather's response when his wife informed him that a particular couple, whom he considered pretentious — 'always dressed as if going to a wedding' — were coming to Sunday lunch. He protested that he could not stand them, to which his wife replied: 'Well, then, tell them so.' They did not show up and Jock's grandmother wondered why, but suspected nothing untoward. About a year later she met the wife who quickly let her know that she was still upset: William Middleton Campbell had, indeed, sent a telegram to the couple — 'Lunch Sunday. Prefer not'.[1]

Jock recalled his grandfather's unfailing punctuality and sense of order; even a suggestion of unpreparedness was anathema. He was a competitive, very ambitious man. Jock's father, Colin Algernon Campbell (1874-1957), was devoted to his father but was perceptibly lacking in the powers of singular concentration and drive which made W.M. Campbell a daunting figure, a success in whatever he did. Like his former partner, Quintin Hogg, W.M. Campbell had a Scottish resolve which brooked no half-measures. Jock was only seven when his grandfather died, but he absorbed his ambitiousness, his competitiveness, the punctiliousness about time and the clarity of purpose.

But it is to his paternal grandmother, whom he saw frequently as a child, that he was most proud to attribute a seminal influence: Edith Angela Bevan, daughter of R.C.L. Bevan (1809–1890), the first Chairman of Barclay's Bank, and Lady Angela Elizabeth Yorke, daughter of Admiral 4th Earl of Hardwicke. Jock's grandmother was of Welsh stock, of high intellectual pedigree. He remembered her as a frail, intelligent, discerning woman. Five of her brothers were Cambridge dons: Trinity College was the family's scholastic home. It was from this lady that Jock acquired the rudiments of an intellectual temperament. It was she who initiated him into the universe of words and shaped his mastery, his genius, at crossword puzzles. It was a boyhood of wealth, servants, Victorian morality and generous affection, but not intimacy.[2]

Jock's father, Colin, and his mother, Mary Barrington, were solidly religious, church-going Presbyterians — firm in their belief in good manners. His father's motto was: 'Do unto others as you would have them do unto you'. Jock says he was 'scrupulously polite', though somewhat aloof: '...although he was a rich man and an eminent man in his way, he was an enormously meek man'. He was thrifty and contemptuous of conspicuous consumption; any form of ostentation was repellent: tawdry. He often told Jock that you could tell how rich a man was not by how much he spent but by how much he saved.[3] There was a feel of every penny as a noble acquisition: there was no other way of protecting wealth. Jock imbibed this attitude to money. My own experience with him underlined for me my inherent incapacity for thrift. Around 1991 he gave me an old, mildewed, zipless rag of a bag, to transport some old papers. I did not realise that this bag was a loan: 'Could you please return my bag, Clem? It is my laundry bag'. I was ashamed to be seen with this derelict acquisition again; meanwhile, my wife could stand it no longer and had dumped it. A couple of reminders followed: 'Oh! That bag, Clem!' I ignored him. However, he was generous in other ways: food, wine, enthralling conversation — books, words, politics, people (from the Queen to his cane-cutters), places and their smells; Guyana over and over; humour. It was his common sense and intellect, his generosity of spirit and amazing powers of discernment to the end, that were so captivating.

He must have inherited this from his grandfather — his rationality, circumspection, clarity of thought, persistence — what he deemed 'the Scottish side'. He often said that an interminable battle was being waged in him: rationality versus emotion. He explained: 'I have always felt it to be a great disadvantage to be half Scots and half Irish. One's head and heart are always in conflict.'[4] His mother, Mary Barrington, was of high Irish Protestant stock. She had married his father in 1911 when she was 20 and he 37. She was very Irish and Jock observed, early, that she did not like the English and the Scots

Jock Campbell around 1924, at Eton

very much. He noticed also that although his parents were deeply religious and brought him up to believe in a virtuous life, that while they loved him, they were not intimate parents. They were aloof: one did not touch; the emotions were controlled.

Jock's mother was totally different from his father. She was handsome, with a 'marvellous' figure. He loved her but he could never get close to her, for as will be seen later, she never approved of his bookish temperament as a teenager. However, Jock's exposure to his mother's family in Ireland was to have an enduring influence on his way of seeing. The Barringtons were an old, aristocratic family; they claimed descent from Odo du Barentin who originated in Normandy and came over with William the Conqueror in the eleventh century. The first member of the family in Ireland, Samuel Barrington, settled in Limerick in 1691; he was buried in St Mary's Cathedral in 1693. They had prospered through their copper foundry and clock-making business. His son, Benjamin, became sheriff of the city of Limerick in 1714. Jock's maternal great-great-grandfather, Sir Matthew Barrington (1788–1861), 2nd baronet, built the great Glenstal Castle in County Limerick in the late 1830s. His brother, Croker (1851–1927), was a lawyer, and his youngest one, John

Barrington (1859–1927), Jock's maternal grandfather, was agent for the grand estate surrounding Glenstal Castle.[5]

It was during the First World War, from the age of three to about seven, between 1915 and 1919, that Jock came into the grand world of the Barringtons: the opulence and capaciousness of Glenstal Castle, amidst its cultured 10,000 acres. He was sent over to southern Ireland, safe from the bombings of the German 'Zeppelins'. This opened the little boy's mind to two different universes — that of his aristocratic, loving, but formal, Protestant relatives, on one hand, and the humble, spontaneous and chaotic, but infinitely more intimate one of his family's Catholic game-keepers and farm-hands, on the other. Jock recalls the profundity of this encounter:

> I went over and stayed from when I was three to when I was about seven in southern Ireland where my mother's family lived, in a great castle, and, of course, at the end of that time the trouble started in Ireland and I spent as much time with game-keepers as I did with my grandparents, and I quickly discovered that two sets of people describe the same events from an entirely different viewpoint. I think because of that I was always conscious of social realities.[6]

This perspective on the experience, which Jock recalled throughout his adult life, shaped in him a partiality for the underdog, a kind of socialist instinct. His grandfather, John Barrington, and his brother, Croker, were married to two sisters, their second cousins, Florence and Catherine Bayly. The women in the Barrington family were loving but strict. Their world of plenty was ordered, more 'stylised'. This had its merits: its comforts, its certainties. But to young Jock the eclectic world of the 'other', the Catholic farm-hands, was beguiling, more seductive. He must have started to collect these impressions long after, but they are no less valid. He was intrigued by what he calls their 'non-stylised', 'primary' reactions — a gift for the unrehearsed, the unbridled instinct. He loved their fluency, the embroidery, the humour — a poetic quality in their narration. Jock explains:

I like people who wear their hearts on their sleeves.... People in both places (Ireland and the West Indies) have primary reactions: they laugh, cry, hate, love. In England people are so stylised. Why? Perhaps because we are overcrowded, perhaps because we haven't been beaten in a war, or oppressed .... I don't think *I* fit into stylised reactions.[7]

Jock had arrived at a point of empathy with the 'idiom' of the 'other'; he was also enamoured of what he saw as the 'non-patronising' way of treating children among the Irish farm-hands: 'I was terrified of my Irish [Protestant] grandmother, but the Irish [Catholic] people were absolutely enchanting to be with for a child: they were interesting; they explained things to you; they didn't patronise children.'[8] He observed also their loyalty to the Barringtons, to his grandfather and his elder brother, Sir Charles Barrington (1848-1943), 5th baronet, who lived at Glenstal Castle. This was extraordinary, as they already held forthright nationalist views, at variance with the loyalist sentiments of the Barringtons.

In spite of his family's aristocratic, Protestant, loyalist frame of reference, they retained the respect of their Catholic farmhands and tenants. The reasons were deep-seated. As early as the 1830s, the family had given £10,000 towards the Barrington Hospital in Limerick. Their generosity had been prompted by 'a sense of outrage at human suffering in the slums of the Irishtown and Englishtown of the Limerick of the 1820s. The building of the hospital was a humanitarian response to this suffering and to the lack of even elementary health care'.[9] Moreover, they had sustained a reputation as 'benevolent landlords'. Donal Ryan, whose family were tenants on the Barrington estate, conveys the depth of this esteem:

> The Barringtons were a major landowning family, possessing a large estate of over 9,400 acres in County Limerick. My own people were tenants of the Barringtons, and the high esteem in which the family was held by the older members of the community is indicative of the fairness with which they treated their tenants .... [T]he role of the Anglo-Irish gentry was not always a negative one ... many of their number contributed positively to the development of Ireland.... Much of the credit for maintaining good relations with the community must rest with

Charles Barrington [Jock's maternal grandfather's eldest brother]. By all counts he was a remarkable man.[10]

The generosity of spirit of the man was astounding. His only daughter, Winifred (1898–1921), was mistakenly killed by the IRA in March 1921. Yet in 1942, at the age of 94, Sir Charles Barrington could still see his life at Glenstal as 'a happy one ... [though] chequered by three rebellions and several threats to take his life'. In a vein typical of Jock, he demonstrated the kind of wit that enabled him to negotiate many Irish mine-fields. He recalled that once when he was entertaining some guests, he received a message that the insurgents wanted to blow up Glenstal Castle. He promptly asked that they be informed that he was entertaining his guests and he hoped that they would not 'disgrace' Ireland by behaving irresponsibly. He advised: 'If you want to blow me up, come here again on Thursday when my guests have gone, and you will have a warm reception.'[11] He regarded his Irish workers as 'fine fellows, kind and generous to a fault'. The Irish connection was a seminal force in shaping Jock Campbell's attitudes to the underdog.

When Jock's great-great-grandfather, Sir Matthew Barrington (1788–1861), the great philanthropist, died, *The Warder* carried a eulogy which could well have formed a good part of Jock's obituary, over 130 years later:

He was a man of wise projects, of indefatigable labour, of ready and always active sympathy, and of genuine and unobtrusive patriotism. In social or business intercourse he had none of the tricks by which men force themselves upon attention. He was entirely without pretension, most unaffectedly modest and patient in discourse, a ready and anxious listener, and careful to select and store in memory everything worth preserving.... No one who took the trouble to observe could fail to be struck at once by his simplicity and breath of view — by his faculty of seeing at a glance, and retaining indestructibly all the essential points of a case or a question in which he was in any way concerned.[12]

Something of the spirit of Ireland and the Barrington's place in it lodged in Jock Campbell's impressionable mind — a sense of responsibility to the community: countering the contemporary assumption of 'the rich man in his castle, the poor man at his gate'; the gift for a spontaneously absorbing tale, the manner of telling; a willingness to transcend one's frame of reference. After the War he was taken back to their residence in Kent, 'Underriver', with its impressive acres of cultured space. There, also, enduring notions of the 'other' were acquired, investing this opulent boyhood with an instinct to go beyond the mould. As noted earlier, the loving but aloof relationship with his parents made him see their many servants as allies: it was with them that a degree of intimacy developed; he could confide in them. Jock recalled vividly the situation after he returned from Ireland around 1919:

> When we lived in Kent with my family, with many servants and gardeners ... I was worried about certain things. My parents were very Christian, God-fearing, delightful people, but servants still had a very bad time. They weren't allowed to marry, they hardly had any holidays, they were underpaid, they had to get up very early in the morning. This always made me uncomfortable.[13]

He noted that the kitchen maids had to get up at 4 a.m. to light the kitchen range; often they would cry to him, as he did to them, because of one 'petty tragedy or another'. He also observed that while he and his siblings were told never to be rude to the servants — one could only be rude to one's equals — and that his father never lost his temper with them, he did not bother to learn their first names although many of them had been with him for 30 years.[14] This was a world of order, highly formalised with its certainties and inviolable codes of status and deference. The idioms spoke of compliance, knowing one's place, prescribed behaviour, politeness, control of the emotions, an intolerance of excess. But by 1919–20, through his seminal Irish experience, the boy had already absorbed notions which were slightly subversive of this old order which 'protected and imprisoned', to borrow Naipaul's telling phrase from another context. It is noteworthy that many of the Catholic servants he knew in Ireland would accompany his maternal grandparents periodically to England: he was always delighted to meet them. The influences could percolate.

As in Ireland, Jock was drawn to the antithesis of the established order without appearing to contravene it. He called the servants by their first names; he sought solace from them although he would not touch them. He knew that he could go anytime to Ashford or his favourite Lavinia — oases in his arid emotional landscape; their 'non-stylised' responses, as in Ireland, enabled him to straddle both universes. He recalled that the larder was always locked; money was never left around: servants could never really be trusted. Yet he found nothing but compassion, empathy, respect and reliability in them: 'others' to lean on. From the age of four he had governesses. They taught him Latin and Greek, to read and appreciate the written word. This soon became another haven into which he could escape: from the austere temper of his privileged world to a world of the imagination. Indeed, his relationship with his parents was mediated through nannies, servants, farm-hands and governesses.[15]

His mother did not tell him stories, but she often read to him. Jock felt that although he was devoted to her and she saved his life when he had polio, as noted earlier, she was not enamoured of his passion for books. He reflected on this relationship:

> I always said that all the ambition I've got was a wish to prove to my mother that I wasn't the fool she thought I was.... I was devoted to my mother but she didn't terribly approve of me. It's a silly thing to say but I think she resented the fact that my father wasn't Irish, and I think she slightly resented that I wasn't very interested in the farm.... I was rather bookish and I think I was slightly different from the Irish side of the family. So I had this extraordinary situation where I was rather frightened of her. I always used to say that the phrase, 'she can't but say "no"', didn't apply to my mother; she would say 'no' in a terrifying way.[16]

The world of the imagination, therefore, gave Jock space to retreat; to find himself. It was fired by his early fascination with the spoken word absorbed through the Irish Catholic oral narratives he heard during the War. The first book he read was R.D. Blackmoore's *Lorna Doone*. He soon became immersed in the Golliwog Books, in which the heroes were black. He drew no conscious lesson from this. The flowering of the imagination had been stimulated by his paternal grandmother also. In the 1920s Jock went to Eton, as did his father, grandfather and great-grandfather. He was fortunate to have a wonderful housemaster, A.C. Sheepshanks, a cultivated man with a passion for the English language, ball games, and a brilliant sense of the absurd. Jock absorbed all these attributes; to his last days he would call up little tales from the inexhaustible repertoire of Sheepshanks, extolling the gifts of this great communicator.[17]

This early romance with the imagination was heightened, paradoxically, by a traumatic personal misfortune — he got polio in 1927, at the age of 15. He did make an astounding recovery, but it had a profound effect on him. Although he was not close to his mother she worked hard to help him through the trauma. For over a year he could not go to school; he had a private nurse who massaged his muscles; she worked wonders. Imposed immobility gave him the space and discipline to become immersed in the classics. He read Dickens, Thackeray, Trollope, Hardy, Kipling, Hazlitt, Walter Scott, R.L. Stevenson, Conan Doyle, P.G. Wodehouse, *The Bible*. He was captivated, above all, by Dickens. He thought about words, played games with words, his first romance was with words. [18]

I had found this so fascinating, reflecting on my own experience of going to the 'Public Free Library' in New Amsterdam, British Guiana, touching and smelling the new books — anticipating the reading, then reading them avidly, quickly, and feeling ambivalent that I was nearing the end. I had asked Jock if he read 'library' books. He said that he would not have known what a library was in those early days: they had a substantial collection at home and he could order whatever he fancied. That was the only time I really envied him his boyhood.

In those worlds sculpted by the classics, Jock found space to express his emotions, possibilities for personal adventure and freedom, pursuit of the truth that the severe, Presbyterian upbringing and its certainties tended to limit. He had discovered an instrument of self-realisation, a means of assessing, of shaping a critical instinct. It is interesting that his first conscious 'political influence' came from Dickens, particularly his *American Notes* and *Nicholas Nickleby*. He consciously empathised with the black slave, as he had done, unconsciously, with the golliwog dolls, earlier. He thought then that slavery was a peculiarly American sin.[19] He would not have been able to reconcile it with the romance fed to him of sugar in Demerara — a world of adventure and exotic peoples, an image heightened by his parents' periodic visits to the plantations, captured in family albums and copious film footage. He had no notion whatsoever that his ancestors were once involved with the ghastly system, that they owned slaves in British Guiana; that aspects of the old inhumanity had survived on their plantations.

The recovery from polio fed another passion — ball games and a fiercely competitive spirit. It is noteworthy that the Barringtons were keen sports people, promoters of organised team sports. Jock became an excellent driver of fast cars, expensive ones, and an avid player of games: table tennis (he told me that it thrilled him once to beat Garry Sobers), lawn tennis, darts, golf, squash, croquet, cricket. His father was not a competitive man but he did play one first class cricket match for Sussex when the great Ranjitsinhji played for them; he also knew the elegant batsman Frank Woolley of Kent. It was as if the polio attack and his remarkable recovery demanded some expiation, the assertion of his manly powers. He had been told that his muscles had come close to atrophy. The competitive spirit, his obsession with ball-games and crosswords, the will to win, were like an eternal celebration of the recovery of body (and mind): a triumphal retreat from the abyss. He could never bear to lose; this meant also that he would not dare to venture if there was a likelihood of failure. Conservatism nestled ineluctably with his sense of adventure.

It is interesting that Jock never played contact sport; he could not countenance the possibility of violent contact and the sight of blood. A profound antipathy to crudity and violence lodged in him. He explains:

> I used to hear my grandmother [in Ireland] — a formidable lady
> — talking to her sisters and her cousins and aunts about 'the
> Irish situation'. My cousin, Winnie Barrington, from Glenstal
> Castle was shot dead [by the IRA in 1921] .... I spent most of my
> time with grooms, gardeners and farm-hands, and the splendid
> Glenstal gamekeeper, Tom Hayes. He unintentionally put me
> off blood sports for life by tying a rabbit by its legs onto a long
> piece of string and making me shoot at it with a 4.10 gun....[My

family] liked shooting; I didn't. I loathed blood sports. I hate aggression. I hate roughness. I hate rudeness.[20]

Jock observed that his obsession with sports coincided with his discovery of girls, of falling in love with a girl name Phyllis Alley. Cars, games, girls — these were of a piece. In 1929, aged 17 and recovered from polio, his mother intervened to express disapproval of what she saw as too much time being spent with girl-friends, although it involved no sex: 'pre-marital sex was a deadly sin'.[21] His retort was bitingly quick, with literary aptness. He quoted Ogden Nash: '...one would be in less danger of the wilds of the stranger if one's own kith and kin were more fun to be with'.[22] But the claims of the privileged path, the beaten track of old certainties, were resilient; so too was the call of the 'other'.

In 1964 *The Times* reflected on the character of this fascinating, paradoxical man:

Liberal and radical though he may be, he is not doctrinaire. The whole pattern of his life has been anti rather than conformist and he has rebelled against the conventions of most of his environments.... Except under the closest scrutiny he is a man of contradictions. He hates power but enjoys influence. His dislike of political machines does nothing to quench an abiding interest in politics ... Campbell sent his sons to Eton and admits to the advantages of his own sequestration at Eton and Oxford. He is a member of the Oxford University Appointments Committee and of the Court of Governors of the London School of Economics, but he employs people intuitively without too much regard for their social and academic background. A tense yet kindly man, he drives fast cars very fast and, despite his earlier poliomyelitis, is a good athlete, playing games with a demonic determination to win. Although professing nervousness about making speeches his written work has eloquence, due perhaps to his devotion to 18th and 19th century novelists.[23]

The germ in the making of the man is traceable in this discerning estimate.

Endnotes

1. Jock Campbell, interview by the author, Nettlebed, Oxfordshire, July 23, 1992, Tape 2. (I am grateful to Colin Campbell for a copy of the Campbell family tree.)
2. Ibid.
3. Ibid.
4. Jock Campbell, interview by the author, Nettlebed, Oxfordshire, July 24, 1992, Tape 6.
5. Dom Hubert and Janssens de Varebeke, 'The Barringtons of Limerick', *The Old Limerick Journal*, no. 24 (Winter 1988): 5-10.
6. *Stabroek News* [Georgetown, Guyana], July 8, 1989.
7. Ivor Hubert, *The Way to the Top* (London: Robert Maxwell, 1969), 22.
8. See note 1.
9. 'A family Contribution', *The Old Limerick Journal*, no. 24 (Winter 1988): 3.
10. See Donal Ryan, 'The Barringtons and their Tenants', *The Old Limerick Journal*, no. 24 (Winter 1988): 63-7.
11. Ibid., 67.
12. 'Sir Matthew Barrington, Bart.: Obituary', *The Old Limerick Journal*, no. 24 (Winter, 1988): 18.
13. See note 6.
14. See note 1.
15. Jock Campbell, interviews by the author, Nettlebed, Oxfordshire, May 9, 1990, Tape 1; July 23, 1992, Tape 2.
16. Jock Campbell, interview by the author... July 23, 1992, Tape 2.
17. See note 15.
18. Ibid.
19. Jock Campbell, interview by the author, Nettlebed, Oxfordshire, February 18, 1994, Tape 10.
20. Jock Campbell's biographical sketch (mimeo.); Jock Campbell, interviews by the author, Nettlebed, Oxfordshire, July 23, 1992, Tape 2; February 18, 1994, Tape 10.
21. See note 1.
22. Ibid.
23. *The Times Review of Industry and Technology*, September 1964 [Appendix 1].

Chapter Four

BEYOND THE MOULD: DOWN AND UP FROM OXFORD

I don't like lying on beaches. I'm not very gregarious.
I'm not easily bored.

Jock Campbell

Jock's polio attack had an unforeseen, profoundly beneficial impact on his life. He was unable to take up his place at Trinity College, Cambridge; he went instead to Exeter College, Oxford, in 1930. He considered this a decisive watershed:

> Fortunately because of my polio I couldn't go to Trinity College, Cambridge where my family had been, where I would have been with other Etonians. I was at Oxford in a small college, Exeter, where there were no Etonians, so I got away from my family's terms of reference and that made me more politically aware because there were many politically aware people there.[1]

Jock was at Oxford between 1930 and 1933, during the Great Depression. His family's wealth, built on the labour of Africans and Indians in remote Demerara, insulated him from the pain and insecurity of want. But, as noted earlier, he could make no connection between his own privilege and their Guyanese plantations, which still called up exotic, romantic associations. Oxford of the early 1930s bred a radical temper: because of the Depression, he sought to comprehend unmitigated capitalism, the consequences of business purely for profits, with no moral compulsion, no sense of a broader social responsibility. This was still the time of a relatively unsullied

*Jock Campbell at
Oxford, 1932*

Soviet Union, when it was a kind of beacon, a source of idealism, the promise of the perfectibility of man. As a student of modern greats, politics, philosophy and economics, in a radical environment, he now had an intellectual framework to seek coherence of the range of inchoate ideas which battled for his young mind.[2] Jock's rebellious spirit, already kindled by his Irish experience and his empathy for their servants in Kent, thrived in this arena of freedom.

Oxford *was* freedom — freedom from his family's Presbyterian certainties, the severe moral codes; freedom, also, from his Etonian mould. The latter tended to foster a tribal instinct, suppositions of hierarchy and deference, notions of one's right to a place in the sun. The Campbell clan had its set code; impenetrable. Though not grand, it was rich, secured and confident in its own frame of reference. Business and religion were at its core; but its religion though morally punctilious, would brook no challenge to the established order: class barriers were sacred. The rich man in his castle may meet the poor man at his gate, but he would not invite him in.

Oxford was, as Jock recalls, the turning point in his life. He could savour the world beyond the mould. He encountered a wide range of fascinating, intelligent, imaginative people — British as well as foreign, many from the colonies. He spoke to atheists, people preparing for the clergy, philosophers, Rhodes Scholars, clever, literate, tolerant people. It was a microcosm of solid intellect, cultural and philosophical, beyond the confines of his class. Oxford enabled Jock to give intellectual depth, emotional security, to his immature mind; to build a foundation of embryonic ideas of justice and a vision of broader responsibilities: one could not elude being one's brother's keeper.[3]

He was discovering his limitations, his ignorance; and he was thrilled to do so. Retracing those spacious, exhilarating Oxford days for me, he would become excited, as if he were back there, receiving this gift of illumination: one could feel the mind being shaped. He was becoming aware that the world was a more complicated, complex place than he had thought. It would be wrong to assume that he was becoming political in the conventional sense. In fact, he was having 'a whale of a time'. Away from the discipline of his parents and Eton, he says that he was learning a lot about life. It was an education in the broadest, most comprehensive sense:

> It was getting to know different sorts of people, not in a patronising way; [whereas] the sort of family I grew up in — we weren't very grand but we were quite rich (a large family, the Irish and the Scots) — behaved in a certain way and had certain values. One went to church, and then to Eton, and then Cambridge; life seemed an easy thing: there was a mould there already. It was automatic what one did, and who one married. And then at Oxford I met all these different sorts of people...if I had gone to Trinity College, Cambridge [the family tradition], I would have probably become a banker or something of that sort. But, I think, it was only after the War that I consciously became a Fabian socialist.[4]

Jock continued to read omnivorously, widely: the classics, biography, history, philosophy and the popular writers of the day — Lawrence, Aldous Huxley, Wodehouse, W.W. Jacobs, Conan Doyle. Conscious of a new lease on life, after the polio and a discernible stammer, his senses were sharpened, acutely receptive to intellectual challenge. As noted earlier, he took to games the same consuming assiduity, the will to win. He would rather withdraw than lose or give a mediocre performance. Jock said that he was lazy at Oxford. He went to classes, read passionately, played games obsessively, spoke to radical people, but gave little time to the assigned coursework. That reeked too much of the mould he was seeking to escape.[5]

He had been given a Bentley. He drove it fast. He pursued girls and drove them around, fast, to London; frequently. His passion for girls, he believes, fed his competitive spirit that found expression in his avid pursuit of games as well. He was socially competitive — to impress the girls. Herein lies the paradox of the man: his empathy for Irish Catholics and their servants; his fascination with a radical, iconoclastic outlook stimulated at Oxford, juxtaposed with his love for the good life, the things that came with his upper class heritage. It is interesting also that his going beyond the mould did not vitiate many of the values absorbed through his family's frame of reference: thrift, ambition, and a Christian ethic, 'a sense of religiosity, however frayed it has become'. At the core of the latter was a revulsion for rudeness, an inviolable code of courtesy, and a stern sexual code.[6]

Rebellion and conformity were properties that permeated Jock Campbell's life. This would also be a life-long source of guilt, of angst, conducing to a severe flaw in this fascinating man: capitalist and socialist at the same time, eliciting incredulity from both sides. Jock came down from Oxford in 1933, a wiser, more confident young man but without a degree. He says that he was too 'idle'; he knew he would not get a good degree, so he did not take his finals. It was already a characteristic of the man that if he could not win, he would back away. His constitution, possibly because of the trauma of polio and the emphasis on ambition and winning in the family, could not absorb any suggestion of half-measures: failure was a tragedy; therefore, he would prefer not to play if winning was in doubt. But he would drive himself to breaking point if there were a slender chance of victory.

For a young man in Jock's position the degree was not all. The broader education had extraordinary merits. He now had intellectual gifts, quickness of thinking, considerable charm, a sense of humour, verbal dexterity and a declining stammer, a passion for games and evident mastery at several. His health was completely recovered, and he was born with 'a sugar spoon in his mouth'. He had not made up his mind what he wanted to do after he came down from Oxford, but he had no desire to go into his ancestral calling, the sugar plantation business in British Guiana.

Strangely, it was his family's stern sexual code that was to precipitate his being sent to Demerara (British Guiana), in 1934. Although Jock had had many girl friends at Oxford, his relations were all platonic, innocent petting. The Presbyterian moral strictures and the transcendental rectitude of the family made sexual adventures taboo; guilt also was a built-in sanction to infringement of the prescribed codes. In the context of the time, conformity however testing or frustrating, was easier to adhere to.

One girl, Olga Webb, evoked greater passions in Jock, but a stern reprimand from the family. He was besotted with her. He did go to bed with her, but they did not have sex. Olga was beautiful; she and Jock played tennis all the time; she was so good she had played on the Centre Court at Wimbledon. She was older than him. That was not a problem: the trouble was that she was 'suburban', below his station, certainly not eligible for a Campbell. On this and similar matters of status, he says, his censorious family were still imprisoned in an Edwardian frame of reference: the upper class were always one generation behind in their attitudes. The matter became a crisis in early 1934. His uncle caught him and Olga in a state of heightened passion on their tennis court. Jock was sexually incompetent; he still retained his virginity but the family were resolved to prise him away from this obviously lascivious, common girl: 'My father told Olga's father who was far less surprised and concerned than my father .... [H]er family had a house in Wimbledon, very suburban.' Jock characterised his family's response as 'a lot of pretentious balls', but he succumbed to the pressure from the 'authorities'.[7]

They recommended a cooling off period, a time for introspection. They suggested that he should go out to their sugar plantations in British Guiana. He still had no idea what he wanted to do; he had no interest in sugar; he was reluctant to go out to the colony. He says that he was bribed to do so: he was allowed to go there by a circuitous route, to Hawaii (an important sugar producer), then Hollywood, through the Panama Canal and the Spanish Main to Trinidad and British Guiana.

He deferred to his family. He was instantly fascinated with the sugar culture of Hawaii: sugar really was in his blood. He had a wonderful interlude in Hollywood where, as at Oxford, his enjoyment did not involve sex, alcohol or tobacco. He still retained an abstemious, Presbyterian outlook on the so-called good life. The old certainties had the power to clip recalcitrant wings. He never saw Olga Webb again. She went to India, married a schoolmaster and died in childbirth in the late 1930s. Her son survived and Jock recalled meeting him several times, years afterwards, at Wimbledon.[8]

Jock said often that he was conscious of being a Celt, of not having any Anglo-Saxon blood; that the head and the heart battled constantly, the Scottish and Irish side of his ancestry. Contradictions, paradoxes, were built into the man, so too was the imagination that drove him beyond the mould. That was why young Jock Campbell who landed at Georgetown, British Guiana in 1934 (aged 22), during the Depression, was a potentially uncharacteristic planter. His way of seeing was already shaped by a religiosity leavened by respect for the 'other', a sort of socialist instinct for the underdog, rooted in his experience in Ireland and Kent, and reinforced by his radical sojourn in Oxford and his people's class prejudices in prising him away from Olga. His discovery of the truth about his family's estates in Guyana — unmasking the romance — fortified him in his progressive outlook. He had sugar in his blood; the old authority was sacrosanct; but his roots in it would enable him — even the novice — to challenge many of the sacred assumptions of the plantocracy.

Peter Parker has written on the young man and the illumination the discovery of British Guiana planted in him:

> Jock had been born rich...[He] went to Eton and graduated into a bit of a tearaway with fast cars and fancy-free ways. He had a wild temper and a stammer that can only have fuelled the rages. Half-Irish, he never lost a rebelly-boy look about him, ever. Then he was sent to British Guiana and had the shock of his young life; his romping life of plenty had been based on the poverty he now saw. Those were the hard times of the Thirties when a ton of sugar sold for as little as the price of a cricket ball. All Jock's abundant energy was converted to a faith that Booker had to mean something in a new deal for the West Indies .... Demerara was his Damascus. And the stammer disappeared, almost completely.[9]

Endnotes

1. *Stabroek News*, July 8, 1989.
2. Jock Campbell, interview by the author, Nettlebed, Oxfordshire, May 9, 1990, Tape 1.
3. Jock Campbell, interview by the author, Nettlebed, Oxfordshire, July 23, 1992, Tape 2.
4. Ibid.
5. Ibid.

6. Jock Campbell, interview by the author, February 18, 1994, Tape 10.

7. Jock Campbell's biographical sketch (mimeo.), n.d.; Jock Campbell, interviews by the author, May 9, 1990, Tape 1; July 23, 1992, Tape 2.

8. See note 3.

9. Sir Peter Parker, *For Starters: The Business of Life* (London: Jonathan Cape, 1989), 99.

Part 2

The Guyanese Sugar Plantation and the Making of a Reformer: 1934-1940

Chapter Five

DEMYSTIFYING THE ROMANCE OF DEMERARA SUGAR: CAMPBELL'S APPRENTICESHIP IN BRITISH GUIANA, 1934-37

When Jock arrived in British Guiana in 1934, he felt 'totally different' about life. The contrast between Guyana of the imagination — shaped by old family narratives, the boyhood fantasies, the 'romance' of Demerara — and the reality of plantation life was stark. He explains:

> I so clearly remember the moment I arrived in Guyana: the smell, absolutely everything; it was the most extraordinary thing to feel that this was my spiritual home, then the extraordinary contrast between the romance, the vision and the reality; but enough closeness for me to try to turn the vision into reality. It was very odd; it was almost like a sort of spiritual experience.[1]

The reality was dismal. The Campbells owned La Penitence Wharf, on the Demerara River, to the south of Georgetown, the capital. They also owned Plantation Ogle (East Coast Demerara), and the larger estate, Albion, on the healthier, less malarial Corentyne Coast in Berbice. His first job was at the wharf where he worked on steamers' claims, a rather prosaic task involving the assessment of requisitions by merchants who had their merchandise broached, broken or stolen. The Campbells were agents for the Harrison Line of shippers. Jock recalled a claim from a 'B.G. Pawnbrokery'. He thought it was an Indian name; he had no notion of a pawnbrokery. Nothing in his world would have prepared him for such an institution: pawning one's personal belongings in return for a small sum of money to tide one over perennial financial crises. Jock replied promptly: 'Dear Mr. Pawnbrokery': 'I just thought the people had a lot of funny names.'[2]

*The Curtis Campbell wharf at La Penitence, British Guiana, in the
early 1930s: men unloading barrels of molasses. Jock worked here
first during his Guyanese apprenticeship in 1934-37.*

He was soon introduced to the two worlds of British Guiana: that
of privilege, of planters and their attorneys and merchants, and the
harsh world of African and Indian labourers. The Georgetown Club,
the epitome of white, affluent colonial society, was located next-
door to the Campbell family home, 'Colgrain House', on Camp Street,
Georgetown. He visited often and was 'outraged' by the obscurantism
of this institution, where the plantocracy and the colonial rulers
shared an intimacy. He was constantly told: '[Y]ou can't trust a coolie
and I remember ... almost everything anybody said to me shocked
me'. At their wharf, however, he befriended several African workers:
Joe White, Hendricks and the coopers. He found these men, contrary
to what he had been told about them, competent, most interesting,
loyal workers. They soon confided in him: 'I got to know the wharf
workers [by name] quite well, because they used to come and talk to
me and unburden themselves, and I used to get them out of
difficulties.'[3] He always believed in getting the name right — a lesson
he learnt from his own family who never bothered to know the first
names of servants.

After a few months in Georgetown, Jock was sent out to Plantation
Albion, on the Corentyne, where he spent 18 months in 1935–37.
This was probably the single most important experience in the young

man's life. For the first time he experienced a collision between his idyllic images of the sugar estates, the romance of his boyhood, and the poverty of Indian coolies, a word with bleak associations of servitude. He was appalled and stimulated immediately by the world of sugar. The life-long fascination was taking shape. He was quickly enthralled by sugar agronomy: the bewildering man-made environment, the complex hydraulic system which owed everything to the Dutch colonisers and their African slaves in the latter half of the eighteenth century, when the Campbells acquired their slave plantations. The engineering complexity of the factory and the delicate art of sugar manufacturing also claimed young Jock's inquisitive mind; he learnt to boil a pan of sugar. But he was quickly 'conscious of the awful conditions'. He would recite a version of the seminal tale, over and over, the signature of his Guyanese awakening: 'I remember saying to James Bee [the manager of Albion]: "Why do you have much better stables for the mules than you do housing for the workers?"; and he said "Because it costs money to replace mules."'[4]

James Bee profoundly shaped Campbell's awakening. He recalled that he was a 'very narrow-minded, dictatorial man ... a hard-headed Scottish autocrat'.[5] Jock spoke often of the authoritarian character of the sugar plantations where the managers and overseers and other supervisory personnel lacked 'imagination'. He recalled: '[T]he smallest things were treated as crimes ... the most extraordinary things people were sacked for, or made off for ... [things] they had never done or somebody else had done; it was absolutely incredible.'[6] Campbell added that the workers often were still treated as chattels; it was therefore difficult to erase the culture of mutual suspicion.

Jock lived with the Bees during his Corentyne sojourn. He would study the autocrat at close range. Old Bee would recline in a 'Berbice' chair with a bell attached to it. He rang it to demand another drink of his servants or to command instant service for the most absurd errand: once installed in his chair, he would do nothing for himself. This appalled Jock. He would often intervene to ask Mr and Mrs Bee to temper their chronic rudeness to their servants. He noticed also that the overseers, poor young Scots, who boarded with the Bees, were assigned to a corner of the dining room, during meals.

Campbell said that although Bee ran a successful estate at Albion, he was, even as a young novice, determined to mend little things, to try to foster more civilised attitudes. Many of the managers and overseers were Scots, farmers' sons who were good planters of cane but rather unpolished, with accents that were unintelligible to the workers. They were 'the salt of the earth in industry; we never could have done without them in field or factory; they were marvellous but they were tough'. They were paid about £100 per year and lived in 'appalling lodgings ... no nonsense about clubs and houses when I started'.[7] They were 'not confident', and this insecurity was reflected in a demonstrable coarseness, a crudity of manner in their dealings with workers. The insecurity showed.

Jock had the authority in Curtis Campbell and Co, to 'get a lot of little things put right quite quickly'. He was the young boss at Albion and Ogle in 1935–37, the estates being the property of his father and his father's brother. He gave an example of what he would later see as a motto, 'the importance of small causes': 'I was able to start ensuring that the wharf workers had water to drink on tap, little things like this.' As noted above, he firmly opposed rudeness to workers. He found that especially reprehensible. An upper class boy, it was taught to him that one must never be rude to servants. His parents never deviated from good manners, reinforcing the idea, however conceited, that one could not be rude to those below one's class. Jock noted: 'They'd never be rude to them; they might fire them; they might make them cry, but they would never be rude to them.'[8] This was imbibed, too, during his early years in Ireland, where rudeness to game-keepers and farm-hands was totally unacceptable.

This was a moral imperative to Jock. He extended to his employees what he always lived by — courtesy and good manners:

This, I think, I got from my mother who was very Irish and she was very tender-minded .... I think ... if you are half-Scot and half-Irish your head and your heart are always at war with each other and I think my heart is uppermost really and I find it difficult to hurt anybody. I've always said I loathe power, I like influence; I hate power and aggression; I hate roughness; I hate rudeness.... [O]f course, seeing overseers being rude to work people in Guyana and managers being rude and managers' wives being rude, I couldn't help my hackles rising really, and I was in a position to change this, which I never would have been able to do if I hadn't been who I was [a Campbell] .... I would have been sacked in the first week if I had been an ordinary employee.[9]

Campbell visited Port Mourant regularly, the estate next to theirs on the Corentyne. There, uncharacteristically, the manager, J.C. Gibson, was an Englishman. Jock saw him as 'a tough manager but a just man .... [H]e was feared but he was respected and he was different altogether from Bee'. He met Gibson often (he had a beautiful daughter). Jock learnt a lot from him about management. Gibson had built a small railway to transport workers to the distant cane-fields. He had provided land on the plantation for the workers to grow rice and rear cattle. Jock felt the people at Port Mourant were discernibly more independent, confident and ambitious. He was sure that Gibson's initiatives, coupled with a healthier climate and a less malarial environment, bred a vastly superior type of worker, less cringing, more assertive: 'I was ...very impressed with the physique and ability, the resolution and [a] sort of independence of the front-line workers.'[10]

Gibson was a better organiser of a big concern; he was more self-assured than many of the Scottish managers; he brought a more 'conscious attitude' to his relations with his workers. This impressed Jock. However, Gibson was no great reformer and Jock recalled that he 'tangled with him over my views for reform, even in those days ... [although] my reforming zeal didn't come into play until after the War', by which time Curtis Campbell had been absorbed by the conglomerate, Booker Bros, McConnell and Co. But Gibson's self-confident workers at Port Mourant stayed with Campbell, a vivid demonstration of possibilities for change.

In 1929, five years before Jock went to British Guiana, the Olivier Commission (headed by the Fabian socialist thinker and administrator, Sydney Olivier), visited the Caribbean to examine conditions on the sugar plantations, on the eve of the Great Depression. They inspected several Guyanese estates in November 1929. The secretary of the Commission was a Colonial Office official and scholar, Sydney Caine, who later became a friend and virtual mentor of Jock Campbell. He, also, had Fabian socialist tendencies, which influenced Jock when he worked with him at the Colonial Office during the War. Caine was appalled by the conditions under which women, in particular, worked in British Guiana. After visiting Plantation Diamond (this was not a Campbell estate), he wrote to his wife in London:

> We passed a group of women lunching by the bank; they were engaged in weeding amongst the canes ... it was a difficult and hot job as the canes at that stage grow 8 to 12 feet high and their leaves are closely interlocked. After we had passed these women we saw them all wading waist-deep across the trench or canal — all the fields are practically surrounded by the trenches and intersected by smaller ones for drainage. *So the population is practically amphibious* [emphasis added].[11]

Of Blairmont Estate, on the estuary of the Berbice River, Sydney Caine had a brighter view. He noted that it was owned by the Davson family, 'a very wealthy family with brains as well, who largely run New Amsterdam', the town on the other side of the river. Col Ivan Davson represented the family in the colony. Caine observed in November 1929:

> Blairmont is well organised on the scientific and accounting side and they do a lot in trying out new ideas. I suspect Col. Davson of being a bit of a theorist and the place is hardly large enough to carry the expense of some of his highly organised methods, but it is good to meet someone who is really anxious to progress and the place has quite cheered Semple [a member of the Commission] up .... Blairmont itself has 'model' cottages ... it also goes in for a light railway to carry the labourers 'up back', i.e. from the main road to the fields miles away, so saving them a long walk and a few wades through canals and trenches. Altogether an enlightened place.[12]

Only two estates had constructed these light railways, the other being Gibson's Port Mourant. The Olivier Commission had commented on the difficulties posed for plantation workers by the absence of this facility elsewhere:

> The labourers on the sugar estates live on the 'front lands' of the estates ... along the seashore or river front, and as the cane-fields are often many miles inland, they must walk along the 'dams' which are often muddy and almost impassable and, in many cases, wade waist-deep through irrigation trenches to reach their work, returning the same way in the evening.[13]

Jock visited Blairmont often in 1935–37, when he was based at Albion. Like Caine he was impressed by the reforming temper of the Davsons. As early as 1920–21 they had initiated a cricket tournament, the Davson Cup, which remained the symbol of cricket supremacy in Berbice until the 1970s. In 1933, the year before Jock went to Guyana, they had brought an eminent Italian malariologist, Dr George Giglioli, to Blairmont, to begin research on the dreaded malaria. This great man was responsible for its eradication by the end of the 1940s. The Davsons were the pioneers of reform on the sugar plantations — the beacon that guided Jock Campbell's reforming temperament.

He used to drive from Albion to the Davson's mansion in New Amsterdam. They had been old friends: like his own family, several of them had gone to Eton. They were of 'a sallow complexion'; Evelyn Davson was 'quite coloured'. Even they could not escape the racial prejudices of the real whites. Jock relates:

> When my father was at Eton, my grandfather [W.M. Campbell] wouldn't have one of the Davsons [stay over]; he was called 'Nigger Davson' [Evelyn]. [Years later] he was reading one of the Littlehowser books in the White's Club and read a bit about 'They do these things better in the West Indies; the coloured families like the Davsons' have done this, that or the other. So he rushed off to his lawyer and said he was going to sue Littlehowser for libel. And so the lawyer had to tell him that (1) calling a man 'coloured' wasn't libellous; (2) it was true.[14]

In fact, Sir Edward Davson's father had married a black lady. Jock admired them immensely. As noted above, it was largely through their imagination in taking Dr Giglioli to Blairmont that malaria was eventually conquered. Theirs was the first estate with glass windows in workers' cottages; the first to dismantle the logies, the abysmal ranges (Jock likened them to pig sties); first, too, to have clubs and swimming pools for workers. From their enlightened managers at Blairmont, Gordon and Guy Eccles, and Sir Edward Davson himself, Jock learnt an 'enormous amount' in his early years, in the 1930s, as he reflected on how to change life on the sugar estates. He recalled:

> Oddly enough Gordon and Guy Eccles and Edward Davson were very, very staunch Conservatives yet they were doing things in health, housing and so on. They regarded this simply as a social thing ... they didn't see it as a political issue at all — they were just jolly good employers ... they were extremely helpful to me.[15]

Jock Campbell's apprenticeship in British Guiana, in his early 20s, between 1934 and 1937, shaped his outlook decisively; it gave him a mission:

> I had been brought up with such a romantic idea of the sugar industry in Demerara and to go out and find not only the way people were treated but the terrible houses, tumbled down factories — dirty, no gardens, no trees — these awful houses, these awful logies (planters despising the coolies and blacks)....
> The whole thing so totally disgusted me I did have to make a conscious decision: shall I pack it in or shall I try to make a go of it? This was a very profound experience.[16]

Campbell now felt impelled to change the plantation culture he encountered in British Guiana.[17] The discovery of that dark world, past and present, inspired guilt which nourished his vision: 'I have always been conscious of the shame of my family having been slave-owners; we weren't, fortunately, slave-traders.'[18]

But without the exemplary reforms of Sir Edward Davson and Guy Eccles, at Blairmont, Jock might not have 'put down his bucket' in British Guiana in the 1930s. These were a solid demonstration of what was possible. It is noteworthy, therefore, that while he was serving his apprenticeship in Berbice, *The Berbice Chronicle*, in February 1936, welcomed Sir Edward as if he were a native son: 'Sir Edward has assured us that he is always happy whenever he is among us. We can assure him that the feeling is reciprocal, for all Berbicians are intensely proud of the connection of the Ancient County with so distinguished a family. There is only one grievance, and that is, that these visits are much too few and far between'.[19]

Nearly four decades after Jock had been fired by the energy and progressive temper at Blairmont, he reflected on what it meant to him — it was the road to Damascus for the young apprentice. It was such an obviously decisive, seminal experience, and the imagery is so rich, I reproduce it in its entirety:

> It was windows in sugar workers' cottages 37 years ago in British Guiana that first made me aware of Guy Eccles. I had gone out to start working in my family's sugar business; and I was disillusioned by what I found.... [T]he labourers were treated as though they were sub-human. The most outward and visible sign of this inhumanity was housing conditions, which were deplorable beyond belief. After I had been in the colony for some months, I went to visit a sugar plantation called Albion [a Campbell estate] which meant crossing the Berbice river on a ferry. The ferry started from a sugar estate called Blairmont belonging to another family business — the Davsons. After a long and dreary journey [from Georgetown] through increasingly desolate surroundings on unspeakable roads, I was suddenly aware that we were on a surprisingly good road, and before I had a chance to ask how come this sudden stretch of civilised road, I saw a row of neat, well-painted cottages with glass windows — cottages the like of which I hadn't seen before. Other sugar workers had to live in ranges or huts. They certainly had no windows — only holes in the walls, to be covered against night or weather by boards or sacks. 'What', I asked, 'were these?' I was told they were Blairmont sugar workers' cottages — recently built. 'Crazy', I was told, 'They'll break the glass in no time.... There's a young manager at Blairmont called Eccles who thinks he is going to change the sugar industry'. But there was more to come. We soon came to a great expanse of mown lawn with houses for the overseers. And a club. And tennis courts. And a swimming pool. And incredibly, a gleaming, shining white factory. And in many ways, he understood the scourge of malaria in the sugar industry and employed an Italian malariologist, [Dr George Giglioli], to cure it. Now it was Guy Eccles at only 33 who, with

the support of the Davson family against all the odds, against all advice, had wrought this transformation. And, of course, *he hadn't only opened windows in sugar workers' cottages — he opened windows in men's minds including my own* [emphasis added].[20]

The workers themselves would ensure that Campbell's awakened outrage did not slumber.

Endnotes

1. Jock Campbell, interview by the author, Nettlebed, Oxfordshire, February 17, 1994, Tape 9.
2. Ibid.
3. Ibid.
4. Jock Campbell, interview by the author, Nettlebed, Oxfordshire, May 9, 1990, Tape 1.
5. Ibid; July 23, 1992, Tape 3.
6. See note 1.
7. See notes 1 and 4.
8. See note 1.
9. Ibid.
10. See note 5.
11. Sydney Caine to his wife, writing from Georgetown, British Guiana, November 1929. I am grateful to his son, the late Sir Michael Caine (1929–99), for providing me with photocopies of several of his letters from the colony.
12. Ibid.
13. *Report of the West Indian Sugar Commission* (Lord Olivier, Chairman), (London: His Majesty's Stationery Office, 1930), 94.
14. Jock Campbell, interview by the author, Nettlebed, Oxfordshire, July 24, 1992, Tape 6.
15. Ibid.
16. See note 1.
17. Jock Campbell, 'Development and Organisation of Booker Brothers, McConnell & Company Limited', Paper presented at The London School of Economics and Political Science (LSE), November 24, 1959, (mimeo.), 4-5; see also 'Speech by Lord Campbell of Eskan [to] the Fabian Society', October 22, 1969, (mimeo.).
18. Jock Campbell, interview by the author, Nettlebed, Oxfordshire, February 18, 1994, Tape 10.
19. *The Daily Chronicle*, February 19, 1936.
20. Jock Campbell, 'Eulogy at Memorial Service for Mr. Guy Eccles', (mimeo.), July 20, 1971.

Chapter Six

TROUBLE ON THE PLANTATIONS, 1935: WORKERS DEMAND CHANGE

Ian McDonald started to work for Jock Campbell, with Booker in British Guiana, when he graduated from Cambridge in 1955. He has tried to locate the source of Jock's crusade:

> [I]t seems what made a decisive impression on him was an extensive visit he made to Guyana [1934–7].... He says he was appalled at the state of the people on the sugar estates. That was the trauma if you like, the 'religious' experience, that made him determined that something must be done about the conditions on the sugar estates.[1]

This characterisation of Campbell's awakening, as a 'religious' experience, was no exaggeration. Indeed, for the rest of his life, virtually in every article, speech and interview, he would underline what amounted to a road to Damascus illumination in the mid-1930s, the foundation of his crusade for reform. Speaking in April 1966, on the eve of Guyana's independence, Campbell returned to the awakening inspired by this sojourn in the colony: 'Such radical political and social views as I now hold were formed by the shock to me, of recognition, of the conditions in which past members of my family had made considerable fortunes.'[2]

As noted before, his great-grandfather had left £1 million, while his grandfather, W.M. Campbell, who died in 1920, left £1.5 million — most of this the fruits of their plantations in British Guiana. Without the chastening experience of the years in the colony in the 1930s, Jock would not have comprehended the foundations of their wealth. For the rest of his life, he would repeat:

Conditions of employment in the sugar industry were a disgrace. Wages were low; housing unspeakable; workers were treated with contempt — as chattels not as human beings — animals and machinery were in fact cared for better than the workers because they cost money to replace.[3]

Campbell located the continuing unconscionable conduct of many managers in older forms of oppression on the plantations in Guyana:

The plantocracy had great power in Government — did all they could to prevent other industries in order to maintain a surplus of labour. This was an industry founded on slavery, continued on the indenture system, maintained on the exploitation of African and Indian workers.[4]

It was in this context of poverty and oppression of workers, a situation aggravated by the Great Depression, that his hitherto 'vague feeling of rebellion ... [became] a coherent force'. In late 1965 he pointed a correspondent to the same fount of his disgust: 30 years after his first visit to Bee's Albion, he could still remark that workers' housing was 'far worse than the stables in which the mules and horses were kept'. The correspondent added:

It was then that John Middleton Campbell ... who had no intention of becoming a permanent member of the family plantocracy [sic], changed his mind. He decided to mount a reformist 'crusade' from within the company, converting less sympathetic executives to his point of view by arguing that reform was in the company's own interests. The labourers, he contended, would not always be satisfied with the status of hewers of cane and drawers of rum, and the company would be the rightful target for revenge if it did not contemplate this emancipation.[5]

Indeed, the workers themselves were demanding change, although they had no recognised bargaining agent, since the so-called protector of immigrants, the Immigration Agent General, had lost his authority to represent Indian workers with the cancellation of the last indentures in April 1920. Indeed, while Campbell was still in the colony, the workers had ventilated their disgust, in a most militant fashion, at the appalling conditions on many of the estates. In September 1934 workers at Plantations Leonora and Uitvlugt, on the West Coast Demerara, went on strike. Their main grievances were inadequate wages; that task-work was not determined in advance; that the head-driver, Hassanalli, was 'overbearing and did as he pleased'; and that 'overseers generally and the deputy manager in particular cursed labourers unnecessarily'.[6] This was precisely what Campbell was referring to — the crude attitudes to workers, the absence of basic decency: a moral void.

In January 1935 the Acting Governor, C. Douglas-Jones, remarked of the strike on the West Coast that at 'no time did the disturbances get out of hand', although there were several threats of violence. He remarked perceptively: 'There is a growing spirit of unrest amongst the labourers on sugar estates in the colony.' He concurred with the workers that since the end of indentureship the practice of informing workers of the rate of pay for task-work, at the time the task was being assigned, had 'not been strictly observed'; this was a 'fruitful source of dissatisfaction'. Douglas-Jones exhorted the plantocracy to change their attitudes in view of advances in the educational level of Indian workers and their growing assertiveness. This would not have eluded young Jock Campbell undergoing his apprenticeship in British Guiana. The Acting Governor had warned:

> I incline to the view that the sugar interests are slow to realise the change which has taken place with regards the educational advancement of the younger East Indian labourers and, unless they are prepared to readjust their methods of dealing with their estate labourers, it is certain that labour troubles will increase.[7]

While conceding that the Depression dictated 'the most rigid economy' in order to stem the collapse of plantations, he deplored the award of 'considerable bonuses', over the previous two or three years, to managers and senior employees. He added: 'This fact is known to the labourers, and it is not unnatural that they should claim that if it is possible to pay these bonuses, it should be also possible to increase slightly the wages paid to them.'[8]

Douglas-Jones was forthright. He cautioned the planters to desist from premature requests for police intervention in disputes between management and workers, advising them to seek the help of the relevant civil authorities. He was trying to alleviate the infamous reputation of a colony, where the indiscriminate shooting of plantation workers had become a tradition. He was perspicacious in his admonition:

> Only as a last resort, and if the management is satisfied that life and property is threatened, should police protection be sought.... It is well known that serious trouble, which might otherwise have been avoided, may be created by the premature interference by Police Forces.... I do suggest that those controlling the sugar interests in this colony should appreciate the marked sociological change which is gradually, and even in some instances rapidly, taking place amongst the labourers.[9]

Campbell's seminal ideas for change were certainly driven by the recognition that the old attitudes could not be sustained: the plantocracy must change or perish. In 1935, however, they were not in a reforming frame of mind. Rooted in slavery and indentureship — the latter had only ended 15 years before — their instinct to navigate the hazardous economic times on the backs of the Indian and African workers was overpowering. Most of the factory workers were Africans, as were many of the seasonal task-gang cane-cutters, who did not reside on the estates.

In September and October 1935 the plantations were engulfed by a wave of strikes. It had started at the infamous Leonora Estate, West Coast Demerara, as was the case the previous year. The allegations with regard to the rates for task-work and the failure to declare such rates at the commencement of tasks were repeated. Allied to these was the charge of 'constant abuse by Mr. Rigden, the Head Overseer'. Other sources of disaffection were the apparently excessively long hours of work in the factory and even worse conditions for mule boys, who handled the mules hauling the cane-punts from field to factory, over many miles: 'sometimes only having two hours of sleep in 24 hours, when they got home at 1 o'clock in the morning and had to be out again at 3 o'clock'. Some complained that older women had to walk 'long distances' to get to the fields, while pregnant women were not offered light work.[10]

There was an epidemic of strikes on the East Coast Demerara plantations: Vryheid's Lust, La Bonne Intention (LBI), Enmore, Lusignan, Ogle (a Campbell estate); Farm, on the East Bank Demerara, also struck. Although the Berbice estates did not experience the same militancy, the task-gang cane-cutters, largely African, struck in October 1935, at Skeldon, Port Mourant, Albion (a Campbell estate) and Blairmont. What was extraordinary was the inordinate prominence of African workers in the strikes of 1935. As the Commission Report of the following year observed: 'A feature of the disputes and disturbances which we think is worthy of notice is that while the resident population is still predominantly East Indian [approximately 54,000 of 136,000 in the colony], the most active parts, particularly in the disturbances, were taken by Black Villagers.'[11]

In October 1935, at Plantation Ogle, a Campbell estate, the deputy manager, Mr Rausch, was manhandled by the workers. The manager reported his humiliation thus: '[Mr Rausch was] marching in front of a mob carrying a red flag. [He] reported to him having been beaten by the mob and made to carry the red flag. The crowd was comprised of East Indian and Blacks — about 200–300 waving cutlasses and sticks and carrying red flags'. These red flags were popular among African workers of the British Guiana Labour Union in Georgetown; from time to time this union sought to extend its influence on the plantations near to the capital.

At the same time, at Albion, where Jock was based in 1935, a strike of task-gang workers from Fyrish and Gibraltar, predominantly African workers, occurred. A labourer was prosecuted and convicted for assaulting a rural constable. The strike ended quickly but it probably dispelled whatever 'romance' with the plantations that might have survived Jock's Demerara awakening.

The Report of the Commission on the troubles of 1935 was published the next year. Campbell had attended some of its sittings in January 1936, as did J.C. Gibson, the manager of Port Mourant. The indictment of the plantocracy was scathing. In February 1936 the Director of Agriculture, Professor J. Sydney Dash, remarked that in spite of the Depression there had, in fact, been an increase in production and productivity in the sugar industry. Although sugar prices had declined from around $70 per ton in 1925–28, to $45.20 per ton in 1933, and $42.90 and $39.80 per ton in 1934 and 1935 respectively, the yield per acre rose steadily: 1.7 to 1.8 tons sugar per acre in the early 1920s; 2.18 tons per acre in the late 1920s; 2.61 and 2.54 tons per acre in 1933 and 1934 respectively.[12] In 1935, as Nigel Bolland observes, 'the yield of sugar per acre reached 3.02 tons and the total output was a record ... 178,041 tons, compared with the previous record of 148,634 tons in 1932.... The sugar workers were producing more sugar, and producing it more efficiently, but they continued to receive the same low wages.' He notes that there was an ethnic division of labour on the estates: resident workers were predominantly Indian; most of the factory workers and some of the cane-cutters were African. This had implications for wages earned: 'Whereas the average wage for all workers in the sugar industry in 1935 was said to be $112, that for Indians was less than $98, so that the majority of sugar workers who were of African descent were better paid'.[13]

It is important to note that the African minority in the plantation workforce demonstrated greater militancy in 1935. Most of the task-gang (cane-cutters) resided away from the estates and resorted to estate labour only during the cane harvest — 'a means of augmenting their incomes' from agricultural pursuits in the village. Africans generally were perceived as having a 'superior physique' to Indians. They were very conscious of their crucial role in harvesting cane, especially at a time when the yield and overall production were a record. Declining prices for sugar, however, had forced a reduction in wages. Meanwhile, unlike many resident Indian workers, as several Africans informed the Commission, they did not live rent-free, neither were they entitled to free medical attention on the estates. Moreover, as the Report observed, the Italian invasion of Ethiopia in 1935, the free ancient kingdom in the fatherland, exacerbated the discontent and sharpened anti-European sentiments. They could have added that since the 1920s Garveyism had helped to shape a deeper pride in their African antecedents. The Depression and the invasion of Ethiopia added fuel to the rebellious spirit ignited by Garveyism.[14]

The preponderance of Africans in the resistance of 1935, notwithstanding, the Report observed that Indian workers had many grievances as well: declining wages aggravated by surplus labour; the absence of a union or any other authority to articulate their discontent and seek redress. On the latter point, they elaborated: 'The interests of the proprietors of the sugar industry are watched and protected by the highly organised Sugar Planters' Association. On the other hand, labour is entirely unorganised, and is incapable of formulating its grievances in proper logical and reasonable form, and without the organised power which is necessary for securing a reasonable and just consideration of its representation by employers'.[15] Moreover, workers, including women, often had to walk six miles to get to the cane-fields, where there was no shelter from rain or sun. Access to these fields, as Sidney Caine had observed in 1929, invariably required 'wading through drainage and irrigation canals ... and jumping over numerous drains and banks'. Only two plantations had light railways to take their workers to the fields, the comparatively better Port Mourant and Blairmont, in Berbice.

The Report cited the evidence of an extraordinary overseer, Mr Pile, who was deeply sympathetic to the workers. He had remarked that punt-loaders, employed during the harvesting season, would normally work from 5 a.m. to 8 p.m. and mule boys (responsible for taking and returning punts between factory and field), from 4 a.m. to 10 p.m. or midnight. Cane-cutters in Berbice tended to work from 5 a.m. to 4 p.m.; those in Demerara 7 or 8 a.m. to 5 or 6 p.m.; while children from 7 a.m. to 5.30 p.m. Days of 16 hours were routine for factory workers in the grinding season.

Possibly the most serious indictment of the plantocracy during Campbell's sojourn in British Guiana in the mid-1930s, was the endemic fear of the estate czars like Bee and Gibson, harboured by workers, especially the Indians residing on the estates. The Report was damning:

> During our investigation *no resident estate labourer came forward voluntarily to give evidence.* We believe the cause to be fear — the fear of retaliatory action and possible eviction from house and subsistence plot with but three days' notice as provided under

the Employers and Servants Ordnance, and the knowledge that no alternative means of earning a livelihood is readily available [emphasis added].[16]

Jock Campbell was conscious of the fear that prevailed at Albion, under Bee's despotic regime, and had tried to counsel the authorities to be courteous to workers. The Commissioners, too, were so disturbed by the fear that permeated the plantations that they underlined its centrality to the pervasive incomprehension between the two worlds:

> Throughout our inquiry, in reply to interrogations as to why a labourer had not made known a grievance to his Manager, the reason given has in every instance been fear to do so; either fear of subsequent victimisation by Drivers [foremen], or fear that the labourer might be regarded as a ring-leader and evicted from the estate. To what extent such complaints are justified it is difficult to say, but admission by all Managers of estates who gave evidence before us that they had no knowledge whatever that trouble was impending on their estates, and that neither then nor since had they been able to discover the causes that gave rise to them, forces us to the conclusion that the complaints of the inaccessibility of the Managers to labourers are not entirely unjustified.... Although Managers may be willing to listen to and adjust grievances brought to their notice, we are of the opinion that under the present system, fear of incurring disfavour, resulting in retributory action and eventual eviction, deters labourers from making complaints.[17]

In October 1935 *The New Daily Chronicle* had contended that while discontent over the wage-rate permeated every dispute, the crude attitudes of white managers and overseers to their workers were underestimated as a contributory factor to the troubles. The paper cited the case of an 'East Indian girl' on an East Coast Estate, to enhance its submission. The 'girl' in question was a single-mother with two children. She earned four shillings per week. The overseer, having neglected to ascertain the quality of her work, paid her only two shillings, pending an inspection later. She implored the overseer to give her the full sum and if on examination her work was considered inadequate, a deduction could be made from her next earnings. The paper continued: 'The poor girl's distress did not touch the heart of the overseer whose neglect of his own duty was imposing hardship on her. Instead, the girl was rudely and shamelessly told by that overseer that if she wanted more money she could travel to Georgetown and try one of the brothels in the city! The news of this spread like wild fire on the estate and, we are informed, things started to happen.'[18] A few days later the paper repeated its stance: '...rates of pay were not always responsible for trouble arising, but very often the bullying and unkind treatment meted out to the labourers led to disturbances where otherwise the labourers most probably would have remained quiet'.[19]

This was the context of Jock Campbell's awakening in the mid-1930s. What would he have grasped from these seminal events that impelled him to stay with sugar, that linked him inexorably with the future of British Guiana? To the young man with inchoate ideas of change, they dramatised the inevitability of reform: the workers had had enough; change or perish. The business was at stake; he was ashamed of his family's record from slavery to the present; but without a thriving business nothing could be done to initiate change. He had grasped, however, that mild reforms, such as at Blairmont and Port Mourant, were already being attempted: structural and social — far too little, but a star by which to steer.

In February 1936 the Director of Agriculture, J. Sydney Dash, had explained the greater efficiency on sugar plantations since the start of the Depression in 1929 — better husbandry informed by scientific research. He noted the spread of the practice of flood-fallowing, in conjunction with constant monitoring of the results; detailed soil surveys of over half the acreage under sugar-cane, especially with regard to drainage and the application of fertilisers; improved irrigation systems; pest control; and the replacement of the old variety of cane, D.625, by higher yielding ones, Diamond 10 and P.O.S.2878. Dash underlined how important this new attitude to husbandry was to the survival of sugar culture on the hazardous coastland of British Guiana:

But for the remarkable increase in yield per acre the Colony's sugar industry would have already disappeared. This increased yield together with reduced expenditure [including lower wages] and the receipt of preference from the Imperial Government have combined to permit the continuation of the Colony's premier industry.[20]

Jock would have been impressed with the extolling of the reforms at Blairmont and Port Mourant in the Commission Report of 1936. These had already suggested to him the parameters of change. They observed that the resident population at Port Mourant was 5,878, of whom 2,188 were still living in the old ranges, the logies, while 3,690 had been re-housed in new, separate cottages: 127 of these were owned by the estates; 634 by the labourers themselves; the latter had an average of 4.84 persons. They explained the basis of the housing reform: 'In order to encourage labourers to own cottages the Estate advances the material for building, which is repaid on easy terms, the labourer paying a ground rent of one shilling per annum, and undertaking not to dispose of his house except to an approved purchaser. This scheme of housing, we were informed, has been in course of progress for 25 years and is giving very satisfactory results.'[21]

The Report noted that on some of the bigger plantations efforts were being made to replace the derelict ranges with their mud floors, with modern ones raised from the ground, even cottages, as at Blairmont and Port Mourant. It was not all darkness; the outline of a reformist spirit, though dim, was discernible: 'Practically all estates are now provided with artesian wells, a great improvement on the open canals that at one time provided the drinking water supply of estates. The medical care of labourers appears good, the hospitals in good repair and clean and efficiently run.' They concluded, perceptively: 'Plantation Blairmont appears to us a model of what an estate's hospital should be.'[22] No wonder Jock would point, time and again, to the example set by the Davsons on this progressive plantation which was pioneering research into malaria when the government doubted the possibility of ever eradicating the dreaded disease.

In February 1984, 17 years after Campbell had resigned as Chairman of Booker, he was reflecting on the prompting of his reformist vision in Guyana to Ian McDonald, shortly after the publication of Shahabuddeen's book on sugar. He wrote to him:

> I suppose I could claim that if I could not get the confidence of shareholders and bankers I could not do all the things I wanted to do. But the truth is that Guyanese pressures forced the pace; and enabled me to gain acceptance of reforms that never would have been accepted in a quiescent Guyana.[23]

Guyanese sugar workers and the occasional leader had a profound influence on the reformist philosophy of Jock Campbell, as did his first encounter with poverty in British Guiana in the mid-1930s. Among these indigenous shapers of change was an Indian goldsmith turned publisher and trade unionist, Ayube M. Edun.

Endnotes

1. Ian McDonald, interview by Frank Birbalsingh, February 5, 1992. See 'Brain Drain Hurting Guyana', *Indo-Caribbean World*, Toronto.
2. Jock Campbell, 'The Clash of Immigrant Coloured Races in British Guiana', Address to the Ministry of Education Commonwealth Course, [London], April 15, 1966, (mimeo.).
3. Ibid.; 'Speech by Lord Campbell of Eskan [to] the Fabian Society', October 22, 1969.
4. Ibid.
5. *The Scotsman*, December 7, 1965.
6. CO111/726/60036 [1935], Report by County Inspector, J. Nicole, October 3, 1934.
7. Ibid., C. Douglas Jones (OAG) to Cunliffe-Lister, no. 29, January 24, 1935.
8. Ibid.
9. Ibid.
10. CO111/732/60036 [1936], 'Report of the Commission of Inquiry into the 1935 Disturbances', (Legislative Council Paper No. 15 of 1936), [Appendix 1].
11. Ibid.
12. CO318/421/3, Northcote to J.H. Thomas, no. 66, March 5, 1936, encl.: 'Report on the Sugar Industry of British Guiana' by J. Sydney Dash (February 24, 1936).

13. O. Nigel Bolland, *On the March: Labour Rebellions in the British Caribbean, 1934-9* (Kingston: Ian Randle Publishers, 1995), 72-3.

14. See note 10; see also CO111/726/60036, Northcote to MacDonald, no. 238, telegram (confidential), October 17, 1935; Northcote to MacDonald, no. 241, telegram (confidential), October 23, 1935.

15. See note 10 [paragraph 66].

16. Ibid. [paragraph 64].

17. Ibid. [paragraph 10].

18. Leader, *The New Daily Chronicle*, October 26, 1935.

19. Leader, *The New Daily Chronicle*, October 30, 1935.

20. See note 12.

21. See note 10 [paragraph 53].

22. Ibid. [paragraph 47].

23. Jock Campbell to Ian McDonald and M. Shahabuddeen, February 9, 1984. I am grateful to Ian McDonald for copies of his correspondence with Jock Campbell in the late 1970s and early 1980s.

Chapter Seven

AYUBE EDUN, THE *GUIANA REVIEW* AND THE BIRTH OF THE MPCA, 1936-39: SUGAR WORKERS FIND A VOICE

Ayube Edun, founder of the Guiana Review *and the MPCA*

Ayube M. Edun (1893–1957), an Indian Guyanese of Muslim extraction, was the foremost champion of sugar workers in British Guiana from the late 1930s to the late 1940s, before the rise of Cheddi Jagan. His grandfather, Edun (1822-1904), was an indentured labourer who became 'head driver' at Plantation Philadelphia, West Coast Demerara. He later bought Orangestein Estate, but he remained a popular mediator in disputes between management and labour. When he died in March 1904, Hindus, Muslims and more than 200 Africans attended his funeral — a testimony to his integrity.[1] His grandson, Ayube Edun, absorbed his empathy with the underdog in spite of his middle-class status.

Edun became a jeweller but he was determined to educate himself. He read voraciously to prepare himself to be a representative of his people. He was secretary of the British Guiana East Indian Association in 1927 and 1928 and visited London in the latter year. This visit gave him the vision that the British Empire was in urgent need of regeneration. Although Britain had been a leader of world civilisation she had 'ceased to lead for a decade. The progress of the British race has been cramped into definite gnomes and channels, archaisms and cul-de-sac....'[2] The travels in England gave him his book of 1935, *London's Heart-Probe and Britain's Destiny.*

Although Edun was a great admirer of Gandhi and was proud of the Indian struggle for *swaraj*, freedom, he retained a robust patriotism towards the Empire: 'I am a British citizen by birth — a fact in which I glory. I was born of pure-blooded Indian parentage in a distant outpost of the British Empire, on a sugar plantation, far away in British Guiana ... in a home that had for its floor the bare earth [a logie] ... [but] I think and feel pre-eminently British.'[3] For Edun the change had to be within the empire; reforms, however, required a transformation of the character of the state.

Capitalism, he felt, had contributed to the degeneration, but he was not enamoured of the redemptive powers of religion or communism. With regard to the former, he contended that 'civilisation has been possible in spite of [it].... It is the outcome of the slow growth of man's intellect, which was able to discard superstition and unrealities for rationalism.' Neither was he enthralled by Russian Communism, Stalin's utopia, 'a regime of unique terror and extreme violence in its method of adaptation and procedure'. It stood 'condemned as a regime that had no heart, no human ideal'. But Edun was not devoid of a utopian vision of his own. He advocated a peculiar instrument for regeneration, for the shaping of the new man — the Rational-Practical-Ideal [RPI] State. It would comprise the following divisions, to which its citizens would be assigned, following 'accurate scientific statistics': 'Supreme Council of Intelligentsia — Intelligentsia — Transitory Intelligentsia — Man-Power Citizens (man-power of brains and hands) — Women-Citizens — Children of the RPI State — Disabled Citizens of Mental, Physical, Social Disabilities — Retired Citizens.'[4]

Ayube Edun's ideal state bore a fearfully uncanny resemblance to the Communist, Stalinist state: it would be the 'inviolable controller' of production and distribution, catering to 'each citizen's equal need'; 'no non-essential luxury must be permitted in the R.P.I. state'. Moreover, no parent must 'tamper with the child's imagination. The R.P.I. state must be solely responsible for children's educational career, which must be constructed on R.P.I. principles'. Apparently the Supreme Council of Intelligentsia would provide the core of the leadership, in order to 'mobilise the citizens' man-power according to the general need of all'.[5]

However bizarre and impractical were Edun's ideas, the idealism, the visionary in him, paradoxically, elicited a pragmatic response to the challenge thrown up by the sugar workers strike in 1935. He launched a radical newspaper, *The Guiana Review*, in November 1936. It provided an ongoing critique of colonial society and was untiring in its indictment of the plantocracy; it was the voice of the sugar worker. In September 1935 a popular Indian correspondent had bemoaned the poverty of leadership among Indians, and called for the revamping of the British Guiana East Indian Association to enable them to advance their political rights. He felt that the predominantly African British Guiana Labour Union was 'not qualified' to represent Indian workers — it was, indeed, 'a sorrowful reminder' of the activities of that Union at Ruimveldt in 1924, when 12 Indian sugar workers were killed.[6] In October 1935, in an open letter to 'our Indian people', he cautioned them not to be duped into violent protest again by African agitators:

> You have had your grievances and have in this particular manner shown your disapproval of conditions under which you live. Strikes are no good; but if you must strike, then I exhort you to follow in the footsteps of our beloved Mahatmaji in India. Do not use force...I can understand your feeling. I have lived under identical conditions nearly all the days of my life...[but] I exhort you to resort to no other force than reason. The Indian people with its thousands of years of culture have always been noted for their docility and reasonableness; and I expect that you will at this crisis show the meekness and readiness to reason that have made our people so famous. I warn you Indians of the estates not to listen to trouble-mongers. I warn you not to pay attention to the villagers who come to incite you [Africans]. I warn you not to pay any attention to emissaries of the Labour Union.[7]

On the eve of the convening of the Labour Commission, in January 1936, the correspondent observed that the lacuna in leadership was especially deplorable because it was the field labourers, predominantly Indian, who were 'the real producers of the wealth of the estate'; they, therefore, deserved a better deal. This perceptive commentator predicted that 'fear of expulsion' from the ranges on the estates would deter Indians from appearing before the

Commission; they were 'hopelessly organised'; they could not present a coherent case — they had no money, no union.[8]

The colonial state was transparently remiss in its attitude to workers' representation. Even after the troubles in October 1935, the Governor, Sir Stafford Northcote, could not elude the plantocratic mould. In December 1935 he informed the Colonial Office that he was nominating two of the most senior representatives of sugar to the crucial, policy-making body, the Executive Council, of which he was chairman. They were F.J. Seaford, head of Booker in the colony, and M.B.G. Austin, senior attorney of Jock Campbell's family firm, Curtis Campbell. Northcote rationalised Seaford's nomination on grounds that he was 'the best informed man with regard to drainage and irrigation' in the colony, with the possible exception of the Director of Public Works, whom he was *not* renominating.[9] That the plantocracy were notoriously obdurate in opposing drainage and irrigation, as Jock discovered in 1934–37, that this was a chronically emotive issue (a chasm between planter and people), did not seem to bother the Governor; neither did the popular assumption of entrenched collusion between the state and the sugar planters.

The Colonial Office detected this planter bias and noted that 'it was a little unfortunate ... that so many members of the Legislative and Executive Councils have interests in sugar, but I suppose the reason is that most of the ablest unofficials in the colony were interested in the industry'.[10] Northcote had anticipated objections to these nominations from the British Guiana Labour Union, representing African workers in Georgetown, and the British Guiana East Indian Association, two prominent ethnic organisations, which had secured no nominations to either of the Councils. With typical condescension he contended that 'the best way in which they can serve members of their communities is to give full and frank evidence on all points which they consider relevant to the Commission and leave it to a highly competent and impartial Commission to probe them'.

In August 1936 the Commission bemoaned 'the non-existent machinery for mediation' on the plantations since the end of indentureship, but they did not recommend the formation of a trade union, following the precedence of the British Guiana Labour Union, which was registered in 1919 and recognised in 1922. As noted earlier, they regretted that workers could not articulate their grievances in a 'logical and reasonable' manner, with the 'organised power' to secure a 'just' response from employers, while the Sugar Planters' Association was a 'highly organised' instrument. However, their conclusion was rather innocuous: 'In order to remedy the unequal situation ... we recommend that Government takes early steps to create some authority clothed with some powers as are considered necessary for the efficient safeguarding of the interests of both employed and employer'.[11]

This, therefore, was the context in which Ayube Edun founded his newspaper, *The Guiana Review*, in November 1936, a prelude to the launching of his union for sugar workers, the Manpower Citizens' Association (MPCA), in November 1937. The Union sought immediately to fill the void in leadership, addressing a range of problems that so shook the planters' complacency that the Sugar Planters' Association deemed it subversive, refusing to concede recognition. 1936 and 1937 had been years of quiescence, with two and four strikes respectively; but 1938 brought an epidemic of strikes, as the MPCA battled for recognition, although this was articulated within the parameters of industrial issues. Basdeo Mangru summarises the events:

> [There were] widespread strikes and violence in the colony's sugar belt and in several Caribbean islands. During the first nine months of 1938 there were 32 disputes in British Guiana involving approximately 12,500 resident field labourers out of 13,000. Of these disputes 25 originated in inadequate pay, 3 in other wage questions and 4 in the employment of certain headmen. During the strikes 177 workers were convicted; 102 for disorderly conduct, 43 for assaults, 20 for malicious damage to property, 11 for obstruction of justice and 1 for threatening behaviour. Among those convicted, 3 were imprisoned, 60 signed bonds to keep the peace and the remainder paid fines ranging from $2.50 to $26.00.[12]

Mangru elaborates on the context of this militancy. Although the MPCA had been registered on November 5, 1937, it was 'extremely difficult' to recruit members, as the planters were inclined to 'intimidate, victimise and evict' those who tried to join the union.

He adds that the violence in 1938 at Port Mourant, Albion, and Cane Grove 'resulted directly from eviction notices served on local organisers ... [of] trade union activities'. At Albion, the Campbell estate on the Corentyne, the police had considered the situation one of 'general intimidation and disorder': the overseers' quarters were looted; vehicles denied access to the estate; telephone wires were cut; people were prevented from leaving.[13]

Yet *The Guiana Review* claimed on November 6, 1938, the first anniversary of the MPCA, that the union had a membership of 'not less than 10,000'; but added that 'its success has resulted in a kind of panic on the part of Vested Sugar Interests [sic], and every conceivable kind of tactics — mean and otherwise — had been employed in order to crush the Association in the bud. Our members have been victimised, repressed, black-listed and provoked, the Executive had been maligned, abused and cursed, and despite all these pernicious practices, the Association has emerged triumphant.'

The Review emphatically denounced the bigotry of the plantocracy. It had no doubts that the workers were setting an agenda for change; they were unstoppable: 'No matter what the tin-gods of Sugardom may do, the workers have been injected with the lofty theme of co-operation, collective bargaining, and the need for economic redemption into their very souls'. The paper dramatised the resilience of the old attitudes of the planters, citing the reaction of even the reformist G.M. Eccles, the manager of the progressive Blairmont Estate, to the MPCA. It alleged that he offered financial help to his Hindu workers to stage a 7-day religious festival, *Bhagwat*, on condition that they keep away from the union. The leader continued:

> While this clever manager will be willing to feed the workers on 'spiritual grace' — for the After Life, he was not eager to give them money as increase on their wage so as to nourish their bodies to sustain their Physical Life.... As a matter of fact we have learnt that he has threatened a working lad with trespass prosecution for selling *The Guiana Review* on Plantation Blairmont. Mr. Manager Eccles has become so desperately afraid of shadows that he will not allow the people to read. It's a peculiar mentality indeed.[14]

This mentality was entrenched, as was evident in the interpretation by the chairman of Booker in London, Sir Alfred Sherlock, of the proliferation of strikes since the formation of the MPCA. In his address to the Annual General Meeting of Booker's shareholders, in January 1939, he argued: 'Two years ago I attributed our labour troubles to outside agitation of a malicious character, and today I am more than ever convinced that Communistic propaganda is really the principal cause; because, although conditions are not by any means perfect, our labourers are certainly very much better off than they have been at any time in the past twenty years.'[15]

Campbell was correct: the planters' attitudes to workers were deeply rooted in the old forms of oppression, slavery and indentureship. The prejudices against their workers surfaced even before the celebrated Moyne Commission, in Georgetown, in February 1939. The Sugar Producers' Association, in its memorandum, had reproduced a despicable excerpt from an article in the *West Indian Review* (June 1938), on the Jamaican peasant, alleging that it was 'substantially true' of their own workers in British Guiana:

> The Jamaican peasant is essentially a gay, light-hearted, emotional person, fatalistic in his attitude to life, and as a rule taking no thought for tomorrow. His main requirements are food, shelter, bright and attractive clothing, a little spare money for rum or gambling, and the opportunity for easy love-making. He does not wish to work too hard.[16]

The principal representatives of the planters before the Commission were Hon F.J. Seaford, the head of Booker in Guyana, president of the SPA and member of the Executive Council, and Col Ivan Davson, Chairman of S. Davson, the owners of Blairmont. The general secretary of the British TUC, Sir Walter Citrine, subjected Seaford to a clinical examination because of the obnoxious excerpt in the SPA memorandum. The famous exchange is reproduced in its entirety because it illuminates the attitudes Jock Campbell said he found so repellent when he lived in the colony in the mid-1930s. (Citrine was a firm advocate of trade unionism in the colonies and did much to stimulate interest in it during the Commission's travels around the British West Indies):

Citrine: What you have done, apparently, is to take the description applied by a newspaper— a West Indian journal — to the Jamaican peasant, and state that it is substantially true of the labourer here.... This is not a very complimentary description?

Seaford: Not complimentary?

Citrine: You say ... that as a rule this man (labourer) 'is essentially a gay, light-hearted, emotional person, fatalistic in his attitude to life, and, as a rule, taking no thought for the morrow'?

Is that true of the East Indian you employ?

Seaford: This is more true of the Negro than of the East Indian.

Citrine: Yes, but you employ the East Indian, don't you?

Seaford: Yes, but we employ quite a bit of Negroes, also.

Citrine: I have seen from a document here that you employ only a few.

Seaford: This is not quite true.

Citrine: Is it that you differentiate? Does it refer to the West Indian labourer?

Seaford: That refers to the West Indian.

Citrine: How can you say that it applies to the West Indian when you say in the memorandum that it also applies to the labour here?

Seaford: That is taken from *West Indian Review* — from Jamaica.

Citrine: How can you compare the East Indian with the West Indian, when you yourself say that they 'take no thought for the morrow'? You quote on page 4 of the memorandum the money they have in the Savings Bank?

Seaford: No.

Citrine: I do not want to fence with you if you would withdraw this description.

Seaford: As far as East Indians are concerned; yes.

Citrine: I don't like it even about the remainder. You say you endorse this description but, incidentally, you know this description was not put forward by any other employer organisation in the colonies?

Seaford: I do not know about that.

Citrine: No employer has come forward and described his employee in these terms; not in Jamaica or anywhere else.

(Seaford did not reply.)

Citrine: You have spoken about them (the labourers) in this description: 'All they want is food, shelter and a little spare money for rum and gambling'.

Seaford: You must not take the words in that way.

Citrine: Well, let me read exactly what you say: 'His main requirements are food, shelter, bright and attractive clothing, a little more spare money for rum and gambling, and the opportunity for easy love-making (laughter)'. Is that the description you want to see of the labourer you employ here?

Seaford: That is stated there, but it is not true in the case of a labourer.

Citrine: Well, why put it in?

Seaford: It is to show that this country is like all West Indian colonies generally.

Citrine: Don't you think we could have found that out for ourselves? I want to know if you maintain that description because if you do, I want to ask you many more questions about it.

Davson: I was not in British Guiana when that was put in.

Citrine: I want to know why it was put in. What was the purpose?

Davson: I can surmise that it was not intended to be so disparaging, as in cross-examination it has turned out to be.[17]

It was a measure of how disconnected the plantocracy were from their environment that on February 14, 1939 — they had appeared before the Moyne Commission on February 9 — F.J. Seaford, in his capacity as President of the Sugar Producers' Association, wrote the Secretary of the Commission, protesting against the manner of Citrine's cross-examination. He argued that the impression created would 'probably have serious repercussions on the good relations hitherto existing between employers and employed in this colony'. Seaford explained: '...some of his [Citrine's] questions were calculated by their nature and the language employed unnecessarily to belittle in the eyes of the general public the Sugar Industry and what it is doing for its employees....' The planters, having grasped, belatedly, the implications of their own bigoted perceptions of their employees, were now trying to displace the people's outrage unto Sir Walter Citrine. This is evident in Seaford's conclusion: 'I would point out that, in a cosmopolitan community such as this where public confidence can be maintained only by a common harmony among the different races making up the population, Sir Walter Citrine's apparent setting up of labour against capital cannot but be most disturbing to the well-being of the colony.'[18] There was a deeper foundation to the objection, as the reference to 'labour' and 'capital' betrayed: they were antagonistic to Citrine's public support for trade unions, especially Edun's MPCA.

Indeed, it was the plantocracy's own bigotry towards their workers which had created the rift between capital and labour, precipitating the strikes of 1934-35 and hastening the formation of the MPCA in 1937. As Campbell argued throughout his life, and as the MPCA observed perceptively in their memorandum to the Moyne Commission: 'The system of work, of working hours in the fields and factories are all based on irrational and traditional customs and usages of the past which do not allow room for modern progressive methods.'[19]

The Union elaborated on the context of disaffection on the sugar plantations at the end of the 1930s. The workers' grievances were genuine: they were not actuated by communists or other outside influences, as the planters were asserting. The MPCA noted that the white overseers, invariably poor, young Scots, were 'mostly unmarried men living in barracks and are open to all sorts of bad designs of sex'. There were several Eurasian children on the plantations, evidence of the pressure exerted by these desperate men for sexual favours from Indian women, in the cane-fields. The Union empathised with the overseers' condition, as Jock Campbell did with those he had encountered on their estate under the draconian Bee. They paid board to the managers who made 'handsome profits' from them. Edun's union even showed compassion, before the Moyne Commission, for these overseers — in their telling phrase, the 'sucked oranges of sugardom': 'As buffers between their bosses and the workers, they suffer mental agony, economic serfdom, and grave social disabilities which are grossly unfair for human beings to endure'.

The MPCA deplored the housing, the poor sanitation and the absence of potable water on many estates; these made workers even more vulnerable to malaria, hookworm and intestinal diseases. They were graphic in their depiction of the abysmal environment:

> The latrines are built on open drains through which water runs. The excreta lie about, and pigs, ducks and fowls feed on them, and these roam about the compound of the barracks [logies] with the consequence that sewage is carried into the very homes of workers. Further, the pigs and ducks enter into the open trenches and people are seen to bathe and wash clothing therein. It is not conceivable to find anything worse.... Apart from the defective latrine system, in the rainy season, as there are no roads leading to the workers' houses, the mud dams become liquid mud ... and the mud also is carried into their ... homes. In hot seasons the barracks covered as they are with galvanised roofs are nothing but ... ovens. In the nights they are cold. While the staff compounds carry electric lights, the workers' compounds are devoid of light.[20]

The Union spoke also of pervasive illiteracy on the plantations, the 'chief obstacle' to the growth of trade unionism. They asserted that the restricting of education was still the policy of the plantocracy: 'the less the workers were educated the easier it was for them to be controlled'. Workers often had to walk seven miles to the place of work on the estates, apart from Blairmont, Port Mourant and another estate where a light railway relieved them of this burden. The MPCA amplified: 'In wet seasons the mud does become impassable and trudging in one or two feet of mud is a harrowing experience, with the result that when the destination is reached the worker is exhausted.'

But it was the working conditions of women on the estates, often reminiscent of indentureship, which underlined the necessity for fresh attitudes by the planters, a culture of reform, if the instability of the late 1930s were not to become chronic. The continuing degradation of women workers in the weeding gangs was the signature of the intransigence, and the Union documented it vividly, to the Moyne Commission, in February 1939, as Sydney Caine had done in 1929:

Men and women have ... to wade and cross the canals and trenches to get to their work. As the men and women proceed in their hundreds on the dams, the women, as soon as they reach their destination [the cane-fields], will have to get into the trenches. These trenches are sometimes breast-deep and other times shallower, but in any case they have to lift their clothing before they enter and they tell the men: 'Brothers, hide your faces that we may cross'. Invariably it has been found that overseers, drivers and others have been in the habit of amusing themselves on the novelties of the unhappy scenes aback. Numerous complaints have been received by the Association [MPCA] and strong recommendations have been made with the result that boats have been recommended, but the process seem to be so slow that the abuses have not yet been eliminated on several estates. In addition to this abuse of women in the cane-fields, they are given tasks to weed the parapets of the trenches where they have to wade in breast-deep water for days and, strange to say, that with all the representation made, these pernicious systems are still in vogue.[21]

It is noteworthy that the MPCA, apart from advocating the 8-hour day and a minimum wage of $1.00 per day for male agricultural workers, the right to peaceful picketing, old age pension, workmen's compensation, security of tenure for resident estate workers, were also demanding constitutional change. They observed that as most workers did not have the vote, their right to articulate their grievances was vitiated further. The Union therefore recommended adult suffrage, an elected majority in the Legislative Council, the end of financial prerequisites for legislators and that they be paid as in the UK. At this time, of course, the MPCA still had not won recognition as the bargaining agent of field workers on the sugar plantations, but they appreciated the centrality of the vote in advancing the workers' cause.

It would take another tragedy on one of the estates before recognition was conceded. On February 16, 1939 — the Moyne Commission was still meeting in Georgetown — striking workers at Leonora, West Coast Demerara, an estate belonging to Sandbach Parker, were gunned down: four were killed, including one woman, Sumintra; four were admitted to hospital with bullet wounds; six were injured. Ayube Edun's influence was neutralised by the Sugar Producers Association's stubbornness in withholding recognition of the Union. The Commission appointed to investigate the shootings concluded that the strike at Leonora was caused by 'a general feeling of discontent with wage-rates, earnings, hours of labour and conditions of living', coupled with rising consciousness generated by the MPCA and the reported militancy of workers throughout the British West Indies in 1938-9. Moreover, they concluded that the absence of leadership 'on the spot' exacerbated the crisis, leading to 'individual and concerted acts of violence'. They then virtually made the case for the SPA to recognise the Union: '...the presence of the trade union leaders could have done no harm and might have served a useful purpose...[I]n the absence of any communication from the Association [MPCA] the estate authorities should have themselves assumed responsibility for securing the presence of the trade union leaders'.[22]

The Commission added that the deliberations of the Moyne Commission in British Guiana — Citrine was an instant hero after he had brought Seaford to earth — fed notions of the quick redress of grievances. Indeed, it ensured the recognition of the MPCA by the Sugar Producers' Association on March 2, 1939, less than two weeks after the shootings at Leonora. Nigel Bolland observes: '[T]he S.P.A. agreed to recognise the M.P.C.A. "for purposes of collective bargaining, giving it the right to negotiate in any case of dispute, and to hold meetings on plantations"...One positive consequence of the strike and the subsequent recognition of the M.P.C.A., which was surely not intended by the S.P.A., was the facility and encouragement it gave the union to organise and unite field workers throughout the colony'.[23] The mainly African factory workers were represented by another union, the British Guiana Workers' League, which was recognised in 1931. So that there was precedence for recognising union activity in the sugar industry; the planters were trying to stop the inevitable. It was to Jock Campbell's credit that he was temperamentally inclined to change; he was therefore able to discern the portents, to see the inevitability of reform, as early as the latter half of the 1930s.

Endnotes

1. See my Introduction to *Joseph Ruhomon's India; The Progress of Her People at Home and Abroad and how Those in British Guiana may Improve Themselves* (Kingston: The UWI Press, 2001).
2. Ayube Edun, *London's Heart-Probe and Britain's Destiny* (London: Arthur H. Stockwell, n.d. [1935]), 190.
3. Ibid., viii.
4. Ibid., 133, 199.
5. Ibid., 183, 201-2.
6. See Lala Lajpat [pseud.], 'Indian News and Views', *The Daily Chronicle*, September 29, 1935.
7. Ibid., October 20, 1935.
8. Ibid., November 3, December 1, 1935.
9. CO111/726/60036, Northcote to H. Beckles (Colonial Office), December 4, 1935.
10. Ibid., Beckles to Northcote, January 13, 1936.
11. CO111/732/60036, Report of the Commission of Enquiry into the 1935 Disturbances [paragraph 66].
12. Basdeo Mangru, *A History of East Indian Resistance on the Guyana Sugar Estates, 1869-1948* (Lewiston, NY: The Edwin Mellen Press, 1996), 238.
13. Ibid., 238, 242.
14. Leader, *The Guiana Review*, November 6, 1938.
15. *The Daily Chronicle*, January 30, 1939.
16. CO950/649, Memorandum of the Sugar Producers' Association [1939].
17. *The Royal Commission in British Guiana, 1939* (Georgetown: The Daily Chronicle Ltd,1939), 176-7.
18. See note 16.
19. CO950/675, Memorandum of the Manpower Citizens' Association [1939].
20. Ibid.
21. Ibid.
22. CO111/762/60270 [1939], encl.: Report of the Leonora Enquiry Commission, 1939, p. 20.
23. O. Nigel Bolland, *On the March: Labour Rebellions in the British Caribbean, 1934-9* (Kingston: Ian Randle Publishers, 1996), 187.

Chapter Eight

CAMPBELL, MILD REFORMS AND THE BEGINNING OF THE BOOKER 'CAUSE', 1938-40

Campbell worked in British Guiana in 1934–37. He returned briefly in 1938. He had made up his mind that his future was in the sugar industry of the colony. The association between his family's wealth and sugar, *not* the romance of it but the darker side — slavery, indentureship, and continuing exploitation — had shocked him; it gave him a mission. He told me in 1990, more than 50 years after he first went out to Guyana, of the emerging angst that determined his calling:

I remember that I once found in the office archives [Curtis Campbell's], which was all burnt during the blitz in London and Liverpool (we had microfilms in Liverpool)...I found an inventory of slaves, which my old secretary, [who had been] my grandfather's secretary, Mary, was looking at, and she became very excited because she saw a woman slave was worth more than a man slave. But when I explained to her why, because of child-bearing, she was very shocked. I always remember that I became aware of slavery as a child: I remember reading Dickens, Dickens's *American Notes* ... about American slavery; there was this whole thing about reading Dickens on American slavery. I was a tender-minded person and I became very conscious of slavery, but in an odd sort of way I hadn't connected the romance of sugar in British Guiana with slavery in America; I wasn't really conscious until the day I got there [in 1934]. And on the day I got there I was conscious that this had all been built on, first of all, slavery, and then cheap labour — that's how it got there. My grandfather left £1.5 million and my great-grandfather left about £1 million, and virtually all this was made out of sugar.[1]

In 1938 young Jock Campbell took his bride, Barbara, to British Guiana. Here again, parental intervention had won out, preventing him from marrying the other woman he loved. In 1936 he had met an attractive, intelligent woman from a business family in British Guiana. Her name was Philomena D'Aguiar. Jock recalls: 'I was desperately in love with Phil. She lived in Georgetown; she was a very attractive girl, and we used to play tennis together.' Indeed, Phil (like Olga Webb) was an athlete of considerable merit in the 1930s, and she had transcended her gender and ethnic limitations, as Sister Menezes has established:

> By the 1930s, [Madeiran] Portuguese women became leaders on the tennis courts; some excelled. The *Christmas Annual* of 1934 [Jock's first year in British Guiana] observed: 'Of all the girls who have indulged in sports in this country it cannot be denied that Phil D'Aguiar is the best all-round sportswoman that British Guiana has known.' She was classed as a brilliant hockey player, a hard-hitting tennis opponent, oarswoman and horseback rider, a walker and a cyclist, while her sister, Monica D'Aguiar, was ranked as the country's tennis champion. By the turn of the century, a few women, chiefly from the upper middle class, had begun to assert themselves and no longer meekly accepted a home-bound existence.[2]

So Phil was of good pedigree and she had the same passion for sports as Jock. He wanted to marry her, but he soon had to face old family attitudes: the resilient codes, so subtle, yet effective, in eliciting conformity. Phil, whose brother, Peter D'Aguiar, became a business magnate and politician, was of Madeiran Portuguese extraction; worse, she was Catholic; that necessarily collided with Jock's family's Presbyterian creed. The religious chasm and the taint of Phil's Madeiran roots — it spoke of indentured servitude and huckstering — a perceived flaw at the fount of white Georgetown society who welcomed Jock's parents during their visits — could have been surmounted if Jock had the will. But the moral code bred by unstated, resilient Presbyterian assumptions, kept him in its orbit throughout his life although he was not a man of faith. It triggered guilt; it was in some ways inhibiting: this was another battle he was not prepared to fight. His explanation for the end of his relationship with Phil, who never married and remained a friend for over 50 years, even if credible, shows the lack of resolve: 'I was very much in love with her. My parents would have been very shocked by a Roman Catholic marriage but they would have been understanding; but Phil and I gently came to the understanding that it wouldn't work.'[3]

Jock had again succumbed to the family's power to define: they chose the wife *they* thought was good for him and he went along with it. In 1938, aged 26, he married Barbara, the mother of his four children born between 1940 and 1948. Barbara was 'the girl my family approved of; the family found her for me; she was totally suitable; she was pretty; a good games player, but it never worked from the word go ... but I got married because I wanted to leave home really.... My family knew her family and so on and she was totally eligible in every way but I suppose I was rather spoilt — domineering; and she was very naive and it never really worked'. Jock adds that Barbara and he never talked about business, never discussed serious things, unlike his second wife, Phyllis, whom he married in 1948. Jock confided in Phyllis; he saw her as handsome, intellectually sharp, elegant, sophisticated and confident enough to move with ease at any level. Barbara, his family's choice, was 'very keen on the garden, very keen on the house, cooking, the children, nannies and servants. We lived in Kent ... quite near my parents'.[4]

Jock had met his parents all the way: with Olga Webb and Phil D'Aguiar, the sacred family assumptions of class, creed and blood, were not violated. The chosen wife did suffice, for a time: four off-springs in eight years. Barbara's conventional preoccupations probably gave Jock the freedom to concentrate on his work, building a niche in the sugar business, as he quickly stamped his presence on Booker. It was there, in the sugar business, with its roots in British Guiana, that he found the space, the autonomy he did not have in his private affairs. In Booker, he felt he could win: the experience in the colony, in 1934-37, had given him a cause; he had the will, a moral imperative, to seek change. By going along with the family's choice of a wife, he had secured the ground to enable him to make demands of them elsewhere. He could make a case, first, to initiate changes in the family firm, Curtis Campbell; then, in Booker, from 1939 (more so after the War), he was adroit in deploying the authority of six generations of Campbells in sugar in British Guiana, to coax them into a more enlightened course as demanded, increasingly, by a militant workforce and the nationalist promptings of post-War politics.

In their memorandum to the Moyne Commission in January 1939, the Manpower Citizens' Association had focused on a case of flagrant cheating by management at the Campbell estate at Albion. They pointed out that punt-loaders had been working to 'an inaccurate and deliberate' tonnage mark. They were being deceived into thinking that the 10 inches mark on the punts constituted 4 tons of cane. After a strike by the cane-cutters at Albion, it was discovered that 'by placing 4 tons of manure in the punt, it was found to be 8 inches and not 10 inches'.[5] The workers had, in fact, been loading an excess of one ton cane per punt, for a period of two and a half years years, with no remuneration.

However, by the end of the 1930s an adumbration of change was discernible; young Jock Campbell was already shaping a new attitude, as the workers were demanding. He explained it to me:

> I knew that the housing was terrible, that the conditions were terrible, that the treatment of the people was terrible, that coolies and blacks couldn't get promotion; I...[became] aware of all that when I went out there [1934-37]. It worried me and I talked to people about it; I talked to my family when I got back [to England]. I don't think anybody had seen it from that point of view, but I had seen it from the inside; and yet again oddly enough, sugar workers would talk to me.[6]

This fresh outlook probably explains why the MPCA inserted in its memorandum to the Moyne Commission in 1939 the case of Plantation Albion, where a range of grievances with regard to wage-rates and working conditions had been ventilated and a number of agreements reached with management, even before the Sugar Producers' Association had recognised the Union. These included increased remuneration for forking and the provision of time on

Mondays for the hearing of complaints from workers by the manager. With regard to the estate hospital at Albion, the Union stated: 'Pigs which roam about the compound to be got rid of; kitchen, bedding and general sanitation to be improved. G.M.O.[Government Medical Officer] to make recommendations for the improvement of the hospital, equipment, dietary, etc., and general administration'. The provision of a better burial ground, also, would be considered when the manager, James Bee, returned to the colony. Some important agreements bore the distinct imprint of Jock's hand: '[the] use of offensive language by members of the staff [was] to be forbidden'; abolition of market fees to be 'sympathetically' considered, as was the reduction in rent for rice-beds from $3 to $2; women crossing canals were to be provided with 'floates' and poles; the provision of 'pure drinking water' for field workers was also under consideration.[7]

These reforms were already being implemented at Blairmont and Port Mourant, the prototypes that had so impressed Campbell in those early years. He said he was appalled that James Bee looked at his workers at Albion as mere coolies, and because his father and his father's brother, Henry, owned the plantation, he had extraordinary authority to seek change, although he was very young. Theirs was a small concern; there were, therefore, severe limits to what he could achieve, especially during the Depression. But he said he was challenging the old bigotry in order to initiate a culture of reform: 'I had great sympathy with the workers and they knew that, and I made great friends with some of them. I was aware of the great injustices ... there were injustices towards the overseers too — Bee ruled them with a rod of iron'.[8]

This then was the context in which Jock was instrumental in convincing his father and uncle, Henry Campbell, that a merger between Curtis Campbell and the biggest sugar company in the colony, Booker Bros, Mc Connell and Co, was inescapable if they were to survive. He was equally conscious that change — structural and social — could not be delayed much longer. Reforms had to permeate the whole industry; amalgamation with Booker was imperative: '[I]t was largely my idea,' he remarked.

Sir Alfred Sherlock was the chairman of Booker; Jock's father and uncle were on the Board of Booker; so they negotiated a take-over of Curtis Campbell in 1939: 'We did an exchange of shares mainly and I went into Booker and right from the beginning I sat in Sherlock's room in London.' Sherlock, like his chief lieutenant in British Guiana, F.J. Seaford, was wedded to old notions of colonial peoples. They were both most uncomfortable with ideas of reform on the plantations, as the latter's infamous exchange with Citrine underlined. Sir Alfred, Jock recalled, was set in his ways. He used to say that 'anti-semitism was hating Jews more than was strictly necessary.... He was very shrewd but he really wasn't interested in anything else except the firm making money: no sense of social obligation. He lived a narrow life'. Another senior member of the management of Booker was Alistair Armour, whose father was Booker's director in Liverpool, 'hopeless chap'; another was Pat Sherlock, Sir Alfred's son, who Jock also deemed 'hopeless'. He added, with no trace of arrogance: 'I came in and was treated on the same level as them, but I could run rings round them.'[9]

Jock Campbell's financial independence — he told me often, almost apologetically, that he was 'no hostage to fortune'; he was 'born with a sugar spoon' in his mouth — gave him the confidence to assert himself quickly in Booker. Moreover, he submits: 'I was intelligent. They were never any threat to me.... I did quite well because I was quite orderly and quite organised.' He soon mastered the intricacies of the sugar trade; he was not interested in the shop-keeping side of Booker's business. He knew many of the big sugar people in London and he rose rapidly: 'I was right in the thick of it and so I was very quickly put on committees.'[10]

Jock brought an imaginative dimension to the affairs of Booker, and a clear vision for Booker in Guyana where most of their assets were invested. He was not intimidated by Sir Alfred Sherlock, who was a creole white born in British Guiana and had been with Booker for some 50 years; nor by A.V.C. McConnell, whose family firm in the colony had amalgamated with Booker in 1900. For him business sense demanded reform — a moral imperative — and he had the will to win when it came to shaping a culture of change. The energy sublimated in acquiescing to his family's dictates with regard to his relationship with women and his marriage, found an outlet here. The authority acquired through his family's old roots in sugar, and his own financial independence, enhanced his reformist vision. He had no doubts that he was endowed with the intellectual means to win this argument:

> I felt I was pointing out things, having ideas that hadn't occurred to them, and I felt right from the beginning that I was a lap ahead. Sherlock had never really thought it out even in the way I had at that age [late 20s and early 30s] — the vision wasn't there. He was a good man in his way; he was a kind man. This is a bit difficult to describe but they hadn't had the same background as I had; they hadn't been to Eton and Oxford; they hadn't known the sort of people my family knew and I was in a way a lap ahead. This sounds awful, but it was so....I had a certain Irish blarney about me: I used to be able to get on with people and get my own way....I was always a good gamesman in an argument. I was always good as a chairman. I always dominated the meeting right from an early age.[11]

But Sherlock and Seaford were no pushovers; they were temperamentally rooted in a framework of reaction: they could see only subversion behind reformist notions, not the spirit of genuine change, the belated reshaping of attitudes to redress ancient wrongs. Indeed, in June 1939, only three months after the sugar producers had recognised the MPCA, Hon F.J. Seaford, on a visit to London, confided to a Mr Beckett at the Colonial Office that the sugar producers felt that there was 'the urgent need for someone to assist in the establishment of a bona fide trade union locally, to replace the M.P.C.A. which was nothing more or less than a political body'. He contended, rather spuriously, that their position was arrived at after the Union intimidated anyone who was prepared to give evidence to the Leonora Commission, following the shootings of February 1939: the MPCA were boycotting it.[12]

Shortly afterwards, in 1940, the Sugar Producers' Association tried to destroy the Union by giving its treasurer, Hon C.R. Jacob, a monthly bribe of $480. Some years later the organ of the MPCA reported the sordid affair:

[I]t has been proved beyond any doubt that the Hon. C.R. Jacob, during his term of office as President of the British Guiana East Indian Association and Treasurer of the Man-Power Citizens' Association used his offices to secure employment with the British Guiana Sugar Producers' Association for £100 ($480) per month under a contract — the gist of which was published in the *Labour Advocate* of 11 July 1943, which Mr. Jacob has made no attempt to deny or correct thereby establishing the veracity of the accusation....Mr. Jacob has not only acted contrary to the wishes of the members of these two organisations by giving the assurance that he would continue to muzzle these two organisations in the interest of the S.P.A. of this colony, but also has allowed members of these two organisations totally to lose confidence in him.[13]

The credibility of the Union was undermined, but the worst consequence of the affair was the hardening of perceptions among sugar workers that one could never trust the plantocracy. Booker, the old devil, could never mend its evil ways, hence the resilience of the pejorative appellation, 'Booker's Guiana'. That was the legacy of Quintin Hogg, William Middleton Campbell, Alfred Sherlock, F.J. Seaford and James Bee.

Jock Campbell was a young director of Booker in 1940, when the bribe was made to C.R. Jacob to curb the militancy of the newly recognised MPCA. He, apparently, knew nothing of the machinations, although he learnt later that the chairman of Booker himself, Sir Alfred Sherlock, was involved in the matter. Jock recalled the scandal:

I remember him [Ayube Edun] well. I rather liked him .... I was in sympathy with the sugar workers wanting a union, and I think they were a fairly responsible union....The allegations are true [about the SPA and the bribe to C.R. Jacob]. I don't think I knew it then, but the S.P.A. were much more worried about the M.P.C.A than I was, and I got on fairly well with Edun ... but I was fairly junior in those days. All this scandal came out and I felt it was almost certainly true that the S.P.A. were paying Jacob....I was appalled when I heard about it ....[Sherlock] never told me about it; he did it and then came back and reported it, and I was appalled. I remember it distinctly.[14]

The rottenness was pervasive and deep-seated; but the workers under Ayube Edun, throughout the latter half of the 1930s and the early 1940s, sustained an unremitting fight for the reform of the sugar plantation culture. Jock Campbell knew that the plantocracy had to change or be consumed by the seething fire of workers' indignation.

Endnotes

1.   Jock Campbell, interview by the author, Nettlebed, Oxfordshire, May 9, 1990, Tape 1.
2.   M. Noel Menezes, 'The Madeiran Portuguese Woman in Guyanese Society, 1830-1930', in *The Colonial Caribbean in Transition: Essays on Postemancipation Social and Cultural History*, eds. Bridget Brereton and Kevin A. Yelvington (Kingston: The UWI Press, 1999), 172.
3.   Jock Campbell, interview by the author, Nettlebed, Oxfordshire, July 23, 1992, Tape 3.
4.   Ibid.
5.   CO950/675, Memorandum of the MPCA [1939].
6.   See note 3.
7.   CO950/675, Memorandum of the MPCA, Appendix B [1939].
8.   See note 3.
9.   Ibid.
10. Ibid.
11. Ibid.
12. CO111/762/60270, 'Note of an Interview with F.J. Seaford, OBE (Booker Bros), Elected Member of the Legislative Council of British Guiana', June 20, 1939.
13. *Labour Advocate*, September 24, 1944. See also Ashton Chase, *A History of Trade Unionism in Guyana, 1900-64* (Ruimveldt, Guyana: New Guyana Co, Ltd, n.d., ca. 1964), 70.
14. Jock Campbell, interviews by the author, Nettlebed, Oxfordshire, May 9, 1990, Tape 1; July 23, 1992, Tape 3.

Part 3

Getting into Stride:
The Case for Reform Vindicated,
1941-1949

Chapter Nine

CAMPBELL WITH SYDNEY CAINE AT THE COLONIAL OFFICE: A MODEL FOR REFORM DURING THE WAR

It is arguable that the entrenched, conservative forces in Booker, Sherlock and Seaford in particular, would have been impossible to shift had it not been for a concatenation of factors in the early 1940s. It was in this context that Campbell was able to propound his vision of reform, in Booker and in British Guiana. His radical perspective stimulated change, as it in turn was driven by the radicalisation of the colonial environment. A culture of reform took root in the 1940s. This was reflected in the following: the work of Edun and the MPCA; the emergence of a young Marxist politician, Cheddi Jagan, shaped by his plantation boyhood at Port Mourant; the cataclysmic impact of yet another shooting of workers, at Plantation Enmore, in June 1948; and the recommendations of the Venn Commission in 1949, following this debacle — a blue-print for reform which Jock embraced as a virtual primer for his chairmanship of Booker in the 1950s. All of this had been stimulated in one way or another by the shaping of an ethos for reform, a touch of iconoclasm, by the radical Governor of British Guiana between 1941 and 1946, Sir Gordon Lethem, an indomitable Scot. He was despised by the plantocracy but Jock was buoyed by his energy and imagination; he saw him as an ally. For him this was a most propitious environment: after the War he could press his case for reform of the Guyanese plantations.

Of all the people involved with sugar in Guyana none had the credentials to change plantocratic attitudes like Jock Campbell. As noted earlier, his ancient background in sugar in the colony, going back to the 1780s, to slavery, had inspired guilt; it also conferred a unique stature, connections which imbued his thoughts, his actions, with gravitas — old authority. He explains:

> I was able to do things, right from the beginning, as the young master, the son of Curtis Campbell and afterwards Curtis Campbell/Booker. I was able to say and do things that I couldn't possibly have got away with had I not had sugar in my blood. Any other employee would have been sacked for some of the things I said and did.[1]

Jock was no revolutionary; he was, however, moving towards a kind of Fabian socialism, a notion of the inevitability of change and the merits of gradualism: 'I thought there was a lot wrong with British Guiana when I first went there [in 1934], but I didn't terribly intellectualise it; I just felt it was wrong. There were things I didn't like at all. I enjoyed talking to Indians and Africans and found the plantocracy rather boring; but I think it was only after the War that I consciously became a Fabian socialist.'[2] He was essentially pragmatic: he did not want to alienate too many crucial players in the contemporary world of colonial politics and sugar economics. He was committed to the cultivation of influential allies and what he later called the 'greatness of small causes'. One such ally in the early 1940s, possibly the most important intellectual force he encountered, was Sir Sydney Caine, Head of the Economics Division of the Colonial Office during the War, the principal architect of a philosophy of reform for the colonies.

Caine had, as noted earlier, a good grasp of the problems of the British West Indies, especially the technicalities of the cane-sugar industry and the abysmal working conditions of many on the plantations. As Secretary of the Olivier Commission which toured the West Indies in 1929–30, to examine the parlous state of the sugar industry, he came under the spell of Olivier's robust Fabian socialist principles: protectionist measures to ensure the survival of Caribbean sugar; crop diversification; peasant settlements; improved housing and sanitation; unionism. Caine's impressions of British Guiana permeate his letters to his wife, sent from the colony in late 1929. The acuteness of perceptions and discernment, the moral outrage, would have been congruent with Jock's own emerging outlook when he lived there in 1934–37. Sydney Caine had remarked:

> This is an extraordinary country, flat as a pancake, large parts of it, including Georgetown, below sea-level and protected by sea-walls; everywhere water-logged so that all the fields are intersected every 10 yards or so by drains a yard or two wide and several feet deep. Once you leave the main road you are constantly crossing drains and canals ... by bridge or by little punts, and all the sugar-cane is carried to the factories in punts. In the wet season the whole fields become seas of mud, and the labourers have to walk and wade through it, sometimes as much as 7 miles, to their work. You can imagine the effect on their health![3]

A few days later Caine spoke of the sugar planters' perennial lament, the shortage of labour. As usual he could quickly unmask the ruse, getting to the core of a matter: 'As employers do everywhere, they complain here of shortage of labour because the people don't want to work. In the first place nobody would want to work in the conditions here; in the second the labourers have to cultivate plots of their own and the women have to do washing, etc., so they can't work every day. But the factories themselves are grossly over-manned. Even I could see lots of things done which a machine could do better and cleaner.' Caine asserted: 'The Demerara planters are simply living in the slave tradition. They organise their estates and factories on the assumption of abundant labour at no cost and then blame the labourers' laziness when they don't get it.'[4]

Caine's insights were discernible in the Olivier Commission Report of 1930; the comments on estate housing, for instance, were identical to Jock's indelible impressions of housing on their own estates, four or five years later. The Report noted:

> [T]he introduction of indentured Indian immigrants established, under Government sanction, a very low standard of housing for estate labourers. Habitually it was deemed sufficient that they should be housed in long ranges of single rooms with floors on the ground [logies].... On many estates on which indentured coolies

were settled the old ranges remain, ruinous, decrepit, and full of dirt and vermin. Their survival ... perpetuates a low standard of living which there is a common tendency to regard as being all that the West Indian labourer, whether Indian or creole, needs or desires. That this psychological assumption is an error is proved wherever West Indian or East Indian labourers have been able to own, build, and maintain their own houses.... There appears further to be very little if any supervision of the sanitary conditions of estates by the local Governments, either through deficiency in public health laws or to such powers of inspection and remedy as exist not being exercised.[5]

It is not clear precisely when Jock Campbell first met Sydney Caine, but they became very good friends. They had, among other things, a common interest in colonial issues and a passion for crosswords. Jock's gifts were astounding; he would complete the *Times* crossword in ten minutes: 'a speed which is downright insulting to those who compiled them'.[6] Caine's was an outstanding intellect — a brilliant economist, widely published, now in a position to shape colonial policies, especially social and economic reforms in the wake of the Moyne Commission's recommendations. It was he who had given Jock the idea of working in the Colonial Office as a contribution to the War effort. Campbell spent two years there, and the younger man befriended Sir Sydney, gaining immeasurably from the latter's wide learning, experience of Government and the labyrinthine ways of the Whitehall bureaucracy. It was a vital ingredient in Jock's development and it came at a crucial time, for Caine's reforming instincts would have strengthened his own resolve.[7]

Campbell considered Caine 'one of the cleverest men I have ever known', noting that after he left the Colonial Office he became head of the London School of Economics and, later, head of the University of Malaya. It is not surprising, therefore, that he would confide in him, seeking solace in the late 1940s when his arranged marriage to Barbara was on the brink of collapse. Jock was always enthralled by a nimble intellect, an imaginative mind grappling with the complexities of a problem; the challenge of ideas; the delicacy of assessing options, the risks, too, if he felt he could win; the chasm between conception and execution; the dexterity and sagacity — the gamesmanship —

required to get a team to cohere, getting the key people on your side, working towards your goals. Sydney Caine's work at the Colonial Office had all these ingredients and it provided Jock with the framework to learn the rudiments of administration; not just the doing, but the clinical reflection on the doing.[8]

What was Campbell's job at the Colonial Office? He explains: 'I was responsible for the allocation of cargoes and convoys to the colonies, particularly Malta; I worked with the Admiralty. Being a non-drinker and non-smoker, I was shocked by the amount of space given to beer and cigarettes when Malta was under siege; and I wrote a minute about this and it came back to me with an awful scribble from Churchill saying: "Who is this lunatic?"' The experience at the Colonial Office, he reflected, 'gave me an understanding of how the Civil Service worked. I was very tempted to become a civil servant'.[9] More important, he made vital contacts in Whitehall and he absorbed the nuances at the heart of government, the modus operandi of many people who would matter as he pursued the business and politics of sugar after the War. He would keep in touch with people at the Colonial Office, periodically sending them clippings or private correspondence that he felt would gradually help to shape perceptions, or clinch the argument in an issue which mattered to him. He was an adroit operator: much subtly of manoeuvre was learnt from his mentor, Sydney Caine.

Although Campbell had arrived at a kind of Fabian socialism during the War, he never anchored his reformist ideals within a discrete ideological framework. He was not comfortable with creeds, dogmas, hard-and-fast theoretical constructs. However, his philosophy, such as it was, had definite promptings, as we have seen. If we venture to categorise it as Fabian socialist it is primarily because of the crucial influence of Sydney Caine and his mentor, the eminent Fabian thinker and administrator, Sydney Olivier, whose connections with the British West Indies were very wide and probably deeper than anyone in colonial administration. Jock had read Olivier's books on Jamaica, in the 1930s; they stayed with him.

Caine's commitment to reforms in the sugar industry, as noted above, had shaped the Olivier Commission Report of 1930, as Olivier himself had influenced the progressive Norman Commission Report of 1897. In January 1937, shortly after the Report on the 1935 troubles on the Guyanese plantations was released, Caine wrote an internal minute that called up the reformist temper of Olivier. He argued that the UK government 'cannot escape a particular responsibility for conditions in that industry because, quite apart from their general responsibility for Colonial administration, the sugar industry is maintained in existence only by the support of the UK Exchequer, given by way of preferences'.[10] Olivier, in his 1930 Report, had quoted from the 1897 Report to underscore the necessity to honour responsibilities to the West Indies. The following argument would become central to Campbell's thesis; even in the early 1990s, he would remind me, in similar language, of this key contention of the Fabian socialists:

> We cannot abandon them [the British West Indies], and if economic conditions become such that private enterprise and the profits of trade and cultivation cease to attract white men to the Colonies, or keep them there, this may render it more difficult for the British Government to discharge its obligations, but will not in any case diminish the force of them. We have placed the labouring population where it is, and created for it the conditions, moral and material, under which it exists and we cannot divest ourselves of responsibility for its future.[11]

Caine, too, in 1937, was making the case for price security and Imperial responsibility, but he was determined that reforms, the percolation of benefits to the sugar workers, be an integral part of the granting of preferences, citing the especially bad conditions on plantations in British Guiana. He wrote in his internal minute:

> If in fact the price of sugar is raised and the preference maintained, I think we should have every justification for pressing for some action to improve working conditions throughout the sugar producing colonies. I am not sure that any definite programme of specific conditions could be put forward. It may be only a matter of using pressure through the dependence of the Colonial industry on U.K. policy. I would urge, however, that this question should be kept prominently in mind, and that if more satisfactory conditions for the industry are established and stabilised every endeavour should be made to

ensure that a full share of the benefits of those improved conditions is passed on to the labourers, partly in increased wages, and, perhaps more important, in better conditions, shorter hours, etc., throughout the Colonial sugar industry. Present conditions vary no doubt, and they are perhaps not everywhere as bad as in British Guiana, but I am sure that they are everywhere capable of improvement.[12]

The commitment to reform at the heart of Imperial government at the end of the 1930s enhanced Campbell's vision. The location of this new resolve, in the Colonial Office in particular, lent urgency to this perspective and gave credibility to his ideas for change; it bolstered his approach and challenged the conservatism at the heart of plantocratic thought. Immediately after the War, sugar prices were remunerative and, as Jock acknowledges, it was his friend, Sydney Caine, who piloted the first wave of reforms in the West Indies and British Guiana by way of the Colonial Development and Welfare Grants, as recommended by the Moyne Commission of 1939. It was he also who, as will be seen later, devised a framework in the late 1940s to ensure that some of the gains from higher prices for sugar reached the plantation workers.[13]

Although the Moyne Commission Report was completed in 1940, it was not published until after the War, for fear that some of its damning criticism of conditions in the British West Indies would provide fodder to the German propaganda machine. However, some of its recommendations were published and governors had access to the unpublished Report, while the Colonial Office were already acting on its Colonial Development and Welfare proposals (the empowering Act was passed in 1940), to guide its new culture of providing grants-in-aid to initiate social and economic reforms. Moyne had been categorical that the spate of labour troubles of the late 1930s had firm roots in chronic deprivation; only an ongoing programme of reform could provide long-term stability.

Campbell notes that the initial reforms on the estates had begun during the War: the building of community centres and the provision of recreational facilities were facilitated by the Colonial Development and Welfare Grants. These mild reforms bred a culture demanding more reforms. The political environment, indeed, was now permeated by a passion for reforms. Michael Swan has written on the scale of Imperial grants to the colony in the aftermath of the Moyne Report:

> In relation to size and population, British Guiana has had more help under the Colonial Development and Welfare Act than any other British dependency. Between 1st April 1941 (when the CD&W Act came into force) and 30th June 1956, direct grants and loans, grants from central allocation from which British Guiana benefits, and grants from research on behalf of the Colony have totalled £7,928,139, or more than £16 for every man, woman and child of the population [over £2 million was allocated to drainage and irrigation].... Even this list does not include some regional schemes, such as that for the University College of the West Indies, from which British Guiana benefits.[14]

Endnotes

1. Jock Campbell, interview by the author, Nettlebed, Oxfordshire, May 9, 1990, Tape 1.
2. Jock Campbell, interview by the author, Nettlebed, Oxfordshire, July 23, 1992, Tape 2.
3. Sydney Caine (Georgetown) to his wife, November 16, 1929.
4. Ibid., November 21, 1929.
5. *Report of the West Indian Sugar Commission* (Lord Olivier, chairman), (London: His Majesty's Stationery Office, 1930), 52-3.
6. 'London Office: History and Biographies', *Pepperpot* 2, no. 5, (August 1948).
7. Michael Caine, interview by the author, London, July 19, 1995.
8. Jock Campbell, interview by the author, Nettlebed, Oxfordshire, July 23, 1992, Tape 3.
9. Ibid.
10. CO111/732/60036, Minute, S.Caine, January 22, 1937.
11. See note 5 [p. 25].
12. See note 10.
13. Jock Campbell, interview by the author, Nettlebed, Oxfordshire, February 18, 1994, Tape 10.
14. For details of these CD&W allocations to British Guiana, see Michael Swan, *British Guiana: the Land of Six Peoples* (London: Her Majesty's Stationery Office, 1957), 211-5.

Chapter Ten

GOVERNOR LETHEM AND THE PLANTOCRACY IN BRITISH GUIANA, 1941-46: ANOTHER MODEL FOR CAMPBELL

Sir Gordon [Lethem] was a progressive governor, certainly, as governors go. His efforts to have his term of office extended were blocked by the planters and the Colonial Office, for he was much too liberal and outspoken for their liking.

CHEDDI JAGAN, The West on Trial

For a colonial official to receive approbation, however qualified, from Cheddi Jagan, the Marxist politician in British Guiana, he had to be extraordinary. A Scot from Dumfriesshire, Sir Gordon Lethem (1886–1962) was probably the only Governor of British Guiana who empathised with the working class. His support for drainage and irrigation for the small farmer was antithetical to the sugar planters; and during his years in Guyana, 1941-46, he went against the official and plantocratic grain by advocating the use of state funds to implement such projects. Moreover, he was seen to be obdurately opposed to the old notion that every cause in the colony had to defer to the demands of King Sugar.

Lethem said that the Imperial Government was obligated to the empoldering (reclamation) of the coastland, as he could not conceive of African and Indian farmers being able to execute such financially taxing, hydrologically complex, but inescapable work. Indeed, as Jagan observes, Lethem had argued 'bluntly of the obligation of the British government to adopt a policy for the provision of a comprehensive scheme of water control'. Jagan quotes the following from one of Lethem's despatches to the Secretary of State for the Colonies, in 1943:

> I may be pardoned if I speak with complete candour. His Majesty's Government should, in my view, accept now in one way or another the obligation of a long-range policy to finance major drainage and irrigation schemes on this full scale; or if this obligation cannot be accepted, a frank statement should now be made that it is impossible to foresee the time when adequate steps can be taken to ensure living conditions for the population of the coastlands.[1]

For a couple of years of Lethem's governorship, Jock Campbell, as stated above, worked at the Colonial Office. It is likely that he had access to some of the progressive governor's despatches to that office. He got to know him well and supported his stance on most issues, contrary to the men involved with sugar in the colony. He recalled that, traditionally, with most governors, the planters had a 'fairly good consensus, but with a reforming governor like Lethem the relationship wasn't nearly so good. I got on with Lethem because we rather agreed about things'.

Already a director of Booker in the early 1940s, Jock would have known the negative perceptions of Lethem held by Sherlock and Seaford, at the highest level of the firm. Lethem did not endear himself to the plantocracy or the Colonial Office: the inevitability of gradualism was not his guiding principle. Jock recalls: 'Lethem was very unusual, rather left-wing, very controversial; [he] really was shocked by what he found in British Guiana: by the power of the plantocracy and about the bad conditions and [he] really wanted to do something about it. I felt I had an ally in him and I think he felt he had an ally in me. He was a splendid Governor and in fact was not very popular at the Colonial Office because he tried to do too much too fast'.[2]

In a despatch to the Secretary of State for the Colonies in September 1943, Lethem briefed him on the forthcoming visit to London of F.J. Seaford, the managing director of Booker in Guyana. He knew him well, as an elected member of the Legislative Council and a member of the crucial policy-making body, the Executive

Council. Lethem was not enamoured of what he saw as the mischievous hand of Sir Alfred Sherlock in London, issuing some 'dogmatic instruction', which tended to 'prejudice' Seaford's judgement on local issues. He cited two examples: 'A special instance appears to be that of bonuses, when the view locally has been that it is impossible to accept recurring rises in prices without giving something more to labour whereas London appears categorically to prohibit anything....Again, in the steps taken to procure some production of food on estates ['Grow More Food'

Sir Gordon Lethem: 'progressive' Governor: 'very unpopular with the plantocracy'.

campaign during the War], while things have worked pretty well here and I have been pretty satisfied with the results achieved, I gather that Sherlock persists in saying that we are trying to push the estates into mixed farming'.[3] It was the 'Grow More Food' campaign which had enabled local consumers to reduce dependency on foreign food at a time of shortages and escalating prices, thus dampening demands for higher wages on the plantations. Much to the chagrin of people like Sherlock, however, it also demonstrated to farmers and estate employees the viability of options for the diversification of agriculture. This was poison to the sugar planters, insatiable in their claim on local labour, and implacable in their lament on the shortage of labour.

Lethem warned the Secretary of State that Seaford's principals in London would argue that rice prices were too high, a temptation to their workers to desert the estates. He countered this, noting that the old rice prices were 'hopelessly low and that a rise was necessary not only to stimulate production but also to cover the cost of production'. Moreover, he argued that it was indefensible to keep down rice prices when sugar and other products were receiving better prices and the cost of imports had seen 'enormous rises'. Indeed, the price per ton of sugar exported was undergoing a boom during the

War: £9.55 in 1939 to £11.95 in 1943; this rose from £12.85 in 1944 to £15.20 in 1945.[4] Lethem was taking a longer view of the colony's development, beyond the plantocracy and its obsession with stifling other enterprises in order to retain control of labour. He was an ally of the rice grower, small farmers generally:

> My own view is that we can hold it [rice prices] as at present if we continue subsidisation of other things; and that generally we have got the rice business on something like an economic basis now, i.e., a fair price to the producer and a not too high price to the consumer both here and in the islands, and that if we can hold this and in the next two or three years get down costs of production by greater efficiency, use of machinery, etc., then we shall have a fair chance of keeping the industry going successfully after the war.[5]

Lethem was determined to resist the planters' old habit of bending all authorities, local and in London, to their procrustean mould. He cautioned: 'If the position is that *everything* must be sacrificed to sugar, as Sherlock would argue, then of course no doubt Government should have kept down and prevented all rises in prices of rice and ground provisions. I think any fair man will appreciate that that would have been outrageous ... *if we are to sit back and do nothing except where sugar comes into the picture, this place will remain one of the blackest spots of the Empire* [emphasis added]'.[6]

The foundation of Sir Gordon Lethem's strategy to develop British Guiana beyond a sugar plantation colony, beyond 'Booker's Guiana', was a comprehensive drainage and irrigation system. The perennial problem of water control had epitomised the small farmer's nightmare here; it was the source of the latifundist character of sugar in the political economy of Guyana. In his despatch of September 1943, Lethem had remarked that F.J. Seaford, who was a member of the crucial Drainage and Irrigation Board of the Legislative Council, had done 'a prodigious amount of work free, in the general interest'. Moreover, Seaford, in his discussions with him, had contended that the chronic hydrological problems must be 'put ... in order'. Lately, however, Lethem had discerned a 'dampening' of his stance, indeed, a retraction, based on the exhausted pretext that 'we haven't got the population and can never get the machinery and so on'. He added that Seaford had even deceived the Board in advocating an 'overstatement as to [the] labour' requirements of the sugar industry.

The Governor sought to explain Seaford's volte-face: '[The] fulminations of Sherlock against anything being done for non-sugar interests has been having effect and Seaford himself is getting uneasy that schemes which will cater for rice, provisions, pasturage, etc., are going to mean more and more difficulties for sugar — shortage of labour....' Of course, buoyant sugar prices had resurrected all the ancient prejudices against the promotion of any activity deemed to be detrimental to King Sugar. But Lethem's resolve to carry out a comprehensive drainage and irrigation scheme was not lessened by Seaford's opposition. He observed: 'Seaford tends to harp pessimistically that this can never carry any of the capital costs and probably never for many years fully carry maintenance charges. I am not going to deny this, but I would go on hoping that some of them would pull out not so badly and I certainly don't want to be deterred from the obvious thing to do....' Then, alluding to the established practices of the plantocracy, the Governor concluded: 'I am a little anxious lest sugar interests may try and pull every possible wire against any big drainage and irrigation projects which are not principally or largely "sugar".'[7]

Lethem's instincts about the plantocracy were unimpeachable. When Seaford met Secretary of State Lloyd, towards the end of October 1943, the main issue raised by him was a newspaper report in which Lethem had argued thus with regard to raising revenue for reform in 1944: 'If we are to carry out our ambitious schemes of social reform and pay our fair share of the cost it will mean specific taxation of capital, of profits going out of the Colony and of other new sources'. Lloyd had requested clarification of this from Lethem, 'if the point should be raised by any of Seaford's business colleagues', in London.[8]

On November 5, 1943 Sir Alfred Sherlock (and F.J. Seaford) met Beckett and Sydney Caine at the Colonial Office, where Seaford again raised the issue of Lethem's tax proposals on repatriated profits. He argued that 'the attitude of outside investors would obviously be affected by such a measure'. However, it was the question of drainage and irrigation schemes and land settlements for farmers that ignited Sherlock's and Seaford's deepest fears. Booker were opposed to

Lethem's scheme for empoldering the coastland, and Seaford proceeded to underline only its limitations: the cost had been underestimated; the labour available in the colony was 'insufficient'; it had reached 'saturation' point as far as rice-growing was concerned — even with mechanical drainage, rice could not be 'profitably produced', except on a large scale; the people were not capable of maintaining the internal drainage. Then Seaford gave away the real ground for his objections, the ancient preoccupation with the loss of labour to sugar: land settlements were doomed unless people were in a position to supplement their incomes with plantation work. What he really meant was that if Lethem's scheme could not be halted, then 'land settlements must ... be in close proximity to sugar estates'.[9]

Lethem had read the plantocracy correctly and he continually apprised the Colonial Office of their machinations; but it was evident that even there no commitment to a comprehensive drainage and irrigation scheme was forthcoming. In February 1944 he wrote to the Secretary of State:

> [M]y impression is that opposition to drainage and irrigation projects in areas other than sugar areas is stiffening with more and more insistence on the uneconomic character, the excessive demand for labour and so on. I have now been asked by the Sugar Producers to emphasise officially the importance of the sugar industry to the colony — perhaps in a broadcast — and also to limit the progress of drainage and irrigation works where there is any likelihood of this affecting labour supply on the estates.

He also reasserted the argument from his speech, cited by Seaford at the Colonial Office, where he had embraced direct taxation rather than the beaten path of the old colonial mantra of indirect taxation. The latter had fallen inordinately on the working class. Lethem was therefore advocating 'steep increases in direct taxation', including on 'profits going out of the colony', in order to undertake 'ambitious schemes of social reform'.[10]

In April 1944 Lethem submitted a comprehensive plan for the drainage and irrigation of the potentially prosperous, healthier Corentyne Coast, where the population had been increasing 'substantially' in recent years: from 58,260 in 1931 to 75,694 in 1942.

This was most impressive in this malarial colony. The Governor was applying for a grant of $3,100,000, under the Colonial Development and Welfare Act (1940), for the empoldering of an area of 443 square miles, between the Berbice and Corentyne Rivers, for rice, provision, food crops and cattle. In his rationale he adroitly submitted that the scheme would also benefit the *surplus* population on sugar estates, which the planters would like 'to diminish'. The problem, therefore, was not the shortage of labour on estates, as Sherlock and Seaford contended, but fear of a shortage if workers were provided with options away from the plantations. On this matter nothing had changed since the regime of Quintin Hogg and William Middleton Campbell in the 1890s. Lethem had explained:

[A feature of the Corentyne] is the increase in the East Indian population, several large villages being now practically entirely populated by East Indians. One of the reasons for the large scheme being so necessary is precisely to accommodate the growing population. The four large sugar estates in the area [Rose Hall (East Canje), Albion, Port Mourant, Skeldon — all Booker estates by the 1940s] present a picture of well-drained and irrigated land, and these have had their reward in being amongst the most well-doing in the colony. The same satisfactory picture, however, does not apply generally to the lands apart from the sugar estates, and in times of flood, from rain in the rainy season and the over-flow of the savannah water in the back-lands, the picture in many of the villages is lamentable: not only provision lands suffering heavily but sanitation being deplorable for a period of several weeks on end.[11]

Lethem had high hopes for the Corentyne: if drained and irrigated, it would facilitate a better distribution of the population, and he underlined the point, subtly but tactfully, that the estates could also benefit. He noted that they 'are themselves already carrying an excess population which they desire to diminish', thereby seeking to nullify the perennial refrain about the shortage of labour. He argued further that despite some handicaps, 'the Corentyne area is in many ways the most promising agriculturally in the colony....[N]ot only have the sugar estates been doing well ... but the rice crop has become more and more successful in recent years, while some areas are particularly suitable for pasturage, as well as for certain kinds of ground provisions which do not do well elsewhere'. He saw this scheme as a major advance for British Guiana: 'Large and expensive ... as the scheme put forward may appear, there is very substantial ground for belief that the economic as well as the sociological benefits will materialise not unsatisfactorily given due time, though this will mean a considerable period of years...' Lethem was unequivocal that the small farmer who could no longer earn a living on the sugar estates should be provided with land that was drained and irrigated: 'sugar estates are no longer able to accommodate the increasing population, by which ... the claim for land is insistent and must in future be met.'[12]

Less than a month after Lethem's despatch, in May 1944, Seaford wrote him to express his objection to the Corentyne Scheme. He paraded all the old arguments planters since the nineteenth century had marshalled, to resist the development of any alternative to sugar. He did not believe that any crop but sugar could bear the expensive overheads for drainage and irrigation and the heavy labour costs. He could see no merit in the Corentyne Scheme being undertaken until 'pressure of population warrants it, and when some economic crop suitable to the Colony has been found to justify the large expenditure proposed'. In fact, Seaford felt that Boerasirie and East Coast Demerara could accommodate 'any expected surplus' population. According to him the colony was nowhere near that position, as the Corentyne only had a population of 55,000 [Lethem spoke of 75,000], and only 18,000 were available for work. The creation of alternative employment would further denude what he considered an inadequate labour supply for the sugar estates. Seaford gave no credence to Lethem's repeated assertions of surplus labour on the plantations: 'Allowing for the expected natural increase of population, it will be many years before the area of the Scheme can be even partially beneficially occupied — bearing in mind that the sugar estates on this Coast are today suffering from a severe lack of labour.'[13]

In 1944 the King Committee (Legislative Council Paper No.2 of 1944) concluded that the reason why work on the sugar estates was not fully taken up was because resident workers found it 'more profitable' to cultivate their rice fields and farms, while non-resident workers, also, were opting for more remunerative employment. This had scared the plantocracy at a time when sugar prices were very attractive: $57.32 per ton in 1943; $61.58 per ton in 1944. Meanwhile the total value of sugar produced had climbed from $7,519,000 to $10,962,000; the area cultivated rose from 192,733 acres to 201,060 acres. Their apprehensions had hardened, too, because of the buoyancy of the rice culture. 1944 was a good year for rice farmers. The export price in 1943 was $98.95 per ton; the following year it had reached $108.38, while the acreage rose from 85,984 to 91,729 respectively.[14] No wonder the sterile plantocratic dogmas were being resurrected: for them rice was subversive of King Sugar.

Jock Campbell was deeply impressed with the indomitable Scot. Sir Gordon Lethem filled a large portion of the colonial stage on which Jock found himself. The following portrait of the man in 1962, the year of his death, by one who knew him well, explains why Jock was so enthralled by him:

> [Lethem] was a lion of a man — great-hearted, formidable when aroused, of bounding energy and vitality. Large-minded and generous, he was the antithesis of everything petty, mean, meticulous, pedantic. The wide, rough colonial stage of his time was an ideal field for his qualities. His facility with languages and liberal and sympathetic spirit kept him in closest contact with high and low among the diverse people with and for whom he worked so devotedly and who in their turn loved and venerated him. His *vividia vis animi*, the faultless verbal memory and power of declamation; his humour and gusto, made him a fascinating leader and friend.[15]

Jock reiterated that Lethem's imagination and zeal for reform were congruent with his own revulsion at the old order; but that, inevitably, he made enemies among entrenched interests: fear of change drove them to bring his governorship to an end, the prime issues which impelled him unresolved. In 1946 Lethem tried to seek a second term as Governor of British Guiana, in order to implement those reforms that he had so fervently embraced during the War. He received great popular support in British Guiana but the Colonial

Office refused him. Jock Campbell believed that the plantocracy might have blocked him, behind the scenes: 'They all thought he was barking up the wrong trees, but he and I really agreed about everything.'[16] As Jock's own capacity for action in Booker, in 1946, was still circumscribed by people like Seaford and the old order, he could commune with the spirit of Sir Gordon Lethem: '[H]e was a remarkable man; I was the only businessman who got on well with Lethem. He and I had common objectives ... he was very unpopular with the Colonial Office and the plantocracy, but he and I got very close together.'[17]

Jock saw Lethem as an ally in his long battle for reform in Booker. His final assessment of the man, therefore, comes with such deep empathy that one may see it as Jock's own reading of the British Guiana situation towards the end of the 1940s, a testament of his own mission:

> I think...[Lethem] was trying to do what any sensible man would have done: he was trying to relieve conditions and pressure on the sugar estates. He was trying to make the plantocracy see the writing on the wall more clearly — that one day there would be political development and one day there would be independence, so they had to come to terms with reality instead of behaving like ostriches and that made him very unpopular with the plantocracy, of course....[They] really resented Lethem and all his views which were for reforms because he understood the workers' resentment.[18]

Lethem's purity of motives in British Guiana enlarged its people's sense of the possible, their conception of a fuller life. But this environment — a capricious landscape requiring irrigation now, drainage soon afterwards; chronic malaria; the latifundist character of sugar: 'Booker's Guiana'— also bred a deep-seated hurt and a radical temperament. High hopes and their abrogation during the Lethem years, coupled with the optimism spawned by the Moyne Commission Report and its advocacy of change (1945), expanded the rebellious spirit.

Endnotes

1. Cheddi Jagan, *The West On Trial: My Fight for Guyana's Freedom* (London: Michael Joseph, 1966), 112-3.
2. Jock Campbell, interview by the author, Nettlebed, Oxfordshire, May 9, 1990, Tape 1.
3. CO111/778/60493 [1943], Lethem to Lloyd, September 23, 1943.
4. Dwarka Nath, *A History of Indians in Guyana* (London: self-published, 1970 [1950]), 251.
5. See note 3.
6. Ibid.
7. Ibid.
8. CO/111/778/60493 [1943], Lloyd to Lethem, personal, December 20, 1943.
9. CO/111/778/60493 [1943], 'Notes of a Conversation in Mr. Beckett's Room...on Friday, 5 November 1943'.
10. CO111/778/60493 [1943], Lethem to Lloyd, February 26, 1944.
11. CO111/785/60466/13 [1944], Lethem to O.F.G. Stanley, no. 74, April 17, 1944.
12. Ibid.
13. Ibid., F.J. Seaford to Lethem, May 10, 1944.
14. See note 4 [pp. 252,257].
15. *The Times* [London], August 20, 1962. See also the issue of August 16, 1962 (Obituary).
16. See note 2.
17. Jock Campbell, interview by the author, Nettlebed, Oxfordshire, July 23, 1992, Tape 3.
18. See note 2.

Chapter Eleven

RACE, CONSTITUTIONAL CHANGE AND THE PAC: EDUN, LETHEM AND THE MAKING OF JAGAN'S MARXISM, 1944-48

British Guiana, after the Second World War, was dominated by two big actors: the Marxist Cheddi Jagan (1918–97) and the Fabian socialist/capitalist Jock Campbell (1912–94). Campbell's reforming zeal was constrained by the essential conservatism of the Booker Board and its shareholders; but it was Jagan's Marxism and immense popularity among Indian sugar workers, from the late 1940s, which impelled Campbell to persist with his reformist vision. The perceived purity of motives of Jagan created an imperative for change; this enabled Campbell to persuade his colleagues of the inevitability of reform. The mould had been set: 'bitter sugar', the implacability of Booker, could not continue because the notion of Booker's Guiana released rebellious impulses in colonial society. Change was inescapable. At the end of the War, with India as the beacon of freedom to most sugar workers, the old order could no longer be sustained.

As noted earlier, the reformist outlook of Governor Lethem, between 1941 and 1946, evoked fear and intransigence from the plantocracy; among the Guyanese sugar workers, though, it released high hopes and eventual disillusionment. A deeper frustration took shape: so much was promised but the possibilities were exhausted by plantocratic reaction and official dilatoriness. Into this already bleak landscape of the promise of change and the despair of reaction was thrown the ingredient of racial politics: the growing apprehension of African Guyanese at what they saw as the threat of domination by Indian Guyanese. This was rooted in the notion that Indians, since the end of indentureship in 1920, were rising inordinately in agriculture, commerce, even the professions, where Africans had had a head-start; the fact that many African landowners had sold out to Indians, also, bred an undercurrent of resentment. Moreover, the demographic increase of Indians, to about 42 per cent by the 1920s, enlarged African fears, already aggravated by irresponsible demands by some Indian leaders, in 1919, that British Guiana be made an 'Indian Colony', a part of 'Greater India'.[1]

The rising tide of Indian nationalism and the ascendancy of Mahatma Gandhi to virtual sainthood among Indians in Guyana, had fed Indian self-confidence and possibilities of their own political domination. This was the context in which Africans had turned to Garveyism in the early 1920s. A bifurcated nationalism — African and Indian — developed from the 1920s. This was sharpened in the 1930s by the Ethiopian (Abyssinian) issue which deepened African consciousness, while the stature of rebel India and its heroes, Gandhi and Nehru (to a lesser extent Tagore), possessed the Indian Guyanese imagination, heightening Indian consciousness. Indeed, one could argue that Indian nationalism in Guyana, fortified by economic progress and Indian nationalist prompting, was more triumphal; African nationalism was reactive, a reflex of perceived, creeping Indian domination and continuing colonialism in Africa.[2]

Since the 1930s the British Guiana East Indian Association and the predominantly Indian MPCA and its president, Ayube Edun, as well as most prominent Indians, had been advocating universal adult suffrage. It is true that the father of trade unionism in Guyana, the founder-president of the British Guiana Labour Union, Hubert Nathaniel Critchlow, since the 1920s, also, had championed universal suffrage. He and Edun were nominated to the Legislative Council by Lethem, in 1943, as representatives of the working class. But ominous for the future of race relations in the colony, the next year, during the debate on the Franchise Commission's Report, Hon Hubert Critchlow, reflecting deep African apprehension of Indian ascendancy, voted against universal adult suffrage. He had appropriated the old plantocratic ruse that literacy was indispensable for the granting of the franchise in order to ensure effective execution of that privilege: many Indians were still illiterate in the 1940s. In 1925 Critchlow had spoken in favour of 'manhood and womanhood suffrage'. He had maintained this position at the British Commonwealth Labour Conference in London, in 1930:

> [N]othing short of adult suffrage and the sweeping away of all qualifications for election as a member of the Legislature will assure to labour sufficient control of the Legislature to ensure adequate laws for the protection of the proletariat. Thus must be finally destroyed all possibility of the nominated 'employer' members combining with the nominated official, always strongly pro-planter in sentiment, to defeat any measure designed for the protection of the masses, and that cannot be achieved unless the elected members are in a permanent majority.[3]

In 1944, in what may be considered a retrograde step, Critchlow voted with several legislators who were 'pro-planter in sentiment' against universal adult suffrage. Jamaica was granted it the same year and the spirit of Lethem would have been in favour of similar advance in British Guiana. Yet, speaking in the Legislative Council on July 7, 1944, Critchlow repudiated his commitment to adult suffrage, supporting even a contraction of the franchise. Fear of Indian domination had reached even this great labour leader:

> With regard to the question of universal adult suffrage I would inform this Council that at the time of my visit to the British Commonwealth Labour Conference held in London [in] 1925, the B.G. Labour Union, on behalf of the workers of this Colony, strongly advocated the introduction of universal adult suffrage, but it was defeated. Our reason for advocating universal adult suffrage at that time was because at elections in this Colony some of the candidates spent a lot of money on drinks and the bribing of voters. As the number of voters was small we advocated the introduction of universal adult suffrage with a view to preventing bribery of the small man. Since then, we have found out that many people believe that if we were granted universal adult suffrage the East Indians would out-vote us in this Council. Even in England I was asked if I was not afraid that some section of the population would out-vote the others and put in whom they liked. My reply to that at the time was 'no', because it was

not so much a colour question. I feel if the Commission recommends that we should reach universal adult suffrage by stages, and that at present we should have a reduction of the franchise, I certainly agree with that because we cannot get all we ask for at once. We must accept what we are given and come back again. I see now that it is really a dangerous thing to allow certain people to exercise the franchise [illiterate Indians] and permit other people to tell them any kind of thing and fool them.[4]

Critchlow's volte-face had so antagonised Ayube Edun of the MPCA that he pronounced it a betrayal of Indian workers:

If we are to compare Comrade Critchlow's recent pronouncement during the Franchise Committee debate — when he said although he supported universal adult suffrage since 1925, he has changed his mind and would support the majority Report which definitely planked for income, property and literacy qualification — with the one of 1925, we would have no alternative but to accuse him of inconsistency; and Comrade Critchlow happens to have been elected recently as President of the Trades Union Council and Member of the Executive Council. How on earth will this labour leader expect East Indian labour to co-operate with the TUC when he, as its head, will change his opinion as if changing a coat? Maybe as a member of the Executive Council, now, he has had to fall in line with the majority bourgeois Councillors, leaving the proletariat to fend for themselves. We are indeed perturbed about this *volte-face* of a man in whom we had the most implicit confidence.[5]

Edun interpreted Critchlow's capitulation as a ruse to keep Indians off the electoral roll. He was especially perturbed, since many members of his union, the MPCA, were affected by the literacy and income qualifications:

We might be permitted to ask what has been the cause for this change of opinion on the part of the Hon. Hubert Critchlow when he himself had admitted as long ago as ... 1925 that the state of East Indian labourers on the sugar estates was tantamount to that of a depressed class. Would relegating the sugar workers, many of whom are Indians and most of whom are illiterates, to the political scrap-heap be any gesture of uplift to equality of standard?[6]

Earlier, in the debate in the Legislature on the Franchise Commission Report, Edun had pleaded the case for Indians in the colony, against the literacy prerequisite. (As late as 1946, 44 per cent of Indians were still illiterate; less than 3 per cent of Africans were.) He felt that it would deprive sugar workers of an elected representative and precipitate a demand for ethnic representation; and that it constituted an insult to India. Edun cautioned:

> Because these illiterate persons are Indians and cannot read and write the English Language, they are to be disregarded.... Do you know what that would mean?... These Indians would have the right to ask for representation in proportion to their economic strength and who can blame them if they do? Let us get out of this rut. Let this country be free from the stigma of what happened in Kenya, South Africa and other countries.[7]

Edun then resorted to pride in his racial identity to advance his case. The problem here was that the emerging bifurcated nationalism in British Guiana made people march to different drums, while the expansion of democracy required a degree of consensus and the de-emphasising of ethnic prompting. However, Ayube Edun's rebuttal of Critchlow, though aimed at allaying African apprehensions, probably aggravated them:

> Let us be Americans in conjunction with being British and give the people the right of representation when taxed. I happen to be an Indian. I am proud of the fact and take infinite pride in the fact I am full-blooded Indian and a member of the British Commonwealth.... I am proud to be an Indian and a British subject, but if as an Indian, there is this stigma against me and my people because they happen to be illiterate, though intelligent enough to work and carry on, I must oppose it.[8]

Edun believed that the literacy requirements would have the desired effect of prolonging the disenfranchisement of most of the sugar workers. The race issue was already permeating politics in

British Guiana. This had evoked a hostile response from Edun against Hon J.A. Luckhoo, the only Indian member of the Executive Council, for failing to support adult suffrage. Edun deemed him a traitor to his race. The temper of the place in which Campbell had put down his bucket was, even in the mid-1940s, veering ominously towards racism in its political culture; but the perceived defence of sugar workers' interests was the foundation of political credibility among Indians in the colony:

> [T]his Executive Councillor [J.A. Luckhoo], appearing as it were as the mouthpiece of the East Indian community in that august Council Chamber, never cared 'one jot or tittle' to aid in lifting the depressed classes on the sugar plantations to a station of economic and political equality with that of the others.... [W]e are sure that the day will come — sooner or later — when this hoax of his nomination to the Legislative Council and elevation to the Executive Council will be a matter of severe censure for the people who are the essential units of the state — seeing that although it is accepted by Government that he represents East Indians in the Executive Council, yet hardly any Indian in British Guiana has any confidence in the man's political honesty towards them.[9]

What was most disturbing about the political culture of this colony in the 1940s, as Jamaica led the way to constitutional reform and the rest of the British West Indies followed, was the tendency for fundamental democratic principles to be subordinated to the reservations and fears inspired by racial insecurities. After the War and the independence of India and Pakistan, the question of the devolution of power was ineluctable, but the racial insecurities sublimated within the context of Imperial trusteeship, were now about to be released. The colony's bifurcated embryonic nationalism gave shape to disparate fears; post-war politics and the end of Empire aggregated and aggravated them.

Yet Governor Lethem persisted throughout his administration, between 1941 and 1946, in framing the political debate in terms of fundamental principles of democratic rights and constitutional evolution. He did not seem daunted by the emerging discordant racial forces. In his speech to the Legislative Council on July 3, 1945, he argued that it was necessary to introduce democratic institutions in order to achieve 'real self-government of the colonies by their own peoples'. Then, in what could be interpreted as a repudiation of Crown Colony Government and the conservative stance of the Franchise Commission — a vindication of Edun — he asserted:

> However well-intentioned and competent any Government machine may be, it will always lack one fundamental basis for effectiveness unless it is ensured that the interests of the great bulk of the population are effectively being given their full weight in the Legislature.... It has been left far too much for Government to stand for the interests of the mass of the people as a whole.... All interests of course must be adequately represented, but the day is past when Government officials or a few important interests, however well-intentioned or competent in themselves, can claim to speak and act for the people of any colony.[10]

Lethem believed that programmes for economic development had to be 'socially acceptable'; that required 'much more adequate representation of the classes presently unfranchised in the Legislature, and with its influence adequate on the Executive'. Then, anticipating his critics who would equate enfranchising the working class with chaos in government, he conceded the likelihood that this process would engender 'the most appalling mistakes', but people had to learn to work democratic institutions however painful or protracted the exercise. As usual, Lethem was optimistic that the people of the British West Indies were capable of governing themselves: '[T]he cure for irresponsibility was responsibility and I see no reason to believe that that principle would not work in these countries as in others'.

For Lethem, like Jock Campbell and Cheddi Jagan, political reform, and economic and social reform were inseparable. He therefore advocated a simultaneous programme of 'rural reconstruction', involving, as seen above, a comprehensive drainage and irrigation scheme for the coastland, in addition to land reform, security of tenure, and rural education to promote cooperative agricultural methods, scientific husbandry and marketing. This question of rural reconstruction, he emphasised, was the foundation of democracy; it had to be considered 'the first and absolute priority'.

Lethem was acutely aware of the plantocracy's resistance to his reformist philosophy (so was Campbell); but he never capitulated to their unrelenting drone about the scarcity of labour. Indeed, he acted on the assumption that there was a surplus population on the sugar plantations which had to be relocated, hence the importance of rural reconstruction. In a recommendation which must have struck a responsive chord in Jock Campbell, Lethem argued: 'The more I look at this coastland question the more it seems to me to come back to one fundamental thing, that is, to get land in order, drained, if possible irrigated as well, and gradually to transfer the surplus population off sugar estates and congested villages to such land where adequate conditions of land tenure and co-operative local government organisation can be established.' He recalled that he had often advised 'the heads of the sugar industry that it will be in the interests of their own industry to hand over land for such purposes as housing rather than for the sugar estates to remain landlords of housing areas'.[11]

In what may be seen as the guiding philosophical principle of Campbell's reforms later, in the 1950s when he had acquired the authority, Lethem defined the broader purpose which he thought should animate the sugar industry, in order to synchronise it with the national interests of British Guiana:

> Sugar is regarded as the sheet anchor of our economics and that is true, but to be fully so it must be a national industry with a real share in it for every section of our people engaged in it. Its set-up must be such as to secure the willing and directly interested co-operation of the Guianese as a whole.[12]

Lethem's frustration grew as he reluctantly approached the end of his tenure. He had defined the fundamental problems which bedevilled this backward colony, but very little would be done to alleviate them: the plantocracy and the Colonial Office, as noted earlier, rejected popular demand to extend his tenure. Nevertheless, by 1946, he had exerted much influence on the young director in Booker, Jock Campbell — the germ of Lethem's enlightened vision had permeated his radical mind; it energised him and fortified his resolve to redress ancient wrongs on the plantations. At the same time Lethem's fortitude in challenging the plantocracy and his definition of the parameters of change, the engendering of a culture of reform, also impressed another young man, who grew up on J.C. Gibson's progressive estate on the Corentyne, Port Mourant — the American-trained dentist, Cheddi Jagan. He had returned to British Guiana in 1943, with his wife, Janet Rosenberg, a Marxist of Jewish Czech-American extraction.

In his July 1945 speech Lethem, in expressing his hopes for the evolution of democratic institutions in the colony, anticipated — prophetically as it turned out — the kind of leadership the tasks ahead might require: maturity; the eschewing of sectional or private interests; the subordination of emotional appeal to reason:

> I am a most confident believer in the establishment more and more of democratic institutions, for this means sharing responsibility and the participation in the ordering of our affairs throughout our community and on the common man. Yet in itself that contains no divine principle and it can only successfully live for the common good if sustained by reasoning men working to serve with all their capacity; it is for people who are adult and who have learned to judge for themselves and not betray their minds and their reasons to emotional appeal or private interests.[13]

Uncannily, on Wednesday November 6, 1946, the last time Lethem presided over the Legislative Council, on the eve of his departure from Guyana, four people brought out a four-page cyclostyled paper (the first of 43 issues; the last was on December 26, 1949) — the *PAC Bulletin*, the organ of the Political Affairs Committee (PAC). This study group comprised the young US-trained Indian Guyanese dentist, Cheddi Jagan (1918–97), his wife, Janet (1920-), H.J.M. Hubbard (1911–72), a labour leader of European Guyanese extraction, and Ashton Chase (1926-), a young African Guyanese trade unionist based in Critchlow's BGLU. For the next 50 years Cheddi Jagan was at the centre of the politics of Guyana; the small group, the PAC, was the nucleus of what became, from January

1, 1950, the People's Progressive Party, the first mass-based political party in the colony.

The *PAC Bulletin* was the forum through which Jagan articulated his vision of a new Guyana, challenging the plantocracy and other capitalists, as well as perceived collusion between the colonial administration and 'vested interests'. He was a partisan of the working people whatever their race. His remorselessly critical eye focused on high rent and exploitation by landlords; land-hunger and insecurity of tenure; the plantocracy and their fear of land reclamation and alternative industries; collusion between union and management in the sugar industry; the 'exorbitant' profits of those he deemed the 'sugar gods' or the 'sugar barons'; the problems of Amerindians. Indeed, he was driven by a passion to eradicate the evils that he believed 'bitter sugar' had perpetuated on the working people of British Guiana. Jagan brought to his politics the zeal of the crusader, incorruptibility in prosecuting the sugar workers' cause, implacability in fighting the plantocracy and the colonial rulers. He had no parallel in the British West Indies, few, indeed, anywhere in the former colonial world.

Reading the *PAC Bulletin*, from November 1946 to December 1949, one is overwhelmed by the zeal of this foremost Marxist of the Anglophone Caribbean — his obsession with the evils of king sugar and its principal representative in the colony, Booker. As I will argue in the next chapter, Jock Campbell's reformist vision, although it predated Cheddi, could not elude his frame of reference; indeed, Jock tried to shape a compromise between the reaction of the old planters and Jagan's uncompromising Marxism. One apprehends in the 43 issues of the *Bulletin* the universe of fundamental beliefs of Jagan, which remained essentially unchanged until the collapse of Communism in the late 1980s. In the first issue, on November 6, 1946, he established his Marxist credentials, his belief in 'scientific socialism' (Marxism); the use of 'scientific political analyses' (Marxist methodology) to comprehend society; and the dissemination of Marxist literature to foster discussion and 'propaganda' (the latter, a noble endeavour in the Marxist lexicon) — all aimed at preparing the way for a communist party in British Guiana. There was no doubt that the USSR and the 'People's Democracies', its Eastern European satellites, were the model for Jagan's socialist utopia. The masthead of the first four issues of the *Bulletin* read:

The aims of the Political Affairs Committee are:-

To assist the growth and development of the labour and Progressive Movements of British Guiana, to the end of establishing a strong, disciplined and enlightened Party, equipped with the theory of Scientific Socialism;

To provide information, and to present scientific political analyses on current affairs, both local and international; and

To foster and assist discussion groups, through the circulation of Bulletins, Booklets and other printed matter.

The inaugural issue, in advocating the promotion of cooperative societies in the colony, rejected the 'individualism and greed' that characterised capitalist societies. This was what perpetuated the very low standard of living, while capitalists extracted 'large profits'. They felt that a 'well planned collective, industrial system' was a 'vital necessity'. It is significant that this same issue carried an item on one of the 'people's democracies', Czechoslovakia, where the oil refineries were being nationalised. They noted that no foreign investment would be permitted in key industries; all of these would be publicly owned: 'This was one way of safeguarding the country's independence from foreign big business'. Foreign capital was inherently exploitative and detrimental to progress.[14]

The second issue of *PAC Bulletin* was even more forthright in its advocacy of the communist way in eliminating poverty in Guyana. Responding to Governor Lethem's farewell address to the Legislative Council on November 6, 1946, when he had restated his support for workers' rights and their fight against entrenched interests, as well as the necessity for racial unity if the colony were to progress, the *Bulletin* underlined the importance of the latter in the struggle to end the exploitation engendered by the capitalist system. The example to follow was the Soviet Union, where 'various ethnic groups participate in their own cultural institutions, [while] at the same time working together as comrades in the same socialistic economy, from which the evil hand of capitalistic exploitation had been removed'.

The *Bulletin* then contrasted this socialist idyll with conditions on the plantations of British Guiana, where the workers were deemed 'wage slaves'. Their labour was compensated by 'a mere pittance', the equivalent of a fraction of their day's work; the remainder of their day's labour — surplus value — was appropriated by the 'absentee capitalist'.They supported Lethem's call for empoldered land for the small farmer, as this was one means of stifling capitalist oppression: '[The farmer] working for himself or in co-operation with other farmers on free or relatively free land does not produce any surplus value for parasitic capitalists or landowners'. Here again the Soviet Union was the guide to action, to workers' emancipation. All land had become the property of the state; the 'kulaks', the land-owning class of big farmers had been 'eliminated'. Farmers were now producing collectively, with the aid of machinery and technical expertise rendered by the state.[15] Cheddi Jagan's utopian vision was rooted in the Soviet experiment: armed with 'the theory of scientific socialism', this total system contained all the answers to liberate the Guyanese worker from the evils of capitalism.

Lethem had deprecated the conduct of the commercial class in British Guiana. He quoted a source, to underline their exploitative role in a poor colony: 'too large a class which has fattened in spite of the mass of poverty-stricken citizens ... existing on imports from which the merchant importers have gleaned an easy harvest through percentages, commissions and profits'.[16] This reformist criticism could not satisfy the ideological fervour of Jagan. His response was grounded in sterner theoretical propositions, in loftier Marxist certainties. These were to inform his attitude to sugar throughout his life:

What the Governor failed to point out was that there is inherent in capitalism all these modes of exploitation, whether by the sugar and bauxite capitalists, the commercial, the land-owning or the money-lending class. All these parasitic exploiters are sharing among themselves in varying proportions the surplus labour value created in production by the wage-earning working class. Only with the complete elimination of the capitalist mode of production and distribution, and its consequent surplus labour value and the substitution of socialistic means of production and distribution will this exploitation cease.[17]

Towards the end of 1946 some were arguing that the standard of living of sugar workers would be improved substantially if a 50 per cent increase in sugar prices could be negotiated with the importers of Guyana's sugar. The *PAC Bulletin* rejected this, contending that because the sugar companies were foreign-owned, any increase in prices, as happened during the First World War, was quickly appropriated by these capitalists; only strike action enabled the workers to gain a small concession. Moreover, the PAC argued, capitalists were masters at inflating 'expenses', over-invoicing, to preclude having to make concessions to workers; besides price increases would encourage 'over-production' with the consequent decline in prices. Finally, they asserted that greater reliance on Imperial subsidies to sugar would compound the colony's dependence on Britain, thus retarding advance towards self-government.

The PAC had no stomach for reforms. They advocated rapid mechanisation of the sugar industry to boost productivity and reduce the unit cost of production. To alleviate the unemployment that this measure would necessarily entail, they recommended diversification. Nothing was said about the marketing of sugar, beyond rejecting 'an artificially high price', British subsidies:

> The permanent raising of the living standards of the sugar and other workers of the colony depends, not on the attainment of an artificially high price for sugar, but on the reorganisation of the industry so as to achieve a higher technical level of production and a consequent reduction in the costs of production. Mechanical tillage and reaping would increase the output per worker and so permit the payment of a higher wage without creating an artificial price level that is dependent on the good will of the 'mother' country. Side by side with this mechanisation of the industry there must be an expansion of industry and trade over

the whole colony to allow of employment being created for those workers displaced by the introduction of machinery.[18]

This, however, was a short-term measure: there was no room for even a reformist capitalism in Jagan's construction. Arguing from what PAC called 'scientific' premises, they asserted that the productive process was dependent on four broad elements — land, raw materials, equipment and labour power. Labour was the only 'dynamic' component, the others being 'static' until labour power was organised to work upon land, raw materials and equipment. In capitalist society, however, man is separated from ownership which is vested in the exploiter, who appropriates surplus value: the worker's wages being 'the minimum price required by [him] for performing the function of vitalising the inert elements.'

The unreconstructed Marxist dogma enabled them to dispense with the capitalist: '[He] is not essential to the [productive] process'; the state alone ensures his survival under capitalism. The socialist revolution would give the workers control of the state and the productive process, now no longer the monopoly of this exploitative capitalist class. This is how Jagan saw the 'struggle' ahead:

> The workers seek to protect themselves and their interests by setting up suitable collective organisations, the chief of which are Trade Unions. Later the workers set up political organisations aimed at taking control of the state and Government apparatus out of the hands of Capitalists. The reality of the Social Organisation, therefore, is that two classes confront each other and contest for supremacy....[T]here can be no 'middle road' between capital and labour, and individuals must take sides in a struggle that is fundamental to their existence [emphasis added].[19]

For Cheddi, the reformist outlook of Ayube Edun, Sir Gordon Lethem (and Jock Campbell later) was a distraction from the fundamental, irreconcilable class division in colonial society, between workers and capitalists. The logic of the class struggle would overcome the false divisions in British Guiana, racial and religious, fostered by the capitalists. The first task for workers was to mobilise their efforts, in trade unions, as a prelude to the formation of the Communist party, which would bring real power to the working class, by giving them control of the state and the means of production to be monopolised by the state (the people): 'the dictatorship of the proletariat', a transitional phase to the perfect communist society.

Nearly 40 years later, in 1985, though languishing in the political wilderness since 1964, Jagan was still proclaiming his monopoly on 'scientific communism' in Guyana, while depreciating the 'eclectic', 'opportunist' Marxist credentials of the party of the late Dr Walter Rodney, the Working People's Alliance:

> Marxist-Leninist science teaches that 'class dictatorship' exists in a bourgeois (capitalist), a transitional (petty bourgeois, bureaucratic and military strata), and a proletarian (working class) state. 'Dictatorship of the proletariat' is a specific form of state rule at a particular period in the revolutionary process, the transition period from capitalism to socialism. In essence, it is a higher type of democracy than bourgeois democracy (dictatorship of the minority capitalist class) since it has replaced the rule of the minority capitalist class by the majority working class and its allies, the peasantry (farmers) and other non-proletarian strata of working people. *This revolutionary process evolved, as in the Soviet Union, into a socialist democracy, a state of the whole people* [emphasis added].[20]

Endnotes

1. See my *'Tiger in the Stars': The Anatomy of Indian Achievement in British Guiana, 1919-29* (London: Macmillan, 1997).

2. See my *India and the Shaping of the Indo-Guyanese Imagination* (Leeds: Peepal Tree Press, 1993); and 'The Shaping of the Indo-Caribbean People: Guyana and Trinidad to the 1940s', *Journal of Caribbean Studies* 14, nos. 1&2 (Fall 1999-Spring 2000): 61-92.

3. CO111/687/75080 [1930], British Commonwealth Labour Conference, 1930: British Guiana Labour Union Memoranda.

4. Legislative Council of British Guiana, Debates (The Franchise Commission Report), July 7, 1944.

5. Leader, *The Labour Advocate*, July 30, 1944; see also 'Report of the British Guiana Franchise Commission, 1941', (Legislative Council Paper, No. 10 of 1944), Minority Report by the Hon A.M. Edun.

6. See note 4 [July 6, 1944].

7. Ibid.

8. Leader, *The Labour Advocate*, July 23, 1944.

9. Leader, *The Labour Advocate*, September 24, 1944.

10. CO114/237, 'Speech by His Excellency the Governor (Sir Gordon James Lethem), July 3, 1945'.

11. Ibid.

12. Ibid.

13. Ibid.

14. *PAC Bulletin*, no. 1, November 6, 1946.

15. *PAC Bulletin*, no. 2, November 20, 1946.

16. Ibid.

17. Ibid.

18. Ibid.

19. *PAC Bulletin*, no. 9, May 7, 1947.

20. Cheddi Jagan, 'No Future for Pragmatism and Rightist Opportunism', in *Yes to Marxism — No to Pragmatism and Rightist Opportunism* (pamphlet issued by the PPP [1985]).

Chapter Twelve

'BITTER SUGAR' AND UNIONISM: JAGAN, THE MPCA AND THE ROAD TO ENMORE, 1944-48

Jagan's Political Affairs Committee was unequivocal: strikes were a means by which the working class under capitalism could extract minor concessions from the exploiters. As long as exploitation continued — an inherent feature of capitalism — strikes were endemic. They argued in July 1947: 'As long as the worker is working to put profits, no matter how small, into the hands of capitalists, so long will there be strikes. Only under a changed political-economic system, as in socialism, where the means of production are owned by society, where profits for individuals are eliminated, where there is no contradiction between production and distribution will there be an end to all strikes'. They were not dogged by uncertainty: 'To outlaw strikes, we must first outlaw capitalism.' A potentially dangerous simplicity permeated Jagan's formula.[1]

The PAC identified what they saw as a concrete case of the veracity of this maxim — Czechoslovakia, now under communist control. Cheddi Jagan quoted a Canadian labour leader in his formulation of the Marxist utopia he thought he could create in Guyana: 'Unions here (Czechoslovakia) are so powerful today that they don't need to use the strike weapon.... The unions could tie up the country if they wanted to, but matters are quickly settled.' Czechoslovakia was already shaping the new man; it struck a millennial chord in Jagan: '[It] has worse housing troubles than Canada or the US, but this is how they tackle the problem: space is allocated on the size of the family. If you have a lot of space and no family, you move out to make room for somebody who has a big family but no space.'[2] As simple as that! This was socialist man in the making. Why should one brook half-measures?

For Cheddi Jagan, the trade union was the precursor to the building of a disciplined Communist Party, the weapon for the dismantling of the capitalist state. He therefore saw control of the union as indispensable to the political culture he wanted to forge; indeed it was central to his struggle against 'imperialism'. The biggest union in British Guiana was Edun's Manpower Citizens' Association (MPCA) which, as seen earlier, had gained recognition since March 1939 as the bargaining agent for the mainly Indian field workers on the sugar plantations. Jagan, an Indian from the plantation, was quickly drawn to the MPCA, after he returned to British Guiana in December 1943. In fact, he became its treasurer in 1945, during Lethem's governorship. He could not tolerate reformism in trade unions or in politics: he soon became disillusioned with what he interpreted as its 'collaborationist' tendencies. He was dismissed in 1946 and was quickly 'convinced of the necessity for having a theoretical organ and political platform' — hence his creation of the Political Affairs Committee (PAC) and the *PAC Bulletin* in November 1946. He recalled his brief, turbulent relationship with the MPCA:

> The union machinery was against me.... Pressure was brought to bear upon me for two reasons. Firstly, because I objected to what I considered to be the high level of expense allowances from the funds of a poor union, and secondly because of the tendency to collaborate with the sugar planters. Actually the MPCA was already set on its course of being a company union. A few years before [1940], one of its founder-members [C.R. Jacob] had been taken on to the payroll of Booker Bros., Mc Connell and Co. at £100 per month....This had shakened the confidence of members in the union. Round the bargaining table where I sat for brief intervals I saw clearly that the union leadership was not prepared to fight for the workers.[3]

These perceptions by Jagan, and the later sordid role of the MPCA in the 1960s, have gravely detracted from Ayube Edun's own pioneering effort on behalf of the sugar plantation workers. The conduct of Jacob and at least one other of his senior officers, also, has tended to diminish Edun's formidable contribution. As Jock Campbell recalled, he had no doubts that the chairman of Booker, Sir

Alfred Sherlock, was instrumental in giving Jacob the bribe. I recall seeing a document from Jacob to Booker during the War, stating that as his son was studying in London, the termination of his 'contract' would put him in severe difficulties. In 1941 this issue had led to Jacob's expulsion from the MPCA; two other founder-members, were also expelled: Pile and Rashid. The following year the secretary of the Union, Harri Barron, too, was compromised by the Sugar Producers'Association (SPA). On November 6, 1942 Edun had reprimanded Barron thus: 'I have protested against your receiving as a gift from the SPA a "wallet" file — and I have asked you to return it to Mr. Bayley [secretary of the SPA]; you refused. I consider this kind of thing eventually leads to bribery like the kind to which Mr...[Jacob] yielded, and as General Secretary your action is detrimental to the trade union...' Barron, claiming to speak for the Executive, retaliated; he informed Edun, the president of MPCA, that his salary had been reduced from $60 to $40 per month.[4] These cases of collusion between key officials and the plantocracy gravely impeached the credentials of both union and planters in the eyes of the sugar workers.

King Sugar found the reality of mobilised workers fighting for their rights most repugnant. This image of the sugar industry as an enemy of genuine unionism was to dog Jock Campbell's reforms, constantly vitiating the bona fides of his reformist programme of the 1950s. The SPA, however, never saw the MPCA as collaborators. Indeed, one could argue that its sordid overtures were designed to stifle what it saw as militancy. As noted earlier, the union had waged a relentless struggle for recognition, and had it not been for the presence of the Moyne Commission in the colony during the Leonora shootings in February 1939, the plantocracy would have resisted recognition longer. Nearly a decade later, in its memorandum to the Venn Commission in 1948, after the shootings at Plantation Enmore, the SPA still saw the MPCA's early work, in 1937-39, as 'a campaign of agitation', a 'propaganda campaign', which sowed 'the seeds of dissatisfaction'. They rationalised what the union saw as a policy of victimisation, a regime of fear, thus:

There followed stoppages of work, refusal to accept job work at usual rates and on customary terms, and a general opposition to all forms of authority and discipline which left the Management no alternative but summary dismissal and eviction [from estate ranges] if discipline was to be maintained. During the next six months the position gradually deteriorated, culminating in the serious disturbances of 1937 and the fatal shooting at Plantation Leonora [1939]. During that period there was much confusion, complete lack of any policy on the part of the so-called trade union.... On almost every estate the preaching and subversive activities of the officials of the trade union had had the effect of bringing to the fore as local leaders the undesirables and blacklegs [ironic!] among the working population.[5]

The SPA perceived a change after 1942, when the Labour Department was organised and a commissioner of Labour, W.M. Bissell, appointed. There emerged a policy of inculcating democratic principles in the MPCA, conducing to better industrial relations. Consequently, since 1945, the establishment of Estates' Joint Committees, representing both sides, had lifted the quality of negotiations. This conciliatory tenor would have been repugnant to Cheddi Jagan, for whom ongoing militancy, manifested in the use of the strike weapon, was inseparable from the class struggle: unionism was an instrument for destroying the capitalist state. The SPA, however, had described the new approach of the MPCA thus: '[T]he old system of stopping work as a first indication of dissatisfaction has been gradually eliminated and the new principle of negotiation while the member remains on the job has slowly been established.'[6]

By 1948, with the Jagan-backed Guiana Industrial Workers' Union (GIWU) challenging the MPCA for recognition, the SPA were already making a distinction between the Marxist Jagan and the reformist Edun, extolling the virtues of the latter's responsible leadership since 1945. The Estates' Joint Committees were lauded for the 'prompt on-the-spot settlement of disputes'. This, they contended, had redounded to the workers' advantage: increase in the cost-of-living bonus from 10 per cent in 1940 to 33.3 per cent in 1948; increased minimum rates of pay in factories and for daily paid field workers; increases in cane-cutting and punt-loading rates; improved working conditions in the factories, with reduction in shift-work, from 12 to 8 hours, 'without any loss of pay'; increased overtime rates to time and a half and double pay; along with 'many other concessions'.[7]

This contrasts sharply with the summary response of the SPA in 1944, when they had suspended the recognition agreement with the MPCA because of an editorial, 'Sugar Estate Economics', in the union's organ, *The Labour Advocate,* on June 18, 1944. The SPA dubbed it 'extremely misleading and subversive'. Earlier they had denounced what they termed the anti-sugar attitude in several articles in the same paper, which was 'not in conversance with the spirit of co-operation professed by the Union in the conference room'. The SPA informed the MPCA that unless they were 'prepared to give a written undertaking to discontinue all propaganda forthwith' and publish their letter in *The Labour Advocate,* 'together with a public retraction of the article' satisfactory to the SPA, it would take steps 'at once' to repudiate the recognition agreement of March 2, 1939.[8] This letter had been sent to the union on July 4, 1944 and recognition was suspended until the publication of a letter from the MPCA on August 21, acknowledging 'inaccuracies' in the leader of June 18, while regretting whatever 'inconvenience and annoyance' they had caused the SPA. The letter from the SPA appeared in *The Labour Advocate* of August 27, 1944.

Ayube Edun, it will be recalled, was in an embattled mood at this time, deeply incensed by what he considered the timidity of people like his old ally, Hubert Critchlow, on the sensitive adult suffrage issue. Indeed, on April 16, 1944, in a leader in *The Labour Advocate,* 'Sugar and B.G. Export Economy', Edun had deplored 'the abominable living conditions prevalent on sugar estates'. He accused the plantocracy of 'economic sabotage of every kind', a result of the 'sinister influence of the absentee proprietors prevailing in the Council of Government, here and in England — seeking a perpetual preservation of 30 million dollar sugar property, ensuring a cheap labour reservoir'.

Edun elaborated on conditions on the plantations, in imagery that virtually anticipated Cheddi Jagan's 'bitter sugar' motif from the late 1940s. He argued:

There must be a rational solution of this economic problem now or never for sugar workers are not prepared to remain helots any longer — living in hovels 10 x 10 feet where 7 to 10 persons are huddled, not earning enough to keep bodies and souls together; their wives, their children and themselves remain as illiterates in order to secure dividends, profits, swimming pools and palatial residences for the parasites. They live in an atmosphere where Rumshops abound. There are no recreation facilities available and they fall prey to the very Rum they themselves manufacture, thus passing through a benighted existence while the parasitical classes prosper at their expense. If this status quo will have to be preserved to satiate a sugar export economy then it is in their interest that every sugar plantation collapses and they turn their attention to Rice and thus a mass of human beings will find Economic Redemption. All the sugar workers have to do is take courage like the people of Windsor Forest, La Jalousie and Hague, Essequibo and the villages and build their economic patterns on self-sufficiency and rice export.

Edun's declamation in April 1944, during the War, was a testament for change: both Jock Campbell and Cheddi Jagan would be moved in their own way to respond; but that had to wait until the end of hostilities. 1947 was a momentous year. On October 30, 1947 Jock Campbell, aged 35, was appointed vice-chairman of Booker — the biggest owner of plantations in British Guiana, with interests in such a wide range of other activities that the expression 'Bookers Guiana', as noted earlier, had acquired pejorative associations: domination, greed, and the worse form of colonial exploitation. On November 24, 1947 Cheddi Jagan, aged 29, was elected to the Legislative Council, the member for Central Demerara, in which were located virtually all the sugar plantations on the East Coast Demerara — Non Pareil, Mon Repos, LBI, Ogle, Enmore — all Booker estates. These two men of very contrasting backgrounds were to be the key players on the same stage for the next 20 years: the Marxist and the reformist capitalist (Fabian socialist) — one committed to the building of a communist state in which no foreign-owned plantations would exist; the other committed to reforming the sugar plantation culture, sweetening the bitter legacy, which evoked in him guilt and remorse.

What was clear by the late 1940s was that 'bitter sugar' was inextricably intertwined with the broader nationalist debate in post-war Guyana; indeed Booker, was the fulcrum around which the Jaganite/Marxist vision revolved. For Jagan, sugar could not be sweetened. Booker became the instrument which quickened and aggregated his own working-class/nationalist credentials; while the MPCA's tarnished image — perceived as supping with the enemy; in Booker's palm — would be the unvarying backdrop against which he would imprint on the popular Indian imagination his impeccable motives, his pure Marxist vision. Jock Campbell's reformist outlook was shaped by his experiences in Guyana in the 1930s, but it was Cheddi's zeal, his unfaltering identity with the sugar worker — a political agenda which, from the beginning, threatened the very existence of Booker — that gave urgency to Jock's mission. He undertook the reforms as a necessary good in their own right, but he was astute enough to seek to undermine the source of the Jaganite appeal, in order to give Booker breathing space.

Jock Campbell told me that with the death of Sir Alfred Sherlock, the chairman of Booker, in 1945, and the elevation of Major A.F.V. McConnell to his position in 1946 and he to the vice-chairmanship in 1947, his authority rose significantly. However, he still had to contend with a resilient conservative tradition which permeated the Board: McConnell himself, A.M. Armour, Drake, A.E.V. Barker, Sherlock's son, N.P. Sherlock, and his own father, C.A. Campbell. But he had a free hand in writing all the Chairman's Annual Statements between 1947 and 1966, the year before he retired, with the exception of 1961 when he was very ill. He often remarked that those statements are a barometer of the evolution of his ideas on sugar, politics and Booker's role in British Guiana and its growth in other parts of the world.

The statements for 1946/7 and 1948 have a discernibly cautious feel, a testing of the ground: modernisation; greater efficiency; the necessity to improve workers' standard of living. In the former Campbell announced that the net profit of Booker after tax, for the 18 months to December 31, 1947 was £180,229, compared with £96,562 for the preceding 12 months. He intervened: 'This, you will agree, is not unsatisfactory.' Shareholders were given a dividend of 3 per cent and a bonus of 2 per cent, both free of income tax. Taxation had claimed £285,000, comprising UK income and profits tax, colonial income tax, and excess profits tax (UK), which was payable up to the last six months of 1946.

Campbell remarked that nearly half the profits came from British Guiana, from sugar: '[I]t is the foundation of our business.' However, unfavourable weather in 1947 had resulted in a fall in production of sugar from 120,347 tons in 1946 to 111,568 tons. Prices had been good, but it was necessary to reduce the cost of production to accommodate a possible decline in prices in the future. The statement has nothing radical in it, although he does acknowledge the obligations of Booker to its employees in British Guiana. He was unambiguous that the cost of production had to be reduced; this required modernisation — a change in methods of production; the assimilation of scientific techniques; the urgency of sharpening their competitive edge. But Campbell knew that the necessity to reduce costs must not obviate their responsibility to their workers. He was cautious in the late 1940s, he told me, because he wanted to get the conservative shareholders on the side of reforms:

> We, for our part, are doing all in our power to reduce costs. You know of many of our plans to increase output, to enhancing efficiency, to obtain new plant and equipment in field and factory, to improve production technique, to seek more technical advice and to strengthen organisation. It must be admitted, however, that in the case of Colonial industries the real need to improve the living standards of the people introduces an element of inflexibility in costs of production of which wages represent over half and the provision of better amenities for workers a further material proportion.[9]

Campbell commented tangentially on the 1948 strike on the East Coast Demerara estates (the matter was *sub judice),* noting that if the cost of producing sugar in British Guiana outstripped its value because of strikes, that would be 'a sure road to ... disaster', not only for sugar workers but 'almost to anyone who earns a livelihood' in the colony. It is clear, therefore, that he was not sympathetic to the Jagan-backed GIWU, which had called the strike on the East Coast: 'I only hope that the workers on our Estates, wisely advised by their established Trade Union [MPCA] and by the Government of the Colony, will carry on peacefully with their daily tasks while the Inquiry [Venn Commission] proceeds'.[10]

In 1948 Booker reported a profit, after taxation, of £157,162; shareholders were paid a dividend of 5 per cent and a bonus of 3 per cent, both free of taxation. The output of sugar was 120,000 tons, compared with 117,500 tons in 1947. This, as Campbell observed, was 'not unsatisfactory', given adverse weather and the six months' strike on the East Coast Demerara, which accounted for a loss of about 6,000 tons. It is noteworthy that Campbell made no mention of the fatal shootings at Plantation Enmore on June 16, 1948 when five workers were killed — supporters of the GIWU. This event was to have cataclysmic implications for the politics of decolonisation in British Guiana.

However, he did not abandon his commitment to reform in the sugar industry, remarking thus of the impending Venn Report (published in 1949): 'Your directors can have nothing to fear from it, indeed they believe that a full and impartial statement of the position of the Sugar Industry in British Guiana will do great good.' Campbell then advanced what may be seen as his case for reform, to the Booker shareholders. He argued that sugar was so crucial to British Guiana that the prosperity of the latter was inseparable from that of the former; and that the success of the industry depended on three main factors: 'the efficiency of the Industry'; 'the price paid for its products'; and 'the human relationships within the Industry and within the Colony'.[11] The latter, he implied, could not be improved without the success of the others. This, in fact, was Jock's broad and unemotional summary of the mechanism for change on the plantations: productivity; stable prices; good industrial relations.

He expressed optimism that the impetus for improving efficiency and expanding production could be sustained with better sugar prices in the UK. This had increased by £2 16s per ton in 1948 over 1947; and although the Ministry of Food, the buyer, had rejected the suggested price for 1949, he was not discouraged. He felt that as a result of a meeting between the British government and British West Indian producers (Edun was present, as was Bustamante, the Chief

Minister of Jamaica), the future of the sugar industry could be secured. Quoting a release on the meeting from the producers' organisation in London, the West India Committee, he underlined his optimism:

> His Majesty's Government assured the delegates that they recognise that the prosperity of the Sugar Industry is vital to the maintenance of an adequate standard of living in sugar producing colonies such as the British West Indies. It is their intention to make long-term arrangements which will give to the efficient producer of sugar in these areas and elsewhere in the Commonwealth firm assurances of markets for agreed tonnages of sugar [quotas], at reasonably remunerative prices negotiated with the producers.

Campbell observed that this was 'essentially a declaration of principle', but he had no doubts that it was made in good faith. A good atmosphere was being created for the impending negotiations, which could give the producers in the British West Indies 'the real security which they justifiably seek and without which the Colonies where they operate will be devastated by social and economic disintegration'. He felt that the sugar producers should be able to convince the British government that quotas and prices must have a duration of at least ten years 'to be of real value'.

Campbell's strategy for reforms was totally dependent on a formula of stable prices and quotas. Prices had improved markedly in the post-war years — from £11 per ton in the early 1940s to £17 8s, £21 9s and £25 2s per ton in 1946, 1947 and 1948 respectively[12] — but these were still based on an ad hoc approach to pricing. A policy of reform, therefore, must be grounded in solid, long-term agreements with the UK government. 'Human relationships' in British Guiana were crucial, but Campbell regretted that their efforts to alleviate working conditions were met with a lack of comprehension in the colony. Then, obviously misreading the mood of many sugar workers and the rising stature of Cheddi Jagan, in the aftermath of the Enmore shootings of June 1948, he asserted: '[T]his atmosphere [of suspicion] is generated not by our employees, but by certain sections of the general community including, I regret to have to say, some Government officials.'[13]

In an attempt to improve their image, they appointed a manager for the Sugar Producers' Association, W.A. Macnie, the former Colonial Secretary of the Windward Islands, a white Guyanese. But Campbell was still not in favour of recognition of the Jagan-backed GIWU, nor was he sympathetic to its leaders who were challenging Edun's MPCA. He claimed that the workers were 'organising themselves', presumably within the latter, and he commended the participation in the sugar talks in England, 'on their own initiative', of Ayube Edun and A.A. Thorne, president of the predominantly African factory workers union, the British Guiana Workers' League (BGWL).

Already, by 1947-48, Campbell's reformist vision was becoming enmeshed in the interstices of the nationalist campaign that was coming increasingly under the influence of the young Marxist legislator, Cheddi Jagan. At the end of August 1947, for instance, Jagan's Marxist colleague in the PAC, H.J.M. Hubbard, an ex-serviceman, had picketed the offices of Booker in Georgetown; his picket read: 'BOOKERS HAVE JOBS FOR ENGLISHMEN BUT NONE FOR GUIANESE'. *PAC Bulletin* endorsed this, noting that with every ship which landed from the UK, came between 10 and 30 people to fill vacancies at Booker, thus augmenting the European elite at the expense of Guyanese. The following assessment would have struck a chord in the colony, at the end of the War: 'These people soon get themselves integrated into the autocratic social class and go around in limousines, while hundreds of local men and women — some of whom fought for King and Country — languish in the streets unemployed. This is a situation that needs tackling and it is time that the importation of these people cease, until local unemployed suitable for these posts are absorbed.'[14]

As noted earlier, Jagan was elected to the Legislative Council in November 1947. He had outlined the qualities he possessed which he felt would make him a good representative: 'open and continuous identification with labour grievances and aspirations' and 'sincerity and honesty of purpose'.[15] He did not deviate from his Marxist frame of reference; his was no mere youthful exuberance; it would be a creed for the next 50 years. He immediately challenged orthodox notions of the relation between labour and capital. He noted that one victorious candidate at the 1947 elections had argued that capital was entitled to its share of profit, while workers must work hard to earn a decent wage. In December 1947 Jagan countered this, repeating that the capitalist was, in fact, superfluous to the productive process: 'Such a statement forgets that all profits come from the sweat of labour and that to tell labour that it must work hard for a decent wage is to fully misunderstand the real needs of labour. Labour wants now a decent wage for the present hard work carried on under conditions of malnutrition and poor housing'.[16]

Jagan saw no role for the capitalist, the appropriator of 'surplus value'; society could do without this parasitic impostor. He then turned to the race issue and labour's task in its eradication in Guyana. His was a simplistic formula:

Labour...will have to solve the question of race. This it can only do by *replacing* the question of race by the one of class. The rich and the poor of one particular race do not have the same interests. It is the poor and exploited of all races who have a common interest — that of improving working and living conditions [emphasis added].[17]

For Jagan, the theory, the Marxist truths, had a transcendental power; he was not encumbered by history, the intractability of the concrete situation: the problem could be theorised out of existence — deemed a false one. The truth, 'the scientific teachings of Marxism-Leninism', would allow him to 'replace' race with the sacred notion of class. The dogmas were reality; and there was enough deprivation in 'Booker's Guiana' to give them credibility, a continuing plausibility.

The December 1947 issue of the *Bulletin* carried an article captioned, 'Victimisation': it was observed that Booker had announced that new agistment fees for grazing stock on estates' land were being introduced. Under the old system workers paid only for their cattle, at 8 cents per head per month. The new scale was harsh: cattle and donkeys at 36 cents per head per month; horses at 60 cents per head per month; goats at 12 cents per head per month. These fees were double for part-time workers. The PAC interpreted this as a retaliation by Booker for the defeat of 'Big Business' in the general elections of 1947: F.J. Seaford, the head of Booker in Guyana, had lost, but the Government quickly nominated him to the Legislative Council. They noted, however, that the sugar workers were 'openly defiant; [they] are prepared to neither pay the increased fees nor to dispose of the livestock, their only independent means of livelihood'. Then alluding to Cheddi's election as the representative for Central Demerara, where several of the Booker estates were located, they discerned a fresh attitude: 'The people have gained political victory at the polls; now they seem prepared to struggle for their economic freedom'.[18] Jagan's fight against the plantocracy had begun.

In January 1948 the PAC denounced 'low slave wages' on the plantations: 8 cents to 20 cents per hour, hardly an incentive for people to do a full week's work; and they blamed the government for allowing the 'iniquitous wage rate' to continue, attributing this to a resilient 'plantation psychology' in the colony:

> A labourer lives in an estate house — in most cases dilapidated ranges. His small wage does not permit him a saving, with the result that he perpetually lives in the fear of insecurity. Should he refuse to do any work to which he may be assigned, he can be given notice to quit [the range]. This he cannot afford, consequently he submits to the dictatorship of the system, revolting only to the extent of mild passive resistance to the detriment of increased production.[19]

The PAC called on government to intervene so that large tracts of land could be acquired by small farmers, easy credit provided, fertilisers made available, as well as advice on marketing, locally and overseas. 'Government', they argued, 'is more bent on aiding the landed proprietors and capitalists than the farmers who actually need the help'.[20]

Dissatisfaction with the MPCA festered, as allegations persisted that it had 'sold out' to the sugar producers, Edun's own integrity notwithstanding. As noted earlier, Jagan was expelled from the union in 1946. This was the context in which the GIWU was formed, as a potential replacement for the MPCA. Its two principal leaders were not Marxists: Dr J.P. Lachmansingh, president, and Amos Rangela, secretary. It is noteworthy that they occupied the same positions in the principal Indian organisation in the colony, the British Guiana East Indian Association. The GIWU was registered on April 5, 1948. Most of its pioneering work was concentrated on the Booker estates on the East Coast Demerara (accessible to its Georgetown-based leaders): Ogle, Non Pareil, Lusignan, Vryheid's Lust, LBI and Enmore. Jagan became involved with the Union as he sought election to the Legislative Council for this district, Central Demerara.[21] When he won it in November 1947, his commitment to ousting the MPCA became an imperative of his political mission.

Shortly after its registration, GIWU had unsuccessfully tried to gain recognition from the SPA as the sole bargaining agent for field *and* factory workers. Although their grievances were numerous — lack of potable water ('trenches over which people bathed and washed their clothes provided drinking water'); the ranges, often, were in an advanced state of dilapidation; long distances to and from work, aggravated by muddy dams and inordinately long hours in the fields; pregnant women had to work in water to their waist; child labour; insufficient land on the estates for farming — it was the replacement of the 'cut and drop' method of cane harvesting by the 'cut and load' method which the GIWU chose to prosecute its claim for recognition.[22]

Introduced in 1947, it marked a change in the character of cane-cutting. Formerly, cane-cutters cut the cane and fetched it in bundles to the bank of the canal; loaders then deposited the bundles in the punts, the flat-bottom tugs. Cane-cutters were now required to perform both tasks at the combined pay of 60 cents (45 cents for cutting, 15 cents for loading). At a MPCA conference in February 1948 delegates voted for the new system on condition that management approved a hike from 60 cents to $1.00 per ton. In mid-April a conference of the MPCA, SPA and the Commissioner of Labour agreed to an increase of 4 cents per ton and a boost in the cost of living bonus from 30 to 33 per cent This, in fact, amounted to an increase of 7 cents per ton. The MPCA signed the agreement.[23]

The GIWU denounced this as another demonstration of the MPCA's degeneration into a company union, and called a strike on April 22, 1948. Ashton Chase, a founder-member of the PAC, admitted that the issue was a ruse to prosecute the union's bid for recognition: 'The Enmore strike started on 22 April 1948, by cane cutters ostensibly over the system of cut and load as against cut and drop. The real object of the strike, however, was to secure recognition of the GIWU as the bargaining agent on behalf of field and factory workers in the sugar industry.'[24] Cheddi Jagan, the legislator for the district, and his wife, Janet, were deeply involved in the strike and the provision of strike relief. For Jagan, this was the foundation of the political mission — control of the largest union in the colony, a major step towards eventual control of the state and the economy in building his Communist society.

When, by mid-June 1948, the strike seemed to be flagging, the GIWU stepped up its propaganda in an effort to give the exercise a broader racial appeal. It planned to win support from predominantly African factory workers: on June 16, several Indian field workers at Enmore tried to advance this strategy, with no success. Meanwhile, several armed policemen had been dispatched to the factory compound to protect it. When some Indian field workers crossed a canal encircling the factory and entered the compound, apparently to persuade the African factory workers to join the strike, the police opened fire. They claimed that the property and their own lives were endangered by the strikers who were armed and agitated beyond control. Five of the invading workers were killed, most while apparently trying to retreat over the canal whence they had come — they were shot in the back.

The funeral of the five workers, on June 17, 1948, was a momentous event in the shaping of the anti-colonial movement in British Guiana. The conduct of the colonial police impugned the colonial state, as an agent of oppression serving King Sugar; but it also reinforced the perception that the plantocracy, Booker especially, were not responsive to change. Enmore brought sugar to the heart of the embryonic nationalist campaign; it meant that henceforth Campbell's reforms would necessarily be enmeshed in the emerging volatile political discourse, on the eve of the end of Empire. The intemperate response of the police at Enmore had played into Jagan's hand, softening the way his Marxist ideology would be seen even by some who were inclined to stress its totalitarian implications. He was handed a cause and the PAC marked that with this evocative headline, written by its activist, Sydney King (Eusi Kwayana): 'THEY ASKED FOR BREAD; THEY GAVE THEM BULLETS'.[25] Jagan recalled the time:

> The Enmore tragedy affected me greatly. I had personally known the young men who were killed and injured. My wife and I, Dr. Lachmansingh and the other leaders led the funeral procession ... it became a tremendous protest demonstration. We left Enmore on foot and marched to the city 16 miles away, taking the bodies there for burial.... At the graveside the emotional outbursts of the widows and relatives were intensely distressing, and I could not restrain my tears. There was to be no turning back. There and then I made a silent pledge — I would dedicate my entire life to the ... struggle of the Guianese people against bondage and exploitation.[26]

Cheddi Jagan's politics now had a remarkable clarity of purpose, an assiduity in assailing perceived injustices on the plantation: there could be no compromise, no middle road, no *modus vivendi*. His implacability, an obsessive hatred for the 'sugar gods', would have a fatal impact on him and his country. But it had its heroic phase, such as his early years in the Legislature, between 1948 and 1952. He had warmed to the role of gadfly:

> I soon learnt to play the game in the same determined way that Seaford did his job for Bookers and sugar — sweetly and suavely with a smile ... it was my task to find out how in a multitude of ways, overtly and covertly, the sugar 'gods' ruled. Mine was the role of 'politics of protest', with the weapons of exposure and struggle. If the legislature was my forum, the waterfront, the factories, plantations, mines and quarries were my battleground.[27]

Ashton Chase recalls Jagan's presence, a virtual voice in the wilderness in the Legislature of 1947-53. It was an unfaltering effort, animated by the workers' problems and his Marxist certainties. Chase makes us feel the zeal, the passion of Jagan's politics; one could even see him transcending the racial divide by sheer will, 'replacing' race with class:

The solemnity of the Legislative Council was rudely shaken by his vigorous advocacy of the cause of workers. He had a passion for statistics. He used these in his pungent and forceful arguments to expose reaction and to lay bare before the workers the vicious system that exploited them. At sitting after sitting, he assaulted the vaunted privileges of the capitalists. On many occasions, single-handedly, but nevertheless most heroically and inspiringly, he fought for the workers' rights.[28]

In Jagan's passion, there was no space for reforms on the sugar plantations — the sugar gods had to go; foreign ownership was deeply anathema to him. Even before the Enmore shootings *PAC Bulletin* had carried an article on the front page, captioned, 'A People's Government', a tribute to the new government in Czechoslovakia, headed by the Communist Party. They were contemptuous of the 'totalitarian' label stuck to it by the 'capitalist class', countering that it was 'a new and genuine democracy': land was being handed over to the peasantry, no one could own more than 125 acres; industries were being nationalised; the press was coming under the control of trade unions, cooperatives and political parties. To Jagan the Czechoslovak experiment was a model worthy of emulation in British Guiana. He imagined:

> Transposing this situation to British Guiana would mean that the present slave plantation system of the sugar estates would be completely smashed. The estate land would be divided up and the sugar workers instead of merely working for miserable wages would be the producers of their own sugar cane on their own land. The sugar factories would be owned and operated by the Government. The other large landed proprietors who are today making an easy and comfortable living by money-lending, share-cropping and land-renting would be forced to earn their bread by performing actual work. The local capitalist press now owned by, controlled and operated for the preservation of private profit would be replaced by a people's press fighting for the real needs of the people.[29]

After the killings at Enmore the strike on the East Coast Demerara continued for several months, as the plantocracy became more obdurate in their resistance to the GIWU campaign for recognition. However, Jagan's reputation was enhanced by Enmore as he skilfully built on the foundation sanctified by the 'blood of the martyrs'. He and his colleagues were weaving a politics of protest in which hatred of Booker was the animating force. The *PAC Bulletin* was distributed free at all his meetings. It pitted Cheddi, the selfless Indian sugar worker's hero, against the Goliaths of privilege, the white sugar gods— the antithesis, yet creator and sustainer, of the coolie. This was the central motif of the awakening on the plantations at the end of the 1940s.

On August 26, 1948, at Grove, East Bank Demerara, Cheddi reportedly remarked that there were two kings in the colony, King George and King Sugar, and that the Governor, Sir Charles Woolley, supported King Sugar. Dr Lachmansingh, president of the GIWU, remarked at the same meeting that the strike would continue until they were able to run the estates themselves: 'We are to strike and make as much trouble as possible until we get what we want.... We are out to destroy the sugar industry either by giving each worker 5 acres of land; the worker plants the canes and sells to them, or ask Government to scrap up [the] sugar estates and give us as land settlements, and we will grow rice and get good prices for our rice.'[30]

The Jaganite vocabulary spoke of collision: sugar was a red rag to this generally charming man and the language would quickly become intemperate. On August 29, 1948, at Good Intent, West Coast Demerara, he told workers that strikes were going to be the weapon for winning their rights and that the next strike would last one year. He added: 'We have to hit the sugar producers one after the other; we are going to cripple the bitches....They say sugar does not pay; well, why the hell keep planting it — divide the land and give the people to plant their own canes and the mills will be owned by them or Government.'[31]

In the mid-1960s Janet Jagan reportedly told a British journalist, Peter Simms, 'Enmore made us',[32] referring to their ascendancy and unassailable stature among Indian sugar workers and Indians generally, after the shootings of June 16, 1948. Enmore was a millstone, too. Already, by 1948, Cheddi's and Jock's positions on the role of sugar in the future of Guyana were irreconcilable. Cheddi's

Marxism could not accommodate the perpetuation of the sugar industry as anything but a nationalised industry. Jock, on the other hand, believed that with ongoing reforms the dark history of sugar could be redeemed, to the benefit of Guyana and its workers; moreover, that Booker and the government could forge a partnership as joint owners of the industry. But Cheddi was not amenable to compromise with the 'sugar gods': although this was judged by his Indian supporters as a heroic quality, rendering him indispensable, it would contribute to their country's degeneration into poverty, racial strife and a massive flight overseas. He could see only black and white, not the nuances which constitute reality; he lacked the flexibility of temperament, subtlety of perceptions and judgement, the imagination, to move beyond the role of crusader — he was not a statesman.

'Enmore made us':
Cheddi Jagan addressing workers in Georgetown
after the Enmore shootings, 1948

Endnotes

1. *PAC Bulletin*, no.12, July 9, 1947.
2. *PAC Bulletin*, no.13, July 23, 1947.
3. Cheddi Jagan, *The West on Trial: My Fight for Guyana's Freedom* (London: Michael Joseph, 1966), 88.
4. Ashton Chase, *A History of Trade Unionism in Guyana, 1900 to 1964* (Ruimveldt, Guyana: New Guyana Co Ltd, n.d., ca. 1964), 112-3.
5. Memorandum of the Sugar Producers Association [to the Venn Commission, 1949], mimeo., pp. 22-3.
6. Ibid., 24.
7. Ibid.
8. Booker File: BGSPSA Industrial Relations Department, Labour Report, February-June 1944.
9. See 'The Chairman's Statement' in Booker Bros, McConnell and Co Ltd, *Report of the Directors and Statement of Accounts, 1946-7*.
10. See 'The Chairman's Statement' in Booker Bros McConnell and Co Ltd, *Report of the Directors and Statement of Accounts, 1948*.
11. Ibid.
12. See Dwarka Nath, *A History of Indians in Guyana* (London: self-published, 1970 [1950]), 251, Table 11.
13. See note 10.
14. *PAC Bulletin*, no.16, September 3, 1947.
15. See note 4 [p.125].
16. *PAC Bulletin*, no. 20, December 17, 1947.
17. Ibid.
18. Ibid.
19. *PAC Bulletin*, no. 21, January 14, 1948.
20. Ibid.
21. See note 4 [pp.148-9].
22. Ibid., [p.142.]
23. Ibid., [p.146-7].
24. Ibid., [p.141].
25. Eusi Kwayana, interview by the author, Georgetown, Guyana, September 22, 1992.
26. See note 3 [p.109].
27. Ibid., [p.95].
28. See note 4 [p.126].
29. *PAC Bulletin*, no. 25, April 14, 1948.
30. CO111/797/60270/5/5 [1948], 'Report on a GIWU Meeting held at Grove, East Bank Demerara, 26 August 1948'.
31. Ibid., 'Report on a GIWU Meeting held at Good Intent, West Coast Demerara, 29 August 1948'.
32. Peter Simms, *Trouble in Guyana: An Account of People and Personalities as They were in British Guiana* (London: George Allen and Unwin, 1966), 95.

Chapter Thirteen

'BITTER SUGAR': THE VENN COMMISSION AND ITS CONTEXT, 1948-49

In July 1948, a month after the Enmore shootings, the *PAC Bulletin*, in an article captioned 'Bitter Sugar', demanded a commission of inquiry to undertake a comprehensive examination of the sugar industry. With the continuation of the strike after the shootings, several estate residents were served eviction notices while six of the leaders of the GIWU, including Cheddi Jagan, the legislator for the district, were given trespass notices in an effort to cripple the strike on the East Coast Demerara. The *Bulletin* argued that the terms of reference of the commission should be 'to enquire into and report on the organisation of the sugar industry, including means of production, profits and their distribution, and wages and conditions of work'. They argued that pending the arrival of the commission and as a precondition to the resumption of work, the workers must be assured of the following:

(i)   No victimisation
(ii)   Withdrawal of all eviction notices
(iii)   Removal of all trespass notices
(iv)   Elective system of cut and drop or cut and load
(v)   Cane-punts to be marked showing tonnage displacement
(vi)   For collective bargaining purposes, employers be made to recognise the union enjoying a majority of members [GIWU][1]

There is no doubt that Cheddi Jagan was the force behind this initiative; indeed, his authority and vigour as a legislator were deployed abundantly to the sugar workers' cause. His crusade became the most potent instrument for change, driving the circumspect Campbell towards reforms. Cheddi was able to dramatise their grievances and, unencumbered by party or other sanctions, he was free to attack the plantocracy from his Marxist standpoint. This scared many in this colonial backwater but gave urgency to the issues. Campbell, however, always had to acknowledge the position of the Booker people 'on the spot', the Booker Board and even the shareholders, essentially conservative forces. This required considerable flexibility, manoeuvring, gamesmanship, at which Campbell was already adroit. Paradoxically, it was Cheddi's revolutionary ideas and his growing popularity among the sugar workers that made Jock's ideas of reform, however repugnant to some of his colleagues, increasingly palatable.

Jock's changing responses to the Venn Commission are a good measure of his modus operandi, as he sought to mollify the resisters of change. On June 25, 1948, nine days after the Enmore shootings, W.S. Jones, the director of Booker in British Guiana, had written to the Governor, Sir Charles Woolley, objecting to a commission of inquiry into the sugar industry, as demanded by the PAC. Such a step, he argued, would lend respectability to 'the pirate union [GIWU]' and the 'agitators', who were 'activated purely by political motives'. Jones was not in a conciliatory mood: 'If Government were to accede to the request for a commission at this stage their action would be construed as a sign of weakness and appeasement' to the forces of subversion. He said that pandering to 'agitators' was a 'palliative', which would embolden other agitators to seek notoriety. Jones could see no merits in Jagan and the GIWU: 'A lasting solution can only be obtained by discrediting the leaders of the "pirate union" in the eyes of the workers by demonstrating that their followers obtain none of their promises and that the unruly elements are liable to eviction. If Government and the British Guiana Sugar Producers' Association combine to isolate the area from subversive elements, this can be done.'[2]

On July 15, 1948 W.S. Jones informed the directors of Booker in London that the 'agitators' were still holding meetings in order to prolong the strike on the East Coast Demerara, while the Jagans, Cheddi and Janet, were also visiting West Bank Demerara. He said that they were apprehensive that the local Boland Commission, examining the Enmore shootings, was going against them — their lawyers had 'walked out' of it, alleging that it was pro-planter — and that they were desperate to prolong the strike and use the issue of the Report to 'rouse a colony-wide disturbance'. He noted also that eviction notices were being served on the East Coast estates as a deterrent; he had remarked to Governor Woolley that 'past experience has shown that such action is the most feared by estates' residents'. Jones concluded with a brief sketch of one notable 'agitator', Janet Jagan — 'an American (from Chicago) of European descent, who met her husband [Cheddi] at Northwestern University while they were both students there.... This lady is reported to have some interesting political connections in the USA'.[3]

On July 20, 1948 Jock Campbell forwarded these letters from Jones to the Colonial Office with a covering letter. He, also, noted that several Indian lawyers representing relatives of those killed in the 'Enmore incident' had walked out of the Boland Commission hearings because the case was going against them. Campbell added that to 'this particular clique of agitators' no commission, including the one contemplated to examine the sugar industry, would prove satisfactory, unless it was demonstrably partial to them. He continued:

> Our British Guiana Directors point out that one of the original declared intentions of the agitators was to force the appointment of a commission, and that the Strike and Riots have been engineered to this end. The Governor is being forced into falling in with the original plan of the agitators, which seems disastrous.[4]

Campbell argued that the appointment of a commission of inquiry into the sugar industry of British Guiana would be a 'catastrophe', as the 'deadlock', the continuation of the strike on East Coast estates, required 'a display of firmness on the part of the Government'. He was therefore recommending that the government issue 'a strong public statement' that they would not tolerate any longer 'this threat to the economic foundations' of the colony. He had no doubts that most of the workers had no sympathy with the strike; in any case if they had 'legitimate grievances' they should channel them through the 'established' union (Edun's MPCA). Campbell then attacked Jagan's communist propaganda: he felt that the Governor should 'consider the possibility of banning the subversive literature, which is at present being circulated on the Sugar Estates by these agitators'.[5] G.F. Seel, at the Colonial Office, replied to Campbell stating that the Governor was 'not unmindful' of a public statement on the primacy of sugar to the economy, but they had to exercise caution with regard to the dissemination of subversive literature, as he had already made a statement on 'communist propaganda' and 'the closest watch was being kept upon speeches and printed matter'.[6]

Campbell's fear of communism had such strong resonance in the colony that it elicited a quick response from Jagan's PAC. In July 1948 the *Bulletin*, in an article, 'The Red Scare', observed prophetically:

> British Guiana seems destined for its share of the present British-American anti-communist Red-scare. Within the past month the established order of the Press, the organised Church and Government officials had been exposing their true colours as upholders of the capitalist system and enemies of peace and progress.

Then, citing a Catholic 'Sword of Spirit' meeting in Georgetown, where a speaker had declared that 'to the communists human life is of no value', the *Bulletin* countered:

> Who did the shooting at the Enmore Rifle Ranges? Here is a clear demonstration of the force and violence at the disposal of the sugar lords of British Guiana — remember Lance Corporal Jones and his firing squad reported to the Manager of Plantation Enmore as soon as they arrived there.[7]

Indeed, Campbell's Booker, could not elude the escalating, increasingly bitter, nationalist debate, and Jagan's Marxist frame of reference would brook no half-measures. When the government's co-operative organiser, G.C.L. Gordon, argued that unless democracy [capitalism] 'proves that it is superior to communism', it was doomed to failure, the PAC quickly rebutted the assumption that 'communism is not democratic'. They cited an article, 'Scandinavia: Decline of the

Middle Way', to demonstrate that the 'ills' of capitalism, insecurity, unemployment and so forth, had not been conquered in spite of the so-called socialism and reformism in Sweden. They concluded: 'Mr. Gordon, like President Truman, will stop the spread of communist teachings by wiping out poverty, disease and insecurity.'[8] So Campbell was being pushed into an increasingly anti-communist stance, while Jagan's political stature thrived on what seemed like a crusade against him, spawned not by his communist philosophy but by his uncompromising challenge of the plantocracy.

This was the context in which the Secretary of State for the Colonies announced the appointment of a Commission of Inquiry into the sugar industry of British Guiana, on July 27, 1948. Its terms of reference were: 'To enquire into and report on the organisation of the Sugar Industry in British Guiana, with particular reference to means of production, wages and working conditions and any other relevant matters, and to make recommendations.' In October 1948 the members of the commission were announced: Professor J.A. Venn, president of Queen's College, Cambridge and Gilbey (University) lecturer in the History and Economics of Agriculture, chairman; R. Sudell, agricultural journalist, with B.G. Smallman of the Colonial Office, secretary.

The Venn Commission conducted its investigation in the colony from December 15, 1948 to February 19, 1949. The hearings were held *in camera*: 192 witnesses were examined in Georgetown and New Amsterdam. Many of these were workers, including several women; over 300,000 words of oral evidence were taken. Meanwhile, 20 memoranda were submitted by organisations and private individuals. The Commission toured all the main plantations, inspecting conditions in fields, factories, hospitals and the homes of workers on the estates:

> We went aback, by mule, launch, punt, estate train and on foot, and familiarised ourselves with every aspect of plantation life and work ... and talked individually and in groups to some 1,500 estate workers.... We thus reached the end of our eight weeks of investigation in the Colony with what we felt to be a wealth of first hand knowledge of all aspects of the sugar industry and a clear insight into its problems.[9]

The British Guiana East Indian Association had protested to the Secretary of State for the Colonies their decision to hold the hearings *in camera*, arguing that labour was 'entitled to know the facts advanced by the sugar proprietors and others, and vice versa'; they threatened to boycott.[10] It is significant, however, that for the first time in the colony's history there was effective representation of workers' views: 99 estate workers gave oral evidence before the Commission. In the past, fear of victimisation had precluded such participation; now, with the anonymity provided by private sittings, workers felt safe to speak their minds. The Sugar Producers' Association, The Manpower Citizens' Association, The Guiana Industrial Workers' Union, The British Guiana Workers' League and many prominent individuals appeared before the Commission — Guy Eccles of S. Davson and Co; Dr Cheddi Jagan, the elected member of the Legislative Council for Central Demerara; F.J. Seaford, the head of Booker in the colony and a nominated member of the Legislature; Jai Narine Singh, a prominent Indian leader from the British Guiana East Indian Association; Mr and Mrs R.B. Scargall, Social Welfare Organiser of the SPA and social welfare worker among estate women respectively; Dr George Giglioli, the eminent malariologist of the SPA.

This was without a doubt the most comprehensive scrutiny of the sugar industry ever done in British Guiana; it was symptomatic of a changing environment. On New Year's Day 1949, during the Commission's stay in the colony, *The Daily Chronicle* acknowledged the phenomenal work of Dr Giglioli in the recent eradication of malaria, the 'plague' which had stunted the population of the colony since its colonisation. The paper was effusive: 'No man in the world has accomplished so much in the eradication of malaria as this Scots-Italian doctor, and generations of Guianese will learn to bless his name.' Jock Campbell respected Dr Giglioli deeply, and recalls that, ironically, the great malariologist was interned during the Second World War because of his Italian background; but that did not deter him: he continued his research on malaria, under internment, and evinced no bitterness to the end of his life in Guyana. Jock's eulogy also was effusive: 'He did such wonderful work and he did it with such resolution.'

This was a colonial society that, by the late 1940s, demanded change. The eradication of malaria made all workers healthier; the independence of India had inspired Indians in the colony to feel good about themselves, to seek a better life; Lethem's plans for development, though stymied by the plantocracy, had fed notions of self-government and economic expansion beyond the ancient obsession with sugar. A healthier body was more receptive to radicalism, ideas that spoke of a better future. Ground down for so long, when the lid was lifted after the War, the possibilities seemed illimitable: moderation, circumspection — the Fabian socialism of the rest of the British West Indies — would seem like a betrayal. It was not a society for half-measures: gradualism was suspect.

Cheddi Jagan was already a man for the time; but his communist rhetoric inspired and repelled. Amidst the escalating Cold War, the anti-communist crusade from the late 1940s, his vision was already the source of deep apprehension. In January 1949 *The Daily Chronicle* regretted the Enmore tragedy in which, it asserted, people 'foolishly' followed 'self-style leaders with little record of service (a reference to Jagan and Lachmansingh of the GIWU)', instead of Ayube Edun of the MPCA of whom they said 'few leaders have accomplished so much in so short a time'. Then advancing what could be seen as a representation of Jock Campbell's position after the War, the paper contrasted genuine socialism and responsible unionism with the 'mouthings of [the] new and ambitious politics', the communism of Cheddi and Janet Jagan:

> Good Socialism and Trade Unionism endeavour to find a common meeting ground between employer and employee. A meeting place where, on an equal footing, representatives of both parties may reach agreements which are mutually satisfactory. On the other hand, the Communist method is to label the Socialist as a 'blackguard', the Trade Unionist as a 'traitor' and the employer as a vampire, sucking the blood of workers. No solution is sought. Only the downfall of our way of life, and the creation of a new slavery, in which Communist leaders will be masters and the rank-and-file will be servants. The Guiana Industrial Workers' Union may not be a communist organisation — but its methods are strangely similar, and, most assuredly, bear little relation to good Trade Unionism.[11]

It was a measure of the perceived energy, resolve and charisma of young Cheddi Jagan that he could evoke revulsion and admiration in the same people at the same time. A few days before the leader cited above, *The Daily Chronicle* named Cheddi 'Labour's Man of the Year' for 1948. Such was the consistency of purpose and indefatigability of this 'enigma' that the paper thought it necessary to recognise his contribution, while deprecating this 'volatile labourite with whom we have frequently crossed swords and whose political beliefs we thoroughly detest'. They explained the paradox:

> A political enigma, Jagan, young and ambitious, is chosen, not because we believe he has accomplished any good by his work among the working population, but because as a labourite he has undoubtedly 'made news'. His choice, in contradistinction to Hubert Critchlow, our 1947 choice, will not be popular among all sections of the community. We trust that in 1949, 1948's Labour man of the year, will devote his undoubted talents to co-operative effort for the good of the whole community.[12]

Jagan brought a thoroughness and discernible selflessness to his work. The Venn Commission expressed their gratitude for his well-researched memorandum and his extensive, useful evidence before them on January 14, 1949. This is what he had observed of the abominable logies or ranges on the plantations:

> Housing for sugar estate workers is perhaps the most depressing of their privations. For the most part, they are low-lying, dilapidated ranges built without much plan, usually on uneven ground. These compounds are usually badly drained and are in no way to be compared to those provided for the Staff — Managers, Overseers, etc. There are very few proper streets and consequently in rainy weather, communication is made very difficult. The common latrines, built over a drainage trench are, in many cases, in a state of disrepair offering very little privacy.[13]

In his memorandum, Jagan had argued from the classical Marxist position to demonstrate 'the rate of surplus value' in the industry or the 'degree of exploitation' of sugar workers. He calculated this at 142 per cent! He said that in a ten-hour day the worker's remuneration (wage) was, in fact, covered by four hours work, the sale of his labour power; the other six hours, constituted 'surplus value', profit extracted by the sugar capitalist. He repeated his argument that the capitalist was superfluous to the productive process, that his was a parasitic role: 'They could afford to pay increased wages, regardless of any increase in price.' He had rejected the contention of *The Daily Chronicle* and Ayube Edun that the local selling price of sugar should be increased to meet the demands by sugar workers for better wages.

Jagan's Marxist creed and his sincerity of purpose fortified him against all opposition, however powerful. In his memorandum to the Venn Commission he had even advocated the breaking up of the sugar plantations into smaller holdings of about 25 acres, with the government assuming responsibility for drainage and irrigation and the disbursement of machinery. In the following exchange with R. Sudell he made his case for the dismantling of the plantation structure of the Guyanese sugar industry:

Jagan: [T]he estates should be divided and the small people have their own land, say 25 acres or so. If mechanisation comes, the people would be able to work on a bigger scale ... the same mechanisation which is going to be used for the estate, should be taken over under Government's supervision and utilised to mechanise the smaller units. It must be under Government's supervision because if you leave the small farmers to themselves they would not be any better off.... In view of the fact that mechanisation will come and that we are striving for efficient production, I feel that we must have some control by Government.

Sudell: I see your point, Dr Jagan, although I cannot say I agree with it. I do not think it would be a wise policy to break up these large units into small scale units. We have been on several of the estates and we have seen much progress made along the lines of mechanisation and I cannot see how it will be good to break them up.

Jagan: Take a small family having 25 acres, they will not be producing on their own but they will be working according to a set plan under the supervision of the Government. I do not see how the efficiency of the industry will be impaired; it is being tried out in Puerto Rico and is working successfully there.... I would like to refer to absenteeism [of the plantocracy]...[it] is tied up with this point of dividing up the land. Very many people will be able to improve themselves and more money will be left in the colony. Most of the capital is sent out of the colony at the present.

[Venn]: I do not think you should go beyond saying 'presumably sent out of the colony'.

Jagan: Well, sir, that must be investigated by you.[14]

Dr Jagan then referred to the fact that during the Enmore strike he was served with trespass notices, prohibiting him from entering the sugar estates on the East Coast, although they were in his constituency. These had been suspended but were reimposed during the strike of 1948. Jagan advocated one union for the industry; at the time the MPCA represented predominantly Indian field workers, while the British Guiana Workers' League spoke for the mainly African factory workers. He felt that this compounded the ethnic division of labour on the plantations, exacerbating the racial division. He noted that this was the case during the tragic strike of 1948, as 'field workers [Indians] were out and factory workers [Africans] were in'.[15]

Jagan was asked whether the GIWU had as much support on the West Coast Demerara as it had on the East Coast Demerara. He responded that they had a 'preponderance' on the latter but was unaware if they had done much work elsewhere. He had no doubts that their progress would be similar wherever they worked. As a prominent leader of the 1948 strike on the East Coast he would have been knowledgeable of the focus of its work. Obviously the GIWU had not established itself beyond this area, with easy access from the capital, where most of its leaders resided. Therefore, Jagan was claiming recognition for the GIWU, to replace the MPCA, purely on its success in one district.

Jagan, as his PAC comrade, H.J.M. Hubbard, had demonstrated earlier, was not happy with the dominance of the key offices in the sugar industry by European importees from the UK. Reflecting on his own father's stagnation at Port Mourant, where he could not gain elevation beyond a 'driver', a field foreman, he observed: '[He] always told me many of the overseers who come here know actually nothing [about sugar] and have to be taught. And that is another trouble in the sugar industry: local people can only rise to certain positions in the sugar industry, and there is no future for them.'

It is paradoxical that Jagan still saw the Imperial Government as central to the development of the industry, that they should provide a market for 10 to 15 years. In a somewhat convoluted way he argued:

> The sugar producers may say that unless they are assured of a continued market ... they would be hesitant to proceed with mechanisation, to erect mills, etc., as the future of the industry would be uncertain to them. That is why I placed the figure in there [10 to 15 years], because I can see if they are not assured of a market it is no use spending money under capital expenditure. They would prefer to spend the money as it is going now, most of it on the workers — invaluable capital — and see the betterment of the Industry as a whole.[16]

When asked about his emphasis on a time but not a price guarantee on the UK sugar market, Jagan remarked that in the past sugar producers appropriated most of the benefits from price hikes; in fact, they were still insisting that there could be no wage rise without an increase in prices. He disapproved of this: profits should be curtailed to facilitate better wages. This was congruent with the orthodoxy of the *PAC Bulletin* that in the Soviet Union, where the means of production were owned by 'the people', prices were controlled in the workers' interest, because the profit motive was not dominant — rarely exceeding 4 or 5 per cent. Moreover, even this small margin accrued to the people's benefit through distribution by the state budget. The Marxist truths were unassailable: '...prices in the capitalist countries keep rising, while in the Soviet Union they fall....'

It was strange, indeed, that Jagan expected the sugar producers to continue to invest in British Guiana when, as the PAC advocated and he reinforced to the Venn Commission, they could see no role for the sugar capitalist other than as a parasite, a mere appropriator of 'surplus value', a dispensable foreign millstone. Meanwhile, his call for the break up of the sugar plantations would not have inspired confidence in Jock Campbell and others in the sugar industry. Essentially Cheddi had no intention of meeting the 'sugar gods' halfway, as the *Bulletin* constantly underlined, because the 'people's democracies' of Eastern Europe were demonstrating the futility of trying to reform capitalism: tomorrow belonged to communism. There could be no middle road.

Jagan's stance was unique in its ideological intensity; no other witness manifested such political fervour or inflexibility. The SPA, in their memorandum to the Venn Commission, underscored the centrality of negotiating a secured quota and remunerative prices with the UK government. They noted that inadequate prices between the Wars had retarded the drive for efficiency on the plantations and efforts to improve the social and economic position of the sugar workers. These were unattainable without 'an assured outlet at economic prices' for the next ten years at least. The SPA also wanted a higher local selling price for sugar: a rise of 50 per cent was considered necessary to bring it in line with production costs. They argued that the rehabilitation of workers' houses and hospitals on the estates should become colonial responsibilities; the exorbitant drainage and irrigation costs on plantations, crucial to survival in British Guiana, rendered these 'unfair overheads' punitive.

Ayube Edun had told the Venn Commission that in recent years the demolition of the ranges on the plantations had progressed; there had been a 'vast improvement' in housing. Another MPCA representative had identified housing at Plantation Blairmont, the Davson estate in Berbice, as an example of the kind of improvement desirable and possible. The evidence of several women before the Commission was indicative of a fundamental change in attitudes taking place on the estates at the end of the 1940s. One such witness, Sanichari, a field worker from Non Pareil and a member of the GIWU deputation, was especially illuminating:[17]

| Sudell: | Do you think it would be a good thing to have some women drivers on the estates? |
| Sanichari: | I would like to see women drivers and women overseers because sometimes my clothes get wet |

when I am in the field and if I am stooping down and
I see the overseer coming I have to go and hide myself
until he passes. The women have to work very hard
on the estates. Sometimes we have to leave home at
4 or 5 o'clock in the morning when it is still dark and
walk very long distances in order to get to work. I
have to leave my young children at home without
anyone to feed them and when I return at night-
time I do not know whether they have eaten or not.
We do not want to do weeding gang work because it
is dangerous for women.

Sometimes we have to go to work in a pregnant
state and we get injured by having to jump across
drains and so on. Only the other day a young woman
got injured this way and lost her baby.

Then reflecting what was perceived to be the condition of middle-
class Indian women, an index of mobility, Sanichari concluded: 'We
do not want to work in the field anymore. We want to stay home and
care our children and send them to school, and also send hot breakfast
[lunch] for our husbands in the field.'

It is noteworthy that the appointment of women drivers did not
meet with the approval of the president of the British Guiana Drivers'
Association, Lionel Luckhoo. When asked by Sudell if he
comprehended the embarrassment felt by women field-workers in a
'state of semi-nudity', in the presence of a male driver, Luckhoo
replied:

Quite candidly I do not think that should have aroused that
degree of criticism, for this reason, that most of the women on
the estates live together in a kind of native state. I am not saying
that they go about nude but their environment is of such a nature
that they are in constant contact in their natural state with
males. For that reason I would hardly expect them to urge that
as a form of criticism ... it is not an unfamiliar sight to see them
by the side of trenches washing their clothing and even taking a
bath.[18]

One is not sure what Lionel Luckhoo meant by women being 'in constant contact in their natural state with males', but his response underlines the sexist bigotry which shaped perceptions of women in this society in the late 1940s and beyond. The language itself speaks of the obscurantism which claimed even this distinguished Indian lawyer and trade unionist — a stark contrast with Jagan's Marxist vision with its progressive idiom, whatever the limitations.

On January 19, 1949 three women from Plantation Enmore — Baichanie, Bhoodia and Jagranie — testified. Baichanie complained of the condition of the creche on the estate, where they left their children while at work in the fields: the building was in disrepair and children got wet when it rained. Bhoodia stated that they were expected to do too much work: 'What they are giving us for a day's work is only to kill us out. Sometimes I have to get my son to help me work.' She informed Dr Venn that whereas in 1939 the estate had provided them with farm and rice land to supplement their wages, most of this land had since been retaken. The following remarks by Baichanie on housing at Enmore, a Booker estate, struck a chord with Venn and Sudell:[19]

Venn:	What about the houses?
Baichanie:	They are in a very bad condition, sir.
Venn:	Are you living in a range?
Baichanie:	Yes, sir, all of us.
Sudell:	I have seen the ranges on your estate.
Baichanie:	I was at work when you went there, sir, but my husband was at home. My husband came many years ago as a 'bound coolie' [over 30 years] and met the range we are living in and it is in the same condition up to now. When we report the condition of the range to the manager he promises to get it repaired but nobody is ever sent to do it. *Even when we are sleeping the rain comes through the roof and would wet us* [emphasis added].
Venn:	Mr. Sudell has seen your houses and we are aware of their condition but, of course, we cannot promise anything this morning.
Sudell:	There is a scheme whereby workers would be able to buy houses; do you know anything about that?

Baichanie:	No, sir.
Sudell:	In that scheme you will get a plot of land and for $25; you can buy the old range and use the materials along with whatever new ones you can buy to build your own house.
Baichanie:	We can only do that if we get regular work and better wages. *The wages we are working for cannot even buy food. Last week I only worked for 10s [$2.40] while the food I buy every week-end costs about $5* [emphasis added].

The hearings, as noted earlier, were heard *in camera*. This unusual situation meant that many field workers who were traditionally intimidated into silence, as was so evident in 1935, were now emboldened into speaking the truth, given the confidentiality of their testimonies. Campbell quickly recognised that this was a most comprehensive inquiry and reposed implicit faith in Dr Venn: the workers themselves were demanding change.

On April 1, 1949 Jock Campbell wrote to Dr Venn,[20]drawing his attention to the fact that Booker had spent £1 million in British Guiana since 1945 on rehabilitation. This had been facilitated by grants under the Colonial Development and Welfare programme and the Sugar Industry Labour Welfare Fund. The post-Moyne environment at the Colonial Office was amenable to reforms — to the provision of imperial grants and higher prices for sugar, to alleviate chronically depressed social and economic conditions in the British West Indies. However, Campbell seemed anxious about long-term sugar prices and was skilfully anticipating Venn's recommendations by suggesting core ideas that were amenable to the industry. In short, he was trying to shape a less demanding outcome by suggesting devolution of some of the responsibility for social reform to the colonial administration; moreover, he was hoping for 'pressure to be brought to bear upon His Majesty's Government for the payment of a fair price for West Indian sugar'. He was also expecting that some 'inequitable taxes' be removed, the local price of sugar be increased, that 'the housing of "nuclear" (key) workers only be the responsibility of the industry ... overhead expenditure such as housing, hospitals and taxation we hoped might be reduced as a result of your enquiries, rather than increased'. He was anticipating greater financial demands on the sugar companies as a result of the impending recommendations, but if the UK government were to refuse a 10-year agreement for a quota and better prices for sugar, it was imperative that 'specific financial assistance' be granted to British Guiana to enable them to implement the reforms.

Campbell was also hoping that the Report would strengthen the 'slender confidence', an allusion to the growing stature of Cheddi Jagan, which the sugar workers had in their employers. At a strategic point in the composition of the Report — Jock had discussions with Venn on these matters on March 31, 1949 — he was deftly ensuring that a few key ideas were lodged with him. This was one of his many skills as a leader, the negotiator par excellence, a master at anticipating, the inveterate gamesman.

But the spectre of Jagan on the plantations was relentless. On May 21, 1949 the Commissioner of Labour in British Guiana, W.M. Bissell, informed B.G. Smallman at the Colonial Office (the secretary of the Venn Commission)[21] that Jagan had accepted membership in the British Guiana Workers' League (Rose Hall Branch) and had consented to be chairman of the proposed district committee for the Corentyne area. Bissell noted that the SPA were 'up in arms' against the idea and had threatened to terminate relations with the League, which represented the mainly African factory workers, if Dr Jagan became an officer. He cautioned that if they did — although Jagan's accession to office in the union would have been legitimate — because 'they don't like [his] politics', they would be seen to be in favour only of biddable men.

Bissell was apprehensive that the SPA's threat would bolster the growing assumption that the MPCA was a company union; that it would poison industrial relations on the plantations, exacerbating the volatile situation spawned by the Enmore shootings. On June 8, 1949 he wrote again to Smallman that the Jagan-backed GIWU were apparently anticipating that they would not emerge well from the Venn Report. He was, in the manner of Campbell, now suggesting to him that the GIWU would 'feel quite satisfied if the report offers a little of the many things they are seeking'.

Bissell was, however, disturbed by Jagan's irrepressible concern with plantation affairs. He told Smallman that Jagan's and the League's positions remained obscure, and that he could not rely completely on 'old Thorne's' (the president of the BGWL) professions of dislike for Jagan. He reflected: 'Now, I am not quite so sure. It may be, of course, that Thorne realises that he cannot prevent Jagan from being a District Officer, and that once there he may move to have the rules altered so that he can become an Executive Officer within less than the two years now stipulated in the rules.'[22]

Nothing came of Jagan's apparent attempt to infiltrate the BGWL, in keeping with his aim to seek to bridge the racial divide on the sugar estates. But this 'political enigma' was unremitting in his resolve to redefine the space within which King Sugar operated. He could not be bought. His passionate hatred of the plantocracy and his belief in the utopian vision of deliverance promised by communism, would not leave him.

Endnotes

1.   *PAC Bulletin*, no. 28, July 20, 1948.
2.   CO111/797/60270/5/5 [1948], W.S. Jones to Woolley, June 25, 1948.
3.   Ibid., W.S. Jones to Woolley, July 15, 1948.
4.   Ibid., Campbell to G.F. Seel (Colonial Office), July 20, 1948.
5.   Ibid.
6.   Ibid., G.F. Seel to Campbell, July 21, 1948.
7.   See note 1.
8.   Ibid.
9.   *Report of a Commission of Inquiry into the Sugar Industry of British Guiana* (J.A. Venn, chairman), Col. No. 249, (London: His Majesty's Stationery Office, 1949), iii-iv.
10. *The Sunday Chronicle*, January 2, 1949.
11. Leader, *The Daily Chronicle*, January 9, 1949; see also the following issues of this paper: January 26; February 2, 3, 1949.
12. *The Daily Chronicle*, January 1, 1949.
13. CO946/1, Evidence of Cheddi Jagan, January 14, 1949.
14. Ibid.
15. Ibid.
16. Ibid.
17. CO946/1, Evidence of Sanichari, January 10, 1949.
18. CO946/1, Evidence of Lionel Luckhoo, January 17, 1949.
19. CO946/1, Evidence of Baichanie, January 19, 1949.

20. CO946/3, Jock Campbell to Dr J.A. Venn, April 1, 1949.
21. CO946/3, W.M. Bissell to B.G. Smallman, May 21, 1949.
22. Ibid., June 8, 1949.

Chapter Fourteen

THE VENN
COMMISSION REPORT, 1949:
BLUEPRINT FOR CAMPBELL'S
REFORMS

I think I would like to be remembered as a successful reformer.

Jock Campbell

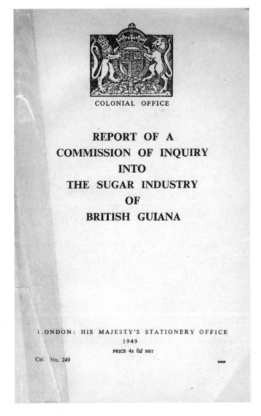

COLONIAL OFFICE

REPORT OF A
COMMISSION OF INQUIRY
INTO
THE SUGAR INDUSTRY
OF
BRITISH GUIANA

LONDON: HIS MAJESTY'S STATIONERY OFFICE
1949
PRICE 4s 0d NET

Col. No. 249

The Venn Commission Report, 1949

By August 1949 the assurance that the UK government had recognised the necessity for reforms in the sugar industry of the West Indies and were prepared to assist by way of better prices and quotas for cane sugar, had buoyed Jock Campbell. A comprehensive programme of reforms on the plantations could be sustained only if this came to fruition.

The Venn Commission Report was, as noted earlier, the most penetrative study ever undertaken on the sugar industry of British Guiana. Their intellectual grasp of the perennial effort necessary for the maintenance of drainage and irrigation on the plantations, and of the complex social forces impinging on the plantations at the end of the 1940s, established the base for a rigorous assessment. They underlined the centrality of the water problem with an evocative, classic quote from James Rodway's *History of British Guiana*:

> Every acre at present in cultivation has been the scene of a struggle with the sea in front and the flood behind. As a result of this arduous labour during the centuries, a narrow strip of land along the coast has been rescued from the mangrove swamp and kept under cultivation by an elaborate system of dams and dykes. Scattered along the rivers and creeks lie a thousand abandoned plantations, most of them indistinguishable from the surrounding forest; these represent the failures of the early settlers. At first sight the narrow line of sugar estates seems but a very poor show for such a long struggle with nature, but when all the circumstances are taken into consideration it is almost a wonder that the Colony has not been abandoned altogether.[1]

The Report dramatises the achievement by citing the astounding findings of Dr F.C. Benham (Legislative Council Paper No. 11 of 1945)[2], who calculated that 'each square mile of cane cultivation involves the provision of 49 miles of drainage canals and ditches and 16 miles of high level waterways. If these figures are raised to cover the whole area under cane the sum total approaches 5,000 miles. Some estates do, in fact, have more than 300 miles of waterways to maintain'. Dr Benham had observed that the cost of maintaining the drainage systems in 1943 was $459,000 or $2.79 per ton of sugar produced. Guyana is no El Dorado. The Commission had captured the essence of the place.

Their recommendations were wide-ranging. They supported greater mechanisation of field work. Given the heavy overheads required to maintain the complex hydraulic system, they felt that the use of drag-lines for dredging and clearing canals would reduce the high production costs. They were not in favour of continued use of human labour (including women) to clean canals. They deplored the engagement of women for this onerous task: '[M]en and women, up to their waists or even higher in the water, were everywhere pulling out weeds with their hands or removing mud and debris in small buckets'. Women and girls, they argued, must not work in water; an ordnance should be introduced to enforce this. They also advised that when women and girls worked in the fields, their gangs should be supervised by a forewoman. They believed that 'drivers' (foremen) — a term they deemed offensive and wanted discarded — should be trained to facilitate and accelerate their elevation to the post of overseers; these were still mainly young Scots who were, in fact, usually shown the ropes by local 'drivers'. The latter should now be educated to 'instruct', not merely to 'control'.[3]

They thought that productivity could be improved by the introduction of new varieties of cane: higher yield per acre to boost output was preferable to increasing acreage to achieve this end. So too would the greater use of creeper tractors (TD 18) and other machinery, to accelerate performance in the field and the transportation of cane to the factory. To sustain the mechanisation programme the Venn Commission recommended an apprenticeship scheme for young employees to acquire technical competence in various fields: mechanical and electrical engineering, tool-making, agriculture, book-keeping, and so on.[4]

The Commissioners also made several recommendations with regard to the working conditions of labour on the estates. For instance, no child under the age of 14 should be employed, in accordance with the Education Ordinance of 1946. They elaborated:

> We ... saw several small boys running with the mules and gathered that they were the children of the mule-boys [sic], but it was strongly maintained by some witnesses that in not a few cases such children or others like them in the Creole gang would be actually on the pay of the estate .... [A mule-boy] .... cannot

knock off until he has brought in the last punt train of his section. His hours therefore depended on the often extended hours of the cutter. To a lad in his middle or late teens twelve hours a day is more than enough, to anyone younger it cannot but be harmful. Further, should any child below age be injured at work there is no legal ground for a claim for compensation ... we were told of one case where a leading boy had been bitten and, it was alleged, had been refused compensation because he was under age.[5]

The Commission recognised (so did Jock Campbell), the importance of seemingly small things. In this spirit they advised that some form of transportation by canal, preferably punts, be available for workers who often had to walk 6 or 7 miles to the fields — a nightmare journey in the rainy season, in knee-deep mud. The provision of light shelters and potable water in the fields, also, would alleviate many of the grievances. Campbell has called this 'the greatness of small causes' (from *Dr Zhivago*). The Report was permeated by this sentiment:

In the changing relations of today between employer and employee, trust and goodwill are essential to successful co-operation and disregarded grievances, however large or small they may be, and even if they are imaginary, are the easiest sources of discontent and mistrust ... but the exercise of patience, good humour and sympathy in an attempt to remove genuine grievances is repaid a hundred fold and it is no exaggeration to say that the attitude of management and staff in this respect is immediately reflected in and can be judged by the atmosphere of the whole estate.[6]

The Commission also recommended changes in the factories: shower baths and changing rooms to allow workers 'to clean up and change out of their working clothes'. They called for the setting up of clean canteens, with cooking facilities to provide a warm meal for the workers.[7]

They felt that claims for workmen's compensation should be backed by statutory authority so that 'unnamed wives' and 'illegitimate children' could benefit. However, the initial compensation for workers in the sugar industry earning up to $50 a month should be reduced from 100 per cent to 75 per cent — in the rest of the British West Indies it was 50 per cent. Meanwhile, inspectors should be appointed to report all accidents in field and factory.[8]

On the contentious issue of the 'cut-and-load', as opposed to the 'cut-and-drop' system of cane harvesting — the ostensible cause of the prolonged strike on estates on the East Coast Demerara in 1948 — the Venn Commission were unreservedly in favour of the former. They were, therefore, not sympathetic to the Jagan-backed GIWU's stance. They countered that 'cut-and-load' led to 'a steady output and relatively good earnings', and did not agree that the strenuous work should preclude consideration of its merits. But they conceded that elderly workers or those with inadequate physiques should not be assigned to cane harvesting. They concluded: 'We heartily approve the use of planks for loading [punts] and, to avoid the possibility of accidents, consider that they should be slatted and at least 18 inches in width. They should be freely available at the site and should not ... have to be carried to and from the field by the cutters themselves.' These slatted planks eased immeasurably the potentially dangerous task of lifting the cane-bundle from the embankment into the punt.[9]

With regard to wages, they noted a progressive increase in earnings per ton of sugar produced in recent years: $22.52 and $24.90 in 1938 and 1939 respectively; $41.30 and $43.73 in 1945 and 1946 respectively; $55.32 and $62.38 per ton in 1947 and 1948 respectively. Between 1939 and 1948 the daily average earnings of male piece-workers rose from 76.2 cents to $1.97. They recommended the establishment of a wages board or council, comprising 6-8 employers' representatives, 6-8 trade unions' representatives and two neutral members. Its task would be to fix weekly and piece-rates, holiday provisions and general conditions of labour. They were also in favour of a contributory pension scheme. Workers' contributions were to be deducted from weekly earnings at the rate of 2.5 per cent; the sugar estates would contribute to the scheme at the rate of 5 per cent. Benefits were payable as a lump sum on reaching the age of 50, providing the worker had contributed for a minimum of ten years.[10]

They endorsed the retention of the Estates' Joint Committees, comprising representatives of the employers and those of the workers drawn from the recognised unions, as the instrument of arbitration. These unions were the MPCA for the predominantly Indian field workers and the BGWL for the mainly African factory workers. But they advised that three other specialised unions in the industry, also, be recognised: the Drivers' Association, the Sugar Boilers' Union and the Sugar Estates' Clerks Association.

With regard to the Jagan-backed GIWU, they were unequivocal that its demand for recognition was 'completely unwarranted'. The Union had grown out of 'disputes and turbulent action' on the East Coast Demerara; it was 'duplicating' the work already being done by the MPCA and the BGWL, while 'taking every opportunity to discredit their achievements and organisation'. The GIWU, they observed, also opposed the work of the Labour Department and tried to undermine the Estates' Joint Committees. The Commissioners were categorical that no trade union should serve as a platform for the political ambition of any individual. In what was an unmistakable rebuke of Jagan's conspicuous involvement in the GIWU, they observed:

> Its members and officers complained to us that the established Unions were ineffective and that therefore their own was founded. The idea that the moment a serious dispute occurs a new union should be formed must be strenuously opposed. Such is the way in which a new leader may achieve power but not the Trade Union movement progress.[11]

However, the Venn Commission did extend a thread of hope to the GIWU, suggesting possibilities for a role in the industry, in the future. They advised that if their strength and financial membership will have been established for between three to five years, then the basis could exist 'for considering whether its influence justifies its being given the recognition that the steady work of past years had brought to the established unions'. They added: 'At the moment its claim is premature and made no less unwarranted by the persistence with which its leaders press it'.[12]

On the question of the background of trade unionists, they repeated their opposition to trade unions as instruments for 'political ends'. They argued that there were sufficient educated workers to obviate their dependence on outside leaders with political axes to grind. Only people who had worked in the industry for three years should hold office in the union. The allusion again to Cheddi's union activities was hardly veiled. Given the fact that in other British West Indian territories trade unions were an integral part of the emerging party political culture, the conclusion is inescapable that what was being repudiated was not outside leadership per se, but the perceived Marxist orientation of Jagan's politics: Fabian socialist unionists were fine, Marxist unionists were anathema.

The Commission also recommended the promotion of peasant cane farming, possibly on cooperative lines, identifying the banks of the Berbice River as a potential area for its introduction. On health matters, they observed that the Corentyne estates, Albion, Port Mourant and Skeldon, were 'naturally healthy plantations', with a low malarial index. Elsewhere, also, this endemically malarial colony had registered an astronomical decline in the disease. For this they were effusive in their acclamation of Dr George Giglioli, OBE, medical adviser to the Sugar Producers' Association. The DDT spraying campaign had reduced not only the incidence of malaria, yellow fever and filariasis, but had raised resistance to others as well. They cited Giglioli's assessment of the broader consequences for British Guiana: increased fertility, with an immediate rise in the birth-rate and a simultaneous fall in infant mortality. But they noted that Giglioli had drawn attention to the prevalent rudimentary hygiene among estate residents: 'their conception of the distinctions between drinking water, bathing water and sewers is of the vaguest'.[13] This ignorance, in conjunction with the insanitary conditions in the ranges, rendered residents susceptible to diseases from contaminated food and water. They therefore advocated regular inspection of estate ranges and factories by the Government Medical Department, to monitor sanitation, water supply and housing.

The Commission recommended the dismantling of the obsolete hospitals on the estates, the establishment of four to six state hospitals along the coast, at points accessible to estates and adjacent villages. However, the sugar estates would still be responsible for the medical provisions of their resident nuclear population. It was suggested that they should establish fully-equipped dispensaries to handle accidents and emergencies, while providing an ambulance on each estate to convey patients to the nearest state hospital.[14]

The Venn Report made a fundamental connection between poor housing and health on the plantations and recommended the demolition of all the obnoxious logies, the derelict ranges, by 1953. The estates were deemed responsible for the rehousing of their nuclear workers only, their key employees; whereas the government should undertake the re-housing of the others, in addition to assuming responsibility for the provision and maintenance of schools on the estates. Meanwhile, defective ranges, pending demolition, should be made weather-proof. This was a specific request by the three women witnesses from Enmore Estate, a point underlined by Mr Sudell following his inspection of the ranges on that estate. They were graphic in their depiction of the scale of dereliction of the infamous ranges:

> We inspected many of the ranges. In quite a number the corrugated iron roofs were leaking and the fabric of the buildings was in a general state of decay. In numerous instances temporary sheets or awnings had been fixed over the beds to keep off the rain. They had mud floors and consequently, with the rain dropping from the roofs, these were made slippery and dangerous; in many cases we found [jute] bags laid over the [mud] floor to prevent slipping. They are built without any plan on low-lying uneven ground. There are few, if any, footpaths and in rainy weather communication is difficult. The common latrines, often built over a drainage trench, are frequently in a bad state of repair, with little privacy.[15]

The Commission addressed the issue of social welfare, recommending that each plantation should provide a creche, a community centre and a sports ground with suitable facilities. A welfare officer should be appointed on each estate. The Venn Commission was impressed with the social welfare programme initiated on some estates, but stated that much more had to be done:

> The Social Welfare programme, and, more important, the changed attitude of the Companies and managers which is

backing it, has already begun to make its mark on the habits of
the estate population. Much remains to be done, but the clubs
and organisations, the excellent new community centres put up
on some estates (and shortly, we hope, to be seen on all), the
increase in sports facilities and similar amenities, are all showing
the worker how to make the most of his leisure time, and, by
widening his interests and outlook, and helping him to take his
place as a worthy member of a progressive community.[16]

The Commission emphasised the importance of sports to the
cultivation of a stronger community spirit. They observed too that
cricket was unrivalled in its supremacy: by 1949 it was an obsession
on most plantations. In that year, the first cricketer from a sugar
estate, John Trim (1915–60), from Port Mourant, played Test cricket
for the West Indies. It was in this context that they reported thus:
'Wherever we went on the estates there would be small boys with
improvised bats and wickets practising or playing "pick up" matches
[impromptu games]. A member of the last West Indies Team [which
toured India in 1948–49] had come from one of the estates we visited
and this did not surprise us when we saw the enthusiasm there was
for the game'.[17]

But this shaft of sunlight on the estates was often clouded by the
dark shadow of rum-drinking and alcoholism. The ubiquitous rumshops, they contended, should be closed immediately. Every effort
must be made to inculcate a spirit of independence among workers,
to foster ambition, to improve their standard of living. They rejected
the assumption of the plantocracy that low wages and the severe
limiting of land for rice and cattle were essential in order to anchor
workers on the sugar estates. That sacrosanct idea had had its day:

> [T]he worker's ambition must be stimulated for himself and his
> family; he must be encouraged to strive for a higher standard of
> living and therefore not be denied opportunities of earning money
> to pay for it. From the proceeds of a successful rice crop he may
> be able to put down money for a new house. A new house will
> bring the need for better furniture which in turn can only come
> as a result of harder work on the estate. Further the man who is
> working for the independence and betterment of himself and his

family will not only work harder but more contentedly as he sees an object in his labour.[18]

They therefore advocated that 'full encouragement' be given to workers to become 'self-reliant', to augment their earnings by growing rice and provisions on estate land. Rice-land allotments should not be less than one acre and, as a precaution against malaria, they should not be located near the houses.

The Venn Commission was recommending a substantial programme of reforms, but who would pay for it? Since 1942 a Sugar Production Tax of $1 per ton, which brought in $180,000 per year, had been paid by sugar producers in British Guiana. This, they argued, should be abolished, along with two minor taxes — a Distillery Tax yielding $15,000 per year and a Cane-Acreage Tax accounting for $19,000 per year. They also asked the Imperial Government to subsidise British Guiana's sugar to the tune of £1 ($4.80) on each ton of sugar produced. They noted that between 1945 and 1947 the average profit per ton of sugar produced in the colony was $8.11; in Barbados it was $15.43 — a reflection of the heavy overheads necessitated by the high drainage and irrigation charges on the coastland of British Guiana. The Commission also recommended that the local selling price of sugar be raised to the level of the export price. These two measures would raise $1,150,000, along with an estimated $214,000 from the proposed tax relief to the producers. This was considered the minimum necessary for the implementation of the reforms.[19]

The Commission suggested another source that could be exploited to finance the reforms. Since 1947, with better sugar prices, the Industry had devised a three-tiered mechanism (an idea advanced by Sydney Caine, Jock Campbell's friend at the Colonial Office) to provide for its own development. This comprised the following: a deduction of £1 5s per ton towards a Price Stabilisation Fund; £1 per ton towards estate rehabilitation; and 10/- per ton for labour welfare (Sugar Industry Labour Welfare Fund, SILWF). By the end of 1948 these had yielded $1,714,000, $1,365,000 and $682,000 respectively. The latter, as B.G. Smallman of the Colonial Office (and secretary of the Venn Commission) observed, had not been clearly identified with specific projects although they were told

Campbell, vice-chairman of Booker, around 1949

in British Guiana that it would be used for housing primarily. The Commission suggested a broader focus, that the SILWF should contribute partially to the cost of implementing the following reforms: the provision of artesian well water, shelters in the fields, creches, sports grounds, as well as the training of apprentices in various technical fields.[20]

On December 28, 1949 Jock Campbell wrote to Dr Venn expressing 'the profound respect and admiration of my colleagues and myself' for the Report. He reproduced a quote from a letter he had sent to the managing director of Booker in British Guiana, R.R. Follett-Smith, to underline his approbation:

> My personal reaction to it is that it is an absorbingly brilliant analysis of the British Guiana Sugar Industry and its environment. It seems to me to be a much better diagnosis and statement of the condition of the Industry than any other I have read.... It is dispassionate and passes no moral judgement.[21]

Campbell had asked Follett-Smith to assemble the recommendations into four categories: (i) those which they accept and will implement as soon as possible; (ii) those which they would implement if they get the subsidy recommended (which he knew they would not get) or if they received 'reasonably remunerative prices' for a large portion of the sugar exported; (iii) those recommendations which the government was expected to implement and which they would welcome; (iv) those for action either by government or the industry which they were unable to accept and the reasons for it. Campbell astutely sought the harmonisation of the position of the two other sugar firms in the colony on the devolving of responsibility to the government for certain provisions hitherto the responsibility of plantations. He felt that by a specific date they should agree that they intended to 'spend no more money on hospital and extra-nuclear [non-essential] housing assets'.

Campbell said that the Report was 'of far more value' than they had had reasons to anticipate and therefore they should make 'the fullest use of it'. He explained how this could be done:

(i)   by ourselves using it as terms of reference for further action, improvement and development.
(Incidentally, I think that the three senior people on every Sugar Estate should have a copy of the Venn Report and study it);

(ii)   by using it as the platform or base for establishing a new and better relationship between the Industry and its environment, Government, Labour and 'the man in the street'.

He concluded that 'a very large proportion' of the Report they had already embraced, for 'our policy for putting matters right coincides very largely with the Commission's'. Nevertheless, Campbell emphasised its merits: '[I]t is invaluable to have an outsider and unprejudiced observer's report, particularly when it has turned out so constructive'. Follett-Smith concurred: 'I think the Venn Report is the best and most readable I've seen and I've seen and read a good many. As soon as I looked through it I realised it was going to be my bible for a long time to come.'[22]

Indeed, Campbell appreciated the devolving of responsibility to the government for the re-housing of extra-nuclear workers and the provision of hospitals. He also welcomed the removal of all direct taxation (apart from income tax), especially the Sugar Production Tax of $1 per ton of sugar manufactured. But of decisive significance for him, was to have the ultimate authority, the Venn Commission, come out in favour of 'reasonable' reforms. It was the culmination of everything he had witnessed in British Guiana since 1934 — the resistance and radicalisation of the work-force; the Moyne Commission; the shootings at Leonora (1939) and Enmore (1948); the Political Affairs Committee and Jagan's agitation against 'bitter sugar', shaped by his Marxist passion. These had all spoken of the inevitability of reforms on the plantations. The unimpeachable authority of Venn, however, spoke now of moral imperatives. Campbell was handed the blueprint, the mandate to demand from the Booker Board and their shareholders fundamental change in attitudes.

On February 18, 1950 J.E. Markham of the Colonial Office wrote to Governor Woolley that he was informed by Dr Venn that Campbell's first reaction indicated a willingness on the part of the employers to implement, 'in their entirety', the recommendations for which they were responsible. He said that he did not want to be 'unnecessarily sceptical' or 'unjust to Campbell' but he wondered whether 'things were as simple as all that'. Was that feasible given that His Majesty's Government had rejected Venn's proposed 20/- (per ton) subsidy to the colony?[23]

Governor Woolley replied to N.L. Mayle at the Colonial Office on April 3, 1950, noting that Campbell's enthusiasm for the Report was 'interesting', as he had expressed opposition to its appointment. He felt that the sugar producers 'naturally liked it' because if it were adopted it would relieve them of all direct taxation except income tax. Woolley remarked that although the proposed 20/- subsidy had been rejected, sugar prices had risen by £3 per ton in 1950. He noted that in his preliminary meeting with the SPA, they were opposed to a Wages Board; neither were they in favour of the pension scheme as recommended by Venn, although they expressed interest in a modified scheme. He felt that the SPA would probably cite failure to gain the Report's suggested 'minimum contribution [from subsidies and higher prices]'as the reason for not implementing their proposals, for stalling on reforms. The Government, also, was likely to find it 'extremely difficult' to fulfil their new obligations with regard to schools, hospitals and extra-nuclear housing on the estates. But Woolley did have one cause for optimism: 'I believe that Campbell is really anxious to do everything possible to improve the lot of the labourer.' [24]

Endnotes

1. *Report of a Commission of Inquiry into the Sugar Industry of British Guiana* (J.A. Venn, chairman), Col. No. 249 (London: His Majesty's Stationery Office, 1949), 1-2.
2. Ibid., 9
3. Ibid., 9, 12.
4. Ibid., 29, 42.
5. Ibid., 53-4.
6. Ibid., 57.
7. Ibid., 61.
8. Ibid., 64-5.
9. Ibid., 72.
10. Ibid., 77-8,86,88.
11. Ibid., 100.
12. Ibid.
13. Ibid., 115.
14. Ibid., 119-120.
15. Ibid., 122.
16. Ibid., 136.
17. Ibid., 135-6.
18. Ibid., 140.
19. Ibid., 164.
20. Ibid.; CO111/796/60270/5, (Ordnance No. 20 of 1947) and B.G. Smallman (Colonial Office minute), August 17, 1949.
21. CO111/813/10, J.M. Campbell to J.A. Venn, December 28, 1949 (personal).
22. Ibid. [The excerpts by Campbell and Follett-Smith are quoted here.]
23. CO111/830/10, J.E. Markham [CO] to Gov Woolley, February 18, 1950.
24. Ibid., Gov Woolley to J.E. Markham, April 3, 1950.

Part 4

Revolution or Reform?: Jagan's Marxism *v.* Campbell's Reformism

Chapter Fifteen

'BITTER SUGAR':
UNEARTHING THE ROOTS
OF JAGAN'S MARXISM

When the Venn Report appeared, Campbell told his people at Booker in Guyana: 'This is the key document'[1]; but commitment to reform could not elude the Marxist frame of reference of Cheddi Jagan. The Enmore shootings of 1948 (the creation of martyrs) and the radical politics Jagan had brought to the Legislative Council since 1947, enhanced his stature as a revolutionary anti-colonialist — he had no time for half-measures. Jagan's reaction to the Venn Report epitomised his antagonism to the reformist approach. His *PAC Bulletin* responded to it with evident disdain in 1949:

EXPLOITATION TO CONTINUE IN SUGAR INDUSTRY: BASIC QUESTION UNTOUCHED — REFORMS SUGGESTED — BURDEN SHIFTED TO GOVERNMENT[2]

While Campbell defined the Report as the blueprint for change, Jagan saw it as papering over the cracks, offering palliatives to prop up the old order. The *Bulletin* noted that whereas in Britain nationalisation was acceptable, in the West Indies and British Guiana state ownership of the sugar industry was repugnant to all commissions of inquiry. It elaborated, reflecting Jagan's commitment to nationalisation: 'The Report does not suggest any basic changes in ownership, production and control of the sugar industry. The sugar 'gods' [an unmistakable Jaganite idiom] are to continue to run the whole industry and enact their toll.'[3]

PAC Bulletin concluded that no good could come from the Venn Report and was cynical about the SPA's statement that 'most of the suggested improvements in the Report have been, are being or will be implemented by the sugar producers'. As the PAC saw it, many of the recommended reforms, if implemented, would impose 'burdens' on taxpayers, as responsibility had been thrust upon the government. As early as 1949 the Jaganite interpretation of the Report was rooted in implacable suspicion, thus questioning the character and doubting the motives of Jock Campbell's reformist mission:

> The Report in great detail strives at two objectives: firstly, the stability and preservation of the sugar industry for the sugar capitalists; secondly, a harmonious accommodation by the workers to capitalist exploitation.[4]

From the beginning, therefore, Jagan's Marxism had foundations in antipathy to plantation sugar and the domination of the colonial economy by the 'sugar gods', Booker in particular. No progress could be made as long as this giant controlled British Guiana, its economy and government.

In November 1949 Jagan expressed his disgust at the crux of the Annual Statement by the chairman of Booker for the year 1948. The company announced profits of £157,162 after taxation, the payment of ordinary dividends to shareholders of 5 per cent and a bonus of 3 per cent (tax free). Meanwhile, £60,000 were transferred to the company's reserves. Captioned 'Good Sweating — Bookers', his article underlined that the rewards accruing to their British shareholders and their elite British employees in the colony, were acquired through the exploitation of their Guyanese workers:

> Most of the profits together with the large amount which are expended in palatial homes for the imported staff are a result of the sweating and exploitation of the ill-clad, ill-housed and ill-fed workers on the sugar estates.[5]

Then reacting to the chairman's assertion (in fact, the statement was written by Jock Campbell, the vice-chairman, and reflected his perceptions) that there was in British Guiana 'an atmosphere of suspicion of our motives' and 'a hostility' which 'depreciates if not thwart our efforts and our aspirations', Jagan was emphatic that the grounds for suspicion were unimpeachable: the people's union, the GIWU, was still not recognised, while its president, Dr J.P. Lachmansingh, and the legislator for Central Demerara (himself), had been served with trespass notices for visiting the sugar plantations. Jagan was sued for $5,000, by Booker, for trespassing on an estate located in his constituency. The spirit of revolt, Jagan was telling the plantocracy, could no longer be assuaged by palliatives — belated, mild reforms: 'The workers will continue to be suspicious so long as they are herded together in semi-slave conditions in the sugar estates and are denied their human rights of freedom of speech, assembly and association. Your suits and intimidation will be of no avail.'[6]

At the Imperial level, too, Jagan could envisage no benefits for the workers from the 'so-called socialist' government of Clement Atlee. Like its Tory predecessor which had given a knighthood to the former chairman of Booker, Sir Alfred Sherlock, Labour had just knighted F.J. Seaford, Booker's chief in Guyana, with whom Jagan had crossed swords many times in the Legislature since 1947. He was appalled that Seaford, who was defeated in the General Elections of 1947, had been nominated by the Governor to that body as well as the crucial, decision-making Executive Council. *PAC Bulletin* even ridiculed the idea that the Secretary of State for the Colonies, Arthur Creech-Jones, a Fabian socialist of repute in the colonies, with whom Campbell empathised, was a 'true friend of Colonial peoples'. He was a 'true friend of the sugar capitalists'. Until true socialism (Marxism-Leninism) is established in Guyana, Booker would 'continue to extract its toll of blood, sweat and tears from the workers'.[7] The economics of sugar was necessarily a political question.

Jagan's politics was already enmeshed in Soviet dogmas; it was contemptuous of reformism or democratic socialism. On the eve of the formation of his party, the People's Progressive Party (PPP), in January 1950, its precursor, the PAC, was immersed in propaganda work. The titles of some of the literature they distributed mirrored Jagan's Marxist illumination: *Essentials of Lenin, Vols. 1 and 2; Case for Communism; Communism and Labour; USSR and China; Russia Revisited with Dean of Canterbury; Soviet Strength by Dean of Canterbury; New China, New World; Land Reform in Czechoslovakia; Social and State Structure of the USSR.*[8]

In the final issue of *PAC Bulletin*, in December 1949, before it was superseded by *Thunder* — organ of the PPP — one is treated to 'Fighting Words', quotations from communist sources, a guide to 'practice'. This reflected the tenor of the Jaganite mission. One excerpt, from *West Indian Newsletter*, on the task of educating the masses, extolled 'the study of Marxism, the widespread popularisation of Marxist teachings, [and] the carrying on of their work in a Marxist way by the advanced members of the working class'. Then, seeking validation from a prominent non-communist source, they cited this gift to the propagandist, from the Dean of Canterbury's *Soviet Strength*: 'Russia's achievements rest on moral foundations. Russia's beliefs have affinity with religion.'[9]

In October 1949, on the eve of the third anniversary of the PAC and the birth of the PPP, Cheddi Jagan was proud to announce that the 'progressive movement was advancing in spite of lies and slander which beset it at every turn'. Political discussion circles had emerged at Kitty (where Jagan lived), Buxton (Sydney King's village) and Plaisance, suggesting a multi-racial appeal. They were urged to study a range of topics: the colonial question, imperialism, wages, prices, profits, capitalism, socialism, American foreign policy. Marxism held all the answers; thus Jagan could argue in the Legislative Council that 'the piling up of surplus value (profits) continues as long as industry remains in private hands', as was evident, for instance, in the sugar industry. He elaborated: '[I]t could afford to double the present rates of wages because the rate of exploitation of sugar cane field workers was about 142%. That is, in a working day of 10 hours the worker gives 4 hours of labour for payment received and 6 hours of labour to the sugar capitalists.'[10] The trade union struggle, therefore, was pivotal, as the fight for higher wages leads eventually to 'the abolition of private ownership of industry and the establishment of socialist ownership. Nothing less will solve the problem'.[11] The fight for recognition of his union, GIWU, in the sugar industry, a protracted one, was the corner-stone of his Marxist political vision.

Jagan's hatred of capitalism was profound. For the rest of his life, for nearly 50 years, his pro-Moscow communist passion was inexhaustible. Removed from power because of his communist faith, languishing impotently in opposition between 1964 and 1992, ridiculed by his arch-enemy — L.F.S. Burnham — his Marxist rhetoric, his claim to possession of the purest version, reached millennial heights, especially after he had 'grounded' with his comrades at the conference of world communists in Moscow in 1969: 'a kind of homecoming', he called this particular arrival. It would sustain him even after the end of the Cold War when, ironically, American conciliation and Jimmy Carter's personal commitment to democracy in Guyana helped him regain power after 28 years, in October 1992. The Marxist veins in the man were inviolable, although belatedly, with the demise of his comrades in Eastern Europe, pragmatism was thrust upon him. He died a communist, in March 1997. What were the sources of his faith?

It is ironic but significant that Jock Campbell was so definitive in identifying the forces that shaped Jagan's Marxist passion. He locates them in the 'latifundist', highly centralised character of the sugar culture in British Guiana: the domination by the Booker colossus of a small colony; and the virtual absence of local people — poor or rich — in the sugar industry. Jock explains:

> Anywhere else [in the West Indies] the sugar industry and business had nothing like the perceived power of Booker because the sugar industry had a lot of [small] cane farmers; they had a lot of people who diversified and fragmented [it]. [In British Guiana] Booker practically owned the colony; it was a state within a state. Barbadians ran the estates in Barbados, [whereas] they were all absentee proprietors in Guyana, apart from the Brassingtons and Vieiras. Booker actually commanded a state within a state.[12]

The lives of these two remarkable men were to intersect almost ineluctably after 1934, when Jock first went to British Guiana, to their family estate at Albion, three miles from Cheddi's home plantation, Port Mourant. The same conditions of deprivation and hurt, aggravated by the depression of the 1930s, which triggered Campbell's reformist instincts, bred the uncompromising Marxism, the millennial vision, of Jagan. Campbell's outlook, however, was tempered by the natural limitations of the coastland of British Guiana, where all the sugar plantations were located, where over 90 per cent of the people lived; where, too, the legacy of oppression, self-deprecation and racial suspicion, between Africans and Indians, was to precipitate an explosion at the end of Empire.

In October 1953, shortly after the British had suspended the Constitution, Campbell wrote to the left-wing weekly, *The New Statesman and Nation* (he became its chairman later), arguing that it is a miracle that life was possible on the hazardous coastland of Guyana:

> British Guiana is a most imperfect place. But its imperfections are of nature — not Britain or Bauxite or Bookers, who are doing their best in formidably difficult physical and economic conditions. The wonder is not that life in British Guiana is not Utopian, but that life and production can exist there at all. Its coastal belt lying below sea-level, a man-made environment reclaimed from the sea by great technical skills and at huge capital expense, fighting a perpetual battle against water, and for years against starvation prices for colonial produce — it is remarkable that inhabited British Guiana can support its ever-growing population at even the present standard of living, low as it is compared with more fortunate countries.[13]

Campbell's stark assessment was disdainful of El Dorado; it was aimed at Jagan: 'Owing to its physical uniqueness there can be no alternative in British Guiana to large-scale planned agriculture. Destroy confidence, drive out capital and skills, and you leave nothing but swamps and starvation.' He was also countering the instinct to dream big in this colonial backwater. The El Dorado myth runs deep in the Guyanese psyche. To do anything on this unforgiving land, to sustain effort, people needed fantasies — grandeur around the next bend.[14] To temper this, to ask them to face reality, the Venn Commission, as noted above, reminded them in 1949 of the hard land, the monumental task of growing cane: '[E]very square mile of cane cultivation involves the provision of 49 miles of drainage canals and ditches and 16 miles of high level waterways. If these figures are raised to cover the whole area under cane the sum total approaches 5,000 miles.' They located the human dimension amidst this surreal imagery, noting that the original shaping of this landscape, under slavery, must have entailed the moving of at least 100,000,000 tons of stiff, heavy coastal clay: no El Dorado.[15]

Only the Dutch, with their peerless mastery of hydraulic systems, could have crafted this amazing tapestry of drainage canals and perfect rectangular fields, veined with ordered drains, ditches, sea-walls and dams, a geometrical wonder — Holland in the Tropics. The Atlantic is above the land and water from the rain forests is a perennial threat. The notion of El Dorado, then, must have helped to lessen despair, feed ideas of possibilities beyond this tenuous grasp on life, on this strip of land, between high water and *terra incognita*, the vast rain-forests watered by mighty rivers which must lead to mountains of gold and the moon. The discovery of pockets of gold and diamond — always tasters — perpetuated the myth of fecundity, of wealth awaiting development. This is what shaped the Guyanese psyche.[16]

Hyperbole abound: fact and fantasy — 'the magnificent province'; 'my Guyana, El Dorado', land of the highest waterfall in the world and rivers so big that Barbados could fit in them many times — masks for insecurities in this place of spacious dreams and puny harvests. The millennium is always about to come. No figure epitomised this more than the pork-knocker, the folk figure who animated the African Guyanese world. This anarchic, rugged individualist, gold prospector, profligate patron of rum shops and whore houses, could transcend the despair. His escape into the unknown interior with the promise of riches, could negate the frustrations of the harsh coastland, where it was so difficult to elude the planters' frame of reference. Fantasy was made in this largely unknown land. The absence of roads or tracks, the navigation of the vast rivers blocked by waterfalls, heightened the mythical associations of the interior. Very few ever got there. The pork-knocker gave it special resonance, a motif of deliverance, and fed the idea of this space as an area of freedom, the antithesis of the slave plantations and the hard land of floods and drought, the cemetery of many dreams. But the pork-knocker's own perilous adventures frequently reaped failure: the dream was always bigger than the find. On the coast and in the interior the myth helped to lessen the harsh reality. As Michael Swan observed, after his travels in British Guiana in 1955:

There is gold in the hills of Guiana; the El Dorado of Sir Walter Raleigh is not a delusion. Many Guianese believe that one day reefs of gold comparable to those in South Africa will be found and with this vast natural wealth the problems of the Colony will be solved. Gold in alluvial deposits have been found in many areas and there have been rushes or 'shouts' as they are called, even in recent years; but by now most of the alluvial pockets have been worked out by lone prospectors and what remains can only be extracted by heavy machinery.[17]

The late Jamaican novelist, John Hearne, has spoken of the way the land shapes its people: '[W]e must never underestimate the significance of landscape on our lives and perceptions. Like the first stories of childhood, it fashions us in a thousand secret ways.'[18] The harsh coastal landscape bred pessimism among the early African farmers. Despair made the legacy of slavery even more resilient, as the plantocracy bent the colony to its procrustean mould. The plantation with its advanced technology and amazing reshaping of the landscape stood in stark contrast to the African and Indian land, ill-equipped to cope with the recurring floods and droughts. The plantation, more so than in Trinidad where the kinder land allowed small farmers to become cane-growers — partners in sugar — remained the focus of Guyanese antagonism.[19] However, this did not diminish the racial mistrust: African and Portuguese; African and Indian. The harsher economic realities, indeed, tended to aggravate the fear, sharpen the divide, especially after 1945, as the Empire was disintegrating.

The plantocracy, Booker, was the sole pivot for tenuous nationalist promptings. As Michael Swan discovered in 1955, anti-Booker sentiments were a Guyanese instinct:

Everywhere in British Guiana one is liable to hear attacks on Bookers.... But such unpopularity is inevitable when one firm has a monopolistic control of the country's main product and can be held as scapegoat for all shortcomings in the Guianese standard of living. Almost every attack on Bookers which I heard was an emotional one; the criticisms may frequently have been justified, but at their root lay a reluctance to reason or accept the causes of distress as coming from any other source other than the wicked exploitation by Sugar, and the 'sugar-coated government', as Dr. Cheddi Jagan wittily describes it.[20]

But the racial instincts of this backward colony were more resilient, more corrosive, than the anti-Booker ones. Yet, in a place where the foundations of a national purpose were so flimsy, hatred of the external colossus was virtually the only potent instrument for contriving a broader vision. Jagan understood this very well. He recalls his fledgling legislative role in the late 1940s, when F.J. Seaford, the head of Booker in the colony, also, was a legislator:

I soon learnt to play the game in the same determined way that Seaford did his job for Booker and sugar — sweetly and suavely with a smile. Politics, it is said, is the science of 'who gets what, when and how'. It was my task to find out how in a multitude of ways, overtly and covertly, the sugar 'gods' ruled.[21]

The Marxist message simplified the task; it fed into the millennial reflex, the El Dorado propensity of the Guyanese psyche; it allowed Jagan to theorise the bedevilling race question out of existence, to see it as a concocted problem, a ruse of the imperialists. 'Bitter sugar' could carry all the blame for the colony's history of pain, as Michael Swan observed:

[Jagan] denies that the Colony's difficulties arise from the problems of its geography. This is an excuse invented by imperialists to explain why they have not made a greater success of the Colony. The difficulties 'are man-made and made by alien control'... Dr Jagan's answer is ruthlessly to destroy the power of 'King Sugar'. He was himself born and brought up on a sugar plantation...and his political principles are guided by a violent hatred of the sugar interests.... Generally a courteous and pleasant man in conversation he will become excited, indignant and lose all powers of proper reasoning when the subject of sugar is discussed.[22]

Jagan's boyhood was firmly rooted in the sugar plantation. His grandparents were taken to British Guiana in 1901 as indentured labourers when his father and mother were babies. His parents

The birth certificate of Cheddi Jagan: name stated as 'Chedda' ('Illegitimate' [in smaller letters in the same column])

became child-labourers: his father at Albion, one of the Campbell plantations; his mother at Port Mourant, where Cheddi was born on March 22, 1918, the eldest of 11 children. His people originated in Basti, in eastern Uttar Pradesh, and were of Kurmi caste, farmers. He has observed that there was no rebel like him in his family tree. What, then, made this unique rebel, in British Guiana?

Jagan read no significance into his caste background. However, throughout the nineteenth century, colonial officials in the United Provinces [Uttar Pradesh] were effusive in their celebration of the Kurmi's agricultural gifts, although most were landless. They spoke of their industry, thrift, refined husbandry (especially the women's meticulous farming methods), consistency of purpose and their ingenuity in pursuing many activities simultaneously. In 1897, four years before Cheddi's people left India, an agricultural authority wrote thus of the Kurmi of Uttar Pradesh:

Nowhere would one find better instances of keeping land scrupulously free of weeds, of ingenuity in device of water-raising appliances, of knowledge of soils and their capabilities, as well as the exact time to sow and reap, as one would in Indian agriculture, and this not at its best but at its ordinary level. It is wonderful, too, how much is known of rotation, the system of mixed crops, and of fallowing. I have never seen a more perfect picture of careful cultivation, worked with hard labour, perseverance and fertility of resource.[23]

Those were the qualities his people cultivated in their new homeland. Cheddi's mother, in particular, was industrious, thrifty and completely dedicated to the family. Jagan recalls the formative influence of his mother: '[S]he taught me the rudiments of finance, of thrift, of how to get along and make do, to survive.' And like the inventive Kurmis of UP, his father's earnings as a 'driver', a field foreman at Port Mourant, were supplemented with rice growing, a few heads of cattle and a kitchen garden. Cheddi's life was inevitably an abstemious one; there were 10 other siblings.[24]

It was from his father that Jagan acquired his leadership qualities. He rose from being a menial cane-cutter, at the age of 14, to a driver, on merit. Cheddi said that he was a good cane-cutter, a strong man, and a good driver; but he could go no further as the next step up, the position of overseer, was reserved for young whites, often Scots. He did not want his son's life to be stunted on the sugar plantation. Cheddi explains: '[H]e sacrificed everything to give me an education; he realised the value of education. If you wanted to get out of the estates you had to be educated, so he sacrificed everything to give me a high school education, to go to Queen's College [in Georgetown], and then later on, to give me enough money to go abroad — a small amount but to him it was a lot of money'.[25]

Jagan attended Queen's College between 1932 and 1935. He had returned to Port Mourant for a year, 1935-6, as he was unable to get a job with the government because of 'a paucity of godfathers'. These jobs often went to light-skinned, coloured people, with the right connections. It was a world hemmed in by prejudices and for the coolie — the Indian from the sugar plantation — the fence was virtually impenetrable. Those crucial years were precisely the time Jock Campbell was learning the ropes, discovering the world of sugar and the Guyanese reality, 1934-37. Cheddi left for Howard University, Washington, in 1936, to do dentistry. He recalls that J.C. Gibson, the manager of Port Mourant, was 'czar, king, prosecutor and judge', an awesome figure. The paths to the planter's mansion and the workers' ranges (logies) did not intersect. This had created in Cheddi a curiosity, a compulsion later, to discover the universe of the 'other'. He used to tell a powerful tale from his boyhood, etched in humiliation:

I recall vividly my curiosity about the manager's mansion. I wanted to know what it felt like to be inside the gate. I wanted to know what was going on inside. I must have been about eight or nine years old [1926–27]. I joined the creole [child-labour] gang and went to share in the largesse of the manager. The manager's wife, Mrs. Gibson, stood at the window of the top floor of this imposing mansion. She threw coins down to us and enjoyed seeing the wild scramble for the pennies. This is the way our manager's wife offered gifts to workers' children at Christmas time on a sugar plantation.[26]

This was what shaped Jagan's life-long obsession with King Sugar, to storm the gates of the world of plantation sugar. This image of the manager's wife tossing pennies to child-labourers in a frenzied scramble, must have lodged in his imagination, the motif of his eternal crusade to cripple the 'sugar gods'. This, in conjunction with the racial ceiling imposed on his able father's ambition on the estate, nurtured the rebel in Cheddi, to fight for the underdog. Although his father was a 'driver' he retained links both with the workers as well as those on the higher rungs of the administration, but he noted that he 'never completely identified with [the latter]; he always fought for the workers in his own quiet way, without jeopardising his position'. Cheddi said that he acquired a boldness and a moral perspective, of right and wrong, from his indomitable father; his capacity for hard work, too, but he rejected his father's penchant for hard drinking. He recalls: 'At week-ends he just drank; this was the only past-time he had.'[27] Cheddi never drank: in this land of big drinkers this would even be seen as a flaw; he never really had personal friends; he never got close to any one.

His father's position on the estate did not affect Cheddi's relationship with ordinary boys at Port Mourant. Through his cricket he retained their respect; but his father's status, in the lower middle stratum on the estate, gave him ambition. He was the first from his family to go to high school, at Port Mourant then Queen's College; he was the first from his area to go to the latter. He had to succeed. The fear of failure, the financial burden on his parents, imposed an intensity of purpose. There would be no frills, no broader interests, no diversion from the academically stilted curriculum. The education at Queen's College was about preparing for and passing examinations — to get a good job, preferably a profession, to escape the sugar plantation.[28] It could not accommodate loftier intellectual designs; it lacked relevance in many ways, but worse, it could not provide the means of self-assessment.

In Georgetown, as a Kurmi (an agricultural caste) lodging in the home of a high caste Kshatriya, he had to know his place: he was made to sleep on the floor although there was a spare room with a bed. When he moved to the home of another Hindu he had to perform many chores before and after school, including 'cutting grass for goats'. Cheddi's mother was a Hindu but she was not fastidious about it.[29] Rituals were performed, festivals celebrated, but the intensity was not there: one could lapse and catch up when necessary. Those Georgetown humiliations, however, at the hands of high caste Hindus, probably turned him away from religion, for good. It alienated him from his Indian frame of reference.

When Cheddi left Queen's College in 1935 and returned to Port Mourant for a year, he was 'relatively unscathed', though armed with an Oxford and Cambridge School Certificate. I pointed out to him in 1992 that during his Georgetown sojourn, 1932–35, there were several vibrant Indian organisations in the city, such as the [Wesleyan] East Indian Young Men's Society headed by Peter Ruhomon, an Indian intellectual; that they debated cultural and political issues; that they were drawn to a resurgent India and its ancient culture as well as the contemporary, militant Gandhian nationalist mission. Cheddi replied casually that he was ignorant of such activities, read no newspapers and did not follow the early Indian independence struggle: he read his school-books, nothing more. He did not have the intellectual means to absorb much; to comprehend such activities. He recalls:

> There was no bridge at all, no association — [I was] just going to Queen's College to pass exams; there was no way to mobilise young people like me into that kind of stream. Things were happening but at that stage my consciousness and awareness weren't developed.[30]

Martin Carter (1927–97), the poet and Jagan's young Marxist protege in the late 1940s and early 1950s, has tried to grasp what the collision of the world of the sugar plantation and that of Georgetown would have meant to Cheddi in the early 1930s. He was talking to V.S. Naipaul:

> The sheer area of experience was too much for a young man from a plantation background to deal with. We were even more remote than we are today from so-called metropolitan centres. You could imagine — 'Martin Carter looks for a word' — the lostness of a young man in those days coming out of a background without a literary culture. It froze him into attitudes which have lasted. This freezing affected him personally. At the same time it brought home to him in a very powerful way the kind of society and community he had come from.[31]

The labour troubles on the plantations, in 1935, as I have argued, brought home to young Jock Campbell the depth of the grievances on the estates, the culture of poverty. The young Jagan, also, could not have been oblivious of this avalanche of protest the year before he left for America. This had affected his own estate, Port Mourant, as well as Jock's Albion. These two men, from diametrically opposite backgrounds, inhabited the same plantation universe between 1934 and 1936. As in Ireland, so in Guyana, Jock was aware that perspectives, ways of seeing the same thing, could vary, depending on the viewer's circumstances. On the question of J.C. Gibson, the manager of Port Mourant, whom he knew well, he concurs with Cheddi on his authoritarian style and adds that Mrs Gibson was 'a terrifying woman'. However, he remembers another dimension of the man: he was 'a tough manager' but 'a just man'. Unlike the Scottish managers who predominated in British Guiana, tough Highland Scots usually, Gibson was an Englishman of some sophistication. He was 'feared', but the workers at Port Mourant respected him; Jock felt he was 'a class ahead of the others'.[32]

Gibson had made good land available for workers on the estate to grow rice and rear cattle; housing was generally better, many having built their own cottages with earnings from supplementary farming. Gibson had also constructed a narrow-gauge railway to transport workers to the canefields several miles 'aback'. He was a keen cricketer and had promoted the game vigorously on the plantation. Even in the 1920s Port Mourant had a flourishing cricket club. The people played the game with a passion; although under the inescapable scrutiny of Gibson, they had some autonomy in organising the club. The annual horse-racing meeting on August 1 had become an august event, stimulating interest throughout the colony; the Governor would travel from Georgetown to open it. By the early 1930s this healthier estate, in this notoriously malarial colony, had shaped a discernibly independent, bolder set of Indian workers and Gibson's role was paramount. Jock Campbell elaborated for me:

> Port Mourant was a very, very well-run estate. [The people] were big and they were healthy in that area because of the salt [air]. There was no doubt about it, they were particularly healthy and the malaria was less serious. I think I told you that when we started [peasant] cane farming in my day [1950s], the Port Mourant cane farmers were way ahead of any other workers in the industry — they were marvellous people.[33]

The spirit of independence (Jock says that 'the labour force was confident') must have quickened whatever rebellious instincts were taking shape in young Cheddi Jagan. His father's 'boldness' and 'humanity', he told me, stayed with him; but his father's life spoke also of hope and its limitations, as eloquently as the plantation evoked social and racial distances: knowing one's place. He had gone from menial cane-cutter to 'driver', but could go no further because of his race. This became imbedded in Cheddi's colonial psyche, as did the fact that he could not get a job in the colonial service after he left Queen's College in 1935, for the same reason. Out of sheer frustration he left for Washington in 1936, aged 18, to do dentistry. As he had no means of assessing his colonial environment, the raw emotions were submerged. Naipaul, paraphrasing Martin Carter, reflects: 'Cheddi had no literary culture, nothing that would have helped him to see and understand, and put things in their place. He had simply taken things as they had come.'[34]

But he had the passion, shaped by the hurt and the injustice of plantation society, the intensity that makes for single-mindedness. However, despair never claimed him. The comparatively progressive character of Port Mourant gave him ambition, while something of the millennial, the El Dorado instinct of the Guyanese temperament, bred by the hard landscape, fed a penchant for escapism. It gave rise to the hyperbolic, a bravura persona, masks for fear and self-doubts rooted in the intractability of the Guyanese condition: the land and its diverse peoples. The literary void, the slight intellectual gifts — for self-assessment and critical evaluation — left Cheddi with no facility for reasoning, of analysing, judging on merits, filtering things; the imagination and flexibility were not there when needed.

The intensity never eased. Indeed, the struggle to survive while he trained in dentistry in America, between 1936 and 1943, hardened it; the narrow, utilitarian focus of his education was reinforced. He admired Gandhi and Nehru, who called up pride in his Indian antecedents, but he was devoid of Indian culture. He had no Hinduism, no conception of or feel for the secular gifts of that great tradition: its poetry, art, music, philosophy, the diverse ancient achievement. He knew nothing of Guyanese history either; very little had been written as late as the 1930s; in any case he did not read what was not schoolwork. He had no frame of reference to make sense of his world.

He became very ill in 1943 and was sent to a sanatorium to recuperate. The enforced rest made him reflect on the limitations of his education. He decided to go part-time to YMCA College in Chicago. There, under Professor Sinha, an Indian, he became interested in political science. He read on the American War of Independence, Nehru's biography, too; *Robber Barons* brought him to an understanding of how American capitalism worked. As he told Naipaul: 'What I do I do very intensely.'[35] The intellectual void deepened the intensity: there was no space for eclecticism, for exploration of human motives or individual motivation.

That is why literature — the probing of deeper personal recesses, an inquiry into the range of human emotions, the complexity of things, human frailties and the absurdity of much that passes for wisdom — meant nothing to him. It never would. The world of the imagination, the intellectual probing, did nothing for him. He was after total knowledge; he had a passion for the primer, 'how to' texts: *How to Win Races*; *How to Play Bridge*. The urgencies, the procrustean demands of a hard boyhood and the fear of failure as a student — he was the first child; so much was invested in him — in Georgetown, Washington and Chicago, bred in him a narrow, rigid, utilitarian frame of mind. It also gave him the drive, the sense of mission, the sincerity and consistency of motives — the inflexibility, too. The learning, later, in his late 20s, after the dental training, could not break out of this utilitarian mould. He was looking for certainties not the means of inquiry.

1943 brought him to Janet Rosenberg (born 1920), a young Jewish American whose parents were of Czech stock. Like many youths during the Depression she was disillusioned with American capitalism. She became a communist. She had read some of the Marxist classics. Her beauty ('love at first sight', Cheddi recalls) and her knowledge of 'scientific socialism' struck a chord immediately. His sojourn at YMCA College had given him 'a peep into socialism'. He was soon to be given the rudiments of a frame of reference to understand the world; besides he had married this 'exceedingly beautiful woman'. Both would give him strength to take on the plantocracy in British Guiana. He recalled that on the plantations 'intermarriage was strictly forbidden'.[36] He had violated that code: his battle with the 'sugar gods' was about to be joined.

He returned to the colony in 1943. Janet joined him later that year, in December. She brought some Marxist primers which gave him 'total understanding of the world'. In 1991 he explained to V.S. Naipaul, in a clean, rehearsed narrative, that illumination of nearly 50 years before:

> It was Janet who, when she came here [British Guiana] in 1943, brought me Little Lenin Library books — little tracts, pamphlets. It was the first time I read Marxist literature. And then — as with the bridge books — I began reading Marxist books like mad. I read *Das Kapital* after the Little Lenin series. And that helped me to have *a total understanding* of the development of society. Until then, all the various struggles — Indians, blacks, the American people — had been disjointed experiences. To put it in a way that was *totally* related to a socio-economic system came

from the reading of Marxist literature. For instance, the woman question was dealt with in Engels's book, *The Origins of the Family.* The Marxist theory of surplus value brought a *totally* new understanding of the struggle of the working class — not only that they were exploited. It was exciting to me, an intellectual excitement because a whole new world opened to me, *a total understanding of the world* [emphasis added].[37]

From the beginning Campbell's reformist 'cause' was pitted against this Marxist mission, marked by its intensity, a purity of motives and an incorrigible naivety. This could have been innocuous, but ominously for Campbell, the simple and simplistic message, with its messianic strain, had powerful resonance on the plantations of British Guiana. 'Bitter Sugar' was the motif animating the mission; it also drove Campbell's efforts at righting ancient wrongs, to meet Jagan part of the way, as he saw it, but he was already immersed in a quagmire. For Cheddi the 'new science' was the way to the promised land; it could not be delayed by Jock's half-measures. In his memoirs of 1966, after he had lost power because his Marxism had scared President Kennedy into subverting his government, Cheddi could still conclude thus: 'Difficulties there will be; the battle will be long and hard. But win we will. History and time are on our side.'[38] The Marxist truths were inviolable.

Eusi Kwayana (Sydney King), who was a disciple of Cheddi in the heady days of the late 1940s and early 1950s, has tried to trace with Naipaul the source of the Jaganite passion, his faith in the Soviet lie:

> I think he had a cultural problem. If he had been a devout Hindu, even in his youth, he would have had a more workable, a more human, frame of reference. But, having rejected imperialism and all its works along with its culture [the Western intellectual tradition], he got attached to another metropolis which was the Soviet Union. He understood it as it presented itself. So everything he did had to be explained, in his own mind, in the culture of that other metropolis. Once he could do that he felt vindicated.[39]

Cheddi had no internal reverences. The passion was there, floating. His illumination, in the mid-1940s, gave him 'total understanding': inquiry was not required. Everything worth knowing was now known: he had arrived at scientific truths. The passion could be sustained. Nearly 30 years later, in 1974, in his address to the eighteenth Congress of the PPP, he saw no reason to revise his outlook:

> The PPP's socialism [is] based on the science of Marxism-Leninism.... Practical political work will succeed only when based on *correct theories and ideas* — the ideology of Marxism-Leninism.... We must fight for *scientific truths*.... Long live the International Communist movement...Marxism-Leninism is a scientific ideology. It will endure. Our party too will endure provided we set our course on this scientific ideology [emphasis added].[40]

Endnotes

1. Jock Campbell, interview by the author, Nettlebed, Oxfordshire, July 24, 1992, Tape 6.
2. *PAC Bulletin*, no. 43, December 26, 1949.
3. Ibid.
4. Ibid.
5. *PAC Bulletin*, no. 42, November 26, 1949.
6. Ibid.
7. Ibid.
8. Ibid.
9. See note 1.
10. *PAC Bulletin*, no. 41, October 18, 1949.
11. Ibid.
12. Jock Campbell, interview by the author, Nettlebed, Oxfordshire, May 9, 1990, Tape 1.
13. Jock Campbell to the Editor, *The New Statesman and Nation*, October 24, 1953.
14. See my article, 'The Shaping of the Indo-Caribbean People: Guyana and Trinidad to the 1940s', *Journal of Caribbean Studies* 14, nos. 1-2 (Fall 1999/Spring 2000): 72-3.
15. *Report of a Commission of Inquiry into the Sugar Industry of British Guiana* (J.A. Venn, Chairman) (London: HMSO, 1949), 9.
16. See note 14 [pp. 67-8].
17. Michael Swan, *British Guiana: The Land of Six Peoples* (London: HMSO, 1957), 183.
18. See John Hearne, 'What the Barbadian Means to Me', *New World Quarterly* 3, nos. 1-2, (1966-67).
19. See note 14.
20. See note 17 [pp.89-90].

21. Cheddi Jagan, *The West on Trial: My Fight for Guyana's Freedom* (London: Michael Joseph, 1966), 95.

22. See note 17 [p. 90].

23. Quoted in my *'Tiger in the Stars': The Anatomy of Indian Achievement in British Guiana, 1919-29* (London: Macmillan, 1997), 13.

24. Cheddi Jagan, interview by the author, University of Warwick, Coventry, May 10, 1992.

25. Ibid.

26. See note 21 [pp. 18-9].

27. See note 24.

28. Ibid.

29. See note 21 [pp. 23-4].

30. See note 24.

31. V.S. Naipaul, 'A Handful of Dust: Return to Guiana', *The New York Review of Books*, April 11, 1991, 18.

32. Jock Campbell, interview by the author, Nettlebed, Oxfordshire, July 23, 1992, Tape 3.

33. Ibid.

34. See note 31.

35. Ibid. [p.19].

36. See note 21 [pp. 62-3, 19].

37. See note 31 [p. 19].

38. Ibid. [p. 454].

39. See note 31 [p. 16].

40. Cheddi Jagan, 'Address to the 18th PPP Congress', *Thunder*, (October-December 1974): 21, 26.

Chapter Sixteen

CAMPBELL'S RESPONSE TO JAGAN'S POLITICS: ANTI-COMMUNISM, 1947-56

Cheddi Jagan's 'total understanding', which came with his Marxist illumination, collided immediately with Jock Campbell's reformist capitalism. For the latter, whose outlook was permeated by an imaginative, infinitely more tentative, apprehension of human nature inspired by nineteenth century literature and Fabian socialism, this 'total knowledge' spoke of fanaticism, an absence of inquiry, the antithesis of compromise — the inevitable give and take — politics as 'the art of the possible'. Between 1947–48 and 1960, before racial violence engulfed Guyana, clouding over ideas of development, Campbell's changing perceptions of Jagan constitute a fascinating chapter in the politics of decolonisation. These two men, along with L.F.S. Burnham (and Peter D'Aguiar), became enmeshed in the tortuous, volatile, increasingly turbulent temper of a bifurcated Guyanese nationalism, African and Indian.

Campbell's changing responses to Jagan's politics may be divided into four phases: (i) 1947–52, when he was vice-chairman of Booker, under the ailing and ineffective A.F.C. McConnell, but wrote all the chairman's annual statements. Jock became chairman in 1952. This period was characterised by circumspection of Jagan's motives and mounting apprehension of his Marxism; (ii) 1953–56, Campbell's most anti-communist phase, when he tried to encourage an anti-communist alternative, following the suspension of the constitution in 1953; (iii) 1957–60, when, after Jagan's re-election in August 1957, Campbell tried hard to work with him, arguing that he was the only credible force in Guyanese politics; (iv) 1961–64, the final phase, the years of racial turbulence in the colony, when Campbell remained largely sympathetic to Jagan, but Guyanese affairs had become fatally enmeshed in Cold War politics and racial violence. Campbell felt defeated and became increasingly aloof. Amidst virtual civil war, in 1963–64, the local Booker people had become somewhat autonomous and tended to be more sympathetic to Jagan's opponents, Burnham and D'Aguiar. Campbell was noticeably absent from British Guiana; his authority was in decline.

In this section I assess the first two phases. Campbell was perturbed by the shooting of workers at Enmore in June 1948, the killing of five men active in the Jagan-backed GIWU's strike for recognition. He recognised the 'real need to improve the living standards of the people' in British Guiana, noting that that obligation made the cost of producing sugar inflexible. Wages alone accounted for half the cost, while 'the provision of better amenities for workers' in this hazardous environment with heavy drainage and irrigation charges, increased it appreciably. But he cautioned that those who were 'sincerely concerned' about the welfare of Guyanese must recognise the necessity to ensure that the cost of production did not increase beyond the price obtained for sugar. That would be disastrous for the whole colony. It was in this context that Campbell assessed the GIWU strike on the East Coast Demerara in 1948:

> For the cost of producing sugar in British Guiana to outstrip its value would be a disaster for the people of the colony. Strikes — bringing in their train reduced output and other, but less easily definable, ill consequences — are a sure road to such disaster and I only hope that the workers on our estates, wisely advised by their established Trade Unions [the MPCA mainly] and by the Government of the colony, will carry on peacefully with their daily tasks.... He is a brave man who would attempt to prophesy the future when international conditions and indeed political conditions in the Colonies are unpredictable. We cannot ... expect that trading activities and values will remain at their present high levels, but, given peaceful conditions, I hope we can look forward with sober confidence to steady if not to spectacular progress.[1]

In May 1949, as noted earlier, the SPA were fearful that Cheddi was manoeuvring to become president of the BGWL, which represented the predominantly African factory workers on the estates. They threatened to terminate relations with the League if that should happen. The Commissioner of Labour, W.M. Bissell, had recommended a less precipitous approach, 'defer[ring] this step until Dr. Jagan committed a breach of the Agreement between the Association and the League, as he was bound to do at an early date if he pursued his object of destroying the sugar industry'. G.M. (Guy) Eccles of the SPA was not placated, and he warned Bissell that it would be impossible to work with Jagan, 'an avowed communist' who had made it clear that 'he intended to do his utmost to destroy the sugar industry'. Consequently, the Association were 'determined to fight communism wherever it reared its ugly head'. A report of the meeting was sent to Campbell who, in an internal minute to F.J. Seaford, observed:

> (a) I strongly agree with Bissell; (b) I doubt whether Jagan is a real communist — he is a self-seeking politician who might well become moderate if in power. His wife is, of course, another story. Still I think it would be most unwise to disregard Bissell's advice.[2]

In June 1949 Jagan's *PAC Bulletin* advanced what they saw as the liberating potential of strikes in the context of the wider mission, the class struggle as the instrument of emancipation from capitalism. They were philosophical about its inherent virtue, drawing the lesson from a recent postal strike:

> There is no strike which is not a victory. The very striking is a victorious action of a class. It is either a victory or a failure to the particular union concerned. Whether the strike of the Postal workers was successful or not in its immediate demands, the working class considers it a victory since it is a progressive step in the class struggle of British Guiana.[3]

A few weeks earlier the *PAC Bulletin* had denounced the Bishop of Guiana on two counts: for accepting a gift of $55,000, presumably from capitalists, for the building of a convent; and for his attack on the communist government of Hungary for its treatment of Cardinal Mindszenty. They argued that the early apostles had tried to 'launch a communist society' by encouraging people to sell their properties and divide the proceeds 'according to the need of each individual'.

Such egalitarianism, however, would be repugnant to the Church, to the Bishop, too. Then alluding to their own beliefs, they concluded: 'People who try to create a proper distribution of wealth and to see that hunger, oppression and slavery are done away with, are called "communists" and servants of Moscow.'[4]

This was the context in which Jock Campbell took up the fight, 'a great cause', to counter the communism of Cheddi Jagan. His reforms on the plantations were at the core of this cause. In a confidential letter to R.R. Follett-Smith, chairman of Booker Sugar Estates in Guyana, on July 21, 1949, he asserted:

> We must remember that we fight Communism not alone on grounds of dogma, not alone to protect a European minority in British Guiana, not alone to safeguard the interests of shareholders in the sugar industry and other commercial undertakings; we fight Communism, above all, to make British Guiana a place fit for *all* its people to live and work in, in the greatest attainable degree of prosperity, happiness and freedom. That is a great cause and one that fully justifies the efforts of yourself and your colleagues, however discouraging the fight may often be.[5]

The single-mindedness, the passion and sincerity of purpose of Cheddi Jagan, in the Legislative Council and in the villages and on the plantations, were an extraordinary feature of post-War politics in the colony, a serious worry for the plantocracy. As noted earlier, Booker had issued a trespass writ on Jagan for his activities on Plantation Ogle. Jagan countered that their action infringed his rights as a legislator: the estate was in his constituency. Campbell was aware that 'human relationships' on the plantations were 'the most difficult problem', but he was also apprehensive of Jagan's energy, commitment to his cause, and his meteoric rise after the Enmore shootings. He could not be ignored. Campbell's Chairman's Statement for 1948 reflected that growing unease with the Jaganite enigma: 'On the part of the Industry much has been done, is being done and will be done to improve the condition of our workers. I must confess, however, that there exists in the colony an atmosphere of suspicion of our motives and even of hostility which often depreciates if it does not actually thwart our efforts and our aspirations.'[6]

Then, repeating what he had written to Follett-Smith earlier, in July 1949, Campbell elaborated on the task ahead: 'We all wish to make British Guiana a place fit for all its people to live and work in, in the greatest attainable degree of prosperity, happiness and freedom, but we shall surely fail unless we all strive in concert to that goal — unless everyone concerned believes that "We are all in the same boat"; unless, in short, we, all of us, realise the identity of our interests.'[7] This was an invitation to all non-Marxist forces in the colony to fight the virus of communism. The cold war had begun.

Meanwhile, Jagan's *PAC Bulletin* was resolute in its anti-Booker stance, denouncing its practice of employing white expatriates mainly, as managers and overseers on the estates and as administrators at its head office in Georgetown. This prevented Guyanese from gaining employment while diverting valuable funds oversees, to Britain, to cover holidays and pensions. A correspondent deemed this an affront to Guyanese dignity, castigating those 'importees who barricade themselves behind a superior "British ruling class" attitude and sneer at Guianese aspirations'. He applauded Jagan's vigorous campaign for 'Guianisation' of the workforce and concluded: 'I personally am sick and disgusted of these British who do not belong here and whose intelligence and desire to do a real job are suspect. There are hundreds of intelligent and resentful Guianese who admire what you [Jagan] are doing and in a short while they will begin to add their voices to yours.'[8]

Reviewing the performance in the sugar industry in 1949, Campbell observed that the MPCA and the BGWL, the recognised trade unions, had secured 'outstanding advances in conditions of employment of workers', adding that 'better industrial relations' had contributed 'very largely' to the greater production achieved.[9] However, Jagan's work on the sugar plantations, especially his commitment to the removal of the MPCA ('a company union'), was central to his political mission: in 1950-51 the Jagan-backed GIWU had accelerated their campaign on the estates. Campbell resented this:

It is never safe to prophesy about the labour situation for unfortunately political agitators and self-seekers are always with us. They aim for their own ends and directly, contrary to the interests of workers, to inflame opinion against the Industry and bring about major stoppages of work. Happily in 1950, their attempts were largely abortive; thanks to the good sense of our workpeople, and thanks to the fact that normal Labour negotiations with the recognised Trade Unions [MPCA included] were conducted in that atmosphere of mutual understanding and goodwill which alone can inspire successful human relationship.[10]

Campbell feared what he saw as Jagan's dangerous utopianism. In December 1951, *The Guiana Sunday Graphic*, virtually the organ of the sugar producers, also rejected Jagan's activities among sugar workers. They considered it intolerable that 'irresponsible organisations', an obvious reference to the PPP and the GIWU, should be allowed to operate freely on the estates, disseminating 'malicious tales and flamboyant promises of Utopian conditions they can obtain for them'. They argued that 'firm measures' should be taken to protect a 'struggling industry from wanton attacks by persons who are really not interested in industrial relations'. These people, they asserted, 'infiltrate' for purely opportunistic reasons, to boost their own political influence.[11]

This uncompromising editorial was probably prompted by a piece, 'Message from Comrade Jagan', in the PPP's organ, *Thunder*, of December 1951. Jagan had just returned from Eastern Europe, 'the People's Democracies', as he unfailingly called them. He had seen tomorrow; it was a journey to see what he wanted to see — vindication of the Marxist illumination. He now sought to debunk the 'lies' that these 'Democracies' were characterised by forced labour and the denial of freedom. Indeed, he contrasted conditions of work there with conditions in capitalist Britain:

I have seen the people at work with my own eyes and on many occasions by myself and not 'led by the nose' as we are made to believe. I have not seen any evidence of forced labour. Rather, everywhere there was enthusiasm and spiritedness. This was no doubt born of the knowledge that the Government was their Government, that the factories were their factories, that they were building a new and bright future for themselves. I did not witness the same enthusiastic spirit among the British working class.[12]

Jagan had seen the Communist utopia: it worked. A true believer, with 'total understanding', he knew this was the path for British Guiana once freedom from British imperialism was won. He would brook no reformist palliatives. He concluded: 'We will always be underfed, ill-clad and ill-housed so long as we are tied hand and foot and allow ourselves to be delivered as booty to the imperialists. Let us resolve to make every effort to strengthen the PPP and fight for self-government and the establishment in British Guiana of a People's Government'.[13] The USSR, under Comrade Stalin and 'scientific socialism', was leading the way to the promised land. Cheddi was not persuaded by an avalanche of evidence to the contrary.

By 1952 A.F.V. McConnell[14] had resigned as chairman of Booker. He was only 49. His family's business in British Guiana, John McConnell and Co, had been absorbed by Booker in 1900, as Jock's was in 1939. McConnell had succeeded Sir Alfred Sherlock in 1946, but as Campbell told me, he did not have his heart in the business. Jock had virtually been in charge since 1946 and in 1952, aged 40, he became chairman of Booker. He explained: 'It was thought wise that the Chairmanship should be held by someone actively concerned and experienced in the everyday management and affairs of the Company.' No one was better equipped for the task than Jock Campbell, but it is arguable that the rising stature of the young Marxist, Cheddi Jagan, on the sugar estates, on the eve of the colony's first elections under universal adult suffrage (1953), hastened the elevation of Campbell. He had no doubt of his capacity to handle the situation; he had piloted the negotiations towards the Commonwealth Sugar Agreement in 1951 with admirable dexterity and success; his life had become interwoven with sugar and British Guiana since 1934: 'For my part I feel particularly honoured at being made Chairman because to me Bookers is not merely a business — it is a cause.'[15]

However, the raw, unmalleable Jaganite communist faith collided with Campbell's reformist temperament, bred on the gradualist instincts of Fabian socialism. A Booker portrait of 1948 recorded: 'Literature takes pride of place among Mr. Campbell's less strenuous recreations and he has a wide knowledge and sincere appreciation of the classics.'[16] As noted earlier, his sensibility was shaped by his immersion in great literature and permeated, since the mid-1930s, by the social awakening on the plantations of British Guiana. Although he acquired a natural empathy for the underdog, for the 'other' generally, his intellect and sense of proportion were repelled by 'utopian fantasies'. As Ian McDonald, who worked for Campbell for many years and shared similar intellectual interests, observes of him: 'Imagination and enthusiasm were more vivid in him than in anyone else I ever knew well.' He recalls a quote from the contemporary American thinker, Irving Howe, which Jock once sent to him. His aversion to the millennial is clear; one could also discern the germ of his contempt for the received Jaganite nostrums: 'There is utopia and utopia. The kind imposed by an elite in the name of an historical imperative; that utopia is hell. It must lead to terror and then, terror exhausted, to cynicism and torpor. But surely there is another utopia. It cannot be willed into existence or out of sight. It speaks for our sense of what may yet be'. McDonald reflects on the pragmatic, but creative, mind of the man and his ability to inspire:

> Jock Campbell himself had a profound sense of what could be attempted and what might be achieved in the cause of a better society. All his working life he strove pragmatically to improve the lives of people whom his decisions touched .... I never met Jock Campbell and came away without feeling that life held a glorious promise I had not thought about before, a potential for exciting endeavours and worthwhile accomplishment which had previously been missing.... He made a good difference in thousands upon thousands of lives.[17]

That was why Campbell saw his work with Booker in British Guiana as a cause; and in 1952 he elaborated on the broader context of that 'cause'. He saw the world as an arena for 'a turbulent interaction of forces, good and evil, creative and destructive'. One of the 'creative' forces was the British Commonwealth: 'Upon the triumph or ruin of the ideals which the Commonwealth represents, and which inspire it, depend whether civilisation — the ability of men to live in creative concert together — or chaos will prevail'. In this context of partnership, Campbell believed that colonial peoples, as independent nations, could make a substantial contribution: 'the mighty influence of colonial peoples for progress and for good can, as we believe it will, decisively weigh the balance on the side of civilisation'. There were, however, 'formidable' social, economic and political problems to resolve before these peoples could play their full part. In this process, colonial companies, such as Booker, were crucial: 'Without them there could have been no colonial economic development — thus no social or political development.'[18]

Campbell's lofty expectations of the British Commonwealth, its elevation as an instrument of 'civilisation', therefore, could be seen as the posing of an alternative post-colonial framework to Jagan's communist vision: the end to 'exploitative' foreign capital; a complete break with 'imperialism'; the creation of a 'People's Democracy' with strong links to the Soviet Union and its East European satellites. This polarity dogged the Campbell–Jagan discourse throughout the early 1950s, into the crucial general elections of April 1953. The PPP's victory, however, evoked instantaneous moderation and circumspection from Campbell. He extended a pragmatic, conciliatory hand to the new Jagan government: 'As in the past, it will be the policy of the Booker Group in British Guiana in the future to work constructively and with goodwill with the Government of the colony for the interests of the people'. He reaffirmed Booker's identity with its main area of investment, while rejecting the popular opprobrious local appellation, 'Booker's Guiana':

> We resent this; we like to think of ourselves as 'Bookers of British Guiana'. We are proud of belonging to British Guiana and proud of the contribution we have been able to make, and mean to go on making, to the health, wealth and happiness of its people .... [H]owever much in recent years Booker may have spread their interests elsewhere in the world, British Guiana remains the source of our existence and the foundation of our structure. If British Guiana prospers, we prosper.[19]

It is reasonable to argue that, like many officials at the Colonial Office, Campbell hoped that power would moderate the rhetorical excesses of the PPP, that responsibility would breed reason and reasonableness. The problem was that the party had deemed the Waddington Constitution (1951), under which they were elected, a retrograde instrument to perpetuate capitalism, and were resolved to make it unworkable:

[T]he British will write any constitution for a colony except a free constitution. For a free constitution never descends from an imperialist overlord into the arms of an exploited people but is won and written by the people themselves in the face of battle.... [I]t is more likely for a dog to surrender a bone, more likely for a crow to relinquish carrion than for an imperialist power voluntarily to hand over control to the peoples of the colonies.[20]

Speaking in the Legislative Council on January 23, 1952, on the new constitution, Jagan underlined that it must be assessed in terms of what it meant for the future of the sugar industry. He elaborated:

We have first of all to stop the flow of profits going abroad. In order to stop the flow of profits going abroad we have to do certain things, and in order to do those things we must have political power.... If we take the sugar industry, there is definite need for reorganisation of the industry either on the basis of complete nationalisation or reorganisation in the sense that the estates are run on a co-operative system.[21]

Although Marxists were in a minority in the PPP, Cheddi's zeal for the communist utopia was irrepressible, and his short-lived administration (133 days), between May and October 1953, demonstrated no sensitivity to American Cold War susceptibilities, gravely exacerbated by the dreadful paranoia of McCarthyism. In May 1953, the party's organ, *Thunder*, reported the death of Stalin thus: 'PPP Mourns the Loss to Mankind of J.V. Stalin': 'The Third Congress of the PPP observed two minutes silence on the sad occasion of the death of J.V. Stalin, the leader of the Soviet people, the liberator of free Europe and the acknowledged pathfinder of peace.'[22]

In a radio broadcast on August 9, 1953, Jagan, as Leader of the House of Assembly and Minister of Agriculture, Forests, Lands and Mines, made no attempt to conceal his Marxist credo. Having found the truth, he was evangelical about it, as if he were reciting from his primer:

I have made no effort to disguise the fact that I believe in the superiority of the socialist system. Capitalism proved itself more efficient than feudalism and slavery and so replaced them. So will the capitalist system in due course be changed into a higher

and more efficient socialist system. Likewise socialism itself will
evolve into the higher communist stage of society.[23]

This was no posturing by Jagan; it was an illumination fed by his
belief that his comrades elsewhere were already building the road to
communism: 'Unlike some socialists I have not hidden the fact that I
am a great admirer of the Soviet Union, People's China, and the
People's Democracies [of Eastern Europe].'[24] This was the star by
which he would steer. It was therefore imperative that the people be
mobilised, be educated for the bigger task of 'building socialism'. He
would say later that they were 'in office but not in power'. The
immediate task, therefore, was to destroy the Waddington
Constitution, to generate popular resistance to it: 'The weakness of
our Constitution must be thoroughly exposed. You must carry out a
continuous agitation against the reactionary State Council [the Upper
House], the two official members of the Executive Council and the
dictatorial veto and reserve powers of the Governor.'[25] In short, the
PPP were behaving as if they were the opposition (not the
government) — and a most virulent one at that — an unprecedented
occurrence in the decolonisation of the British West Indies. Elsewhere
in the region, a milder Fabian socialism, generally, was at ease with a
measured, incremental approach to self-government, more
congruent with Jock Campbell's reformism.

In August 1952, in response to Campbell's Chairman's Statement,
Thunder had rebutted his argument that Booker and other colonial
companies had an important role to play in the progress of colonial
peoples. The PPP countered sarcastically:

Without the imperialist companies 'there can be no colonial
economic development, thus no social or political development
[quoting Jock]'. The sequence has been turned upside down —
the cart has been put before the horse. Surely every infant knows
that in order to put their economy on a sound and democratic
footing, the subject people must FIRST capture political power
now in the hands of the rulers. The truth is that there has been
no real economic development because of these companies and
the loot and plunder and the perpetual drain into the coffers of

the British Treasury and into absentee owners of these plantations and trading companies.

In July 1953, Jagan, now in government, gave the House of Assembly a civics lesson in world politics: 'Communism and Socialism are in the same camp, so that to all intents and purposes the world is divided into two camps — the Socialist or Communist camp, which is the people's camp, and the camp which today calls itself the Democratic camp, but which is really the capitalist camp.'[26] In August 1953 he was more passionate on the subject. He conceded a role for local capitalists for some time yet, but did not indicate where foreign capitalists stood in his Marxist scheme, nor did he reassure them. In fact, he made a projection of dire austerity, as they faced the possible consequences of nationalisation of foreign assets: 'In the past, canals were dug and dams were constructed with bare hands. If we cannot get the money and the machines, we must undertake to do these things again with our bare hands.'[27] Such was his faith in the doctrine: no sacrifice was too great, for the millennium will come. There was danger in this passion — the potential for self-destruction.

In this context, then, the second claim for recognition by the GIWU, in 1953, while the PPP was in government, becomes comprehensible. Its president, Dr J.P. Lachmansingh, was the Minister of Health. In June 1953 the GIWU, through the PPP's Minister of Labour, Ashton Chase, had written to the SPA seeking, as it had done unsuccessfully in 1948, to replace the MPCA as the sole bargaining agent for all workers in the sugar industry. After some delay, the SPA replied to Chase on August 20, 1953, agreeing to recognise the GIWU as the bargaining agent for the overwhelming majority of workers in the sugar industry, the field workers, most of whom were Indians, while the MPCA would remain the union for the minority factory workers, most of whom were Africans (the BGWL was defunct). This was a major concession, granted possibly because the Venn Commission had suggested reconsideration of the recognition question after a few years, providing the GIWU could demonstrate substantial support. Jagan's ascendancy among Indian sugar workers had been irrefutably proven in the elections of April 1953. Campbell told me that he had supported recognition in 1953.

However, the SPA submitted that this would be done on the terms agreed to with the MPCA. GIWU rejected the offer of recognition, without responding to the SPA. On August 31, the union called a strike in the sugar industry for recognition as the sole agent for all workers, field and factory.[28]

Cheddi Jagan (right) with Forbes Burnham, in London, early 1950s

A principal architect of the rejection of the SPA's terms was Sydney King [Eusi Kwayana], Minister of Communications and Works. His reason for doing so is convoluted but fitted into the broader purpose, the class struggle as an instrument of racial unity. He told me that he had warned Jagan and Burnham in 1953 that they would win the elections. He was apprehensive that this could be a Pyrrhic victory, because the party was still a coalition between the races, Indians and Africans; the class struggle was still in its infancy, so it could quickly be subordinated to passions triggered by racial insecurities.[29] He probably saw the SPA's withholding of the representation of African factory workers from GIWU, the PPP's union, as potentially detrimental to the class struggle. Another reason for rejecting the terms of recognition was that this issue was the arena for the PPP to wage relentless struggle against imperialism, as was the Waddington Constitution. It would undermine the capitalists — all strikes did — while, supposedly, forging working class consciousness and undermining racial discord. For the Marxists, trade unionism was the foundation of their mission to seize the state from the capitalists. The strike in the sugar industry lasted 24 days, from August 31 to September 23, 1953. This was the single most important issue that impelled the British to suspend the Constitution on October 9, 1953.

Jock Campbell had received several letters from senior Booker people in Georgetown denouncing the PPP leaders. On September 8, during the strike, Henry Seaford of Bookers Shipping, the brother of Sir Frederick Seaford, wrote to Jock in a desperate mood: 'Their aim is to get rid of all white officials and make life so unpleasant for other whites that they will get out. Unless something drastic is done, Bookers will cease to exist in five years. This is a serious statement to make but I do it in all sincerity and because of my love for this firm. I consider that the future of Bookers is at stake.'[30]

Campbell forwarded this letter to the Colonial Office, to Philip Rogers and N.L. Mayle (West Indian Department), both of whom he knew well. He went to see them at the Colonial Office on September 17, 1953. Nothing definitive seemed to have emerged from this meeting, other than his ventilation of the panic that the conduct of the PPP leaders had ignited among the ruling class. The following day Campbell forwarded a letter to the Colonial Office from another desperate representative of sugar. This letter, from H.L. Steele of the Demerara Company, a smaller sugar company in the SPA, spoke of 'unscrupulous communist gangsters', who had created a 'cancer' in British Guiana; their patron was Russia. Campbell observed in his covering note that 'H.L. Steele is a local "white creole". A letter not to be taken too seriously; but an interesting expression of local opinion'.[31] In fact, however antagonised he was by the PPP's intransigence, there is no evidence that Campbell recommended suspension of the Constitution, although the possibility of suspension was intimated to him by Rogers and Mayle, before the decision to do so was made in late September. In his letter to Jock, Henry Seaford had noted that a deputation from British Guiana would be going to the Colonial Office soon, and that he (Jock) would probably be asked to lead it. On September 15, Rogers minuted thus on this matter: '[I]t would be most unfortunate to give the impression to those sitting on the fence in British Guiana that if the constitution has to be suspended, the Secretary of State's decision was taken because of a deputation from one group concerned.' He noted: 'Mr. Campbell fully agrees.'[32]

It is arguable, therefore, that Campbell was certainly not enamoured of Jagan's Marxist philosophy nor impressed with his brief leadership in government; and that his personal relationship with Rogers and Mayle over many years, and his ventilation to them, in September 1953, of the local sugar leaders' apprehensions and growing panic, enhanced the case for suspension of the constitution. Although he did not recommend suspension, he certainly was aware of the likelihood of the Colonial Office ousting Jagan's government and he did nothing to oppose it.

The Colonial Office, in fact, minuted on September 21, 1953, four days after Jock visited Rogers and Mayle, that the clinching argument for suspension had come from two sources: the Governor of British Guiana, Sir Alfred Savage, in a letter of September 13; the other from Sir Stephen (Timmy) Luke of the Colonial Office, writing from Barbados on September 12, following his visit to the colony. The minute was definitive:

> It is becoming clearer every day that a break with the [PPP] Ministers is going to be, sooner or later, inevitable. We had already been coming to this conclusion in the Colonial Office and we have been confirmed in this view by two letters received today [21 September], one from Sir Alfred Savage and the other from Sir Stephen Luke to Mr. Rogers.... Sir Alfred Savage refers to the 'countless directions in which the foundations of society are being attacked insidiously almost without check', and he concludes: 'I am rapidly coming to the conclusion that unless the opposition elements in the country rouse themselves quickly and wake up to their obligations and opportunities, then to retain British Guiana in the Commonwealth we shall have to go back on the new Constitution which would mean the use of force and the maintenance of military forces here for some considerable time'. Sir Stephen Luke refers to the thorough going communist totalitarianism with which the Ministers and other leaders of the PPP are organising themselves. It is now not so much a question of whether or not a break with Ministers is to come but when and how that break is to me made.[33]

On September 24, N.L. Mayle minuted that a decision was reached to proceed with the suspension: 'It was decided at the meeting with the Secretary of State yesterday that in view of the most recent developments in British Guiana we should have to take action now.'[34] On September 25, Secretary of State for the Colonies, Oliver Lyttelton, recommended to the Cabinet suspension on grounds that the PPP government had taken every opportunity to 'undermine the constitution and to further the communist cause'. He cited the strike in the sugar industry, which had undermined business confidence in the territory, as a prime example of this. He concluded: 'Their sole aim appears to be complete totalitarian dominance, which they are seeking to achieve by the classical Communist technique of penetrating trade unions. Their leading figures are in close touch with the World Federation of Trade Unions [a Communist front] in Vienna.'[35]

The Constitution was suspended on October 9, 1953 but rumours of impending developments had abounded. On October 6, as the warship *Superb*, was reportedly heading for British Guiana, Campbell expressed consternation at the rumours: 'I am concerned about these reports but the major trouble in the colony is surely over. Strikers have returned to work [they did on September 23] and what looked like a Constitutional problem has now apparently been settled. I find it hard to understand what this is about.'[36] Yet shortly after the Constitution was suspended he gave decisive support to the action, recalling that although he had demonstrated earnestness in cooperating with the PPP government, it quickly became evident that they were not interested in his initiative. His indictment was, in fact, virtually a paraphrase of the official rationale for suspension:

It soon became clear that the Government was dominated by bad men and women who, far from working in the interests of the people, were enemies of the people, planning to subjugate and sacrifice them for foreign political ends; and clear too that they were ready utterly to destroy the economy of the Colony, the very means of livelihood of the people, to achieve those ends.[37]

Two weeks after the suspension Campbell observed that a programme of reform had already been initiated in the sugar industry. He remarked that under the Commonwealth Sugar Agreement of 1951, two-thirds of British Guiana's sugar now had secured prices in the UK, and as a consequence the industry had expended over £5 million on capital works leading to discernible social improvements for workers. He added that malaria, once endemic in the colony, had been eradicated, largely through the excellent work of Dr Giglioli, the industry's malariologist, and that they were trying to encourage alternative industries. In short, he was saying that at a time when his reforms were beginning to work, Jagan was sabotaging them in pursuit of his communist creed.[38]

Campbell, as noted earlier, attributed most of British Guiana's problems to the hazardous natural environment, contending that without foreign capital the precarious coastland would be reclaimed by the bush. Then, countering the PPP's lament over the paucity of small cane-farmers, he argued that there was no alternative to large-scale agriculture in British Guiana, given the great expenditure on hydraulic works and the necessity for centralised control to execute ongoing maintenance. He explained: 'Owing to its physical uniqueness there can be no alternative in British Guiana to large-scale planned agriculture. Destroy confidence, drive out capital and skills, and you leave nothing but swamps and starvation.'[39]

In October 1953, the West India Committee, of which Jock Campbell was chairman, remarked on the fact that British Guiana was not a 'settlers'' country, presumably alluding to the paucity of indigenous people with the requisite skills in a difficult natural environment. They then underlined Jock's argument — without foreign capital and skills British Guiana would revert to bush and sea. There could be no quick fix:

> Without the expenditure of vast capital sums and the constant employment of a considerable body of highly skilled technicians, [it] could never be anything but a desolate waste of jungle and sea. Accordingly it is not difficult to see how the action of Dr. Jagan and his associates could only have led, and led most speedily, to the undoing of the skilfully planned work of generations and the reduction of the people of the colony to a condition of abject poverty and misery.[40]

The West India Committee, paraphrasing Campbell, observed that Jagan's government was led by 'malevolent men' who sought to deceive the people with 'illusions of quick prosperity'. To give such men responsibility for governing was a 'mockery'; their only goal was the 'fruits of corrupt power'. They had no time for Jagan's communist ideology — a subversion of the reform programme of Jock Campbell, 'whose personal warm interest in the well-being of the people of the colony has been so strongly in evidence from the day when he joined the company [Booker]'. They concluded on a note of disappointment, which was congruent with Campbell's own frustration at the PPP's 'unpracticality':

> It had been hoped that the exercise of responsible government by freely elected representatives of the people, and a drive to extend and improve the welfare arrangements, particularly in the realms of education and housing, supported by the management of the sugar estates and the other employers through their own welfare organisations, would have seen the dawn of a better day in a colony where ruinous prices for sugar over many years had, until recently, stood in the way of all progress.[41]

By 1954, when Campbell presented his Chairman's Statement for the year 1953, his anti-communism had hardened to the extent that he virtually became an actor against 'the forces of evil', in the turbulent politics of the colony. He explained:

> Friendly critics told me last year that my Chairman's Statement [for 1952] was 'too political'. I am afraid it is more political than ever this year. But colonial businesses, indeed I suspect all businesses, are nowadays inevitably girt about by politics. It is with the political environment that you have to come to terms. If the Booker Group could operate in a vacuum, I could tell you that you had no cause for concern .... But we cannot operate in a vacuum .... With the future of British Guiana so uncertain...if the sugar crop does not suffer too badly from last year's interruption of field-work [the GIWU strike] or from bad weather, and if political turbulence does not again acutely infect industrial activity.... your Board can hope that the financial results will continue to command your confidence in Booker.[42]

He denounced the PPP-led 'futile political strikes', to gain recognition for their union. The fact that the Union had rejected the SPA's terms of recognition — a substantial concession — without any communication to that effect, must have convinced Campbell that the whole issue was an aspect of the Party's Marxist agenda. He observed that the 'politically dictated' strike of September 1953 had resulted in a loss of £250,000 in wages to workers. He felt that British Guiana needed British 'understanding' and money more than ever if it were to progress. He could see nothing redeeming in Jagan's Marxism, a recipe for chaos. Campbell elaborated on the PPP's agenda: ' [Their] highest aim seems to be to overthrow and to destroy all that is established, all that is creative and constructive, all that is good and all that is British in British Guiana in order to achieve for themselves personal power in a social and political structure utterly foreign to the Guianese and bound, I believe, to lead to their ruin.'[43]

Jock emphasised that Booker did not fear Guianese nationalism. In fact, they were committed to the independence of the colony, and looked forward to participating in the country's development. However, their support was tempered by the 'evil' of politicians who 'wait with slobbering jaws to strengthen themselves upon their unsuspecting prey'. He wished for a progressive government, with which companies such as Booker could work:

> We would welcome a progressive Government of Guianese for Guianese able to offer leadership, generate confidence, harmonise the qualities and the aspirations of the African, Indian and the other peoples there, and create the conditions in which Booker — and other providers of the external capital and skills which British Guiana will need for many a day — could play their full part for the good of all.[44]

Campbell was censorious of the tendency to succumb to the spell of El Dorado, the millennial allure: Guyanese assumption that tropical fecundity was synonymous with inexhaustible tropical fertility. He cautioned incessantly that it was a most 'imperfect place', severely limited by its 'imperfections' of nature. A responsible government must acknowledge this and temper its utopian excesses: 'Such a Government, realising the physical obstacles to their country's becoming an independently viable economic unit would surely regard it as being overwhelmingly in British Guiana's interest to remain within the British Commonwealth.'[45]

He was certain that Britain was prepared to assist places like Guyana on the road to social and economic development, as there was an 'immense fund of goodwill' in Britain towards them. As noted earlier, between April 1941 and June 1957 Britain did provide £7,928,139 in Colonial Development and Welfare grants to British Guiana, as recommended by the Moyne Commission.[46] Campbell envisaged a partnership between the old country and the emergent ones:

> Nowadays Colonial development need in no way be identified with Colonial domination. But Colonial peoples cannot have it both ways; they cannot clamour to 'go it alone' and, in the same breath, complain that Britain is not sufficiently assisting them with grants and loans and other enlightened and indispensable measures such as the Commonwealth Sugar Agreement. Neither, of course, can Great Britain have it both ways; she cannot expect statesmanlike and well-disposed Governments in these territories, and fruitful markets for British exports, unless she gives ungrudgingly the economic assistance essential to raise their living standards.[47]

As I have argued earlier, Jock Campbell was temperamentally ill at ease with extremism, but he appreciated its power to seduce in conditions of deprivation. This made him apprehensive of the emerging political culture in Guyana: 'It is difficult to see what constitutional forms of devices can enable honest, truthful, progressive politicians of goodwill to woo the undiscriminating voter from the quite unattainable material promises of politicians unencumbered by the truth, who are ready to mislead and intimidate him, or her, with distortion and misrepresentation of the attitudes and actions of all save themselves.'[48] He was worried that his reforms and his motives would never be understood by the people he was trying to help.

This fear permeated a lecture he gave at Cambridge on July 12, 1954. It was the most conservative speech he ever delivered: he told me that he came to regret it, in parts, over the years. He argued that Guyanese inexperience, industrial and political, made them antagonistic to foreign capital and skills and susceptible to the lure of an instant utopia. He located this millennial reflex in the unforgiving nature of the land, its natural 'imperfections' — the floods, droughts and threats from the sea, requiring capital, skills, discipline, and managerial efficiency. These environmental hazards inevitably made the sugar industry the preserve of big companies: the daunting hydrological overheads shut out the small farmer. The plantation, therefore, remained the most potent symbol of Guyanese deprivation, the epitome of historical wrongs. This was aggravated by the dominance of Booker.[49]

Booker's colossal growth in the colony was achieved by default, over nearly a century and a half, as it acquired plantations and stores because of the multiplication of bad debts and consequent foreclosures: 'Nobody in their senses could have designed to involve themselves in British Guiana to the extent that Booker have done.' Campbell then assessed the anatomy of the vulnerability of European capital in this environment, with 'fertile grounds for the seeds of Communism'.[50] It is difficult to improve on his exposition:

> Sugar is overwhelmingly the mainstay of the economy of British Guiana. The production of cane sugar is a fascinating and multifarious economic activity. It presents the problem of agriculture, of engineering, of chemistry, of marketing and of finance and wherever it is grown it tends to dominate the economy with resultant wide political and sociological impact. This large scale economy, dominated by European capital and technicians, is very politically vulnerable. Its vulnerability is increased by the absence of a peasant farming class. Peasant farming in the normal sense of the term has proved impossible owing to the fact that no peasant farmer could have the capital to drain and irrigate his land, and that one incompetent or idle farmer who failed to clean his canal at the right time can flood thousands of acres. So here you have this artificial man-made environment with its extraordinary heterogeneous and almost wholly imported population largely dependent at present upon external capital and skills for their very existence.[51]

He regretted that many politicians were magnifying the grievances of the workers, attributing them to exploitation by foreign capital, while promising deliverance by extolling the communist system without 'letting them know the conditions of agricultural workers under the ruthless impersonality of Russian communism'.[52] Campbell was countering Jagan's Marxism with his reformist capitalism:

> Nobody would argue that it is a perfect system but is there any better alternative? The ignoble politicians were willing for the sake of personal power and in some cases, abstract theorising, to destroy the system without having anything better to put in its place. Capitalism *is* the system — the instrument which has been used to generate Colonial economic development; just as parliamentary democracy is the system which has been introduced to generate social and political development. They may not be the best systems or instruments, but I know of no evidence which suggests that any other systems existing or which have existed in the world might be better.[53]

Against this backdrop of grave uncertainties, he remarked that they had to continue to build 'hedges', in the UK, Africa and the Caribbean, in order to insulate themselves against 'catastrophe in British Guiana should the worst come to the worst, the forces of evil prevail there, and British interests be expelled. We do not believe this will happen, but we must guard against its happening'.[54]

Between 1954 and 1956 Campbell's fears for the political evolution of Guyana found expression in a virtual campaign to find a 'responsible' alternative to 'those ignoble politicians of the PPP'. The presence of British troops in the colony and the wholly nominated Interim government which had replaced the deposed PPP, constituted a 'marking time' approach, a stop-gap to prevent 'open subversion and indiscriminate agitation'. For Campbell, this was most unsatisfactory: if the country were to advance, the political vacuum must be filled. In 1955 he noted that some 'sound and sensible' politicians were trying to create a 'responsible, progressive party', a reference to the faction of the PPP under the African Guyanese leader, L.F.S. Burnham, which had broken away from the PPP of Cheddi Jagan in February of that year. The Robertson Commission Report of 1954 had deemed Burnham a socialist, as opposed to the doctrinaire Marxist, Cheddi Jagan. This, however, was still a tentative step, which Campbell felt would not seriously deflect support from Jagan's PPP, with its 'quite unattainable material promises, misrepresentations and intimidation'. What worried him most was the undiminished stature of Cheddi among the predominantly Indian plantation workforce. His capacity for mischief, Campbell thought, was probably enhanced by the suspension: something of the martyr's syndrome would redound to his benefit.[55]

Jock Campbell was a great admirer of the Jamaican leader, Norman Manley, the Oxford-educated lawyer and intellectual, equally so his wife, Edna, the gifted sculptor. He told me what he thought of Manley: 'I was devoted to him. He was a great scholar with an enchanting wife, and he really felt very strongly about the things I felt strongly about.' Jock also had great respect for the Trinidadian leader, the historian, Dr Eric Williams, although he was not enamoured of the little man's unfailing arrogance.[56] It was the reasonableness, flexibility and nimbleness of intellect of Norman Manley which made him yearn for a similar leader in British Guiana:

> [It] will not prosper until she can produce a leader of the calibre of those other British Caribbean leaders who have held ministerial office with high distinction; a Guianese who can form a clear vision of the good Guiana, strive for it, convey it to the public imagination, and, when he has gained election, lead government and people, constructively and progressively towards their goal — with a true sense of responsibility and in terms of the possible.[57]

In early 1956 Campbell was still bemoaning the absence of imaginative leadership in British Guiana. Moreover, the fact that support for the 'communist-dominated' PPP of Jagan seemed undiminished, troubled him. He reflected:

> This is not because more than a handful of people [there] would vote for Communism or for the destructive features in the Party's programme — any more than they did in 1953; but because, being human they would vote for the unattainable material

promises of the PPP in default of any other coherent Party with a straightforward, constructive, reasonably practical and intelligible programme likely to capture the public imagination; and in default of real leadership.[58]

Campbell's visit to British Guiana in early 1956 left him with the belief that the politicians were still motivated primarily by petty ambition, reflected in the perpetuation of several small parties. He had hoped for an anti-Jagan coalition, for people to subordinate self-interest to a broader purpose — 'a coalition against Communism'. But he did not desire a conservative government in British Guiana; he was in favour of a radical party inspiring the people to work cooperatively, imaginatively, for attainable goals: a social democratic party, like Norman Manley's People's National Party in Jamaica:

> It is only by cohesion and concerted action that the many politicians of goodwill and good sense will be able to avoid a small Communist clique driving a horse and coaches through them at the next elections as they did in 1953 — to the disaster of British Guiana. We are not looking for some sort of conservative Government [here]. Nothing but a progressive, radical and nationalistic party — with virile leadership — can capture the imagination of the people. We shall make it our business to work with any such Government — and leader — that will work for the real good of the people.[59]

This was the context in which Lionel Luckhoo, a lawyer from the most professionally distinguished Indian family in the colony, founded the National Labour Front in 1956: a welfare-oriented party, advocating self-government, more jobs, schools, land for the tillers; it as also robustly anti-communist and anti-Federation. Jagan attributed its birth and professed programme to the desperate campaign to wean Indian support away from his PPP after the suspension had failed to do so. He added that the 'lead' for its creation was given by Jock Campbell during his 1956 visit, when 'he had declared that there was no place for a conservative party, and that any party thinking of capturing the imagination of the people must talk in terms of a welfare state'.[60]

Nothing, however, could put out Cheddi's communist ardour. In March 1956, while he was still restricted to Georgetown, he sent a confidential address to the PPP Congress held in New Amsterdam, 'behind closed doors'. It was leaked to *The Daily Chronicle* and published in its entirety, nine months later, on December 22, 1956, under the caption: RED MOVE TO TAKE OVER B.G. It was an exhortation to enhance the Marxist orientation of the PPP, while, paradoxically, urging the need for an alliance between 'the working class and the revolutionary bourgeoisie against imperialism'. The latter was interpreted as a charge to consolidate the Indian presence in the PPP by attracting Indian businessmen.

As noted above, Jagan detected the hand of Campbell in the emergence of Luckhoo's National Labour Front, an 'imperialist-backed' party. Then, as if responding to Campbell's persistent advocacy of a reformist, social democratic leadership, he remarked proudly: 'Our party is unique in the history of national movements: from its very inception it was under left-wing, Marxist-inspired leadership, uncompromisingly championing the cause of the working class. The right-wing, representing the middle and professional class and native capitalists, was in the distinct minority.' He contrasted this with Manley's People's National Party (the brightest light in Campbell's firmament), in which the right-wing dominated. There

Cheddi and Janet Jagan, Georgetown, 1957

were several quotes from 'Comrades' Lenin, Stalin and Mao to underline that 'Marxism was not a dogma, but a guide to action'. From 'Comrade Stalin', he discovered, also, what the PPP's role must be in the struggle against the imperialists in British Guiana: 'In order to smash these powerful enemies, it is necessary to have a flexible and well-considered policy of the proletariat, to take advantage of every crack in the enemy's camp, [and] skill in finding allies.'[61]

In January 1957 the West India Committee in London, of which Jock was president, applauded *The Daily Chronicle* for publishing Jagan's 'secret' speech, which had been outside of the public domain for nine months. They reported that several key members had left the Jagan faction of the PPP — Sydney King, Martin Carter, Rory Westmaas — because Jagan's 'attitude towards them [was] too dictatorial'; and that the speech revealed that his faction was 'just as Russian Communist as it ever was'. The defectors had been castigated by Jagan for 'left-wing deviationism', but they had countered that his quest for new allies, the so-called 'revolutionary bourgeoisie', was a design to consolidate the PPP as an instrument for Indian domination.[62]

Shortly afterwards Campbell observed that the new constitution under which general elections would be held, in August 1957, the first since the suspension, was restrictive and politically circumspect. He deeply regretted that it was a regression from the one suspended in 1953: the Legislative Council would comprise 14 elected members, 3 officials and 11 nominated members. Depressed by the dogmatic, pro-Soviet speech of Jagan to the 1956 Congress, especially after the Hungarian crisis, Campbell looked with foreboding to the impending elections:

> The political situation in British Guiana remains dreadfully clouded.... All of us in Booker are longing for the day when restrictive constitutional devices will be unnecessary in British Guiana; and when a properly elected and responsible Guianese Government can join the rest of the West Indies in their confident, vigorous and orderly march forward to independent status as a fellow member of the Commonwealth. It is our earnest hope that there may be elected in British Guiana a Government approaching the quality of those of Barbados, Jamaica and Trinidad. We unreservedly pledge our intention to do all we can to serve such a Government.[63]

Campbell and his wife, Phyllis, leaving British Guiana, mid-1950s

Endnotes

1. Booker Brothers, McConnell and Co, Ltd, Report of the Directors and Statement of Accounts, 1946–47 (Chairman's Statement) [Hereafter cited as The Chairman's Statement with relevant year], pp. 14-15.
2. BGSPA, Notes of a meeting between the council of the BGSPA and the Commissioner of Labour held on Monday, May 9, 1949, to discuss the Association's attitude in the event of Dr Jagan becoming president of the British Guiana Workers' League.
3. *PAC Bulletin*, no. 38, June 30, 1949.
4. *PAC Bulletin*, no. 37, May 29, 1949.
5. *Bookers Sugar, 1954* (Supplement to the Accounts of Booker Brothers, McConnell and Co, Ltd.), p. 91.
6. The Chairman's Statement, 1948, p. 17.
7. Ibid., 18.
8. *PAC Bulletin*, no. 36, April 13, 1949.
9. The Chairman's Statement, 1949, p. 18.
10. The Chairman's Statement, 1950, p. 17.
11. Leader, *Guiana Sunday Graphic*, December 30, 1951.
12. Quoted in *Report of the British Guiana Constitutional Commission, 1954*, Cmd. 9274 (James W. Robertson, Chairman), (London: HMSO, 1954), Appendix I, p. 79.
13. Ibid.
14. See Booker's in-house journal in British Guiana, *Pepperpot* 2, no. 5, (August 1948).

15. The Chairman's Statement, 1951, p. 18.

16. See note 14.

17. Ian McDonald, 'Jock Campbell: Obituary', *Sunday Stabroek*, January 1 1995.

18. The Chairman's Statement, 1952, p. 23.

19. Ibid.

20. Sydney King [Eusi Kwayana], Foreword, Cheddi Jagan, *Fight for Freedom: Waddington Constitution Exposed* [pamphlet], n.d. [1953], p. 30 (a).

21. Ibid. (See text of speech to the Legislative Council, January 23, 1952), 45.

22. See note 12 [p. 79].

23. Text of Speech by Dr Cheddi Jagan Broadcast on Radio Demerara, (mimeo.), August 9, 1953.

24. Ibid.

25. Ibid.

26. See note 12 [p. 81].

27. Taken from unmarked Booker File [Campbell Papers], n. d. [1953].

28. BGSPA, 'Labour Unrest, Commencing 31 August 1953', Strictly Private and Confidential, September 13, 1953 [Campbell Papers].

29. Eusi Kwayana, interview by the author, Georgetown, September 22, 1992.

30. CO1031/121, Henry Seaford to Jock Campbell, September 8, 1953.

31. See CO1031/118 for H.L. Steele's letter and Campbell's covering note.

32. CO1031/121, minute, September 15, 1953 [E.F. for P. Rogers].

33. Ibid., minute, September 21, 1953 [James W. Vernon]. Savage's and Luke's letters are in this file.

34. Ibid., September 24, 1953 [N.L. Mayle].

35. CAB129/63 — C.(53)261, Memorandum by Secretary of State for the Colonies [Lyttelton] to Cabinet, September 30, 1953, Top Secret [dated September 25, 1953].

36. *The Daily Chronicle*, October 7, 1953.

37. See note 27 ['Short Statement by Mr J.M. Campbell'], (mimeo.), n.d. [October 1953].

38. Jock Campbell to the Editor, *The New Statesman and Nation*, October 24, 1953.

39. Ibid.

40. *The West India Committee Circular*, October 1953.

41. Ibid.

42. The Chairman's Statement, 1953, p. 26.

43. Ibid., 24.

44. Ibid., 25.

45. Ibid.

46. Michael Swan, *British Guiana: The Land of Six Peoples* (London: HMSO, 1957), 211-5.

47. See note 42.

48. Ibid.

49. See my article, 'The Shaping of the Indo-Caribbean People: Guyana and Trinidad to the 1940s', *Journal of Caribbean Studies* 14, nos. 1&2 (1999-2000): 61-92.
50. Jock Campbell, 'British Capital in the Changing Conditions of the Colonies', Speech delivered at Cambridge University, July 12, 1954, (mimeo.), pp. 2, 5.
51. Ibid., 3-4.
52. Ibid., 5.
53. Ibid., 8.
54. See note 40.
55. The Chairman's Statement, 1954, p. 24.
56. Jock Campbell, interview by the author, Nettlebed, Oxfordshire, July 24, 1992, Tape 6.
57. See note 40.
58. The Chairman's Statement, 1955, p. 36.
59. Ibid.
60. Cheddi Jagan, *The West on Trial: My Fight for Guyana's Freedom* (London: Michael Joseph, 1966), 213.
61. *The Daily Chronicle*, December 22, 1956.
62. *The West India Committee Circular*, January 1957; see also note 60 [pp. 212-3].
63. The Chairman's Statement, 1956, p. 40.

Chapter Seventeen

BELATED ALLY?: CAMPBELL'S MODUS VIVENDI WITH JAGAN, 1957-60

Jock Campbell was a pragmatic businessman with a social conscience. He realised that Booker could not extricate itself quickly from the colony: 'So many of our eggs still remain in British Guiana — despite the success of our hedge-building policy',[1] the diversifying of some of their investments away from the colony, after 1953. Booker still needed the time and capital to be able to continue the process. Besides, Campbell still retained his personal commitment to the 'cause' of reform, his way of repaying old debts incurred by his family (no other Chairman of Booker ever held those sentiments). Booker's transactions in the colony were profitable; they would continue to reinvest, providing the political culture did not degenerate into total hostility to the company.

Jagan won the elections held on August 12, 1957 because of his unassailable support among Indians. His PPP won nine of the 14 seats in the Legislative Council; this gave him a majority in the Executive Council as well, the principal decision-making body. Burnham's PPP, still a fledgling party, won only three seats. Campbell knew that he had to seek a modus vivendi with Cheddi Jagan. He dropped his anti-communism and extended conciliatory gestures immediately. Shortly after the elections *The Economist* had observed that during the campaign Dr Jagan had 'insisted' that foreign capital was needed and that it should be given 'maximum encouragement'. The correspondent even sought to make a distinction between Cheddi's sincerity towards foreign capital and those of his 'more fanatical' anti-capitalist followers. In fact, it was Jagan's instinct for parading his Marxist, pro-Soviet rhetoric, as reflected in his party's organ,

Thunder, which had engendered the latter's intransigence. However, *The Economist* was optimistic that he was maturing:

> Dr Jagan is fully aware that British Guiana under him is not a good investors' risk. This partly accounts for the sweet reasonableness of his tone; he is anxious to impress everyone with his moderation and devotion to democratic processes. There is little doubt that his own views on foreign investment are sincerely held, but it is less certain if he can restrain his more fanatical anti-capitalist followers. It was significant that neither sugar nor bauxite [the second major export] became issues in the election campaign. Prospects for investors are probably better than they may appear at first sight. For whatever the outcome, another 1953 is extremely unlikely.[2]

This positive assessment must have inspired Campbell's perception that Jagan could be weaned from his irrational Marxist excesses. Out of his deep foreboding and his anti-communism, shoots of optimism were discernible: that rationality would accompany the PPP as they re-entered government. He tried to allay the fears of his colleagues, noting that Jagan's PPP was 'not the Government but is sharing in a Government led by the Governor'. However, he contended that the restricted constitution presented 'no obstacle to imaginative and progressive Government'.[3] Campbell was advocating radicalism rooted in realism. As noted earlier, he had, before Jagan's re-election, called for a government 'approaching the quality' attained in the rest of the British West Indies. That obviously did not include the PPP. By 1958, however, he was astutely, deftly accommodating Jagan's party in his conception of responsible governance: 'Last year [1957] I unreservedly pledged Bookers' intention to do all we could to serve a properly elected and responsible Guianese Government. The present Government and the majority Party [Jagan's PPP], have done nothing to lessen our faith in the rightness of this policy.'[4]

In fact, Campbell had hoped for an alternative to the PPP. Lionel Luckhoo's National Labour Front, possibly even Burnham's PPP, were more palatable than the perceived Marxist nullity of Jaganism. Both had failed and he was not impressed with either of these men:

the former was 'bogus'; the latter was a 'crook', by Jock's definition.[5] His belated acceptance of Jagan was *realpolitik*, coming to terms with the inescapable. He moved into a positive frame of mind quickly: public confidence was improving; the government was encouraging the community and industry to cooperate for the good of the country. His optimism, though, carried one portentous note: he detected 'disquieting signs of racial conflict and bitterness between Indians and Africans'. He had a remarkable sense of discernment.

Jock began to cultivate impressions of a fledging Jaganite maturity, as if he were seeking, belatedly, to shape a more emollient, rational persona. As usual, he reminded Guyanese that their country was not the El Dorado with which their politicians had deluded them; and that foreign capital must play an enlightened role in its future:

> This is certainly the only way in which Guianese can make the most of the limited natural resources with which nature has endowed their country; only by giving evidence of constructive co-operation will British Guiana be able to raise the capital which she needs for development to maintain, let alone increase, the standard of living of her fast-growing population. There are healthy signs throughout the West Indies and British Guiana that Governments and people, in their rising self-confidence, are adopting a far more robust and realistic attitude towards Capital than in the past. In short, they are learning to live with Capital. And Capital, which must equally learn to live with them, is showing increasing adaptability towards the evolving economic, social and political pressures of these countries.[6]

This went against the grain of Jaganite Marxism, but Campbell, as in 1953, was hoping that responsibility would moderate the romantic excesses of Cheddi, that he could still be persuaded that the Soviet way was not the best option for his country. It is interesting that in June 1958, he challenged the Marxist assumption that in nineteenth-century Britain there was a convergence between economic power and political power. Campbell conceded that European industrialisation did place considerable wealth in the hands of individual capitalists who exerted 'great influence in politics', but these people did not run the governments of Gladstone or Bismarck. He believed that some form of liberal government flourished even under classical capitalism, whereas 'the countries of state-sponsored industrialisation', past and present, were invariably characterised by 'political despotism'. He was saying that even nineteenth century British capitalism had created a more open society than the centralised regimes in post-war Eastern Europe, the 'People's Democracies', which had so impressed Jagan. Campbell felt that his reformist capitalism, even in its most paternalistic mode, offered infinitely greater space for the flowering of the imagination than communism:

> There was room in nineteenth century Great Britain for the expression of public conscience by writers and artists and philanthropists, by trade unions, and by paternal employers. The paternalism of, say, the Cadburys and the Courtaulds at the time, although now fashionably forgotten, or even belittled, set a pace in the practical provision of social services. These fatherly pioneers provided a flexibility and resilience in the social system which is tragically absent in the State of Big Brother.[7]

The ideological dimension of the Campbell-Jagan discourse was somewhat muted in 1957–58, but Jagan was still impermeable to liberal suasion: years later he would celebrate this grandiloquently, as 'political flexibility and ideological implacability', a testament to his Marxist purity. In his New Year's message of 1959 he had invited foreign companies, especially insurance companies and banks, to invest in British Guiana; but he bemoaned the negative impact on development of continuing colonial status. He had to get 'ideological clearance', he claimed, before he could engage certain scientists or economists. He was alluding to the official resistance he apparently encountered when he tried to employ specialists in development planning deemed to be Marxists or of East European origin. Jagan attributed this to the 'cold war atmosphere'. Yet, as if to demonstrate that there was no tergiversation implicit in his invitation to foreign investors, he offered illumination from his Marxist primer, in welcoming in the New Year: '[T]he forces operating in society work exactly like the forces operating in nature. Once we have recognised them and understood how they work, the gradual subjection of them to our will and the use of them for the attainment of our aims, depend entirely upon ourselves.'[8] Scientific socialism was the answer to all the ills of humankind.

The next day the *Guiana Graphic* carried a leader questioning Jagan's statement about 'ideological clearance'. They countered that it was the Soviet Union which placed barriers to freedom, as demonstrated in their refusal to grant the author of *Dr. Zhivago*, Boris Pasternak, an exit visa to receive his Nobel Prize for Literature. The paper argued that Dr Jagan was creating 'smoke screens', a ruse for his unreconstructed Marxism. They advised:

> What we want in British Guiana is to cut out ideological propaganda, however subtle it may be, and get on with the business of running the country for the benefit of its people. Screaming for wolf when there is no wolf around cannot serve any useful purpose. The wolf is far away in the eastern end of Europe.[9]

On January 3, 1959 a correspondent to the same paper, with a Russian pseudonym suggestive of the nationalisation of sugar [V. Sagaroff], questioned Jagan's sincerity in calling for foreign investment, hard work, self-criticism, avoiding waste and so on. This was a deceptively 'bourgeois' stance, no different from that of past governors of the colony, whereas Jagan's 'teachings were in lineal harmony with those of the "venerable" Karl Marx and his disciples, Lenin and Stalin'. Indeed, Jagan attributed all ills to one source only — 'wicked Imperialist exploiters, the blood-sucking capitalists'.

Jagan then played right into the hands of the *Guiana Graphic* and its perceptive correspondent. The press relations officer of the PPP, C.R. Jacob, proceeded to challenge the paper's assessment of Pasternak as a writer who had won 'the award on merit'. The PPP claimed that the Nobel Academy were not interested in Pasternak, the artist, but Pasternak, 'another cold war crusader'. Then quoting *The Economist*, that his was 'a nostalgic voice of Russia's past', the Party asserted that this writer had 'earned the indignation of his people': it was, therefore, as an enemy of the USSR that he was being exalted.[10] The PPP were still fundamentally inspired by the Soviet example; they were not prepared to change their spots, however conciliatory their postures in the late 1950s, however potentially self-destructive their belief in the superiority and inevitability of communism.

Indeed, the early months of 1959 were heady times for Jagan and his Marxist followers. For the first time, a potential Marxist ally had come to power in the region: Fidel Castro's Revolution inspired grand hopes in the inner circle of the PPP. They were quick to congratulate their new hero. The cable sent by the General Secretary of the Party, Janet Jagan, read: 'People's Progressive Party of British Guiana sends congratulations victory democratic forces Cuban people.'[11] It is against this back-drop of the emergence of an increasingly manifestly Marxist regime, an ally of the Soviet Union in the backyard of the United States, that Jagan's shedding of his circumspection of 1957-58, his affected moderation, may be seen.

In May 1959 Cheddi reprimanded the TUC and the MPCA for 'crawling' to the capitalists, instead of 'battling' against the extractors of 'surplus value'. The 'imperialist interests', he contended, still controlled the 'state machine and political superstructure.' This was the source of the country's low wages, starvation and suffering. He explained: 'This backwardness is due to the colonialist-imperialist system. But the PPP's objective is to break that system, which is deep-rooted. To do so it must secure political independence, it must capture the political superstructure'. He was, in fact, already implicitly repudiating his invitation to foreign capitalists to invest in British Guiana, expressed in his New Year's message of 1959. He really had no sympathy for 'the imperialist interests and those associated with them', whose 'main concern is to extract as much surplus value, profit, interest and rent as possible, most of which is shipped abroad'.[12] Even Jock Campbell's reformist capitalism, therefore, had no place in Jagan's vision of a free Guyana.

Pragmatism was anathema to him; his mission was still clear: he enjoined the trade union movement not to struggle against the PPP and the government; 'its duty to the working class is a struggle against colonialist-imperialist interest'. He elaborated: 'Its clear duty is to help the PPP break up the present political superstructure, the state machinery, so that a new economic order will emerge.'[13] Jagan was not one for secrets; he harboured no Machiavellian designs: his 'total understanding' simply would not permit him to meet Jock Campbell half way, to see him as a potential ally — he had few. In fact, Fidel Castro's triumph in 1959 emboldened him, hardening the ideological certainties.

This seemed to have dampened the cautious optimism Campbell had articulated after the PPP victory of August 1957. His Chairman's Statement for 1958 (delivered in early 1959), was the least overtly political he had ever written. He praised Booker's senior management in British Guiana, European and Guyanese, for their 'practical capability and imaginative humanity', in fulfilling their four-fold responsibility to fellow workers, customers, shareholders and the community — the foundation of his programme of reform in the colony. But a note of frustration was discernible; it was triggered by Cheddi's resurgent utopianism:

> We are wholly confident in the ability of our management colleagues in British Guiana to minimise the effects of the hazards of tropical agriculture. And I believe that we can rely upon our workpeople to play their part to the full again this year [1959]. This is not to say that the hazards will not occur.... Even though we all realise that any big business anywhere is fair game for criticism, it is often discouraging to them that so many Guianese seem to carp and snipe at every imperfection; and to take all the good for granted.[14]

However, Jock could not conceive of an alternative to Cheddi after 1957 great though his imperfections. By early 1960 the British government, too, were prepared to take a chance with Jagan, as the leader to rule an independent Guyana. Iain Macleod, the Colonial Secretary, was very supportive of him, although many Tories still deemed him a communist. Macleod was not enamoured of L.F.S. Burnham, the African leader of the People's National Congress (PNC), whose paraded moderation, though evident since 1953, had not dissipated his apprehensions of Burnham's machiavellianism. In March 1960 Jagan secured internal self-government under a new constitution to be introduced after elections not later than August 1961. To his advantage, the British retained the 'first past the post' electoral system. They also 'accept[ed] the principle of independence for British Guiana ... at any time not earlier than two years after the first General Election held under the new constitution'.[15] Jagan reacted bitterly to the delay; after the Constitutional Conference in London he denounced Macleod's constitutional proposals: 'We are totally dissatisfied with the outcome of the discussions and I have said so clearly. We came here with a mandate for Independence. We are going back still as colonials with Crown Colony status.'[16]

Campbell thought differently: internal self-government was 'a great constitutional stride forward'; Booker would work with any government elected under the new constitution. Then, making his usual assertion that British Guiana could not do without foreign capital in its development drive, he appealed for reason and reasonableness:

> British Guiana and her leaders and people are going to need all the help they can get from all over the world to enable them to strengthen and to build upon the economic foundations of this country. But in the last resort it is only the confidence of the Government and people themselves in the future progress and prosperity of this country that can generate external confidence towards British Guiana.[17]

Ominously, *The Daily Argosy* had cautioned, before the Conference, that racial unity in the colony was indispensable, and that independence could be not be granted if it were not attained.[18] With the granting of internal self-government to Jagan, the paper was more forthright on the race issue, arguing that his party could not be 'entrusted with Independence':

> [I]t is our belief that the UK Government has granted one of the most liberal constitutions it could venture to permit under the circumstances. Let those who bellow for Independence remember that [the British] have a responsibility to minorities in its colonial territories. And it would not be discharging its duty faithfully if it pulls hurriedly and completely out, leaving those minorities to an uncertain and perilous fate. Political leaders can do more than clamour for Independence — they must qualify for it.[19]

A former minister in Jagan's government, Edward Beharry, joined the debate, arguing that since India gained independence the British were committed to giving independence to all colonial peoples, providing their leaders demonstrated maturity. It was there for the taking; but he was not optimistic for British Guiana. He attributed the continuing 'backwardness' of the colony to Jagan's lack of statesmanship: he 'yet has to grow up and realise that a stable government is the prerequisite to economic prosperity'; he was incorrigibly 'demagogic', incapable of comprehending that political purpose, constitutional progress and economic prosperity were inseparable. Depressed by Cheddi's Marxist rhetoric, Beharry concluded that sober government was urgently needed: 'It is better to have a Crown Colony constitution under Britain, than to have a Crown Colony constitution under Communism which denies freedom.'[20]

Campbell and Macleod thought that Jagan was acquiring a measure of sobriety after his return to office in 1957; with the rise of Fidel Castro in 1959, however, it was evident that their assessment was prematurely optimistic. He was not prepared to accept that independence was there for the taking, that internal self-government was a prelude to it. He would seek confrontation with the 'imperialists' when all that was required was knowing how to wait. As his reaction, in March 1960, to the new constitution demonstrated, it was as if raging against the British had cleansing properties, an imperative dictated by his Marxist purity.

After the Conference he belittled the new constitutional proposals in unstatesmanlike language that could not have enhanced his reputation among many of his non-communist supporters, who still admired his sincerity of purpose: 'They [the British] were prepared to adorn me with the title of Premier and I threw it back in their faces, because I was not asking to become Premier but to have Cabinet status as in Trinidad.' He advised colonial leaders to 'stay outside' of such 'imposed' constitutions and 'agitate by other means' against them: they should 'refuse to attend official functions or resort to boycott'. Compromising with the 'imperialists' was unconscionable: 'There is a clear lesson here for all colonials to learn — that we cannot rely fully on the words of the Colonial Office and that freedom will not be won by mere pleading and peaceful protestation but by direct action'. He would not be delayed by the piecemeal approach of Macleod and Campbell, political or economic. He promptly announced that he was going to Cuba to see how Fidel Castro was doing things.[21]

Obviously buoyed by what he saw there, Jagan alluded sarcastically to Prime Minister Macmillan's recently delivered 'wind of change' speech with regard to Africa, to proclaim his renewed faith in his Marxist illumination: 'The East wind was blowing over the West and because of this the West are forced to liberate colonial peoples. The British are breaking up fast, not because they want to make us free.... Two years from now there will be no more colonies'. Yet, paradoxically, he cautioned that although some people believed that independence was going to be secured easily, the examples of Ghana and India demonstrated that 'bloodshed was experienced before independence came'.[22] Cheddi was not a statesman.

By early 1960, it was clear that the debate over Guyana's freedom was already enmeshed within the parameters of African racial insecurities and Portuguese Guyanese fear of Jagan's communism, following his acclamation of Fidel as 'the greatest liberator of the 20th century'. More ominously though, he had taken his little colonial backwater into the Cold War: he would have to take on the Americans too. This was the context in which Jock Campbell had sought to allay the fears of those, at home and abroad, who had become apprehensive, again, of Cheddi Jagan's Marxist adventures:

> It goes without saying ... that Booker will continue to do everything within their capacity to serve and to work with the Government and the people of the country. Booker's vigorously sustained confidence in British Guiana and her future will, he hoped, give encouragement to others... to invest in her developing economy....The opportunities and the challenge of self-government and the great fresh measure of responsibility must work to inspire new unity and purpose, and a new will in the whole community to plan and work together for the good of all. [23]

Endnotes

1. The Chairman's Statement, 1957, p. 43.
2. *The Economist*, August 24, 1957.
3. See note 1 [pp. 43-4].
4. Ibid. [p. 44].
5. Jock Campbell, interview by the author, Nettlebed, Oxfordshire, February 17, 1994, Tape 8.
6. See note 1.
7. Jock Campbell, 'Paternalism — Good or Bad?', *Optima*, (June 1958): 68.
8. *Guiana Graphic*, January 1, 1959.
9. Leader, *Guiana Graphic*, January 2, 1959.
10. *Guiana Graphic*, January 7, 1959.
11. *Guiana Graphic*, January 17, 1959.
12. Cheddi Jagan, 'Instead of Battling, They Crawl' [Straight Talk], *Thunder*, May 16, 1959.
13. Ibid.
14. The Chairman's Statement, 1958, p. 43.
15. *Report of the British Guiana Constitutional Conference Held in London in March 1960*, Cmnd. 998 (London: HMSO, 1960), 5,9.
16. *The Daily Argosy*, April 1, 1960.
17. The Chairman's Statement, 1959, p.8.
18. *The Daily Argosy*, March 4, 1960.
19. Ibid. [Leader], April 3, 1960.
20. Ibid.
21. Ibid., April 1, 1960.
22. Ibid., April 15, 1960.
23. The Chairman's Statement, 1959, p. 8.

Chapter Eighteen

JAGAN (AND BURNHAM) IN 1960: CAMPBELL'S CONFIDENTIAL ASSESSMENT

Jock Campbell's annual visit to British Guiana was a successful one in 1960. His reforms were beginning to bear fruit and he was anxious to communicate his impressions to his colleagues, but he was 'depressed' by the politics. In a confidential address to the Booker Board and other senior executives in London, on March 22, 1960, he expressed genuine interest in working with the Jagan government, whatever the difficulties and uncertainties, because, as he saw it, for the foreseeable future there really was no credible alternative.

In January 1960, on his way to British Guiana, Campbell visited Jamaica. As usual, his assessment of the Jamaican leader, Norman Manley, celebrated his statesmanship: '[He] is a great leader in world terms and his party is firmly in the saddle. Broadly speaking Jamaica is now a well-governed country and, of course, they have a substantial degree of self-government.'[1] Unlike British Guiana, however, Booker's investments in Jamaica were marginal to its overall interests: Estates Industries Ltd. which made 'Tia Maria' liqueur.

Campbell also went to Trinidad where he met Eric Williams, the leader of government, whose support came almost exclusively from the African population. The Indians were firmly opposed to him. Jock's perception of the man is one of the most discerning I have encountered:

> Eric Williams is something of a dictator. He [has] tremendous intelligence and ability and drive, but a man greatly lacking in charm. He's a very small man, he's deaf, he has chips on his shoulder about colour and he's a man it is very hard to get close to even for his own colleagues; he rules his cabinet with a rod of

iron — and it is a highly authoritarian Government at the moment in Trinidad. The Opposition and many of the older-fashioned business people and planters there are very frightened by what they call Dr. Williams's 'radical politics'. I, myself, rightly or wrongly, am perfectly satisfied that he is simply a left-wing capitalist politician. He has no truck with Marxism or Communism at all, but he is a great believer in government planning and government control.[2]

Booker's investments in Trinidad, like Jamaica, were minimal: two department stores, Fogarty's, and Stephens and Todd, and W.C. Ross and Co, which ran their chemist shops. In 1960 Booker still had most of their eggs in the precarious British Guiana basket: Campbell's assessment was substantially bleak. Although he was very proud of Booker's achievements, he could see no silver lining on the political horizon. He was not fazed by communism, but he was perturbed by what he considered the rudderlessness of local politics, a consuming nihilism. It was darkening the pride he felt about his Booker mission. He explained to his colleagues: 'I have come back from this visit to British Guiana more depressed by the political and the economic situation in [the colony]. This is not because I believe that there is going to be a communist coup there or because I think there is going to be a Communist government or a dictatorship, but because there is a sort of vacuum. Nothing is happening and everybody is going round in ever-diminishing circles.'[3]

Campbell proceeded to explain this stasis, Jagan's dilemma in colonial society: the angst of the true believer, marooned between the dead-end of 'imperialism' and its arch-representative, Booker, on one hand, and the allure of Soviet communism and the impossibility of its pursuit in a colony, on the other. Jock tried to unravel this bedevilling condition:

There is the extraordinary position of Dr. Jagan and his wife [Janet] — he the convinced ideological Marxist, she the highly effective organiser, the two of them head and shoulders above any alternative leaders in British Guiana in every way, particularly in capturing the public imagination. They are balanced precariously on a tightrope — trying to maintain their

Marxist integrity but at the same time trying to run a capitalist society in which they don't believe; and wooing Britain and America and Bookers for money with the strong feeling that if they could come to terms with Russia they would not have to live with capitalist enterprises. This results in a hopeless sort of dichotomy in their minds. I very often feel that if only Jagan would be a good Communist, then we would know where we were. But he will not do either because, though he completely believes in Communism as the right form and organisation of human society, and genuinely believes that Capitalism is destructive and exploits the people, he knows he is running a capitalist society.[4]

Jagan had informed Campbell, in London, after the Constitutional Conference in March 1960, that he was going to visit Cuba to see how Castro was changing his country. As noted earlier, he was buoyed by the success of the Cuban Revolution: the beacon had come very near to home; the millennium was not the preserve of remote places like the USSR and China. As early as March 1960, Cheddi had no doubts of the Marxist pedigree of Castroism. So that Campbell's contention that Jagan was 'intelligent enough' to realise that he was isolated from international communism, and would not attempt to build a communist state unless Latin America and Cuba paved the way, was not accurate. Jagan's problem was not lack of zeal; his problem was his colonial status and the increasing determination of America to dictate the character of change in the Hemisphere. Therefore, the more transparent Castro's Marxist credentials became, the more dangerous was Jagan's pursuit of his dream.

Campbell also argued that Jagan could not really embrace communism, as most of the communists had deserted him (a reference to the departure of Sydney King [Eusi Kwayana], Martin Carter and Rory Westmaas in 1956). Moreover, he observed that the urban intelligentsia, predominantly African, which might have thrown up new Marxists recruits, were 'solidly' opposed to him on racial grounds. Campbell noted that the wealthy Indians who financed the PPP, did so primarily because Cheddi was on the winning side; should he dare to implement Marxist policies, they would ditch him. Jagan, therefore, was in a quandary: 'People ask what Dr Jagan is going to do when he achieves self-government. The answer is that he does not know any more than the next man.' Here again Campbell was minimising Jagan's obduracy and his capacity for self-destruction. He was also underestimating Jagan's singularly mesmeric influence on his rural Indian supporters, in the villages and on the sugar plantations. This remained undiminished throughout his life, thus unwittingly underwriting his Marxist excesses.

What is most difficult to comprehend in Campbell's confidential address of March 1960, was his failure to recognise the potential strengths of L.F.S. Burnham, the premier African leader, although he detected 'growing racial conflict' in British Guiana. He spoke with his usual perspicacity on the impending Indian dominance and its impact on Africans. At the end of the Empire Campbell saw ominous signs:

> The Indians are trading on their numerical majority and the Africans are finding it hard to accept that; having for two centuries been dominated by Europeans, they have now got to be dominated by Indians, who for a long time they have called 'coolies' and who they have had a great deal of contempt for — I think quite wrongly. The Indians, of course, are thrifty, they are growing in numbers, and they have a hearty contempt for Africans, who they regard as thriftless and incompetent. There is really no inter-marriage at all between the races. The Africans are developing an obsessional neurosis and anxiety about what will happen to them under Indian domination, which there seems bound to be in British Guiana because almost inescapably it is going to be Indian-governed.[5]

So the political culture, rendered hazardous by Jagan's ideological pertinacity, was now compounded by this 'appalling conflict' between Africans and Indians. Campbell observed that this was reflected in the pervasive tendency to dichotomise: 'they' and 'we':

> In the rest of the West Indies people will talk about 'we' all the time. They will say 'we' have our differences. In British Guiana the word 'we' is apparently not in the dictionaries at all. It is

always 'they' (Bookers) or 'they' (the Africans) or 'they' (the Indians) or 'they' (the Europeans) or 'they' (the sugar industry), and you are always thinking how you can get the better of somebody else, some other group, or not to be done down by them. And one simply cannot see how they are going to break out of this vicious circle.[6]

However, he felt that a greater measure of self-government, from 1961, could be beneficial, as Guyanese have always 'sheltered' under somebody else: officials, Booker or the Colonial Office. Greater responsibility, therefore, could stimulate more realistic attitudes: 'They have always been in a position to criticise and destroy and never to do things themselves. It is always somebody else's fault in British Guiana.'[7]

The future, according to Campbell, was most unpromising. Jagan would probably try to get aid from Russia, on the assumption that such an initiative would induce the Americans and the British to compete with the Russians. He told Campbell that he was already seeking Cuban help to gain access to Russian credits. That did not worry Jock. The 'real bogey' was not a Communist state; few in the colony wanted that. The problem was the paucity of people around Jagan with the intellectual calibre to lead him towards a decisive position on anything. Jock could not credit Cheddi with the ability to build anything; unlike most, after 1957, he was not afraid of the Jaganite Marxist rhetoric:

> I think they will continue to go around in ever diminishing circles of incompetence, because one of Cheddi Jagan's problems is that he is administratively very incompetent and he has not got anybody to help him. [H]e knows that he wants money, and unless he is perfectly certain that he can get enough money from Russia to keep the country going, he is the first to say that he cannot risk anything that is so obtrusively Communist, that it will antagonise the people from whom at the moment his money has to come.... I do not myself believe that Communism is the bogey in British Guiana. I think the bogey is economic stagnation and a sort of nihilism.[8]

But Jock was committed to Booker remaining there; he still believed that it had an 'invaluable and inescapable' contribution to make in the evolution of an independent society — while continuing its 'hedge-building', reinvesting in the West Indies, Canada and the UK, a bulwark against the vagaries of British Guiana. This was pragmatism, for Booker, as noted earlier, still had the bulk of its capital invested there; but Campbell's own sense of guilt, too, of ancient debts unpaid, impelled him to honour 'obligations of the past', to stay on, however 'ugly a woman' the colony was. He said that no 'half-hearted' approach to Booker in British Guiana was acceptable. They either had to pull out — *'this over my dead body'* [emphasis added] [9] — or they must increase their productive capacity and efficiency, adapting imaginatively so as to retain the confidence of their workers and the support of the Guyanese people. As I have argued throughout, no other person in the sugar business had the passion or the authority to sustain this argument. It was, indeed, a cause. Nothing, not even the threat of nationalisation, would detract him from this mission. As Jock said to me often, if any other person in Booker had pursued this line, he would have been fired.

This civilised man whose wealth and intellect gave him the freedom and instinct to be magnanimous, concluded his confidential address, in March 1960, to the Booker Board and senior administrators with a balanced assessment of Booker's role in British Guiana:

> We cannot operate in British Guiana as we would like it to be. What we must operate in is British Guiana as it is. We would be reactionary if we were not flexible and adaptable to the aspirations, the changed values, the hopes and the fears of Guianese, and I think we would be lunatic if we made a completely blind act of faith and went far ahead in the circumstances. What we have got to do is to maintain our strength and our investment and to continue to combine the greatest possible efficiency in our business in British Guiana with a flexibility and adaptability to whatever the society and circumstances may bring and this does mean continuing our hedge-building. [10]

Campbell still harboured a basic fount of goodwill towards Jagan, his inflexibility notwithstanding. He was, more than his colleagues, prepared to minimise Cheddi's communist proclivities, as Colonial Secretary Iain Macleod had done:

Marxism and Communism mean so many different things to so many different people, and in the last resort it is a game of follow-the-leader (if he is an outstanding leader), but he is in difficulty because he has not got any really Marxist lieutenants. Nevertheless I think people will continue to vote for him and what he stands for, even if it can be logically shown that it is against their own interests as capitalists and landowners. As far as the small man is concerned, as long as he is still a peasant farmer, he will tend to vote for Cheddi, because Cheddi is a very attractive and effective politician, and anyone in this room who was not half-witted would vote for Cheddi Jagan if he lived in British Guiana, because there is effectively nobody else to vote for.[11]

It bears repeating that nowhere in the 23-page text of his crucial speech, which may be seen as a retrospective assessment after nearly ten years at the helm, does Campbell mention Burnham. This omission, amidst almost prophetic observations on the colony in 1960, was extraordinary. I was to learn why, as I interviewed Campbell many times between 1990 and 1994, the last years of his life. In May 1990 I suggested to him that Jagan must bear some responsibility for the destruction of Guyana. He agreed, but remarked that he always had more time for Cheddi than any other politician there. He added that while he was never enamoured of his ideological fantasies, he understood why he felt strongly about the workers. Jock sketched something of the strange, symbiotic link between himself and Jagan: 'I had been brought up with sugar in my blood, born with a sugar spoon in my mouth but was pretty left-wing myself. I was on the whole on the side of the workers. My views matured and I think I got more radical as time went on.' Indeed, he acknowledged that Jagan's extremism drove him to the left and that although he disagreed with his Marxism, he respected him: 'I think he really believed in what he was doing; he was a completely honest man and he worked for the Indians, but I don't think he worked for them racially. I had very strong feelings about Cheddi.' But he was always aware of Cheddi's potentially fatal political fragility: '[H]e never recognised politics as the art of the possible at all; he was unpractical (sic).' I enquired: 'He had no idea how to run a business?' Jock retorted: 'He had no idea how to run anything.'[12]

Campbell would return time and again to the 'unpracticality' of Jagan. The word spoke of an inherent, unconquerable failing: politics by the primer — the inviolability of the received wisdom, Cheddi's 'total understanding'. Jock underlined this for me, citing the experience of an Indian economist who had worked briefly with Jagan in the early 1960s. This man had told him: 'Cheddi is so impractical that I've written down six do's and six don'ts; he has done a few of the don'ts but has not done any of the do's.'[13]

Campbell said that he hated the things that Jagan hated, and appreciated why he was determined to change that. However, he regretted that when, belatedly, he was trying to put certain things right in the sugar industry, Jagan's ideology made it impossible for him to see any merits in what he was doing. He recalled: 'I always remember when I first met him I liked him; I found him an attractive person and I felt a certain affinity with him, and I understood why he disliked the sugar industry. There was a lot to dislike which I was trying to put right and it did begin to worry me how extraordinarily *unpractical* he was.'[14]

Campbell has tried to locate the source of Jagan's 'unpracticality'. This is what he came up with:

> I always felt that he never entirely grew up. I think being entirely impractical is always a sign of [a] certain immaturity and when you are young you tend to be totally idealistic. I've become more practical as I've got older because I know what's possible and what isn't; and Cheddi never understood that politics is the art of the possible. This is a psychological thing because some people never learn the art of the possible. But my tendency to be for the underdog, to be for the persecuted, which is very Irish, to be against oppression, to give people a chance, made me go for Jagan and we did try very hard to work with him.[15]

Campbell spoke often of the difficulty of reconciling his pursuit of reform in the sugar industry with Jagan's unconquerable romanticism. He said that he tried to meet the PPP government half way. He elaborates: 'I felt impressed with their idealism, their eloquence and self-interest. Just as they were impressed with me as a human being who understood their view.' He observed, however, that they 'didn't recognise the art of the possible — what they were expecting us to do — and I didn't realise their total lack of co-ordination and impracticability. So the meetings of individuals, however well they got on [an allusion to himself and Cheddi], couldn't bear any fruit, because I hadn't got the understanding and backing of my own people'.[16] He was saying that entrenched interests in Booker were not imbued with his legacy, his sense of historic wrongs and the need for reparation. Moreover, Cheddi's fundamental opposition to what he saw as Jock's piece-meal, tendentious reforms, did not enhance his cause to his more pragmatic colleagues in Booker.

He was on a losing wicket: while he sought to comprehend Jagan's motives and succeeded, the reverse was not the case, because Jagan could not go beyond the mould of his doctrinaire Marxist frame of reference. His was a political culture rooted in a virulent hatred of sugar. Jagan's crusade against sugar gave his politics its passion, its inflexibility, too. He could see nothing but machiavellian motives in Campbell's reforms. By the early 1960s the futility was wearing Jock down; it contributed to his nervous breakdown in the summer of 1960, which kept him out of Booker for nearly a year (see Part 8). He explains the source of his pain:

> He [Cheddi] was clearly unself-interested; he wasn't on the make. One great difficulty in those days was that because I had always had the guilt about the evils of slavery and oppression in the sugar industry, and the social and economic injustice, I always understood what the 'slave' was trying to do and why he was trying to do it [but] we were never quite on an even keel because they just assumed that I was only trying to protect the profits of the sugar industry. I always understood what they were at; they just *assumed* what I was at. Cheddi once said [to me]: 'It's nothing to do with you; I can't hate you.' I knew what he meant.[17]

This wall of incomprehension had foundations, too, in Campbell's perceived role in the 1950s, when he was an avowed anti-communist. He said that in his Chairman's Statement for 1953 and his speech at Cambridge in July 1954, after the suspension of the constitution, he had portrayed Jagan as a force for evil. He regretted this and wanted to clear up any impression that because the plantocracy panicked in 1953 and pressured the Governor, who also panicked, that he also was involved in the suspension. He was not; neither did he make any such recommendation when he visited Mayle and Rogers at the Colonial Office on September 17, 1953:

> I am absolutely sure that the suspension of the constitution wasn't discussed at that meeting and I never would have suggested it. Moreover, I was astonished when I heard it on the wireless. When someone rang me up to say that it had been suspended (the press rang me up), I said I thought it was absolutely mad and quite unnecessary. I always thought that the Governor [Savage] was as wet as hell. I think the plantocracy panicked; I think they kept on clamouring to Savage who panicked as well; and I think he asked for the constitution to be suspended.[18]

As observed earlier, Governor Savage recommended suspension on September 13, 1953, four days before Campbell went to the Colonial Office, but the role of the plantocracy in the process and his own anti-communism and defence of the suspension at Cambridge in July 1954, made it natural for Jagan and the PPP to implicate him in the machinations surrounding the issue. It would never be erased, even by his conciliatory attitudes after 1957. Campbell admitted to his fear of communism in the early 1950s. This was prompted by apprehension that the dogmatic excesses of the PPP and Jagan's ideological rigidity would stifle his programme of reform on the plantations which was bearing fruit. He explains:

> I had become pretty disgusted with communism, but certainly not with socialism. And I did feel that when we were trying hard, so that there was a real chance of getting Guyana run by Guyanese, [and] masters of their fate — all the sorts of things I wanted to see in training Guyanese — that this had been messed

up by a group of Marxists. What I regret is that I made Cheddi out to be an evil man and I never thought he was an evil man; I thought he was a misguided man. But the more I got to know him the more I realised his attraction but his impracticality.[19]

Campbell said often that he regretted the picture he painted of Jagan in his speech at Cambridge in 1954.[20] He had described Jagan's PPP as a hive of 'ignoble' politicians, motivated by 'personal power' and 'abstract theorising', pursuing 'mischievous and evil ends'. He told me that he would have liked to erase this image: 'Months later I would have worded it in a different way: I would have made the point that that group could not get the future for Guyana as all Guyanese wanted it to be; but I wouldn't have put it down to absolute sheer viciousness. I think I would have put it down to impracticability.'[21]

He believed that although Janet Jagan was infinitely more astute as an organiser and politician than Cheddi, she, also, was deeply rooted in the Marxist creed. Therefore her capacity to moderate Cheddi's rhetorical excess and impracticability was limited. Jock recalls a meeting with Janet sometime in the late 1950s; the encounter suggests that fundamentally she, too, was so certain of the communist millennium that an inflexibility, a hardness, possessed her as well: 'I remember once saying to Janet that if you do that [impose communism] you will have a great many Guyanese unemployed and possibly dying of starvation; and she said it would be worth many Guyanese unemployed and dying of starvation to have communism in Guyana.' He felt that the power of the creed and belief in its superiority as the instrument of human organisation, had clouded out notions of the individual; freedom of the individual was a 'bourgeois' concept:

They were not thinking of individual Guyanese; they were thinking of a political system which she, rootedly, and he, by acquisition, worshipped; and Booker, whatever we'd done, offended that creed entirely. It was almost like an acquisition, a religion, and that's why I don't think there could ever be a meeting of minds or a compromise.[22]

In 1994, the year he died, Jock shared with me a final reflection on Cheddi Jagan:

> He did do what he did with the best will in the world and was totally unself-interested, but he was a political maniac, like a religious maniac, and everything that conformed to this religion was right and anything that didn't conform was wrong and there could be no meeting of minds at all. Capitalism was an oppressive and outdated creed; colonialism was oppressive and outdated; and communism was the answer. British Guiana because of its latifundia [the plantation structure] could have been right for communism.[23]

It is interesting that after 1957 Campbell never accommodated Burnham within his scheme of leadership, despite his professed anti-communism. He harboured a cerebral antipathy for the man that no ideological moderation could palliate. As will be seen in Part 8, it was only when Jagan's communism took British Guiana into the Cold War, in the context of Cuba's ascendancy as a pro-Soviet state in the Western Hemisphere, that the belated rise of Burnham to power was engineered through Anglo-American collusion, in 1963–64. Only after this did Campbell seek a modus vivendi with him; but he left Booker, after 28 years, shortly after Guyana became independent under Burnham in 1966. The volatile political maelstrom had taken its toll: what his friend, the economist, Kenneth Boulding, in a Christmas card he sent to him in the early 1960s, described as 'poor B.G. divided against itself on the road to nowhere'. Burnham had skilfully and ruthlessly (with Peter D'Aguiar's crucial support) played to America's Cold War fears in unseating Jagan, but Jock could see no silver lining; his dreams had dried up:

> The trouble was that Burnham was entirely corrupt — a very, very nasty man; Peter D'Aguiar [the Portuguese leader of the United Force and the brother of Jock's girl friend in the 1930s, Phyllis], was a sort of anti-Castro crusader; and Cheddi was a well-meaning, good, unself-interested, totally unpractical Marxist. My difficulty with Cheddi was that he always had good intentions, [but he felt] that Marxism was [creating] a better

world, [removing] the injustices of life, the glory of the Cuban
Revolution — he believed it all, however naively, and he did
very few vicious things. [Then, setting Jagan against the persona
of Burnham, he found something redeeming]. [Jagan] was never
corrupt; he was never cruel; he was naive, immature and
impractical. He made mistakes — he never made anything but
mistakes — but was all very well-intentioned, whereas Burnham
was a criminal, an absolutely beastly man in every way.[24]

This was why he would try to work with Jagan until the Cold War
made the question academic. He felt that Jagan's Marxist frame of
reference was not 'touching the real hopes and fears of the people'; it
was principally 'a political creed', rooted in antagonism to the arch-
colonialism/capitalism of Booker. Jagan would never 'have
considered compromising with the devil'. Campbell has reflected on
this journey to nowhere: 'I don't think, even if we had been the
Archangel Gabriel, or if we had been the blackest of black companies,
it would have made any difference because the mixture of the three
politicians and the political incitement [between 1962 and 1964],
with the background of slavery and indentureship and Booker's
latifundist role in B.G., produced this totally destructive force.'[25]

But even with the bleakness of hindsight, Campbell maintains, he
would still have done what he did: reform Booker in order to pursue
social advances for workers which, though too little, too late, he
nevertheless felt were necessary and worthy in themselves. As I have
argued throughout, his guilt, his family's part in sugar in British
Guiana, under slavery and indentureship, impelled him to embrace
reform, however difficult the political context. For this, ironically,
he acquired a reputation for being beyond the pale as a businessman,
among some people in Booker and business people in London: 'It
hurt me in a way that I got the reputation of not only being a socialist
but of being impractical. Fortunately Booker was a success but most
people would have said they wouldn't touch me with a barge-pole.'[26]

'Bitter sugar' had given Cheddi a cause; Jock as well. But given
the dominance of King Sugar and Booker in the political economy of
British Guiana, Campbell could do no more than try to sweeten the
bitter legacy.

Endnotes

1. Booker Brothers, McConnell and Co, Ltd, [Jock Campbell], 'The Group Chairman's Visit to British Guiana and the West Indies — January-March 1960', [March 22, 1960], (mimeo.) confidential, p.2.
2. Ibid., 3.
3. Ibid., 6.
4. Ibid., 6-7.
5. Ibid., 7.
6. Ibid., 8.
7. Ibid.
8. Ibid., 8, 22.
9. Ibid., 19.
10. Ibid., 18.
11. Ibid., 23.
12. Jock Campbell, interview by the author, Nettlebed, Oxfordshire, May 9, 1990, Tape 1.
13. Ibid., July 23, 1992, Tape 4.
14. Ibid.
15. Ibid.
16. Ibid., July 24, 1992, Tape 5.
17. Ibid.
18. Ibid.
19. Ibid.
20. See Jock Campbell, 'British Capital in the Changing Conditions of the Colonies', Speech delivered at Cambridge University, July 12, 1954, (mimeo.).
21. See note 16.
22. Jock Campbell, interview by the author, Nettlebed, Oxfordshire, July 24, 1992, Tape 7.
23. Ibid.
24. Ibid.
25. Ibid.
26. See note 13.

Part 5

Sweetening 'Bitter Sugar' I: Shaping the Instruments for Reform

Chapter Nineteen

'PRACTICAL IDEALISM': CAMPBELL'S PHILOSOPHY ON REFORM

Jock Campbell was always ready to explain the source of his radical temperament. For most of his mature years he would begin a speech or an article with what he considered the central prompting of his effort:

> I felt — perhaps as the sixth generation of my family connected with sugar in British Guiana — a heavy sense of debt unpaid; a compelling need to do something about the situation — to do what could be done to improve the health, wealth and happiness of the people of British Guiana. Any progress depended on getting the backing of one's shareholders, who were in any case hardly likely to be eager to invest new money in tropical agriculture in British Guiana. All these problems led me to an agonising reappraisal and to question 'What is Bookers for?' I was not satisfied with the answer: 'Make profits for the shareholders.'[1]

Time and again he would remark that his forefathers had grown rich from slavery and indentureship. This engendered a life-long guilt; a slight consolation came from the fact that 'mercifully they were not slave traders'. Another factor that inspired him was that he was deeply committed to the development of West Indian peoples. He argued that ethical historical considerations dictated that Britain help these island communities, for she was the architect of their existence from the very dark beginnings. In July 1958 he explained:

> It was this country which started the West Indies on their present course. It was we who settled in the islands, and who built up industries on slave labour. It was we who set the social patterns

which have created present demands. In short, on any reading of history we owed the West Indies a debt which had not been fully paid off. They did not want to be dependent on UK economic aid. They did, however, want this country's support in building their industry and commerce — which it was emphatically in our self-interest to give them.[2]

Campbell's work and annual visits to the region since 1934 had bred an empathy for its peoples, a comprehension of their fears and aspirations. He knew their leaders personally and spoke and dined with them regularly: Cheddi Jagan, Forbes Burnham, Norman Manley (his favourite, his exemplar), Alexander Bustamante, Eric Williams, Grantley Adams, V.C. Bird, Robert Bradshaw, Ebenezer Joshua. Jock recalls a defining encounter with the irrepressible Bustamante (Busta) in London around 1942, as well as his regular meetings — intellectual discourses — with Eric Williams and Norman Manley, and a memorable lunch with C.L.R. James:

> I asked Busta to dinner at the Traveller's Club ... he was a natural actor and performer; I don't think he ever thought before he spoke (Norman Manley thought everything out). Busta had a lot to drink and he had his Attorney General with him: just me, Busta and his A.G. There were few people at the Club and we stayed later and later, and Busta was talking louder and louder. He was saying he would shoot Manley because he would set up a one-party state; and therefore it would be better for Jamaicans that he be shot. The A.G. intervened: 'Mr. Bustamante, you are being most unreasonable, considering I had been twice in a position of indicting you for murder; I think I have been most tolerant'. Busta was undeterred. I mentioned to him that Sir Frank Stockdale, Chairman of the Colonial Development Corporation, had died in his sleep, adding: 'That's the way I want to go: peacefully.' Busta retorted: 'I don't agree. I want to be assassinated....' He had immense charisma, a very big, enormous man, about 6 ft. 4 ins — very good-looking, Spanish-looking. Busta was absolutely spontaneous in everything he did ... beautiful voice, very dramatic.... I will always remember that the first time I met Busta he put a revolver down in front of him and he said to me: 'That's to show we're friends....' I met C.L.R.

James with Eric Williams, at a cocktail party. I had lunch with James: it was the most wonderful lunch I've ever had .... James was a most fascinating man. I got on very well with Williams. We used to have very long lunches at the Hilton Hotel in Trinidad. One day we had lunch there when they were building an extension and he was Prime Minister, and we walked out together and there must have been about 300 workmen — he never took any notice of any of them. I was fascinated by this; extraordinary man. But he was a very clever man: I have seen him at a couple of those Woodford Square meetings, haranguing an enormous crowd for about two hours .... I would talk to him about slavery; I would talk to him about calypso; I would talk to him about sugar; I would talk to him about the Spanish days in Trinidad .... there were so many things .... You couldn't have a conversation with Busta at all. You could have a wonderful conversation with Norman Manley. He was totally different: a much smaller man, very intellectual, very sensitive. More like Stafford Cripps, rather aesthetic (Busta was totally unaesthetic); a Rhodes Scholar; lovely wife [Edna].... Manley was a marvellous man; I adored him as I adored Edna.[3]

Jock always adored Edna. But it was a measure of the intellectual breadth and curiosity of Campbell that he took time, too, to meet many of the region's rising artists, thinkers and sportsmen in the 1950s: Mittelholzer, Lamming, Naipaul, Jan Carew, Sylvia Wynter, Arthur Lewis, Martin Carter, Edna Manley, Aubrey Williams, Clyde Walcott, Garry Sobers, McDonald Bailey. A refined man of discerning literary tastes, he read widely on the Caribbean, including the novels of the artists he befriended. He felt that there was something exhilarating about the West Indies at the end of Empire and he wanted to help in the shaping of these young, vibrant societies. As he observed in 1958, at the time of the inauguration of the short-lived West Indies Federation:

For me, the great attraction of the West Indies is the opportunity to be able to do new and creative things in new ways with the willing help and enthusiasm of a vigorous new community, unhampered by the burden of tradition and of an Establishment dedicated to resistance to change. The opportunity of the West

Indies is the opportunity to cultivate fresh and fruitful soil, to get on with the job and get it done.[4]

He was optimistic that the people's vigour could be channelled into productive enterprises; in this venture he was confident that an enlightened capitalism had a crucial role, as a shaper of a progressive community, beyond the old static attitudes of the plantocracy. He argued in June 1958:

> It would be a mistake to forget, or to play down, the significant part which the character of the West Indian peoples, their gaiety and warmth and freshness and enthusiasm, will have to play in attracting the capital they need to live a fuller life. I for my part — and I think this is true for most people who have worked in, and who know and love the West Indies — find there a purpose and a sense of engagement and responsibility which go deeper than economic and financial considerations.[5]

Unfortunately, as I have argued above, among British Guiana's leaders, Jock encountered an antithesis of the creative energy he felt in the British West Indies. In Cheddi, however attractive and sincere, he discovered a single-mindedness that fused everything into entrenched categories, a static universe at variance with the carnival of the imagination and intellectual nimbleness celebrated in the region's politics, arts, popular culture and sport. As he said of Jagan (Margaret Thatcher, too): 'Sometimes people have to be single-minded to get what they want, but they very often spoil their own market by the inflexibility of their single-mindedness.'[6]

This assessment of Jagan went beyond a capitalist's aversion to the rigidities of a communist mind; it came from a civilised man's vision: his cultivation of the imagination, his sensitivity to nuances, and instinct for tolerance and compromise. That is why although he was amused by the histrionics of Alexander Bustamante, he was never enamoured of him. Jock recalled that in the late 1940s when he dined with him at the Traveller's Club in London, he had propounded, in his compelling way, that illiberal actions were justifiable in forestalling 'greater illiberalism'. Bustamante contended that such measures were essential in containing his arch rival, Norman Manley, who if he were to come to power, would set up a Communist police state.[7] Jock said that when he first met Manley and his gifted wife, Edna, in Jamaica, he could see no trace of the monster that Bustamante had contrived. Jock met them regularly over the next 25 years; indeed, he had come to see Manley as the epitome of refinement, a totally civilised being, and for Edna he showed abundant respect and adoration, which had intellectual and, possibly, erotic foundations:

> I met a man who at once impressed me as an exceptionally civilised human being. Norman Manley is often referred to as the Stafford Cripps of the Caribbean. Certainly he had the brilliance and the quality of intellect; and all the powers of analysis and exposition of a great advocate. But Cripps struck me as almost a disembodied intellect: Norman Manley was far from disembodied. His Military Medal in the First World War, his prowess as an athlete [a Rhodes Scholar at Oxford], his wit and his charm — and indeed his marriage to Edna — were all evidence of the abundance of his humanity. He was an unusually attractive man with an unusually attractive wife — herself the embodiment of civilisation too.[8]

In British Guiana, among its crop of leaders, he could discern no such embodiment of civilisation. Yet Campbell could rise to the severest of tests; he saw change as a 'challenge', not a 'threat', whereas many in Booker were inclined to resist change. He always had to fight on two fronts: hostile Jaganite Marxism and the resilient conservatism in Booker, especially those 'on the spot'. It was a measure of his own flexibility, tolerance and powers of persuasion that he could observe in 1968, the year after he left Booker, that although Jagan lived by 'the cliches of an impassioned quasi-Marxist, anti-colonialist socialism', he was able to get Booker to work with him. He added that it was imperative for the foreign company to adapt, to be imaginative, 'to understand the outlook and policies of the government with which it had to deal'. For Campbell, there was still a place for enlightened capital overseas:

> Booker continued to trade successfully in British Guiana under Dr. Jagan's rule [late 1950s and early 1960s] and never failed

to maintain a reasoned and reasonable dialogue with his Government, in spite of its highly vulnerable position as by far the largest commercial enterprise in the country. But this, perhaps, is an unusual case. More commonly it is a question of coming to terms with an unfamiliar situation rather than a hostile one. It is part of Booker's thinking that private enterprise in the developing world must always be ready for a more direct, obvious and involved participation by Government in a country's economic advance.[9]

As I have argued, from the mid-1930s, Jock Campbell tried to read the pulse of British Guiana, especially the changing moods of the sugar plantation workers. During and after the War the case for reform had been persuasively made by the Moyne Commission (1940/5), the progressive, though thwarted, Governor, Sir Gordon Lethem (1941–46) and the Venn Commission (1949). The Colonial Development and Welfare grants since 1941, recommended by Moyne, also, had created heightened expectations, which fed a rebellious spirit in the colony clamouring for a new order. This was magnified by the formation of Cheddi Jagan's Marxist Political Affairs Committee (PAC) in late 1946, his meteoric rise as the obdurate defender of the working class in the Legislature, after 1947, and the shooting of sugar estate workers at Plantation Enmore in 1948. Yet many in the sugar industry were still averse to change. But Campbell's own rise in Booker, paralleled by the rise of Jagan, allowed a culture of reform to percolate through the company. From 1947, when Campbell became vice-chairman (virtually chairman, as McConnell was a lame-duck), he gradually persuaded Booker shareholders and senior executives that reform was inescapable: with most of their eggs precariously placed in the Guyanese basket, they could not pull out. This was the context in which Jock was able to build his case for corporate responsibility in British Guiana, a veritable moral crusade. The fact that it was pitted against the consuming Marxist fervour of Jaganism, on and off the plantations, gave urgency to his cause while reducing opposition to his 'practical idealism'.

It is an aspect of the intellectual history of the Caribbean, the charting of the evolution of Campbell's ideas, his reformist capitalism, between the late 1940s and 1960, in an environment that was very hostile to Booker — a passion encapsulated in the popular, pejorative phrase, 'Booker's Guiana'.

In 1949, shortly before the Venn Commission Report was published, Campbell observed that the prosperity of British Guiana and that of the sugar industry were intertwined. Therefore, the progress of both could be sustained only if efficiency were improved in the industry, if long-term remunerative prices were secured for sugar and its by-products, and if good 'human relationships' were fostered.[10] Indeed, he was trying to create the foundation for his policy of reform in British Guiana: (i) technical efficiency as the basis of greater productivity; (ii) stable, remunerative prices to sustain profits and fund reforms on the plantations; (iii) harmonious industrial relations conducing to a more enlightened worker/management ethos.

Campbell noted that although much was being done to alleviate working conditions on the estates, he was disturbed by the 'atmosphere of suspicion of our motives and even hostility' of some sections of the community.[11] By 1949, as I have argued, the Venn Commission had provided a framework for reform, identifying specific measures which should be taken in a programme of comprehensive change. But two years earlier, in 1947, Campbell had exhorted his subordinates in the colony that 'everything possible must be done to engender the spirit of goodwill between the industry and its labour population. It will be uphill and heartbreaking work, but without goodwill the industry cannot survive'.[12] In 1948 he remarked that while they were trying to reduce costs their capacity to achieve this was restricted because of 'the real need to improve the living standards of the people'.[13] In July 1949 Campbell informed R.R. Follett-Smith, the chairman of Booker Sugar Estates in British Guiana, that it was crucial for sugar producers in the colonies to negotiate a long-term purchase agreement with the UK government to 'enable us to maintain, if not improve, the present standard of living in the colonies'.[14]

The Commonwealth Sugar Agreement (CSA) was signed in December 1951; Campbell was the chief negotiator for the sugar producers; without it his reforms would not have been affordable. The guaranteed prices and quota gave him the ammunition to bring even some of the most reactionary people in Booker around to a degree of support for reform. No less effective in shifting obdurate defenders of the old order, was Cheddi Jagan's communist message and his growing stature on the plantations. In July 1949 Campbell, seeking to win over his more reluctant colleagues in Booker, had deftly linked his pursuit of change to the communist threat which, he admitted, did scare him at that stage.[15]

It is noteworthy that at the end of January 1950, the month that Jagan's PAC became a full-fledged political party, the People's Progressive Party (PPP), Campbell was exhorting his staff in British Guiana to study and absorb the policy of Booker. This was crucial, the philosophical underpinning of their work, in an environment where the Marxist definition impugned the company for the exploitation of the colony: its extraction of 'surplus value' and the repatriation of profits, at the expense of the worker. As he would often ask of their work: 'It works in practice, how about the theory?'[16]

The necessity to give theoretical grounding to his reforms led Campbell, gradually, to ask why Booker was in business. In March 1953, shortly before the victory of the PPP in the first elections under universal adult suffrage, he communicated on this matter to his administrative managers in the colony:

> Obviously the main purpose of Bookers — and it has to be faced — was to pay a proper return to the Shareholders on the capital employed in their business. Put as simply as possible, the policy of Bookers and the responsibility of the Directors at all levels throughout the Group was to secure maximum possible return on capital employed after making full provision for the maintenance of all productive assets; the greatest possible return on capital employed compatible with the fair and reasonable payment to staff and to labour and the fulfilment of the Group's responsibilities to the peoples of the countries in which it operated.[17]

What is significant in this definition is the centrality, still, of dividends to shareholders and the maintenance of capital assets. Even when he includes 'reasonable payment' of staff and labour and responsibilities to the community, he emphasises the need for 'the greatest possible return on capital employed' — profits. The focus on responsibilities to shareholders was evident also in September 1953, during the PPP-inspired GIWU strike for recognition in the sugar industry. In an address to the Booker Board, Campbell, after denouncing the 'illegal strike' and the 'overtly hostile' attitude of the Jagan government, stated that they would not run away but remain to ensure that Booker survived and that they would continue to contribute to the 'health, wealth and happiness' of British Guiana. This was, he concluded, 'the only lasting way' to protect 'the real interests of Bookers' Shareholders, the owners of the Business'.[18]

The emphasis, up to 1953, in spite of his conviction that reform was inescapable, still spoke primarily of shareholders' interests and the maintenance of capital assets. From late 1953, however, after the dismissal of the PPP from office, Campbell started to articulate a more inclusive philosophy for Booker, with sharper focus on 'human relations' in the company. As he would argue consistently, time was not on their side; they had to get it right. To counter the big ideas of the Marxists, the impersonality of man in the mass, he embraced a more humanist approach: 'the ability to understand human beings (including oneself), both as individuals and as members of groups, and to act on that understanding in a way that will bring the best out of everybody for the common good, to seek the good qualities in men and women and to direct them to good ends — by by-passing as far as possible their shortcomings'.[19] A crucial dimension of his 'practical idealism' — the greatness of small causes — was taking shape. He wanted to respond to the fears and hopes of individual workers, cautioning against the Marxist passion for theorising in the mass, its facelessness:

> I am frightened of too much theory and writing on these matters. What we want is effective efforts and action now in thousands of small ways which can help a discontented community in turbulent conflict to become a happy people working together for the common good. We must strive for harmony against discord.[20]

In early 1954, in his Chairman's Statement for 1953, as was seen earlier, he remarked that business was 'inevitably gird about by politics': to survive they had to come to terms with the political environment; they could not operate in a 'vacuum'. Then, for the first time, he began to sketch what became known as his four-fold responsibility of business (sometimes five-fold): the exercise of 'sound judgement and enlightenment' in fulfilling responsibilities to shareholders, staff, labour and the community.[21]

In April 1954, in a letter to Follett-Smith, the head of Booker in the colony, pointedly to counter the reservation, if not opposition, of some of his own people (including Follett-Smith), to this new ethos, Jock wrote sarcastically: 'I always fear that our vision and good intentions may be frustrated by the *unimaginativeness* of others, who will not understand the importance of doing what is to be done with expedition and good grace nor realise that *time is not on our side* [emphasis added].'[22]

The attitude of some of Campbell's key people in British Guiana was not an asset to the cause. As he told me on several occasions, he was not at ease with Follett-Smith, who was 11 years older than him, had trained as a chemist in London and Trinidad, joined Booker in 1937 as consulting chemist, became a director in 1946 and since 1951, was the Chairman of Booker Sugar Estates Ltd.[23] This was what Campbell thought of his chief in British Guiana:

> Like all chemists he saw everything in black and white or true or false, and he was very reactionary. He never liked me and I never liked him. In fact, one of the most embarrassing moments in my life was when he died in retirement in Sevenoaks [Kent]. I obviously went to the funeral. As I arrived at the church the cortege was drawing up, and as I went up to the church the parson said: 'Lord Campbell, where do you want to stand for the address?' And I said: 'What address?' He replied: 'Mrs. Follett-Smith said you are going to do the funeral oration.' (The nightmare was, I detested the man and he detested me and never disguised it.) So I said I would go outside for ten minutes and think. It was the most difficult speech I ever made. I will never tell a lie about people; I will leave out some of the truth, and I did get away with it.[24]

Follett-Smith: Campbell said of him: '[V]ery reactionary... He never liked me and I never liked him'

Campbell and the Head of Booker Sugar Estates in British Guiana, R.R. Follett-Smith, late 1950s: an uneasy relationship

Jock recalled that in the early 1950s he wrote a report which got back to Follett-Smith, stating that he was a valuable man as long as you 'don't make him a chemist-manager'. (He was a fine chemist, an active researcher.) That had upset him and, obviously, poisoned their relationship. However, there was apparently no other person in British Guiana at the time with the experience to become chairman of Booker Sugar Estates. Campbell's assessment of the man reflected fundamental differences in temperament: 'He was very hardworking, totally humourless. Follett-Smith was a very great problem but he did the job; he was totally honest but he wasn't popular. He was a very limited man.'[25]

Follett-Smith lacked Jock's intellect, imagination, enthusiasm for change, his unfaltering sense of mission. Jock, however, tried his best to work with him: 'One of my dictums was you take people as you find them, and you have to build on their virtues and bypass their shortcomings.'[26] But in the context of the volatile political climate of British Guiana in the early 1950s, and Booker's infamous reputation, Jock's efforts at reparation could not have been enhanced by Follett-Smith. He was too symbolic of the old order; a programme of reform required a new face. This would bedevil Campbell's cause even after Follett-Smith retired: image mattered.

He argued that while his reforms would alleviate the material conditions of workers, they must be seen to do so. For, as he informed Follett-Smith in May 1954, it was essential that the workers begin to identify with Booker, that they see their future as inseparable from the progress of the company. Guyanese must have access to jobs at all levels of Booker. Campbell explained:

> A 'foreign' industrial undertaking imposed upon the life of a people cannot gain their confidence — and ward off their hostility — however good conditions of service, unless a sense of the undertaking belonging to the country and the people can be achieved; unless, above all, the people can be brought to understand their identity of interest with the undertaking. [W]ould it be true to say that materialism cannot alone solve the problem; that the people and the industry must have an industrial sense of purpose and cause?[27]

Jock was very sensitive to the mercurial political culture of British Guiana; he was deeply suspicious of extremism, its arousal of volatile passions, and fearful of violence as an instrument of change, as he showed in his Cambridge lecture of July 1954. He felt that while discontent is rooted in material deprivation, frequently it was inflamed by the fallacious notion that illimitable gains were procurable if 'violent or large-scale change' was forced upon society. He contended that people had to be educated to grasp what was realistically attainable in given circumstances. He always believed in the 'greatness of small causes': '[H]istory has surely shown us that great and humanitarian upheavals designed to revolutionise the material lot of man have led to bitter disappointment, if not to tyranny; while personal efforts to solve the small problems of small men can bring about such contentment.'[28]

He untiringly sought to wean people away from the allure of utopianism. He did not suggest that capitalism and parliamentary democracy were perfect, but they were the best tools available. Campbell remarked that while it was 'arrogant and impertinent' to posit European superiority over subject peoples, it was the 'duty' of the former to 'guide' the latter, to prepare them for self-government.

This did not have to be marked by European dominance, it could be a partnership: 'I personally have no reason whatever to believe that Africans and Asiatic peoples, either in partnership with Europeans or inter-married with them, are not, or cannot become, just as fit to look after their own affairs. [W]ithout racial partnership and integration there must always be suspicion, distrust and conflict.'[29]

He argued that for the foreseeable future European capital and skills had a place in the economic development of poorer countries. But it was imperative that the latter should acquire the skills which are indispensable for true self-government, prominent among them being 'that indefinable something awkwardly called "entrepreneurial ability" which I suppose is industrial genius'. This was not sheer altruism on the part of Europeans: they could not do without the products and the markets of these places. Always optimistic that a genuine partnership could be forged, Campbell observed: 'Our western civilisation cannot survive without the help and strength and ever-growing vigour of the young peoples.'[30]

European companies still had much to do to earn the respect of non-European peoples. As he was arguing since late 1953, that required a 'wide and fairly balanced' responsibility to staff and labour, to the peoples of the countries in which they invested, as well as their shareholders. This four-fold responsibility became the guiding motif of Campbell's cause — repeated and embroidered upon just as passionately and as often as Jagan expounded on the superiority of Marxism and the glory of the Soviet system.

In early 1955, in his Chairman's Statement for 1954, Campbell repeated that it was necessary to cultivate 'a sense of identity between the people of the country and Booker'. Toward this crucial end, in 1954, he had appointed Antony Tasker Director of Public Relations in British Guiana; a Chief Personnel Officer, also, was appointed. He asserted an identity of interest between Booker and British Guiana, noting that Guyanese had a vested interest in Booker's capacity to serve the country as 'an efficient and prosperous enterprise'. This identity of interest had to be promoted.[31]

In early 1956 Jock Campbell went a step further, arguing that it was not enough for Booker to do good towards British Guiana: the recent political troubles made it necessary to 'blow our own trumpets' as well. He then recommended Tasker's dictum with reference to public relations — 'behaving well and taking the credit for it'. He believed that Booker was behaving well, that they were 'guided by a deep sense of purpose and responsibility toward the people of British Guiana', but it had to be a two-way process: Guyanese, also, had 'real responsibilities' towards Booker.

To facilitate the permeation of his philosophy in the company, Campbell created an umbrella organisation, Booker B.G. Group Committee, under the chairmanship of Follett-Smith. This brought together the various, independent companies in Booker to ensure that the financial competence of these largely discrete companies was not achieved at the expense of the cohesion and ethos of the Group. He cited the main terms of reference of the Group Committee: 'ensuring that the long-term ethic and policy of the Group is known, understood and applied by the Booker Group of Companies in British Guiana; in particular that the Group's *five-fold* responsibilities to *Shareholders, Staff, Labour, Customers and the Community* are properly fulfilled and *balanced* [emphasis added]'.[32]

By 1956 the four-fold responsibility of 1954, to shareholders, staff, labour and the community, had become a five-fold, 'balanced' responsibility, in Campbell's evolving 'practical idealism'. He had added 'customers' to his list, reflecting the contribution of the shop-keeping sector in the Booker Group. Although he was depressed at the failure of a responsible political leader to emerge in British Guiana after the suspension of the constitution, he never wavered in his belief that Booker had to persist in trying to do good in British Guiana, while 'building hedges' in other countries.

In February 1956, during his annual visit to the colony, he gave what amounted to a virtual manifesto of change for the society, while linking Booker unequivocally to a progressive development of British Guiana. Departing from the old plantocratic mantras, he stated that for the foreseeable future agriculture was the key to economic progress but that Booker would welcome a diversified economy: 'It was not a good thing that the company should be so large a factor in British Guiana's economic life.' Campbell advocated the creation of land settlement schemes, to provide small farmers space for development and independence. This would help them not merely to 'exist' but to 'live abundantly'. He welcomed a diversified agriculture, while acknowledging that there were problems with finding a range of remunerative crops. However, with land settlements and adequate drainage and irrigation, he could see new agricultural enterprises flourishing. Campbell was buoyed by the record sugar crop of 1955. Booker's factories had produced 201,931 tons, 80.7 per cent of the colony's output, compared to 168,117 tons or 70.1 per cent of output in 1954. He observed that this had enabled them to award the workers a good bonus, which he hoped would persuade them that their 'personal interest was inseparable from those of the industry'.[33]

Campbell then delivered a memorable line, which became the veritable slogan for his reforms, the defining maxim, the signature of Booker's new way in British Guiana. Asked by a reporter what he meant by the centrality of 'human relations' in Booker's scheme of things, he said:

> *Our basic policy is that people are more important than anything else: ships, shops or sugar estates.* Good human relations are essentially the responsibility of management [emphasis added].[34]

In March 1956 he quickly hitched his new slogan to his notion of the five-fold responsibility of Booker as a progressive enterprise in British Guiana. He explained that ships, shops and sugar estates are 'built and run by people, with people's money, to provide goods and services for people'. People could have no 'moral responsibility' to ships, shops and sugar estates; they could have moral responsibility to people only. He elaborated for the benefit of all Guyanese:

> The obligations that those who work in a business have towards the land, the sugar cane or the machine, to the ship or the shop or the goods in it are really obligations to people — a moral responsibility to the owners of business, to fellow workers at all levels — managers and staff to labour, no less than staff to managers — to customers and to the community. It is the interest of people and not the interest of things that matter.[35]

He explained that in a business, as he understood it, the interests of all people were interwoven. He was making the case that a capitalist concern like Booker was not an enemy of the people: in his scheme their responsibilities to shareholders, staff, labour, customers and the community were 'equally balanced responsibilities'. In his inclusive, people's capitalism, all elements were crucial: 'Our business cannot exist without any one of them and we cannot fulfil our responsibilities towards one without, or at the expense of, the others.' Everyone should have a stake in Booker, for the future of British Guiana and the company were inseparable. Guyanese, therefore, could have nothing to gain from a failing company:

> An unprofitable and inefficient business is an enemy to the community, demoralising, and likely to bring with its inevitable ruin much more hardship to its workpeople and the community than its shareholders. On the other hand an efficient and profitable business in generating production and employment, in providing food and services, in circulating money, can make a positive and inspiring contribution to the well-being and satisfaction of everybody concerned with it.[36]

In March 1956 Campbell articulated what was an act of faith in British Guiana. In spite of the turbulent politics of recent years Booker was prepared to continue its work as long as Guyanese wanted them to. This was tantamount to a plea to give his reformist capitalism a chance, to eschew the seductive road of Jaganite 'scientific socialism':

> [A]s head of Booker, I can tell you that despite all difficulties and problems, and in the face of much discouragement, we mean to go on planning, investing and working for the health, wealth and happiness of the people so long as we are allowed to do so, and so long as it is not made impossible for us to fulfil these balanced responsibilities to our shareholders, to our staff, to our workpeople, to our customers and to the community at large.[37]

Brian Scott observes that in the context of the 1950s and Booker's reputation in the colony, the seemingly trite slogan, 'people are more important than ships, shops and sugar estates', constituted a 'revolutionary statement', and that 'Jock Campbell encapsulated this fundamental shift in [Booker's] outlook'. Scott has assessed the deeper implications of Campbell's slogan for their operation in British Guiana:

[T]he slogan's importance for Booker was more than a recognition
of the social dimensions of its operations — a means of making up
for past wrongs with investment in more efficient processes,
humane management, and an enlightened personnel
department. It signified also the beginning of a self-conscious
effort to redefine the meaning and role of Booker as a company
engaged in tropical agriculture. Inevitably, this demanded a
thorough examination not only of internal operations — seeking
ways to improve efficiency and to make employees' work more
meaningful and more satisfying to them — but also of the relation
of the company to its total environment; and, indeed, an attempt
to understand what that environment consisted of.[38]

In early 1957 Campbell observed that in the five-year period,
1952–56 (since he assumed the Chairmanship of Booker), nearly two-
thirds of their profits still came from British Guiana and the West
Indies, primarily the former. In 1956, though, the proportion had
fallen to 56 per cent, 'the effect of our policy and plans to build hedges
against the political hazards of British Guiana'. He was very cautious
about the political question, suggesting that Guyanese would do well
to elect a government 'approaching the quality of Barbados, Jamaica
and Trinidad', in short, a social democratic or socialist government,
but not a communist one.[39]

Campbell's 'practical idealism' allowed him, however, to continue
to work in the colony as long as that was possible, while 'building
hedges' in other areas. Profits there were still good: that enabled
them to diversify away from Guyana, while increasing their
investments there, thus allowing him to pursue the reforms which
meant so much to him. Shortly after Jagan's victory in August 1957,
Jock observed that he had 'unreservedly pledged Booker's intention
to do all we could to serve a responsible Guianese Government',
astutely adding, now, that the new government 'have done nothing
to lessen our faith in the rightness of this policy'.[40] Booker started to
increase their investment there.

Jock often remarked that a good leader had to overlook the
weaknesses of key people, building on their strengths: whether it was
Follett-Smith or Jagan. The lack of a perceived alternative — he

detested Burnham — led him to a more accommodating stance with regard to Cheddi. It is noteworthy, also, that from 1957 to 1958 until his illness in the summer of 1960, he never lapsed in his philosophical endeavour to propagate his reformist capitalism. He had come to recognise that he had to live with Jagan (as he did with Follett-Smith), and hoped that responsibility and age (Cheddi was now 40), would guide him towards a more moderate socialism — towards common sense. He always insisted that a conservative government could not address the fears and hopes of Guyanese; and he constantly tried to stimulate progressive, radical, potentially intersecting strands in his ongoing debate with Jaganite Marxism while underlining the congruence of their ends.

In July 1956, at the Duke of Edinburgh's Study Conference at Oxford, Campbell had delivered his clearest exposition of his conception of progressive capitalism and the basis of human endeavour. In seeking an explanation why people worked, he came to the conclusion that self-interest was the principal motivator — obligations to one's family — however lofty the proclaimed motives. That was why, later, he spoke so often of 'the greatness of small causes', of the importance of the individual and the centrality of small things in people's lives. He was repelled by the leviathan — all-encompassing total systems; by the forcing of people's fears and hopes within universal 'scientific' moulds, however professedly liberating; by the misguided assumption of the possibility of 'total understanding' and infinite perfectibility. However, his was not a cynical construct of crass materialism: self-interest, if guided properly, could intersect with broader social responsibilities. The more individuals are made to feel fulfilled in their private endeavours, the more likely it is that they could be persuaded of the merits of broader social obligations. Within the interstices of the personal and the social, there was room for the cause, for idealism. For him, this was realism:

> To all but the high-and-mighty mortals it is not high-and-mighty problems that seem real. To the ordinary man it is the ordinary problem — affecting him and his family and friends — that counts. He may now and then have an uneasy feeling that there is

something in what the politicians tell him about the national interest or the company chairman about the competitive position of the industry. But it isn't the natural interest or the company interest that is really going to influence him or his attitude to his work. What is going to influence him are the factors that immediately impinge upon him.[41]

He then explained how self-interest could be harnessed for higher social objectives: by stimulating the individual worker, improving working conditions, conferring meaning on his/her work by praise where it is warranted, fostering a sense of his/her importance. Good leadership helps the individual worker gain self-respect. Campbell thought it paramount that such leadership must strive to give workers doing humdrum jobs meaning beyond the motives generated by self-interest. He was saying that self-interest combined with social responsibility were attainable in the context of an enlightened capitalist framework:

[W]e may deceive ourselves that we are influenced by transcendental motives and high moral principles; but in truth self-interest predominates however well it may be disguised, even from ourselves. Of course, what we have to learn and remember is that in the long run and in the last resort self-interest cannot be separated from the rest of the community. We must start by getting the right man in the right job, and he must be properly trained for the job. He must have reason to think that he is fairly paid in relation to his requirements. There is no doubt that money matters to all of us.[42]

Campbell felt that the workers' sense of identity with the company had to be cultivated through good management. Leadership of a high order was crucial to guide self-interest into the broader stream:

[Workers] will be stimulated by good leadership, a sense of cause, a sense of purpose, a sense of challenge, a sense of importance of their jobs, by interest, by self-regard, by ambition and scope for advancement — by praise when they deserve it; they must never be criticised or blamed without explanation and understanding. Indeed, explanation and understanding are imperative in all things in industry.' In other words, man was not exclusively economic-man, strong though the self-interest. To reach the good in people, however, management must 'engender their self-respect'.[43]

Jock would often remind his managers that everybody mattered. He told me that he respected the smallest worker because he had a 'total feeling of inferiority', presented with the peculiarities of each job and the practised competence of each worker, whatever his rank: 'I knew I couldn't do a single estate manager's job; I knew I couldn't do an advertising man's job; I knew I couldn't do a salesman job. I had the greatest respect for other people.' He was gifted, also, with abundant tolerance. One had to take people as one found them, 'build on their virtues and bypass their shortcomings'. He said that he was 'genuinely interested' in what work other people did and wanted to know how they did it, what problems, what joys they had. On his annual visits to the estates, he spoke to everybody, in field and factory. He said he was enthralled by the myriad tasks, the bewildering coordination of effort that went into making a spoon of sugar. In his notion of good leadership, the primacy of good manners, especially to workers (one could be rude to equals), learnt from his family, was a special ingredient:

> [A]part from being sensitive and intelligent and quick on the feet, and knowing what you want to achieve and knowing what you think, of being able to express what you think, I think the important thing is respect for other people. I mean never think what does the worker think of me; think of what he thinks I think of him. I mean so many people show off and say that he will think well of me; the important thing is what you think I think of you.... I was genuinely interested in what they did and how they did it. I really wanted to know. I genuinely respected them.[44]

This was the way of engendering the worker's self-belief: good material benefits; the chemistry between manager and himself which makes the smallest worker think that he or she is important. In my many interviews with Booker workers who met Campbell on one or more of his annual visits, a constant recollection was that he made them feel that they mattered: he knew how to listen, however brief the encounter. He could ask them simple questions which suggested that he cared; they felt that he had genuine interest in their work, however small in the bigger scheme — an extraordinary gift.

In early 1959, on the Third Programme of the BBC, Jock Campbell challenged Professor Theodore Levitt's thesis that 'the business of business is making money', and that welfare was not its business.[45] He was contemptuous of this formulation, arguing that there was no inherent conflict of interest between an enterprise seeking 'profits, efficiency and production' and a community seeking 'truth, beauty and goodness'. Indeed, business could not afford to be oblivious of 'human relationships and social responsibilities'. He explained the social obligation of business in the context of his four-fold responsibility:

> I believe that industries and business are groups of people combined together to produce wealth, provide services and distribute goods; that in so doing they generate employment, that their managers must recognise, balance, and efficiently fulfil responsibilities to shareholders, fellow-employees [staff and labour], customers and the community.[46]

Campbell was not against profits. An unprofitable concern was a fraud on the community; it would soon collapse, unable to honour its four-fold responsibility. A business was in business to make profits, but that could not be the monopoly of shareholders only. He explained that shareholders had a right to a reasonable return on their investments and should rise 'in their wrath' if they were not so remunerated. Equally, employees [labour] or customers or the community were 'entitled to rise in *their* wrath to protect *their* interests', if these were perceived to be vitiated.

Having achieved, by 1959, after a decade of social reform in British Guiana, discernible success in many fields, Campbell could, with confidence, expound the theory behind the practice. He spoke now of his 'practical idealism', his reformist capitalism, rooted in what J.D. Bernal called 'a really constructive purpose into which we can now throw the whole of our energies and intelligences'. In fostering a modus vivendi with Cheddi Jagan he was, until Cold War politics enveloped the colony between 1962 and 1964, endeavouring, in practice and in theory, to promote his 'practical idealism' as an instrument to reshape the place that he loved to his last days:

> [M]en and women grouped together in industry, within a free capitalist socicty, to produce wealth, to provide services, to distribute goods; men and women generating employment; men and women recognising and being encouraged to recognise responsibility to each other whether as citizens, customers, employees, or shareholders. Idealism, you may say. But if it is, it is practical idealism. What our free world desperately needs is a sense of human purpose which transcends the awe-inspiring material achievement of modern technology and big business. And individual men and women need inspiration beyond personal material gain. Being bent on merely making money and thinking that the only good is what pays are hopelessly uninspiring and really dreadfully unattractive.[47]

He felt he had a 'great cause' in British Guiana, however piecemeal or seemingly tendentious his philosophy in this environmentally daunting, volatile political environment. But he saw his cause as a radical endeavour, and he was contemptuous of conservatism and the Conservative Party in Britain. In October 1964 — in spite of the Guyanese debacle — he was still proud to reassert his radical promptings:

> [M]y personal background of the West Indian sugar industry and trading in Africa has taught me that the vast majority of people have not got money, privilege, position and power. Most of the population of the world, and indeed of the Commonwealth, are poor, hungry, insecure and underprivileged. And my experience as a businessman has shown me that the benefits to everybody immeasurably outweigh the disadvantages to a few, of striving to raise general standards and conditions of living.... I am a radical (or at any rate I hope I am). What do I mean by a radical? It is partly, I suppose, a matter of temperament, a desire to get down to root causes, an inclination to be sceptical about the conventional wisdom which traditionalists take for granted

.... I believe that most progress, and nearly all reforms, come from radicals. If government was left only to Conservatives we would still be in the Middle Ages.[48]

Endnotes

1. Jock Campbell, 'The Development and Organisation of Booker', Paper delivered at the London School of Economics on Problems in Industrial Administration, November 24, 1959, (mimeo.), p. 6.
2. 'Report of Sir Jock Campbell's Speech to the Cocoa, Chocolate and Confectionery Alliance', *Cocoa, Chocolate and Confectionery Alliance Journal*, (July 10, 1958): 2.
3. Jock Campbell, interview by the author, Nettlebed, Oxfordshire, February 17, 1994, Tapes 8&9.
4. Jock Campbell, 'Opportunity and Investment in the West Indies', *West Indian Review*, (June 6, 1958): 3.
5. Ibid., 2.
6. Jock Campbell, interview by the author, Nettlebed, Oxfordshire, February 18, 1994, Tape 12.
7. Ibid.
8. Jock Campbell, 'Norman Manley', Obituary, October 1969 (mimeo.).
9. Jock Campbell, 'Address to the Education Conference at Missenden Abbey, Bucks.', October 4, 1968, p. 1. [This was published in *International Development Review*, (December 1968).]
10. The Chairman's Statement, 1948, p. 16.
11. Ibid., p. 17.
12. *Booker Sugar* (Supplement to the Accounts of Booker Brothers, McConnell, Co., Ltd., 1954), Jock Campbell to Booker (B.G.), June 26, 1947, p. 90.
13. Ibid., The Chairman's Statement, 1948, p.90.
14. Ibid., F.J. Seaford to Follett-Smith, July 11, 1949, p. 90.
15. Ibid., Jock Campbell to Follett-Smith, July 21, 1949, p. 91.
16. Ibid., Jock Campbell to N.P. Sherlock, January 31, 1950.
17. Ibid., Minutes of a Meeting of the Administrative Managers [with Jock Campbell], March 9, 1953, pp. 92-3.
18. Ibid., Minutes of a Meeting of Booker Brothers, McConnell and Co, Ltd, September 8, 1953, p. 91.
19. Ibid., Jock Campbell to Follett-Smith, December 2, 1953, p. 93.
20. Ibid.
21. The Chairman's Statement, 1953, p. 26.
22. See note 12, Jock Campbell to Follett-Smith, April 16, 1954.
23. Ibid., 4.
24. Jock Campbell, interview by the author, Nettlebed, Oxfordshire, July 23, 1992.
25. Ibid.

26. Ibid.
27. See note 12, Jock Campbell to Follett-Smith, May 18, 1954, p. 94.
28. Jock Campbell, 'British Capital in the Changing Conditions of the Colonies', Speech delivered at Cambridge University, July 12, 1954, (mimeo.), p. 6.
29. Ibid., 9-10.
30. Ibid., 10.
31. *West India Committee Circular*, October 1954.
32. The Chairman's Statement, 1955, pp. 36-7.
33. *The Daily Argosy*, February 5, 1955.
34. Ibid., February 6, 1955.
35. 'Script of a Broadcast Talk Given by Mr. J.M. Campbell over Radio Demerara on 4 March 1956', in Booker Brothers, McConnell and Co, Ltd, *Report of the Directors and Statement of Accounts, 1955*, p.[2].
36. Ibid., [3].
37. Ibid., [4].
38. Brian Scott, 'The Organisational Network: A Strategy Perspective for Development', PhD thesis, Harvard University, 1979, pp. 107-8.
39. The Chairman's Statement, 1956, p. 40.
40. Ibid., 44.
41. Jock Campbell, 'Why Does Man Work?', Address to the Duke of Edinburgh Study Conference, Oxford, July 11, 1956, (mimeo.), p. 5.
42. Ibid.
43. Ibid., 6.
44. Jock Campbell, interview by the author, Nettlebed, Oxfordshire, February 17, 1994, Tape 9.
45. See Theodore Levitt, 'In Defence of American Capitalism', *The Listener*, November 27, 1958, pp. 859-60, 901.
46. Jock Campbell, 'The Responsibilities of Big Business', *The Listener*, January 8, 1959, p. 48.
47. Ibid., 71.
48. Sir Jock Campbell, 'Why I am Voting Labour: Greater Good for the Greater Number', *The Observer*, October 4, 1964.

Chapter Twenty

THE COMMONWEALTH SUGAR AGREEMENT (1951) AND BRITISH GUIANA: THE FOUNDATION FOR CAMPBELL'S REFORMS

*Its strength stemmed from the fact that it provided both the producer
and the consumer with a fair and stable price over a long term.*

John Southgate (1984)

Between 1949 and 1951 Jock Campbell was the chief negotiator with
the British Ministry of Food, on behalf of the Commonwealth sugar
exporters. His task was to secure a guaranteed price for 'efficient'
sugar producers, as well as quotas to provide producers protection
for a reasonable portion of their output. The Commonwealth Sugar
Agreement (CSA), which was signed on December 21, 1951,
established this essential cushion, thus ensuring a degree of security
necessary for long-term planning in the sugar industry. The CSA was
the foundation for the reform of Booker and the programme of social
reform initiated by Campbell; without it the reforms recommended
by the Venn Commission would have remained largely imaginary.
The reform of the structure of the sugar market was vital to the reform
of Booker and Campbell's role in achieving this was a towering one.
The energy he put into these negotiations was driven not only by the
financial imperatives of the sugar business but also by the 'cause' of
social reform.[1]

The abysmal prices of the 1930s meant that even if the will for
change had existed, it could not have been executed because of the
paucity of means. In 1934 and 1935, when Jock first went out to
British Guiana, the export price of sugar was a paltry £8.95 and £8.25

per ton respectively. In 1936 it was £8.10 per ton, while in 1938–39, when the Moyne Commission visited the region following widespread riots fed by dire living conditions, the price was still only £9.55 per ton. The contrast with the 1920s was eloquent: prices fluctuated between £14 and £15, with peaks of £50 and £25.65 per ton in 1920 and 1923 respectively. During the Second World War sugar prices remained stable at around £11-£12, but after that, for the rest of the 1940s, prices rose steadily, from £15.20 in 1945 to £25 per ton in 1948–49.[2] This, however, did not allay the anxieties of producers, bred on a pattern of volatile prices and the absence of any mechanism of price stabilisation. Writing in 1966, in the context of the entrenched security provided by the CSA, Ian McDonald dramatised what price instability had meant for the sugar industry:

> The rapid expansion of production, and all the benefits that flow from it, naturally could not have been sustained if worthwhile marketing arrangements had not been developed over the years. In the history of sugar no problem has been more consistently intractable than that of securing an adequate outlet for production at a stable and remunerative price. The stagnation, low living standards, and deterioration of assets which were the fate of the industry for long periods in its colonial past are a terrible reminder of what would happen if a time came again when the problem could not be solved. The ultimate disaster of depressed markets is well illustrated by the fact that there was a time in the 1930s when sufficient 'world market' raw sugar to keep one person in the UK on a luxury consumption level for five years was worth the price of a cricket ball![3]

This was what had provided the impetus after the War, to do something to foster a degree of stability. It was Campbell's friend at the Colonial Office, the economist, Sydney Caine, who had first devised a strategy to alleviate the hazards of another rainy day in the sugar industry. With good prices ruling after the War, he recommended, in 1947, the creation of three distinct funds from the surplus available, in order to initiate reform in the industry: a Price Stabilisation Fund (to cushion the vagaries of price fluctuation); a Rehabilitation Fund (to facilitate modernisation of capital assets);

and a Sugar Industry Labour Welfare Fund (to sustain social reform on the plantations).[4] These funds were legislated for in British Guiana by Ordnance No.20 of 1947: $13.20 were deducted per ton of sugar exported and allocated thus — $6.00 for price stabilisation; $4.80 for rehabilitation; and $2.40 for social welfare.[5]

Campbell understood immediately the implications of the better prices of the late 1940s. He argued that it was necessary to reduce production costs as much as possible, for to assume that prices would somehow be indexed to escalating costs, was 'a most unrealistic and dangerous attitude'. It was, therefore, imperative to increase production and productivity. Modernisation in field and factory, utilisation of the best technology, was inescapable, if they were to survive as efficient producers of sugar. In 1947 Campbell cautioned that maturity was required to enable them to balance the necessity for competitiveness with their obligations to their workers' welfare:

> [I]n the case of Colonial industries the real need to improve the living standards of the people introduces an element of inflexibility in costs of production of which wages represent over half and the provision of better amenities for workers a further material proportion. At the same time all who are sincerely concerned with the welfare of the people of British Guiana must reflect upon the fact that wages cannot increase *ad infinitum*; that a cost of production higher than the value of sugar will bring disaster not only to the Company but to all who work on the sugar estates and indeed to almost anyone who earns a livelihood in the colony.[6]

After the War, however, an atmosphere of sympathy towards the sugar industry and recognition of the need to right ancient wrongs against plantation workers in the West Indies prevailed at the highest level of the Imperial government. As noted earlier, the Moyne Commission (1940/1945) and the Venn Commission (1949) had advocated some form of imperial support for this crucial industry in the West Indies. Indeed, it was because of the Interim Report of the former, in 1940, that the Colonial Development and Welfare Act was passed, providing for the allocation of grants from the Imperial Treasury to the British West Indies. Between April 1941 and June

1956 British Guiana was to receive £928,139 (£16 per capita), for a range of programmes, including rural and urban housing, drainage and irrigation, the expansion of rice cultivation, health centres, schools, geological survey, and so forth.[7] The Venn Commission, in 1949, had submitted that if the British government were really interested in reform then they had to provide some form of subsidy to the sugar industry:

> [T]here is only one possible method by which the prices of the Colony's sugar can be raised, and that is by the granting, temporarily, of a subsidy or bonus, either directly or indirectly, from the Imperial Government. [W]e do not hesitate to make a strong recommendation to the effect that a subsidy or bonus, of £1 ($4.80), be granted upon each ton of sugar raised in British Guiana. During the next critical years such assistance would form the only means of meeting the cost of introducing the social improvements we have advocated.[8]

This was the context in which the CSA was negotiated. In 1950–51 Jock Campbell's astute leadership was requisitioned by the Commonwealth Sugar Exporters Association — he was its chairman from 1950 to 1983 — to negotiate a long-term contract with the Ministry of Food. It should be noted that before and during the War, Britain had had to expend scare dollars to procure some of its sugar; it was the contention of many in the ministry that Commonwealth producers must therefore be supported, in order to obviate dollar expenditure on this commodity in future. The problem, though, was that unanimity on any matter was unattainable, a common agenda inconceivable, amongst the claims and counter-claims of this diverse group of sugar exporters: Australia, the British West Indies, Fiji, Mauritius and South Africa. It took the genius of Campbell as a leader to contrive a situation that enabled them to formulate a common position to the ministry.

Campbell and John Southgate, a brilliant sugar economist, were able to get the producers to leave the negotiations solely in their hands because, as Jock often pointed out, if they had all turned up at the Ministry, it would have degenerated into a Babel of irreconcilable positions. He quickly realised that the two fundamental issues for negotiation were: (i) the allocation of quotas to the respective producers; (ii) a formula for constructing a fair price to reasonably efficient producers, and the determining of a sliding scale to be adjusted annually. It was in his modus operandi, however, his skill in shaping and articulating a coherent position out of the disparate, potentially conflicting, stances of his colleagues, on prices, quotas, production costs, and so forth, that the man's intellectual stature shone.[9]

He told me that he would secure the highest common denominator from the sugar producers, which he would then take to the Ministry of Food. He knew his way around Whitehall, having gained invaluable experience through Sydney Caine at the Colonial Office, during the War. He would deliberately inflate his side's demands to the ministry, asserting that that was the minimum they would agree to. The ministry would usually arrive at a position below what Jock had contrived but higher than what he had agreed with his colleagues. He would return to the producers and misrepresent what he had received from the ministry, citing an offer below their demand. They would probably hold out, not aware that Jock had actually got more than they had asked for. He would resubmit to the ministry that the producers were not prepared to accept their offer, at which point they would give a little more, but still below his contrived original demand. The upshot was that he got substantially more for the sugar producers than he was delegated to seek. By so doing he kept them very satisfied while retaining his freedom to manoeuvre. As Campbell recalled: 'The Ministry always used to say to me that if it hadn't been for me they would have driven a coach and horses through the Agreement'.[10] John Southgate, Campbell's astute technical adviser and confidant throughout the CSA negotiations, has extolled Campbell's extraordinary gifts:

Differences between the exporters would leave the Ministry free to pick them off one by one and to get what it wanted out of the agreement while making only minimal concessions. Jock Campbell had been chosen by the exporters as their spokesman. He was to be elected annually as their chairman throughout the duration of the Agreement [1975; in fact until 1983].... He had been converted to socialism by his experience of working on his family's estates in British Guiana. He had inherited privilege, Eton and Oxford and a wall full of Raeburns; he loved fast cars, ball games and good conversation; he was energetic, ambitious and sometimes selfish; and he possessed an art of talking as an equal with men of all kinds and an ability to get his own way by cajolery, persuasion or authority. But he also had what most aristocratic reformers lack: a very clear sense of where he wanted to go, an eye for seeing which ways in that direction could be opened and which could not, an instinct for friendship and a whole-hearted devotion to the cause he had adopted.[11]

As the preamble to the CSA states, it constituted a long-term agreement to supply sugar to the UK, conducive to the development of an efficient sugar industry in the Commonwealth and for 'the orderly marketing' of that sugar. The pro-planter newspaper in British Guiana, *The Guiana Sunday Graphic*, had underlined the centrality of the CSA to development planning in the sugar industry: '[I]t is obvious that a long-term contract is necessary if ... long-term planning and the heavy expenditure it will entail are to be embarked upon. The sugar producing colonies regard as *vital* long-term stability of markets and a system of purchase that will guarantee that the price for their sugar bears some reasonable relationship to the cost of efficient production under local conditions.'[12]

Under the CSA the producers were to limit their exports internationally to 2,375,000 tons in any calendar year, the quota of the British West Indies being the highest, 900,000 tons. The Agreement was to be operative from January 1, 1950 to December 31, 1959. Under this negotiated price, the quota of the British West Indies was set at 640,000 tons, out of a total Commonwealth quota of 1,568,000 tons.[13] The UK government would purchase this stipulated amount each year, 'at prices which shall be reasonably remunerative to efficient producers'.[14]

The prices were adjustable annually, with the price for 1950, £30 10s per ton, as the base for computing the necessary price changes. The latter would take into consideration increases in wages and goods and services, factors affecting cost of production from year to year.[15] The prices arrived at under the CSA for 1950, 1951 and 1952 were £30 10s, £32 17s 6d and £38 10s per ton respectively

— a significant increase from the £9 per ton average for the 1930s, substantially higher, too, than the £25 2s in 1948-49.[16] As Table I shows, although there was still some fluctuation in prices after the CSA, it is clear that stability had been achieved. Meanwhile, the default of one country in honouring its quota, could be taken up by another with a surplus.

Table I
Sugar Prices, 1947-66

Year	Price per Ton
1947	£21 9s
1948	£25 2s
1949	£25 9s
1950	£27 2s
1951	£31 5s
1952	£37 16s
1953	£37 10s
1954	£35 6s
1955	£34 14s
1956	£35 8s
1957	£43 12s
1958	£37 5s
1959	£37 14s
1960	£38 19s
1961	£37 17s
1962	£39 1s
1963	£54 12s
1964	£43 17s
1965	£38 16s
1966	£40 13s

Source: Dwarka Nath, *A History of Indians in Guyana* (London: self-published, 1970), 251.

Campbell spoke often of the transformation engendered by the guaranteed prices and reasonable quotas facilitated by the CSA — the 'orderliness' and security, as opposed to the anarchic price fluctuations under which primary producers had long laboured, for the benefit of the UK, at the expense of colonial peoples. This was no longer acceptable, he argued in 1953:

> [M]any parts of the Commonwealth whose economies largely depend upon primary production cannot support, let alone improve, the living standards of their ever-growing population unless they have remunerative outlets. In the past when the economies and living standards of Colonies and their peoples were of very secondary importance to the production of the commodities required by this country, the dynamic of primary production continued, in good times and bad .... [I]ndeed, *colonial living standards were the unfortunate buffer which enabled the generator of primary production to take risks and carry on from day to day.* [emphasis added][17]

Campbell explained that the changed circumstances demanded responsibility for the welfare of labour on the part of colonial companies. Guaranteed prices were crucial if they were to maintain 'civilised standards of living and employment'. He felt that the CSA, therefore, should be a model to assist other primary producers in the Commonwealth. He was very clear that they were not after 'feather-bedding for the inefficient or artificial protection' for uneconomic producers; they were seeking 'assurance of remunerative outlets' to be able to plan ahead, to meet their obligations as civilised corporate citizens. He never took things for granted, and was punctilious in reassuring the UK consumer and government that sugar producers and the West Indian colonies were not expecting hand-outs.[18]

The West India Committee, of which Campbell was vice-chairman in 1953, also extolled the merits of the CSA as an instrument for implementing reforms in British Guiana. In rejecting the perceived extremism of the deposed PPP government in October 1953 — purveyors of 'illusions of quick prosperity conjured up by malevolent men' — they advanced the case for gradualism, now that sugar had the means to contribute to a programme of comprehensive reform:

> It had been hoped that the exercise of responsible government by freely elected representatives of the people, and a drive to extend

and improve welfare arrangements, particularly in the realms of education and housing, supported by the managers of the sugar estates and other employers through their own welfare organisations, would have seen the dawn of a better day in a colony where ruinous prices for sugar over many years had, until recently, stood in the way of all progress.[19]

They concluded with a quote from Jock Campbell, a plea for the restoration of stability, so that the progress of the people of British Guiana would proceed 'uninterrupted', and Booker could 'play their vital part in the life and development' of the country. As noted earlier, the CSA became a reality in December 1951, with Campbell's leadership a crucial element in its shaping. In recognition of this, and sensitive to the Marxist character of Jagan's politics on and off the plantations, Booker made the 40 year old Jock Campbell its chairman in 1952. He had virtually been running the Company since Sir Alfred Sherlock died in 1945.

I have tried to locate the source of his gift for leadership. When I asked about this in connection with his negotiation of the CSA, he attributed it to the fact that 'I had sugar in my blood and I believed in the sugar industry'. As I have argued throughout, his family's roots in slavery and indentureship gave to his conception of reform the calling of a moral imperative. His financial independence, too, the freedom which the wealth from sugar gave him, emboldened him to challenge many sacred cows, as exemplified in the making of the CSA: 'This wasn't business or money; this was a burning political desire and I reasoned that the ends had justified the means. Secondly, I had no hostages to fortune because I was reasonably well-off. Anybody could have sacked me any time they wanted — I didn't have any constituents. They could have said "Get out", and I would have got out and gone. I didn't give a fuck. That put me in a very strong position.'[20]

Jock elaborated on his modus operandi, his skill at the art of 'gamesmanship'. He was a master at exerting his authority, a knack for getting his own way. He thought that his public school education, at Eton, taught him about authority; and he explained why he could get his own way:

[A]t a meeting I was good at bringing out what I wanted people to say and rather good at shutting up the people who said what I didn't want them to say.... On the whole I was able to win in an argument: I knew when to argue and when to pull back; I knew when to stop the discussion and to deal with people privately afterwards. I knew when to draw out the people I agreed with and how to frustrate the people I didn't agree with. I knew when to be sarcastic. I knew when to be charming. I was quick on my feet and quick-brained .... I wouldn't say it was a gift; it was nothing to do with my quality.... you see I always did have the advantage of not minding personally if I lost.[21]

In fact, he minded very much that he should never lose. As I will show later, he virtually kept out of the fight as Guyana became embroiled in the Cold War, and on the brink of a racial war in 1964. What he did have, though, when he knew he had a good chance of winning, was a certain fearlessness fed by his financial independence and his belief in his cause. This was what he had demonstrated to several Conservative MPs, at the House of Commons, in 1949: 'I was so appalled by how frivolous their attitude was to sugar and to the sugar countries that I stormed out and said I'm never fucking going to trust those people again.'[22]

The CSA was a potentially winning wicket; there, all his abundant gifts were harnessed for the benefit of sugar and the reforms to which he was committed:

I knew my way about Whitehall; I had worked for a short time in the Colonial Office [during the War].... I decided that I, with the assistance of John Southgate, who was very clever and would stop me from making mistakes, would do the negotiation with the Ministry. I said to the Ministry, at the top level, that we can't have negotiations if we all negotiated. We've all got different interests; you've got to let me try to get my people together....I got permission to do it and I don't think they would have found anybody who could do it in the same way, because they were all to some extent in fee to their own constituents, the people who paid them .... I wasn't in fee to anyone. I was also good at changing my mind, to say, 'No; I'm wrong', or start again if I found I couldn't get something ... this was what made the CSA possible.[23]

When exploring with him his gifts as a leader he would return to the security of his wealth: 'not enormous', but it could ensure his independence if he were fired. That, he said, insulated him from the energy-sapping pettiness of many, and the fear of taking chances which dependence and insecurity bred into most people. He said that for much of his younger years he was acutely conscious of his stammer. It was responsibility and having a cause, in British Guiana, which gave him the wings to experiment, to change old ways. He lost his stammer. Why was he better than others in working towards the Commonwealth Sugar Agreement? He paused for a long time: 'It's sort of difficult talking about this .... I do know ... it was partly confidence, partly intelligence, partly being quick-witted, partly enjoying the game, and partly having a certain amount, I suppose, of Irish charm.... It's awful to say this about one's self.'[24]

In 1992, in discussing the CSA, I asked Jock the following: 'How important was your own confidence, your belief in what you were doing?' He paused long again before he responded:

> I think it is all important. It's conviction that what you're doing is right. I'm not normally a conceited person but I really think that I can say that without me there would never have been a Commonwealth Sugar Agreement, because the sugar producers were all inclined to quarrel among themselves. The Ministry [of Food] didn't trust them but the Ministry absolutely trusted me.[25]

It was a measure of the esteem of Campbell among the disparate band of Commonwealth sugar producers that he remained chairman of the Commonwealth Sugar Exporters' Association between 1950 and 1983. In 1969-70, Patricia Jamieson was a young member of the team led by Jock, which was negotiating with the British government to secure safeguards for poor sugar-producing Commonwealth countries, on the eve of Britain's entry into the then EEC. She said that the retention of the level of protection of the CSA within the larger European framework, despite considerable opposition, was largely attributable to Jock's incomparable leadership. She was fascinated and inspired by his gifts:

After a few short meetings with Jock .... listening to him in awe, one could see that he was a leader. He could identify the key issues and was capable of taking clear views and decisions. You were dealing with a very difficult problem: a diverse group of countries with very different approaches, so you had to get someone to drive this lot. It took determination and also the political feel. Jock always kept his ear very close to the ground, had a nose for the politics; he could see the way things were going. He could anticipate — proactive rather than reactive. He was well known and highly respected by civil servants and MPs on both sides of the House, not only his fellow socialists. With his sense of what had to be done to force the hand of the British Government, he actually got to the point where there was a sufficient body of opinion across both sides of the House that if the terms Britain had negotiated with the EEC were unacceptable to sugar producers in developing countries of the Commonwealth, then a majority of MPs would have voted against the European Community Bill. Now, that takes a lot of doing, winning the respect of a very broad base of MPs, from the very right to the very left ... Jock spoke with authority and commanded respect.[26]

Indeed, Jock had been preparing for this battle for many years. He was never complacent about the CSA and the role of British sugar consumers in sustaining it. In 1963, when the world market price had risen precipitously, he was quick to remind them of the benefits of the CSA. He noted that they were paying 9 pence less for a 2 lb bag of sugar, on current world prices inflated by an international shortage. He underlined the reciprocal benefits of the CSA:

There is no shortage of sugar in the UK because the Commonwealth Sugar Exporters are supplying, and will continue to supply, the bulk of this country's market requirements at fair, settled prices — irrespective of world price and supply position. The West Indies sugar industry as we know it today would not exist without the assured markets at stable prices provided by the CSA over the last 10 years; and they remain the foundation for its continued prosperity and expansion. Thus, if and when the world price again slumps below the CSA price, it will be well to remember that for a period the West Indies helped to protect Britain rather than the other way round.[27]

Endnotes

1. Jock Campbell, interview by the author, Nettlebed, Oxfordshire, February 17, 1994, Tape 8.
2. These prices are taken from Dwarka Nath, *A History of Indians in Guyana* (London: self-published, 1970 [1950]), 250-1.
3. Ian A. McDonald, *Sugar in B.G.: Challenge and Change*, (Georgetown: Booker, n.d., [1966]), [reprinted from *New World Fortnightly* (Georgetown), nos.10-13 (1965)], p. 9.
4. See note 1.
5. M. Shahabuddeen, *From Plantocracy to Nationalisation: A Profile of Sugar in Guyana* (Georgetown: University of Guyana, 1983), 120.
6. The Chairman's Statement, 1946-47, p. 14.
7. Michael Swan, *British Guiana: The Land of Six Peoples* (London: HMSO, 1957), 79, 211-5.
8. *Report of a Commission of Inquiry into the Sugar Industry in British Guiana* (J.A.Venn, chairman), Col. No. 249 (London: HMSO, 1949), 155, 157.
9. See note 1.
10. Ibid.
11. John Southgate, *The Commonwealth Sugar Agreement, 1951-74* (London: Czarnikov, 1984), 19.
12. *The Guiana Sunday Graphic*, April 23, 1951.
13. 'The Commonwealth Sugar Agreement [1951]', Chapter II, art. 2.
14. Ibid., Chapter V, art. 13.
15. Ibid., Chapter VI, art. 20.
16. Ibid., Chapter VI, art. 18.
17. Jock Campbell, 'Marketing of Primary Products: CSA as Model', *The Times*, January 1, 1953 [reprinted in *West India Committee Circular*, January 1953].
18. Ibid.
19. Leader, *West India Committee Circular*, October 1953.
20. See note 1.
21. Ibid.
22. Ibid.
23. Ibid.
24. Ibid.
25. Jock Campbell, interview by the author, Nettlebed, Oxfordshire, July 23, 1992, Tape 4.
26. Patricia Jamieson, interview by the author, London, August 1, 1991.
27. Sir Jock Campbell (letter), *The Times*, October 31, 1963.

Part 6

Sweetening 'Bitter Sugar' II: Modernising Booker, 1950–1951

Chapter Twenty-One

SHAPING THE NEW ORDER: CAMPBELL AND THE MODERNISING OF BOOKER, 1950–51

I have argued that even in the 1930s young Jock Campbell had a sense of authority rooted in his family's history in British Guiana's sugar industry; this made it possible for him to initiate change, small things, on their plantations. That had given him the courage to go beyond the mould. After 1939, when Curtis Campbell was absorbed by Booker, he recognised that the latter was 'in a total mess', and 'minded terribly about it'. The War, however, had clipped his adventurous fledgling wings: reforms had to await the peace.

By 1949 Campbell, still only 37, was very optimistic. As vice-chairman of Booker and president of the West India Committee, he was at the core of post-war initiatives to establish a framework for stable sugar prices and adequate quotas — to give security to sugar-producing colonies such as British Guiana. As noted above, the Moyne and Venn Commissions had endorsed this firmly, while the Imperial government, faced with a dollar crisis, were amenable to aiding Commonwealth producers. On August 10, 1949 the West India Committee, reflecting its president's buoyancy, expressed hopes for talks with His Majesty's Government:

> HMG assured the delegation [of sugar producers] that they recognise that the prosperity of the Sugar Industry is vital to the maintenance of an adequate standard of living in sugar-producing colonies such as the British West Indies. It is their intention to make long-term arrangements which will give to the efficient producers of sugar in these areas and elsewhere in the Commonwealth firm assurances of markets for agreed tonnages of sugar, at reasonably remunerative prices to be negotiated with the producers. It is the declared policy of HMG to

maintain and improve the economy of the Colonial territories and where, as in the British West Indies, sugar production is the main and indispensable basis of a healthy economy, this will be given special consideration in fixing the quantities of sugar to be covered by these arrangements.[1]

Campbell had observed that while this was 'essentially a declaration of principles', it was made 'in good faith'. An agreement on prices and quotas soon got endorsement, at the end of 1949, from the Venn Commission. Meanwhile, the urgency for Imperial support was underlined, in British Guiana, by the growing appeal of the Marxist, Cheddi Jagan, since 1947 the Member of the Legislative Council for Central Demerara, a key sugar-growing area.

Campbell, therefore, could grasp both the possibility and the necessity for renewal. He was determined that Booker be equipped to secure maximum benefit from a more stable market environment for sugar. He argued that the sugar industry was the social and economic foundation of British Guiana; its prosperity, therefore, was naturally tied to progress in the industry. He advanced the thesis, in 1949, that the success of sugar had to be grounded in three fundamental principles: (i) the efficiency of the industry; (ii) the price of its products; (iii) the 'human relationship' within the industry and the colony. At the base were stable prices: technical innovation and social reform could not be addressed seriously without this.[2]

When he became vice-chairman in 1947 he set himself the major undertaking of modernising Booker — a massive organisation with its fingers in very many pies in British Guiana. Its industrial practices, also, were tainted by its roots in slavery and indentureship: the phrase 'Booker's Guiana' spoke of the contempt most Guyanese had for Booker. Campbell thought its structure chaotic, and traced this to its haphazard, fortuitous growth going back to the days of slavery and indentureship. He said that in 1815 Josias Booker, from near Carnforth in Lancashire, turned up in British Guiana to have a try at growing sugar-cane. Three of his brothers soon joined him, two were to die very young. The survivor, George Booker, became Josias's partner in the firm of Booker Bros and Co, West India merchants. In 1832 George Booker founded the firm, George Booker and Co, in Liverpool.

It handled the shipping and supplies for Booker Bros, as Josias Booker developed as a planter in British Guiana.

John McConnell went to the colony as a clerk in 1846 and in the 1870s founded the firm, John McConnell and Co. He had worked as a partner of Booker Bros, from London, providing supplies as well as supervising the finances of his own firm and Booker Bros in British Guiana. His sons, A.J. McConnell and F.V. McConnell, entered the firm in 1889 and 1890 respectively. In 1900 the two firms merged, becoming Booker Bros, McConnell and Co, with A.J. McConnell as chairman, a post he held until 1920.[3]

By this time, after nearly a century in the colony, Booker had become a huge, cumbersome, somewhat incoherent company. Jock Campbell believed that its problems in the 1940s were rooted in its eclectic growth, its ineluctable propensity to absorb others, from its early days. It had become a juggernaut:

> I do not believe that at any time the management of Booker have consciously intended to develop to the extent that they have in British Guiana — like the much quoted Topsy, Bookers have 'just growed', largely by the process of pulling other peoples' chestnuts out of the fire. All Booker businesses in British Guiana have been vitally dependent on sugar. Shopkeeping grew through servicing the estates, and the life of our shipping has been the movement of sugar and rum along the coast of British Guiana and from the capital, Georgetown, to Liverpool. What happened in many cases was that Booker, starting as merchants and plantation owners, and backed by U.K. capital, would lend money to a neighbouring plantation in financial difficulties through low prices or other hazards, and would eventually have to take the property over as bad debt. Again they would start an 'estate supplies department'. Proving successful it would develop into a general hardware store with a wholesale branch; the wholesale branch would give credit to a small retailer who, in hard times, went broke — so Booker had another retail shop. So with timber, saw-milling, wharf owning — and my predecessors found themselves with a Booker Group in British Guiana.[4]

This process had continued through the chairmanship of A.J. McConnell, the inter-regnum of Thomas Greenwood and Samuel

Cameron, between 1920 and 1926, and the long reign of Sir Alfred Sherlock (1876–1946). The latter was born in the colony and remained chairman from 1927 to his death in February 1946. Campbell spoke often of the plantocracy's power to define, to shape colonial policies; this was evident in the career of Sherlock who, as managing director of Booker in British Guiana, served as a Member of the Court of Policy from 1911 to 1916 and as a member of the chief policy-making body, the Executive Council, from 1914 to 1926, when he took up the chairmanship of Booker in London.[5]

Even in the 1930s, during the Depression, Booker had continued to acquire more shops and sugar estates. As noted earlier, Jock's family had traded with the colony since the last quarter of the eighteenth century, having acquired slave plantations, as bad debts, in the 1780s, when what became British Guiana in 1831, was still the two Dutch colonies of Essequibo/Demerara and Berbice. Curtis Campbell and Co, therefore, predated Booker in the colony: they were the oldest firm surviving there — the source of Jock's peerless stature in the sugar business. Even Sherlock, that patriarch of the old order, had worked with Curtis Campbell, between 1900 and 1906, before joining Booker.[6] It was largely because of Jock's initiative, based on his experience in British Guiana in the latter half of the dismal 1930s, that Curtis Campbell was amalgamated with Booker in 1939.

Their subsidiary firm, Campbell Bros, Carter and Co, with stores in Rhodesia and Nyasaland, also came under Booker's variegated umbrella. Jock's father, C.A. Campbell (1874-1957), and his brother, Evan Campbell, became directors of Booker, as did Jock, in 1943. He became a managing director in 1945. When Sherlock died in February 1946 the chairmanship of Booker went to A.F.V. McConnell, nephew of the former chairman, A.J. McConnell, and son of his late brother, F.V. McConnell.[7] In fact, Jock Campbell, who became vice-chairman of Booker in 1947 at the age of 35, virtually had the chairmanship thrust upon him. During McConnell's tenure, 1946-51, Jock, though nine years younger than him, was making most of the crucial decisions in the firm. He said that McConnell did not have his heart in the business. This was an excellent apprenticeship for him; besides, between 1949 and 1951, he was deeply involved with the West India

Committee and the Commonwealth Sugar Exporters Association, in their deliberations with HMG towards the negotiation of the CSA. This had enhanced Jock's stature as a leader immeasurably, before he became chairman in 1952.[8]

Campbell knew that crucial though the CSA was, it was not the panacea of all of Booker's or the Guyanese people's ills. Booker had to be modernised if it were to take advantage of the CSA; and only a successful Booker could sustain a programme of social reform and begin to gain respect from Guyanese. It was a problem of image as well as its chaotic structure. Jock said that in the late 1940s, as he started to address these problems, he knew that 'Booker was detested by everybody'. Even in England, its reputation was unsavoury; people with left-wing views would not invest in the company. He said that it was difficult to promote change because a lot of the shares were still in the hands of big families, including his own through the Curtis Campbell take-over. New ideas went against the grain of the old plantocracy.[9] Besides, Booker was a very inefficient outfit, with its eclectic agglomeration of assets: 'It had become unmanageable.' Campbell recalled why a radical reorganisation in Booker had become an imperative, by the end of the 1940s:

> [It was] a shapeless, incoherent conglomeration of variegated activities in British Guiana and the West Indies, Central Africa and the UK. In particular, in British Guiana, one management group was responsible for sugar growing and milling; shopkeeping — wholesale and retail — from provision to motor cars; shipowning, stevedoring and wharfingering; balata bleeding; drug manufacture; printing, owning a hotel and a newspaper [*Guiana Graphic*]; and a host of minor activities connected with gold, diamonds, charcoal, hides, fish glue — with almost every conceivable product in British Guiana. It was almost impossible to make out who and what made a profit or loss, who or what were efficient or inefficient. Hardly anybody was efficient, happy or satisfied. Nearly everybody was frustrated.[10]

Campbell said that the attitude of management was 'geared to the past'. Antony Haynes, one of the young reformers who worked with Jock from the early 1950s, recalls Booker as a 'reactionary company': many of the old hands were afraid of change, but Campbell was adamant that Booker had to adapt, modernise, assume its social responsibilities or disappear. With Jock, the passion was grounded in history: 'I felt perhaps as the sixth generation of my family connected with sugar in British Guiana — a heavy sense of debt unpaid; a compelling need to do something about the situation — to do what could be done to improve the health, wealth and happiness of the people of British Guiana.'[11] No one else in Booker had this consuming prompting or the authority, but without the security of the CSA very little could have been attempted.

Campbell stated that, initially, he made the monumental old mistake of trying to find a 'superman', who would take on all the problems of their diverse companies in British Guiana and solve them. He certainly could not do it himself. The task was beyond human capacity; the structure of the Company had to be changed. They settled for the notion of functional organisations — that 'the advantages of management specialisation in a particular trading activity are greater than specialisation on a geographical or other basis ... [that] there is greater difference between running a shop and a sugar estate than between a shop in British Guiana and one in Nyasaland'. Consequently, from January 1, 1951, Booker's holdings were subdivided into four main divisions — sugar, rum, shopkeeping, shipping — with 50 companies of varying sizes.[12] Each company had a clearly-defined activity, under its own chairman as head of its board. Out of a cumbersome, amorphous Booker, with responsibility so diluted that inefficiency and inertia were a natural adjunct, people could now work in smaller units, with a clearer sense of their goals and individual responsibility, and a healthier environment for accountability and reward. In early 1952 Campbell acknowledged that the financial results had not shown appreciable change, but he identified progress in crucial areas: 'The dynamic and efficiency of management has improved out of all recognition.... The standard and quality of our premises, stocks, salesmanship and display are now second to none in the British West Indies.'[13]And as Jock explained in 1959, eight years after the reorganisation:

A separate company concerned with a particular function derives advantages from the principle of specialisation, and it also has

advantages of personal co-operation and morale which are so
often associated with people working in relatively small groups.
The most important result is that authority and responsibility
are inextricably part of and coincidental with the corporate
structure.[14]

Booker had devised a pyramidal framework with defined goals
for each company, clear structures of responsibility and
accountability, and financial operational plans (fop's), with detailed
accounting procedures to ascertain profits within each discrete
company. However, these were not independent public companies:
the Booker Board in London was still ultimately responsible for all
companies in the four main divisions.

In the management structure, below the Booker Board, came
what later became the Boards of Principal Parent Companies, of which
there were originally four; but by the late 1950s, with hedge-building
away from Guyana quite advanced, there were six — sugar, rum,
shopkeeping, shipping, light industries and engineering, the latter
two reflecting growing investment in the UK. These two boards, the
Booker Board and the boards of the six Principal Parent Companies,
constituted the Group Parent Board. There were also the divisional
boards, reflecting the trading specialisation of the various operating
companies in British Guiana, Africa, UK and, later, Canada.

In terms of responsibility the Group Parent Board retained
exclusive control in certain crucial areas — appointments and
emoluments to directors of subsidiary companies; the sale and
purchase of assets; borrowing; the objectives of the business and its
ethos. Indeed, substantial power still remained with the centre. The
responsibilities of the local boards, on the other hand, were outlined
by Campbell thus: 'The day-to-day business decisions required by
each operating company are firmly and solely a matter for the
management of each company. They are wholly responsible for its
success or failure within the broad framework of finance, policy and
ethos laid down by the Board of Booker.'[15]

To ensure that decentralisation did not result in a 'lack of co-
ordination in policies and purposes', Booker Group Committees were
appointed in the various countries of operation. For instance, in
British Guiana, the terms of reference of the B.G. Group Committee

were 'to be responsible for co-ordination and consultation between the Booker Group of Companies in British Guiana'; and, in keeping with Campbell's four-fold responsibilities, 'to be responsible for ensuring that the long-term ethos and policy of the Group is known, understood and applied by the Booker Group of Companies in British Guiana; in particular that the Group's responsibilities to shareholders, employees, customers and the community are properly fulfilled and balanced'.[16]

Booker's principal enterprise in British Guiana, sugar plantations, was administered by the divisional trading company, Booker Sugar Estates Ltd (BSE), under the chairmanship of R.R. Follett-Smith, between 1951 and 1961. These were Booker Demerara Sugar Estates Ltd, West Bank Estates Ltd, Demerara Foundry Ltd, and Mahaicony Coconut Estates Ltd. The parent board in London responsible for BSE was the London Advisory Committee, chaired by Follett-Smith's predecessor in the colony, F.J. Seaford (now Sir Frederick); Campbell also sat on it.[17]

Shopkeeping in British Guiana was administered by the divisional board, Booker Stores Ltd, chaired by Sir Frederick's brother, H.G. Seaford. It included Curtis Campbell Ltd, British Caribbean Agencies Ltd and Booker Amalgamated Groceries Ltd. The parent board was Campbell Booker Carter Ltd, which covered its UK and African shopkeeping holdings as well. It was chaired by Jock Campbell.[18]

Rum came under Booker Rum Co Ltd and was chaired by Follett-Smith. Its parent company in London was United Rum Merchants Ltd. Shipping in British Guiana was managed by Booker Shipping Transport and Wharves Ltd, chaired by H.G. Seaford. Its parent company, on which Campbell sat, was Booker Bros (Liverpool) Ltd. A miscellaneous collection of companies in British Guiana came under a fifth divisional company, Booker Properties Holdings and Services Ltd. Among these were B.G. Lithographic Co, Ltd, Booker Manufacturing Drug Co, R.D. Balata Co, Ltd and Petroleum Marketing Agencies Ltd. Like sugar, these came under the parent company, London Advisory Committee.[19] It is noteworthy that Jock Campbell was totally in control of the decision-making process — his finger in every pie — certainly up to his nervous breakdown in the summer of 1960.

In 1950, on the eve of the reorganisation of Booker, 41 per cent of its capital was invested in sugar (and 9 per cent in rum), 27 per cent in shopkeeping, 13 per cent in shipping and 10 per cent in properties and miscellaneous enterprises. In the same year 24 per cent of Booker's income was earned from sugar, 35 per cent from stores, 11 per cent from shipping, 14 per cent from rum and 14 per cent from properties and miscellaneous investments. While 60 per cent of its investments were in the West Indies (primarily British Guiana), 46 per cent of its income originated there; from its assets in Central Africa (Rhodesia and Nyasaland), 14 per cent of its investments, came 18 per cent of its earnings; and the UK, with 26 per cent of its assets, yielded 36 per cent of its income. The latter was already becoming a significant area of investment, of hedge-building.[20]

In 1950 wages and salaries had absorbed £1,950,000; taxes took £405,994 and dividends to shareholders £123,097. In that year, after raw materials, supplies and general expenses (working capital) had been paid for, £376,577 were expended on depreciation and replacement reserves, while £311,817 were ploughed back to cover rising costs of operation.[21]

Nearly ten years later, in 1959, Jock Campbell could report positively on the reorganisation scheme, which had created an energised workforce, as people worked in smaller groupings, towards set goals. They could see their place in the scheme of things; he detected a growing sense of belonging:

> The reorganisation ... has worked wonders. Its success, I am sure, is essentially due to enabling men and women, who were previously floundering in a fog of futility and frustration, to understand and to identify themselves clearly with the purposes and results of the business in which they work; and due to their new-found awareness of their dependence on each other — management and workpeople alike.[22]

But, as Campbell told me, it was not all plain sailing: he encountered much resistance to his reforms from the Booker people in British Guiana, in the early years, although he did succeed in winning most over to his perspective:

I think they thought I was a misguided socialist, rather naïve, and I had great difficulty with many of our reforms .... I think they thought I was partly lunatic, partly spoilt, partly I didn't realise what the difficulties were, and that I was threatening their lives and their authority.... In those days there was a formal set-up in Guyana: I mean the Government House set, the whites; 'coolies' and blacks didn't go there and you no more appointed a black man to be director of something or manager.... I was making this all topsy-turvy, and it must have been bloody for them. Here was a young man with no hostages to fortune coming originally from one of the smaller companies, Curtis Campbell, who was really turning the whole thing upside down .... I mean, their wives and their children and the lives they had known in Guyana — their prejudices and their values — were all being upset. I remember the criticism I had at every level ... [but] I was astonished at the way I successfully fought off the challenges.... On the whole, though, I had quite good relations with them (I was aware they thought I was a crackpot and a bit eccentric), but they played along with me.... Yes, I was always confident that what I was doing was the right thing.[23]

No other person in the sugar industry in British Guiana could have demonstrated such resilience and commitment to reform, great though the political momentum for change in the colony in the early 1950s.

Endnotes

1. The Chairman's Statement, 1948, p. 17.
2. Ibid., 16.
3. *Pepperpot* 2, no. 5, (August 1948): ii-vi.
4. Jock Campbell, 'The Development and Organisation of Booker', Paper delivered at LSE, November 24, 1959, p. 4.
5. *Pepperpot* 1, no. 1, (December 1946): 10-11.
6. See note 3, [p. iii].
7. Ibid., [v-vi].
8. Jock Campbell, interview by the author, Nettlebed, Oxfordshire, May 9, 1990, Tape 1.
9. Ibid.
10. See note 4 [p. 5].

11. Ibid., p. 6.

12. The Chairman's Statement, 1951, p. 21.

13. See note 4 [pp. 7-8].

14. Ibid., [8].

15. Ibid.

16. Ibid., [9].

17. Booker Brothers, McConnell and Co, Ltd, *Supplement to the Report of the Directors and Statement of Accounts, 1950*, p. 7.

18. Ibid., 11.

19. Ibid., 13-5.

20. Ibid., 16-9.

21. Ibid., 20-1.

22. See note 4 [p. 9].

23. Jock Campbell, interview by the author, Nettlebed, Oxfordshire, February 17, 1994, Tape 8.

Chapter Twenty-Two

BECOMING AN EFFICIENT SUGAR PRODUCER: MECHANISATION IN FIELD AND FACTORY

In 1952, the first year of Campbell's chairmanship, he underlined that Booker 'is not merely a business — it is a cause'. He then warned that while the CSA brought a great measure of security to the sugar industry, it carried compelling requirements for the 'utmost efficiency'. He elaborated on the responsibility this entailed:

> [I]t has been rightly called a Charter for Commonwealth Sugar ... it carries assurance, for eight years ahead, of 'reasonably remunerative' prices for about two-thirds of our planned production of sugar.... [T]he agreed method for determining each year this 'reasonably remunerative' price is far from being a cost-plus method conducive to inefficiency. It will not protect the high cost producer. On the contrary — it will by its very nature impose the need for the utmost efficiency and will only establish prices sufficient to stimulate the flow of sterling sugar which this country [UK] so urgently needs. Now that by this Agreement the fears and anxieties which have in the past inhibited full production have been swept aside, our objective is to produce the greatest tonnage of sugar from the smallest acreage in the shortest time at the lowest cost. Only by reaching this objective can the future prosperity of the sugar industry of British Guiana, and thus of the Colony, be assured.[1]

The consequences of the CSA — Campbell's reorganisation and modernisation of Booker and his social reforms — were impressive. It is one of the few areas of brightness in the dark reign of 'bitter sugar' in the West Indies. In 1949, on the eve of the CSA, British Guiana produced 174,227 tons of sugar; in 1960, at the height of Campbell's chairmanship, production reached a record 334,441 tons, a rise of 92 per cent. This was obtained from an increase in acreage of only 43 per cent. Ian McDonald explains this astounding achievement:

> The sugar companies in the late 1940s took the decision to aim at rapid expansion in the hope of obtaining more markets, specially anticipating the quotas to be assigned under the CSA which was then under discussion. This was a courageous decision since markets were weak and the future was uncertain. The safe and secure course would have been for the industry to draw in upon itself and not risk considerable financial outlays in respect of which the certainty of even a small return was dubious. Instead, a large-scale drive for increased production was undertaken with such vigour that between 1949 and 1960 the production of sugar in BG increased 92%. This represents a much higher rate of expansion achieved either in the West Indian territories or indeed in the world as a whole in this period.[2]

The output of sugar in 1960 exceeded the previous record, in 1958, by 28,080 tons, and the contribution of Booker Sugar Estates was 81.21 per cent. Much of this was attributable to Campbell's foresight. Being a principal architect of the CSA, he was sagacious in his explication of its intricacies and the minutiae of its provisions. In February 1956 he had advised sugar producers in British Guiana to increase production and productivity, in order to extract maximum benefit from the Agreement. Increased production, beyond the NPQ (Negotiated Price Quota), would enable them to take up the shortfalls of other Commonwealth producers, thus establishing their credentials as reliable and efficient producers, therefore, entirely deserving of a higher quota when the Agreement was renegotiated. Besides, a surplus in output would make them less vulnerable to any 'politically-inspired' strike: they would not be detracted from meeting their quota and honouring their four-fold responsibility.[3]

Earlier, in 1954, on a visit to British Guiana, he had emphasised the importance of efficient sugar production to the welfare of the people. He argued that 'an unprofitable business was an enemy of the state', whereas a profitable one was the obverse, 'generating wealth, employment and exports — and paying taxes, without which modern government could not exist'. Unlike Cheddi Jagan, he saw no conflict of interest between the welfare of colonial peoples and a successful, foreign-owned company, imbued with an enlightened conception of its responsibilities to its workers and the host community. He underlined Booker's role in the future of the Guyanese people:

> [He reportedly stated that] Booker might be regarded as a barometer showing a favourable or unfavourable climate for business and pointing the way to political investment....[H]e knew of no other country where capital and skills, and the good government necessary to foster them, were so essential as in British Guiana — owing to the artificial man-made environment, for the most part below sea-level, in which the main life of the colony existed. Great capital and skills have been required to bring the land into cultivation, great capital and skills were required to maintain it. In other parts of the world life could go on a happy-go-lucky basis with no external capital and no government, but in British Guiana without capital and good government there could be no life for the people.[4]

Efficiency, reliability as producers and distributors, responsible corporate behaviour, these were at the core of his mission in British Guiana. The production and productivity of Booker Sugar Estates (BSE), between 1950 and 1960 (see table II), indicate that he had accomplished much that he had envisaged.

In 1958, for instance, the local sugar target was set at 275,000 tons, with BSE responsible for 225,000 tons; they produced 230,168 tons. In 1960 the local target was revised upwards to 285,000 tons, with BSE allocated 245,000 tons; they produced 246,338 tons of sugar. As Table II shows productivity on BSE had also increased, from 3.04 tons per acre in 1950 to 3.50 tons per acre in 1960, nearly .5 ton per acre.[5] It is noteworthy, too, that largely because of Campbell's initiative, the sugar produced by small farmers had increased by nearly 60 per cent by the end of the 1950s: the Belle Vue Scheme on the West Bank Demerara, a principal supplier, was virtually subsidised by him.

This enviable record enabled British Guiana to meet its CSA quota, while partially meeting the shortfall of some Commonwealth exporters. As a result, as Campbell had advised, they succeeded in getting their NPQ progressively lifted, from 225,000 tons in 1955 to 249,000 tons in 1960 (see table III). It was on this basis that the minimum production target of sugar for 1960 was set at 300,000 tons, with BSE responsible for 250,000 tons, and Demerara Company, owners of two estates (Leonora and Diamond), allocated about 50,000 tons.

Table II
Sugar Production on Booker Sugar Estates (BSE), 1950–60

Year	Acres Reaped	Estates' Sugar [tons]	Farmers' Sugar [tons]	Yield [tons per acre]	Total Production of BG [tons]
1950	30,781	93,719	2,726	3.04	195,651
1951	30,768	102,112	2,958	3.32	217,306
1952	33,037	109,937	3,704	3.33	242,692
1953	34,494	117,058	3,862	3.39	240,176
1954	40,455	124,653	3,869	3.08	238,922
1955	46,714	159,124	7,190	3.41	250,111
1956	45,394	165,524	8,413	3.63	263,333
1957	51,092	187,156	9,031	3.66	284,973
1958	62,720	230,168	11,946	3.67	306,361
1959	63,280	209,165	13,316	3.28	284,425
1960	70,344	246,338	15,420	3.50	334,441

Sources: Chairman's Annual Report of BSE...1960; Ian McDonald, *Sugar in British Guiana: Challenge and Change*, (Georgetown: Booker, n.d., ca. 1966), 8-9

Table III
British Guiana's National Price Quota (NPQ), 1955–60 [tons]

1955	1956	1957	1958	1959	1960
225,000	233,259	233,259	238,765	239, 180	249,661
Allocated Shortfalls					
15,000	50,000	30,000	79,000	16,000	38,000
Quotas Wasted					
8,500	38,000	—	30,500	—	—
	+ 3,000			+ 11,000	+ 9,000

Source: 'Note on Production Policy and Quota Position', Appendix B, BSE Minutes, April 23, 1960.

Campbell was, as I have argued throughout, preoccupied with minimising the negative consequences of British Guiana's hydrological deficiencies. One ignored this dismal reality of coastal Guyana at one's peril. The CSA provided the means to augment the Sugar Industry Rehabilitation Fund (SIRF), to facilitate planning, maintenance and mechanisation to reduce unit costs of production. He would cite for me, over and over, almost verbatim, this quote from the Venn Report of 1949, to dramatise his intimate knowledge of this harsh land and the necessity to coax it into fecundity: '[E]very square mile of cane cultivation involves the provision of 49 miles of drainage canals and 16 miles of high level waterways. If the figures are raised to cover the whole area under cane, the sum total approaches 5,000 miles.' They noted that in 1947 the cost of maintaining this system was estimated at $1,350,000, or over $7 for each ton of sugar produced.[6] No wonder Campbell, in tracing Booker's antecedents, would continually caution Guyanese to be circumspect about utopian ideas, not to lose their heads, for they were not well endowed with natural resources:

> British Guiana, where the Group began, is part of that north-eastern shoulder of South America where Sir Walter Raleigh sought El Dorado, the Golden City, and lost his head for not finding it. Nobody has ever found a Golden City in British Guiana; but by patient, slogging work a narrow coastal strip has been won from intractable swamp and made to provide a sparse living for half a million people. Inhabited and productive British Guiana is an artificial man-made environment brought into existence by outside capital and outside technical skills. Only the Dutch would have started this continuing battle against water in which the sea must be kept out, and a hundred inches a year drained off.[7]

Through the SIRF a complex drainage and irrigation system, the lifeline to the sugar plantations, was revolutionised. Already, by 1954, most of the canals which were originally dug by hand, men using long-handle shovels, had been rehabilitated by draglines. Even so, as a Booker expert warned in that year, 'maintenance is an expensive item — trenches left to themselves rapidly silt up and become choked with lotus lily or water hyacinth — an attractive sight but not appreciated as such by the sugar planter'.[8] Apart from their role in drainage and irrigation, these canals were the only means by which the cane was transported from field to factory; they were high-level waterways on which the cane-punts were hauled. The impressive production and productivity of the Campbell years would have been unattainable without his meticulous approach to the colony's hydraulic system. Ian McDonald explained in 1966:

> An enormous amount has been done to improve drainage and irrigation. At a cost over the last 15 years [1950–65] of approximately $2,600,000, large new pumping stations have been established, modern pumping equipment installed, and old plant completely rehabilitated. The networks of canals for drainage and irrigation have been widened, deepened, extended and strengthened. Large areas that were once flooded for days after heavy rain are now cleared of all water within hours. Crops which would have died because of lack of water are now irrigated successfully until the rains fall again.[9]

Economies were realised with the introduction of tractors to transport the punts from field to factory. This enabled Booker to amalgamate some of its estates while closing derelict, uneconomic factories. Thus when, in 1955, the Port Mourant factory was dismantled, mechanised haulage facilitated quick transportation of its cane to the neighbouring factory at Albion. Thus also was the amalgamation of Ogle with LBI accomplished.[10] The replacement of mules by tractors, 'Farmalls', brought the punts much faster to the fields, seven or eight miles from the factory, shortening the time cane-cutters spent at work. The drinking-water tanks, also, could be replenished faster; workers could be taken 'aback' with despatch.

The use of Caterpillar tractors for ploughing, drain-digging in the fields, and the grading of dams facilitated a rapid expansion in acreage. This entailed the excavation of 1,140 miles of drainage/irrigation and transportation canals, and the digging of 27,500 miles of internal field drains![11] Without the Commonwealth Sugar Agreement this could not have been done; in any case, it would have been unnecessary.

Whereas most of the preparation of the cane-fields was formerly done by hand, by the early 1950s, ploughing, inter-row tillage and drain-digging were all performed with TD 18 Caterpillar tractors, while the digging of the main canals and side-line trenches was done with 'Priestman' or 'Rouston Bucyrus' draglines. Field preparation involved the following:

(i)   ploughing of the land by groups of disc or mouldboard ploughs drawn by crawler tractors (Caterpillar)

(ii)   digging of drains about eight feet apart with heavy ditching machines

(iii)   cambering of beds with bulldozers or graders

(iv)   reploughing to restore top soil tilth spoiled by cambering machine

(v)   the shattering of subsoil to a depth of 18 inches with cultivator tines

(vi)   completion of drain-digging

(vii)   forming rows with a tractor-drawn tool[12]

However, the planting, routine weeding, and reaping (cutting the cane and loading it into the iron punts) remained exclusively manual tasks. The complexity of the hydraulic system, the intricate pattern of drains, ditches and embankments, precluded the introduction of machinery for these tasks.

It is not surprising, then, that Campbell's discussion of British Guiana tended to start with a preamble on its hydrological hazards, or that the Venn Commission would preface their Report with an evocative quote on the same theme, from James Rodway's *History of British Guiana* (1891), or that the chairman of BSE, Follett-Smith, would appropriate it for his Introduction to *Booker Sugar* (1954). It speaks of the tenuous grip man has on this land and bears requoting:

The story of the colonies which now form British Guiana is one of plodding perseverance rather than conquest — every acre at present in cultivation has been the scene of a struggle with the sea in front and the flood behind. As a result of this arduous labour during two centuries, a narrow strip of land along the coast has been rescued from the mangrove swamp and kept under cultivation by an elaborate system of dams and dykes. Scattered along the rivers and creeks lie a thousand abandoned plantations, most of them indistinguishable from the surrounding forests: these represent the failures of the early settlers. At first sight the narrow line of sugar estates seems but a very poor show for such a long struggle with nature, but when all the circumstances are taken into consideration it is almost a wonder that the colony has not been abandoned altogether.[13]

As Jock would often remind Guyanese, the unforgiving land has not changed; if Booker were starting all over again, British Guiana would not be a prime contender for its capital. Only a draconian approach to drainage and irrigation and meticulous scrutiny in maintenance could sustain production. This entailed substantial overhead expenditure for the sugar industry; to remain competitive, therefore, efficiency was paramount; mechanisation and technical innovation were inescapable.

Under R.A. Wilkins, Director of Surveys (BSE), a major drainage and irrigation problem on three Berbice estates, on the Canje River (Rose Hall, Albion, Port Mourant), was resolved. The installation of 12 pumps (three at Rose Hall, four at Port Mourant and five at Albion), with a drainage capacity of 529,000 gallons per minute, enabled them to cope even with the phenomenal rains of 1959: 33 inches fell in seven weeks; 6 inches in a peak period of 36 hours. Foresight and technical innovation ensured that they resolved a major irrigation problem too. These three estates depended on the Canje, the main tributary of the Berbice River, for water for irrigation and manufacturing. A chronic problem was that the Canje tended to become salty for many miles upstream, during very dry spells, as water from the Atlantic moved up the river. The anticipated opening of the Black Bush Polder scheme in 1961 and the demand for irrigation water from the Canje for its 31,000 acres for small farmers, would have aggravated the problem.[14]

Booker integrated the irrigation systems of the three plantations by linking their main canals. They also installed a powerful pump about 25 miles upstream of the Canje, at Brotherson (where the water was always fresh), whence ran a canal to Albion. Consequently, not only Rose Hall, on the lower reaches and more susceptible to salt water — its pumps were only 12 miles from the Atlantic — but Port Mourant, too, were beneficiaries of fresh water, all year.[15] This had major implications for production and productivity. Albion/Port Mourant, as noted earlier, had shaped young Jock in the 1930s; the Corentyne had a special resonance for him.

In September 1960 Booker erected a new pumping station at Strathspey, to service Enmore Estate, the fourth such installation since 1955. As in Berbice, this project had consolidated the immense strides made in water control in the latter half of the 1950s. Follett-Smith placed this work in context in 1960:

> [A]griculture ... has always had to combat the two-fold problem of the sea in front and the flood waters behind, and vast sums of public and private funds are tied up in the construction and maintenance of capital works designed for sea defence and water control. There is also the problem of periodic drought, so that water control in British Guiana is no less concerned with the conservation and provision of water for irrigation than with the removal of water in the form of drainage. Our first aim has been to ensure that each estate has an adequate supply of water for navigation and irrigation. In so far as it is possible for us as a company, this has now been done.[16]

Between 1955 and 1959 nearly $1,000,000 had been spent on three new pumping stations; the one at Strathspey cost another $500,000, while $200,000 were expended on the rehabilitation of old pumps and $200,000 on new sluices, between 1954 and 1959, to improve drainage.[17] Booker had *not* committed the old Guyanese error of separating drainage from irrigation, nor had they emphasised one at the expense of the other. At the technical level, Follett-Smith was at his best.

The same attitude to technical efficiency was brought to the modernisation of Booker's sugar factories, where amalgamation into larger, more productive units had been pursued since the early 1950s. In 1948 there were 16 factories in the colony; by 1965–56, towards the end of Campbell's chairmanship, there were 11, of which eight belonged to Booker; two, Diamond and Leonora, belonged to the Demerara Company, and one, Versailles, was privately owned.

In 1955 the factory at Port Mourant, which had become rather inefficient, was closed and its cane diverted to Albion; Ogle and Houston factories were dismantled shortly afterwards and LBI, with its modern factory, became the grinder of their canes. By the mid-1950s Booker was on such firm ground with regard to its management structure and its technological innovations, that the model plantation of the Davson family, Blairmont, which had made such a great impression on Jock Campbell in the 1930s, was forced to amalgamate with it, in 1955.[18]

By mid-1956 the factory at Rose Hall, Canje, had been modernised and enlarged. Follett-Smith was most impressed with this achievement, the installation of its turbine-driven mill, as he was with the quality of Guyanese workmanship. *Booker News* captured this optimism in mid-1957:

> The extensive modernisation and enlargement of the Rose Hall factory were completed in time for the autumn crop [1956]. The new milling plant, driven by turbines, was officially set in motion ... on 12 August 1956 — a gesture which was highly appreciated by all grades of workers in the plant, who were justly proud of the magnificent reconstruction job which they, by their loyal and united efforts, had finished in the nine short weeks between the two reaping seasons.... Mr. Follett-Smith said ... that this remarkable achievement proves — what so many of us know — that the people of British Guiana can, when properly led and when the reasons for an operation are explained to them and the necessity for it made apparent, do work fully comparable with that of other lands and peoples.[19]

By March 1959 the LBI factory had been completely rebuilt at a cost of $3.5 million; another $15,000,000 had been spent by this time on the modernisation and enlarging of the other sugar factories. The construction of the one at LBI, as Follett-Smith observed, had been done with Booker's own funds, 'without loans or grants from Government or other outside sources'. He interpreted this as a vindication of Campbell's philosophy, his 'enlightened capitalism', generating wealth for many, 'fulfilling our responsibilities to our shareholders, to our fellow workers, and to the community in which we live'. He then amplified on Booker's social contract with British Guiana, paraphrasing Jock: '[T]he success of this joint responsibility [rests] with every one of us. Capital — in the sense of cash or land or buildings or machinery — cannot generate wealth by itself: it must be brought to life and put to work by people — people at all levels who know what they are doing and why.' [20]

By the end of the 1950s Booker could report that they had made great progress in raising their average factory output, as Campbell had exhorted them to do in 1952. They noted that this had reached 25,485 tons in 1959; in 1957 and 1958 it was 23,668 tons and 24, 782 tons respectively. They expanded on their manufacturing success of 1959:

> [T]hree of our nine factories broke production records. Reflecting this growing efficiency of the factories, the average rate of milling increased from 68.9 tons of cane per hour in 1958 to 74.3 tons in 1959; the average grinding week rose from 115 hours to 120 hours ... an increase of 205 over the last six years.... Correspondingly the average time taken to process the crop was reduced from 35.7 weeks in 1958 to 32.1 weeks in 1959. And production time lost in the factories was again cut down, demonstrating the value of the preparatory work already done towards the introduction of a thorough system of planned preventative maintenance. [21]

However, while Booker celebrated their achievements, they were never complacent. In 1963, for instance, George Bishop was emphasising the necessity to maintain and sharpen their competitive edge, in spite of the CSA, and the relative security of the Canadian and American markets which absorbed some 50 per cent of British Guiana's sugar. He argued:

> In the struggle for markets it is those producers who improve their efficiency faster than their competitors, and face up to the need for technical change and innovation, who will survive and prosper. The sugar industry of British Guiana is fortunate indeed in having a safety net.... But if sugar is to make a positive contribution to the further development of the country, and to maintain its place in the Booker Group, it has no alternative but

to modernise and adapt itself as fast as the most efficient of its competitors.[22]

By 1966, the year before Campbell resigned the chairmanship of Booker, in spite of the turbulent politics in Guyana in the early 1960s, all the Booker factories had been modernised; the last one, Albion, Jock's old family estate, was being completely rebuilt. Diamond, too, belonging to the Demerara Company, had undergone considerable modernisation and expansion. Ian McDonald identified some of the key technological innovations encompassed by the comprehensive process of factory modernisation:

(i)   new continuous juice clarifiers and rotary vacuum filters
(ii)   new and enlarged evaporating pans
(iii) new and larger vacuum pans
(iv)   high-speed and semi-automatic centrifugals
(v)   turbine drives for the crushing plants
(vi)   extensive electrification
(vii) improved steam raising plants
(viii) new instruments for measurement and control [23]

Booker had become one of the most efficient sugar producers in the world, thus enabling them to take full advantage of the markets, in spite of the hazards of the Guyanese environment, natural and political. By 1960 it looked as if Campbell was fulfilling his pledge to Jagan, on the eve of the 1957 elections, that 'Booker is prepared to work with any Government no matter how radical'.[24] Indeed, with a record sugar crop, they were demonstrating confidence in the future of Guyana, whatever their reservations about Jagan's communism.

Booker's technical excellence was at the core of its progress. Its chief chemist, J.F. Williams, had shown that efficient factories and a regular, though smaller, work force in the fields and factories, were crucial to enhancing productivity. In 1944-45, for instance, over 30 per cent of the grinding time of factories was lost because of mechanical failures (mill chokes and fall in steam pressure) and inadequate cane supplies. By 1952–53, with the modernisation of the factories advancing, the loss of grinding time was reduced to 18 per cent.[25] Meanwhile, the character of the labour force, too, was changing. Until the late 1940s a characteristic of a larger field force was its irregular attendance; now a smaller force, with better wages and incentive bonuses, had positive consequences for factory operations and sugar production. Williams explained the inefficiency prevailing before the transformation:

> There was [by the late 1940s] .... a growing tendency for those workers still engaged in cane cultivation to work *not* more than three days a week. The general effect was that it became impossible to keep factories regularly supplied with cane, and reaping, which in normal times occupies about 26 weeks in the year went on intermittently over long periods. Less sugar was made in longer grinding periods, and less off-season time was available for factory overhaul and maintenance, which had a carry-over effect on subsequent grinding periods in that more mechanical break-downs occurred than would have been the case had time been available to put the machinery in first class condition during the inter-crop periods.[26]

Better wages and incentives, after the CSA, gave a smaller work-force security, which made them greater consumers with higher aspirations of mobility. This made them better, regular workers. Until then, poor wages and general insecurity were responsible for their unreliability, their eclectic attendance, as they were forced into seeking other sources of subsistence. Campbell's chairmanship, with its focus on rationalisation of managerial and technical operations, competitiveness and social reform, had shaped a more self-respecting, reliable work-force. Holiday with pay was introduced in 1950; special bonuses for cane cutting and loading in 1951; and the following year a weekly incentive target bonus, a crop bonus and an annual production bonus were introduced.[27]

In his Chairman's Statement of 1958 Campbell repeated his case for building 'hedges' against the uncertainties of 'tropical agriculture', a reference to the potentially volatile political environment of British Guiana. The contribution of sugar to the Booker Group's profit had dropped from 48 per cent to 38 per cent between 1950 and 1958, while the capital and reserves of shareholders had risen from $35 million to $65 million, an increase of about 85 per cent.

In the process of 'hedge building', Booker had acquired two of the premier manufacturers of sugar machinery, George Fletcher and Co Ltd (Derby) and Duncan Stewart and Co Ltd (Glasgow), in 1956 and 1958 respectively, as well as Sigmund Pumps (Gateshead), in the latter year. This was an elaboration of two of Campbell's key principles on Booker's growth: efficiency through vertical integration; and the diversification of investments, geographically and qualitatively, in order to lessen their dependence on British Guiana. *Booker News* elaborated in mid-1959:

> As owners ... of twelve sugar estates, Booker Sugar Estates Ltd. should be a sugar manufacturer's dream customer for machinery and engineering requirements, and sugar machinery old and new in the company's factories carry the two well-known sugar engineers — George Fletcher and Duncan Stewart. When Engineering Holdings [a new member of the Booker Group] flexes its young muscles and adds not only these two famous names but also that of Sigmund [Pumps] to its roll, it means that Booker has become a more closely knit and integrated group. It means that as of now, Booker sugar is exported in our own ships after having been manufactured by our machinery.[28]

These ventures, however, did not constitute an abdication of Booker's responsibility to British Guiana, as Campbell saw it. In February 1961 they opened the Demerara Sugar Terminal at Ruimveldt, on the lower Demerara River, on the southern periphery of Georgetown. It cost $7.75 million. This speeded up the bulk loading of sugar vessels: sugar was received by road and sea; the terminal had storage for around 40,000 tons and mechanised facilities for the direct loading of sugar into the holds of ocean-going liners. The terminal was another advance in the efficiency drive, encompassing economy of scale and time, thus enhancing the competitive edge of Booker. The company's newspaper grasped its significance at the time of its commissioning in 1961:

> Over the past ten years the sugar refiners in Britain and North America who are our major customers have swung entirely over to bulk handling of their purchases, so that for some time now

there have been no facilities at the journey's end for receiving sugar shipped in bags. The industry in British Guiana had therefore to resort to the unsatisfactory manual process of slitting the sugar bags above the hatches of sugar ships and emptying the contents into the hold. Undoubtedly, this provided work for a sizeable number of hands, but on the other hand turn around was slow. It would take an army of hands to cut and empty sugar bags at the rate of 500 tons an hour, which is the speed of the sugar terminals installations. Moreover, in shipping, time, literally costs money.[29]

Table IV
Reduction in Field and Factory Workers in the Sugar Industry, 1950–67 (Weekly Employees)

Year	Field	Factory	Total
1950	21,641	6,594	28,235
1951	21,791	6,145	27,936
1952	21,948	6,404	28,352
1953	20,501	5,804	26,305
1954	22,054	5,845	27,899
1955	20,548	5,544	26,092
1956	19,958	4,877	24,835
1957	19,504	5,070	24,574
1958	18,354	5,288	23,642
1959	16,982	4,784	21,766
1960	16,001	4,478	20,479
1961	15,159	4,075	19,234
1962	13,901	3,914	17,815
1963	14,240	3,604	17,844
1964	12,451	3,583	16,034
1965	14,082	3,830	17,912
1966	13,262	3,663	16,925
1967	13,743	3,552	17,295

Source: Clive Y. Thomas, *Plantations, Peasants, and State* (Los Angeles: Centre for Afro-American Studies, UCLA,1984), 52.

Completed in 1960, a year of record sugar production, the Demerara Sugar Terminal demonstrated that Campbell's hedge building strategy was not incompatible with continued faith in Guyana. Indeed, rational economic arguments — with the CSA it was now a good sphere of investment — as well as Campbell's social reform programme justified continued engagement with the Guyana mission. The Governor, Sir Ralph Grey, in January 1961, saw the terminal as a demonstration of Jock Campbell's 'courage and imagination', while alluding to Jagan's compulsive hatred of sugar and his Marxist nostrum:

> The decision to go in for bulk handling ... was born of the stern necessity to remain efficient in business in the face of world competition ... so much of the prosperity of British Guiana depends on sugar remaining in business.... Sir Jock Campbell [has] courage and imagination in unusually full measure ... courage and imagination are sorely needed in British Guiana today.... Have we the courage to take the harder, but the surer, way to a happy future rather than what at first sight is an easier path, even if one is not truly certain where it leads?[30]

Impressive though the progress of mechanisation in field, factory and shipping, and inescapable as this process was to the survival of the industry as an efficient producer, there were negative consequences. As Table IV shows, between 1950, when Campbell embarked on the reorganisation of Booker, and 1967, when he resigned from it, the employees in sugar declined from about 28,000 to about 17,000, a drop of nearly 40 per cent. Field workers contracted from about 21,000 to between 13,000 and 14,000, while factory workers fell from about 6,500 to about 3,500. This had added grist to Jagan's anti-Booker mill, epitomised by his assertion that the dismantling in 1955 of the factory at Port Mourant, his home plantation, was a deliberate tactic to punish his supporters.

On the other hand, Richard Ishmael, the President of the MPCA, the anti-Jagan union recognised by the SPA as the sole bargaining agent of sugar workers, had, in March 1959, endorsed Booker's mechanisation programme: Booker had to modernise or it would disappear; the workers would be in a worse position. Having exerted restraint in wage demands, because it was necessary to made the industry competitive, he was now ready to negotiate a pay hike, pensions and other benefits. Ishmael explained: '[W]e are entering the era when workers must benefit considerably from these technological developments which reduce the cost of production per ton of sugar.'[31]

Booker News approved of Ishmael's strategy, observing that a smaller, better paid labour force was unavoidable; Booker had to adapt to the realities of the sugar trade or face extinction:

> Mr. Ishmael's statement of MPCA policy was not only enlightened, it was realistic.... Obsolete machinery and outmoded processes would lead to stagnation and low productivity in an industry in whose prosperity this Union was vastly interested. Out of a prosperous industry, Mr. Ishmael asserts, he can unhesitatingly demand increasing benefits for sugar workers.... Private enterprise cannot face the challenge of competitive markets when it employs six or eight badly paid and perpetually disgruntled men to do work of which one competent and contented worker could make short shrift.[32]

In February 1960 Jock Campbell addressed the apprehension which mechanisation and redundancy had bred in British Guiana in the 1950s. In a radio broadcast to sugar workers, he reassured them that people were, indeed, more important than ships and shops and sugar estates — people were 'more important than anything else'. That was confirmed by what he saw as 'reasonable improvement in wages, housing and conditions of service' in the sugar industry. However, mechanisation and retrenchment were inevitable in modern industry; they had to cushion the impact of that harsh reality:

> [I]n order to survive, the British Guiana sugar industry must be at least as efficient as sugar industries in other countries. If they use modern machines that produce sugar more cheaply by employing fewer people than we employ, either our wages for each person will have to be a lot lower than theirs; or our sugar will be so much more expensive than theirs that nobody will buy it....[I]t is far better for the people of British Guiana as a whole

that a thoroughly efficient sugar industry should pay good wages to a smaller number of people. The large number of people with bad wages would all be poor and have no money to spend. Fewer people with good wages will have money to spend, which will in turn give employment to others.... I know that some individual men and women suffer in this inescapable process. For them our policy is to do everything we can to help them to find other jobs. Or, if we fail, to give them redundancy payments. There is no more that we can do.[33]

High productivity, technical efficiency, unremitting vigilance to maintain and enhance competitiveness were imperatives of a modern business. Failure to observe these basics, Campbell remarked, would vitiate the company's responsibilities to shareholders, employees, customers and the community. Indeed, in February 1960, at a meeting of the board of Booker Sugar Estates, a recommendation was made for further 'decasualisation of labour', more mechanisation, and the 'pruning' of employment rolls. Jock Campbell, who was present, countered that 'in the interest of British Guiana such efficiencies as these might have to be sacrificed in keeping people in work ... the clear responsibility of business was to be as progressive and efficient as possible. Any other approach by the Company would be irresponsible both in respect of its obligations as a company and in the context of its responsibilities in the social framework'.[34]

Campbell was acutely aware of the limits to retrenchment in the politically volatile environment of British Guiana; besides the economy was severely restricted in its capacity to absorb excess labour. This had spawned a new response by the plantocracy since the early 1950s. Shahabuddeen assesses this 'softening' of their attitude: '[E]conomic diversification and labour deflection were no longer things to be feared ... the industry, having traditionally opposed economic diversification on the ground that its labour supply would be reduced, ultimately adopted programmes directly productive of a degree of redundancy which the economy, by reason of past sugar policies, was not structured to absorb.'[35] Campbell understood very well the terms of this debate. Yet the labour force continued to decline: from 20,479 in 1960 to 17,295 in 1967, when he resigned. It had, however, stabilised at around 17-18,000 for the rest of the 1960s. This was the context in which the sugar industry sought to placate their critics by pursuing a more enlightened land disbursement policy: between 1956 and 1964, 36,000 acres unbeneficially occupied by Booker were disposed of 'to Government, to rice and cattle co-operatives, for school buildings, for residential purposes, for public buildings ... and police stations'.[36]

Campbell believed that considerable savings could be effected by improving the yield and the rate of conversion of sugar: tons of cane per acre and the tons-cane/tons-sugar ratio. The individual worker could become more efficient, too, by the fostering of pride in work through inspired leadership. This, he noted, was clearly lacking in a case he had recently witnessed in early 1960: '[H]e was unhappy to see the lack of pride and morale among the workers in the splendid new L.B.I. factory, and wondered to what extent this was caused by bad management within the factory. This lack of pride undoubtedly affected efficiency. It was very important to ensure that individual standards of efficiency were raised.' [37]

Campbell often cited the exemplary work of Dr Harry Evans, Booker's plant pathologist in British Guiana since 1952. He was fascinated by this man who epitomised his prescription for excellence: pride in work and enhancing output through research and efficiency. As Dr Evans wrote in 1967, in the evening of his career:

> [T]he technology of the Guyana sugar industry is one of the most advanced in the world with a cultural system involving close scientific control at all stages. In spite of the relative unsuitability of the climate in comparison with that optimal for sugar cane ... nevertheless the yield of sugar per acre per annum ranks with the top six of about thirty sugar producing territories. For instance, yields on a comparative basis have been higher than those of Mauritius, South Africa, other Caribbean territories, Louisiana and Florida, Taiwan, and equal to the best mean yields in Australia in years when the industry has not been affected by drought and strife.[38]

Barry Newton has spent his whole working life with Booker and Booker/Tate. He worked for several years in Guyana and remembers Harry Evans as a 'unique' man, 'extraordinarily loquacious' about his technical projects, totally dedicated, 'with a memory so remarkable as to become irritating for people who hadn't done things that they were supposed to have done several years before'. Newton assesses Evans's contribution to productivity in Campbell's Booker:

> Guyana is a very demanding place to grow cane.... It requires a lot of attention to detail, more than many other places, and if you don't do it in a timely manner and an accurate manner, you will suffer dramatically and quickly. If you don't maintain standards you will fall very fast into the abyss. Harry's job was to raise the agricultural standards of the operation. His principal task was to examine the physiology and pathology of the plant, and to raise the standard of cane husbandry to a level where you maximise what you have. The size of the factories is necessarily sub-optimal because of the time taken to transport cane by the water-borne system. So the inherent disadvantages of Guyana are compounded by this factor: factories are the biggest user of capital. Harry's technical excellence went far in removing Guyana's natural hazards.[39]

This had been Jock's aim throughout his chairmanship; Evans's work, therefore, was at the core of his mission in Guyana. But he was perennially enthralled by the myriad tasks required to make a spoon of sugar. He was no less fascinated, he told me, by the thousands of men and women who performed these tasks, and would try to let them know this on his annual visits to the colony.

Endnotes

1. The Chairman's Statement, 1951, p. 20.
2. Ian McDonald, *Sugar in B.G.: Challenge and Change* (Georgetown: Booker, n.d., ca. 1966), 8.
3. BSE [Booker Sugar Estates Ltd.] Minutes, February 28, 1956.
4. *West India Committee Circular*, March 1954.
5. 'Note on Production Policy and Quota Position', Appendix B, BSE Minutes, April 23, 1960.
6. *Report of a Commission of Inquiry into the Sugar Industry of British Guiana* (J.A. Venn, chairman), (London: HMSO, (1949), 9.
7. Jock Campbell, 'The Development and Organisation of Booker', Paper delivered at LSE, November 24, 1959, p. 3.

8. Leonard Hares, 'Field Routine: A Non-Technical Description of Sugar-Cane Growing in British Guiana', in *Booker Sugar* (Supplement to the Accounts of Booker Bros, McConnell and Co, Ltd, 1954), p. 28.

9. See note 2 [p. 13].

10. 'Review of Operations', in Booker Bros, McConnell and Co, Ltd, *Report of the Directors and Statement of Accounts, 1955*, pp. 20-1.

11. Brian Scott, 'The Organisational Network: A Strategy Perspective for Development', PhD thesis, Harvard University, 1979, p. 137.

12. See note 8 [pp. 33-4].

13. R.R. Follett-Smith, 'Introduction', in *Booker Sugar* [1954], p. 8.

14. *Booker News*, August 28, 1959.

15. Ibid.

16. Ibid., September 23, 1960.

17. Ibid.

18. Ibid., (Special Supplement), July 8, 1955.

19. Ibid., (Special Supplement), June 21, 1957.

20. Ibid., March 13, 1959.

21. R.R. Follett-Smith and G.M. Eccles, 'Sugar', in The Booker Group of Companies, *Review of the Year 1959*, pp. 24-5.

22. George Bishop, 'The Markets for Booker's Sugar', in The Booker Group, *Review of the Year 1962*, p. 37.

23. See note 2 [p. 13].

24. *Booker News*, June 21, 1957.

25. J.F. Williams, 'Factory Development', in *Booker Sugar* [1954], p. 59.

26. J.F. Williams, 'The Development of the Sugar Cane Industry in British Guiana', in *Booker Sugar* [1954], p. 123. This is a revised version of an article published in *Timehri*, No. 29 (Fourth Series), (August 1950).

27. M. Shahabuddeen, *From Plantocracy to Nationalisation: A Profile of Sugar* (Georgetown: University of Guyana, 1983), 206-7.

28. *Booker News*, [Leader], June 19, 1959.

29. Ibid., [Leader], February 24, 1961.

30. Ibid., February 24, 1961.

31. Ibid., March 13, 1959.

32. Ibid., [Leader]

33. Ibid., March 11, 1960.

34. BSE Minutes, February 2, 1960.

35. See note 27 [p. 252].

36. See note 2 [p. 3].

37. See note 34.

38. Quoted in 'Report of the Commission of Inquiry into the Sugar Industry in Guyana', [G.L.B. Persaud, chairman], (mimeo), September 1968, p. 6.

39. Barry Newton, interview by the author, London, May 17, 1995.

Chapter Twenty-Three

RESEARCH AND PRODUCTIVITY ON BOOKER SUGAR ESTATES: THE WORK OF DR HARRY EVANS

In mid-1957, on learning of the knighthood conferred on Jock Campbell, *Booker News* pondered on the fact that he had polio in his teens and suggested that this must have given him an inner strength, always to turn adversity into advantage. This, also, must have given him his gifts as a leader, reflected in the great esteem in which he was held in Booker. Prominent among his skills was the knack, often, of selecting the best person for the job. The paper elaborated:

> [O]ne of his qualifications for office ... stands out above all others — his ability to recruit able lieutenants, to inspire them with his zeal and to win their loyalty and genuine affection.... It is a case for wonder that Jock Campbell could have assembled such vast human resources, such a team of men, of experts and managers, all eminent in their chosen fields and have them all defer to him as the real and functioning heart and head and source of inspiration of this great enterprise.[1]

He was still only 45. Since the late 1940s Campbell had been closely associated with the Imperial College of Tropical Agriculture (ICTA) in Trinidad: first, as chairman of its finance committee, then, for many years, as deputy chairman of its governing body. He had believed in the primacy of research ever since he encountered the sugar cane on his family's plantations in the mid-1930s. He had imbibed the cane culture which was already advanced in British Guiana. Indeed, this colony had led the Empire in agricultural research as early as the mid-nineteenth century. The complex hydrological conditions on the coastland of British Guiana, the plantation zone, had made it an imperative; besides, the pronounced monocultural character of its economy and the plantocracy's power to shape policies, had fostered the development of an impressive cane research culture.[2]

The Royal Agricultural and Commercial Society was founded in 1844 in Georgetown; it helped to consolidate the colony's research culture and its journal, *Timehri*, from the 1880s, extended this tradition, giving it intellectual respectability. But, as early as 1846, a distinguished soil pathologist, Dr John Shier, a student of Sir Humphry Davy, was doing research in British Guiana on sugar-cane soils, the use of fertilisers, as well as manufacturing innovations. This work was enhanced by the passion for research of the world-renowned 'chemist, agriculturalist, analyst, geologist, agronomist and soil scientist', Professor J.B. Harrison. Between 1889 and the early 1920s, when he was the Director of Agriculture, he revolutionised sugar agronomy with his Demerara-bred seedlings: D74, D109, D625, D1135. It was his D109, with its special adaptability to high rainfall and the heavy clay on the British Guiana coast, coupled with its drought-resistant features, which had endeared it to Mauritian planters as well; it was the 'father' of their spectacular variety, the M134/32.[3]

This was the culture which had attracted R.R. Follett-Smith, the chairman of Booker Sugar Estates, to the colony in 1929, as chemist in the Department of Agriculture. An Englishman, he had done graduate work in tropical agriculture at ICTA in 1924–25, and had stayed on in Trinidad for four years as a sugar chemist. So that by 1937, when he joined Booker as consultant chemist, he was already immersed in sugar agronomy and the complex world of sugar chemistry. Two crucial developments took place in the early 1950s that were conducive to sustaining the colony's research tradition: (i) Follett-Smith became chairman of BSE in Georgetown; (ii) he was instrumental in bringing to Booker a brilliant Welsh physiological botanist, with abundant experience of the sugar-cane culture of Mauritius (1932–48), an expertise which was enhanced by his research at ICTA (1948–52). In October 1952, Dr Harry Evans became Booker's Agricultural Director in British Guiana. Follett-Smith had met him in Mauritius in 1947 and was impressed with his work.[4] Ian McDonald, who knew Dr Evans well, recalls that he was a passionate researcher, obsessed with every facet of cane culture in the colony, an agronomist of the highest order in the theoretical and applied science of the field.[5] 1952 was also the year of Jock Campbell's ascendancy as Chairman of Booker; he said that he detected quickly a kindred spirit in Dr Evans. He had expressed great optimism at his appointment:

> Mr. Follett-Smith...has wisely decided to appoint as Agricultural Director, Dr. H. Evans, Ph.D, B.Sc., a leading member of the staff of the Cocoa Research Scheme at the Imperial College of Tropical Agriculture in Trinidad. Dr. Evans is a plant physiologist of international repute, who has, moreover, done valuable work on the sugar-cane in Mauritius. We have the highest hopes of what he may be able to do.[6]

Dr Harry Evans, Booker's agricultural director in British Guiana: 'a genius ... a world figure in the sugar industry'

Already, by 1954, Booker could report progress: 'Past efforts to reduce costs, both in field and factory, are now beginning to bear fruit and yields of sugar per acre have risen steadily. Whereas in 1950 our Estates gave a yield of 3.04 tons of sugar to the acre, in 1953 the yield had risen to 3.39 tons of sugar per acre.' Unseasonable weather in 1954 (drought in late 1953 and excessive rainfall the next year), occasioned a fall in yield, to 3.08 tons per acre.[7] But in the spheres of fertiliser application and experiment with new varieties of cane, Booker were effusive in their praise of Dr Evans. Follett-Smith observed that at Plantation Uitvlugt, where the tightly-packed clay soils, under rainy conditions, showed signs of nitrogen and phosphate deficiency, it was the practice to abandon the stunted, yellow fields and replant. Now these fields were being rehabilitated with small 'dressings of nitrogen and phosphate'. The culture of research was enhanced: '[T]he work of the agricultural research branch is already showing returns. Phenomenal yield increases are being obtained on the Corentyne by application of phosphates. New cane varieties are being rapidly tested and extended.... On practically every estate there is an awareness that the future depends on the rapid application of research work.' [8]

However, Follett-Smith observed that the dreaded leaf-scald disease had not been completely eradicated because the old, vulnerable variety of cane, B34104, was not yet eliminated. When that was done, the disease would go. The B34104, which was ideally suited to the heavy coastland clays, had occupied about 80 per cent of the cane acreage when leaf scald struck in 1951.[9] This was the most urgent task that confronted Harry Evans: he had to find a way to replace B34104. He isolated a wide range of varieties which, if not resistant, were at least tolerant of it, while proceeding with research to breed resistant varieties. In 1954 Dr Evans reported:

> From existing relatively untested Barbadian seedlings which would not ... [ordinarily] reach commercial plantations for at least five years, selections of leaf-scald resistant seedlings which showed sufficient promise as commercial varieties were made and bulked up. Occupying a few acres or fractions of an acre two years ago, there are now several hundred acres of these varieties — the best of which may be extended to the degree desired at any moment.... The varietal situation, which looked rather gloomy when leaf scald was first discovered in 1951, has improved immensely and a future supply of high-performance disease-free varieties is now assured.[10]

But he was also immersed in the chemical control of weeds and the application of herbicides through aerial and ground spraying; pest control, too, was an ongoing area of research. Dr Evans observed that weed-infested fields tended to be rat-infested, therefore, weed-free cultivation was most desirable, a deterrent to the rat menace: on one estate, in one year, 204,691 rats were destroyed. He explained the range of the pest control exercise: 'the breeding and releasing of parasites of cane-borer; benzene hexachloride dusting against froghopper and hard-back beetle and insecticidal spraying of caterpillars of various kinds; baiting and anti-coagulants against the two species of rats which can quickly play havoc with cane, particularly in the later stages of growth'.[11]

Dr Evans's work also involved experiments on soil types. He was especially fascinated with soil-plant interaction, noting that this varied not only with different crops on a given soil but with different varieties of the same crop as well. This enabled him to ascertain precisely what nutrients were missing and the rate of degeneration of key nutrients. He was surprised by the ignorance in the industry of the minor nutrients which, in combination, enhanced productivity. He had made good progress in this area and could report in 1954 that they were able to detect factors which were not 'optimal', thus facilitating remedial measures: for instance, 'an insufficient supply of phosphorous, of potash, or of calcium; an excess of iron, of manganese, of aluminium, or of magnesium; a deficiency of the trace element molybdenum and in one instance of boron, are some of the factors which during the last two years have been identified as factors which are limiting the yields of cane and sugar'.[12]

Dr Evans also developed a system to expedite the testing of the sucrose content of cane in each field on the estates. While this could not raise the sugar content of the cane, it was an effective way of ensuring that the cane was cut at the optimum point: output was reduced if the cane was cut too early or too late. He was also deeply involved with extending the ratoons, the cycle of repeating the croppings from the original plants without replanting. More ratoons could be garnered providing the supplementary nutritional measures were practised. He underlined the importance of scientific husbandry: '[C]ane culture is rapidly becoming a highly skilled agricultural technique, in which every activity is scientifically controlled and timed. In much of the Hawaiian sugar industry, a high standard of production has already been reached, but research and improvement continue.' [13]

To counter the effects of soil exhaustion, Dr Evans advocated flood-fallowing, a practice unique to the plantations of British Guiana. When the yield started to deteriorate, it was futile to prolong the ratoon; the land had to be rested under 9 to 12 inches of fresh water, for 6 to 9 months. The water was then drained away and new plants put in. The results were astounding. He explained the process of renewal activated on the heavy clay:

From a buttery, cheesy structureless clay the technique of flood-fallowing produces a structure.... As a result of impregnation of the soil by reduced forms of iron, in particular under the chemically reducing conditions which occur during flood-fallow, and the subsequent oxidation of the reduced iron compounds when the water is drained off, particles of clay become water-proofed by a film of oxidised iron, and so a structure is produced where none previously existed. The development of this structure and the better aeration which accompanies it are the signal for the stepping-up of beneficial biological activity; availability of most nutrients is increased — root growth is enhanced and there is an overall increase of approximately 40% in yields.[14]

Therefore, by the mid-1950s, Harry Evans had developed new varieties of cane; succeeded in extending the number of ratoons by his research into soil types; retarded the rate of soil degradation and introduced measures to improve them; while protecting the cane from parasitic flora and fauna by aerial and ground spraying of pesticides and weedicides.

Dr Evans researched and published prolifically on the sugar cane: by early 1956, only three years after joining Booker in British Guiana, he had published ten scientific papers. He was a world-recognised authority in his field, but those who knew him remember his passion and the contagious curiosity he engendered about his work. *Booker News* assessed his contribution thus:

His three years of work in the laboratory and in the canefields has contributed much to the increased yield per acre in the sugar estates and to last year's [1955] returns of 250,000 which made local history. To Dr. Evans this achievement is not enough.... Even in some advanced countries, he says, there is a lag of twelve to fifteen years between the findings of research and their application in the field: 'we cannot afford this gap'. British Guiana is already in statistical competition with some of the best producers in the world; at present the yield per acre is far higher than Cuba, India, South Africa or Fiji — higher than in Mauritius and Australia, but still Dr. Evans presses on in the race for superiority.[15]

Jock Campbell observed that in 1956 the Booker estates had produced 263,333 tons of sugar — an increase of 13,000 tons over 1955. He attributed this entirely to better yields: 3.63 tons per acre in 1956, compared to 3.41 tons per acre the previous year. While noting the 'staunch and sterling' contribution of management, characteristically, he commended the effort of all, from top to bottom. But he did reserve a special place for 'the inspired researches of Dr. Harry Evans and his team'.[16]

Follett-Smith was more circumspect. In his BSE Report for 1956, reflecting a basic difference in outlook between himself and Campbell, he had worried about the difficulty of achieving an 'acceptable return' on capital employed in sugar while maintaining and improving the assets of the estates. But, like Jock, he gave credit to Dr Evans: 'Without the immense help provided by the agricultural research department under Dr. Evans the present situation and the prospect for the future would be depressing.'[17]

Follett-Smith then demonstrated one case in which Dr Evans's findings were being quickly translated into practice — the foliar diagnostic technique:

[I]t has permitted the examination of 90 to 100 leaf samples a day for nitrogen, potash and phosphate, thus indicating corrective measures within 7 to 10 days of the collection of the samples. When the case is too advanced for ground application of manures, distribution of urea by plane has been successful. During the past 2 or 3 years the widespread phosphorous deficiency has been largely corrected and this enables the cane profitably to use more nitrogen. Certain areas where potash reserves are low have been defined and are being treated by suitably timed, profitable potash dressings.[18]

Between 1956 and 1959 the acreage reaped rose from 74,028 to 87,658, while the sugar produced rose from 263,333 to 284,425 tons. Indeed, in 1958, for the first time, production exceeded 300,000 tons.

In 1959 Dr Evans reported that the varieties, B41227 and B37161, accounted for 80 per cent of the cane cultivated: these were resistant to the leaf scald disease. He had successfully replaced the vulnerable

B34104, which he encountered when he went to the colony in 1952. He remarked that B41227 was being planted at the expense of B37161; another variety, too, B47258, was making inroads into the latter. But complacency was not a feature of Dr Evans's treatment of cane culture. The following from his Report of 1959, epitomised his unfailing vigilance and intellectual alertness:

> [B47258] has some excellent characteristics, performing well in drought years, but suffers from being particularly susceptible to damage by rats and borers, and to aphid infestation. Indeed, were it not for the new organo-phosphorous insecticide, Dimethoate, it would not have been possible to extend the variety B47258 to any appreciable extent. For specialised conditions (silts of poor texture, low-lying badly drained areas, etc.) the varieties, D37/45 and B45137 have proved valuable and some extension of the new variety, D141/46, is being made.[19]

He was equally alert to the drop in production between 1958 and 1959: BSE made 232,000 tons of sugar, 20,000 less than the previous year. He pointed to the problem of drought, as well as inadequate soil aeration on the stiff coastal clay. He observed that plant growth was impeded by inadequate moisture in the soil and the consequent rise in salinity; in excessively wet periods, too, growth was hampered by poor soil aeration. He then identified current shortcomings in dealing with the problem:

> Our present method of irrigation by total inundation of the field, may, whilst supplying the necessary moisture, deleteriously affect the soil oxygen. This is particularly true when inter-bed and in-field drains are not well maintained. In other words it is a prime consideration that the mechanism for quickly draining the excess irrigation water off the land is efficient and that irrigation be only applied when necessary.[20]

In 1960 sugar production in British Guiana reached the record figure of 334,441 tons; Booker estates produced over 270,000 tons, about 20,000 more than the previous record crop of 1958. The yield per acre, however, was below the highest yield, 3.54 tons of sugar per acre in 1958. In fact, although the sugar produced exceeded 300,000 tons in 1960, 1961, 1962 and 1963, productivity declined to 3.42, 3.03, 3.25 and 3.28 tons per acre respectively, in those years.[21] Guy Eccles, a senior Booker executive in London, noted that the yield was not likely to improve, because the Company had decided to prolong the ratoons in order to gain economies: 40 per cent of the cane harvested in 1960 were in their fourth ratoon or older. Dr Evans had recommended that this be done, for with adequate nutritional supplements and efficient drainage and irrigation, the ratoon could be profitably extended. Stable prices in the early 1960s and increased exports made this a prudent strategy. However, as Guy Eccles observed in 1960, this did not constitute a diminution of the meticulous husbandry for which Harry Evans was punctilious:

> Water control is, as we have said time and again, one of the most crucial factors in successful sugar growing in British Guiana. A new pumping station has been built at Strathspey, giving Enmore estate the capacity to remove more than two inches of rain in twenty four hours. At the same time experiments are going forward in the use of plastic-lined and unlined mole drains in an effort to control the water-table while maintaining satisfactory soil aeration. Taking as we do some 11 tons of cane to produce one ton of sugar in British Guiana, we are always conscious that one of the keys to greater efficiency in the long run is the quality of our cane. While chemical treatment can lead to some increase in the sucrose content of the cane, any radical improvement in juice quality may only follow from better control of the water-table and the plant's environment, particularly in relation to the development of cane varieties to suit the peculiar agricultural conditions of British Guiana.[22]

The early 1960s, as will be seen in Part 8, were marked by virtual civil war in British Guiana, between Africans and Indians. The plantations were not affected by the events of 1962 and 1963, but 1964 was a disastrous year and sugar production plummeted from 317,137 tons in 1963 to 258,466. Politically-motivated violence was compounded by a prolonged drought, from August 1963 to May 1964, with a slight break in December only. Dr Evans assessed the impact of both:

A serious effect of the two consecutive years of strife [1963–64] has been the disruption of our normal abandoning [flood-fallowing] and replanting programme. On agricultural and economic grounds we have established a crop cycle of plant cane and six ratoons to be optional for British Guiana conditions. This calls for the replanting of some 15% of our acreage each year; an inability to follow this programme has resulted in estates having proportions of their total acreage varying from 11% to 31% in ratoons older than sixth.[23]

Evans elaborated on the consequences of the political violence on the plantations in 1964 for the crucial drainage and irrigation system: '[T]he unavailability of labour required at the critical periods, led to a falling off in the standard of internal drainage. This has been more particularly serious on those estates characterised by subsoil salinity, since severe drought results in upward movement of salts which deleteriously affects the growth and quality of cane.' Equally, drainage ditches and canals had to be maintained, by periodic digging and clearing of aquatic vegetation, in anticipation of floods. In December 1964, after nearly 18 months of drought, about 30 inches of rain were recorded; one estate, Skeldon, received 14 inches in one week. Dr Evans noted that in this case they were better prepared: '[C]onsiderable ingenuity has been shown by some estates in mechanising the maintenance work, particularly of side-line drainage.... This was invaluable since torrential rains fell in December 1964....Had the main drainage channels not been cleared, considerably more water-logging of the estates would have occurred.'[24]

Ian McDonald was recruited by Jock Campbell when he left Cambridge in 1955. He worked with and knew well all the key people with Booker in British Guiana in the late 1950s and 1960s. He observes that Harry Evans's contribution was 'inestimable', as were several others: '[He] was a great man in his own way; at the scientific level he was a genius ... a world figure in the sugar industry.... We [also] had wonderful technical people like Lionel Birkett, Jack Williams, a first class chemist, and Follett-Smith, who became chairman [of BSE] and had a very good reputation on the chemistry side. Technically everyone was first class.'[25]

McDonald attributed this to Campbell's capacious vision, his belief that people mattered and that one should not be afraid of bright people; they should be respected and given space for their gifts to flourish. He explained why Campbell acquired so many clever people at Booker: 'That comes down to Jock's philosophy — that in this life and in this world you can only really make things happen through people and for people. There is no way you could invest a million dollars in a company if you don't have the right people around you.... [H]e interviewed people personally; he had excellent people.'[26]

But it was the general ethos of the four-fold responsibility fostered by Campbell, after the reorganisation of 1950–51, which shaped an environment conducive to the professional excellence of a man like Harry Evans. This is how a commentator assessed Campbell's Booker in 1960:

> Considerable importance is attached to this question of ethics, which embraces such things as strict opposition to any manifestation of racial discrimination, team work regardless of personal position and, more positively, giving encouragement to local managerial talent and the 'Guianisation' of the business in British Guiana. In addition to upgrading local employees, this involves shaping the business to fit in with national traditions and, soon probably, more financial participation in Booker enterprises. In the chairman's words, this reorganisation has 'worked wonders'. The delegation of responsibility and initiative to the man on the spot has stimulated enterprise, *esprit de corps* and adaptability to the social, economic and political environment ... the reorganisation has not only vitalised operations everywhere but has enabled the group to attract talent — young men, including specialists, who are deliberately encouraged to develop the job to the full extent of their capabilities. For example, an accountant need not be confined to his books but may organise the training of local employees.[27]

As Jock often said, leadership requires a vital ingredient — 'human understanding of yourself and other people'. He adds: 'Running any organisation is dealing with people. When you're near the top of an organisation it's all people.' [28] In 1966, towards the end of Campbell's chairmanship, Ian McDonald summarised Booker's achievement in agricultural research:

> New and stronger varieties of cane have been developed which are more resistant to weather, weeds, insects, and plant diseases. Varieties with different growth cycles have been developed, so that portions of the crop reach maturity in sequence rather than all at once. Great advances have been made in the investigation of soil types and the consequent rectification of soil deficiencies. Richer fertilisers are now being applied and more rational schemes of fertiliser application developed. New weedicides and pesticides, suited to local conditions, have been developed and are now in use. Control of the harvesting programme on estates has been improved through the increasingly sophisticated use of maturity-testing techniques.... This unrelenting effort to keep the industry modern — modern in administration, in field and factory operations, in financial control, in new techniques, and in the new ideas which research reveals — must continue if the industry is even to survive much less grow and prosper.[29]

Jock's optimism of 1952 had not been misplaced; but this was a tribute to Dr Harry Evans as well as Campbell's Booker: technical mastery as a servant of the civilised, broader human endeavour.

Endnotes

1. *Booker News* [Leader], June 21, 1957.
2. Harry Evans, 'Field Research in British Guiana: Past, Present and Future', in *Booker Sugar* [1954], 37-8.
3. Ibid.
4. *Booker News*, March 2, 1956.
5. Ian McDonald, interview by the author, Georgetown, Guyana, September 11, 1992.
6. The Chairman's Statement, 1951, p. 20.
7. 'Review of Operations', in Booker Bros, McConnell and Co, Ltd, *Report of the Directors and Statement of Accounts, 1953*, p. 21; *Report..., 1954*, p. 18.

8. BSE, Chairman's Annual Report [Follett-Smith], 1954.
9. Ibid.
10. See note 2 [p. 42].
11. Ibid., 42-3.
12. Ibid., 44.
13. Ibid., 44-5.
14. Ibid., 39.
15. *Booker News*, March 2, 1956.
16. The Chairman's Statement, 1956, p. 38.
17. BSE, Chairman's Annual Report [Follett-Smith], 1956.
18. Ibid.
19. BSE, Chairman's Annual Report, 1959 — Report of the Agricultural Director [Dr Harry Evans].
20. Ibid.
21. Clive Y. Thomas, *Plantations, Peasants, and State: A Study of the Mode of Sugar Production in Guyana* (Los Angeles: Centre for Afro-American Studies, UCLA, 1984), 110.
22. G.M. Eccles, 'Agriculture in 1960', in The Booker Group, *Review of the Year 1960*, pp. 22-3.
23. BSE, Chairman's Annual Report, 1964 — Report of Agricultural Director [Dr Harry Evans].
24. Ibid.
25. Ian McDonald, interview by the author, Georgetown, Guyana, September 11, 1992.
26. Ibid.
27. 'Bookers: The Transformation of Booker Brothers, McConnell and Co. — Once Static, now Vital and Forward-looking', *Investors Chronicle*, March 25, 1960, pp. 1124-5.
28. Ivor Herbert, *The Way to the Top*, (London: Robert Maxwell, 1969), 22.
29. Ian A. McDonald, *Sugar in B.G.: Challenge and Change*, (Georgetown: Booker, n.d., ca. 1966), 14-5.

Chapter Twenty-Four

BUILDING 'HEDGES': FACING UP TO THE HAZARDS OF GUYANESE POLITICS AFTER 1953

Michael Caine, one of Campbell's young proteges in the 1950s and Chairman of Booker in the late 1970s–1980s (the son of his friend and confidant, Sydney Caine), has argued that Jock Campbell's policy of building hedges, diversifying some investments away from Guyana after the suspension of the Constitution in 1953, gave Booker the financial base and the time to ride the nationalisation of its assets in Guyana, whenever that came. This base was so secure, two decades after, that when the Burnham regime nationalised the assets of Booker in 1976 (with the support of Cheddi Jagan's PPP), the Company could carry on with no discernible effect on its dividends or the value of its shares. Caine states that it was the profits from its investments in Guyana which enabled it to diversify geographically and industrially (especially into the food wholesale business in the UK). Meanwhile, Jock's enlightened social policy enhanced Booker's image somewhat, and gave it crucial time, over a decade into the Burnham regime (1964–76), to strengthen its hedge building. However, Caine observed that during Campbell's chairmanship, Booker continued to invest, to expand operations and diversify in British Guiana, while pursuing the social reforms which meant so much to him.[1]

In 1959, Campbell recalled that at the time of the suspension in 1953, Booker reflected on its options and concluded that there were three: (i) stand still and hope that the antagonism, partially rooted in the perceived record and size of Booker, would disappear; (ii) leave precipitately; (iii) carry on but fortify itself against the risks, build 'hedges'. Campbell decided on the latter because their assets were still based overwhelmingly in British Guiana; besides, he was not prepared to abdicate 'our commitment and obligation to the people of [the colony]'.[2]

Even before 1953, Booker had commenced their hedge building strategy. As Campbell remarked at the time:

> [W]hile the long intimacy of Booker's association with British Guiana must always influence our policy and progress, we have in recent years ... spread our branches. Shop-keeping and agency business in the Rhodesias [Zambia and Zimbabwe], Nyasaland [Malawi] and Trinidad; rum companies in the UK and Canada, with valuable export markets throughout the Commonwealth and in many other countries; Campbell Booker Carter's business as an export, shipping and confirming house, representing clients all over Africa and some in the Far East; groundnut financing in the Gambia — these all show promise and add to the stability and flexibility of the Group.[3]

In 1954, after the suspension, Campbell had rejected what he deemed the irresponsibility of politicians 'unencumbered by the truth', dispensing 'unattainable material promises'. However, Booker had to honour their four-fold responsibility to shareholders, employees, customers and the community. Efficiency and profitability in local enterprises had to be combined with the building of hedges. Against a backdrop of deep pessimism, he advised:

> [D]oubt and uncertainty cloud our vision of the future in British Guiana. But it would not be the wish, or in the interest, of shareholders that we should run away at the sign of trouble. Our policy must be, so long as politics do not make it economically unjustifiable and downright imprudent, to maintain our business in British Guiana as efficiently and profitably as we possibly can.... However, your Board are keenly aware of the need that the Group should continue to build up, in the form of profitable interests elsewhere, 'hedges' against a catastrophe in British Guiana should the worst come to the worst, *the forces of evil* [Jagan] prevail, and British interests be expelled. We do not believe that this will happen, but we must guard against its happening [emphasis added].[4]

In early 1955 Campbell was giving the same advice but he was also quick to observe that hedge building did not constitute a winding down of their assets in British Guiana, nor did it preclude expansion there. He conceded that they were 'forced to accelerate' their hedge building in Central Africa and the UK because of the 'political hazards', but he still expressed optimism in British Guiana. Therefore, he did not wish to apply 'this change of emphasis too rigidly'; wherever possible, they would continue to acquire profitable assets, renew old ones, or operate in partnership with others in the colony.[5]

Table V
Acquisitions of the Booker Group, 1949-59

Year	Company	Description	Location
1949	United Rum Merchants Ltd	Blending and Marketing Rum	London
1951	Norton and Co Ltd	Stores	Northern Rhodesia
1952	Ressouvenir Estates Ltd	Sugar Estate	British Guiana
1953	Davidson and Todd	Department Store	Trinidad
	Balata Ltd	Balata Agency Co	London
	Richard Bondy Ltd	Carpet Wholesalers	Woking, England
1954	Port Mourant Ltd	Sugar Estate	British Guiana
	Motor Car Supply Co of Canada	Automotive Accessories and Appliance Wholesalers	Alberta, Canada
	George Brown and Son, Ltd	Retail Shopkeepers	Northern Rhodesia
1955	Davson Group	Sugar Estates	British Guiana
	Bowman Bros, Ltd	Automotive Accessories and Appliance Wholesalers	Saskatchewan, Canada
	Coe Group	Coasting Shipowners	Liverpool, England
1956	George Fletcher and Co Ltd	Sugar Machinery Manufacturers	Derby, England
	Reliance Manufacturing Co (Southwark) Ltd	Potentiometer Manufacturers	London
1957	Alfred Button and Sons, Ltd	Wholesale and Retail Grocers	London and the Home Counties
	R.J. Rouse and Co Ltd	Coffee Brokers	London
	Estate Industries Ltd	Manufacturers of *Tia Maria*	Jamaica
1958	Enmore Estates Ltd	Sugar Estate	British Guiana
	Duncan Stewart and Co Ltd	Sugar Machinery Manufacturers	Glasgow
	William Fogarty Ltd	Department Store	Trinidad
	Gillis and Warren Ltd	Automotive Accessories and Appliance Wholesalers	Manitoba, Canada
	Sigmund Pumps Ltd	Pump Manufacturers	Gateshead, England
1959	Taylor Pearson and Carson (Canada), Ltd	Automotive Accessory and Appliance Wholesalers	Alberta and British Columbia, Canada

Source: Jock Campbell, 'The Development and Organisation of Booker', Paper delivered at the London School of Economics, (mimeo.), November 24, 1959.

As Table V shows Booker pursued this two-pronged strategy with vigour. In 1953 they acquired Davidson and Todd, a department store in Trinidad, as well as Balata Ltd (London), based on raw materials collected in the interior of British Guiana, and Richard Bondy Ltd, carpet wholesalers, in Woking, England. In 1954 Booker acquired Port Mourant Ltd, a sugar estate in British Guiana which they had previously managed, Motor Car Supply Co in Alberta, Canada, and George Allen, retail shopkeepers, Northern Rhodesia (Zambia). As noted earlier, in 1955, Booker acquired the Davson Group which owned Blairmont Estate in British Guiana; Bowman Bros, car accessories and appliances wholesalers in Saskatchewan, Canada; and Coe Group, coasting shipowners in Liverpool. In 1956 and 1957 Booker made several acquisitions which were to define its character beyond the chairmanship of Jock Campbell: George Fletcher and Co, manufacturers of sugar machinery, in Derby; Reliance Manufacturing Co, potentiometer manufacturers, in London; and Estate Industries Ltd, manufacturers of 'Tia Maria' liquors, in Jamaica.

In early 1956, shortly after a successful visit to British Guiana, Campbell informed shareholders that the building of hedges against the 'political hazards' of the colony was progressing. He acknowledged that although management and workers were doing good work in the colony, and that while their businesses were 'inherently sound', they were still economically vulnerable because of 'grave political uncertainties'. However, he reaffirmed his commitment to Booker's 'five-fold responsibility [often four-fold]', to shareholders, staff, labour, customers and the community.[6] Both in terms of the hedges and the pursuit of his social reforms, he knew that their investments in the colony were crucial. He therefore sought to reassure shareholders that sanity was returning to British Guiana. He could not sustain the two-pronged project without their confidence in him:

I found confidence [he was there in February/March 1956] — I hope not without justification — being restored, and development progressing. In all my visits I have never found the people on the sugar estates, on the wharves, in the street more friendly and co-operative than they were this time; or seeming for the most part happier — although this is not to say that the people of B.G. do not suffer their full share of human frustration and tribulation, or that there are not still wrongs to be righted.... I left, after all too short a stay, with, as always, feelings of deepest affection for that country, of pride at Booker's association with her people, and of confidence that their innate good sense will ultimately carry them through the present slough of political despond. If this be so, then I am sure that, between us all, the economic problems can be solved.[7]

Michael Caine considered Jock an exceptionally able man, with a consuming sense of guilt because of his family's old associations with the bitter side of sugar. This gave him, like no other person in Booker, an unimpeachable social conscience, an unwavering motivation to change the social landscape of Guyana. He said that Jock believed that if he made Booker a socially responsible, humane company, this could enhance the quality of life there. Campbell had often argued that Booker's debts to the place, alone, placed an immense responsibility on them to stay on as long as it was economically profitable to do so, because there were 'still wrongs to be righted'.[8]

In 1963, ten years after Campbell's adumbration of the hedge building policy, he repeated his quote from his 1953 Chairman's Statement, reminding shareholders that Booker could not 'run away at the sign of trouble'. Racial troubles of greater intensity than anything hitherto were brewing now; but his belief in his cause never wavered, however depressed he felt about the country's politics.[9] By 1963 the hedge building and the social reforms had made much progress, bleak though the gathering political storms.

Between 1952 and 1956 sugar, from British Guiana, accounted for 42 per cent of Booker's profits; shop-keeping (mainly in the colony and Central Africa), 36 per cent; shipping 10 per cent; rum, 8 per cent; light industries 3 per cent; and engineering 1 per cent. Sugar's contribution to Booker's profits slipped progressively throughout the late 1950s–1960s: by 1959–63 it yielded 27 per cent; shop-keeping 35 per cent; rum 18 per cent; shipping 13 per cent; light industries 10 per cent; and engineering 10 per cent. In other words, while sugar's contribution had dropped by 15 per cent in the two periods and shop-keeping had remained virtually unchanged, the place of rum, light industries and engineering combined, had risen from 12 per cent of profits in 1952–56 to 41 per cent in 1959–63. This was reflective of the two-pronged policy of reinvesting locally and hedge building overseas.[10]

The character of Booker was changing. The decline of sugar's contribution to less than 30 per cent of its profits was a psychological victory: the vulnerability of the company to Guyanese politics was diminishing, so, too, its older vulnerability, to the vagaries of sugar prices. Equally important were shifts in the contributions to their profits of the various geographical trading areas. Between 1953 and 1957 British Guiana and the West Indies (particularly the former) yielded 65 per cent of Booker's profits; the UK, 19 per cent; Central Africa, 11 per cent; Canada, 5 per cent. By 1959–63 British Guiana and the West Indies (still primarily the former) had dropped to 57 per cent; Britain had reached 25 per cent; Central Africa had declined to about 5 per cent, while Canada was responsible for 13 per cent of Booker's profits.[11] As Michael Caine saw it: 'Booker was coming home, at last'. The foundations of the Company as primarily a UK-based enterprise were being laid, with the acquisition of shops in the wholesale food business.[12] As Campbell observed in June 1964:

> Our wholesale (Alfred Button) and retail (Budgen) food business did well again; their sales and profits showing satisfactory increases. We opened three supermarkets during the year. In March 1964 we bought 23 shops from Teetgen and Company. Our food businesses include various forms of distribution — voluntary group trading, supermarkets, self-service and traditional counter-service shops: we believe we gain strength from this variety.[13]

But Booker was still dependent on British Guiana, with its increasingly violent politics in 1963–64, for over 50 per cent of its profits. Indeed, even after Campbell resigned from Booker in mid-1967, during David Powell's and George Bishop's chairmanship in the late 1960s and early 1970s, Booker was still committed to investing in an independent Guyana. Bishop had a good relationship with L.F.S. Burnham, and had none of Jock's idealism, his vision of the four-fold responsibility of Booker: Guyana was still a profitable area of investment.

Paulette Pierce detects a tendency to shift emphasis with regard to hedge building: when political stability returned to Guyana in the late 1960s, under Burnham (Jock had left Booker), the vigour of geographical diversification was attenuated; the indifferent results from some of the hedges also encouraged this.[14] She contends, however, that the pattern of diversification was already set during Campbell's stewardship; it would accelerate in the early 1970s as Burnham moved to the left:

> Booker's hedging policy was defensive and inconsistently pursued. When political tensions mounted, Booker would quicken the pace of its acquisition in the industrialised countries. Thus during the struggle for independence in Guyana [Campbell's chairmanship], Booker steadily increased its investments in food distribution and engineering in the UK and merchandising in Canada. However, as the political crisis receded [after 1964, under Burnham], the pursuit of a geographical and product mix lost its vigour. Booker ran into many problems during its first major attempt at diversification. The investments in Canada proved a complete failure and Booker's UK shops and engineering companies were only marginally profitable by the end of the sixties. Nevertheless, a diversified foundation had been laid; and, more importantly, Booker had acquired invaluable experience which would serve it well during its next crucial phase of diversification which began in 1970.[15]

Pierce adds that whatever the economic, environmental or political risks involved with tropical agriculture, Booker remained committed to sugar production in Guyana, until the Burnham regime imposed a draconian levy in 1974, which made their continuation there pointless. By then its diversified structure could ensure its survival when nationalisation of its Guyanese assets followed in 1976. Ten years earlier, in his last Chairman's Statement, in May 1966, Campbell had underlined the fact that the hedges had cushioned some of the hazards of sugar in British Guiana. He noted that between 1961 and 1965 Booker Sugar Estates (BSE) made an average profit (after tax) of £287,000, whereas the other companies made an average profit of £964,000. In 1964, because of virtual civil war in British Guiana, drought and the 'ludicrously low' world market price of sugar, tropical agriculture got a reduced profit of £88,000; in 1965 it experienced a loss of £48,000. Campbell explained how they were able to cope: '[A]lthough we have had plenty of troubles with diversification, the savings and the roundabouts have helped to keep profits steady during a dangerous time for Guyana and a poor time for sugar. Had Booker remained solely a sugar company, we should now be worrying not about percentage returns and falling profits, but about losses and passed dividends.' [16]

In 1966, the last full year of Campbell's chairmanship, drought again brought bleakness to the sugar industry. Sugar produced on Booker estates was 237,000 tons, compared to 252,000 tons in 1965 and an average of 250,000 between 1961 and 1965. Union rivalry between the Jagan-backed GAWU and the recognised union, MPCA, also, exacerbated the situation. In the words of David Powell (Campbell's successor from June 1, 1967), and contrary to popular perception, BSE were just breaking even at the time of Guyana's independence in 1966. The idea of super-profits, an axiom in Guyana, propagated relentlessly by Cheddi Jagan, had no basis in fact:

> The disruption following the political and industrial unrest of the early sixties was followed in 1964 and 1966 by two of the worst droughts recorded in Guyana for a hundred years. In recent years it has been difficult for BSE to do better than break even, and in 1965 there was a loss.... Nevertheless, whatever the price, and taking a long-term view, it is essential to make the largest crop possible since markets must be secured and performance established to safeguard future quotas and outlets. BSE have therefore steadily and cautiously increased their acreage in cane over the years. [17]

Campbell's rationale for continued faith in Guyana was rooted in the profitability of overall investments there: sugar, shops and ships; but he was, to the end, resolved to enhance life for the sugar workers. Booker had no plans to abandon the country. As Paulette Pierce argues, from the economic angle, 'Booker were seeking a balance between its investments in the underdeveloped countries and the UK, because of political uncertainties in both parts of the world. Booker was not looking to get out of its traditional business or Guyana.' [18]

In the late 1960s, in an independent Guyana which seemed amenable to foreign capital, Booker still saw a role for themselves in the sugar industry. As David Powell remarked in 1968: '[I]t does not make sense — economically or socially — to believe that any advantage would be gained by diversifying at the expense of sugar.'[19] However, with the proclaimed radicalisation of the Burnham government in the early 1970s, its advocacy of 'co-operative socialism' and its initiatives towards Cuba and China, Booker again moved quickly to build hedges against the perceived resurgent Guyanese uncertainty. They were seeking to earn at least 50 per cent of their profits in the UK: as George Bishop, the chairman from 1972, announced, Booker's aim was 'to have as its core a broadly-based food company'. But they were still hoping to retain sugar as an important plank in their business. Pierce concludes: 'Although George Bishop did not share Lord Campbell's legendary vision of corporate responsibility and adaptation, the new Chairman did recognise that continued success and survival required finding a *modus vivendi* with Third World states increasingly exercising their sovereign rights.'[20] Only Burnham's exorbitant levy of 1974 made them conclude that Booker's long odyssey in Guyana had come to the end.

Speaking towards the end of his chairmanship and the end of Empire, in May 1965, after L.F.S. Burnham had become Prime Minister of independent Guyana, Campbell had said that he was having discussions with him on the 'decolonisation' of sugar. In his precise, philosophical way he explained: 'By this concept we all mean the fuller integration of the industry with the community, to avoid its standing out — in the light of its past history — as an alien organisation superimposed on British Guiana.'[21]

Campbell added that towards this end, they had embarked on a four-pronged programme, two of which were quite advanced: (i) 'Guianisation of management', to ensure that 'there is no job in Booker that is not available to Guianese capable of doing it'; (ii) the expansion of peasant cane farming to dilute the dominance of Booker in sugar, the aim being to bring 12,000 acres under independent cultivation by 1968. Besides, Campbell noted, they were keen to introduce local government institutions in sugar estates communities, to give government greater responsibility for the provision of social services; in short, to extinguish the 'old paternalism, bred of slavery'. Finally, he was encouraging the government of Forbes Burnham — as he had tried with Premier Jagan personally, in 1958 and 1960, without success — to accept majority share participation in the industry. He concluded that while government had indicated no interest in the operational and technical management of sugar, their participation could be exercised through a statutory board, facilitating regular consultation between them and the sugar companies on strategic issues.[22]

To the end of his days at Booker, Jock Campbell never lost sight of his four-fold responsibilities, however depressed he was — 'very depressed', he said — by the racial futility of Guyana. In June 1967, his successor, David Powell, made an assessment of Campbell's achievement after being effectively at the top for 20 years. Powell observed that in 1947, when Campbell became vice-chairman and chief executive, shareholders' capital employed was £2.8 million, while after-tax profits were £208,000, and 800 shareholders received dividends totalling £80,000. In 1966, Campbell's last full year as Chairman of Booker, shareholders' capital was £22 million, after-tax profits were £1.4 million, while dividends were nearly £1 million. Powell added that in 1947 the output of sugar on Booker's estates was 117,000 tons worth £3 million. In 1960, when the highest production was recorded, 272,000 tons of sugar worth £10 million, were produced.[23]

Powell attributed Campbell's achievements to several factors, including Guianisation, based on a cadet scheme to train local managers, and the provision of technical training for workers, to enable them to play a bigger role in Booker. He noted also that sugar workers' earnings had risen four-fold since 1947, in addition to a 'spectacular' improvement in housing, with 11,000 families, former occupants of the derelict ranges, re-housed: 'Relative to the size of population, this is an achievement in housing unsurpassed in the Caribbean.' David Powell concluded:

> In 1947 over one-half of the Group's net profits came from sugar; in 1966 virtually nothing. There have certainly been failures — as well as successes — in our policy of diversification; but without it there would have been cut dividends and no broadly-based

Booker economy to give us the confidence to continue the expansion and modernisation of our various businesses, not least our sugar estates — despite near civil war in Guyana in 1964 and severe droughts in both 1964 and early 1966. In an unguarded moment at an annual general meeting Jock Campbell once remarked 'Booker is a difficult business'. During the twenty years of his responsibility as chief executive he successfully led Booker through several political crises with deep awareness of the social, economic and political problems of developing countries. The stability of the Group today owes much to his vision in seeing that Booker played a steadily constructive part through the birth-throes of nations whose independence he constantly supported.[24]

In 1964 Campbell had explained to a reporter what he saw as the role of foreign capital in poor countries: a partnership, a progressive, corporate citizenship in tandem with an enlightened public opinion — an open mind to transcend the old hurts. Appropriately enough, on May 26, 1966, the day Guyana became independent, *Booker News* reproduced the interview: 'I see large international companies like Booker as linking together metropolitan capital and "know how" with the talents and resources of underdeveloped areas like the West Indies, and by showing it can be done, encouraging others to do the same.... I do think we help to maintain standards of efficiency and enterprise without which the West Indies could not earn their keep. There is quite a lot to be said for just going on doing things well however difficult the circumstances, even if it is not all that glamorous.' [25] The orderly, creative, socially-committed mind could not countenance otherwise.

Between 1955 and 1964 Booker, under Jock Campbell, made a reasonable profit for its shareholders, but an average return on their capital of 2.85 per cent was certainly not super-profits.

In March 1958 *Booker News*, reflecting on the popular perception that 'bloated capitalists' in Booker were exploiting the Guyanese people, contended that this was a mirage: the facts hardly constituted a windfall to its 3,826 shareholders. They elaborated:

358 / Sweetening 'Bitter Sugar'

[T]he last Annual Report of Booker Bros. McConnell and Co. showed that their balance represents the investment of 3,826 shareholders [in 1956] — not one or two robber barons!... [F]or every shilling of net revenue, *three-quarters of a cent* was paid in dividends to shareholders. The remainder went to wages, salaries and other employment costs, which took sixteen and a half cents; taxes; and depreciation and replacement of machinery; together with a cent and a quarter which was ploughed back into the business. In sum, shareholders got less than three cents profit on every dollar invested.... At three cents on his dollar there just isn't enough to convert every shareholder into a 'bloated capitalist'. But since 3,826 persons continue to invest, it would seem that they are attracted more by the soundness of their investment in tropical agriculture and the healthy state of the Booker operations than by the possibility of making a fast dollar.[26]

Jock often said that it was easier for a Campbell to pass through a needle's eye than for the people of Guyana to love Booker, given its latifundist character. He only wished that the new Booker he was trying to build would be understood; he could not expect more. It was assumed in the colony that the profits from sugar were unremittingly exorbitant; nationalisation in 1976 would soon demonstrate that it took immense technical efficiency and professionalism to make sugar profitable, even with a substantially secured market. No golden egg was being returned to the national patrimony; nationalisation quickly disabused Guyanese of images of that version of El Dorado. But the image of Booker as vampire was resilient. Nevertheless, as Sir Peter Parker observes, Jock's social policy earned Booker invaluable time 'to diversify and to balance its assets both by type of business and geographically'. He concludes: '[T]he resilience was there to take the inevitable stresses of transition when the colonies gained independence.' [27]

In the next section I will assess how Booker was able to honour its obligations to its workers, especially its sugar workers, and the community in British Guiana, in the 1950s and the early 1960s, through Campbell's social policy.

Table VI
Summary of Consolidated Figures for Booker, 1955–64
(Figures in £000s)

	1955	1956	1957	1958	1959	1960	1961	1962	1963	1964
Booker Shareholders' Funds Employed	9,341	10,153	11,104	11,970	15,100	15,970	14,350	14,970	15,520	18,680
Profit Before Taxation	1,939	2,360	3,340	2,992	3,365	3,361	3,108	3,331	4,307	3,169
Taxation	1,136	1,465	2,089	1,795	1,855	1,764	1,673	1,834	2,439	1,617
Profit After Taxation	803	895	1,251	1,197	1,510	1,597	1,435	1,497	1,868	1,552
Dividends After Tax: (Preferential)	21	21	21	21	22	22	22	22	22	22
(Ordinary)	191	191	286	286	477	525	590	590	590	590
Profit for Year Retained in Business	492	619	664	984	850	887	354	750	818	608
Dividends Expressed as a Percentage of Booker's Shareholders' Funds	2.27	2.09	2.76	2.34	3.44	3.39	3.36	3.1	2.93	2.83
Number of Shareholders	3,398	3,826	4,525	4,949	5,816	6,340	7,461	8,214	8,753	9,352

Source: Booker Group, Review of the Year, 1964, pp 21-22

Endnotes

1. Michael Caine, interview by the author, London, July 19, 1995.
2. Jock Campbell, 'The Development and Organisation of Booker', Paper delivered at LSE, November 24, 1959, (mimeo.), p. 12.
3. The Chairman's Statement, 1952, p. 24.
4. The Chairman's Statement, 1953, p. 26.
5. The Chairman's Statement, 1954, p. 25.
6. The Chairman's Statement, 1955, p. 35.
7. Ibid., 36-7.

8. Michael Caine, interview by the author, December 10, 1996.

9. The Chairman's Statement, 1963, p. 18.

10. See Chairman's Statements, 1960, 1963.

11. Ibid.

12. See note 1.

13. The Chairman's Statement, 1963, p. 13.

14. Paulette Pierce, *Non-Capitalist Development: The Struggle to Nationalise the Guyanese Sugar Industry* (Totowa, NJ: Rowman and Allanheld, 1984), 143.

15. Ibid., 140-1.

16. The Chairman's Statement, 1965, p. 10.

17. The Chairman's Statement, 1966, p. 27.

18. See note 14 [p.141].

19. Ibid., Quote from Chairman's Statement, 1967.

20. Ibid., [p. 143].

21. The Chairman's Statement, 1964, pp. 17-8.

22. Ibid.

23. David Powell, 'The Booker Group under Lord Campbell's Leadership', in The Booker Group, *Report and Accounts, 1966*, pp. 24-5.

24. Ibid., 24.

25. This interview first appeared in a Jamaican magazine, *Spotlight*, (July 1964), pp.13-4.

26. *Booker News* [Leader], March 14, 1958.

27. Sir Peter Parker, 'Lord Campbell of Eskan', (Obituary), *The Independent*, January 4, 1995.

Part 7

Sweetening 'Bitter Sugar' III: Reforms on the Plantations, 1934-1964

Chapter Twenty-Five

BURNING THE 'BRIDGE TO THE GRAVE': DR GEORGE GIGLIOLI AND THE ERADICATION OF MALARIA, 1933–48

I have argued that Campbell's empathy with his workers and the Guyanese community must be located in his encounter with plantation life, on his family's estates in British Guiana, between 1934 and 1937. I have also argued that the example of reform set by the small family firm of sugar producers at Blairmont, S. Davson and Co, especially under their innovative managers, Gordon and G.M. (Guy) Eccles, made a profound impact on him. This was the spark that had kindled Campbell's notion of possibilities for change. Their pioneering work in the eradication of malaria was a fundamental step in transforming the inhospitable coastland, from the graveyard of indentured workers to one of prolific demographic growth after the Second World War. It was Davson's malariologist, Dr George Giglioli, OBE, (1897–1972), who was to isolate the vector and lead the campaign for the eradication of malaria, between 1945 and 1948.

In May 1966, on the occasion of Guyana's independence, the *Guyana Graphic* attributed the eradication of the dreaded disease almost exclusively to Giglioli. They observed:

> The era of Guyana's growing pains is pock-marked with incidents none the least significant of which has been the battle against the scourge of malaria. And in this battle one man's name stands out boldly — Dr. George Giglioli, famed malariologist whose dedicated service in the cause of ridding Guyana of this dreaded scourge, is a story of single-minded purpose and unflagging determination. In the course of this battle, [he] has helped

Guyana's transformation from one of the world's foremost fever-ravaged countries to the place where the death-dealing disease was first checked, then beaten back until today, victory over malaria has become one of the glorious achievements in the history of Guyana's progress against disease and death. Today Guyana can boast of freedom from malaria, a freedom won largely through the unrelenting campaign of Dr. Giglioli.[1]

The *Graphic's* designation of the malarial experience as a 'scourge' was no exaggeration. In 1943–44 the percentage of school-children with enlarged spleens was astounding, with the wetter Essequibo Coast recording the worse rates: 29 to 78 per cent on East Coast Demerara; 20 to 55 per cent on East Bank Demerara; 37 to 80 per cent on West Bank Demerara; 20 to 43 per cent on West Coast Demerara; and 52 to 90 per cent on the Essequibo Coast. Malaria had had such a devastating effect on population growth that between the 1931 and 1946 censuses, while the drier, malaria-free Corentyne Coast recorded a population increase of 384 per 1,000 and the partially malaria-free West Coast Berbice 249 per thousand, it was a paltry 87 per thousand on East Coast Demerara, and 113 on the East and West Bank Demerara. On the Essequibo Coast the population actually declined by 142 per 1,000. This translates to a meagre natural increment of 36 per 1,000 between 1921 and 1931, and 186 per 1,000 between 1932 and 1946. With the virtual eradication of malaria, by 1950, the natural increment, overnight, was a comparatively prolific 192 per 1,000.[2]

On the sugar plantations, in a population of about 75,000, hospital admissions during the malaria epidemic of 1938 was over 13,000, with 240 deaths directly attributable to the disease. In 1944, over 10,000 cases were admitted to estate hospitals; 200 died. With the eradication campaign launched after 1945, less than 800 were admitted in 1948, with under 30 deaths; by 1950 under 200 cases were admitted to estate hospitals, with less than 10 deaths.[3]

Yet, as late as 1939, the Director of Medical Services of British Guiana, Dr N.M. Maclennan, in an exchange with Dr Mary Blacklock of the Moyne Commission, argued that malaria was so endemic to the colony that it was futile to contemplate its eradication. It was axiomatic that the 'scourge' which stifled the imagination, nullified effort, and killed was a 'sisyphean' task: 'elimination is an utter impossibility':

Maclennan:	[M]alaria is the biggest single cause of death.
Blacklock:	What has been done about malaria in this country? What steps do you propose to take?
Maclennan:	Practically nothing has been done except treatment of malaria. From the preventive standpoint little has been done, because the country is up against great difficulties.
Blacklock:	Is this a difficult problem?
Maclennan:	It is a difficult problem, probably the most difficult problem I have come across....
Blacklock:	Why is that?
Maclennan:	Because of the extraordinary hydrographic condition of the country.
Blacklock:	The amount of water?
Maclennan:	Yes.
Blacklock:	What steps do you take to ameliorate conditions?
Maclennan:	I have now an assurance from the Rockefeller Foundation that they are going to give some assistance towards investigating the problem of malaria in the country. *We believe that malaria cannot be eliminated from this country.* It would be too costly and would not be an economic proposition, but we believe, from certain investigations that have already been carried out by the Health Adviser to the Sugar Producers' Association [Dr Giglioli], that we can reduce its incidence and control it to some extent [emphasis added].[4]

Since the late 1920s, Dr Giglioli's passion for researching the causes of malaria in British Guiana had led him to isolate the *Anopheles darlingi* as the sole vector. Moreover, he was well on his way to identifying the sources of its vulnerability, its potential for self-destruction. In June 1939 a Malaria Research Unit, headed by Dr Giglioli, was established with support from the Rockefeller Foundation, the Sugar Producers' Association and the government.

This extraordinary man was on the verge of possibly the most significant achievement in the social history of Guyana.[5]

George Giglioli was an Italian, born in Naples. His father was Director of the Faculty of Agriculture and Professor of Agricultural Chemistry at the Royal University of Pisa; that was where Giglioli graduated from in 1921 as a Doctor of Medicine. In 1922 he obtained a Diploma in Tropical Medicine and Hygiene from London and in 1925 a Diploma in Dermatology and Venereology from Paris. In 1932 he got a Diploma of the Superior School of Malariology; while in 1933 he was admitted to membership of the Royal College of Physicians, London, as well as becoming honorary lecturer in Tropical Pathology at his alma mater, the Royal University of Pisa.

Dr George Giglioli:
The great malariologist

However, it is his phenomenal achievement in British Guiana, which will endure in the annals of tropical medicine. For ten years, 1922 to 1932, he was Chief Medical Officer with the Demerara Bauxite Company at Mackenzie, Upper Demerara River. His major contribution, in malariology, was still to be established. In 1933, the year before Jock Campbell arrived in the colony to work in his family's sugar business, Giglioli joined S. Davson as medical adviser, at Plantation Blairmont.[6] This estate, at the mouth of the Berbice River, had a fairly high rate of malarial infection; but under its progressive head, Sir Edward Davson, and its imaginative manager, Guy Eccles, Blairmont had become a reforming estate, already trying to sweeten the bitter legacy of sugar. As noted earlier, the Davson example, including Giglioli's bold research on the disease in the Berbice estuary, made a ready impression on Campbell, a frequent visitor to Blairmont in the 1934–47 period.[7]

The reforming temper of the Davsons was at variance with the obscurantism of the Campbells, epitomised by the derelict ranges and the *ancien regime* of James Bee at Albion. Unlike Blairmont, however, Albion was in a salubrious region, generally malaria-free.

It was the former's susceptibility to malaria which had led to the inspired appointment of Giglioli as their medical adviser. He had already done useful research on the Upper Demerara River in the 1920s; this was published as a book in 1930, *Malarial Nephritis*, which won the Davson Centenary Gold Medal in 1932, the year before he joined Davson's at Blairmont.

Campbell recalls the context of Giglioli's early work in the sugar industry, in the mid-1930s: 'When I went there [1934], the infant mortality was about 350 per thousand and the result was that the population ... was going down.'[8] Giglioli's excellent research at Blairmont, between 1933 and 1937, was pursued with equal vigour at Booker, which he joined as Estate Medical Officer, in the latter year. In 1939 he was seconded to the government as Director of the Malaria Research Unit. By then he had published several ground-breaking essays on *Anopheles darlingi* and identified its cardinal behavioural patterns, its feeding and resting routines. By the late 1930s the colonial inertia on malaria was lifting. Workers' militancy after 1934–35 and the low productivity of workers with chronic malaria were eroding the complacency, as did other factors, as I have argued elsewhere:

> By the 1930s sugar prices had plummeted to around £8 to £9 per ton — a reduction of 50% on the prices during the depression of 1921–22. All immigration [from India] had ceased since 1917. The extinction of the industry seemed inevitable. The efforts to beat malaria were spawned by these dire economic circumstances and were an aspect of a vigorous policy of rationalisation on the plantations in the 1930s.[9]

In 1942 Giglioli was named Honorary Government Malariologist and in 1945 he became Medical Adviser to the SPA, a post he held until his death. Campbell recalls his impressions of the man with whom he had many meetings after 1945. He emphasises his single-mindedness as a researcher and his strength of character, amply demonstrated by his lack of bitterness although he was interned for a part of the War because of his Italian background. Jock relates:

I remember him well, indeed. I cottoned on to the importance of [his research] and we added to his salary and his facilities; he was paid by the SPA by then [after 1945]. I spent hours with him. He was a very intellectual man; very anti-Mussolini, very anti-fascist, very well read and he spoke very good English. Everything was very clinical in his approach to people, [but] he wasn't very interested in people's problems at all. I had a row with him because our hospitals were so bad, but he wasn't interested in that. As long as he did what he wanted, clinically, he didn't mind if the hospitals were dirty; and I cared a lot about improving hospitals because he wasn't interested. But he was a first-rate man, totally committed to research, very single-minded.[10]

He concluded with admiration for Giglioli's contribution to the whole anti-malaria culture which took shape in the late 1930s–40s: 'Malaria was the bane of Guyana and he eradicated it in the face of great difficulties because during part of the War he was interned and he discovered what the [malarial] vector was, how it behaved, how you killed it, and he actually eradicated malaria.'[11]

Indeed, Giglioli's research into *A.darlingi*, establishing that it was the sole vector of malarial infection in British Guiana, the assessment of its breeding habits and the astounding eradication of the dreaded disease in the colony, between 1946 and 1948, constitute an epic in tropical medicine. It was an achievement with revolutionary potential economically, socially and politically, at the end of the 1940s. George Giglioli himself has told the story.

Between 1922 and 1932, when he was the Chief Medical Officer of the Demerara Bauxite Co. at Mackenzie, Upper Demerara River, he established that *A.darlingi* could not survive in the excessively acidic, brown water of the Demerara River and the surrounding forest creeks and swamps. When, however, this water was contaminated by the bauxite washing process, leading to precipitation of the brown organic matter the water carried in suspension, thus reducing its acidity, *A.darlingi* was able to breed. This was the start of his journey on the tortuous road to its demise. Between 1933 and 1937, on the Davson's Estates on the Berbice estuary — Blairmont (West Bank), Bath (West Coast) and Providence (East Bank) — Giglioli advanced his work, limiting the breeding and distribution of the anopheles to the pivotal question of water reaction. This was the environment which enabled him to isolate *A.dalingi* as the sole vector of the disease, rampant on most of the coastland of British Guiana.[12]

In 1938–39 those findings were published locally, in four articles. He arrived at four principal conclusions: (i) that *A.darlingi* was the only carrier of malaria of importance in British Guiana; (ii) that it 'breeds selectively in large bodies of water which are clear and slightly acid or neutral in reaction; it does not breed in waters with a marked acid reaction'; (iii) *A.darlingi* does not breed in water of high salinity or brackish water, very common on the Corentyne Coast, in Berbice; (iv) originally a forest mosquito, it likes a humid climate; it does not survive on the wind-swept, drier coastal front-lands of the Corentyne.[13]

On the basis of these crucial findings he was able to recommend to the sugar producers in 1937, when he joined Booker, that the depredations of *A.darlingi* could be tempered if 'sheltered yards, situated within the cane cultivation, were condemned to be gradually eliminated'. He advised that all new residential areas be located on the 'open front-lands, where salt soils, wind-borne sea spray and constant winds offer a naturally unfavourable water and atmospheric environment for both the breeding and survival of *A.darlingi*.' [14]

Giglioli attributed its virulence to the empoldered, man-made environment of the British Guiana coastland. Ironically, it was the reclamation, the humanising of this environment, which had made it vulnerable to *A.darlingi*. He argued that malaria was virtually non-existent on the Corentyne Coast, apart from the occasional epidemic in years of excessive rainfall, because much of its front-lands were still in a primitive state, unreclaimed, with constant incursions by sea water and the consequent high salinity of the land. This gave rise to a sort of scrubland, hard grasses, not trees, thus exposing the coast to high winds; this was antagonistic to the propagation of *A.darlingi*.

Giglioli contended that the highly acidic, organic soils of the 'pegasse' area immediately inland from the coastland clay, as well as the forested sand reefs, interspersed on its margins, were not conducive to this dreaded malarial vector. So both the sea in front and the 'pegasse' lands and sand reefs behind, were inimical to the propagation of *A.darlingi*. They tended to predominate in the less acidic interior regions of red loams and lateritic soils: 'In the red loams and lateritic soils of the interior which contain clay, organic matter from decomposing vegetation becomes precipitated near the surface where it is further decomposed. The waters which drain from these soils are limpid, colourless and only slightly acidic, offering perfect conditions for *A.darlingi*'.[15]

The cultivated coastland, the plantation zone, with its myriad drains and ditches, irrigation canals, flood-fallowed cane fields, rice fields, ponds and borrow pits, provided an ideal habitat for *A.darlingi*. These ubiquitous reservoirs of non-acidic water were a haven for this species — a point dramatised by the malaria-free Corentyne Coast's sudden susceptibility to malaria, in years of heavy rainfall, when the water on the saline front-lands became diluted, as was the encroaching acidic water from the 'pegasse' back lands.[16]

Giglioli calculated that on every square mile of cane cultivation (10 acre fields) there were 16 miles of irrigation canals, 4.5 miles of drainage side-line canals and 45 miles of four feet drains. This complex hydrological environment, in conjunction with the extension of the area under wet-rice culture since the First World War, made coastal British Guiana especially vulnerable to *A.darlingi*. By the start of the Second World War, Giglioli had unearthed most of the key characteristics of this species, including its peculiar feeding patterns. He explained later:

> The very characteristics which made *Anopheles darlingi* an exceptionally dangerous malarial carrier, have also been the cause of its downfall: its selective preference for human blood and its habit of biting and resting in houses, and not in the open, render this mosquito specially vulnerable to DDT, when this powerful insecticide is applied as a thin residual film to the interior of all the houses of the community. The mosquito not only disappears from the houses, but it actually becomes extinct in the surrounding countryside.[17]

At the end of his series of articles on malaria, in 1938–39, Giglioli had concluded that 'certain weaknesses' in the biology of *A.darlingi* 'may be exploited to its detriment'. Though confident that malaria could be 'successfully controlled', he was circumspect about its eradication. His achievements a decade later, by 1948, had exceeded his most optimistic prognostication.[18]

As Giglioli observed (and Campbell repeated to me), it was Davson's imaginative approach to industrial relations, even before the 1930s, which had made the research possible. The higher incidence of the disease at Blairmont gave urgency to the task. Giglioli explains:

[I]n 1933 [I] joined Messrs. S. Davson and Co. Ltd., for the purpose of reorganising medical assistance on this Company's plantations on the Berbice estuary. The latter experiment was introduced for the specific purpose of attracting workers to take up residence on these estates (internal migration).... The Blairmont Estate Hospital was rebuilt and enlarged, and a clinical and bacteriological laboratory erected and equipped. Remarkable results were obtained at Blairmont mainly by the routine application of rational and intensive therapeutic measures, the aim, wherever possible, being a cure rather than temporary relief.[19]

Giglioli remarked that it was here that 'great advances' were made in 'unravelling' the old problem of the transmission of malaria. But he also conducted surveys and treatment campaigns on hookworm on the Davson estates. In April 1934 the infection rate was 73.4 per cent; by December 1935 it had been reduced to a mere 6.2 per cent. Giglioli tackled another common problem, megalocytic anaemia of pregnancy. He observed: '[It was] a very common and disabling disease in East Indians causing a high maternal, foetal and neo-natal mortality, was identified and its complex causes were elucidated; very effective therapeutic and preventive measures were successfully introduced.'[20]

The health of the predominantly Indian resident workers at Blairmont was dire. In 1934, the year Campbell went to British Guiana, 1,075 of its resident population of 1,926 had to be admitted to hospital at least once that year — 55 per cent. That constituted 1,392 admissions, entailing a loss to the estate of 13,388 hospital man-days in 1934 alone. In short, this amounted to 36.5 in-patients per day, with each patient spending 9.5 days in hospital. Besides, 1,185 cases were treated as out-patients and 40,656 minor treatments were administered at the estate's dispensary.[21]

Giglioli observed that the following figures on health at Blairmont between 1914 and 1933, while abysmal, were generally reflective of the condition on the coastland of British Guiana, between the Pomeroon (in Essequibo) and the Berbice Rivers, before the eradication of malaria. Only the drier, windier Corentyne Coast escaped this dire pall of disease, with its discernible torpor.

TABLE VII
Health at Blairmont Estate [S. Davson], 1914-33

Average Population	2,013
Total Number of Births	1,275
Total Number of Deaths	1,472
Average Number of Mortality per 1,000 Live Births	222
Crude Vital Index (Number of Births per100 Deaths)	86.6
Average Annual Natural Increment	-10

Source: George Giglioli, 'Medical Services on the Sugar Estates of British Guiana', *Timehri*, no. 35 (fifth series), (1956): 7.

On the sugar estates of British Guiana, in 1944, just before the start of the anti-malaria campaign, infant mortality per 1,000 live births was 176. This declined progressively to 109, 106, 91 and 82 between 1945 and 1948. It is irrefutable that malaria was at the crux of the stagnant population on the estates. Indeed, it was the foundation of the static Indian population in the colony before the end of the 1940s. For them in particular, more susceptible to the ravages of malaria than African people, the results were dismal. As the Immigration Agent General observed in 1922, of the 238,969 Indians taken to the colony as indentured labourers between 1838 and 1917, 69,803 had returned to India, leaving a balance of 169,166.

However, the census of 1921 recorded 44,228 fewer Indians in British Guiana — 124,938.[22]

I have written elsewhere on the revolution in demographic patterns among Indians, after 1948, with the eradication of malaria:

> The eradication of malaria was magic. Between 1931 and 1946 the population on the malarious East Coast Demerara increased by only 87 per thousand; on the endemically malarious Essequibo Coast it declined by 142 per thousand. The Indian population declined between 1911 and 1921 and stagnated for most of the 1920s. The death rate among Indians between 1921 and 1930 was 28.4 per thousand; in 1946–50, with the eradication of malaria, it dropped to 13.9, declining further to 9.7 in 1956–60. Indian birth rates were 30.3 and 36.4 per thousand; by 1948–9 it had increased to about 48 per thousand. (African birth rate was about 35 per thousand in the latter years). Infant mortality also declined from 175 per thousand in 1921–5 to 110 in 1941–5 and 63.7 in 1956–60.[23]

The implications of this demographic revolution for the social, economic and political evolution of the colony were astounding. Even when taken in conjunction with broader international and imperial developments after the Second World War, the eradication of malaria still represents the most important achievement in the country in the twentieth century. For the Indians, it marked a profound change in self-perception, opening the door to active politics: the rise of Cheddi Jagan.

Jock Campbell grasped its implications immediately, as did the Venn Commission in 1949. The latter commented on the demographic revolution: '[T]hey are amazing enough and when it is considered that on the estates, and therefore among 21% of the colony's population, the birth rate has well nigh doubled [in a couple of years] and infant and child mortality halved, the population problem for the future is evident and clamant.'[24]

As Table VIII shows, by the end of 1948, hospital admissions for malaria on all estate except the non-malarial Corentyne ones (Albion, Port Mourant, Skeldon), had declined from 9,752 in 1945 to 872, a drop of over 90 per cent.

TABLE VIII

Admissions for Malaria, Hospitals on Sugar Estates, 1945–48 [does not include the non-malarial Corentyne estates: Albion, Port Mourant and Skeldon]

Estate Hospital	Pop[1947]	DDT control established	Malarial Admissions			
			1945	1946	1947	1948
[West Coast Demerara]						
DeKinderen	2864	Oct 1947	374	263	67	59
Uitvlugt	5,526	Sept 1947	2,246	420	128	104
Leonora	5,177	Sept 1947	896	490	232	134
[West Coast Demerara]						
Versailles	1,238	Dec 1947	272	233	78	68
Wales	1,608	April 1946	183	65	9	15
[East Bank Demerara]						
Diamond	4,601	June 1947	444	296	48	21
Providence	4,120	July 1946	347	201	47	16
[East Coast Demerara]						
Ogle	2,919	Feb 1947	304	203	87	40
Vryheid's Lust	1,636	June 1947	207	106	57	36
L.B.I.	1,942	March 1946	239	86	7	3
Lusignan	3,938	Feb 1947	407	441	142	41
Non Pareil	2,599	Nov 1947	423	425	287	131
Enmore	3,237	Nov 1947	374	323	171	93
[West Coast Berbice]						
Bath	1,946	June 1946	932	519	22	8
[West Bank Berbice]						
Blairmont	2,299	May 1946	1,337	506	145	35
[East Bank Berbice]						
Providence	272	May 1946	71	21	4	4
[East Canje, Berbice]						
Rose Hall	5,275	May 1947	696	546	229	64
Total		50,749	9,752	5,144	1,760	872

Source: Adapted from the *Report of a Commission of Inquiry into the Sugar Industry of British Guiana* (J.A. Venn, chairman), Col. No. 249, (London: HMSO,1949),179

Dr Giglioli quickly unveiled the short-sightedness of old attitudes, as well as the economic benefits accruing from eradication of the great scourge. He noted that two years after the spraying of DDT on sugar estates, malaria was reduced by 95 per cent. In the three years preceding the campaign, 1943–45, 56,475 man-days were lost to the industry through hospitalisation. With the disease virtually eliminated in 1948, he concluded: 'We suggest $300,000 as a very conservative estimate of the saving realised annually by the effective control of malaria on the colony's sugar estates. This figure is ten times as great as the cost of control by DDT.' [25]

The sugar producers absorbed this. Even after the eradication of malaria, they continued to support the DDT campaign. From the late 1940s they could see the link between increased productivity and the elimination of the disease, for so long the curse of this backward colony. Less funds were now required for hospitals and a range of diseases directly associated with malaria. In 1944, before the start of the DDT campaign, 10,486 estate residents were admitted to estate hospitals; this entailed a loss of 63,693 hospital man-days; besides 19,868 other residents received out-patients treatment. Between 1950 and 1953 no malaria cases were reported on the sugar plantations; in 1953 a mere 30 cases were reported in the whole colony. In 1954 Dr Giglioli assessed the impact for British Guiana as a whole:

The elimination of malaria has had far-reaching effects on the health of the community, as this disease provided the background of all other public health problems and directly or indirectly affected the incidence and course of most other diseases and infirmities. The spectacular transformation of vital statistics is indicated by the following figures:

	1943	1953
Birth rate per 1,000 inhabitants	33.5	44.1
Death rate per 1,000 inhabitants	24.7	13.3
Infant mortality per 1,000 live births	141.0	79.3
Maternal mortality per 1,000 deliveries	14.0	4.0 [26]

Giglioli's work, admired and supported at all times by Campbell, was a gift to the colony from the industry which had itself got so much from it. In 1958, a decade after his great miracle, *Booker News* paid homage to this outstanding man of the twentieth century:

[R]ight here in British Guiana there are men, no less dedicated than other members of their fraternity abroad, who continue man's ageless struggle against famine and disease. Such a man is Dr. George Giglioli, MD (Italy), MRCP (London), Medical Adviser to the Sugar Producers' Association and Malariologist of wide international reputation, whose work in the successful eradication of malaria locally is the chief factor in this country's phenomenal population increase, improvement in general health condition of its workers and heightening of their expectation of life.... [T]he extent of Dr. Giglioli's contribution is best determined by the fact that in 1944 the vital index was 130. That is, 130 births to 100 deaths. And in 1956 the vital index of British Guiana was 387.[27]

It is noteworthy that Cheddi Jagan could see little in this great achievement, nothing beyond the self-interest of the plantocracy. In his pamphlet, *Bitter Sugar* (1953), he interpreted the industry's battle against malaria as another machiavellian device in their pursuit of profits — the compulsion to shore up a flagging labour force. Jagan argued:

Unfortunately for the sugar imperialists, the indenture system ceased in 1917. Later attempts at resettling Assyrians and Jews failed. Other means, therefore ... had to be found not only to maintain the necessary and surplus labour force in and around sugar estates, but also to circumvent the drift away from the plantations. These measures have taken different forms — lack of agricultural diversification, land idleness, inadequate drainage and irrigation, price fixing of wages and farmers' produce, etc. One — control of malaria, has even taken on an humanitarian garb. Malaria coupled with malnutrition was to a very great extent responsible for the decimation of the population.... If the sugar workers were to remain alive — dead men produce no profits — some means had to be found to wipe out the scourge of malaria.

It was in the light of this fact that Dr. Giglioli was appointed as Medical Adviser to the SPA and Honorary Malariologist [to the government of British Guiana].[28]

There is much that is true here. Productivity and attendance certainly rose from the early 1950s. Vastly better health led to Indian workers becoming even more predominant in the industry, dominating the more demanding tasks such as cane-cutting and working in the shovel-gang. This was a major factor behind the stabilising and reduction of the labour force, as healthier workers, earning better wages, tended to be less prone to absenteeism. But it takes an especially bitter view of Booker and the sugar industry not to be magnanimous about the victory over malaria. For it was when Campbell became vice-chairman of Booker (virtually chairman), in 1946–47, with the death of the old autocrat, Sir Alfred Sherlock, that the anti-malarial campaign accelerated and the new spirit of reform started to take shape.

Jagan did give sparing recognition to Giglioli: 'He devoted much valuable time and study in combating this dreadful disease.' Not a word, though, for this great man of the twentieth century, in his autobiography, *The West on Trial: My Fight for Guyana's Freedom*, published in 1966, on the eve of his country's independence. Denis Williams, the late biographer of Dr Giglioli, gives a more balanced assessment of the role of the sugar industry and the great malariologist in eradicating the scourge, at the end of the 1940s:

[T]he history of medicine in Guyana, when it comes to be written couldn't conceivably be approached without regard to the history of sugar: a relationship which in certain instances went beyond immediate economic considerations and produced long-term and lasting benefits to all.... The elimination of malaria was initiated partly with sugar capital and sugar resources...[I]n 1933 Giglioli had found a manager [Guy Eccles at Davson's sugar estate, Blairmont] equipped and prepared to discuss medical problems with intelligence and understanding....[T]hough the interests of the industry, taking into account traditional shortages in labour and its general stamina, could never be regarded (and they weren't meant to be) as wholly altruistic, the sugar industry has done a great deal to be proud of in its general health record in

Guyana.... Giglioli conducted his first DDT field experiment ... in 1945.... By mid-1948 the malaria and yellow fever vectors had disappeared from the sprayed coastlands, and persons chronically infected with malaria had begun, in the absence of reinfection, to progress towards spontaneous cures. By August a mere six years after his release from internment the incredible public health revolution had been accomplished....[T]he generation born since 1945 — the Giglioli Generation — is among the most healthy and most becoming of young people to be found anywhere in the world today. But more than this, our population has doubled itself in the period, a population which, at the turn of the century, couldn't manage to replace itself, let alone show a natural increase.[29]

It is arguable that Jagan's ascendancy in the early 1950s owed much to the demographic revolution spawned by the eradication of malaria and the new outlook, the reforming zeal of Campbell's Booker. The Indian population which had shown less resistance to malaria than Africans, rose dramatically. Their birth rate which had been about 30 per thousand in 1928 climbed impressively, reaching 49 per thousand in 1949, just three years after the anti-malaria campaign had commenced. The birth rate of Africans, too, had risen, but this was still only 35 per thousand in 1949.

TABLE IX
Birth Rates of Africans and Indians, 1928–29 and 1948–49 (per 1,000)

Years	Africans	Indians
1928	26.6	30.3
1929	27.8	36.4
1948	34.9	48.8
1949	35.3	48.7

Source: Dwarka Nath, *A History of Indians in Guyana* (London: The Author, 1970), p.233.

This marked an irreversible rise of the Indian population in British Guiana: from 42 per cent in 1933–34, when Dr Giglioli started his work at Blairmont, to nearly 45 per cent in 1948 and, after the eradication of the disease, reaching nearly 50 per cent by the early 1960s. Cheddi Jagan benefited from this growing demographic superiority of Indian Guyanese ('Giglioli's babies'), as he did from the economic, psychological and political consequences of the conquest of malaria. It coincided with the heightened self-confidence, after the War, of an Indian middle class already established in rice, cattle and business — the base of the Indian professional elite, in law and medicine. This self-belief percolated to other sections of the Indian Guyanese community, too, fortified by their sense of the richness and antiquity of their ancestral culture, and, since the 1920s, the Gandhian nationalist resurgence, culminating in Indian independence in August 1947. This helped to shape a rebellious spirit and an assertive temperament in post-War Guyana, especially on the plantations. This was the context of Jagan's political rise: 'Bitter Sugar' was the catalyst for the sustaining of the vision around which Indian sensibility cohered. Jock Campbell genuinely sought to assuage the offended temper, but his reforms only added fuel to the flames, feeding notions of vast possibilities ahead, if the 'sugar gods' could be brought down.

Campbell has written perceptively on the foundation of the implacable African-Indian incomprehension, while locating the work of Dr Giglioli and its ramifications at the end of Empire. This is his assessment from April 1966, on the eve of Guyana's independence:

During a century of gradual advancement the Africans had established what seemed an unassailable position of security and predominance in the lower and middle echelons of Government service: in the police force, in the judiciary, and in the professions of law, medicine, teaching and Christian religion. For a long time even the economic progress of the Indians did not touch this citadel. There seemed quite enough scope for both middle class Indians growing in wealth and property and middle class Africans secure in their Government or professional jobs — just as there seemed quite enough scope for both the Indian farm workers and plantation labourers, and the African urban workers.[30]

Campbell then assessed the implications of the eradication of malaria on the political culture of British Guiana after the War:

> Malaria was wiped out through the remarkable work of Dr. Giglioli, an Italian malariologist employed by the sugar industry. The Indian population in particular began to explode in the narrow [coast]land. The leisurely pace of life quickened. The consciousness of all men of opportunities to be grasped, or challenges resisted, grew sharper and more insistent. And in this upsurge of change and new aspirations the pressure of the Indians to seize for themselves a fully respected position commensurate with their increasingly weighty economic role, suddenly grew powerfully strong. More and more Indians entered the professions and qualified for government service. The Africans could not help but feel that their Indian fellows — more numerous, more wealthy, attached to seemingly alien cultural and religious loyalties — were now at last putting in jeopardy the position of security, prestige and influence built up so long and so painfully over the years. The Africans' inheritance of the colonial earth was being recognisably threatened. For a time this sharpening conflict was hidden in the larger conflict waged by both races together as underdogs against the entrenched interests commanding the heights of the economy and society. But as soon as it was clear that the mutual antagonist was on the point of being driven from the battlefield, then the deep-down racial rivalry for position was bound to come out in the open.... The Indian Dr. Jagan and his wife had returned from the United States in 1945 [1943] and had brought a fresh fervour and dedication, and a new ideology [Marxism], to political life in the country. Dr. Jagan's undying achievement was to give the Indians, the despised coolies, their sense of identity with the future of Guyana.[31]

Both Cheddi Jagan and Jock Campbell were shapers of these changes. As noted earlier, the reforms initiated by Campbell on the estates nurtured an appetite for even more, thus corroborating Jagan's unreconstructed Marxist beliefs that the belated reforms, palliatives — too little, too late — were a pinch of the 'surplus value' stolen by the 'sugar gods': there was much more there for the workers than the crumbs which the masters were now offering. Taking over the plantations was the panacea; it would even wipe out whatever racial problems existed in Guyana. The Soviet Union was demonstrating that the communist utopia is possible, that the race question could be eliminated: uniting in the fight against 'bitter sugar', therefore, would bring Africans and Indians together as a prelude to the abolition of all notions of racial consciousness. The trouble for Jagan was that Africans were, by the 1950s, already a minority in the labour force on the sugar plantations; even the war against Booker would be seen as another manifestation of Indian self-assertion and ascendancy. The futility notwithstanding, Campbell believed to the end that his own family's part in the making of 'bitter sugar' — six generations — dictated that he should commit his authority in Booker to repay ancient debts to British Guiana, as long as the politics did not preclude them from doing so.

I have remarked on Cheddi Jagan's failure, in his memoirs of 1966, to acknowledge Giglioli's monumental accomplishment in the eradication of malaria: even this great man's work was attributed to the machiavellianism of the 'sugar gods'. The final word, therefore, on Giglioli's achievement in British Guiana must go to his Guyanese biographer, Denis Williams (born 1923), who had lived through the malarial scourge:

> During the first decade of the [twentieth] century more people died in this country than were born — a situation chillingly described by the Census Commissioner, in 1911, as a 'natural decrease'!... But no statistics could record the inexorable sapping of strength throughout the population, decade after decade, from the time of the early Dutch settlers [in the seventeenth century] with the empoldering and land reclamation and man-made marshes, all disrupting the natural balances that had sustained populations here a good thousand years before them. For all of Raleigh's, and later Walpole's enthusiasm for Guyana, the country remained virtually *a bridge to the grave* for all who had suffered it since its colonisation. In such a public health situation, one wonders how many of us could have sustained the energy required for the winning of nationhood; how many would have been fit to carve highways into the Interior, and man the land

by way of feeding ourselves. By the end of the decade following
the Census Commissioner's report of a natural decrease in our
population [the 1920s, before Giglioli joined Davson's sugar
estates in 1933]... [he] had taken the first steps towards
understanding the problem of malaria transmission in the
country. That's to say... [Giglioli] single-handedly set about
trying to keep our peoples alive! [emphasis added].[32]

George Giglioli's work is inviolable.

Endnotes

1. 'Time When Malaria Wreaked Great Havoc in Guyana', *Guyana
    Graphic* (Independence Souvenir), May 1966.

2. Ibid.; George Giglioli, 'Immediate and Long-Term Economic Effects
    Accruing from the Control of Mosquito-Transmitted Diseases in
    British Guiana', *Timehri*, no. 28, (fourth series), (1948): 6.

3. George Giglioli, 'Eradication of *Anopheles Darlingi* from the
    Inhabited Areas of British Guiana by DDT Residual Spraying',
    Journal of the National Malaria Society 10, no.2, (June 1951): 149
    [calculated from Fig. 2].

4. *The Royal Commission in British Guiana, 1939* (Georgetown: The
    Daily Chronicle Ltd, 1939), 154.

5. See my *'Tiger in the Stars': The Anatomy of Indian Achievement in
    British Guiana, 1919-29* (London: Macmillan, 1997), 81-2.

6. *Who is Who in British Guiana, 1945-8* (Georgetown: The Daily
    Chronicle Ltd, 1948), 200-1; George Giglioli, 'Labour Health', in
    Booker Sugar (Supplement to the Accounts of Booker Bros,
    McConnell and Co, Ltd, 1954), p. 75.

7. Jock Campbell, interview by the author, Nettlebed, Oxfordshire,
    July 24, 1992, Tape 6.

8. Ibid.

9. See note 5 [pp. 84-5].

10. See note 7.

11. Ibid.

12. George Giglioli, 'The Influence of Geological Formation and Soil
    Characteristics on the Distribution of Malaria and its Mosquito
    Carrier in British Guiana', *Timehri*, (fourth series), no. 30,
    (November 1951): 49.

13. Ibid., 50.

14. Ibid.

15. Ibid., 53.

16. George Giglioli, 'Malaria in British Guiana, Part III: Breeding
    Habits of *A. Darlingi*. Natural Factors which Limit the Distribution
    of this Species and of Malaria', *The Agricultural Journal of British*

Guiana IX, no. 4 (December 1938): 201. See also 'Malaria and Agriculture in British Guiana', *Timehri*, (fourth series), no. 27, (July 1946).

17. See note 2: Giglioli, 'Intermediate and Long-Term...', (1948): 7-8.

18. George Giglioli, 'Malaria and British Guiana, Part IV: The Distribution of Malaria on the Coastlands. Genesis of Malarial Epidemics', *The Agricultural Journal of British Guiana* X, no. 1, (March 1939): 12.

19. George Giglioli, 'Medical Services on the Sugar Estates of British Guiana', *Timehri*, no. 35, (fifth series), (1956): 5.

20. Ibid., 6.

21. Ibid., 6-7.

22. See note 5 [pp. 75-6].

23. Ibid., 83-4.

24. *Report of a Commission of Inquiry into the Sugar Industry of British Guiana* (J.A. Venn, chairman), Col. No. 249 (London: HMSO, 1949), 114.

25. See note 17 [pp. 5-6].

26. See note 6: Giglioli, 'Labour Health'..., pp. 77-8.

27. *Booker News*, June 6, 1958.

28. Cheddi Jagan, *Bitter Sugar*, (Georgetown: self-published, n.d., ca. 1953), 2-3.

29. Ibid., 3.

30. Denis Williams, *Giglioli in Guyana, 1922-1972* (Georgetown: National History and Arts Council, n.d.), 41, 59-60.

31. Jock Campbell, 'The Clash of Immigrant Coloured Races in British Guiana', Address to the Ministry of Education Commonwealth Course, (mimeo.), April 15, 1966, pp. 37-40.

32. See note 30 [p. 36].

Chapter Twenty-Six

HEALTH ON THE PLANTATIONS: RESEARCH AND PREVENTATIVE MEDICINE

It was only with the advent of the Commonwealth Sugar Agreement in 1950 that a measure of security has been afforded to the industry, which can enable us to plan ahead and to maintain certainly not a ceiling standard of living for its workers but, at least, not too precarious a floor.

Jock Campbell (1958)

The sugar estates' medical scheme is supervised by Dr. George Giglioli, MD, MRCP, Medical Adviser to the SPA, who by conquering the scourge of malaria has given sugar workers new energy and a longer span of life.

Booker News, June 6, 1958

If I have had any new thought during this visit [to British Guiana], it is that people are more important than politics and the press.

Jock Campbell (1963)

Jock Campbell was deeply influenced by the commitment, resolution and phenomenal work of Dr Giglioli. The amazing results of the anti-malaria campaign of the late 1940s convinced him that the sugar industry, however belatedly, could make a difference. He recalled that on his first visit to British Guiana after the War, with Curtis Campbell absorbed by Booker, he felt the urgency for reforms to alleviate abysmal conditions on the estates. He explained how he sought to define his mission after 1945:

I then saw in clear perspective the tremendous amount which had to be done, if the sugar industry was to survive to the benefit of the country and its people. And I realised that in Booker, as the largest company operating in British Guiana, I had the opportunity and the obligation to do something about it.... I found a personal *raison d'etre*. I became convinced that Booker...had acceptable and intelligible purposes; and that 'profits for the shareholders' and 'business efficiency' were only means, although essential means, to valid human ends.[1]

But Campbell was realistic about the extent to which Booker could change its image, given its history and dominance of colonial society. His expectation was different:

Our size made me see how vital was public acceptance. We could not in a small country such as British Guiana expect to be loved or liked — I doubt whether big business can be loved or liked anywhere. But I believed we could at least be understood, and I hoped respected — and worthy of respect.[2]

His reforms, therefore, were aimed at earning that respect. The Marxist politics of Cheddi Jagan gave his reforms an urgency, but, as he pointed out incessantly, his family's roots in 'bitter sugar' imbued him with a moral imperative to pursue them. Health reform, encapsulated by the dramatic success of the anti-malaria campaign of 1945–48, was the beacon of the fresh attitude — what one observer called '[a] reformist "crusade" from within the company, converting less sympathetic executives to his point of view by arguing that reform was in the company's own interests'.[3] Abundantly gifted, passionately engaged scientists, such as Dr Harry Evans and Dr George Giglioli, could sustain the effort even when some administrators were less sanguine about the four-fold responsibilities. But there were limits to what even a progressive capitalist enterprise could do to transform an ecologically hazardous and politically self-destructive country like Guyana. As Campbell said in mid-1963, amidst the political futility and racial hatred, 'no business could assume responsibility for the problems of the country as a whole'.[4]

Under indentureship, the plantation had been virtually a self-contained world. Employers were responsible for the health and housing of their employees, among many other provisions. Since the termination of the system in 1920, the plantations had continued to do so, retaining their old, dilapidated hospitals and the abominable logies, the derelict ranges, often mired in mud and filth during the heavy rains. Some of the beneficiaries were no longer estate workers but had remained there, in their rent-free hovels. The old paternalism bred a resilient dependency. Campbell recalled the practice:

> Every conceivable aspect of their lives and the lives of their families were dominated and controlled by their employers; and housing, food, health and education were all the responsibility — in omission or commission — of the employer.... This led to the extraordinary situation of employers providing housing, hospitals, schools, provision lands, sports fields and so on for their workers — none of which they could afford to maintain properly or to improve.[5]

This was what had inspired the Venn Commission's recommendation in 1949, that greater responsibility for the health and housing of plantation workers be devolved unto the state. They advised that the government should build at least four hospitals at strategic points along the coastland, to accommodate both villagers and residents of sugar estates. They advised further that, in lieu of estate hospitals, each estate should have an equipped dispensary for its resident 'nuclear' workers, to treat cases of 'accidents and sudden illness', and an ambulance to convey patients from the estate to the nearest state hospital. The Commission concluded: 'This proposed arrangement, while emphasising the estates' responsibility for the welfare of their own employees, would also relieve them of much of what is at the moment an unfair charge on their resources.'[6]

Campbell had remarked on the derelict appearance of the estates' hospitals as well as dwindling demand for their services after the eradication of malaria. He wrote: 'The estates' hospitals were great, bleak, ramshackle barns, far too big for present requirements — due to the world-renowned work of the industry's medical adviser, Dr Giglioli, in eradicating malaria from the coastlands of British Guiana.'[7] He was correct: the conquest of the disease drastically reduced susceptibility to a range of other illnesses, but Campbell retained the great malariologist as medical adviser to the Sugar Producers' Association until he retired in 1966.

In 1956, seven years after the Venn Commission had recommended the building of state hospitals, they were still not available: the first one, built at Port Mourant, was opened in 1958. Yet the estates proceeded with the demolition of several of their 'ancient and dilapidated' hospitals, beginning in 1952: Vryheid's Lust, De Kinderen, Wales, Versailles, LBI, Non Pareil, Ogle, Providence (Berbice), Port Mourant, Uitvlugt, Providence (Demerara) and Rose Hall. The only 'obsolete structure' standing, at Albion, was retained because of the imminent opening of the state hospital at neighbouring Port Mourant. Elsewhere, because of the government's tardiness in building the other hospitals, the sugar industry, 'as a temporary measure', decided to 'improve and reorganise' one hospital in each district to meet the needs of their own workers: Leonora (West Coast Demerara), Diamond (East Bank Demerara), Blairmont (West Bank Berbice) and Skeldon (Corentyne Coast). Giglioli reported thus in 1956: 'New properly designed dispensaries and small emergency hospitals have taken the place of the demolished hospitals; in addition eight motor ambulance stations have been established at Uitvlugt, Wales, Diamond, Ogle, Enmore, Bath, Rose Hall and Port Mourant.' [8]

Giglioli observed that the new dispensaries had gone beyond the recommendation of the Venn Commission; they were not merely treating cases of 'accident and sudden illness'. In 1955 alone, at estate dispensaries, medical officers treated 30,683 out-patient cases, while 220,632 cases were handled by dispensers, 'with an aggregate of 867,394 attendances for medicine or minor surgical dressing'. It is obvious that the dispensaries were still providing services for all callers. Giglioli drew attention to another advance in the medical provisions on the plantations: 'The system of clinical records has been modernised, so that any patient who returns to consult the Medical Officer appears before him with his index card summary, his previous medical history. This facilitates examination of and favours continuity in the study and treatment of cases much to the benefit of patients; at the same time valuable clinical documentation is built up.' [9]

In 1951 Giglioli had noted that although the eradication of malaria had reduced morbidity and expenditure 'drastically', the system by which medical treatment was 'handed out' indiscriminately, to all callers, survived. He thought that growing apprehension that the 'old privileges' would evaporate, in light of the Venn Commission's recommendation that their medical provision become the responsibility of the state, could thwart the impending move of non-essential workers or non-workers to extra-nuclear areas. He added: '[I]t may later prove even more difficult to suddenly close the dispensaries to $^6/_7$ of the estate population.'[10] In the absence of a range of basic medical provisions by the state, the plantation retained its paternalism, the dispenser of old largesse.

Campbell was in favour of greater individual autonomy, the evolution of a community spirit: 'As the community develops its own social organisation, management can more and more concentrate on its proper functions of managing industry.'[11] But as Dr Giglioli pointed out in 1956, even non-estate workers were still availing themselves of the medical facilities at estate dispensaries:

> Regular periodical ante-natal clinics are held at the dispensaries on all estates; the attendance by expectant mothers is fair but could be better [4,612 attendances in 1955]. All women residing on the estates, whether belonging to a worker's family or not, can attend at the clinics; women workers and workers' wives get advice and whatever treatment may be required; non-workers get free examination and advice including prescriptions, but free medicine is not issued.

There were 3,494 births registered on estates in 1955: 835 in hospital; 1,213 at home. From January 1, 1956 every worker on the estates' payroll was entitled to free medical treatment at the dispensaries, 'on presentation of his pay envelope for the previous week'.[12]

Throughout the 1960s Booker proceeded with the construction of modern dispensaries. In January 1960, for instance, one such centre comprising a dispensary and two bungalows for the dispenser and his assistant was opened. It was described thus: 'The dispensary carries a covered porch as waiting room, and separate rooms for doctor and dispenser, and compounding staff with a two-bed ward for emergency cases.' [13]

In March 1962 Booker handed over its Skeldon Estate Hospital to the government at a cost of $54,137, to be used as a state district hospital. Dr Giglioli noted that the estate had continued to operate this hospital at an annual cost of about $30,000 because there was no other medical facility on the Upper Corentyne. However, Booker had completed a new dispensary for its own workers, so they were offering the hospital to the government at the cost of the dispensary, although a recent evaluation of the Skeldon Hospital had set it at $100,000. The government's Chief Medical Officer, Dr C.C. Nicholson, thanked Dr Giglioli, 'because of whom malaria had been conquered', and added that 'the time had come for fuller medical facilities to be provided and Government had accepted that responsibility'.[14]

In August 1963, in spite of the growing political turmoil, Booker opened a new dispensary at Blairmont, at a cost of $35,000. The senior dispenser, C. Chung, said that the facilities were 'a hundred per cent improvement on the services which the demolished hospital had provided. The dispensary was an out-patient department and an emergency clinic, and the district medical officer is available for consultations three times a week. On busy days as many as 80 patients may be treated at the dispensary. Cases that need hospitalisation are sent to the Public Hospital [New Amsterdam]'.[15]

Campbell was committed to excellence: intellectual solidity, innovation, imagination — grounded in research and with an ear to the ground, keeping in touch with the environment. Dr Evans, Dr Giglioli and the Estates Director, Dr George Bacs, represented what he saw as vital strands in the business and his social reform programme. Bacs, born in Hungary in 1913, had graduated from the University of Budapest, aged 22, as a Doctor of Laws. He had, for some obscure reason, turned up in British Guiana in July 1939, as an overseer on Plantation LBI, a Booker estate. His modus operandi spoke of the cultivated approach of which Jock was so enamoured. In late 1956 *Booker News* explained:

George Bacs possesses two valuable assets: he is thorough, and he is an educated man. Thorough in the sense that he brings all his faculties to bear on whatever he is committed to, and educated in the sense that what he learns is not pigeon-holed, but becomes integrated and co-related into a very special kind of General Knowledge. He gathers from every kind of literature 'information required to do my work', and such information could include an article on human relationship, on tractors, on government. Education is the sheath, the second skin which covers the man; breeding is the first layer. The breeding which distinguishes George Bacs came to him from a long line of land-owning farmers [in Hungary].[16]

Ian McDonald worked with him for many years. He recalls Bacs's grasp of things, however diverse, as well as the technical excellence of several of the Booker men in British Guiana in the late 1950s and early 1960s:

George Bacs lived next door to me, so I used to see a lot of him.... He was from Eastern Europe: the rumour was that he came from the aristocracy and that he killed someone in a duel over a woman, and that he fled the country and he ended up in London walking the streets; and he saw this advertisement and, suddenly, became an overseer on a Guyana sugar estate. He was a wonderful man; he had a doctorate.... He had such a fine mind and an inspiring personality, that he did well in anything he did. He rose from being an overseer of field staff to the position of Director on Booker Sugar Estates; he was in charge of field operations. Harry Evans did most of the technical stuff but George was on the field side and, of course, because of his personality he was also on the social policy side — how you treated people; what you did about motivating people; wages and so on. So he was very much a key man on social policies.[17]

George Bacs was, indeed, at the cutting edge of Campbell's reforms: technical excellence and the ability to motivate. Moreover, his solid experience in the colony (since 1939), like Giglioli's (since 1922), gave him a powerful sense of nuance for the susceptibilities of the workers on the plantations. But Campbell had recruited many others with enviable technical gifts into his team: Lionel Birkett (a former West Indies Test cricketer, who played four Tests in Australia in 1930–31), Jack Williams, the chief chemist, and Arthur Goodland, technical director of BSE (1958–71). McDonald recalls: '[T]echnically, everyone was first-class. There was John Baxter and Ray Wilkins — [the latter] was the man in charge of doing a survey on the sugar estates and he got very involved with drainage and irrigation as well as surveying the lands. He was first class. The technical people were first class, led by Harry Evans.'[18]

The health reforms, like others, must be located in the context of Jock Campbell's belief in the culture of research as the handmaiden of business and its accompanying ethos of social reform. People are the core of a great enterprise: shareholders, customers, workers and the community — that was the animating motif, he would reiterate; without that there was no point to the effort. Ian McDonald summarises the Campbell project: 'Jock's philosophy [was] that in this life and in this world you can only really make things happen *through* people and *for* people.... [H]e interviewed people personally; he had excellent people'.[19] And, very often, as with the research into public health, the ramifications were far-reaching: the eradication of malaria and the simultaneous elimination of yellow fever. DDT had wiped out not only *A.darlingi* but the *Aedes aegypti* mosquito as well, the yellow fever vector.[20]

In 1948 Dr Giglioli had cautioned that the proliferation of pit latrines, especially in the villages, would accelerate the incidence of filariasis. These latrines were constructed as an antidote to hookworm, to wipe out the habit of men 'defecating promiscuously' in the bush and people stepping on faecal matter in which hookworm eggs thrived. DDT was innocuous against *Culex fatigens*, the main transmitter of filariasis. This vector bred prolifically in pit latrines and cesspools. The much-maligned over-trench latrines on the plantations, with the rapid dispersal of faecal matter, was not conducive to the breeding of *Culex*; therefore, filariasis was rare on the estates.[21]

By 1952, with several 'extra nuclear' sugar workers settlements established, on which pit latrines were mandatory, Giglioli again warned of the hazards: 'It is important to guard the new settlements from the introduction of this disabling disease.'[22] Apprehensive of the proliferation of these pit latrines, he underlined in 1954, the gravity of filariasis with a clarity reminiscent of his old campaign against malaria:

> Filariasis is a common and disfiguring disease caused by a blood-worm; it is transmitted by the *Culex* mosquito and is more characteristic of the towns and larger villages.... It is not a problem on estates at present; its carrier, however, breeds in sullage waters, cesspools and pit latrines, so that the rapid growth of new villages in the 'extra nuclear' layouts on estate frontlands needs watching. The effect of the DDT campaign on the *Culex* has been disappointing; it is less susceptible to the insecticide and its feeding and resting habits in respect to the human dwelling are in no way as clearly defined and restricted as those of *A.darlingi* and *Aedes aegypti*; thus a large proportion of this mosquito fails to make contact with the insecticide.[23]

Having established the potential ravages of filariasis, Dr Giglioli embarked on a programme of research and preventative treatment. The passion, his single-minded pursuit of research, belonged not only to the sugar industry, it was a gift to the whole colony and Campbell was proud of this.

In 1958 a young Guyanese doctor, Dr Harold Edghill, MB, BS (London), inspired by the Giglioli tradition of research, joined the great man in the medical services of the Sugar Producers' Association. He began his research at Plantation Port Mourant where the incidence of filariasis was relatively higher than on other sugar estates. Because of its proximity to Rose Hall Village, where pit latrines predominated, the *Culex* had penetrated that estate. By June 1958 Dr Edghill had already examined 3,400 persons and discovered that the filaria worm could be present in the blood stream with no demonstrable symptom, such as swollen feet. Once tests for filariasis revealed parasites in the blood, tablets were administered to patients for three weeks. A month later a follow-up check was made; recurrence was widespread, necessitating treatment up to seven times.

Dr Edghill's research gave a new perspective on the complexity of the disease, crucial to its diagnosis and treatment:

[I]t seems that the filaria worm comes out into the blood stream only at night, for a person tested at night may show positive evidence and the same person shows negative when tested in the daytime, a few hours later. The presence of filaria worms in the body will not necessarily show any obvious sign, such as swollen feet, for he has found a large percentage of healthy looking cane cutters with blood teaming with filariasis worms, while people with swollen feet have little evidence in the blood. In the second case, this is due to damage caused by the worm to the circulation.[24]

The award of the Davson Gold Medal for 1958 epitomised the attitude to research and public health in Campbell's Booker. They gave it to Dr William Ewart Adams, MB. BCH, an Indian Guyanese from the distinguished Luckhoo family. He was honoured for his preliminary work on filariasis, in 1955–56, including his scientific paper, 'A Public Health Approach to Filariasis in British Guiana'. Dr Adams was magnanimous in his hour of acclamation:

[S]tudies were done on a blood survey of over thirty thousand people and a task of such magnitude could not have been achieved without the help and support of the technicians and the men in the field, for the very nocturnal nature of the disease make it imperative for work to be done during the night and I am happy to recall that these men carried out their duties with great zest and enthusiasm, and the honour bestowed on me today must be shared by those field workers.[25]

Booker's research into preventative medicine, their ongoing medical reforms, though prompted by the urgent needs of their own workers, were in the service of all Guyanese. Among the 11 winners of the Davson Gold Medal since its inauguration in 1919, was Dr George Giglioli, OBE, the recipient in 1926, seven years before he commenced his great work with Davson's in 1933 at Blairmont. The spirit of the man permeated Booker's attitude to preventative medicine after 1939, a vital ingredient in Jock Campbell's culture of reform after the War.

Giglioli's vigilance was unwavering.[26] In spite of, as he said, 'the new crop of healthy, vigorous children now approaching adolescence on the sugar estates where formerly many of them would have fallen victims to the disease', he was not complacent. In March 1962 he reported that there had been isolated cases of malaria on the coastland. Since July 1961 several were confirmed at Diamond, Wales and Canal No.2 Polder. Dr Giglioli quickly noted that the relapse was restricted to settlements on the estuary of the Demerara River. He added that apart from *A.darlingi*, other species of mosquitoes were not vectors of malaria, because they preferred to feed on animals. The main task, therefore, was to ascertain whether *A.darlingi* had returned to the coastland.[27]

He reported that extensive examination in over 1,000 homes, carried out by day and night, had failed to produce a single specimen of *A.darlingi*. The vector had to be located elsewhere. A new one was isolated on the West and East Bank Demerara, the area of recurrence. Giglioli observed: '[A]nother common mosquito, *Anopheles aquasalis*, appeared to be frequenting the houses in abundant numbers where formerly it was rarely found indoors. This mosquito .... is quite capable of transmitting malaria, once it acquires the habit of biting humans instead of cattle. And it would appear that this is what has been happening in restricted areas of the east and west banks of the Demerara estuary.' [28]

These plantations — Diamond (East Bank) and Wales (West Bank) — along with the Canals Polder settlements in the latter district, had very few areas allocated for grazing. Greater pressures on land on riverine plantations and villages meant that livestock was always subordinate to arable farming. With the eradication of malaria and the population boom, the paucity of space for livestock had been exacerbated, with serious consequences for the anti-malarial culture. Dr Giglioli explained clinically:

In the areas concerned great changes have taken place over the past twelve years [since 1950]. The human population has increased by 60%; housing developments and industrial estates have sprung up; cane and rice fields have been extended; pastures have disappeared and draught animals are being rapidly replaced by tractors, lorries and vans. The result is that the livestock population has been halved. On the East Bank [Demerara] in 1950, there were 3.7 persons for every head of livestock, today the ratio is 12 to 1. The *Anopheles aquasalis* require a bloodmeal before it can mature its eggs and, in the absence of livestock, it has shifted its attention to the human population. In so doing it has become a malaria carrier; where once it was harmless, now it has become dangerous.[29]

Giglioli always moved quickly from research findings to application. He implemented a few strategic measures to fortify the coastland from reinfection, from the potentially malarial interior, as well as from *A.aquasalis*: (i) the medicated salt campaign was continued in the interior districts in order to negate the former; (ii) every case of infection from the interior reaching the coast had to be reported and monitored; (iii) a long-term programme to control the behaviour of *A.aquasalis* was devised.

Giglioli recommended an integrated approach to agriculture, rural and urban development and public health. The balance between the human and livestock populations must be improved: 'green belts' had to be accommodated in the development of settlements in order to facilitate livestock rearing — a rational proposition in view of the preference of *A.aquasalis* for the blood of cattle. The potential return of the dreaded scourge was strangled.[30] Preventative measures, informed by vigilance and alacrity in research and implementation — the backbone of Campbell's medical strategy on the plantations — had positive reverberations for the whole of British Guiana. In 1965 Professor Peter Newman of the University of Michigan estimated that the Malaria Eradication Campaign was responsible for 40 per cent of the population increase since the late 1940s. The population was generally healthier, being now less susceptible to other diseases.[31]

Campbell was determined that the workers must remain healthy, so the ongoing focus on research and preventative medicine never diminished. Among the beneficiaries were Booker's workers in Georgetown: about 2,000 monthly-paid staff and 300 pensioners were entitled to free medical attention. Weekly employees, who were not covered by the scheme, could get free treatment for minor ailments from the staff nurse, Mrs Quintena Chapman-Edwards, but they had to pay for medical attention. Her assignment included an annual health survey of all employees in Booker's companies in Georgetown. They were weighed and if found to be underweight, were provided with cod liver oil or 'Mallevol', 'until the scales showed a

return to normal'. In 1954 Mrs Chapman-Edwards had requested
that BCG tests for tuberculosis be introduced; by the late 1950s this
was routine in the annual check-up. In 1966 the medical scheme for
its employees in Georgetown was assessed thus: '[It] seeks to be both
preventative and curative. People who come into Booker are
medically fit; the Companies see to it that they remain so. The result
is fewer hours lost through illness, and increased efficiency. To keep
guard against the depredations of ill-health is not paternalism, but
sound business.'[32]

The medical service in Georgetown was led by Dr D.K. Jardine.
The staff nurse, Mrs Chapman-Edwards, was a former assistant
matron at the Public Hospital, Georgetown. In January 1966 *Booker
News* reported that Sir Jock Campbell had been given a life peerage;
they also announced that their staff nurse was awarded the MBE,
primarily for her work, over 20 years, as chairman of the After-Care
Committee of the British Guiana Society for Prevention and
Treatment of Tuberculosis. In 1961 she had been awarded a medal
by the London Chest and Heart Association for 'outstanding work in
preventing and controlling tuberculosis' in British Guiana.[33] The work
of Mrs Chapman-Edwards was a vindication of Campbell's belief that
responsibility to the community was no less important than those to
their shareholders, customers, employees and workers.

At the core of Campbell's strategy to improve the quality of life
of Booker's workers, given the character of the disease environment
of the hydrologically difficult coastland, was the notion that success
on the plantations was bound to have reverberations nationally. And,
as noted earlier, in Dr George Giglioli, his chief medical adviser, he
had a man whose great attributes included a passion for research
and a facility for quick application of the fruits of such labours. Ian
McDonald recalls his meeting with Giglioli in 1955, years after he had
conquered malaria. What the great man said on that occasion has
stayed with him; it epitomised the ethos of Campbell's cause in British
Guiana:

> [O]ne of the first people I met when I came in 1955 was Dr. Giglioli
> .... a kind, gentle, professional man who was obviously technically
> good at his job; and at the end of the interview he was telling me

what he was trying to do: medical services and so on. He said: 'Do you know, Mr. McDonald, when I first began to look at people on sugar estates [from 1933] and I took their blood count, they were so anaemic from malaria that if you or I had the blood count they had, you would not have been able to walk up those stairs. I am not quite sure how they did it; you literally would not have been able to walk up those stairs.' The impression I got was of (this has not been investigated enough) the enormous improvement in health and, therefore, well-being generally that must have taken place, say, in the 1940s and 50s.[34]

The following exchange I had with Jock Campbell in 1994, the year he died, underlines the resilience of the impression which Giglioli, who retired in 1966 towards the end of Jock's chairmanship, had left on him, too:

> CS: Is there someone ... during the years in British Guiana who really impressed you, somebody whom you thought did a very good job, made an important contribution?
>
> JC: The malariologist.
>
> CS: What was it about Giglioli?
>
> JC: Well, he did such wonderful work and he did it with such resolution, even in internment [1940–42, during the War] and everything else ... he went on working in internment.[35]

Another great exponent of Campbell's belief that the best in Booker could intersect with what was best for Guyana, was Arthur Goodland, the Technical Director of Booker Sugar Estates, from 1958 to 1971. In him were combined a passionate intellect, the pursuit and integration of wide learning and a commitment to excellence. The following are excerpts from an obituary by Ian McDonald in 1986, when Goodland died in his 75th year:

> Arthur Goodland was one of the most remarkable men I have ever known. In his time in Guyana as Technical Director of Bookers Sugar Estates (1958–1971) he was celebrated as a great enlivening, colourful and creative personality. Not only did he

direct with vigour and imagination technical development in the main body of sugar factories in the country in a particularly dynamic era for the Guyana sugar industry, but he also became the foremost amateur archaeologist in the country ... he travelled extensively in the Interior, recording petroglyphs for the Guyana Museum as Honorary Curator of Archaeology, and becoming acquainted with the folklore of Amerindian communities and with the varied flora and fauna ....[He also] developed his talent as a sculptor to the point where he was honoured among Guyana's greatest artists. His massive carving of the slave princess, Imoinda, which now stands in the main lecture hall at the University of Guyana, is perhaps the greatest piece of sculpture in the nation. In Guyana also his interest in Amazonian mythology grew and he began the arduous work of translation which was to bear fruit in his years of retirement near Recife and then in Canada.[36]

Campbell gave to Guyana a marvellous range of creative, committed minds, an indispensable instrument for shaping a young nation. It is an enduring tragedy, though, that Cheddi Jagan could see nothing redeeming in this great Campbell experiment, that he could not go beyond the litany of denunciations of the 'sugar gods', however justified in the past. Indeed, in a broadcast on local radio on February 21, 1960, Jock had exhorted Guyanese to work with Booker to remove the 'overburden' of that past:

[I]f we look at the history of this country — slavery, the indenture system, colonialism, and all the ills and conflicts that went with it — it is easy to understand why Booker, whose roots are two hundred years deep in it all, should be made a symbol of these ills and conflicts. And why so many people in their relationship with Booker, find it difficult not to be suspicious and wary and on guard. It's the overburden of the past. An overburden that sits on the present like the Old Man of the Sea on the shoulders of Sindbad the sailor. The people of British Guiana, and Booker, suffer together from this overburden. It would be stupid and dim-witted to ignore this. But it would, I suggest, be sensible and creative to understand it, and try to handle it in such a way that it would cease to be the hindrance to progress it still unfortunately is.... [I]t is in our interest to struggle against anything that hampers the progress of B.G., because that would hamper us too. This is a simple and straightforward proposition; and yet many people still talk as though Booker has some mysterious interest in inhibiting the progress of this country.[37]

Campbell was beginning to despair of the impenetrable Jaganite faith in the superiority of the communist creed.

Endnotes

1. Jock Campbell, 'The Development and Organisation of Booker', Paper delivered at LSE, November 24, 1959, (mimeo.), pp. 4, 6.
2. Ibid., 6.
3. *The Scotsman*, December 7, 1965.
4. *Booker News*, July 19, 1963.
5. Jock Campbell, 'Paternalism — Good or Bad?', *Optima*, (June 1958): 64.
6. *Report of a Commission of Inquiry into the Sugar Industry of British Guiana* (J.A. Venn, chairman), Col. No. 249, (London: HMSO, 1949), 120.
7. See note 5 [p. 66].
8. George Giglioli, 'Medical Services on the Sugar Estates of British Guiana', *Timehri*, no. 35, (fifth series), (1956): 17.
9. Ibid., 17-8.
10. George Giglioli, 'Reorganisation of Medical Services on the Sugar Estates', July 19, 1951, (mimeo.), p. 2.
11. See note 5 [p. 63].
12. See note 8 [pp. 18, 25].
13. *Booker News*, January 29, 1960.
14. Ibid., March 23, 1962.
15. Ibid., November 29, 1963.
16. Winifred Gaskin, 'George Bacs', *Booker News*, October 26, 1956.
17. Ian McDonald, interview by the author, Georgetown, September 11, 1992.
18. Ibid.
19. Ibid.
20. George Giglioli, 'Labour Health', in *Booker Sugar* (Supplement to the Accounts of Booker Bros., McConnell and Co, Ltd, 1954), p. 78; see also Giglioli, 'D.D.T. Defeats Mosquito in British Guiana', *The Crown Colonist* 19, no. 211 (June 1949): 347-9.
21. George Giglioli, 'The Population and Housing Problem on the Sugar Estates of British Guiana', Legislative Council Paper, no. 11 of 1948, p. 17.

22. George Giglioli, 'Further Developments in the Population and Housing Problems on the Sugar Estates of British Guiana, 1947-51', (mimeo.), 1952, p. 32.

23. See note 20: 'Labour Health', [p. 78].

24. *Booker News*, June 6, 1958.

25. Ibid., June 20, 1958.

26. See G. Giglioli and L.J. Charles, 'Reappearance of *Anopheles Darlingi* Root in a Controlled Area of British Guiana's Coastlands', *American Journal of Tropical Medicine and Hygiene* 3, No. 5 (September 1954): 808-15.

27. *Booker News*, April 6, 1962,

28. Ibid.

29. Ibid.

30. Ibid.

31. *Guyana Graphic* (Independence Souvenir), May 26, 1966.

32. *Booker News*, June 6, 1958.

33. Ibid., January 7, 1966.

34. Ian McDonald, interview by the author, Georgetown, September 9, 1992,

35. Jock Campbell, interview by the author, Nettlebed, Oxfordshire, February 18, 1994, Tape 11.

36. Ian McDonald, 'Arthur Goodland — Obituary', *Kyk-over-al*, no. 35 (October 1986): 6.

37. Jock Campbell, 'The Responsibilities of a Modern Business', *Booker News* (Special Supplement), February 26, 1960.

Chapter Twenty-Seven

DEMOLITION OF THE 'PIG STIES': HOUSING REFORM ON THE PLANTATIONS

No feature on the sugar plantations dramatised the continuing deprivation or perpetuated images of slavery and indentureship as the logies or ranges — infamous hovels which, evocatively, were still called 'nigger yard' well into the 1950s. In mid-1929, five years before Jock Campbell's first experience of British Guiana, Rev C.F. Andrews, Gandhi's friend, confidant and adviser on Indians overseas, depicted these logies with unconcealed revulsion. Those at Skeldon, on the Corentyne River, were most repellent:

> [T]he filth which has been thrown outside the door (where no drain exists at all) must have accumulated in such thick layers that the ground in front of the lines [ranges] were almost like a cesspit.... The buildings themselves were in a dilapidated condition. In some cases the floor was entirely of mud and there had been no attempt whatever to raise the building above the level of the mud outside.[1]

As seen earlier, these derelict ranges had so profoundly shaped Campbell's seminal impressions of their plantations that for the rest of his life, he would quickly locate the source of his reformist cause in the stark contrast between the housing for man and mule. In 1990, during my first of many meetings with him over the next four and a half years, he related the following experience of his Guyana awakening (this or a version of it frequently illuminated his recollections of the 1930s):

> I was only in Georgetown for two or three months [in 1934] and then transferred to Albion where I was for about eighteen months.

Old James Bee [the manager] was there, and I was absolutely fascinated by the whole agriculture and engineering of sugar.... I also became aware of the awful conditions. I remember saying to James Bee: 'Why do you have much better stables for the mules than you do housing for the workers?' And he said: 'Because it costs money to replace mules.' Housing was unbelievable.... *Their housing was like pig sties; it was just a hole* [emphasis added].[2]

In 1959 Campbell, in a lecture at LSE, elaborated on the ethos which had shaped plantocratic attitudes. He observed that even up to the Second World War, in Booker, social perceptions were still distorted by slavery and indentureship — the latter was only terminated in 1920. He encountered these attitudes first hand when he worked in British Guiana in the 1930s:

I was appalled as I was fascinated by the sugar industry there. Material conditions were bad — very low wages, deplorable housing and no amenities. But as bad — and even more frightening — were the moral and social attitudes.... What I saw was almost a textbook form of the Marxist 'property-less proletariat'. The sugar industry was dependent upon, and utterly demoralised by, a system of cheap labour following from slavery and the indenture system. Tentative suggestions on my part that something ought to be done about all this led to the defensive, but unfortunately at the time all too true, arguments that the low price of sugar made any improvement in material conditions impossible; and that as a result little, if anything, could be done for the workers. I was told I didn't understand; or 'you must understand they are [a] different sort of people'. There were then always good reasons why nothing could be done to improve the lot of the Guyanese. On top of all else malaria, at the rate of nearly 300 sufferers per 1,000 of the population, had a further demoralising effect upon the whole society.[3]

For Campbell, therefore, the eradication of malaria and the improvement of workers' housing were to be central planks in his post-War programme of reform. The perception, as articulated in a Report of 1939, that the old ranges on the plantations were 'squalid, dilapidated and overcrowded', was a common one. This condition of dereliction had its roots in Indian indentureship, in its stipulated terms of reciprocal obligations between the worker and the employer. As a condition of free housing, medical provisions and, in some cases, small plots for rice and vegetables, in conjunction with communal pasture rights, the indentured labourer was 'bound' to work for a registered employer for five years. In British Guiana, the massive problems of drainage and irrigation tended to retard settlement away from the plantations; the latter, with their minimal provisions, however primitive, offered a cushion of security. Even after the abolition of indentureship in April 1920, many Indian residents on the estates remained in the logies; indeed, 25 per cent of them were no longer employed on the plantations but continued to live there rent-free.[4]

A 'pig sty': one of the infamous 'logies' or ranges

Campbell's reforms at work: workers build their own houses with interest-free loans.

The symbol of the new sugar worker: a painted house in the early 1960s

Dr Giglioli pointed out that in December 1946, in a resident adult estate population of 45,917, there were 11,735 engaged in 'private trades', non-plantation work. In a population of 71,480, about 15,924 (22.2 per cent) were doing their own work; of this 6,824 still lived in the ranges on the estates. Two of the most populous estates were Port Mourant and Albion. In 1946 Port Mourant had a resident population of 7,547, with 3,889 living in their own houses on estate land, while 3,658 lived in the ranges, of which this estate had 95. Albion, with 7,330 resident population, had 4,138 living in their own houses on estate land, while 3,192 lived in the ranges, of which it had 67. Rose Hall, another Berbice estate, had one of the highest number of ranges still standing in December 1946, 132; only Providence (East Bank Demerara), with 194 ranges, and Uitvlugt (West Coast Demerara), with 145, exceeded Rose Hall.[5]

At the end of 1946, when Cheddi Jagan founded his Marxist Political Affairs Committee (PAC), 1,247 of these derelict ranges still blighted the plantation landscape, the most potent symbol of the unrelieved deprivation of many on the estates, at the end of the War. Like the derelict estate hospitals, these logies were ready casualties of the stern austerities required of the planters for most of the 1920s — a situation exacerbated by even worse sugar prices in the 1930s. Until the eradication of malaria, the plantocracy were paranoid about their supply of labour, therefore, they were obsessed with retaining excess labour on or in the vicinity of plantations. They were not so enamoured of this, when the population started to rise at the end of the 1940s.

It is arguable that Cheddi Jagan's political imagination was permeated by the logie — this motif of subjugation also ignited the political instincts of his American-born wife, Janet. In August 1946 she visited the ranges at Rose Hall; her response was an eloquent indictment of the chronic neglect of workers' housing on the plantations. This was the soil in which the Marxism of the Jagans took root:

> The ranges are in a miserable state of disrepair, and hardly a building can claim a roof that does not leak or a complete door with hinges. The rooms are dark and depressing. Many depend solely on the door for any light or ventilation. The partition separating the dwelling of one family from another is inadequate and does not offer sufficient privacy. It is not unusual to find a mother, father, and nine children living in two small rooms.[6]

Janet Jagan was not impressed with the planters' claim that shortage of building materials during the War had precluded them from rehousing workers: she noted that the residence of the manager at Rose Hall had recently undergone 'extensive and expensive' repairs. She also deplored the sanitary conditions of the ranges, where the latrines were located over a drain, just 250 to 300 yards away. In some cases these latrines were only a few feet from the workers' front door, while fowls and ducks fed on the faecal matter. Moreover, residents had no access to potable water. She explained:

> The only water available for drinking and cooking purposes is so murky and putrid that one wonders how the residents can survive. In the whole estate there is one method of obtaining rain water but this is restricted by location and volume to only a section of the community.... In numerous places there are filthy, stagnant drains with putrid odours, drains which provide excellent breeding grounds for mosquitoes. It is quite evident why the majority of the inhabitants suffer from malaria. Due to improper drainage of the land, in the rainy season it is impossible to walk on the estate without being immersed, ankle-deep, in the mud.[7]

Janet observed that the planters were apportioning blame for the pervasive filth on the residents; that they were 'slovenly and irresponsible'. She felt that this could not be upheld by the facts, for invariably the interior of the logies was clean and neat: most people daubed the floor of the hovels with a 'kind of mud which gives [it] a neat, grey appearance'. She concluded on a grim note — precisely the imagery which would sustain the Jaganite messianic vision. The fact that this incisive article, at the beginning of their life-long political mission, was published in the organ of the British Guiana East Indian Association, gave it special resonance:

> The poverty, malnutrition and sickness of the people can be seen all about. Little children are constantly plagued with large and running sores of the legs; adults are always suffering from fevers and chills [malaria]; and old and young alike look thin and emaciated. Such are conditions on the sugar estates of British Guiana.[8]

This was the signature of the crusade. Although, or perhaps because, Cheddi Jagan grew up at Plantation Port Mourant where conditions were much better than most estates — less susceptible to malaria, with many workers owning their own cottages, even their own land to grow rice and rear cattle, and a locomotive to transport them the miles 'aback' to the cane fields — he and his people were said to be demonstrably more self-assured. It gave his politics an uncompromising edge; it fed on imagery of contrasts, polarity, the light and the dark — the manager's mansion and the logies in its shadow. The insecurity of the Indian, though, just moving away from the logie, compared to the intellectually more experienced Africans and Coloureds, gave to Jagan's politics passion but little flexibility. He sketched the Port Mourant of his boyhood in the late 1920s:

> The plantation was indeed a world of its own. Or rather it was two worlds: the world of exploiters and the world of the exploited; the world of whites and the world of non-whites. One was the world of the managers and the European staff in their splendid mansions; the other the world of the labourers in their logies in the 'nigger yard' and the 'bound-coolie yard'. The mansions were electrically lit; the logies had kerosene lamps. It was not unusual to hear it said that mules were better treated than human beings, for the stables had electric light.... Between the white and non-white worlds there were distances — social (inhabitants of these worlds did not associate) and physical (the mansions were out of bounds). There was also a psychological distance. I recall vividly my great curiosity about the manager's mansion. I wanted to know what it felt like to be inside the gate. I wanted to know what was going on inside.[9]

This imagery shaped the Marxist vision: for the rest of his life he would call it up to explain his way of seeing. Whatever the reforms, it remained resilient; immutable. Nothing could change under the regime of the 'sugar gods'. I got the feeling, often, that he could see nothing redeeming in Campbell's reforms, only cracks being papered over. Those dark lenses from his boyhood would cloud out everything but 'bitter sugar'; the Marxist illumination made him implacable. As he argued in his pamphlet of the same name, issued shortly before the elections of 1953:

> Sugardom is not only running the sugar industry. It is also running the whole colony. The time has come when a People's Government must replace our sugar-coated government and reorganise the economy in the interest of the broad masses of the people. Join the fight against sugar imperialism. Make B.G. British Guiana and not Booker Guiana.[10]

The distance between himself and the world of capitalists, even one as progressive as Jock Campbell, would remain a chasm: unbridgeable.

The Venn Commission was aware of the acute housing problem on the estates, and were rigorous enough to time their visit of the ranges in early 1949 to coincide with the rainy season. The air of dereliction permeates their response, which I cite again because it became a mantra of the Jaganite mission:

> We inspected many of the ranges. In quite a number the corrugated iron roofs were leaking and the fabric of the buildings was in a general state of decay. In numerous instances temporary sheets or awnings had been fixed over the beds to keep off the rain. They had mud floors and consequently with the rain dropping from the roofs these were made slippery and dangerous; in many cases we found [jute] bags laid over the floor to prevent slipping. They were built without any plan on low-lying uneven ground. There were few, if any, proper footpaths and in rainy weather communication is difficult. The common latrines, often built over a drainage trench, are frequently in a bad state of repair, with little privacy.[11]

In April 1953, on the eve of the general elections, in a pamphlet, 'Is Imperialism Dead?', Cheddi cited the above quote in his rebuttal of any suggestion that it was dead. He elaborated graphically, drawing from his own experience; this was a potent issue in his mission against King Sugar:

Imagine the state of sanitation and the condition of the sugar estate workers during the heavy rainfall and flood periods which are frequent. The whole housing area becomes covered with polluted water from the overflowing latrine trenches. This polluted water remains on the land for days and sometimes weeks, during which time boats and canoes have to be used for communication. In contrast to this the manager's and officers' quarters are generally always dry. During the 1950 floods I went to the manager at Lusignan to request that the workers' housing area be properly empoldered and a pump used to get rid of the polluted water. His reply to me was whether I knew that I was trespassing — and this in my own constituency [Central Demerara]! The pump was never given.[12]

In 1992 I conducted a long interview with several officials of the main union in the sugar industry, Jagan's GAWU. One of them, Premchand Das, grew up at Plantation Albion in the late 1940s and early 1950s. His recollections of his estate boyhood are punctuated with resilient images of the logies. His large family was one of the last to vacate the ranges in the mid-1950s. Each range had 10 rooms; each family was usually allocated one; his had two. He still referred to the area as 'nigger yard', as he retrieved fresh images of the mud floors in the hovels, and choked drains, the repositories of stinking refuse. Each room looked out on such a drain, whence emanated a most offensive stench. Das recalled that the problem was exacerbated during the heavy rains: primitive latrines straddled a ditch not six rods away; clumps of turds would escape and float ominously, as if destined for the logies marooned in a sea of polluted water.[13] This was the context in which politicians from Jagan's PPP made an impression on young Das's mind, why he and many others embraced Cheddi as their liberator.

This was the context, too, in which the Venn Commission, in 1949, recommended the demolition of the ranges: '[T]hat an Ordnance should be passed to provide for the clearance of all ranges and the rehousing of their occupants by the end of 1953. Pending demolition, defective ranges should forthwith be rendered weatherproof to the satisfaction of the Medical Department.' They considered it a matter of urgency that the 6,000 families, the residents in these ranges, be relocated in 'extra-nuclear' areas, on estate land in the vicinity of estates.[14] They were emphatic: 'There can be no peace on the sugar estates until this depressing legacy from former days is removed and we consider that rehousing should be given a high priority.' However, while it was the responsibility of the plantations to rehouse their 'nuclear' or key workers — technical or artisanal — they concurred with the Colonial Development and Welfare ruling of 1944, that the rehousing of non-essential (extra-nuclear) workers was the responsibility of the government. To rehouse the 6,000 families by 1953, they advised that the government raise a loan of $7,200,000. In September 1950, as will be seen shortly, the government announced that it could not afford to undertake this project.[15]

It is noteworthy, however, that some rehousing had commenced as early as 1931, at Blairmont, Rose Hall, Albion, Port Mourant and Skeldon — the Berbice plantations. These had found favour with an investigator, Sir William Beveridge, but he was more amenable to the building of cottages. The Industry contended that this would have necessitated considerable dispersal of the houses over a larger residential area, thus diffusing the impact of the mosquito control measures. Given the prevalent approach to spraying, they opted, in 1937, for a more concentrated residential pattern — long buildings on pillars, with four apartments. By 1946, 29,327 or 41 per cent of estate residents were already rehoused in their own houses: 'a large proportion of these had been built with interest-free loans or other assistance from the estates'.[16] The 'non-whinging', independent spirit which Campbell admired in the Corentyne workers, had its roots in the relatively malaria-free nature of the district, coupled with access to land on and off the estates and possibilities for escape from the logies.[17]

The sugar producers had taken steps since 1947 to allocate funds for social welfare. As noted earlier, with good prices for sugar after the War, Campbell's friend at the Colonial Office, Sydney Caine, had recommended the creation of three special funds to give stability to sugar in the British West Indies. In British Guiana, from 1947, these funds were resourced on the basis of a levy on each ton of sugar exported from the colony: £1 per ton for a Rehabilitation Fund, to modernise factories and other assets; £1 5s per ton for a Price Stabilisation Fund; and 10s ($2.40G) per ton for a Sugar Industry

Labour Welfare Fund (SILWF). Social welfare was already being funded from the latter. The Venn Commission had endorsed this, adding that the SILWF should also fund a pure water scheme, shelter in the fields, creches for children on the estates and sports grounds.[18]

By December 1950 the SILWF had accumulated $1.5 million, but the pace of rehousing was not impressive: in 1946 there were 1,217 ranges (a slight underestimate); in 1950, 1090; in 1951, 1,068: only 150 had been demolished in six years. It was not until September 1950, when the government announced that it would not raise a loan to rehouse the extra-nuclear workers, and that such funds had to come from the SILWF, that a concerted programme was launched. In fact, Dr Giglioli had estimated in 1952 that at the current rate of demolition it would have taken 15.7 years to eliminate all the ranges; the 1953 deadline was absurd.[19]

It was the suspension of the Constitution in October 1953, fed by the apprehension, in the heat of the Cold War, that the Marxist virus would take root in the colony, which gave urgency to the rehousing issue. Campbell understood fully that to counter the Marxist appeal of Jagan, reforms on the plantations had to be accelerated, but that the SILWF could not provide all the funds required for rehousing without undermining other reforms.

The Minister of Health and Housing in the short-lived Jagan-led government of 1953, Dr J.P. Lachmansingh, had noted that the Price Stabilisation Fund (PSF) had to its credit $7,000,000 at a time when sugar prices were guaranteed under the Commonwealth Sugar Agreement. He had asked that 'a few million dollars from the PSF be loaned to expedite estate housing': if the SILWF were augmented, this could be achieved.[20]

Responding to another searing indictment of housing conditions on the plantations, Jock Campbell wrote to Follett-Smith on November 6, 1953: 'That this description of housing conditions on our sugar estates can be written — not without justification, despite all that has been done and is being done — is one of the compelling reasons why I have increasingly said that we can never rest satisfied until our workers are properly housed. What is wanted now is a long pull and a strong pull'. He supported the transfer of $2.5 million from the PSF to the SILWF, arguing that extra-nuclear settlements must not become new slums. The maintenance of buildings was important, so too were sanitation, roads, water supply, lighting, and so on. On November 17, 1953, primarily as a result of his intervention, Campbell was able to announce that the sugar producers had agreed that $2.5 million should be transferred from the PSF to finance the rehousing programme.[21]

At the end of 1954, seven years since its introduction, the SILWF was credited with $6,823,579. As Giglioli observed 'every cent of this came from the sugar industry'. The Fund was administered by the Industry and the recognised trade unions, such as the MPCA, under the chairmanship of the Commissioner of Labour. Workers were now able to erect their own houses in designated areas near to the estates, on lots leased at a peppercorn rental of 24 cents per month. They could borrow up to $1,000 interest-free; $750 for construction and $250 for painting. The loans were repayable in weekly instalments of $2.00.[22]

By January 1956 *Booker News* could report that at Uitvlugt (West Coast Demerara), which had the largest number of ranges, Booker had laid out and prepared five areas for extra-nuclear settlement. Ocean View, which was established in 1947, 'offered workers not only escape from the ranges, but a healthy siting for the houses facing the sea wall'. Ocean View was situated on the healthier front lands and was the prototype for the four other housing areas: Zeeburg-De Willem (149 houses); Meten-Meer-Zorg (179 houses); Tuschen (79 houses); the Garrison (128). Initially there were some workers who resisted the move, clinging tenaciously to the familiar, however environmentally dismal. There were deep roots here and a strong sense of community, its rituals and life-cycle rites synchronised with the rhythm of the plantations. By the mid-1950s, though, perceptible success in house-building and pride in home-ownership in the extra-nuclear areas, were eroding the conservatism of the range-dwellers. There were those who had squandered their loans, but this was quickly checked. No cash was given to potential house builders; an order to the saw mill for building materials was provided to those whose building plans had been approved. The SILWF monitored progress in construction.[23]

In January 1957 a correspondent of the *Manchester Guardian* commented on the success in rehousing workers, noting that the 'primitive barracks' were disappearing fast as well-planned settlements emerged. He characterised Booker's relationship to their workers as 'enlightened paternalism'. He explained: 'The estates have become miniature welfare states, the workers and their families provided for almost literally from the cradle to the grave, the local wages negotiated ... are high by colonial standards, the standard of living far in advance of most "underdeveloped" countries'. But he detected, still, an undercurrent of uncertainty, 'bursting out occasionally into open resentment'.[24]

Campbell responded promptly to the charge of paternalism, explaining the context in which the extra-nuclear housing schemes had taken shape:

> After the last War, the sugar industry decided that the disgraceful housing on sugar estates ... must be put right, and that it would be in the best interests of everybody that people should live in their own houses in future instead of estate-owned houses — a positive step away from the paternalistic heritage of slavery and the indenture system. The industry put at the disposal of Government land near their estates at token prices where new villages could be created with Government financial assistance to the people. Government, while welcoming the principle, refused to do anything at all about it, owing to 'lack of funds'. So the industry laid out the land, leased house-lots to the people at peppercorn rents, and lent them money on easy terms, interest-free terms, to build their own houses. Thousands of families have been rehoused in this way.[25]

Campbell observed that government was still not assuming responsibility for the communities created: they had no system of local government; they just lingered as 'no-man's land adjacent' to the sugar estates. He did not desire a paternalistic role for Booker but with no initiative coming from government, they could not view the situation passively, shirking all responsibilities. In any case, his four-fold responsibilities imposed certain inescapable duties. Campbell pondered:

> The declared policy of the sugar industry is opposed to paternalism, which is recognised to be demoralising — apart from being very expensive. But equally the industry recognises its

responsibilities to its employees and to the community — as well as to its shareholders. If Government will not or cannot act, the people cannot raise themselves by their own bootstraps ... without some effective guidance or leadership or assistance. What should industry do? Too much (paternalism and Booker Guiana)? Or nothing?[26]

However the extra-nuclear settlements were perceived, they did enhance people's self-esteem. By vacating the logies they were already easing their dependency, emulating their more successful compatriots who had created village communities since the late nineteenth century. Moreover, by building their own houses, painting and furnishing them, repaying their loans to the SILWF, and sending their children to primary and, increasingly, secondary school, they were claiming the right of citizenship and greater autonomy as individuals. They were beating back paternalism. As Sir Frederick Seaford observed, after his inspection of a few extra-nuclear areas in 1957, workers now had a better standard of living, reflected in new fittings and furnishings in their homes. They owned them; they could take pride in them. He believed British Guiana was experiencing a broadening of the middle class, the heightening of aspirations, 'a desirable objective in the development of any country'.[27]

In February 1960 Jock Campbell, speaking at the opening of the community centre at Plantation LBI, commended the workers for their progress in home-ownership: 'It is a joy to me to see the real homes in which so many of you now live in, instead of those wretched old ranges.' He was also appreciative of the work of the chairman of the Sugar Industry Labour Welfare Fund, Mr J.I. Ramphal, OBE.[28] But government was still unable to assume responsibility for the extra-nuclear areas and bring them under self-government, as adumbrated by the Marshall Plan for the reform of local government. It was, therefore, agreed that the SILWF Committee should take responsibility for these communities from the sugar estates. They would proceed to administer the transfer of the house-lots to the tenants at the nominal price of $1 per lot. The workers were now owners of their houses and the land. Campbell hoped that this would enhance their self-confidence and promote a spirit of cooperation, as they entered the threshold of self-government.[29]

In 1961, consonant with Campbell's idea that preventative maintenance was essential in preventing these settlements from degenerating into slums, the SILWF Committee and the union, the MPCA, agreed to have the ordnance amended to enable those who were reliable rate-payers to borrow supplementary loans: $300 for extension of the house or $200 for repairs.[30]

By the end of 1960 of the 1,247 logies in existence in 1946, the year before the inauguration of the SILWF, only 132 remained, some on non-Booker estates. *Booker News* was very pleased with the progress, noting that the loan scheme had resulted in the construction of 8,927 houses, each on a one-tenth acre lot, taking the place of 'those long, unsightly barns'. Yet the programme was far from exhausted: in 1961 there were still 2,000 new loans available. The paper added that water connections were being made from the mains to workers' houses in the extra-nuclear areas. Additional loans were available for this; borrowers did not incur any hike to their weekly repayment. So by the early 1960s, most sugar workers owned their own houses and house-lots, with access to potable water in their homes or in their yards.[31]

In 1962 the SILWF Committee announced the expansion of its programme to construct 'permanent asphalt-surfaced' roads in the sugar estates housing schemes. They envisaged the building of 60 miles of all-weather roads at a cost of $2 million. This type of work had commenced in 1959, and the SILWF had already financed road construction in 23 housing schemes: 17 miles had been surfaced at a cost of $522,400 or $30,729 per mile. The first piece of work was undertaken in February 1959 at Tain Settlement, near Port Mourant. This had been a successful pilot project, yielding accurate data on construction costs, while facilitating the training of construction foremen. The SILWF bore the cost of construction and maintenance of all road-building programmes, while the management of estates were responsible for the actual work on the new roads. In 1962 similar work was nearing completion at Annandale Housing Scheme, on the Lower East Coast Demerara, near Plantation Lusignan.[32]

By the end of 1963, the reform which Campbell had deemed most crucial was virtually completed — the rehousing of workers away from the abysmal hovels. More than 12,000 families had been resettled in 80 extra-nuclear housing areas; this was equivalent to nearly 25 per cent of the coastal population of British Guiana. Sugar workers had received interest-free loans totalling $10 million. Besides, the SILWF expended $2 million on the development of new housing schemes; another $2 million on water supply; more than $1 million on road building; and $1.75 million on community centres and sports facilities throughout plantation Guyana. Yet in 1965 $11.5 million were still credited to the Fund, and the approved expenditure that year was a record $6.75 million. With the resettlement virtually accomplished, more funds were being allocated to social amenities: $3 million for roads; $1.4 million for potable water, but there were still $1.2 million for housing loans and nearly $1 million for developing 49 new housing areas. Since 1947 the sugar industry had spent $20 million on social welfare.[33] As Jock Campbell told me in 1990: 'It was beyond the wildest horizons of Booker ... and suddenly this idea occurred that why not give them land, build the roads and let them build their houses. Everybody was rehoused in a short space of time. This was a very great social reform.'[34]

On September 3, 1965 *Booker News* carried two pictures along with its article on the progress engendered by the SILWF. One showed a line of trim little houses, painted white and picketed, at Annandale Housing Scheme, an Indian settlement on the East Coast Demerara. The other was captioned: 'The new generation ("Dr Giglioli's children"). Keen bright-eyed children from Ogle Housing Scheme at a local talent show organised by the Ogle Community Centre Council.' The eradication of malaria and the housing reform, these were the shapers of the post-War generation of sugar workers and their children, primarily Indian Guyanese people. The reformist vision of Jock Campbell and the unwavering challenge from Cheddi Jagan's incorruptible, Marxist-inspired mission, were inseparable. The social reforms fed an insatiable appetite for even more reforms; it is a tragedy for all Guyanese that Marxism, in one form or another, won out; that capital was seen as necessarily evil. The English-speaking Caribbean has had no such parallel, not even Bishop's Grenada.

Campbell continually preached 'the importance of small causes'. In 1958 he had reflected on what the housing reforms meant to him.

He probably came nearer, too, to the individual perceptions of the sugar workers:

> I find these new villages tremendously exciting because they are villages; they are a community of the houses of individuals. Many critics — perhaps, particularly critics who have seen the gleaming labour lines of modern mining camps, for instance — may say they look shoddy and amateurish; some houses are painted, some are not, some are absurdly big with fantastic towers, some are ludicrously squat and small. But the point is they do reflect the lives and values of the families living in them and not the values of management — or the expert advisers of management.[35]

In September 1992, when interviewing Premchand Das, the trade unionist from the PPP's sugar union, GAWU, I gathered indelible impressions of what the move from the logie to their own home in the extra-nuclear area at Albion, Jock's old family estate, meant to him. Premchand said that the exodus from the 'nigger yard' (he still used that evocative expression), in the mid-1950s, was not just a physical move; it had profound psychological ramifications. His family's 'estate mentality' was evaporating; their horizon broadened; they became aware of greater possibilities. Education became an obsession, and the facilities at the Albion Community Centre — library, literary and debating club, sports and games — heightened their curiosity as their healthier bodies, too, sought expression. Whereas his four older siblings did not go beyond primary school, the last five in the Das family all went to high school. By the late 1950s he had become an inquisitive young man, strong in mind and body, conscious of the need for even greater changes in colonial society. In 1957, during the election campaign, he had heard Cheddi Jagan speak at Albion. A PPP group for young people already existed on the plantation. The lesson that fired him was 'the exploitative nature of capital'. On September 15, 1960 he joined Cheddi's PPP: he had no doubts that the changes on the estate, crucial to his awakening, were the tip of the iceberg and that Cheddi could get infinitely more for them.[36]

In 1964 racial violence disrupted many SILWF projects in the extra-nuclear areas. However, 1,238 housing loans, totalling

$412,800 were disbursed; 214 houses were completed and 392 were under construction. In 1966, the last full year of Jock Campbell's chairmanship, 1,777 housing loans were granted; $170,000 were allocated to social welfare on the plantations; $1.5 million went to road construction in the housing schemes; $1 million to water supply. It was noted that, over the past 17 years (since 1947), the SILWF had helped 'radically to improve living conditions in the rural areas'.[37] Indeed, between 1947 and 1967, $11,462,861 were allocated as loans to workers to help them to construct their own houses; of 1,247 ranges or logies on the estates in the former year, only 45 were standing in the latter.[38] This, however, had led to invidious comparisons being made between the extra-nuclear areas and the adjacent villages, with no access to funds from the sugar industry. It was a measure of the sugar workers' progress that Booker's Director of Social Policy could report thus in 1964:

> [T]he [Sugar Industry Labour Welfare] Fund's main problem was starkly spotlighted in 1964: funds further increased to about $9 million which ... were nevertheless committed to a continuance of the current pattern of expenditure in the Extra-nuclear Areas. The dangers of the large fund, and the social problems caused by the existence of privileged sugar communities, are obvious.... An examination of ways in which the pattern of expenditure could be altered, to benefit also, if possible, villages adjacent to the Extra-nuclear Areas, was being undertaken by year end.[39]

Endnotes

1. CO111/689/75141, encl.: C.F. Andrews, 'Impressions of British Guiana', (mimeo.), [1930],pp. 66-7.
2. Jock Campbell, interview by the author, Nettlebed, Oxfordshire, May 9, 1990, Tape 1.
3. Jock Campbell, 'The Development and Organisation of Booker', Paper delivered at LSE, November 24, 1959, (mimeo.), p. 4.
4. George Giglioli, 'The Population and Housing Problem on the Sugar Estates of British Guiana', Legislative Council Paper, No. 11 of 1948, pp. 6-7.
5. Ibid., 7, 9.
6. Janet Jagan, 'Sugar Estate Housing', *Indian Opinion*, August 31, 1946.

7. Ibid.

8. Ibid.

9. Cheddi Jagan, *The West on Trial: My Fight for Guyana's Freedom* (London: Michael Joseph, 1966), 18-9.

10. Cheddi Jagan, *Bitter Sugar* (Georgetown: self-published, n.d., ca. 1953), 17-8.

11. *Report of a Commission of Inquiry into the Sugar Industry of British Guiana* (J.A. Venn, chairman), Col. No. 249 (London: HMSO, 1949), 122.

12. Cheddi Jagan, 'Is Imperialism Dead?',(mimeo.), [April 1953], p. 12.

13. Premchand Das, interview by the author, Georgetown, September 9, 1992.

14. See note 11 [p. 124].

15. Ibid., 127.

16. George Giglioli, 'Labour Housing', in *Booker Sugar* (Supplement to the Accounts of Booker Bros, McConnell and Co, Ltd, 1954), p. 82.

17. Jock Campbell, interview by the author, Nettlebed, Oxfordshire, July 24, 1992, Tape 6.

18. See note 11 [p. 148].

19. George Giglioli, 'Further Developments in the Population and Housing Problems on the Sugar Estates of British Guiana, 1947-51', [1952], (mimeo.), p. 17.

20. Ashton Chase, *133 Days Towards Freedom in Guiana* (Georgetown: self-published, 1954), 32.

21. Jock Campbell to R.R. Follett-Smith, in *Booker Sugar* (1954), p. 93.

22. See note 16 [p. 83].

23. *Booker News*, January 20, 1956.

24. Ibid., [quoted in Leader], February 15, 1957.

25. Ibid.

26. Ibid.

27. Ibid., March 15, 1957.

28. Ibid., February 12, 1960.

29. Ibid., July 1, 1960.

30. Ibid., April 7, 1961.

31. Ibid., [Leader], March 9, 1962.

32. Ibid., August 24, 1962.

33. Ibid., September 3, 1965.

34. See note 2.

35. Jock Campbell, 'Paternalism — Good or Bad?, *Optima*, (June 1958): 66.

36. See note 13.

37. BSE, 'Report of the Director of Social Policy', 1964, 1966.

38. SPA, 'Report of the Sugar Industry Labour Welfare Fund, 1967', (mimeo.), pp. 7,12.

39. See note 37, [1964].

Chapter Twenty-Eight

SOCIAL WELFARE ON THE PLANTATIONS, WITH SPECIAL REFERENCE TO THE COMMUNITY CENTRES AND WOMEN'S WELFARE

In 1949 the Venn Commission endorsed the programme of social welfare initiated on the plantations, concurring with the belated pronouncement of sugar planters, 'to foster the self-confidence of their employees and to encourage them to stand on their own feet'. They expressed satisfaction with their 'vision' in piloting a range of welfare projects; they were also 'greatly impressed' with the social welfare organiser of the SPA, Ralph Scargall, with his 'energy and understanding' in initiating many of the social welfare schemes on the plantations since the War. This was one of the first reforms Jock Campbell was able to pursue, with the death of Sir Alfred Sherlock, the Chairman of Booker, in 1946.[1]

The Commission underlined the importance of community centres, with good sports grounds, ample recreational facilities, and welfare officers to coordinate activities. These could engender workers' and children's pride in self, their independence and broader aspirations. They considered this change congruent with the interests of the sugar industry: 'Increased productivity is needed today in the industry and a contented, self-reliant man with an incentive to improve his position is, naturally enough, going to be a keener worker and put more effort into his job.'[2]

In 1946 the SPA had appointed a Yorkshireman, R.B. Scargall (born 1909), as their social welfare organiser. He was an experienced youth worker in British Guiana, having been secretary of the YMCA in Georgetown between 1938 and 1944 and the colony's youth organiser from 1944 to 1946.[3] In March 1946, in exhorting administrative managers of sugar estates to support Scargall's work,

Jock Campbell had focused less on the mechanics, the construction of cricket pavilions and youth centres; rather, he went straight to the human dimension, defining it primarily in terms of attitudinal change on the estates — 'change of thought amongst the people and the arousing of interest in welfare matters amongst members of the estates' [administrative] staff'.[4]

Campbell's initial interest in social welfare, like his belief in reform generally, had its origins in his seminal experience of plantation life in the mid-1930s. The Moyne Commission had advocated it, and the Colonial Development and Welfare grants, since 1940, were demonstrating what was possible. Rising expectations had been fed by the more enlightened attitudes of American employers in the colony during the War. The amalgamation of Curtis Campbell with Booker, since 1939, gave Jock the authority to begin to shape a culture of change, while better sugar prices after the War provided the means to do so. He reflected on his position after 1945: 'I had grown up and become an executive in a larger business because my family business had been taken over by a bigger company... Booker — me with it. So it was more easy to identify the desirable and the possible. More money was available to achieve them. And I had the authority to do something about it all.' [5]

His reforming impulse had been quickened by the Venn Commission Report of 1949, and by the growing influence on the estates of the young Indian Marxist, Cheddi Jagan who, as a legislator since 1947, had won wide appeal as champion of the underdog. Eusi Kwayana (Sydney King), an early disciple of Jagan, recalls the man and his time:

> The exemplary conduct of the Central Demerara representative, Cheddi Jagan, in the Legislative Council, his targeting of Booker as the common enemy, instead of seeking accommodations with the imperialist firm, won the confidence of a large section of the working people and of a large part of those who considered themselves thinking citizens and had been steeped in the planter tradition .... [T]hese developments made it possible for the shooting of the Enmore martyrs to win the response it did from all sections of the society.[6]

Campbell recognised the power of Jagan's seminal message and sought to minimise its appeal by getting to the root of its inspiration — 'Booker's Guiana': 'Booker and the sugar industry — in the light of their history — were detested and distrusted beyond measure, including by their own employees...It is easier for a Campbell to pass through the eye of a needle than for big business to be loved. But it can be understood and respected, and [be] worthy of respect.' [7]

In 1947, with the inauguration of the SILWF, money became available for social welfare. By September 1950, however, F.J. Seaford of Booker was expressing doubts about the commitment of estate managers to social welfare work. He thought it necessary to emphasise that it was not peripheral to other work; it was at the core of the estates' programme. Obviously echoing Campbell, Seaford had written: 'We feel that the work is of such importance that it should be one of the first charges on estates, in the same way as salaries, wages and maintenance, and, in getting out their estimates, Administrative Managers should set aside a fixed amount for this work, which they should use to the best advantage after consultation with Mr. Scargall.' [8]

The Venn Commission's emphasis on this aspect of reform had lent authority and urgency to it. In May 1951 Campbell was contending that social welfare officers were crucial not only for the execution of such work, but for the training of good Indian leaders at the grassroots. He was very conscious of the paucity of leadership among Indians who, under the paternalism of the plantations, had stagnated in this vital area. There was no doubt that fear of Jaganite communism impelled Campbell to try to shape an Indian leadership with 'a sense of proportion': 'I most sincerely hope this experiment will succeed not only because the influence and leavening effect of young Indians who have gained balance and a sense of proportion ... in a position of some authority in the sugar industry would be immeasurably valuable'.[9] In keeping with his admonition of March 1946, he felt that social welfare could speed up attitudinal change, reshaping the minds of young Indians on the estates.

Scargall noted in 1954 that in 1950 they had sent 'two Guianese of Indian origin' to the UK to be trained in social welfare. Since then eight had been trained, seven of whom were still working on the plantations. These provided the nucleus to train others locally. With the suspension of the Constitution in October 1953, the centrality of

(a) (b) (c)

a. *The social welfare team on the sugar plantations in the 1950s: (sitting left to right): Ruby Samlalsingh (social welfare adviser — Women); Dr George Giglioli (medical adviser); W.A. Macnie (managing director, SPA); W.E.V. Harrison (secretary, SPA); Clyde Walcott (cricket organiser); (standing left to right) R.B. Scargall (social welfare organiser); H. Hobbs (statistical officer); J. Jack (sanitation officer); R. Rice (industrial relations officer).*
b. *Clyde Walcott, cricket organiser, coaching at Enmore Estate around 1954.*
c. *R.B. Scargall, social welfare organiser on the plantations.*

this work in shaping people's minds, a counter to the perceived extremism of Jagan, led to its acceleration. It was not fortuitous that the SILWF was augmented by the diversion of $2.5 million from the Price Stabilisation Fund, in November 1953. In 1954 a Women's Welfare Adviser, Miss Ruby Samlalsingh, BSc, an Indian Trinidadian social welfare expert, trained in Manitoba as well as England and India, with eight years' experience in Trinidad, was appointed. In the same year the SPA acquired Clyde Walcott, the great Barbadian and West Indies Test cricketer, as cricket organiser on the sugar estates; so, too, the Trinidadian Olympic medallist, McDonald Bailey, as sports organiser.[10] Scargall was justifiably buoyant: '[T]he welfare sky in British Guiana is bright: the sun is rising. If its warmth has not yet penetrated the whole country it is at least being felt.' [11] The imagery, too, was justified.

In 1954, also, Campbell appointed Antony Tasker, public relations director of Booker in British Guiana. His mandate was 'to interpret the policies and plans of Booker to the community, and the hopes and fears of the community to Booker'.[12] In July 1955 the first issue of *Booker News* appeared in Georgetown. Campbell's message at the time was unambiguous: 'I hope that *Booker News* will help to foster a better understanding by employees of management policies and actions; and, equally important, a better understanding by management of employees' attitudes and problems.'[13] As Campbell would often say, public relations for Booker in British Guiana was about doing good and being seen to be doing good — taking credit for it.

Campbell promoted social welfare as an instrument to fight paternalism. It was not only essential to advance 'industrial welfare' — community centres, sports grounds, canteens, creches — the 'social' dimension of welfare, too, the inculcation of attitudes of initiative and self-help among plantation workers, had to be consciously pursued. Scargall articulated well what Campbell had argued continually since the War: 'By social welfare I mean the guidance, stimulation and organisation of workers' committees and workers themselves to make the most of the facilities provided and by self-help to improve them .... [W]ithout it, without the sense of contribution and partnership which it gives, there is a human tendency to undervalue the benefits which are the inheritance of the worker of today.'[14]

The work pioneered by Scargall was advanced admirably by Clyde Walcott, McDonald Bailey, Ruby Samlalsingh and her successor, Roma Persaud, and many welfare officers, men and women on the estates, as well as the thousands of workers and their children who became enmeshed in the culture of the community centres, especially from the mid-1950s. This strengthened the Indians' sense of community and sealed their identity with the future of Guyana. Paradoxically, Booker's stature among them was not necessarily enhanced, neither was Jock Campbell's, as the example of Premchand Das amply demonstrated. Cheddi Jagan was the principal beneficiary of a vibrant estate culture, the culture of reform since the early 1950s, as Indian workers in particular became increasingly confident of their own possibilities. The political context of reform was inescapable, as Scargall explained, following the augmenting of funds for social welfare in 1954: 'Through the Welfare Plan coupled with improved personnel relations it should be possible to do much to mould the young generation towards *a more moderate political outlook* and a more reasonable attitude towards the Industry [emphasis added].'[15]

The principal areas addressed by the social welfare reforms were (i) the construction of community centres and sports grounds; (ii) coaching and organisation of sports with special reference to cricket and athletics; (iii) imparting various domestic/craft skills, nutrition and games to young women and girls; (iv) drama; (v) creches for workers' children; (vi) the provision of libraries on all estates; (vii) the inculcation of attitudes of independence and self-help and training in leadership.

In January 1949, when the Venn Commission was meeting in Georgetown, Scargall announced that the 'principle of providing a community hall or welfare centre on all estates' had been adopted. He hoped that people would avail themselves of the facilities provided and that they would assume responsibility for the management and organisation of community activities. Three such community centres had already been opened and local welfare officers appointed.[16] By 1954 he could report considerable progress: '[E]very sugar estate ... has a creche, a sports ground and a canteen of some sort or another — nine have fine, modern and well-equipped community centres. Of the creches, be it said that the estates provide free milk daily for the attending children.'[17]

The appointment of Walcott as the cricket organiser of the SPA was an imaginative step. With thousands of people on the plantations already playing cricket (John Trim [1915–60] from Port Mourant played Test cricket for the West Indies between 1949 and 1951), the passion for the game was augmented by Walcott's great gifts. In 1955 two players from Port Mourant, where a community centre and a sports ground already existed, represented British Guiana against Australia: Basil Butcher and Rohan Kanhai. The community centres sowed ambition on the plantations, and Walcott's authority enabled a few brilliant backwoodsmen to gain recognition from the cricket czars in Georgetown. Hitherto they had rarely sought talent beyond the accessible clubs in the city.

Consequently, in 1956, five cricketers from sugar estates on the Corentyne represented British Guiana in the Quadrangular Tournament, the symbol of cricket supremacy in the West Indies: Basil Butcher, Rohan Kanhai, Ivan Madray and Joe Solomon (Port Mourant), and Sonny Baijnauth (Albion). The captain of the national team was Clyde Walcott. All four of the cricketers from Port Mourant, the birth place of Cheddi Jagan, would soon play in Tests for the West Indies: Kanhai made his debut in 1957, while Butcher, Madray and Solomon made theirs in 1958–59. Kanhai (79 Tests), Butcher (44 Tests) and Solomon (27 Tests) were pillars of West Indies batting in the 1960s, as Roy Fredericks (59 Tests) and Alvin Kallicharran (66

Tests), gifted batsmen from Blairmont and Port Mourant respectively, were in the 1970s.

I referred earlier to the enlightened paternalism at Port Mourant, where J.C. Gibson, an Englishman, the administrative manager from 1908 to 1939, had given workers greater self-belief. Many had built their own houses, were rearing cattle and growing rice, while he had installed a small locomotive to transport workers to the fields, several miles into the back-lands. An avid cricketer, Gibson had founded the Port Mourant Cricket Club before the First World War, and had allowed his workers to run it; this engendered a somewhat fanatical pursuit of the game among his Indian workers, feeding the passion kindled by the ascendancy of their great Indian hero, Prince Ranjitsinhji (1872-1933), the master batsman for Cambridge, Sussex and England, before the First World War. It is arguable that at Port Mourant, the spirit of independence and self-help which Campbell sought to foster on the plantations, had already taken shape; and he had recognised that and considered it admirable.[18]

Some years ago I explored the context of the shaping of the amazing drive, the continuity of effort — the energy of the people of Port Mourant. I reproduce it here:

> The Corentyne Coast, in Berbice, is the 'coolie' heartland. It comprises a string of flat, fertile villages ... interspersed among many vast sugar plantations.... From the 1920s through the 1940s, Indians made small, but firm, strides in rice cultivation, cattle rearing, market gardening and the retail trade. Each step constituted a gnawing away at the fetters, material and psychological, which had bound them to the plantations ... the eradication of malaria around 1948, largely through the work of the SPA's malariologist, Dr. George Giglioli, gave to the people in rural Guyana a new physical vitality.... They could now speak and they could run also. The malarial sloth was lifting and a mental and physical regeneration was emerging.... Community centres, with excellent cricket grounds, were built on all estates. Social welfare officers were appointed at each estate — the graceful West Indies batsman, Robert Christiani, was sent to Port Mourant; and in 1954, the great Barbadian [and West Indies] batsman, Clyde Walcott, was acquired as a cricket coach by the SPA.[19]

By the end of 1956, as the Social Welfare Report of the SPA reveals, Walcott's presence and quietly effective leadership already had much to its credit. Training courses for cricket umpires were held on all the estates on the East Coast and West Coast Demerara. It was observed that better training of umpires was producing a generally higher standard of cricket. Indeed, six Berbice players represented British Guiana in Antigua in July 1956. The inter-county matches for that year, between Essequibo, Demerara and Berbice, were played on the Rose Hall Estate Community Centre Ground, 'one of the best grounds in the Colony'. The Berbice team, which defeated Demerara in the final, comprised nine players from the sugar plantations. The quality of the grounds, the availability of facilities for training and relaxation, at the community centres, and the inspiration of Walcott, contributed to a perceptible rise in the standard of play. Cricket on the Berbice estates had reached the pinnacle. The Report concluded:

> The Quadrangular Tournament [between British Guiana, Trinidad, Barbados and Jamaica], held at Bourda [Georgetown] in October [1956], was a tremendous success and fillip to estate cricket as a whole. Six estate players represented the Colony in both games and were particularly outstanding. Three of them [Butcher, Kanhai and Madray] have been selected for the Trial Games in Trinidad in preparation for the West Indies tour of England during 1957.[20]

Clyde Walcott was named vice-captain of that West Indies team which went to England; Rohan Kanhai, also, was selected. In 1958 Ivan Madray, the leg spinner, played two Tests against Pakistan; and in 1958–59 Butcher, Kanhai and Solomon were major contributors to the victory of the West Indies in India.

In June 1957 Follett-Smith observed that social welfare work had progressed, with emphasis on self-help and community development. He regretted that the social welfare organiser, R.B. Scargall, had to retire because of ill-health, at the age of 48, acknowledging that he was 'one of the pioneers of social welfare work' in British Guiana. He identified some of Scargall's achievements: the appointment of welfare officers on each plantation, the development of community councils, formation of tenant associations, club work (especially girls' clubs), libraries, regular film shows, handicrafts and culinary skills, athletics and cricket. He added that the libraries had been a great success and that they were about to introduce more on the estates. He praised Clyde Walcott's work and McDonald Bailey's in athletics, especially cross-country running and road races.[21]

Follett-Smith observed that the women's social welfare organiser, Ruby Samlalsingh, also, had had a successful year. Her staff had been augmented significantly in 1957. Miss Roma Persaud, Miss Ramdeholl (who resigned shortly afterwards) and Miss Maureen Bhagwandeen had returned from Puerto Rico in 1956, having studied home economics and social welfare. Miss Persaud was based at Skeldon Estate where she was appointed women's welfare officer and home economics instructor. Her work was varied: classes in cookery and nutrition for teenagers and young wives; classes in sewing, embroidery, child care, home maintenance, housing, health, sanitation, handicraft and first-aid. She had also formed a Parents/ Teachers Association and a Literary Club where play reading, story telling and poetry reading were pursued. The Report expressed approbation for Miss Persaud's work at Skeldon: 'A good deal of this Officer's time is spent in visiting the homes, campaigning for "clean yards" and "open windows" as well as introducing projects for the improvement of the kitchen, etc. The response to the Woman Welfare Officer on this estate has been very good indeed and the people are very enthusiastic to learn.'[22]

Similar work was being done by Miss Bhagwandeen at Port Mourant and Miss Mary Shackleford (a graduate of the University of Edinburgh) on the East Coast and East Bank Demerara. Three other women had been trained locally and were assigned to Rose Hall, LBI (East Coast Demerara) and the East Bank Demerara. These received further training in Puerto Rico in 1957.[23] This was a significant development, as these pioneers were carving out a space for predominantly Indian women at a professional level on the estates, beyond the cane fields. Moreover, they were demonstrating that Indian women could assume leadership roles in the community, outside of the home. But, as will be seen later, Ruby Samlalsingh's courage, skills and tact were required constantly in order to placate traditionalists, detractors, who preferred Indian women and girls to aspire to nothing beyond housework.[24]

By the end of 1958 all the plantations had community centres, so some aspect of the welfare work in adult education, home economics, handicrafts, drama festivals, sports and games could percolate to all layers of the estate community. In August of that year a residential training course in youth leadership was held at Uitvlugt Community Centre (West Coast Demerara), with Clyde Walcott a principal speaker. On July 31, 1958 a new girls' club was opened at Albion, with funding from SILWF. In mid-August *Booker News* expressed satisfaction with the varied work undertaken among women on the estates, but cautioned against complacency: this task demanded resolution to stem the resistance of the obscurantists.[25] A girls' club was being opened at Rose Hall at the same time, the sixth such club to be built with funds from SILWF. The aim was to complete ten clubs at a total cost of $250,000. Miss Samlalsingh, SPA's Welfare Adviser (Women), considered these clubs a foundation for home management, a crucial task, as 'the culture of the community is based on its women'. Nearly ten years after the Venn Commission, fewer women were working in the fields; she elaborated on the significance of these girls' clubs:

> Conditions of life on the sugar estates ... have improved considerably. Workers now enjoy better wages, and better housing, and it is fast becoming unnecessary for mothers to work in the field. More women stay at home: there is time for leisure and for social work. That ... was why the girls' clubs were being built and handsomely equipped by the sugar industry, and that was why they were staffed with trained and carefully chosen female welfare officers. Girls who had just left school could prepare themselves at the club for the day when they would have to manage their own homes. Women already married could learn to give their families better and more nourishing meals at no extra cost. They could learn to make their homes more attractive by making simple items of furniture and decorations themselves, at far less than they would buy them for.[26]

But some women on the estates were already going beyond the domestic sphere. At the Second Annual Conference of Sugar Estates' Women, in Georgetown, between August 29 and 31, 1958, many displayed the handicrafts and skills which were learnt in the various groups on the plantations. The chairman commended the 'great work' which was done in training 'hands and minds'. Miss Samlalsingh was impressed by the fact that older women were now attending the clubs, participating in home improvement, handicraft and drama classes, while broadening their outlook through educational tours. She interpreted this as 'a continuing education of an informal nature', which could compensate somewhat for the limited formal educational opportunities given most women. Moreover, the Conference was considered an ideal medium to promote racial harmony. In 1958, 61 women participated: Muslims, Hindus, Christians; Indians, Africans and Chinese, 'worked, played and prayed together for two days without incident or friction'.[27]

A couple of weeks later, Ruby Samlalsingh participated in the opening of the Girls' Club building at Port Mourant. She advised the women to develop self-help skills in view of the reduced employment in the area, occasioned by the closure of the sugar factory in 1955. Although there was a preponderance of Indian women in these clubs, reflecting the ethnic imbalance on the estates, several African women were members. By early 1959, for instance, Irma Phillips, the Welfare Officer at Wales Estate, West Bank Demerara, had organised a Club as well as a Women's Institute, comprising African and Indian women from their teens to their fifties. At that time it was announced that two other African women, Vilma John and Waveney Bristol, were being trained in social welfare work.[28]

Campbell always stressed the necessity for national unity in British Guiana and was perturbed by any suggestion of racial bigotry in Booker. When opening the Community Centre and Girls' Club at LBI, in February 1960, he extolled racial tolerance as a national imperative, citing the resolve and imagination of the sugar industry as an example of what was achievable:

> Just as I believe that our British Guiana sugar industry, despite great natural problems and difficulties, is relatively more efficient than other West Indian sugar industries — indeed if it were not we would not survive; so I believe that with national unity and purpose the people of British Guiana should forge ahead of their island neighbours. Unity brings purpose, purpose brings confidence, confidence brings success. Without national unity there can be no progress.[29]

Jock felt that the activities of the community centres and Girls' Clubs could contribute to the building of a 'strong, purposeful, self-confident community'. Social welfare work must proceed, imbued with what he called 'the new spirit': African-Indian unity. He sketched his hope for British Guiana:

> I like to think that a new spirit will be created, nurtured and developed in this Community Centre and Girls' Club. The community spirit — the realisation and acceptance of the fact that no man or woman is an island, and no people or race can live entirely to themselves and for themselves. This is the only solid basis on which a community can be founded, the only structure on which a nation can be built.[30]

But there were many tortuous paths to Guyanese race relations, as Ruby Samlalsingh was constantly reminded. In early 1959, for instance, after conferring with several Indian leaders on the plantations, she discovered that many women were still reluctant to join the Women's and Girls' Clubs, apprehensive that they would lose their Indian culture. She tried to reassure them that many of their activities were, in fact, designed to foster Indian culture: Hindi classes at some community centres; the prohibition of beef and pork in the domestic science kitchens — the focus, often, being on enhancing the preparation of Indian dishes: *pilau*, curried chicken, *pera*, *poolouri, mohanboug* [*prasad*]; teaching women to wear the sari and sari puralees; the celebration of Indian festivals and the learning of Indian songs. Samlalsingh also learnt that some parents were deterred by the possibility that their daughters would 'meet boys' at the Girls' Clubs: boys were not allowed there. She concluded:

> [I]t should be obvious that we do not want to wean you away from your own fine culture, but to help you to appreciate all that is best of both cultures.... In our Centres we do not teach anything which affects your religious beliefs. We do not discourage you from speaking the language of your choice, and we do not teach you to eat foods which are foreign or forbidden to you.[31]

The race factor would obtrude often, although the motives of the sugar estates were unimpeachable: tolerance of others and national unity. Booker tended to be sensitive to racial sensibilities, and in framing their welfare policies towards Indians were punctilious in seeking to identify and enhance the strengths of Indian culture. In 1953 E.N. Edwards, the Industrial Relations Officer of Booker Sugar Estates, had observed that Indians in British Guiana were not a 'primitive people' but one with a 'strong tradition'. Their life was based on 'precept and well-tried observance, sometimes religious and frequently of high objective, and an already well-knit family life'. He cautioned that there were potentially serious consequences of framing a welfare programme directed uniformly at Africans and Indians, as the latter would resist it. Edwards explained:

> The danger in our present policies is that by hammering away at people already handicapped by distant removal from the source of their own culture, we may weaken the less strong-minded ... of their home and family features which are unquestionably good. It is a very serious danger; and until adequately high standards of living justify a complete transition to western patterns of living we have no right to 'episcopate' to them. We must rather evolve welfare instruction that takes account of East Indian views and habits. If necessary there should be a separate and specialised side of welfare.[32]

This was congruent with Campbell's perception of Indian culture as an instrument of self-belief. Booker, he acknowledged, must respect and encourage it or destroy the mutual goodwill which the reforms were designed to promote between the Company and the community. However, he was averse to the fostering of cultural apartheid or the total separation of the sexes. The welfare programmes, though sensitive to racial or cultural peculiarities, must aim at promoting racial harmony. The annual Estates' Women Conference provided an environment for African and Indian women to meet socially and discuss their work and their lives. The Estates' Drama Festival, started by Ruby Samlalsingh in 1955, was an important engagement for both the community centres and the girls' clubs: quietly, it gnawed away at resistance to mixing between the sexes on the plantations.

Before the creation of these drama groups there had been no opportunities for the development of this activity on the estates. Now space was created for Indian girls and women to demonstrate their skills on the stage. In February 1959 Samlalsingh noted that while some prejudice remained, it was refreshing to report a discernible pride among male sugar workers in the dramatic performances of their daughters. She sketched the impact of the annual Estates' Drama Festival thus:

> [T]here are drama clubs on all the sugar estates and dramatic productions have become a regular feature of the programmes in Community Centres and Girls' Clubs. Throughout the year the groups do play reading, acting exercises and acting games, or are engaged in rehearsals for a show. Encouragement is now being given to them to practise make-up, to learn to make wigs and beards, to study period costumes, and to broaden their club programmes so as to include the allied arts of music and painting. All shows given are well supported by the residents, workers and staff, who attend in large numbers. On most estates last year [1958], the Drama Festival preliminaries ran for two nights in succession and were completely sold out. At a few places large numbers had to be turned away.[33]

Social welfare was beginning to reshape the entrenched attitudes of most Indian men on the education of women. Moreover, the fact that a few Indian women themselves had become professionals on the plantations — pathfinders such as Ruby Samlalsingh, Roma Persaud, Agnes Bhagwandeen — inspired other women to contemplate their own potential for mobility beyond the domestic sphere. But, as *Booker News* argued in August 1958, Guyanese society was tenacious of its prejudice against women; only the education of women and their resilience in pursuing careers could undermine the 'entrenched superiority' of their menfolk:

> There is certainly prejudice against the female executive, not only in Booker, but in the Civil Service, in every field and in every community where working women may pose a threat to men's entrenched superiority. This prejudice will not be beaten by sitting down and whining before it. Whenever it has been overthrown, the upset was caused by women who, armed with qualifications equivalent to any a man might hold, have invaded the masculine territory and demonstrated equal ability.[34]

In the field of cricket and athletics, the social welfare work had brought admirable results. After four years as the Athletics Organiser with the SPA, McDonald Bailey proudly announced in March 1959 that there were ten clubs on sugar estates with 100 athletes; these clubs had organised 89 athletics meetings. He was unrestrained in commending the achievement: 'In this role of stimulating competition the estate athletics clubs have made a contribution to sport in British Guiana second to none. These clubs have sparked the movement we now see and they have done this when the general consensus was that they would fail.' [35]

In February 1959 Bailey had announced the inauguration of the first cross-country athletics championship of the Booker estates. The winner, he asserted, would be the recognised no.1 champion of all estates. The winner was a 20 year old worker from Plantation LBI, Moses Dowarka, who completed the six miles in 31 minutes 5 seconds — the best time recorded by a Guyanese or West Indian runner for this event. The extraordinary fact about this champion was that he was a 'barefoot' runner.[36] Bailey noted that while some felt that he could do better if he ran in running shoes, he was sceptical of the merits of the advice, as it would take some time for him to get accustomed to them: 'it could be a psychological handicap' — a grave problem in athletics, no less so than a physical one. Bailey attributed Dowarka's success to his temperament and predicted a bright future for him: 'Among his many good qualities is his ability to maintain a level head, something which I hope many of our athletes, regardless of success, will emulate.' [37]

In January 1960 Dowarka won the second annual Booker cross country championship. He erased 6.6 seconds from his performance of 1959, while Harry Prowell, another outstanding athlete, also from LBI, came in one minute behind him. Jock Campbell witnessed the race, which had coincided with the opening of the community centre at LBI. He quickly drew from it a lesson for race relations in British Guiana: Dowarka was Indian; Prowell, African. Perturbed by the creeping racism in local affairs, Campbell observed:

[L]ast Sunday I had the privilege and pleasure of watching the L.B.I. cross-country championship and presenting the prizes — the first two to those magnificent athletes, Moses Dowarka and

Harry Prowell of this estate — of whom you must all be proud. I could not help thinking then as I watched Indians and Africans running fast and courageously forward together over a very tough course, all knowing clearly where they were going, and intent upon overcoming every difficulty to get there, all in a spirit of perfect goodwill, that this might be a symbol for all of us of national unity.[38]

The same lessons could have been drawn from Booker's promotion of cricket on the sugar plantations, among Africans and Indians. By 1959 Rohan Kanhai, Basil Butcher and Joe Solomon were established batsmen in the West Indies Test team. As noted before, they were all from Plantation Port Mourant; in the late 1960s and early 1970s Roy Fredericks (Blairmont) and Alvin Kallicharran (Port Mourant), also, were first rate test batsmen. This was a unique achievement in the history of cricket in the region. Clyde Walcott's role in this, as well as in the rise of the game on all plantations, was astounding: several other estate players represented British Guiana, in inter-colonial cricket, and the counties of Berbice and Demerara, in domestic cricket.[39] They certainly dominated Berbice cricket: Saranga Baichoo, Charlie Bissoon, Karia Chandrapal, Basil Mohabir, Sonny Moonsammy, Randolph Ramnarace, Isaac Surienarine, Joe Sookwah and others. The community centre grounds were the cradle for the shaping of this extraordinary competence. Meanwhile Joe Solomon, the West Indies batsman, had joined Walcott as cricket organiser on the plantations in April 1961. In a speech in June 1962 Walcott reminded his audience of sugar's admirable contribution to the game:

[C]ricketers on the sugar estates have realised the contribution the sugar industry has made within recent years to cricket in British Guiana. The improvements to, the maintenance of grounds, the appointment of an organiser [Solomon] and coaches, the travelling expenses for cricketers playing in competitive matches — all these contributions by the sugar industry — have made it possible for the sugar estate cricketers to improve their game.[40]

In the county of Essequibo, however, where the last sugar estate, Hampton Court, was abandoned in 1935, sports facilities were non-existent: they have never produced a cricketer for Guyana or the West Indies. Therefore, the stimulus of Campbell's reforms and their ramifications did not reach Essequibo; the county's old, colloquial name, 'Cinderella', never lost its poignancy.

In August 1963, while Kanhai, Butcher and Solomon were helping to forge the supremacy of the West Indies, in their 3-1 victory on their tour of England, Walcott was still dispensing his wisdom on cricket, leadership, good manners, strength of character — technical and psychological aspects of the game. Addressing a week-end seminar for cricket captains from the community centres, he emphasised the importance of discipline, noting that captains must command it; it should not have to be 'imposed'. He declared, drawing on his wide experience of leadership: 'The captain should be confident and he must show confidence in his players in order that they may feel confident in him. He must try to cultivate and show an evenness of temper. He must be composed and, however desperate the situation, his team must never be allowed to sense that their captain is "rattled".'[41]

Walcott's role in the advancement of Guyanese cricket in the 1950s-60s is an epic in West Indies cricket. To Kanhai, Butcher, Solomon, Madray, Gibbs, Lloyd and Fredericks, he contributed much to their technical development, erasing flaws and building the confidence to experiment and grow. But it was also his subtlety of perceptions of the social forces which shaped these men, which endeared him to them, as well as a whole generation of unsung cricketers at club and county levels in colonial Guyana. Ivan Madray probably spoke for them all, in 1987, when, in a moment of inspired recollection, he said: '[Walcott had] no time for race, pettiness or spite.... [He] took a man for what he was worth...I could have walked to the end of the earth for him. He always brought out the best in me.... I never wanted to let him down.'[42] In 1965, after ten years as Social Welfare Adviser to the Sugar Producers' Association in British Guiana, he was awarded the OBE for his services to cricket. *Booker News* paid him the following tribute on the occasion:

Mr. Walcott, with Everton Weekes and Frank Worrell, formed the famous 'W' triumvirate, the scourge of English bowling in the fifties. He came from his homeland, Barbados, in 1954 to work for the BGSPA as cricket organiser. [He] is widely credited for discovering three famous Guyanese cricketers — Rohan Kanhai, Basil Butcher and Joe Solomon. He has successfully captained the British Guiana team to the top of Caribbean cricket, a position this country has held for nine years.[43]

Walcott had retired prematurely from Test cricket in 1960, aged 34, but continued to represent Guyana in first class cricket, as well as playing inter-county and club cricket for most of the 1960s. He was, indeed, the principal architect of the dynamic cricket culture in Guyana from the mid-1950s to the late 1960s. It was another inspired appointment, reflecting the progressive temper of Jock Campbell's time. When the politics started to deteriorate under the authoritarian Burnham regime, Walcott returned to Barbados in 1970. He was knighted in the early 1990s for his services to the game. He became the President of the International Cricket Conference in 1994, but Everton Weekes believes that 'the achievement that has given him greatest satisfaction was the way he revitalised cricket in British Guiana'. Walcott recalls the experience:

[I]n the mid-1950s when I arrived and saw the facilities I realised what a mammoth task I faced to develop the game on the plantations. I had to organise the clubs and the competitions and advise on improving facilities, persuading the owners to put down concrete pitches in the outlying areas that would survive the harsh climate. New grounds were built and such was the enthusiasm of the Indian population that immense strides were made in a very short time.[44]

Gordon Rohlehr has located some of the forces that shaped this cricket culture on the plantations of British Guiana:

Alarmed at the continual striking since 1945, and especially at the Enmore strike of 1948 when the police opened fire on a group of workers, killing five and wounding twelve, the sugar bosses followed the cue of the Colonial Office and entered on a programme of conspicuous welfare, which if it did little to alter the plantation system, sought to modify its natural by-product of degraded and tension-ridden human relationships. Thus, Welfare Officers were appointed on each estate...Cricket Clubs were encouraged for the men, as part of a programme of welfare, sewing classes for the women. Traditionally cricket on the sugar estates had been, like electricity or the riding of horses and mules, a status symbol distinguishing a white managerial elite from the Indian workers. Now that cricket was being used to sublimate the violent energies and protest generated by plantation society, clubs arose out of the estates, and rapidly developed into powerful centres of social activity in communities which had been devoid of physical recreation. A new area had been created in which social prestige could be won. In such compact communities, the struggle for prestige is often keen. In the 1950s, for example, long-distance and cross-country running suddenly became a popular sport on the estates. In two or three years, they produced six or more pretty good athletes. The citizens of the new-look plantations took their cricket with equal seriousness.[45]

Campbell told me that he often had to fight his corner to persuade people like F.J. Seaford and Follett-Smith to appreciate the centrality of his reforms to the Booker enterprise in British Guiana. A researcher of Campbell's Booker, Brian Scott, observes that around 1954 when Campbell was embarking on a four-year programme of social welfare, some of his lieutenants on the Board of Booker Sugar Estates in British Guiana, showed 'considerable opposition to the idea of welfare — "bread and circuses" as it was called'. He added that at the end of the 1950s there were still those in Booker who argued that all the funds accruing from the SILWF should go towards the re-housing of workers, rather than diverting a considerable proportion to social welfare.[46] Conservatism had long roots in Booker. This was the context in which Roy Close, the Director of Social Welfare, was asked to draft his 'Notes on Social Policy', in 1959. Scott argues:

Throughout the period [1954–59], Jock Campbell was a keen supporter of the social welfare effort. However, its larger importance did not become apparent to middle management in Guyana with the end of the 1950s. One of the more important attempts to communicate to company personnel that the social policy, and other forms of outreach to the community, were serious and important parts of Booker's strategy was R.E. Close's 'Notes on Social Policy'.... This reiterated the views which Campbell had been trying to communicate throughout the previous decade: that Booker was constantly being judged as an economic factor in Guyanese society, as a place of work, and as a corporate citizen; that pressing the four-fold responsibilities was an important means of improving Booker's prospects for survival in Guyana.[47]

'Notes on Social Policy', bearing the obvious imprint of Campbell's philosophy, came out at a crucial time: on the eve of the new decade of rapid decolonisation, a few months before the British Guiana Constitutional Conference in London, in March 1960, when the likelihood of Jagan leading an independent Guyana seemed inevitable. It was a reaffirmation of Campbell's commitment to integrating Booker's practices with the broader aspirations of Guyanese nationalism. Besides, as Scott observes, it represented the 'complete acceptance' of the Booker management in the colony of Campbell's reformist philosophy. This 'private and confidential' document could, therefore, be seen as the definitive restatement and projection of his central ideas within Booker, on the eve of Independence:

The continuity of Booker here [in British Guiana] depends on their proper fulfilment [of the four-fold responsibilities].... This means that the Group has special responsibilities in the fields of human relations among its employees at all levels, community relations, industrial relations and public relations. All of these relations have to be improved — if possible to the point where the Group cannot be unjustly accused of economic exploitation of its employees, of bad conditions of work, of discrimination against race or colour, of failing to give Guyanese the opportunity of (or training for) promotion, of an unsympathetic or autocratic attitude towards its employees, or acting without proper regard to community and social developments. If possible, the Group must be willingly accepted by Guyanese not only for the prosperity it brings, but also for its contribution to improved standards in the business community, its contribution to social development and to human happiness. At the very least future attacks or political action against the Group must be seen by the majority of people to be unjustified and so lack full public support.[48]

Booker was hoping for infinitely more than Guyanese society could yield: as I have argued throughout, they could not elude the procrustean mould of Jagan's Marxist frame of reference. But, as Campbell related to me time and again, the debts he felt he owed British Guiana, the lingering guilt, dictated that, at least, an effort be made to atone for historic wrongs, even if it could not be readily acknowledged: 'It is easier for a Campbell to go through a needle's eye than for Booker to be loved. But it should be understood and respected and be worthy of respect.' This was another key premise of his mission in British Guiana.

Campbell appreciated the importance of public relations, and when, in 1954, he appointed Antony Tasker, Director of Public Relations in British Guiana, he quoted Tasker's definition of public relations with evident approbation: 'behaving well and taking credit for it'. He added: 'Booker *do* behave well, and are guided by a deep sense of purpose and responsibility to the people of British Guiana.' [49] Shortly after Tasker was appointed, Campbell started *Booker News,* a fortnightly paper. The first issue appeared on July 8, 1955 under the editorship of R.B.O. Hart, an African Guyanese who had edited *The Clarion*, in the early 1950s. He came with strong anti-Jagan credentials, but in the context of the suspension of the Constitution, Campbell probably saw this as a potential merit. Jock explained to me how *Booker News* was started: 'Robert Hart came to me and said, "I think you ought to know that everyone in Guiana thinks Booker stinks." And I said: "It's no good just coming to tell me about it; you must do something about it. Would you like to be editor of *Booker News?*"'[50] It is noteworthy that the masthead carried the caption: 'A Newspaper printed and published fortnightly for the Employees of the Booker Group of Companies in British Guiana.' In fact, it was aimed at the people of the colony as a whole, although its employees, including some on the higher rungs, had to be kept on track, be divested of their cynicism ('bread and circuses') over Campbell's four-fold responsibilities — to shareholders, customers, workers and the Guyanese community.

Booker News editorialised regularly on the social welfare programmes on the plantations, often citing or paraphrasing the views of Jock Campbell. In February 1959, in what was in effect an assessment of the first five years of social welfare reforms, 1954–58, the paper commended the work of Clyde Walcott, McDonald Bailey and Ruby Samlalsingh in cricket, athletics and drama respectively, noting the deeper reverberations of their accomplishment. It even remarked on the contribution of Robert Christiani, the former West Indies Test batsman, who was the social welfare officer at Plantation Port Mourant, the acme of cricket mastery on the plantations:

> There can be no better yardstick for measuring what has been done by the Booker Group and the Sugar Producers' Association in providing recreational facilities for their workers than the fact that the enthusiasm of these workers has gradually overflowed into the community at large. The seeds sown by Clyde Walcott and Robert Christiani on the cricket fields of sugar estates community centres have produced a rich harvest of international sportsmen. And no one can deny that much of the widespread interest in athletics and the desire to run for the joy of running have been sparked by the work of McDonald Bailey.... [T]he Annual Sugar Estates Drama Festival, now in its fourth year, [is] a brainchild of Miss Ruby Samlalsingh, Social Welfare Adviser (Women) to the Sugar Producers' Association. A roaring success from the start, the enthusiasm that has attended these sugar estate festivals has risen to a crescendo that it is no surprise that the general community has found it infectious. Industry is happy that communal benefits have accrued from the special attention it has given to cricket, athletics and drama.[51]

In early 1960 it was reported that Miss Ruby Samlalsingh, BSc, was on secondment for three months, from February to April, to the Extra-Mural Department of the University College of the West Indies (UCWI), in Trinidad. A Trinidadian, she decided soon afterwards to accept a permanent appointment at the UCWI. However, in just four years, she had done much to change Indian parents' attitudes to their daughters, fostering a more enlightened approach to their education — many were entering secondary schools on Booker scholarships.[52] *Booker News*, in order to promote this new outlook, remarked on Indian women's progress elsewhere, in athletics and dance: Miss Lela Rao, a 16 year old Indian whose participation in the 1956 Olympics in Melbourne brought her 'considerable acclaim'; Miss Indrani Rehman, a world famous dancer from India, who performed in British Guiana in mid-1960. The paper exhorted Indian parents to emulate the fine example being set by several local Indian women, too:

> [W]e have in Miss Roma Persaud, recently appointed Assistant Social Welfare Adviser to the SPA [she succeeded Ruby Samlalsingh], and in the female welfare officers on the sugar estates, young women who have played games, taken part in drama groups and shared in other cultural activities, without injury to their person or their character. We hope, therefore, that just as the parents of the girls we have mentioned and of those other girls who will go to secondary schools, accept the fact that their daughters are helped to a fuller life on the sugar estates today, will realise that what is offered at the girls' clubs is education to fit the progress which is taking place all over the world and right here in British Guiana.[53]

By mid-1962 nearly all sugar plantations had women's and girls' clubs and their impact was seen as 'steadily increasing'. There were three clubs on estates on the West Coast and East Bank Demerara; two on the East Coast Demerara; five in Berbice. There were clubs, too, at Bath (West Coast Berbice), Ogle and Non Pareil (East Coast Demerara) and Cornelia Ida (West Coast Demerara), housed in their community centres, as there was at Versailles (West Bank Demerara). They were all equipped with self-contained kitchens. At Providence (East Bank Berbice) and Blairmont (West Bank Berbice), home economics was taught in similar kitchens although there were no girls' clubs.[54]

In 1962 Miss Roma Persaud assessed the progress made since the mid-1950s. She observed that because women and girls were given the responsibility for the administration of these clubs, members had gained experience in conducting meetings and in public speaking; moreover short training courses and the annual three-day conference for women on estates, had enhanced their competence in a range of skills, while the interaction with women from different districts broadened their horizons as it built their self-confidence. Their achievement was varied, meeting diverse needs in their lives: handicraft, drama, sports (volley ball was popular), childcare, health and beauty care, fashion shows, home improvement and gardening. Persaud summarised the achievement:

> The interior of the houses of sugar workers, the behaviour and dress habits of the girls, the cooking skills of the [women] and the way they bring up their children; the increasing participation of women in community organisations — all these reflect the influence of the girls' club. They are performing valuable service in training and educating women and girls to meet their responsibilities in the changing environment of the sugar estate.[55]

Reflecting Campbell's philosophy that material incentives, alone, could not engender workers' satisfaction, Booker contended that well-conducted, imaginative social welfare would enhance initiative, confidence, self-respect and regard for the rights of individuals. It was Campbell's belief that to lessen paternalism and dependency, it was imperative to stimulate the imagination of workers, to encourage them to expand their vision beyond the estates: the libraries and drama clubs on the plantations had their roots in his own life-long fascination with words, ideas and clear thinking — his hatred of dogmas. This was crucial in shaping loyalty to the new nation about to be born, in the early 1960s. This was how *Booker News* echoed his vision in May 1959:

> The Social Welfare Programme planned by the Sugar Industry in British Guiana aims at evolving on the sugar estates, workers with a spirit of independence who are trained to think and act for themselves, who will accept responsibility with confidence and who know to live the fuller life that comes with improved standards and better conditions of work.[56]

By February 1963 Booker could take a retrospective view based on ten years of social welfare work on the plantations. It was observed that the community centres were run by the workers themselves, with the social welfare officer on each estate as ex-officio member. Indeed, they had demonstrated that they could plan and administer their own affairs[57] — a vital lesson in self-help and self-government, away from the dependency of inhibiting paternalism. At Uitvlugt Estate, for instance, under its experienced social welfare officer, Baljit Ramdin, the Community Centre Council showed initiative and financial stability. In 1962 it had $1,000 in its coffers; by the end of the year it had $2,000, after covering maintenance, repairs, sports and educational activities. It had raised all the funds independently.[58]

Moreover, the 'hunger' for learning, kindled in a community which was until recently mired in its low, labouring status — the universe of the 'bound coolie' — bred conceptions of freedom as it expanded notions of possibilities. In February 1963, on the eve of the slide into racial carnage, *Booker News* pondered on something altogether lofty, an elevating temper, intellectual curiosity shaped by social welfare work:

> One of the most interesting and intriguing groups at the community centre is the adult education council. It is an index of the hunger for knowledge, or the diffidence to it, on the estate. But, whether there are forty people in the audience, or ten, something has been achieved that was not possible before. Every activity of the centre must be viewed in this light. Whether it is the library, the domestic science class, the handicraft section or the drama group, it is taking place in a society which before was almost blank. Therefore, while it is understandable to wish for greater evidence of success, it must be remembered that the important thing is to begin.[59]

Booker had expressed satisfaction that schools in the villages and other extra-plantation bodies were already availing themselves of some of the facilities of the community centres. They envisioned this as a step towards the integration of the estates with the broader rural communities. In March 1963 Jock Campbell, in an address to welfare officers in Georgetown, had exhorted them to try to comprehend the forces that were shaping Guyanese society at the end of Empire, while preparing estate residents to participate in the new society through 'self-reliance and responsibility'. He argued that social welfare must be informed by the needs of the fledgling national purpose. Towards this end workers must be guided to enhance 'personal independence, family unity and civic responsibility'. Campbell elaborated:

> [A]s this important work goes on, and as the re-housed communities find their feet in the larger community, and as the population expands, the division between sugar estate communities and adjacent communities becomes increasingly artificial. And, as this happens, the role of industry in community welfare becomes more anachronistic, and the responsibility for community welfare, must sooner or later — and in my view sooner — pass to Government. And it has occurred to me that the excellent facilities in the women's and girls' clubs might well be made available to the older girls in the new government schools. That, however, should not detract from the important work being done by welfare officers as we all adapt ... to changing circumstances.[60]

However, this vision of growing autonomy within constituted villages, of the end of paternalism, was soon clouded over by despair and pessimism, in 1963–64, as the politics of racial bigotry permeated Guyanese society. All the radical notions of reform, which Campbell had cultivated since the War, were drawn into the morass of racial hatred, as the two major races, Africans and Indians, sought to inherit the post-imperial kingdom. The expanding gloom hovered over every plantation: the futility depressed Campbell to the point where he was unable to pay his annual visit to British Guiana, in 1964. He could not cope with the death of people or the death of reason.

Welfare officer, Baljit Ramdin, at Uitvlugt, reported lucidly on the consuming darkness, of racial hatred degenerating into violence in his community on the West Coast Demerara. It was dissipating all that had been so assiduously built up through welfare work. Ramdin observed that the racial violence of Georgetown (generated by the Burnham-inspired 80-day strike against the Jagan government), had reached his district. The bitter union rivalry, also, between the MPCA, the recognised union in the sugar industry, and the Jagan-backed, GAWU, which most workers supported, poisoned ethnic relations on the estates and in neighbouring villages. In August 1963 Ramdin captured the weight of the hatred:

People [Africans and Indians] who lived like friends, suddenly seemed to have lost their sense of reason and judgement. In a mad chain of action and reaction, people were planning and carrying out actions aimed at the destruction of others.... Workers who drank in the same rum shops and beer parlours and walked the streets together regardless of race, now restrict their activities to people of their own ethnic group.... We hear of children refusing to be punished by teachers of another ethnic group, and parents saying that they do not want their children to be taught by teachers belonging to another ethnic group. There have been cases where people have said they will not play cricket with people of any other race.... Some of the clubs against whom some of our estate clubs [mainly Indian] play are comprised of players of one single ethnic group [African]. Here fears may exist when estates' clubs have to play against them.[61]

In early 1964, as Jagan's political fortunes declined as a consequence of relentless American pressure, his union, GAWU, certain of its overwhelming support among sugar workers, as opposed to the Booker-backed, MPCA, called a massive strike on the estates for recognition. This quickly degenerated into virtual civil war between Africans and Indians. As will be seen in the next section, Booker's continuing support for the MPCA translated into a perceived anti-Indian position, among the predominantly Indian sugar workers, who supported Cheddi Jagan and his union. Campbell's reforms were ineluctably enmeshed in the politics of racial bigotry. This explains the poignant despair in the Report of the Director of Social Policy in 1964:

Use of the estates' community centres was greatly reduced during the year. Even allowing for the disturbed conditions, there is cause for concern at the lack of acceptance of these buildings as real community facilities, in spite of the untiring but thankless efforts of Mr. C[lyde] Walcott, Miss R[oma] Persaud, Mr. J[oe] Solomon, Mr. C[olin] Wiltshire and the Estate Welfare Officers.

Between 1947 and 1967 (the start of Campbell's vice-chairmanship to the end of his chairmanship of Booker), the SILWF expended $31,573,952 on a range of projects to enhance life on the plantations. Of this $11,462,861 were loans to workers to help them build their own houses; $3,783,037 went to the development of the housing areas; $5,583,986 for pure water supply; $546,700 on road repairs in the housing areas; $5,601,869 on the construction of permanent roads; $1,966,706 on community centres, women's and girls' clubs and creches; while $391,748 were allocated to the preparation of recreation grounds.[62] It was an impressive achievement; but as the quote above demonstrates, the ideals of Jock Campbell were foundering on Guyanese political and racial futility.

There was, however, an oasis of purpose and the pursuit of standards — the sugar estates' drama festival, a tribute to the fine work of Ruby Samlalsingh and Roma Persaud. Amidst the racial violence of 1964 two commentators detected something wholly inviolable:

> The Sugar Estates' Drama Festival, part of the Sugar Estates' Welfare Programme, has expanded considerably since its inception in 1956.... Today, associated with almost every estate's Community Centre Council, there is a drama group, representing an encouraging cross-section of estate life. In fact, drama is probably the only leisure activity which regularly draws both sexes, and all sections of the estate community together. Some estates boast more than one drama group.... It is noteworthy that a sugar estate's play won both the 1961 and 1963 National Drama Festivals. In addition, the 1963 runner-up and best producer awards went to estates' groups. This impressive record led one to expect a high standard at this year's finals.[63]

A local literary critic, Frank Pilgrim, attended the sugar estates' drama festival at the Theatre Guild Playhouse in Georgetown in November 1964. He was impressed:

> The three finalists from Port Mourant, La Bonne Intention [LBI] and Wales, were really of a remarkably high standard, and the winning presentation, L.B.I.'s production of 'The Goose and Gander', by Wilfred Redhead, was well up to 'city' standards.... The standard of all three productions was much better than that achieved at the National Drama Festival last year! This is some

indication that the years of trial and error in the world of theatre in Guiana, is at last beginning to bear genuine fruit.[64]

Endnotes

1. *Report of a Commission of Inquiry into the Sugar Industry of British Guiana* (J.A. Venn, chairman), (London: H.M.S.O., 1949), 133.
2. Ibid., 135-6.
3. See R.B. Scargall, 'Labour Welfare', in *Booker Sugar* (Supplement to the Accounts of Booker Bros, McConnell and Co, Ltd, 1954), p. 70.
4. Jock Campbell, Minutes of a Managers' Meeting, March 11, 1946, in *Booker Sugar* [1954], p. 89.
5. Lord Campbell, 'From Demerara to Milton Keynes', Speech given at The Wilderness Club Dinner, (mimeo.), February 25, 1974, pp. 12-3.
6. Sydney King, Foreword, Cheddi Jagan, *Fight for Freedom: Waddington Constitution Exposed* (Georgetown: self-published, [1952]).
7. See note 5 [pp. 13, 22].
8. F.J. Seaford to W. Macnie [SPA], September 25, 1950, in *Booker Sugar* [1954], p. 91.
9. Jock Campbell to W. Macnie [SPA], in *Booker Sugar* [1954], p. 91.
10. See note 3 [p. 72].
11. Ibid., [74].
12. See note 5 [p. 26].
13. *Booker News*, July 8, 1955.
14. See note 3 [pp. 72-3].
15. Ibid.
16. SPA, R.B. Scargall, 'Memorandum on Welfare on the Sugar Estates', (mimeo.), January 3, 1949.
17. See note 3 [p. 73].
18. See my '*Tiger in the Stars': the Anatomy of Indian Achievement in British Guiana, 1919-29* (London: Macmillan, 1997), 310-23.
19. See my 'The Tiger of Port Mourant — R.B. Kanhai: Fact and Fantasy in the Making of an Indo-Guyanese Legend', in Frank Birbalsingh and Clem Seecharan, *Indo-West Indian Cricket* (London: Hansib, 1988), 50-2.
20. SPA, Report of the Proceedings of the Board of Directors, 1956, Appendix 1, Social Welfare Report, 1956.
21. *Booker News* (Special Supplement), June 21, 1957
22. See note 20.
23. Ibid.
24. *Booker News* (Special Supplement), July 4, 1958.
25. *Booker News*, [Leader], August 15, 1958.
26. Ibid., August 29, 1958.

2 7   Ibid., September 12, 1958.

2 8   Ibid., February 13, 1959.

2 9   Ibid., February 12, 1959.

3 0   Ibid.

3 1   Ibid., March 27, 1959.

3 2   SPA, 'Welfare on the Sugar Estates', by E.N. Edwards, Industrial Relations Officer, BSE, in W.A. Macnie (managing director, SPA) to Demerara Sugar Board, London, August 14, 1953.

33   *Booker News*, February 13, 1959.

3 4   Ibid., [Leader], August 15, 1958.

3 5   Ibid., March 13, 1959.

3 6   Ibid., April 24, 1959.

3 7   Ibid., August 28, 1959.

3 8   Ibid., February 12, 1960.

3 9   See note 19.

4 0   *Booker News*, June 1, 1962.

4 1   Ibid., August 16, 1963.

4 2   See note 19 [p. 123].

4 3   *Booker News*, January 8, 1965.

4 4   Clyde Walcott, *Sixty Years on the Back Foot: The Cricketing Life of Sir Clyde Walcott* (London: Orion, 2000 [1999]), viii [Weekes]; 65.

4 5   Gordon Rohlehr, 'Rohan Kanhai', in *Kanhai/Gibbs: Tribute to Two Great West Indians* (Port of Spain: self-published, 1974), 25.

4 6   Brian Scott, 'The Organisational Network: A Strategy Perspective for Development', PhD thesis, Harvard University, 1979, p. 158.

4 7   Ibid., 160-1.

4 8   BSE, Board paper, November 2, 1959.

4 9   The Chairman's Statement, 1955, p. 36.

5 0   Jock Campbell, interview by the author, Nettlebed, Oxfordshire, July 24, 1992, Tape 5.

5 1   *Booker News*, [Leader], February 13, 1959.

5 2   Ibid., February 12, 1960.

5 3   Ibid., [Leader], September 23, 1960.

5 4   Ibid., August 24, 1962.

5 5   Ibid.

5 6   Ibid., [Leader], May 8, 1959.

5 7   Ibid., February 22, 1963.

5 8   Ibid., August 24, 1962.

5 9   Ibid., [Leader], February 22, 1963.

6 0   Ibid., March 22, 1963.

6 1   Ibid., August 16, 1963.

6 2   SPA, 'Report of the Sugar Industry Labour Welfare Fund, 1967', p. 7.

6 3   Antigen [pseud.], 'Sugar Estates' Drama Festival', *New World Fortnightly*, no. 3 (November 30, 1964): 34-5.

6 4   Frank Pilgrim, 'Senior Plays: Sugar Estates' Drama Festival [1964]', *New World Fortnightly*, no. 3 (November 30, 1964): 37-8.

Chapter Twenty-Nine

WAGES AND SOCIAL AMENITIES IN FIELD AND FACTORY

In March 1959 the president of the MPCA, Richard Ishmael, expressed support for the sugar industry's policy of mechanisation in field and factory. He observed that obsolete machinery and outmoded processes contributed to stagnation and low productivity. As a trade unionist he was most concerned that the industry should be prosperous and that productivity be improved. As *Booker News* editorialised: 'Out of a prosperous industry, Mr. Ishmael asserts, he can unhesitatingly demand increased benefits for sugar workers. He could also negotiate for severance pay, pensions and other forms of relief provided by management for retrenched workers.'[1] Antony Tasker, the Public Relations Officer of Booker, had argued in the Legislative Council (he was a nominated member) that although technological innovation required some retrenchment, it was indispensable to the sustaining of the competitive position of the sugar industry — a vital prerequisite for the provision of better wages and other amenities for workers. This, indeed, was what had inspired Jock Campbell, in the early 1950s, to work for the CSA and the consequent reorganisation and modernisation of Booker. The guaranteed prices for over 50 per cent of British Guiana's sugar enabled him to do this, thus enhancing the company's competitive edge, the basis for improved conditions of employment. Booker sought to rationalise this approach and the attendant contraction of labour:

> The principle of spreading out employment so thinly that it hardly justifies the name has long been proved to be uneconomic to industry and unfair to workers. Private enterprise cannot

face the challenge of competitive markets when it employs six or eight badly paid and perpetually disgruntled men to do work of which one competent and contented worker could make short shrift. Surely the answer to employment could not be to keep workers in industry on wages which can stand comparison only with the dole. There is, moreover, insufficient justification in an emergent country of vast size and small population — such as British Guiana — for cheapening honest toil, or impeding industrial progress with the kindling wood of frustrated workers.[2]

The changes in the sugar industry, after the War, reflected the cumulative effect of Campbell's strategy for survival: price and quota stabilisation, reorganisation of Booker, modernisation and mechanisation, stabilisation of the workforce, and social reforms. By 1960, with the workforce in the fields stabilised at around 18,000 and annual production of sugar at around 300,000 tons, the yield per field labourer had risen impressively, from 7.68 tons in 1941–45 to 16.21 tons of sugar per worker in 1956–60.

TABLE X
Changes in Productivity in the Sugar Industry, 1941–45/ 1956–60

Years	Production	Acreage	Field Worker	
	(tons)		[avg. weekly]	[tons sugar per worker]
1941–45	161,663	61,710	21,039	7.68
1946–50	176,282	60,215	21,404	8.23
1951–55	237,841	74,307	21,375	11.13
1956–60	294,318	86,338	18,159	16.21

Source: J.R. Mandle, *The Plantation Economy: Population and Economic Change in Guyana, 1838-1960* (Philadelphia: Temple University Press, 1973), 72-73

Brian Scott has characterised these advances as 'dramatic' and has ascertained what they meant in economic terms. He elaborates: production more than doubled; between 1950 and 1960 company profits almost tripled; fixed assets grew 4.5 times; taxes paid to the government of British Guiana increased from £406,000 to £1,765,000. Benefits to workers were considered 'substantial':

'Between 1948 and 1960 wages rose by approximately 300% while the cost of living index increased by less than 40%'. By 1966 field workers on time-rates and unskilled factory workers earned about $3.60 per day, compared with a wage of $2.06 per day in 1956. Cane-cutters on piece-rates were paid $2.14 to cut and load a ton of cane, in conjunction with a cost of living allowance negotiated between the MPCA and the SPA. Their daily earnings, therefore, tended to exceed the minimum time-rates. Many of the grievances related to remuneration of labour were discussed between management and the MPCA, in the Estate Joint Committee on individual plantations.

With a stabilised labour force by the late 1950s, a number of material incentives complemented the social ones; fringe benefits were an established practice — holidays with pay; annual production bonuses; a cut and load bonus for cane-cutters; and, from 1957, an annual 'once-for-all' bonus tied to production targets. Holidays with pay were awarded each crop to those who had worked 75 per cent of the days on which work was available, and the award was computed on the basis of the worker's average gross weekly earnings per crop, added to 25 per cent of such earnings. The annual production bonus was awarded to those who had worked not less than 82.5 per cent of the days on which work was available per crop. They received three days' pay; if the industry's production target was reached, they got six days' pay. A cut and load bonus, devised as an incentive to encourage workers to harvest cane on week-ends, offered an additional 35 cents per ton of cane cut on Saturdays and Mondays (absenteeism was rife on the latter), providing they worked on the Friday of the previous week and one other day of the current week. The 'once-or-all' bonus was paid in 1957, 1960, 1961, 1962 and 1963; it was based on the annual production target, the weekly wages earned and the level of sugar prices, especially the more remunerative prices obtained on the US market in the early 1960s.[4]

It was, as noted before, the CSA which provided long-term security for over 50 per cent of the sugar produced in British Guiana; that was the foundation of generally better wages in the industry. As Diane McTurk, an employee of Booker, argued in 1966, the CSA brought stability but also established the basis for efficiency:

This Agreement provides the underpinning of the whole industry in Guyana. By securing to the efficient producer a guaranteed remunerative price for over half of his sugar for a period running eight years ahead, it enables long-term planning to take the place of hand-to-mouth improvisation, it breeds confidence and stability in the place of dire uncertainty, and it means the difference between relative prosperity and depressed standards of living. Experts in commodity agreements throughout the world recognise the CSA as the most successful and the most beneficial Agreement to be negotiated in international trade.[5]

McTurk emphasised that it offered a remunerative price only to 'the efficient producer'. Indeed, in May 1956, when the SPA and the MPCA had reached a deadlock in negotiations over a cost of living allowance — the latter were asking for a 20 per cent increase — the SPA went ahead with an award of 7.5 per cent, the same as in 1955, approximately $750,000. They submitted that although there had been no increase in the price of sugar, they felt that the benefits accruing to the industry should be passed on to the workers. These had been won through increased efficiency, stemming from their policy of 'applied research and rehabilitation which had led to increased yields and better factory production'.[6]

In February 1957 Booker countered allegations that their approach to reform was a 'paternalistic' one, asserting that they were making a more self-reliant worker by offering him incentives to work regularly and with commitment: the tradition of casual employment and eclectic attendance was no longer tenable:

[R]ewards go to those who earn them by hard work. Those who work for 82.5% of available working days are entitled to a fortnight's holiday with pay. If the estate produces a given amount of sugar the worker earns a bonus. If the colony as a whole reaches its target, then the worker gets another bonus. That is not paternalism. That is demonstrating that management and workers are partners in effect.[7]

It is arguable that, paradoxically, because the MPCA, for political reasons, was deemed by the sugar producers to be infinitely more 'responsible' than a PPP (Jagan-backed) union in the industry, they were more inclined to accede and be seen to accede to the demands of the MPCA. In December 1957 the MPCA announced that they had negotiated a sick benefit scheme with the SPA, costing approximately $250,000. It recalled that the SPA, earlier that year, had agreed to spend $1 million on workers' wages and other benefits, including the 7.5 per cent cost of living allowance. The MPCA were clearly impressed with the new sick benefit scheme, which provided another margin of security for a workforce now the recipient of better wages and amenities. The Union observed of the scheme:

> Those workers who during any year qualify for participation in the scheme by a certain degree of regularity in attendance at work are credit[ed] at the beginning of the next year with six days' wages, which they may draw as sickness benefit if they are sick for one week or more. If in any given year the worker does not draw the sickness benefit which lies at his credit, the credit is carried forward to the next year — that is, sickness benefit accumulates when it is not drawn. Accumulation continues without limit until death or retirement, provided that the worker continues to qualify annually and remains in the employ of the estate. This means that a worker who does not draw sickness benefit for some years may in three years accumulate credits which will see him through a long illness later on, or that a lump sum will be available on his retirement, subject to certain qualifications.[8]

Richard Ishmael, president of the MPCA, an arch-enemy of Cheddi Jagan, had contested the PPP's assertion that the scheme was a sop to him, a ruse by the SPA, designed to prop up his bogus leadership. He argued that if the local selling price of sugar were increased by 2 cents per pound — a reasonable and long-overdue hike, he contended — this would result in an annual increase in expenditure of $4.16 for a family of six, whereas the sugar worker would get a minimum wage hike of $31.20. In late 1957 Ishmael called on Jagan to sanction the price hike, as this would give the workers a rise of 7.5 per cent, independently of any increases won from the sugar producers in 1958. He said that the freeze on the local selling price of sugar was a political decision by the Jagan government; this was indefensible, for sugar workers should not have to subsidise the rest of the country with sugar sold below the cost of production. Ishmael concluded that this issue underlined the hazards implicit in the rise of a political union in the industry: the specific grievances of its workers would be subordinated to the defined political objectives and ambition of the political leader.[9]

By the end of 1958, the first year of operation of the sick benefit scheme, 22,703 workers had qualified for it, with an earned credit of $375,150. In that year $283,700 had been expended on sick benefits, $33,700 more than when the programme was inaugurated at the beginning of the year. In September 1959, twenty months after its commencement, the SPA announced that in order to save their sickness benefits, they were offering an interest of 3.5 per cent on all credits accumulated under the scheme.[10]

In March 1960 Jock Campbell assured sugar workers that they were, indeed, 'being treated as more important than shops and ships and sugar estates'. He added: '[P]eople are more important than anything else. I should have thought that the remarkable improvement in wages, housing amenities and conditions of service on the sugar estates in British Guiana during recent years bear full witness to our policies'. But he observed that to survive as a remunerative producer of sugar, even with the preference provided by the CSA, mechanisation was indispensable, although this, inevitably, brought the pain of redundancy, as witnessed at Port Mourant in 1956. These stringent measures were inevitable in the drive for efficiency and competitiveness — survival. Campbell explained why redundancy was unavoidable in the industry:

> [I]t is far better for the people of British Guiana as a whole that a thoroughly efficient sugar industry should pay good wages to a smaller number of people. The large number of people with bad wages would all be poor and have no money to spend, which will in turn give employment to others .... I know that some individual men and women suffer in this inescapable process. For them, our policy is to do everything we can to find other jobs. Or, if we fail, to give them redundancy payments. There is no more that we can do.[11]

Wages were, indeed, better and there was demonstrable improvement in the overall condition of life, even for cane-cutters, the traditionally despised section of the plantation workforce. Nothing epitomised this more than the dramatic rise in painted houses in the late 1950s (often coterminous with the payment of the annual once-for-all bonus), as well as the escalating numbers of their children attending secondary school. In December 1960, for instance, it was announced that the 'once-for-all' bonus would be computed on the following terms: if the final production figures for 1960 were 317,000 tons of sugar, workers would get seven days' pay; if 326,000 tons were reached, they would be awarded eight days' pay. To qualify for the bonus the worker had to make 82.5 per cent of the days for which work was available. In 1960 British Guiana produced 324,441 tons of sugar, a record.[12]

In November 1960 Campbell had demonstrated how the CSA had fostered a greater sense of security among management and workers. He noted that Commonwealth sugar exporters had increased their exports by 100 per cent since 1950–51, while £250 million had been reinvested to modernise the sugar industry. He explained: 'The astonishing increase in production has not been brought about by depressing wages or inflating prices. On the contrary, workers' wages, well-being, amenities, housing and their whole living standards have improved. Their security is greater and their future far more assured'.[13]

In February 1963 Senator Antony Tasker, OBE, now chairman of the Booker B.G. Group Committee, told the Senate of British Guiana that the sugar industry could not be considered 'a fading industry', because between 1949 and 1960 production had nearly doubled, from 174,227 tons to 334,441 tons, while the acreage under cultivation had increased by only 25,000, from 68,533 to 94,103. The yield per acre had improved markedly: in the 1920s it was 2 tons per acre, in the early 1960s it was 3.5 tons per acre. Scientific husbandry now permeated all layers of sugar cane culture, exemplified best in the modern drainage and irrigation systems on all estates. Between 1954 and 1961 pumping equipment had cost more than $1.2 million; by the latter year $5 million were being expended annually on the modernisation of field and factory assets.

Tasker observed that between 1954 and 1961 the 20,000 sugar workers benefited from a wage hike of 50 per cent; besides the 'one-for-all' bonuses between 1957 and 1961 totalled $5 million. He elaborated: 'A comparison of wages paid in September 1955 and 1962 showed that the average weekly earnings of cane cutters ... had increased from $16.77 to $27.82 and factory workers from $18.44 to $31.36. A sickness benefit scheme was introduced in 1958 and sugar workers could have had a pension scheme already.'[14]

Tasker estimated that the medical scheme on the sugar estates cost nearly $500,000 annually. The housing programme, incorporating 90 new housing areas established on land provided by the sugar estates, and the interest-free loans provided by the SILWF (financed from a levy on sugar exports), had facilitated the re-housing of 10,000 sugar workers and their families. By November 1962 the SILWF had allocated $10.8 million on housing loans; $2.1 million on the preparation of housing areas; and $4.7 million on water supplies, roads, community centres and sports fields. Tasker noted also that in pursuing Booker's policy of 'Guianisation' — of which Jock Campbell was the architect — a 'comprehensive training programme provided at all levels of management and technical responsibility', to equip Guyanese for high-level jobs, was far advanced. His argument was that Campbell's reformist capitalism had transformed Booker's practices in the colony, increasingly harnessing Guyanese talent in reshaping the industry at the core of Jagan's Marxist passion.

Tasker elaborated on the impact of these reforms on the national income: $4.4 million annually in income tax; $292,000 annually, since 1959, in export tax ('a discriminatory tax imposed on no other agricultural product', he contended); $640,000 annually in subsidies to the local consumer, facilitating the 'sale of sugar ... at a Government-controlled price below the cost of production'; $600,000 from duties, every year, on imported goods used in sugar production; and $1.7 million annually on welfare projects for sugar workers. Between 1956 and 1961 the after-tax profits were 6 per cent of capital employed; the latter was assessed at $38.6 million. According to Tasker, Booker was no massively successful company yielding super-profits,[15] a fact confirmed after the company was nationalised in 1976: Guyanese were quickly disabused of notions of sugar as the goose with golden eggs. This has been reinforced since the PPP came to power in 1992, for the union in the industry since nationalisation, the GAWU, an arm of the PPP, has been chastened by the fact that its gargantuan demands for profit-sharing under the previous Burnham regime, would soon bankrupt the industry if they were conceded. At last they were growing up: the Jaganite idea of King Sugar's blood-sucking propensities was vastly exaggerated.

In 1968, the year after Campbell retired from the chairmanship of Booker, the MPCA submitted to the Persaud Commission that sugar workers were not being adequately remunerated for what they saw as an increase in productivity. They argued that the reduction of the workforce, from 24,835 in 1956 to 16,925 in 1966, and the consequent increase in output per worker — from 10.41 tons of sugar to 16.42 tons — had not redounded to the workers' advantage: '... the labour force had not benefited from greater regularity of employment nor had their incomes increased significantly'.[16] They also contended that the wage rates of cane-cutters 'did not adequately reflect the time used in travelling from estate pick-up points to the field or assigned work-place'. Further delays were encountered as frequently the punts into which the cane was loaded arrived late. The MPCA submitted that the means were available for further remuneration: workers were contributing inordinately to 'replacement reserves', capital expenditure that was 'too ambitious and unwarranted'. The Union explained how better wages could be afforded:

> The sugar producers had not sought capital from outside sources with the result that the Industry had been built from Guyanese resources; workers had therefore made a significant contribution to the development of the Industry and to its assets. The pace of modernisation could be slowed, so that workers could be given additional income to improve their existing standards.[17]

TABLE XI
Output per Worker (Field and Factory), 1956–66

Year	Avg. no. of Workers	Tons of Sugar Produced	Avg. Tons of Sugar per Worker
1956	24,835	258,615	10.00
1957	24,574	280,177	11.39
1958	23,642	300,419	13.00
1959	21,766	280,097	12.86
1960	20,479	329,044	16.00
1961	19,234	319,938	16.63
1962	17,815	320,381	17.98
1963	17,834	311,588	17.46
1964	16,034	253,559	15.81
1965	17,912	299,809	16.73
1966	16,925	278,010	16.42

Source: 'Report of a Commission of Inquiry into the Sugar Industry in Guyana', (G.B.L. Persaud, chairman), (mimeo.), September 1968, p.83

TABLE XII
Average Weekly Earnings of Field Workers on Sugar Estates, 1956–66

FIELD (MALE)	($)										
	1956	1957	1958	1959	1960	1961	1962	1963	1964	1965	1966
Resident and Non-Resident Piece Workers	13.28	15.25	16.41	16.56	18.78	22.20	21.82	24.93	25.05	25.47	26.60
Resident and Non-Resident Time Workers	8.83	10.50	13.41	12.30	13.54	16.77	16.97	20.39	22.91	21.55	22.15
Young Persons	4.88	5.90	7.15	7.51	8.89	10.16	10.17	12.14	11.24	11.72	12.53
FIELD (FEMALE)											
Resident and Non-Resident Piece Workers	5.92	6.05	6.58	6.59	7.82	9.05	8.89	10.72	11.18	11.56	11.20
Resident and Non-Resident Time Workers	4.37	4.58	5.04	5.21	6.09	8.17	8.75	10.77	10.85	10.43	10.64
Young Persons	4.78	4.88	5.32	6.18	7.39	8.19	8.38	10.25	11.19	9.81	11.10

Source: 'Report of a Commission of Inquiry into the Sugar Industry in Guyana', (G.L.B. Persaud, chairman), (mimeo.), September 1968, p.85.

Campbell's reforms at work:
a truck transporting workers to the cane-field (in background)

It is noteworthy that the largest wage hike occurred between 1960 and 1963, when the benefits from the modernisation of the late 1950s were being felt. Productivity increased by 3.2 tons sugar per ton per worker, between 1959 and 1960; production increased by 30,000 tons from 1958 to 1960, 300,000 tons having been reached for the first time in the former year. Although workers benefited from these achievements, the MPCA and the PPP government were not satisfied with the wages received. The diminution of the workforce on the estates, however, did not necessarily mean that field and factory workers became full-time employees: the seasonal character of the cycle of production on plantations precluded this. Most of the workers, especially Indians, were enmeshed in various niches to tide them over the 'slack' period, when the sugar factory closed for annual maintenance. Indian sugar workers were never really a rural proletariat. By the early 1960s, with the establishment of extra-nuclear settlements away from the estates, and the rice industry booming under the Jagan government, invigorated by the opening of the Cuban market, many became small rice farmers, having bought front-lands from the sugar estates. This was satisfactory both to the workers as well as the sugar producers: the former had their own means of subsistence during the 'slack' season, while the estates retained the labour of satisfied workers at no extra cost. Sugar and rice could co-exist.

It is interesting that the Persaud Commission of 1968 made no definite statement on the exploitative character of the sugar industry, neither did they seek to curb the presumed 'super-profits' of the sugar producers. But they did recommend a 30 cents increase in the basic daily wage of unskilled workers, with corresponding adjustments in other categories, retroactive to January 1, 1966. This expenditure, they submitted, should be drawn on the Price Stabilisation Fund, to which the SPA had been contributing since 1947, but which had not been utilised for its original purpose as the CSA had offered competitive prices since 1951. As noted earlier, funds had been drawn from it to augment the SILWF in the 1950s, for social welfare purposes; its balance stood at $7.2 million in 1968. The Commission, on the other hand, rejected the MPCA's contention that funds from the Rehabilitation Fund should be diverted to cover wage increases because capital projects undertaken by the SPA were often 'ambitious and unwarranted'.[18]

SILWF received the commendation of the Commission for their 'substantial work towards the alleviation of the harsh living conditions of the sugar worker who hitherto was compelled to raise his family in ranges in surroundings which could hardly be described as healthy by any standard'. They were unequivocal in recommending continuation of its funding at the rate of $4.80 per ton of sugar exported, paid by the sugar industry.[19] They could not endorse the government's recommendation that it be reduced. They were well aware of its sterling contribution in changing the social landscape of the plantations, and concluded: '[T]he Fund is already functioning effectively at present in meeting claims upon it from established and well recognised sources. In the circumstances we feel unable to recommend any reduction in the present rate of cess.'[20] The SPA had asked for no such reduction: it had been the base of Campbell's reform programme.

It is my contention that in assessing these reforms, their range, after the CSA of the early 1950s, it is erroneous to seek to determine the condition of the sugar worker merely by reference to wages earned. It is difficult to quantify the benefits of Campbell's reforms, but they had transformed plantation life by the early 1960s: free house-lots and loans for house-building; land sold at reasonable rates for cultivation; diverse social amenities, including potable water, dispensaries, good roads, community centres with excellent sports facilities, girls' clubs and libraries; free transportation to and from work; technical training for workers and their children, including many high school scholarships; sick benefits and workmen's compensation, and so on. As Campbell reflected to me: 'paternalistic, maybe; too little too late, perhaps; but necessary', given the domination of the economy by sugar. J.B. Raghurai, who grew up at Plantation Rose Hall (East Canje), and rose from humble beginnings (at New Dam) to became head of the estate in the early 1990s, recalls: 'We were hearing more and more of Jock Campbell's plans for development and we were literally seeing it on the estates, manifesting itself: the changes, though gradual, were quite obvious.'[21]

In 1949, the Venn Commission had recommended that sugar estates provide potable water and light shelters for workers in the fields. By the early 1950s water-tanks, mounted in punts, took fresh drinking-water into the remotest cane-fields, where water-carriers distributed it at intervals to the workers. However, the industry deemed the recommendation for the erection of light shelters, one to every 10 or 12 fields, impracticable because of the necessity for constant mobility in field-work, whether cane-cutting, forking, weeding or manuring. Because of the size of the cane-fields, too, it was an impracticable proposition to expect workers to seek shelter, during their lunch-break, under a structure located 10 or 12 fields away.[22]

Another recommendation of the Venn Commission was that dams on the plantations be graded to enable workers to cycle to work. By the mid-1950s lorries transported workers from their homes to the fields. As the SPA reported in 1966:

> Although the provision of transportation is not a condition of employment, estates provide a measure of free transportation for field workers. On many, this consists of a fleet of lorries which run a shuttle service through the neighbouring villages right into the estate back-dam. Two estates [Port Mourant and Blairmont] have a railway for transporting labour, and in many

cases passenger punts, drawn by tractors, transport workers to the work site in the cultivation.[23]

On the question of conditions in the sugar factories, the Venn Commission had called for the installation of showers, changing rooms and a canteen with cooking facilities. They had also advocated the introduction of workmen's compensation.[24] In 1966, in their assessment of the state of industrial welfare in Guyana, the SPA concluded:

> Rising wages have been paralleled by improvements in the industry's industrial and social welfare programme. Measures have been introduced to improve work conditions, provide canteens, guard against accidents, give the sugar worker greater security in the event of injury, and in old age. Sickness Benefit and Severance Pay Schemes are operated. Pending the establishment of a Government Pension Scheme, the sugar industry spends a considerable sum each year in ex-gratia payments to retiring sugar workers.[25]

The Sickness Benefit Scheme was introduced in 1956; by 1966 it had cost the sugar producers nearly $3 million, or about $500,000 per year. Between 1955 and 1961 $280,000 had been spent on severance pay to workers who had been made redundant by the contraction of the workforce, the closure of factories, such as that at Port Mourant in 1955–56 and by the implementation of the bulk-loading of sugar at La Penitance. However, the most resilient problem confronting sugar workers was a comprehensive pension scheme.[26] Here, as with so many issues relating to sugar in British Guiana, the efforts of the SPA and the MPCA became mired in the intractable politics of sugar and the imponderables of Guyanese nationalism — the intransigence of Jagan's government. In 1966 Ian McDonald remarked on the stalemate:

> So far as provision for workers who have grown old in the service of the industry is concerned the sugar companies have exerted themselves for years to introduce a properly funded pension scheme. Such a scheme has been worked out with the trade unions [including the MPCA], and has the general approval of a UN

pension expert ... who has visited British Guiana on behalf of the Government. But the scheme has been stalled for want of the necessary legislation.... In the meanwhile the sugar companies are paying annually directly out of revenue the sum of $500,000 in purely ex-gratia pensions to retired employees.[27]

In 1949 the Venn Commission had recommended the establishment of a contributory pension scheme in the sugar industry. It should have applied to all adult male workers who would contribute 2½ per cent and employees 5 per cent of their weekly earnings. Workers were to be eligible for benefits at the age of 50 after a minimum of 10 years' service. The Commission stipulated further:

> Any worker withdrawing, being discharged, or reaching the age limit before the ten years had elapsed would have all his own contributions (with accumulated interest) returned to him together with 10% of the employer's total contribution, plus interest, for each year of completed service. The relations, or legal heirs, of employees dying during the ten-year period would receive the full benefits (viz., contributions plus interest) derived from the two sides; so, too, would those workers becoming hopelessly incapacitated.[28]

They advised that a committee should hold in trust and administer the funds on each estate.

By 1966, as McDonald observed, no progress had been made. The workers were still dependent on ex-gratia pensions of $2 or $3 per week. As Ashton Chase, the Minister of Labour in the short-lived PPP government of 1953, remarked in 1964: '[Workers] depended on the whim and caprice of their respective employers. These miserable pittances were hardly enough to upkeep a manager's dog.'[29] But both the interim government (1954–57) and the PPP governments (1957–61 and 1961–64) seemed in no hurry to legislate for any such scheme for sugar workers. By 1966, when the PNC-UF coalition was in office, the momentum had drained out of the issue.

In November 1957 Richard Ishmael, President of the MPCA, told sugar workers in Berbice that ever since 1953 government had failed to implement the Pension Plan for sugar workers. He estimated that this tardiness had resulted in their losing about $4¼ million; this money was irretrievable. He remarked that the MPCA and the SPA had agreed to implement a Pension Plan since January 1, 1955, assessed at $1¼ million or 7 per cent of their total wage bill per year. The Interim Government (1954–57), however, had brought out an expert to conduct a survey of sugar workers, and it was suggested that the new pension plan, the Richardson Plan, could start from January 1, 1956. Nothing had been done. Ishmael added that they had agreed, also, to a Pension Plan for old, retired sugar workers, enabling them to use funds from the industry's Price Stabilisation Fund. The SPA had agreed to divert $2 million along with $320,000 to service the Pension Trust. He concluded that if the new PPP government (elected in August 1957) were not prepared to implement the Richardson Plan, then he would seek exemption from it so that they could revert to the old Plan.[30]

Ishmael had written to the relevant PPP minister to expedite matters, but had received no response to several letters. He wrote again, in November 1957:

> To this date there has been no reply even though more than a month has elapsed and even though it was pointed out quite clearly to you that this matter was pending for over two years. Does not a Pension Scheme for sugar estate workers which has been secured by the MPCA warrant prompt attention?...Already sugar workers have lost the sum of approximately $4¼ million which would have been paid into a pension scheme by the employers, and this amount can never be recovered. This is a result of the indecision and dilatoriness of Government and the Union vehemently deprecates it.[31]

In his letter of October 22, 1957 to the PPP minister, Ishmael had explained that the SPA and the MPCA had agreed in principle to 'the diversion of $2 million from the Price Stabilisation Fund (PSF)', in addition to an annual diversion of 20 per cent towards the Pension Scheme, to enable old, retired sugar workers to have access to benefits, as it was too late for them to join any new scheme. He was appalled by the government's silence: '[T]he Union ... regrets profoundly that Government to this date has not seen fit to treat this pension Scheme for sugar estate workers as a priority matter.'

Indeed, Jagan's government was not interested in this or any other manifestation of social reform emanating from the sugar planters. Moreover, the fact that the pension scheme was an initiative of the MPCA, which the PPP deemed an illegitimate outfit, a company union bereft of a base among sugar workers, hardened the obduracy of the government: there could be nothing of merit in such a measure.

As late as 1961 the PPP government was still not interested in legislating for the pension scheme, neither did they suggest how its perceived flaws could be removed. In January 1961 the SPA and the MPCA agreed to another scheme to start on July 1, 1961. The MPCA expressed reservations on some of its provisions, but conceded that it should be delayed no longer as the Pensions Trust could address possible revisions once the scheme was in operation. They therefore submitted the scheme to the PPP government in January 1961, giving them five months to introduce enabling legislation for the transfer of funds from the PSF to the Pensions Trust. Nothing was heard from the government until June 1961, two weeks before the scheme was scheduled to be implemented. Meanwhile, the SPA had proceeded with the preparation of legal documents and the printing of booklets explaining the scheme to sugar workers.[32]

The SPA said that Jagan announced that they could not agree to the transfer of funds from the PSF to inaugurate the scheme. Indeed, as Ashton Chase observes, the government could see nothing worthwhile in it and objected to virtually every provision: its trustees; their jurisdiction over the funds; the rate at which the pensions were to be computed; the equality of contribution between employees and employers — 1¾ per cent on both sides. They contended that the latter constituted a saving on the part of the sugar producers of $100,000.[33] Moreover, as Shahabuddeen points out, the PPP government's principal objection was that it was not legitimate to transfer funds from the PSF and the Rehabilitation Fund to cover pension liabilities: 'The proposed pension scheme, it was thought, should instead have been established by the industry at least in part from its own resources outside of the special funds. These doubts related in particular to the PSF, intended, as this had been, to stabilise prices during periods of low demand and ... indirectly to serve as a resource to maintain wages when sugar prices fell.'[34]

As a consequence of the PPP's prevarication on the Pension Scheme, no enabling legislation was ever introduced, and as the government became mortally wounded during the virtual civil war between 1962 and 1964, the issue disappeared from the agenda: a genuine pension scheme for sugar workers was never implemented. However, the ex-gratia pension payments were revised continually as late as 1974, a little before the sugar industry was nationalised: then the maximum and minimum weekly payments for men were $9.60 and $4 respectively; for women $6.40 and $3 respectively.[35] The sugar workers were the losers, pawns in the politics of sugar, throughout Cheddi Jagan's political career — from the late 1940s to the late 1990s.

In 1965 the Cummings Commission recommended that the SILWF be the source for the initial funding of the pension scheme; nothing came of this either. In 1968 the Persaud Commission recommended that the PSF be used for funding ex-gratia pensions. Although the PPP had objected to this in 1961, there was a precedence: after the suspension of the Constitution and the removal of the first PPP government in 1953, resources were diverted from the PSF to augment the funds of the SILWF, in order to accelerate housing and social welfare reforms. The Sugar Industry was confident that the guaranteed prices under the CSA ensured that the reforms initiated in the early 1950s, would not be affected, neither would there be any extraordinary demands on the Price Stabilisation Fund.

This, therefore, leads one to question the premises on which the Jagan government throttled the pension scheme negotiated between the SPA and the MPCA. As noted earlier, the Marxist PPP were irreconcilable to the 'reformism' of Jock Campbell's philosophy. And in mid-1961, on the eve of the general elections, which were considered the last before independence, Jagan could not countenance any compromise with his arch-enemies, the 'sugar gods' — no trucking with Imperialism. Buoyed by the ascendancy of his hero, Fidel Castro, his aim was control of the 'commanding heights' of the economy, nationalisation of sugar and expulsion of the 'blood suckers'. Statements to the contrary, in October 1961 in Washington, were a ruse designed to placate President Kennedy. Besides, Jagan was deeply wounded by Booker's continuing recognition of the MPCA, whose president, Richard Ishmael, was a foremost enemy. He was not amenable to any measure which would have given tacit legitimacy to the MPCA. It is significant that shortly after his victory in the 1961 elections, he resurrected his Party's union, the Guiana Industrial Workers Union, which had sought recognition in 1948 and 1953 as the sole bargaining agent for sugar workers. Now, as the Guyana Sugar Workers' Union (from 1963 the Guyana Agricultural Workers' Union [GAWU]), it was considered indispensable in the anti-imperialist struggle. His Marxist frame of reference could not accommodate the Fabian socialist programme of Campbell, its mild reforms, deemed another imperialist ruse to perpetuate capitalist exploitation. If the sugar workers did not get a pension scheme that was a minor set-back in the longer, heroic struggle to create his communist utopia — no quarter must be given to the enemy.

In 1964 Ashton Chase, who was the Minister of Labour in the first PPP government in 1953, commented on the impact of Cheddi and Janet Jagan on the fortunes of sugar workers. This is, indirectly, a verdict on the Venn Commission of 1949 and the reforms of Jock Campbell as well, in the 1950s and early 1960s. He wrote:

> The Enmore Martyrs [five workers shot on June 16, 1948, during the first GIWU strike for recognition] did not die in vain. The glorious struggle of the East Coast [Demerara] ... sugar workers under the inspiring leadership of Dr. and Mrs Jagan and Dr. Lachmansingh [then president of GIWU] was still to be crowned with important advances on several fronts. It is to the heroic struggle of these workers that sugar workers owe so much. The vast improvements in housing on the sugar estates and other social amenities, and certain changes in working conditions owe their derivation to the Enmore strike.[36]

Jock Campbell reflected frequently on the promptings of his reformist vision; on what made him stay on in turbulent British Guiana:

One could have said, let's give the whole thing up. We probably could have sold it to the other sugar companies or abandoned it. This is where I started to think of the enormous social obligation. I realised that we ... were almost the only visible means of support of the country at that time. So I came to the conclusion that one couldn't simply contract out at that stage. And it seemed to me that one had got to get it right .... I suppose in my own mind, there was an unpaid moral obligation to stay. But I was Scottish enough to realise that this could be made to work.[37]

As I have argued throughout, there was no other person in the sugar industry of British Guiana with the moral compunction, will and authority to frame and sustain a programme of reforms. He believed that reformist capitalism could work in this colonial backwater: that the four fold responsibility to shareholders, customers, employees and the community, could intersect with the nationalist aspirations of its peoples. Jock Campbell's unique empathy was, indeed, crucial to the development of a progressive Guyana on the threshold of independence. However, Cheddi Jagan, certain of his Marxist creed as the instrument of liberation from Imperialism and enthralled by Castroism after 1959, could see nothing redeeming in this. The evidence ever since would seem to vindicate Campbell's philosophy of gradualism.

Guyanese economist, Wilfred David, has assessed the achievement of Campbell's reforms to the early 1960s. He looks first at wages on the sugar plantations:

Despite technological labour displacement, the industry still remains one of the major employers of labour in the country. In 1956 sugar companies accounted for 20 per cent of the labour force, but by 1960 this figure had fallen to 15 per cent, the workers remaining in employment having substantially increased their real earnings in sharp contrast to the stagnation in real wages during the 1939–49 decade. Between 1948 and 1960, annual money earnings per worker tripled while the cost-of-living index rose by less than 40 per cent. Between 1954 and 1960 average earnings increased by over 85 per cent, the cost-of-living index rising by 11 per cent, leaving real wages 67 per cent higher than in 1954. This is an increase of nearly 9 per cent a year in the purchasing power of the average sugar worker. The rise resulted not only from increases in basic wage rates but rather from raising the cost-of-living allowance every year from the introduction of bonuses and holiday with pay.... When in 1963 the world price of sugar reached record peak, the workers shared the fruits of negotiated increases in wages amounting to 15 per cent over the two years, 1962 and 1963, and over $500,000 was paid as a special bonus for the 1962 crop. Thus not only are sugar workers one of the highest paid groups of workers in the country, but real wages have shown significant increases.... Thus the industry has made a real contribution to the generation of purchasing power, consumption demand and, as a corollary, investment demand within the country.[38]

David adds that the sugar industry also subsidised the local consumer of sugar with over $1 million per annum, while providing 45 per cent of government revenue through income tax and excise duties. As an example of a good corporate citizen he thought that the industry's credentials were admirable: employees' welfare, skills, new technique, efficiency, production and planning. Their record was especially commendable, given the peculiarly hazardous hydrological conditions of coastal Guyana:

The two-fold problem of sea and floods is still with us; hence the necessity for a system of high and low canals, the low for drainage the high for transportation and irrigation. Sugar cultivation in Guyana involves special techniques, extra effort, and more urgent timing than production on most other countries. The unique necessities of water control involves the extensive building of sea walls, digging of canals and ditches, and maintaining them. Similarly the heavy soil requires much preparation, and the superabundance of weeds and pests calls for intensive tillage and chemical control measures. These local peculiarities have necessitated heavy overhead investment prior to and during the cultivation of cane, with consequent high production costs and the weakening of the competitive position of sugar produced in the country.[39]

Obsessed with the notion of Booker's domination of their land — 'Booker's Guiana' — and the sordid record of sugar in the colony, the monumental effort, the unrelenting discipline required for producing sugar on that hard land, was missed completely. This had tragic repercussions for the country when the sugar industry was nationalised in 1976 by the Burnham regime (with Jagan's support): production fell to nearly half that of the early 1960s and most of the benefits to workers, gained through Campbell's reforms, quickly evaporated. In a confidential note to the chairman of the Guyana Sugar Corporation (GUYSUCO), Harold Davis, in 1989, Ian McDonald explained the basis of the decline:

> Ten years ago, in 1979, one ton of export sugar in Guysuco yielded $860. In 1989 one ton export sugar yields $17,000: the Guyana dollar value has multiplied 18 times. Yet the minimum wage in 1979 was $11.85 and in 1989 is $32.69; it has increased less than 3 times. One day's pay incentive to sugar workers in 1979 cost $0.4 million = 465 tons of sugar then, and in 1989 costs $1.2 million = 70 tons of sugar. A middle manager in sugar in 1979 was getting, say $20,000 p.a. = 20 tons of sugar then, while in 1989 he gets, say $50,000 p.a. = 3 tons of sugar...[W]e have to get over the fact that sugar workers and sugar managers have been seriously short-changed and must be given a much better deal if increased production and exports are to be achieved.[40]

In Campbell's Booker, however, there could be no margin for error, hence no space for infantile rhetoric. That was why Jock felt it was crucial to procure high quality technical people, such as Dr Harry Evans, Dr George Giglioli, Ray Baxter, Dr George Bacs, and Arthur Goodland, to undertake and enhance the range of inescapable, complex scientific work, if sugar were to survive and carry the heavy responsibilities with which it was saddled in a most difficult natural and political environment: to shareholders, employees, customers and the Guyanese community. In this process Campbell had started to train and employ Guyanese to replace expatriates: the 'Guianisation' of labour, too, was key to his reforms. As two Canadian scholars observed in the mid-1970s, Campbell's Booker tried to honour their obligations to Guyana and wished to be seen to do so:

> In the 1960s [under the Burnham regime] two government commissions studied the sugar industry in Guyana and supported its [Booker's] contention that profits and shareholders' dividends were modest.... Built into Booker's corporate strategy...was an acceptance of its social responsibilities, which were portrayed by its management as an integral part of the company's *raison d'etre* .... [But] as the industry overhauled and retrenched its operations, much unemployment resulted. The outcome was that sugar production and workers wages shot up, making the mainly East Indian sugar employees one of the highest paid occupational groups in Guyana.[41]

Endnotes

1. *Booker News* [Leader], March 13, 1959.
2. Ibid.
3. Brian Scott, 'The Organisational Network: A Strategy Perspective for Development', PhD thesis, Harvard University, 1979, p. 125.
4. Diane McTurk, *The Oldest Industry: Aspects of Sugar in Guyana* (Georgetown: SPA, 1966), 9.
5. Ibid., 17.
6. *Booker News*, May 11, 1956.
7. Ibid., [Leader], February 15, 1957.
8. *Labour Advocate*, December 15, 1957; see also *Booker News*, December 20, 1957.
9. *Labour Advocate* [Leader], December 15, 1957; Ibid., December 22, 1957.
10. *Booker News*, September 11, 1959.
11. Ibid., March 11, 1960.
12. Ibid., December 2, 1960.
13. Ibid., March 14, 1961.
14. Ibid., February 8, 1963.
15. Ibid.
16. 'Report of a Commission of Inquiry into the Sugar Industry in Guyana', (G.L.B. Persaud, chairman),(mimeo.), 1968, p. 28.
17. Ibid., 31.
18. Ibid., 129.
19. Ibid., 130.
20. Ibid., 31.
21. J.B.Raghurai, interview by the author, Rose Hall Estate, September 14, 1992.

22.   *Report of a Commission of Inquiry into the Sugar Industry of British Guiana*, (J.A. Venn, chairman), Col. no. 249 (London; HMSO, 1949), 78.

23.   See note 4 [p. 10].

24.   See note 22 [pp. 61, 64-5].

25.   See note 23.

26.   Ian McDonald, ' Sugar in B.G.: Challenge and Change', (mimeo.), 1966, pp. 16-7.

27.   Ibid., 17.

28.   See note 22, [pp. 88-90].

29.   Ashton Chase, *A History of Trade Unionism in Guyana: 1900 to 1964* (Ruimveldt, Guyana: New Guyana Co, Ltd, n.d., ca, 1964), 158.

30.   *Labour Advocate*, December 1, 1957.

31.   Ibid.

32.   *Booker News*, May 29, 1964.

33.   See note 29 [pp. 158-9].

34.   M. Shahabuddeen, *From Plantocracy to Nationalisation: A Profile of Sugar in Guyana* (Georgetown: University of Guyana, 1983), 196.

35.   Ibid.

36.   See note 29 [p. 152].

37.   See note 3 [Quoted on p. 124].

38.   Wilfred L. David, *The Economic Development of Guyana,1953-64* (Oxford: Clarendon Press, 1969), 123-4.

39.   Ibid., 125.

40.   Ian McDonald to the Chairman, GUYSUCO, n.d., [1989], private and confidential.

41.   Isaiah A. Litvak and Christopher J. Maule, 'Foreign Corporate Social Responsibility in Less Developed Economies', *Journal of World Trade Law* 9, no. 2 (1975): 123, 128, 131. See also (by the same authors), 'Foreign Firms: Social Costs and Benefits in Developing Countries', *Public Policy* XXIII, no. 2 (Spring 1975): 167-87.

Chapter Thirty

'GUIANISATION' OF SUGAR: PLACING GUYANESE AT THE HEART OF BOOKER

In an interview in January 1960 Jock Campbell made a number of significant remarks about the role of British business in poor countries. He underlined the necessity for flexibility, while acknowledging the difficult political environment in which they often had to operate: 'In British Guiana, for example, we have to deal with a quasi-Marxist if not a Communist government.' He elaborated:

> In my view British firms will not succeed in maintaining themselves in these countries unless they are able to project themselves completely into the local community. They have got to learn the language in every sense of the phrase; and try to learn to see their undertaking through local eyes. And though their shareholders' interests must, of course, be efficiently promoted and protected, they will have to regard the local interest as paramount, and vary their policies in the context of the particular country in which they are operating.[1]

Campbell then turned to the crucial issue of the appointment of local people to strategic positions in the company, technical and managerial. He could not envisage their continual exclusion; the alternative was extinction of the firm in the inexorable claims of nationalist politics. He explained: '[W]e should not recruit non-specialists from this country [UK] when we can obtain people on the spot to do the job. We should bring far more of the local people over here for training schemes of one kind or another.' He drew a parallel between the eventual boldness in devolving political power to people in the ex-colonies and the inevitability of decentralising and training local people to take control in business. Campbell was realistic and optimistic:

We must try and create a real sense of partnership, a genuine international business .... I certainly don't think we can afford a drastic reduction in efficiency, but I do think that the risk is often exaggerated. The [British] Government has had to face up to this problem. There was a great deal of head shaking when it began to hand over responsibility to the local people, plenty of stories of inefficiency and corruption. But they had to do it more hurriedly than they thought it wise perhaps, in order to keep the goodwill of the countries concerned. And we in business will have to do the same if we do not want to be thrown out. We will have to decentralise, and in my experience it is remarkable how easily and quickly the local people can be trained to take control at all levels.[2]

Indeed, he was committed to 'Guianisation' in British Guiana. Since 1956 Booker had pursued what they termed a 'vigorous policy of management by Guyanese': 'When a management vacancy occurs, the position is filled by a suitably qualified and experienced Guyanese, unless it is proved quite impossible to find a Guyanese with the necessary technical qualifications.'[3] In fact, as will be seen in the next section, Jock Campbell had taken a bigger step: in 1958 and 1960 he had actually offered Cheddi Jagan the option of the government, the unions and local capitalists acquiring 51 per cent of the shares in Booker. He did not receive a reply.

A crucial facet of Campbell's programme of Guianisation was the enhancement of the professional competence of Guyanese. This was achieved in a variety of ways: on-the-job training to equip workers to assume roles as field and factory supervisors, at the level of middle management; as apprentices at the Booker Training School at Port Mourant or at the Government Technical Institute in Georgetown, to prepare them for diverse technical jobs; and, at the highest level, as cadets trained in management, agriculture and engineering, at university or colleges overseas. This policy, over a twenty-year period culminating in the nationalisation of Booker in 1976, had produced a stream of technically competent people, many of whom were to become pathfinders in the Guyanese diaspora in North America, as life was disfigured by the Burnham dictatorship in the late 1970s and early 1980s. Clive Thomas observes that many of the technical graduates did not stay long with Booker but moved into more remunerative positions elsewhere, maximising their options because of a paucity of trained personnel; these people, too, were better placed to secure visas as permanent migrants to Canada and the United States when the post-colonial flight escalated.[4]

This is how the sugar industry assessed their achievement in education and training, in 1966, the year before Campbell's retirement from Booker:

> The sugar industry is playing an important part in the national programme, to expand and improve educational and technical training. It maintains three Apprentice Training Schemes which have together enrolled 270 apprentices since 1961. Of the 107 apprentices enrolled prior to that date, and have completed their five years' training, 69 are still employed by the Company to which they were apprenticed. In addition to a variety of employee, supervisory and management training courses organised by the Education and Training Officer, employees at all levels are sponsored for specialised courses abroad. Correspondence courses in such subjects as accountancy and book-keeping, are financed by loans which are refunded and, in addition, monetary awards are given, if the candidates successfully complete their courses. During the past ten years, 75 Guyanese have been sponsored by the sugar companies for training in universities and technical colleges abroad; 171 secondary school scholarships have been awarded to the children of sugar workers.[5]

This was an impressive undertaking. A good example of how this culture of technical advancement had percolated to the middle stratum of Booker is provided by James Ramdeholl. Having joined the company as a time-keeper in the Maintenance Department, he took a three-year study course through Bennett's College, London. In 1957 he passed his final examination in Road Construction and Maintenance. He had studied the following subjects: testing and uses of materials, design and construction of roads, road maintenance, road services, mechanical and hand plants and road works organisation. These equipped him for promotion to the supervisory level in the SILWF roads building project.[6]

In 1959 Campbell explained the centrality of Guianisation to the Booker enterprise in British Guiana. He noted that 'through no fault of their own' there was a paucity of qualified Guyanese and West Indians to fill the many administrative and technical jobs that were available in Booker. However, they were resolved to accelerate the process of training. He elaborated:

> 'In order to play our part in putting this right, we are building up a concerted campaign for education and training for all kinds and levels of management; universities, colleges, schools and formal internal and external courses all enter into our plans.... As well as a wide range of training experience within our own Companies, we have found a wonderful willingness on the part of other small and big companies in the United Kingdom to offer training experience for Booker men and women from overseas.

Campbell underlined the policy: 'In British Guiana and the West Indies it is our absolute policy, resolutely pursued, not now to appoint anyone from outside those countries to any job for which we can recruit a Guianese or West Indian with the necessary qualifications and experience.'[7]

A fine example of the role of Booker in facilitating the development of excellence is the case of Ann Jardim, the 1955 Guyana Scholar. In 1959 she was awarded a scholarship in personnel management by Campbell Booker Holdings (London). She was required to spend three months with the Personnel Department of the Booker Group in British Guiana in order to gain practical experience. After that she proceeded to the London School of Economics to complete her management course; she had secured her BSc (Hons) in Economics there in 1957.[8] Ann became a prominent, if controversial, member of Booker in Georgetown in the early 1960s, as will be seen later.

But at the secondary school level, too, Booker were making a contribution to the education of young Guyanese, thus radically changing the character of the sugar plantations. In 1959, for instance, Booker Sugar Estates awarded 15 secondary scholarships to children of sugar workers, boys and girls under the age of 12, tenable for five years at a school of their choice. The award covered tuition and a maintenance allowance. Several of the winners over the years were children of field labourers: cane-cutters, shovel-men and female weeders.[9] Booker's commitment to education was acknowledged by one of Jagan's ministers, Brindley Benn, at the opening of the Corentyne High School, at Rose Hall Village, on August 1, 1960. He reportedly congratulated them for their role in 'higher education within the sugar industry through higher qualified staff, and in British Guiana as a whole'. But it was the principal of this school, which produced hundreds of outstanding students in the 1950s–60s, J.C. Chandisingh, who was more magnanimous:

> Much has already been said about the contribution of Booker, but in view of their substantial assistance, too much cannot be said. Their gift of Albion Estate Hospital [the main structure of the school was remodelled from it], their offer of ten acres of drained and built-up lands, their loan of equipment in the course of construction, and the interest shown and encouragement given by several members of the estates' staff were important factors in the successful completion of this $98,000 project, at a cost representing considerable saving. The value, however, of community effort does not lie so much in building sites and materials, but rather in what this gesture symbolises — a gratifying relationship between industry and the community it serves.[10]

Booker had initiated a cadetship scheme in the mid-1950s, to prepare Guyanese for senior management responsibilities, through training overseas. One of its first recipients was Pat Thompson, in 1955. He had worked briefly with Booker in Georgetown before going to the UK for on-the-job training with various subsidiaries of Booker in London. In 1959 he returned to British Guiana as Secretary of Industrial Holdings (B.G.), a subsidiary of Booker.[11] In 1960, after a three-month visit to British Guiana, Jock Campbell said that Guianisation was 'going forward very fast indeed', and that they were approaching a situation where 'in a very few years all but the top stratum of jobs will be held by Guyanese'. However, he expressed reservation that the necessity to work their way up through a pyramid of practical jobs, in most cases, would retard the pace at which they could rise to the top management positions — chairmen and managing directors of the companies in the colony.[12]

A year later Booker announced what seemed like the beginning of the 'concerted campaign' (Campbell's characterisation of 1959) to recruit skilled Guyanese. The focus was the UCWI: Campbell had been a member of its Council since 1959, addressed the students periodically and met the Principal, Professor Arthur Lewis, often. In March 1961, in a veiled reference to Jock, Lewis remarked that he had 'not realised the acuteness of the shortage [of trained people] in British Guiana until I heard employers on the subject'. *Booker News* explained:

> To encourage graduate recruitment Booker have embarked on a policy of publicity to put the facts about the Group and the opportunities offered within it before Guyanese and West Indian undergraduates in their last year at UCWI. We have also made our requirements known in the United Kingdom so that more and more Guyanese go to Booker first after they qualify. In addition, 'talent scouts' of the Group Social Policy Committee keep a sharp look-out for promising Guyanese. Efforts have also been made to discover how many Guyanese are qualifying in the USA to the standard required by Booker.[13]

Between 1958 and 1967, the year Jock retired from the Chairmanship of Booker, the number of expatriates on the senior staff of Booker Sugar Estates had declined from 54 per cent to 29 per cent. In 1967, in the factories, 40 of 58 senior staff were Guyanese, as were 74 of 105 in the fields, 18 of 20 in Accounts, 12 of 16 in Personnel; of the administrative managers, the most senior position on the estates, four of nine were Guyanese.[14] This was remarkable progress, as Clive Thomas, the Guyanese economist, has acknowledged:

> At the higher managerial levels, the estates have promoted a policy of Guyanisation. This...was designed in part to resist the pressures for nationalisation and to assuage nationalist sentiment. The effect, however, has been to speed up the number of higher-level Guyanese on the managerial staffs on the estates ....[The] data show a substantial increase in Guyanese staff relative to expatriate staff. Some of the Guyanese staff have been recruited on the open market, but in several cases appointments

have been offered to persons whom the estates sent abroad for university and other forms of higher education.[15]

A culture of scientific inquiry and technical proficiency, central to the modernisation of Booker and the sustaining of the competitiveness of the sugar industry in a hazardous ecological and political environment, was at the core of Campbell's thinking. In March 1956, in a radio broadcast in British Guiana, he had explained the importance of a successful business in the context of the four-fold responsibility he had charted for Booker: '[A] business must be efficient and profitable because if it doesn't make a profit it will collapse and thus be unable to fulfil its responsibilities to staff, workpeople, customers and the community.' [16]

This is especially significant, as one of the main criticisms made of Booker in the context of the nationalisation negotiations in 1976 was that the company, in pursuing its modernisation and expansion programmes during the Campbell years, had brought no new money into the country.[17] It is arguable that such financial prudence in achieving 'self-generated surpluses', reflected the quality of management obtained in the company, the merits of which the architects of the nationalisation programme should have recognised, studied and sought to emulate, rather than denigrate as another demonstration of the venality of imperialism. At the heart of Campbell's Booker was attention to technical excellence and recognition of people's efforts, big or small. As he framed it in his celebrated dictum of 1956: '[T]he central theme of all our plans and policies is that people are more important than ships and shops and sugar estates.'[18]

In January 1965, one month after Jagan's PPP had lost the elections under PR, Booker's senior executive in British Guiana, Antony Tasker, observed that, after ten years, 'progress had been made with all of our policies and there is no facet of the Booker image that has not been improved'. But he conceded that it was 'still easy enough to get depressed about the subject because our progress must inevitably appear slow': the history of sugar, the size of Booker in the colony and its expatriate origin had all contributed to the perpetuation of negative images of Booker.[19]

Perceptions of Campbell's reforms were still being refracted through what Lloyd Searwar, in an address to Booker executives in

1960, characterised as 'scratches on the mind' — 'a historic [negative] image of Booker which ... [most Indians] held in their minds and which was an important source of their political energy'. He felt that that image probably owed 'very little to reasoned judgements'; it had a 'reality of its own which might not correspond to the true facts'. He added: '[but] what a man carries around in his head is more real for him than the hard facts outside'. Searwar illustrated what Campbell was up against by reference to the 'scratches' on his own mind — 'the stories and folklore which shaped... [his] image of Booker': (i) that the Company was *the* government of British Guiana and that the Booker men in London controlled the Colonial Office; (ii) that Booker could 'buy out' any politician who challenged them, and one such Indian [probably a reference to C.R. Jacob in 1940] had 'fallen into appalling silence' through bribery; (iii) few Guyanese could get big jobs in Booker unless they were Portuguese or light Coloured. That these assumptions could still impress Searwar, although his people were urban Christian Indians with over a century's residence in Georgetown and no direct connection to the plantations or Booker, demonstrated the residual power of those 'scratches on the mind' inflicted by sugar.[20]

Searwar argued that until 1953 most Guyanese shared those conceptions of Booker, but that the bifurcation of the national movement, into racial wings — the PPP (Indian), under Jagan, steeped in rural, plantation Guyana, culturally entrenched, inflexible in their sense of hurt, on one hand; the PNC (African), under Burnham, urban, better educated with 'wider flexibility', on the other — had by the late 1950s and early 1960s, spawned diverging images of Booker. For Indians the motif was unmitigated oppression ('we prapa punish [we really suffered]'). This was what fed the political passion of Cheddi Jagan, which in turn reinforced the source of its prompting. He elaborated: 'It is the often expressed opinion of the leading Minister of the Government [Jagan] that Booker and the PNC [Burnham] are acting in collusion. The Minister usually goes on to provide several proofs of his contention, the main one being that the chairman of the PNC is a senior employee of Booker [Winifred Gaskin, editor of *Booker News*].' But, Searwar observed, the fact that Gaskin could hold such high office in the PNC, while remaining a senior Booker employee, seemed to indicate that to Africans 'the bad historic image of Booker had changed and given place to a far more favourable image'.[21]

It is true, as we will see in the next section, that Jagan was inclined to make a distinction between Jock Campbell and his senior executives in British Guiana. Searwar explained:

> [T]he PPP still believes that Booker has enormous power for good or ill over the political affairs of the country.... On the other hand, there is some evidence that changing conditions [the reforms] are having some little effect on the traditional PPP stand. And this I believe, among other things, has caused Dr. Jagan to make his well-known distinction between the vision of the good intentions of Sir Jock Campbell in London and the malevolent local Directors who are apparently unwilling to carry out Sir Jock's policy.[22]

However mitigating, this did not change the fundamental Jaganite conception of Booker as an exploitative imperialist enterprise.

By late 1963 Jagan was mortally wounded, ground down by racial warfare orchestrated by the African and Portuguese leaders in 1962 and 1963. This culminated in American intervention at the highest level, to stop 'communism' and remove Jagan from office, a process virtually guaranteed by the infamous Sandys Plan of October 1963 (see chapter 31). On January 12, 1964, *Mirror*, the PPP newspaper, carried on the front page a story purporting to link Booker with the rabidly anti-communist Portuguese leader, Peter D'Aguiar, of the small, but vibrant, opposition party the United Force. The PPP reproduced a letter in which the head of the security force of Booker, V.J. Fitt, was purported to have recommended to D'Aguiar a certain pandit, a Hindu priest, who could do 'some useful work in either arranging demonstrations [against Jagan] or getting at the East Indian people'. This caused the PPP to ask: 'How far is Booker involved?' They intimated something sinister on the part of the Company, noting that three of its senior staff were key members of the opposition parties: Winifred Gaskin and Dr Ptolemy Reid (PNC) and Ann Jardim (UF). In the leader of the same issue of *Mirror*, the PPP sought to suggest even Jock Campbell's complicity in the escalating activities, 'intrigue' against the Jagan government:

If they [Booker] are logical and clear-sighted they will accept and understand the policy of our Government.... They will co-operate with the Government in the interests of the country and will refrain from participating in petty or major conspiracies with unscrupulous enemies of the state, to bring about its downfall. This we understand to be the position which was taken up by Sir Jock Campbell when desperate efforts were being made in 1962 and 1963, by traitors of many hue, to bring about the suspension of the constitution. The story of our front page shows very clearly the extent to which, in the leadership of Booker at the local level, top employees of the company are co-operating with hostile elements in the community to damage and destroy the Government. If this was an isolated incident it would not be too difficult to believe that the hostility at the top level of the local leadership of the Company was unknown to Sir Jock Campbell and his co-directors in London. We would like to believe that this is so, that a realistic understanding with our Government, which is also in the best interests of the Company, will not be discarded in favour of war. But in view of this succession of events and circumstances, something more tangible than a pious declaration of impartiality is now necessary. Things have gone too far, in recent times, for words to be a tolerable substitute for deeds.

The fact that several prominent anti-Jagan politicians (including the chairman of the PNC, the editor of *Booker News*) could continue to work at the highest level of Booker, was not conducive to revamping its image among the majority of its workers, Indians on the plantations, unwavering supporters of Jagan since the late 1940s. In August 1962, for instance, *Thunder*, the official organ of Jagan's PPP, could effortlessly link Booker to the PNC because of Gaskin's position in both organisations:

Now in the United States, Mrs. Winifred Gaskin, PNC Chairman and Editor of *Booker News*, is on a slanderous campaign vilifying the name of the Premier [Jagan] in the hearty tradition of her leader [Burnham], whitewashing Booker's capitalist empire, attempting to drive fear in the minds of US citizens, saying that the PPP will turn Guyana over to Russia. By this, she hopes to persuade the US to stall aid for our country.[23]

Retaining such partisan executives, like Gaskin, Reid and Jardim, was counter-productive and gave strength to the argument that Campbell was not in total control, that Booker's directors in the colony were anti-PPP, tending to a diminution of his reformist credentials and impugning the purity of his motives. Besides, his reforms became enmeshed in Indian intransigence, shaped by their sense of historic hurt at the hands of King Sugar and aggravated by the unrelenting political crusade of Cheddi Jagan. They were being strangled, too, by the violent racial politics of British Guiana at the end of Empire. Sugar could not even escape the Cold War: President Kennedy, obsessed with the spread of communism in the Hemisphere, through Castroism, and humiliated by the Bay of Pigs fiasco of April 1961, demanded that the British get rid of Jagan, an admirer of Fidel Castro. Through it all, Jagan remained implacable to the reformism of Campbell's Booker, unwavering, too, in his certainty that communism was the key to human perfectibility and that the Soviet Union was paving the way to utopia. No one could really sweeten 'bitter sugar', no reform, however effective, was acceptable; no one could divert Cheddi from his Marxist calling.

However, as Canadian economists, Litvak and Maule, argue 'Guyanisation' was not a utopian conception to placate Guyanese nationalists; it was integral to Booker's programme, under Campbell and beyond:

> By the 1950s foreign companies were expected to begin 'Guyanising' their management staff. Such positions within Booker's companies required high technical and managerial skills. To assist in implementing this programme Booker established a training centre in Guyana, organised management courses and awarded scholarships. Booker vigorously executed this policy, but more important, 'Guyanisation' in Booker included top staff positions, from chairmen and chief executives on down. It is largely because of its success that Booker has been able to display sensitivity to Guyanese aspirations. Booker has also served as a focal point in enlarging the pool of technical and administrative skills available in Guyana, since only a portion of the participants in the management courses returned to Booker. A result has been a cross-fertilisation of former employees of Booker in numerous responsible positions within the Guyanese public and private sectors. [24]

But as Searwar contended, in the absence of an authentic Guyanese identity beyond the passions of its ethnic components, even Guianisation became enmeshed in the bedevilling racial proclivity of the Guyanese mind. Booker had reflected on this problem and opted for a long-term solution:

> What does Guianisation mean to Guianese? To an Indian it may mean the employment of more Indians in senior posts; to an African it may mean the employment of more Africans in senior posts, and so on for Chinese, Portuguese and each of the minority groups living in British Guiana.... The Booker answer to this problem is to put the accent on qualification for the job, and to leave it to time and nationhood — and education — to produce a Guyanese who could feel his national aspirations fulfilled in the person of any other person born in British Guiana who accepts British Guiana as his motherland.[25]

They should have asked, though: 'Do Guyanese know how to wait?' But Booker were not complacent about the race issue. They noted, in November 1960, that several of their key personnel would be participating shortly in a symposium at Plantation Albion on 'Race Relations in a World Context with Special Reference to British Guiana'. They expressed the optimistic view that current 'racial stridency' was the 'birth-cry of nationalism', and that it would wane with the responsibility of nationhood. But, ominously, they also echoed the 'more widely held opinion that British Guiana is moving towards a disintegration of the social harmony for which we have long been noted'. They observed: 'While we are not alarmist nor pessimistic about race relations in British Guiana, we accept that there is a problem and that it needs to be faced. The fact that the challenge is being taken up with ready assistance from Booker executives, is another illustration of how to interpret our motto of service to the community.'[26]

Endnotes

1. *FBI Review*, January 1960.
2. Ibid.
3. Diane McTurk, *The Oldest Industry: Aspects of Sugar in Guyana* (Georgetown: SPA, 1966), 12.
4. Clive Y. Thomas, *Plantation, Peasants, and the State: A Study of the Mode of Sugar Production in Guyana* (Los Angeles: Centre for Afro-American Studies, UCLA, 1984), 79.
5. See note 3.
6. *Booker News*, January 6, 1957.
7. The Chairman's Statement, 1958, p. 47.
8. *Booker News*, June 19, 1959.
9. Ibid., September 11, 1959.
10. Ibid., August 12, 1960.
11. Ibid., September 25, 1959.
12. Booker Bros, McConnell and Co, Ltd, 'The Group Chairman's Visit to British Guiana and the West Indies, January-March 1960', confidential, (mimeo.), p. 17. This was delivered to the Booker Board and other senior executives in London on March 22, 1960.
13. *Booker News*, [Leader], March 24, 1961.
14. 'Report of a Commission of Inquiry into the Sugar Industry of Guyana', (G.L.B. Persaud, chairman), (mimeo.), 1968, pp. 19-20.
15. See note 4.
16. Script of a Broadcast Talk Given by Jock Campbell over Radio Demerara [Georgetown], on March 4, 1956, Appendix, Booker Bros, McConnell and Co, Ltd, *Report of the Directors and Statement of Accounts, 1955*.
17. M. Shahabuddeen, *From Plantocracy to Nationalisation: A Profile of Sugar in Guyana* (Georgetown: University of Guyana, 1983), 276 [L.F.S. Burnham, February 22, 1976], p. 279 [Gavin Kennard, Minister of Agriculture, March 29, 1976]; see also note 4 [pp. 160-1].
18. See note 16.
19. Antony Tasker, 'The Manager and Our Image', (mimeo), restricted, January 28, 1965.
20. Lloyd Searwar, 'Bookers Guiana: A Study in the Development of an Image and the Implications for Independence', (mimeo.), n.d. [1960], p. 3.
21. Ibid., 2.
22. Ibid., 7.
23. *Thunder*, August 25, 1962.
24. Isaiah A. Litvak and Christopher J. Maule, 'Foreign Corporate Social Responsibility in Less Developed Economies', *Journal of World Trade Law* 9, no. 2 (1975): 128.
25. *Booker News*, [Leader], October 7, 1960.
26. Ibid., [Leader], November 18, 1960.

Part 8

Jagan, Campbell and the Politics of Sugar in the Context of the Cold War, 1960-1964

Chapter Thirty-One

KENNEDY'S OBSESSION: JAGAN, CASTRO AND THE DECOLONISATION OF BRITISH GUIANA, 1960–63

Cheddi Jagan's problems — largely of his own making — began shortly after the 1960 Constitutional Conference in London. In November 1958 Under-secretary of State for the Colonies, John Profumo, had told the House of Commons that since the elections of 1957 the government of Jagan, 'despite their dissatisfaction with present constitutional arrangements, have been co-operating fully with the Governor in the general administration of the colony'.[1] During the elections the PPP had spoken of their interest in expanding trade with Brazil and Venezuela, while fostering foreign investment:

> The party feels that in our present stage of development there is no need to nationalise private industries. Like the Governments of India and Ghana we reserve the right to nationalise and will pay just and adequate compensation. We feel that the development of industries, particularly in the fields of mining and hydro-electricity should be the responsibility of Government. To this end we advocate the establishment of these industries either completely by Government or jointly with private enterprise.... Foreign capital for the development of the real interests of the colony will be encouraged.[2]

But buoyed by the rise of Fidel Castro in Cuba, in early 1959, Jagan was emboldened into repudiating his comparatively moderate posture of 1957–58 ('responsible', as the British saw it); he now had regional vindication of the inevitability of communism, indeed, its imminent realisation. In spite of virulent American anti-Castro sentiments, twice in 1960 he visited Cuba. In September 1960 he was interviewed by the Cuban newspaper, *Revolucion*, and he was proud to proclaim that 'the only Government in Latin America which was openly supporting the Cuban Revolution is ours'. Cheddi observed that Suez (1956) was a 'turning point in the history of Imperialism which is now on the defensive and is losing more and more positions every day. The process will grow not in arithmetic, but in geometric progression'. He predicted that socialism — the communist utopia — would 'emerge triumphant', as capitalism was 'becoming a moribund system'. Jagan was ecstatic about the Cuban Revolution; it was the new beacon for his own country: a home-grown October Revolution:

> I completely support the Revolutionary Government of Cuba....
> [It] has the support of most of the Cuban people. I have no doubt
> the revolution will achieve all its objectives. Any revolutionary
> movement such as this which is tending towards social and
> economic emancipation will obviously have enemies both inside
> and outside the country, but if we take into account the times in
> which we are living, the speed with which the progressive forces
> of the world are advancing, and the great support of the majority
> of the Cuban people I have no doubts about the Cuban Revolution.[3]

He concluded with a eulogy on the leader of the Revolution, repeating virtually what he had said some weeks before in British Guiana: 'Fidel Castro is not only the liberator of the American continent but also the liberator of this century.'[4]

Cheddi Jagan had taken his country into the Cold War. The Americans would now see him as an enemy, and an independent Guyana as a potential beachhead for communism in Latin America. As will be seen in the next chapter, Jock Campbell's reforms would be relegated to a footnote as racial violence — fomented by Burnham and D'Aguiar (1962-63) and aided and abetted by the United States, to delay independence; and by Jagan (1964), in despair of losing power — ravaged the colony between 1962 and 1964. Booker necessarily would be at the centre of the cauldron, but Campbell, virtually to the end, gave moral support to Jagan while, in vain, seeking to caution him about the dangers of becoming embroiled in the Cold War. Neither reform nor revolution, but racial violence, was what Guyana was experiencing on the 'threshold' of independence.

Fatal Attraction: Cheddi Jagan and his hero, Fidel Castro, Havana, 1961

The crusade against Jagan started shortly after his return to British Guiana from Cuba, in September 1960, his second visit in less than six months. Since his victory in 1957 the British, as reflected in Macleod's granting of internal self-government to Jagan in March 1960, were prepared to give him the benefit of the doubt about his communism. Not so the Americans: they objected as early as September 6, 1960 to Jagan's acceptance of a loan from Cuba. This loan of $5 million at 2 per cent was apparently procured from Russia at 2½ per cent! It was to be repaid with timber, over ten years. The loan evoked immediate suspicion, at the State Department, of Cuban motives. The American Embassy in London promptly informed the Colonial Office of their concerns: they were unequivocal that 'the Cuban offer to Jagan presaged a Russian campaign for the economic and cultural penetration of Latin America'. The State Department hoped that the British would not 'fall for this Russian attempt to use Cuba as a spring-board for the subversion of British Guiana and, in its turn, the use of this British colony for subversion elsewhere'. The Colonial Office, in keeping with the liberal outlook of the Secretary of State for the Colonies, Iain Macleod, were not persuaded by this drastic interpretation of the situation and minuted confidentially: 'This one sounded like a threat of heavier artillery in the background', as they tried to temper American anxieties with the sober submission that 'what Jagan seemed to want most was a source — any source — of cheap loans to develop British Guiana'. They noted that while the Americans were prepared to cut off all future aid to Jagan if he accepted the Cuban loan, they were not prepared to make a compensatory offer to 'buy over' Jagan: '[T]he US Government as a matter of policy has decided that it will in no circumstances be jockeyed into pre-emptive aid programmes. There could, therefore, be no question of the US Government attempting to "top" the Cuban offer.'[5]

Ominous for Cheddi Jagan, the American official at the London Embassy had concluded his 'recital', as the Colonial Office noted sarcastically, with the suggestion that they should collaborate on the Jagan–Castro affair: '[T]he Department of State were anxious to co-ordinate as closely as possible with us in developing a line of policy towards this incident that would avoid "presenting an anti-colonial issue" to Castro — or to Jagan.' The British were not too enamoured of American passion over Jagan's communism and argued that they did not want to 'limit... [their] chances of proceeding by persuasion', adding that if they were 'left solely with the use of constraints under the present Constitution, there was no knowing where this situation may lead in terms of "anti-colonial issues"'.[6] The Americans, however, were relentless: the same US Embassy official who had 'recited' to the Colonial Office on September 6, 1960 returned there on September 13, having received a further communication on Jagan from the State Department. They now raised a crucial point, relating to the anticipated independence of British Guiana as adumbrated at the 1960 Constitutional Conference. Independence was there for Jagan to take, consequently the Americans were worried about 'the presence of communist technicians in British Guiana', who they thought had a 'dual role', alluding to subversive activities. They feared also that Jagan would 'use the Cuban [loan] offer to blackmail the UK and the USA'. Already, in September 1960, the State Department were urging the British 'to reconsider the independence date' for the colony — to delay it.[7]

This growing American apprehension of Jagan's communism, however, did not temper him into caution, to affect a more pragmatic stance. Such was not the nature of the man, as the Governor of British Guiana, Sir Ralph Grey, who understood his instincts more than most, observed in September 1960, when the controversy over the Cuban loan was brewing. He tried to convey to the Colonial Office something of Jagan's mind:

> Throughout a long conversation on this and other topics I deliberately avoided expressing any opinion on the merits of the various schemes Dr. Jagan explained to me. I have learnt that with him the first necessity is to try and unravel from the tangled skein of all he says just what is fact and what is fantasy. He is an eternal planner but... very shy of the moment of decision. He loves concerting plans with anyone and everyone that he thinks is sympathetic and he thinks nothing of dropping the whole of an elaborate scheme to which others have devoted much serious thought if something comes along that appeals to him more. I, therefore, contented myself with asking what would be the mechanics of this Cuban affair. [8]

Their own reservations notwithstanding, the British continued to play by the rules, frequently giving Jagan space, virtually imploring him, to try to redeem himself in the eyes of the unrelenting Americans, who had the power and the will to destroy him. As noted above, independence was there for him to take, as the Foreign Office reminded Secretary of State, Iain Macleod, in a brief prepared for him before his meeting with the US Ambassador in London, on September 18, 1960:

> There is a good deal of sense in the State Department's fears. Castro may well regard Dr. Jagan as a useful agent for the promotion of revolutionary ideas throughout the area. Dr. Jagan is a left-wing extremist.... He has come out openly in support of Castro and the Cuban Revolution. There is no strong unified opposition in British Guiana to his party and it is likely he will be in power for some time. Her Majesty's Government has agreed, if the British Guiana legislature so wish, to hold another conference to discuss independence within a year or two of 1961 [when elections under the new constitution were due]. [9]

They noted that Jagan had criticised the size of the five-year development plan, 1960–64 (the Berrill Plan), in the order of £23 million. They, however, thought that the colony could not bear a heavier debt burden and that British aid had 'not been ungenerous'. The funding was ascertained as follows: £4.6 million grant from the UK through Colonial Development and Welfare Grants and possible Exchequer loans up to £8 million. It was anticipated that the rest would come from the small revenue surplus of the colony, local loans, the Development Loan Funds, the World Bank and other international agencies.

While not condoning the proposed Cuban loan to Jagan, they could not see a way to reject it unless they were able to demonstrate that 'some harmful strings were attached to it', or if they could provide 'an equally attractive alternative'. The latter was not likely as neither the UK nor the US were prepared to 'outbid the Cuban offer'. The Secretary of State for the Colonies was advised to inform the Americans that while they realised 'the force of objections to the [Cuban] loan', they could see no way of rejecting it. They observed:

> Dr. Jagan's position is extremely strong. If HMG agree to the loan, he will gain credit locally. If not, HMG will incur considerable political odium, which will not be confined to B.G., and Dr. Jagan's anti-colonial cause will receive a boost. He might even go ahead and sign a loan agreement unconstitutionally, thus provoking us to suspend the Constitution once again.[10]

By October 1960 American 'anxieties' were still not assuaged by this latest British response to the Cuban loan but, ominously for Jagan, the spectre of suspension was suggested. The Colonial Office repeated its position to the American Embassy in London, that they would 'shed no tears if the whole thing came to nothing', but that it would be difficult for them to veto it, if it was clear that the loan 'contained solid advantage and no discernible economic or other real danger for British Guiana'. For the Americans, however, the mere fact that Jagan saw Castro as the greatest liberator of the century made him an enemy. Towards the end of 1960 they were, in fact, considering the possibility of refusing him a visa to the United States. The Colonial Office did not see any merit in this and told the Americans so: '[I]t would be a great mistake.... [A]ny advantage which the Americans might think that they would obtain by so doing would be less than the damage which would flow from such a course'. They also reminded them that Jagan was likely to lead the next government under the new Constitution effective from 1961, and the Americans 'at once saw the implications of that'.[11]

This probably explains why the Sate Department met with Jagan in mid-November 1960 for talks on technical assistance, although he had gone to New York on a speaking engagement with *National Guardian*, a pro-communist newspaper which supported the Cuban Revolution. This had elicited a portentous reflection from the Colonial Office: 'Perhaps this is an indication that sweet reason has prevailed in the State Department — or is it a temporary gesture pending the installation of the new Administration [Kennedy's in January 1961]?'[12] Indeed, as the British Embassy in Washington soon informed Governor Ralph Grey, American anxieties were far from being assuaged: 'The State Department delivered itself of no *obiter dictum* about Castro or about those who dealt with him, though privately they were relieved to know that Jagan was returning... [home via] Trinidad and so, unless he changed his booking subsequently, is not proposing to call in at Havana.'[13] The mould was already set: Jagan's perceived communism, like Castro's, would be at the heart of Kennedy's foreign policy for those thousand days of his Presidency.

In January 1961, at the time of Kennedy's inauguration, the British Embassy in Washington informed the Colonial Office that the Cuban loan 'remains a cause of great apprehension' to the State Department. They were perturbed that nothing had emerged to strangle it: '[T]hey are hopeful that we will succeed somehow in ensuring that it finally runs into the ground; they will be interested in almost a blow by blow commentary.'[14]

In February 1961 Adam Foster of the State Department paid a visit to British Guiana to ascertain the character of the Jagan administration. What he told a senior Colonial Office official was most deceptive, given that the plan to invade Cuba (Bay of Pigs, April 1961) was probably at an advanced stage — but it did underline the centrality of the question to the new administration. Foster said that there was a possibility that President Kennedy would raise the future of British Guiana with the British Prime Minister because of the Cuban issue. They felt that Castro was losing support, with pockets of resistance in Cuba and growing disaffection with him in Latin America. He reportedly argued:

> In these circumstances the best policy for the US is to sit back as far as it can, even to the extent of appearing passive in the face of attacks on US business interests, in the belief that the tide will turn against Castro. It is an important part of this process that he should not be able to add to his reputation by any sort of diplomatic coup. One such coup would be if British Guiana appeared to be turning to Cuba and looking to Castro for inspiration and leadership.... He referred to the publicity which had been given to Jagan's visit to Havana some months ago and to the Cuban loan proposals.[15]

It is remarkable that the British consistently sought to deflate American passion on the matter, even seeking to minimise or detract from Jagan's Marxist obsessions. Governor Grey, for instance, had tried, in his discussions with Foster in February 1961, to get to the source of America's fears of 'exportable Castroism', while seeking to rebut their contention that this was a possibility in British Guiana:

> There are no large landlords (other than the two sugar companies) to be dispossessed by landless peasants; the small Indian landholder aspires to be a large Indian land owner; and it seemed far-fetched that during the next few years Jagan could or would expropriate the sugar companies, much less the Demerara Bauxite Company. One of British Guiana's tragedies ... was that it did not lead anywhere. Although it had long frontiers with Venezuela and Brazil, communications were almost non-existent and the parts with which it marched were among the wilder parts of those countries. This sad fact was at least this much of consolation that it made this country unattractive to Castroism or Sino-Soviet Communism as [a] jumping off place for Latin American adventures.[16]

Grey had therefore counselled that the United States 'refrain from treating Jagan as a villain', as, admittedly, the State Department were 'disposed' to. He added that while he did not wish them to compete with the USSR in providing aid, he hoped they would help to bring the country to 'greater economic stability'.

As late as April 1961, around the time of the Bay of Pigs fiasco, the British were still inclined to be relatively liberal in their attitude to Jagan's passion for seeking trade links and loans from the Eastern Bloc countries and Cuba. While noting his 'excessive admiration for Castro', the Colonial Office stated that they were trying to 'educate' him and his ministers 'away from their earlier irresponsibility and to prepare them for internal self-government'. They had no doubts that Jagan would win the elections in August 1961; he would then have the power to negotiate and conclude trade agreements with other countries. The British position was stated thus:

> It is not our intention to take a dog-in-the-manger attitude over any commercial negotiations they wish to undertake with Eastern Bloc countries, particularly as it is already HMG's general policy to encourage the liberalisation of trade, but we do intend, for so long as we retain any responsibility of the colony, to stand firm against anything inimical to HMG's foreign policy or relations with other countries ... and to veto anything which results in British Guiana becoming enmeshed in undesirable political strings.[17]

The Colonial Office did not take as remotely sanguine a view of Jagan's trading with Castro as the United States did. In fact, they were inclined to make a distinction between trade with Cuba, on one hand, and more powerful communist countries, especially Russia, on the other: '[W]e do not think there is the same danger in a commercial deal between Cuba and British Guiana, of the latter becoming politically tied up in a way we could not accept.' They concluded that control of the colony's trade links would only last another three, possibly two, years, as presented in a formula at the 1960 Constitutional Conference, presided over by Iain Macleod.[18]

This was anathema to the United States, especially after the failure of the Bay of Pigs invasion in April 1961. Kennedy was obsessed already with any manifestation of communism in the Hemisphere: little British Guiana was soon to acquire disproportionate notoriety in US–UK relations. This was communicated to Secretary of State for the Colonies, Iain Macleod, by the President, in the White House in early 1961. As Nigel Fisher, Under-Secretary of State for the Colonies, recalls:

President Kennedy told Macleod of his anxieties during a long talk in the Oval Room of the White House. He said he understood our policy but he hoped we would not move too quickly towards independence. Macleod replied: 'Do I understand, Mr. President, that you want us to decolonise as fast as possible all over the world except on your own door-step?' President Kennedy laughed and said: 'Well, that's probably just about it'. Macleod answered that he appreciated the President's point if view, but that our policy to bring Guiana to independence would continue. The American attitude did not slow down his own approach, although the serious racial strife between the African and Indian communities in the colony a year or two later, and the difficulty of getting an agreement on an Independence Constitution between Cheddi Jagan and Forbes Burnham, did impose an inevitable delay.[19]

Fisher observed that Macleod was 'never afraid to use power', and that he had 'the courage to take controversial decisions against official advice'. Jagan could not appreciate this, for in 1960 although Macleod had granted him internal self-government (with, in principle, independence after the next elections), and responsibility for internal security and the police, he proceeded to diminish the advance. He said he was 'totally dissatisfied' with the outcome, and accused the Colonial Office of 'wielding the big stick': 'an unsatisfactory formula for independence had been forced down the throats of the delegation'. He wanted immediate independence. He announced that he would take his fight to the UN, whence he was going to Cuba. Such was the lack of proportion, the paucity of statesmanship in the man; he later threatened to resign from the government, so he could be free 'to carry on the struggle, to increase the tempo both at home and abroad'. He added, tactlessly, that Fidel Castro had told him that he was prepared to help British Guiana, 'in keeping with his policy for the liberation of the hemisphere'.[20]

Dazzled by Castroism, his 'unconquerable naiveté' got out of control. He could not see that independence was a gift awaiting collection: no 'struggle' was needed to claim independence from the 'imperialists'. But Cheddi would court ideological confrontation when none was required — continually asserting his anti-imperialism, to establish that he was not a lackey like the social democrats, the Fabian socialists in the region. Reflecting the outlook of Jock Campbell (he was its President), the *Chronicle of the West India Committee* had cautioned Jagan, after the 1960 Conference, to show maturity:

> It is no exaggeration to say that all this has distressed those who have the good of British Guiana at heart ... the real cause for concern now is the light that Dr. Jagan's statements shed on his own willingness to undertake increased responsibilities and to promote British Guiana in Britain and elsewhere.... He knows perfectly well that those with large investments in ... [the colony] are as anxious as he is to see a prosperous and dynamic country governing itself. Yet despite these favourable conditions, some people are beginning to wonder if Dr. Jagan is getting a trifle apprehensive about having complete responsibility for the future of his country. Does he think it easier to travel than to arrive?[21]

The journal underlined that independence was there for the take; that was hardly an issue; the question was the calibre of leadership in the pursuit of development:

> Now that independence in 1963 has been pencilled in on the timetable, the character of the country's political leadership assumes a new importance; and the only way by which it can be judged will be by the actions taken between now and 1963. For the real challenge is not wresting independence from a British Government which already accepts it as a working principle .... The real challenge is the job of establishing sufficient confidence in the outside world that an independent British Guiana is a good place to go to and put money in.[22]

It would take monumental ineptitude to squander what Jagan had achieved by 1960; yet he succeeded in doing so. His adulation of Castro compounded his tactical weaknesses, as he walked into the

Cold War, daring to take on the Americans. This gave ammunition to his arch enemy, L.F.S. Burnham, the African leader of the People's National Congress (PNC), and it led, too, to the emergence, in late 1960, of the rabidly anti-communist crusader, the Portuguese entrepreneur and leader, Peter D'Aguiar of the United Force (UF). He brought with him the anti-communist passion of the Catholic church and the apprehension of the mercantile community. Burnham and D'Aguiar were to become allies of the United States as the Cold War engulfed this little sugar colony towards the end of 1961.

However, as will be seen in the next chapter, there was still a fount of goodwill for Jagan coming from Jock Campbell; and although the Americans had grave reservations about him, the British were still prepared to coach him to comprehend how perilous was the environment he had drifted into, propelled by his pro-Castro revolutionary euphoria. The Governor, Sir Ralph Grey, was rather philosophical at the opening of the Constitutional Conference in London in March 1960, alluding to the visionary strand in local politics: 'British Guiana ... is a country of considerable romance. Romance gathers about mundane things. Perhaps ... sometimes it softens the harsh outlines of facts that might better be seen in the raw.' [23] Cheddi's irrepressible Marxist instincts, his 'unpracticality', as Campbell often put it, precluded him from ever seeing things in the raw: *realpolitik*. That was the foundation of the tragedy that would unfold after the general elections which he won in August 1961, having defeated Burnham and D'Aguiar.

Maurice St. Pierre notes that the American Secretary of State, Dean Rusk, on August 26, 1961, a few days after the elections, had informed the British Foreign Secretary, Lord Home, that they considered the results 'unpalatable' and had suggested that their representatives meet to discuss 'the covert side'. On August 30, President Kennedy's special assistant, the eminent Harvard historian, Professor Arthur Schlesinger, had recommended to him a mixture of aid and covert work in British Guiana, in order to destroy the communists. St. Pierre notes, however, that on September 4, 1961 American gestures towards Jagan suggested a distinctly conciliatory chord:

[P]resumably in view of Rusk's unhappiness with the 'unattractiveness of the available alternatives', the Americans decided 'to make a college try to tie Jagan to the West', and to make 'a wholehearted across-the-board effort' to work with the new Jagan Government. The decision was based partly on Burnham's inept showing during the 1961 election campaign ... [and] the dearth of effective political leadership apart from Jagan and the recognition that coldness towards him and withholding aid could only result in his 'gravitation towards the Soviet-Castro bloc'.[24]

In fact, a few days after the elections Jagan had approached the American Consul-General in British Guiana, Everett Melby, to 'explore the possibility of meeting with the President or people at the top'. Governor Grey thought that he genuinely wanted 'to get on working terms with the US Administration'.[25] With the visit to Washington approved, he remarked on how prejudicial the reporting on Jagan had been in the US press, with communism clouding out any rational assessment of the country: 'It is fascinating to see how details, trifling in themselves, are twisted from the truth .... Always, of course, such twists are against Jagan ....' Grey met Jagan on September 23, 1961 and counselled him against 'acts or words likely to bring unfavourable publicity'. He tried desperately to prepare him to meet the Americans as a statesman worthy of respect. He advised him to stay in a 'reputable hotel' and not with Mr Felix Cummings, his somewhat unkempt representative-of-sorts in New York, to go up-market a bit. Knowing that Kennedy was keen to scrutinise his ideological credentials, he cautioned Jagan to be tactful: 'If he wanted to be treated by the US Administration as a person of consequence, he must behave like one. He made some demurring noise about being himself — I sympathised and said that it was not pleasant to have to be less than sincere in all one's dealings — but ... the pursuit of Absolute Truth is remarkably difficult and must in a man of affairs occasionally yield to expediency.' [26]

It was all water on a duck's back! This belated lesson in diplomacy could not reach Cheddi. On October 24, 1961, for instance, in an address in Washington to the National Press Club, with President Kennedy seeking assiduously to measure the man, Jagan could not conceal his fundamentally Marxist formulations, his meandering notwithstanding. As this speech was seminal in Kennedy's assessment of Cheddi in the context of the President's obsessive anti-Castro, Cold War crusade after his Bay of Pigs fiasco of that year, several excerpts are cited below:

> I am a passionate anti-colonialist. I, like your forefathers, believe that colonialism is wicked. I believe so strongly that colonialism is utterly wrong that I would gladly accept any help from whatever quarter to help me in my fight against it.... British Guiana today in fact represents the typical pattern of a colonial economy. It is little more than a raw material base and a market for industrial products with the drain of wealth abroad which perforce results in stagnation and poverty. I am dedicated to the task of changing this pattern.... Second only to my passion for the independence of my people is... dedication to their economic advancement, so that their life may be more abundant. By this I mean that I am in favour of the workers reaping the full fruits of their labour through public ownership of the means of production, distribution and exchange. This will ensure a fairer distribution of a country's wealth than any other system. But I also have to recognise things as they are. While I reserve our right, as any sovereign state does, to nationalise whatever industry we think should be nationalised in the public interest we have explicitly stated that we have no intention of nationalising the existing sugar and bauxite companies. These companies today dominate our economy, but British Guiana is still largely under-developed. We are resolved to diversify our economy and to industrialise it rapidly so that as we launch new enterprises the proportion of our national income produced by expatriate enterprise becomes smaller and their present command of our economic life weakened. If on the other hand it ever becomes necessary to nationalise any industries, fair and adequate compensation would be paid. In carrying out our programme of industrialisation the state will play an active and direct part .... *I believe ... that the economic theories of scientific socialism [Marxism] hold out the promise of a dynamic social discipline which can transform an underdeveloped country into a developed one in a far shorter time than any other system.* We may

differ from you in the way we organise our economic life. You have as your dominant philosophy private enterprise but let us not forget that your development took place in a different political historical epoch [emphasis added].[27]

Indeed, Jagan was unique among politicians in the Third World; his romantic vision was not tempered by power. So uncritically did he absorb his Marxism, 'scientific socialism', as the instrument of political and economic liberation, so total his immersion in the received doctrine, that he drifted, unconsciously, straight into the Cold War. After the rise of Fidel, he had no doubts that the communist utopia was achievable in the region: with little ammunition, therefore, he would seek to fight 'American Imperialism'; British colonialism, too, although the latter was on the verge of termination. His party's organ, *Thunder*, founded in 1950, was a Marxist tract tirelessly extolling the beauty of life in the Eastern bloc; so, too, was *Mirror*, the party's other paper, founded in 1962.

On October 15, 1961 with President Kennedy watching the programme, he told Laurence E. Spivak, the celebrated moderator of 'Meet the Press', of his political beliefs: Cheddi's capacity for tripping on his own banana peel was astounding. Thomas J. Spinner observes: '[T]hough he enjoys the question ... [his] instinct for self-destruction erupts when he is asked about his political creed. Able to escape when he generalises, he cannot resist the urge to verbalise and define. This verbosity leads to lengthy discussions about communism, Marxism and Leninism.'[28] Responding to Spivak's question whether there really was freedom in the Soviet Union and China he ensnared himself in the web Kennedy had spun for him:

All I can say — I haven't been to China, I haven't been to Russia, but the experts who have been there who have said — for instance, you have this chap who is a writer on this question, an expert, apparently, who writes for the London *Observer*, I can't recall his name right now, but he has said in his latest book that life in the Soviet Union is growing day by day better and better. The standards of living are improving, and as such, we are concerned. We want to know how this is done.[29]

He was then lured ignominiously towards a definition of his creed, which only confirmed, as far as Kennedy was concerned, that an independent British Guiana under Jagan would herald the expansion of communism in South America:

> [I] would like to say from what I have read from the text books, socialism means, or the slogan under socialism is, from each according to his ability, to each according to his labour, the work that he gives. Under communism as under the early Christian set-up, all persons were supposed to share equally, and so I see the communists say, in that period to come, there will be distribution according to needs. Each one will contribute according to his ability, and from my point of view this is good. This is a good thing that all persons should get from society what they need, regardless of whether he is a cripple or whether he is able to produce more or less.[30]

As Lloyd Searwar, Jagan's information officer, who accompanied him to America, recalls: 'Spivak shafted him. That was a mistake. Sir Hugh Foot, Head of the British Mission at the U.N., had cautioned me against it: they rather liked Cheddi and hated Burnham's guts. I should never have allowed Cheddi to go on that programme; but I thought that it would give him a visibility which would have constrained Kennedy. It was a disaster.'[31] Kennedy's fears were not assuaged, so that when he met Jagan on October 25, 1961 he was even more resolved to locate the ideological underpinning of Jagan's politics. As noted above, in the aftermath of the Bay of Pigs fiasco, the President was obsessed with the spread of communism in Latin America. He believed that his re-election could be determined by this issue. Therefore, this little colony of 600,000 people had assumed geopolitical significance in Kennedy's hemispheric thinking out of all proportion to its size or economic significance. Until then, the Americans had, in spite of grave reservations, concurred with the British assessment that there was no readily identifiable alternative to Cheddi Jagan.

Maurice St. Pierre argues that considerable indecision then crept into the Administration's estimate of Jagan. He notes that a document dated October 17, 1961 had recommended a harder line towards Jagan on the question of independence, if he were seen to be going the way of Castro. It is not possible to ascertain whether this was prompted by his less than satisfactory performance on 'Meet the Press'. However, in the short run, the President hoped to 'gauge the character and turn of Jagan's mind and exert influence on it'.[32] There was, therefore, some slight hope, as far as the Americans were concerned, that Jagan could be rescued from the communist proclivities that he had demonstrated. It was certainly his last chance to redeem himself.

This, then, was the context in which John Hennings, the colonial attache at the British Embassy in Washington, sought to prepare Jagan for his meeting with Kennedy on October 25, 1961. Four days before, Hennings had advised him to improve on the impression he had created so far on the trip, and proceeded to explain why Kennedy was giving inordinate attention to him:

> I told him that he now had while he was in Washington the opportunity to make a forthright and unambiguous statement of his political credo, which would sweep away these equivocations.... I told him that he was an intensely controversial figure in this country, and he might wonder why America should appear to be so excited about such a small country as his. I said that Americans were not really interested in British Guiana as such; they were interested in it as a symbol [of communism]. Americans by and large were a very simple people: they saw things as broad issues, and they believed in action to right wrongs; they believed, too, that America had the power, or should have the power, to put matters right. They were therefore perplexed by the complex and threatening world scene [a perceived communist threat]; they were exasperated that there were not quick answers to these problems; they were frustrated by not being the first nation to put a man into space which their belief in the superiority of their system of economic organisation suggested to them to be right and proper. [33]

He told Jagan that the President was a liberal but was facing a small but vocal conservative element in his country, people who were especially perturbed by what they considered weak leadership against the communist enemy. Hennings did not say that this was exacerbated by the Bay of Pigs disaster, but he noted, perceptively, that such people were looking for a soft spot where a lesson could be taught to the enemy and credibility restored to the American way: '[T]hey were yearning for some small issue on which swift and firm action could be taken. British Guiana seemed to them such an issue — small, isolated and easy, if only the leaders of the country were brave enough to take the plunge.'

The British obviously understood how crucial this meeting with Kennedy was for Jagan, and the fact that they put so much effort in trying to tutor him into a projection of statesmanship, should disabuse us of the popular notion that they were simply pawns in American hands, and that their stance, since the suspension of 1953, was one of unwavering hostility to Cheddi. In fact, Hennings even tried to explain to him that his vocabulary — words and their American connotation — must be scrupulously considered if he were to rescue his reputation. He provided examples:

A Communist, for example, was not a man who believed in scientific socialism as a method of economic organisation. When Mr. Spivak [on 'Meet-the-Press'] asked him whether he was a Communist, he meant was he a lackey of Moscow, Peking or Havana. It was therefore no use saying he was a socialist, rather than a Communist, because Communists also called themselves socialists, and the strongest believers in free enterprise in this country regarded any extension of Government endeavour as creeping socialism, which would lead inevitably to Communism. It was no good either saying he was a democrat, because Communists called themselves that as well.... To Americans generally, a Communist was the dedicated agent of an international conspiracy, controlled by Moscow and Peking, in the interests of the new Communist imperialism.[34]

Hennings concluded with the observation that Americans could not comprehend the attraction of Marxist 'economic doctrines' in poor countries, nor the appeal of Cuba: 'Thinking Americans recognised ... [the] disequilibria and instabilities in Latin America; they recognised the Cuban Revolution was due to them, but they felt that Castro has betrayed that revolution. I warned him against trying to score runs for Castro; he had enough troubles of his own and should concentrate on the interests of British Guiana.' He was really imploring Jagan to desist from any complex ideological discourse with the President. His appearance on 'Meet-the-Press' had already made a poor impression on Kennedy. Professor Schlesinger, the special assistant to the President, recalls that he had 'resolutely declined to say anything critical of the Soviet Union'. He adds: 'This appearance instantly diminished the enthusiasm for helping his Government. The President who caught the last half of the show, called for a re-examination of all aspects of the problem, saying he wanted no commitments made until he had seen Jagan himself.' [35]

Jagan's future was now in the hands of President Kennedy, who was determined 'to draw out his visitor's political ideas'. Cheddi did nothing to redeem himself. In fact, he would not have comprehended the thrust of the British counsel to him, prior to the meeting with the President. He was quickly lured into an ideological morass which convinced Kennedy that they had to find an alternative in British Guiana; and that he had to pressure the British, as he had sought to do with Iain Macleod, to renege on their pledge to grant independence to the colony under a communist. Schlesinger was present at a part of the meeting of Kennedy and Jagan at the White House on October 25, 1961. He thought that Jagan, though 'personable and fluent ... [was] endowed, it seemed to those of us present, with an unconquerable romanticism or naivete'. Indeed, during his meeting with Hennings on October 21, he had admitted that 'saying too much was a besetting sin of his'. He did not seek to correct this; in fact, he later celebrated his tactless performance in his memoirs, grandiloquently titled, *The West on Trial*, published in London in 1966, about 18 months after Kennedy's machinations had secured his demise:

> I recall, on this question of underdevelopment, my hour and a half interview with the late President Kennedy in November [sic], 1961 ... and my conversations with some of his 'Harvard brains trust' aides [Schlesinger and George Ball, for instance]. I gathered the impression that they were realists who understood the problems confronting them and who as good defenders of the faith [capitalism] recognised the necessity for change to prevent a 'powder keg' from exploding.[36]

Jagan elaborates on his exchange with the President — he would have us see it as something of a conquest, David and Goliath:

> Kennedy and his aides attacked me on the grounds of our trade with Cuba and associations with socialist countries [the Eastern bloc]. I took the counter-offensive and attacked them for preventing countries like British Guiana from making an economic break-through. I referred to their opposition to non-alignment as evidenced by their overthrow of the government of President Janio Quadros of Brazil, and pointed out that the increasing difficulties which faced poor countries ... could only be overcome by a planned, balanced industrial-agricultural economy and free trade with all countries. I referred to our own position and asked Kennedy point-blank: 'What would you do, were you in our position?' This philosophy of the West, I argued, could not help the underdeveloped countries. I cited our negotiations with the Cuban Government which not only bought our rice at prices favourable to us, but was prepared to lend us initially $5 million (US) for a wood-pulp project, and the steel, cement and generators for a $32 million (BG) hydroelectric plant. The $5 million was to be a soft loan at 2 per cent interest to be paid for in wood pulp produced locally .... I was told there were dangers in this kind of arrangement. [37]

Fatal Meeting: President Kennedy and Cheddi,
the White House, October 25, 1961.

Jagan's certainties were inexhaustible; one could not write a script for him, neither was he amenable to counsel. He proceeded to put the President in his place, as he saw it:

> I accused the US Government of overthrowing Quadros because he was pursuing a path of non-alignment in attempting to solve his economic problems. I was told that the US had nothing to do with the overthrow of the Quadros government.... I then asked "if this was so, why was President Goulart forced to assume office with less powers than he was constitutionally entitled to". The reply was that it was the wish of the Brazilian Congress. Kennedy and his aides, forced on the defensive, said that they were not opposed to genuine non-alignment, not even to nationalisation.... They said, however, that what they were opposed to was a total commitment to the Soviet bloc and the denial of freedom! [38]

Lloyd Searwar recalls the context of Cheddi's self-destructive encounter with the President. All the coaching by the British was forgotten in the informality of the White House lawn:

> I was with Cheddi when he met Kennedy in October 1961. Kennedy had with him Pierre Salinger and Arthur Schlesinger, but this meeting lasted a short time. Then the President took Cheddi out through the French windows unto the lawn — out of earshot of anybody. And they talked at great length, for a long, long time. His staff became very upset because Robert Frost, the great poet, was waiting to see him, and was kept waiting for the better part of an hour. Then Schlesinger and I had to produce some kind of a communique; we found it hard to agree on a form of words....Cheddi was naïve, he never acquired the sophistication required of a statesman. He never really left the plantation.[39]

It was not an impressive performance — White House officials deemed the talks 'delicate and controversial'[40] — and the President made no definite commitment to grant Jagan any aid, the main reason for his visit. Instead, a vague communique was eventually constructed to enable Jagan to save face: he committed himself to parliamentary rule, while the US promised to send a team to assess the needs of British Guiana. But the visit would soon lead to a firm decision by Kennedy to support Burnham. In an interview with the editor of the Soviet newspaper, *Izvestia*, on November 25, 1961 Kennedy had remarked that he opposed Castro because he had not honoured his pledge to hold free elections and uphold the freedom of his people:

> Until the present Government of Cuba will allow free and honest elections ... it cannot claim to represent the majority of the people. That is our dispute with Cuba. Mr. [Cheddi] Jagan, on the other hand, who was recently elected Prime Minister of British Guiana [August 1961], is a Marxist, but the United States doesn't object — because the choice was made by an honest election, which he won. If the people of any country choose to follow a Communist system in a free election, after a fair opportunity for a number of views to be presented, the United States would accept that.[41]

Kennedy did not really mean what he said. As Schlesinger observed, '[T]he President, after meeting Jagan, had grown increasingly sceptical, but he was impressed by the British contention that there was no alternative. The British advanced the argument at every opportunity, though one always suspected that their main desire was to get out of British Guiana as quickly as possible and dump the whole problem on us.'[42] He then drew attention to the fact that by February 1962 'frightening race riots' had broken out in Georgetown; the equation was changing; they were increasingly able to identify an alternative to their communist enemy — the African leader, L.F.S. Burnham. Schlesinger was at the cutting edge of Kennedy's policy towards the colony, so his interpretation of events leading to the fall of Jagan in 1964 deserves scrutiny. As will be seen later, his rapid rendition of developments, though on the surface accurate, conceal the depth of Kennedy's machinations, his unrelenting pressure on the British, in 1962–63, to force them to reverse their commitment to grant independence to Jagan: the riots orchestrated by the opposition parties in Georgetown on February 16, 1962 with American support, and the CIA's subversion in 1963 of Jagan's government were the pretext. Schlesinger recalls:

Thus far our policy had been based on the assumption that Forbes Burnham was, as the British described him, an opportunist, racist and demagogue intent only on personal power. One wondered about this, though, because the AFL-CIO people in British Guiana thought well of him; and Hugh Gaitskell [Leader of the Labour Party] told me that Burnham had impressed him more than Jagan.... Then in May 1962 Burnham came to Washington. He appeared an intelligent, self-possessed, *reasonable* man, insisting quite firmly on his 'socialism' and 'neutralism' but *stoutly anti-communist...* In the meantime, events had convinced us [Jagan's visit] that Jagan, though perhaps not a disciplined communist, had that kind of deep pro-communist emotion which only sustained experience with communism could cure ... [but] the United States could not afford ... [that] when it involved a quasi-communist regime on the mainland of Latin America. Burnham's visit left the feeling, as I reported to the President [June 21, 1962], that 'an independent British Guiana under Burnham ... would cause us many fewer problems than an independent British Guiana under Jagan'. And a way was open to bring it about, because Jagan's parliamentary strength was larger than his popular strength: he had won 57 per cent of the seats on the basis of 42.7 per cent of the vote [under first-past-the-post]. An obvious solution would be to establish a system of proportional representation. This, after prolonged discussion, the British Government finally did in October 1963; and elections held finally at the end of 1964 produced a coalition government under Burnham. With much unhappiness and turbulence, British Guiana seemed to have passed safely out of the communist orbit [emphasis added].[43]

The failure of the Americans to offer any concrete assistance to Jagan deflated the optimism that had inspired him to go to America after his election victory of August 1961. This would not have enhanced his image at home, and must have lifted his opponents, Burnham and D'Aguiar, from the despair of defeat. He aggravated the situation on November 3, 1961 when he announced in the House of Assembly, prematurely, that the US had refused his request for financial aid, and had told him 'in effect, to get it where he could'. He said that it had been confirmed 'at the highest levels', in the US and

Canada, that while they were concerned with the 'preservation' of the democratic way of life in developing countries, 'it is no concern of theirs how these countries organise their economic life'. The US Government expressed surprise at Jagan's announcement, stating that they had opted for 'modest and venturesome' financial support, in an effort to keep him 'within the Western fold and the inter-American system'. Jagan's statement that he had been refused aid and told to look elsewhere was rejected as 'not hopeful'. They felt that this was a ploy by him to ascertain whether the Communist bloc would provide aid to his country, due to become independent in a year or two.[44] No American aid of consequence was to come Jagan's way for the three turbulent years he remained in office.

Burnham and D'Aguiar were energised by the perceived rebuff of Jagan by the Kennedy administration. Although there is no evidence that the President had already opted for an alternative to Jagan, implicit in Jagan's failure to get American aid was the notion that the way was still opened for a 'moderate' alternative. It is of great significance, therefore, that Burnham made a very strong case for a change of the electoral system to proportional representation, with an implied call for the delay of independence, only two days after Jagan made the announcement about his failure to get American aid. Burnham was already testing the ground, distancing himself from communism and suggesting to the Americans a way of defeating Cheddi Jagan: in 1961, with 42.7 per cent of the votes Jagan won 20 seats; with 41 per cent Burnham won only 11; D'Aguiar won 4 with 16.2 per cent. Burnham also linked race and implied violence unambiguously to the core of the question of power in an independent Guyana. He told his Party's Congress in Georgetown on November 5, 1961: '[T]he PPP victory, regardless of what its leaders may say or think, represents to its adherents and supporters, as well as to their opponents, an Indian racial victory at the polls on 21 August [1961].... The PPP leadership has recognised that their victory has been the victory of a minority in peculiar circumstances [the first-past-the-post system].' Then, ominously, with loaded imagery, he dramatised what he saw as Indian racism at the heart of Jagan's politics:

[T]hey have been pouring forth declarations about the necessity for a single nation, while the acts of their supporters and some of [the] lieutenants ... of the PPP are in the habit of making such remarks as 'we pon top' [we are on top] — and more especially to the African people — 'You been come fo' cut cane and pull punt [slavery]'. On the other hand, we have had the bombast from the Minister of Natural Resources on more than one occasion that 'heads will roll'. In the midst of the bombast he did not make the mistake of specifying any PNC [African] heads. That, comrades, is more than a coincidence. That is, I submit, because we of the PNC have shown such great solidarity and determination, have shown especially on the Corentyne Coast [predominantly Indian] that we can give better than we take. [45]

Burnham then challenged what he saw as Jagan's racist interpretation of the history of the colony, and suggested how his African people must respond to a potential Jagan government after independence:

I have noticed that he gives the economic history of this country starting with its introduction of [Indian] indentured labour. There is no reference made of the contribution which our forefathers, the Africans, made, who came here not to farm on better plantations [than] those which existed in their lands, but came here under compulsion and made the chief contribution to this country. There is no mention of the contribution of the African people to the economy of this country in the interior, and what they did in effect to advance the sugar industry is ignored. The Leader of the PPP went so far in his petition [to the UN] ... to tell them that the Africans dominate the Civil Service and the professions. Obviously he does not see the lawyers; obviously he does not see the doctors at the Public Hospitals [Indians]... Comrades, there is one question I will ... ask you: 'Are we mice or men? Will we sit down and allow Jagan ... to rape our Constitution?... [I]f he attempts to make these changes without the referendum to the electorate a revolutionary situation is created, and I believe that we can learn a lesson from our members and supporters on the Corentyne Coast [resort to violence]. That is why I continue to emphasise at all times and at all points that we have now entered a new phase of our struggle ... you will recall that Jagan talked about sharpening cutlasses. We have been accused in the past of talking not doing. Comrades, let us think and reason and let us be prepared to do when the time comes.[46]

In October 1961, Sydney King [Eusi Kwayana], the expelled general secretary of the PNC, had set the tone for an African political resurgence with his creation of the African Society for Racial Equality (later African Society for Cultural Relations with Independent Africa [ASCRIA]). Its principal aim was stated thus: 'To put forward ideas which can, even now, save the African descendants and secure their heritage, in a racial situation which means permanent election victory for the majority racial party [Jagan's Indian PPP].'[47] The Americans would have been buoyed by the resurgent vigour of Jagan's principal opponents, even if it contained the potential for a racial confrontation. They would also have been encouraged by the ferocity of the anti-Communist crusade of Peter D'Aguiar's United Force and the rabid anti-Castro stance of his two newspapers, the *Sun* and *The Daily Chronicle*, as well as the Catholic Church. Indeed, it was D'Aguiar who had invigorated the rather ineffectual opposition, which Burnham had provided between 1957 and 1960. He brought resolve and passion to the anti-Jagan campaign and dramatised it in a manner that galvanised the urban, African population, apart from his loyal Madeiran Portuguese and Coloured devotees, between 1961 and 1964. Ironically, it was the PPP which had rescued the United Force from potential extinction at the 1961 elections: by not contesting two Georgetown seats and a few elsewhere, and getting their Indian supporters to vote tactically against Burnham's PNC, D'Aguiar won two of his four seats and a crucial 16 per cent of the popular vote. But the principal beneficiary of the rise of the UF was, in fact, Forbes Burnham:

[F]rom the very beginning D'Aguiar developed the theme of anti-communism as a major factor in his anti-Jagan campaign.... It is no exaggeration to say that despite its small representation in the House, the UF has been the guiding force in the opposition. The reason is, of course, that D'Aguiar had a clear ideological basis for his opposition as opposed to the ambivalent and opportunistic attitude of the PNC.... And so D'Aguiar led the way. In November 1961, he opposed immediate independence in the House and called for a referendum or new elections on this issue. In February 1962, he led the opposition to the Budget which culminated in the Budget riots. At the November 1962 constitutional conference ... he led the opposition to Jagan's claims for the transfer of residual powers ... and supported the PNC in its claim for elections before independence and PR. The result was a deadlock. In 1963 he was very active in the opposition to the Labour [Relations] Bill which resulted in a long strike. Later in the year he again triumphantly supported the PNC in its claim for elections and PR at the 1963 [Sandys] conference in London.... His anti-communism has become a kind of hysteria ... the UF, militant and decisive, led the way and the PNC, often hesitant, but never failing to seize an opportunity, followed.[48]

The American government, therefore, had the makings of an anti-Jagan coalition in the PNC and the UF. However, a serious problem was posed by the resolve of the British to grant independence to Jagan in 1962. In November 1961 Jagan had got the Assembly to pass a resolution in favour of independence the following year, and Burnham's PNC had supported it. Grave though his reservations, the latter could not be seen openly to be opposed to independence. The Americans, too, were in a bind. In April 1961 Dean Rusk, the American Secretary of State, had expressed concern to Iain Macleod, Secretary of State for the Colonies, that an independent British Guiana might produce 'another Castro-type situation'. Macleod had recognised the paradox in that: while, as a general principle, the US were committed to early independence for subject peoples, they wanted them to 'put the clock back' in the case of Cheddi Jagan. He would not concur with that exception. He therefore recommended a 'reasonably generous ... technical, economic and financial aid' to thwart Communism and ensure political stability in British Guiana.[49] By late 1961 the stance of the British had not changed, in spite of greater American apprehension after the visit of Jagan in October. In December 1961 the British proposed a formula 'with the aim of completing the transition to full independence by the end of 1962', subject to the agreement of the Americans. In early January 1962 Prime Minister Macmillan was informed: 'The Americans have now been consulted and are prepared to agree with this proposal.'[50]

For the opposition in British Guiana the announcement from London on January 14, 1962, that the British government had agreed to convene a conference in May, 'to discuss the date and arrangements to be made for the attainment of independence for British Guiana', must have seemed like the end of the road.[51] However, both Burnham and D'Aguiar were galvanised by the impending transfer of power to Jagan, to seek to delay independence. They proceeded to construct opposition to the 1962 Budget, with the help of the TUC, in order to mobilise workers in Georgetown, to challenge the legitimacy of Jagan's government. The PNC canalised public servants' protracted disaffection with the government over long-overdue increases in salary, as they did that of lower-level government employees, and brought these to bear on the budget. The UF, too, representing business interests and the small Portuguese and coloured community, exploited the fear of communism to launch street protests. The 'sense of fear that the country would obtain independence under a Government with obvious Communist leanings', was very effectively manipulated.[52] Workers in Georgetown came out on strike, and a volatile political atmosphere was fomented with such rapidity that the African and Portuguese communities mounted a tremendous show of force, culminating in the riots of February 16, 1962: 56 premises were destroyed by fire; 87 were damaged, 66 of these were looted.[53]

It is of significance that the TUC had come out clearly on the side of the PNC and the UF. The president of the TUC, Richard Ishmael, was also president of the sugar workers union, the MPCA, which was seen by Jagan's PPP as a company union. It was irrefutable that most sugar workers, Indians, voted for the PPP and that if a poll were held in the industry, an overwhelming majority of those workers would have voted for the PPP's union, the Guyana Sugar Workers' Union, which was registered in September 1961; it was called the Guyana Agricultural Workers' Union (GAWU) from 1963. In short, on the basis of a bogus check-off system negotiated with the Sugar Producers' Association, the PPP argued, and in the name of workers whose loyalty to Jagan was unimpeachable, Richard Ishmael, in league with Burnham and D'Aguiar, were subverting the democratically elected government.

The upshot was that the Independence Conference scheduled for May 1962 was postponed to July, then to October, in order, ostensibly, to facilitate the inquiry into the riots launched by the British government, the Wynn Parry Commission, which sat in British Guiana in May-June 1962. The hearings were probably more memorable for the fact that Cheddi Jagan, again, was lured into the anti-communist web which confronted him everywhere. In Georgetown, in mid-1962, with his political future in grave danger, he faced his old enemy, the Indian lawyer and discredited politician of the old order, Lionel Luckhoo:

Jagan:	I believe the tenets of communism to be 'From each according to his ability, to each according to his need'.
Luckhoo:	That is your conception of the tenets of communism and you believe in that?
Jagan:	Yes.
Luckhoo:	That represents your communist belief?
Jagan:	Yes.

Jagan had expanded on his communist creed before the Wynn Parry Commission, typically tortuously but categorically:

If you look at a Webster dictionary, one would find a definition of communism which will compel me to say that I am not a communist because the assumptions are that liberties and freedom will be denied under such a set-up.... [I]n this country the people who have been accusing us for many years on this question have always assumed that communism is evil. That is why I have always refused to give a 'yes' or 'no' answer to this very complicated question. I have always said that I am a Marxist. Marxism is a science of the laws of development of society from one stage to the next.... Now, sir, by saying that I am a Marxist, I could be at one and the same time anti-colonialist, an anti-Imperialist, a democrat, a socialist, a humanist and a communist.

In a lecture on July 3, 1962 he had remarked that although Castro had to resort to arms to win freedom that did not mean that he was not a democrat; he was forced to employ revolutionary violence in order to achieve change and democracy. Jagan, alluding to liberal democracy, added that he did not believe in 'gradualism', for '[w]hile you are going gradually, the press, the capitalists, the imperialists are always undermining your position. They are always trying to get you out of the way'.[54]

The exchange with Luckhoo cited above was reproduced in his party's organ, *Thunder*, on June 30, 1962. It was interpreted as another triumph in the anti-Imperialist struggle. The next issue of the paper attributed the fomenting of violence in February, in part, to the Americans who had become active since the announcement was made that independence talks would convene in May 1962:

> [T]he anti-independence forces in British Guiana, aided and abetted by American provocateurs from the Christian Anti-Communist organisation of Dr. Schwarz and certain trade unionists well supplied with finances, started to flood this country. They used money and influence and pressures to help bring about the February riots. The trade union movement here, heavily financed by foreign funds, were strengthened in their efforts to defeat or delay independence. Britain quickly rose to the situation and delayed independence talks.[55]

Thunder also carried an article by Cedric Belfrage, the British Marxist writer, elaborating on American involvement in the violence of February 1962:

> The hope of overthrowing *the hemisphere's second socialist regime* lies in creating chaos — a fact evidently digested in Washington's dark corners where international subversion is plotted. Missionaries of chaos are sent in the guise of 'Christian anti-communists' (two of these, Messrs Schwarz and Sluis, have now been officially excluded), and 'delegates' and 'advisers' from the International Confederation of Free Trade Unions (ICFTU) [emphasis added].

He listed a number of 'visitors' to the colony shortly before the February riots: ICFTU Latin American Division's education director, Palladino; William McCabe of the US Public Services International; Ernest Lee of the US Chemical and Commercial Workers Union; and Alan Hargraves of the British TUC International Affairs Committee. On a post-riot 'return visit' was Serafino Romaualdi, top ICFTU man for Central America and the Caribbean, a rabid anti-communist and self-confessed enemy of Cheddi Jagan. He had boasted in Georgetown: 'More US trade union officials have come here in the past six months than have visited my whole area in six years.' [56]

This damning information did not feature in the Wynn Parry Commission Report; there is no reference whatsoever to the role of the United States. So apart from getting the Independence Conference postponed, the opposition had extracted from Jagan, in dramatic circumstances, an unambiguous statement that he was a communist, precisely what the Kennedy Administration wished to establish. The Commission did not state the obvious — that the opposition parties, in league with the TUC and US-based subversive organisations, were undermining the Jagan government in order to delay independence. Moreover, although they blamed the PNC, the UF and the TUC for fomenting the disturbances, they did not exonerate Cheddi Jagan:

> The personal political belief of Dr. Jagan is relevant only in so far as his deeds and declarations caused certain reactions among the people and brought about a state of affairs in which tensions grew and spread.... [T]he utterances of the Premier had conveyed to many people in British Guiana and to the outside world that he was indeed a communist.... There is very little doubt that many of his speeches and some of his deeds gave rise to the apprehension that despite his evasions and professions to the contrary, he was acting as a communist.... The trade unionists, although professing to be completely free from political taint, made common cause with the Civil Service Association and with the politicians, and a gathering together of all these forces was made possible by the fact that Dr. Jagan was not endowed with the breadth of vision which would have enabled him to foresee that his purpose was progressing towards a lamentable end. Nor did he possess the nimbleness of intellect, or the dexterity of political manoeuvring which allows a politician to change his

plan of action without incurring the odium of his supporters or inviting the derision of his opponents.[57]

Violence had paid off; the involvement of the TUC even gave it a degree of respectability — grass roots authenticity; and the PNC, the UF and the US government now had more ammunition in their resolve to pressure the British government to ensure that independence was not granted to Cheddi Jagan. Locally (with American help), anti-communism and violent sabotage, would enhance the case for delay, while, externally, Kennedy would harness his anti-Castro obsession to this programme of sabotage, to extract the same end from the British. Jagan stood virtually alone, armed solely with the erroneous notion that 'history and time' were on his communist side.

Uncannily, two days after the riots, on February 18, 1962 the US Assistant Secretary of State for European Affairs informed Secretary of State, Dean Rusk, that no assistance had so far been given to Jagan because of 'factors beyond our control' and Jagan's attitude towards the United States. He was pessimistic that a rapprochement could be reached with Jagan 'which would prevent the emergence of a communist or Castro-type state in South America'.[58]

The next day, in the House of Commons, Reginald Maudling, who had succeeded the more independent-minded liberal Tory, Iain Macleod, as Secretary of State for the Colonies, remarked ominously that the riots 'had considerable implications for the future of British Guiana'. Nigel Fisher, a senior member of the Macmillan government, gave a darker prognosis — a message which Burnham and D'Aguiar could not have missed — when he advised Maudling to consider the following when the issue of independence is discussed: '[W]henever Dr. Jagan gets power in British Guiana it leads to trouble — now, as in 1953. Will My Right Honourable Friend weigh this when considering the danger of giving independence to a Government which may become the first Communist government in the British Commonwealth?' Maudling replied: 'I would not like to comment on these important and far-reaching issues at this stage. We are urgently examining the implications of recent developments.' [59]

At this stage the British government must have known precisely how the Americans interpreted the riots and the role that US trade unionists and other anti-communist forces played in the events. If there was any equivocation, this was quickly dispelled when a firm, blunt letter from Dean Rusk, dated February 19, 1962 — three days after the Georgetown riots — reached Lord Home, the Foreign Secretary. As it constituted a definitive reversal of US policy, hitherto informed however, tenuously, by British perception that there was no viable alternative to Jagan, it is necessary to reproduce Rusk's letter to 'Dear Alex [Lord Home]' almost in its entirety. Jagan had to be removed before independence:

> You know from my correspondence of [26] August of last year of my acute concern over the prospects of an independent British Guiana under Cheddi Jagan. Subsequent to his victory in the August elections [1961] we agreed to try your policy of fostering an effective association between British Guiana and the West.... In pursuance of this programme the President received Jagan on his visit to this country in October. I must tell you now that I have reached the conclusion that it is not possible for us to put up with an independent British Guiana under Jagan. We have had no real success in establishing the basis for understanding with him due in part to his grandiose expectations of economic aid. We have continued to receive disturbing reports of Communist connections on the part of Jagan and persons closely associated with him. Partly reflective of growing concern over Cuba, public and congressional opinion here is incensed at the thought of our dealing with Jagan. *The Marxist-Leninist policy he professes parallels that of Castro which the OAS ... declared incompatible with the inter-American system. Current happenings in British Guiana [the February riots] indicate Jagan is not master of the situation at home without your support .... [T]he continuation of Jagan in power is leading us to disaster in terms of the colony itself, strains on Anglo-American relations and difficulties for the inter-American system ....* I am anxious to have your thoughts on what should be done in the immediate future. In the past your people have held, with considerable conviction, that there was no reasonable alternative to working with Jagan. I am convinced that our experience so far, and now the disorders in Georgetown, makes it necessary to re-examine this premise. It seems to me clear that new elections should now be scheduled, and I hope we can agree that Jagan should not accede to power again [emphasis added].[60]

It is a fallacy that the British meekly acquiesced to what became a campaign by the Kennedy administration to remove Jagan. On February 26, 1962 Home replied to Rusk — 'a very good letter ... pure Machiavellianism' on the part of Rusk, Macmillan noted — asserting that the process of independence had become irreversible largely because of pressure from America: within the universal framework of decolonisation, British Guiana alone could not be made an exception because of Jagan's communism. He could hardly have been more forthright: '[I]t was your historic role to have been for long years the first crusader and the prime mover in urging colonial emancipation. The communists are now in the van. Why? Amongst other things because premature independence is a gift for them. What I do not think possible is to beat them by cancelling the ticket for independence and particularly if this is only to be done in the single instance of British Guiana'. Home then posed the difficulties implicit in effecting a constitutional coup against Jagan:

> You say it is not possible for you to 'put up with an independent British Guiana under Jagan', and that 'Jagan should not accede to power again'. How would you suggest that this be done in a democracy? And even if a device could be found, it would almost certainly be transparent and in such circumstances if democratic processes are to be allowed, it will be extremely hard to provide a reasonable prospect that any successor regime will be more stable and more mature.[61]

Home was saying that as long as they played by the rules of democracy Jagan would win again. He asserted: 'So I would say to you that we cannot now go back on the course we have set ourselves, of bringing these dependent territories to self-government. Nor is it any good deluding ourselves that we can now set aside a single territory such as British Guiana for some sort of special treatment.'

It was clear that fear of the spread of Castroism to British Guiana, on the eve of the mid-term elections in the United States [1962], made it imperative that Kennedy be seen to be tough on communism. He was even prepared to affect supposed 'strains' in Anglo-American relations to pressure the British to remove Jagan: 'pure Machiavellianism', indeed. This had driven the Colonial Attache at the British Embassy in Washington, John Hennings, to suggest toeing the American line. He wondered whether 'our agreeing to control Jagan for some longer period and assisting in his downfall' could not be tied to the American commitment to 'a really imaginative aid programme in British Guiana'.[62] But at the highest level, the British were still holding the line against Kennedy. A few days later, in early March 1962, Secretary of State for the Colonies, Maudling, requested that Macmillan send the under-secretary, Hugh Fraser, to assess the situation in British Guiana, in order to expedite the removal of British troops from the colony, and 'to ensure an orderly transition to independence, with the least damage to Anglo-American relations'.[63]

American pressure was relentless. On March 8, 1962 the British Embassy in Washington informed the Foreign Office that Kennedy had phoned that day to say 'he was worried about the future of British Guiana. He was not satisfied that ... information on developments there was accurate'. Kennedy added that he would like to see Hugh Fraser, on his return from the colony, to discuss British policy with regards to Jagan.[64] Buoyed by recent American success in fomenting trouble for Jagan, Kennedy was saying that the British had to reverse their policy of working with him whatever the risks, because the equation had changed. Maudling had told Schlesinger that 'responsible people' had suggested that the CIA were involved in fomenting the recent troubles against Cheddi Jagan, and he did not see how Britain could 'consistently' seek to remove a democratically-elected government.[65] By March 1962, then, Jagan's communism was at the core of US-British relations: the President was implacable in his assertion that Jagan had to be removed; the British, on the other hand, still held to the notion that the process towards independence was irreversible and that there was no credible alternative to Jagan. By May-June 1962, however, Kennedy's pressure was permeating British resolve; while Jagan's unveiling of his communist creed before the Wynn Parry Commission, in June, had undermined his case — irretrievably.

The British were still trying to resist Kennedy's pressure, but an ambivalence towards Jagan was taking shape. Hugh Fraser, the Under-Secretary of State for the Colonies, visited British Guiana in March 1962 and reported to President Kennedy (and officials of the State Department, the head of the CIA, McCone, and Attorney

General, Bobby Kennedy). The President gave him more than two hours of his time: '... it [is] clear that the problem of B.G. in American eyes is regarded as one of critical importance'. Fraser informed Kennedy that British policy towards the colony had not yet been decided, and he sought to render some balance to the Jagan issue: (1) to 'tone down' the impact of the Rusk/Home exchange [February 1962]; (ii) 'to get the Americans to accept our policy of a fairly swift withdrawal from B.G. as the best'; (iii) to change American attitudes to British Guiana: to 'damp down [its] importance' and to get them to end the 'present policy of boycotting' Jagan and 'reneging' on pledges of aid to him.[66]

Fraser had played into American hands. He conceded that to proceed to independence with Jagan commanding only 42 per cent of the votes was 'not morally acceptable', adding that Burnham and D'Aguiar would press for a system of proportional representation in order to defeat Jagan. Fresh elections before independence were 'inevitable'. While not putting it 'authoritatively' to the Americans, he had suggested that the constitutional conference scheduled for May 1962 was 'almost certain to break down'. They would then have to contemplate whether to impose or negotiate a constitutional solution. He advised the Americans to try to win Jagan over, as the Indian population was growing fast:

> I think I have made it clear to them that over the next ten years the Portuguese will remain a minority and the Africans will become one, and that therefore their policy must be whilst helping minorities to look to the Indians as the centre of power to concentrate on weaning Jagan and the moderates away from the communist apparat. This is run, I think, by Mrs. Jagan, and I hope I have made it clear that a line can be drawn between these types of international communists and what I would call the anti-colonial type of communist [Cheddi] which, as I pointed out to them, Jefferson might well have been if the Communist Manifesto had been written in 1748 instead of 100 years later.[67]

The Americans had no time for such intellectual distinctions — Jagan had to be removed. On March 12, 1962 in Geneva, Rusk had impressed on Home that the United States was 'really terrified of another Cuba on the continent', adding that all the South American countries were united with them in 'stopping Jagan from taking his country into the communist orbit'. Home remarked that Fraser's impending report to Kennedy was crucial: that should be the basis on which 'to decide on a line on the possibilities of independence'. But he noted that he 'did not see how we could delay it all that long'. It is significant that in spite of Fraser's advocacy of support for Jagan in his meeting with Kennedy, he had given the Americans clear hints that the conference would fail, therefore independence would be delayed; that the case for proportional representation would be advanced by Burnham and D'Aguiar; and that elections would have to be held before independence. He also left them with vital ammunition — that 'British Guiana was really now more their responsibility than ours and would increasingly become more so'.[68] Embedded in these propositions, unwittingly, were the constitutional parameters to weaken Jagan's electoral strength, coupled with the notion that such changes could be 'imposed' to achieve the demise of Jagan. Therefore, while superficially Fraser's report to Kennedy appeared supportive of the old British line of taking a calculated risk with Jagan because he was the best of a bad lot, it contained the germ of his destruction. The resolute anti-communism and fear of Castroism at the heart of Kennedy's foreign policy in Latin America was not amenable to moderation, British intransigence notwithstanding; but after Fraser's visit, this resolve seemed to be giving. Kennedy would now insist on concrete concessions from them in his anti-Jagan crusade. These would be congruent with the political ambitions of Jagan's opponents, Forbes Burnham and Peter D'Aguiar.

But even before Fraser's arrival in Washington, as Arthur Schlesinger informed Kennedy, 'both State and CIA are under the impression that a firm decision has been taken to get rid of Jagan'. He advised that nothing be done until the President met Hugh Fraser and concluded: 'British Guiana has 600,000 inhabitants. Jagan would no doubt be gratified to know that the American and British governments are spending more man-hours per capita on British Guiana than any other current problem!'.[69] Kennedy's preoccupation with Jagan would soon take effect on the British. By early May 1962 Macmillan had arrived at the position that they had to cooperate with Kennedy on British Guiana. Reflecting on Fraser's talks in Washington, he noted that the Americans 'attach great importance' to the British Guiana issue, adding that this was driven by internal politics [the mid-term elections] 'as much as by genuine fear of communism'. He concluded: 'It is surely to our advantage to be as co-operative and forthcoming as we can. In the future the Americans will have to carry the burden of British Guiana and so it is only fair that they should have a share in shaping its future.'⁷⁰

Macmillan's private secretary, too, advised a revision of their policy towards the colony, that they must work 'in close concert' with the Americans. He was critical of the Colonial Office and, by implication, the former Secretary of State, Iain Macleod: 'The Colonial Office still treats the place as if it were in Africa or Asia whereas *it is in the US backyard* and politically very important to the Administration with the mid-term elections coming in the autumn [1962] [emphasis added].'

This then was the context in which Macmillan wrote to Kennedy ('Dear Friend'), on May 30, 1962. He sought to tie the British Guiana issue to the future of British Honduras (Belize), as Lord Home had done in his response to Dean Rusk in February. It seemed like the offer of a quid pro quo, with Kennedy being asked to temper Guatemalan territorial ambitions with respect to Belize in return for his having a free hand in British Guiana. Macmillan then explained to Kennedy their 'latest thinking' on constitutional development in British Guiana:

> Previously, we had been thinking in terms of an Independence Conference in May [1962], to be followed by independence within a few months. We have now decided to postpone the Conference until July, and we intend to persuade the leaders of the political parties to agree that elections should be held before the territory becomes independent. This will give us a little more time and also, perhaps, a further opportunity to try to establish whether, under a democratic system, there is any alternative to Dr. Jagan's Government. If, however, it becomes clear, by a further expression of electoral opinion, that Dr. Jagan's party is the choice of the people, I hope that we shall be able to persuade you that the best line for both our Governments to follow is to do our best to

keep that Government on the side of the West by co-operating fully with it and giving it the economic support which it requires.[71]

The Constitutional Conference was subsequently convened in October 1962, but by then the United States had already chosen their alternative to Jagan: L.F.S. Burnham. The opposition parties knew this; they therefore brought several constitutional demands to the Conference on which there could be no compromise, while the British government obliged by demanding unanimity as a precondition to independence. As St. Pierre observes, Schlesinger and others in the US government had met Burnham in Washington in early May 1962. The latter left with his hosts a sense of a fundamental distinction between himself, a democratic socialist, and Cheddi and Janet Jagan. He had categorised them as 'thorough-going communists ... [who] not only supported communism ideologically, but also received instructions from the international communist movement'. This was precisely what the Americans wanted to hear. Their assessment of Burnham, therefore, reflected the man's nimbleness of intellect and his mastery of the nuances of Cold War politics, the antithesis of Cheddi Jagan's ponderous doctrinaire style. Burnham's hosts had characterised him as 'unemotional and precise', 'lucid', with 'the restrained manner typical of a British barrister' — all superlatives.[72]

Kennedy's determination to destroy Jagan would rescue Burnham from the brink of political oblivion. American pursuit of a non-communist alternative to Jagan would settle on him, while he feigned support for independence and paraded a spurious autonomy and an unsullied nationalism. Kennedy had dispatched Schlesinger to British Guiana in mid-June 1962 for this specific purpose. He even visited Jagan's home plantation, Port Mourant. The trip is memorable for Schlesinger's concurrence with the portentous perceptions of Burnham he encountered in British Guiana: *'[T]here is considerable feeling here, which I am inclined to share, that British Guiana would be worse off with Burnham than with Jagan* [emphasis added].' Yet on June 21, 1962 he sent the definitive memorandum to Kennedy, which established clearly that L.F.S. Burnham was their man in their crusade to destroy their communist enemy, Cheddi Jagan. Schlesinger argued:

[T]he evidence shows increasingly that Jagan's heart is with the Communist world. He is quite plainly a Marxist nationalist who sees the West in terms of the old stereotypes of capitalism and imperialism and who is deeply persuaded of the superiority of communist methods and values.... The alternative to Jagan is Forbes Burnham .... [A]s an African, [he] is the representative of the ethnic group deemed by its low birth rate to minority status in British Guiana. On the other hand, Burnham is regarded more favourably by the AFL-CIO people who have had British Guiana contacts [they advised local unionists in the February riots] and by some people in the British Labour Party [including Gaitskell] .... [H]e made a good impression on his visit to Washington [May 1962]. All alternatives in British Guiana are terrible; but *I have little doubt that an independent British Guiana under Burnham* (if Burnham will commit himself to a multi-racial policy) *would cause us many fewer problems than an independent British Guiana under Jagan* [emphasis added].[73]

Cheddi Jagan was doomed. On July 12, 1962 these sentiments were reinforced by Dean Rusk in a memorandum to the President. He noted that a national security assessment of Jagan, on April 11, had concluded that he was a communist and that his government, once independent, 'would probably lean in the Soviet direction'. He observed, too, that on June 22, Jagan had admitted to the Wynn Parry Commission in Georgetown that he was a communist. Rusk advised: 'I believe we are obliged to base our policy on the premise that, once independent, Cheddi Jagan will establish a Marxist regime in British Guiana and associate his country with the Soviet Bloc to a degree unacceptable to us for a state in the Western Hemisphere .... It is my view that a policy of trying to work with Jagan, as urged by the British will not pay off. Jagan is too far committed emotionally [to communism] and suspicious of our intentions.'[74]

Cheddi had left no doubts of his communism when he was examined by his arch-enemy, Lionel Luckhoo, before the Wynn Parry Commission on June 22, 1962 as the following exchange illustrates:

Luckhoo: Dr. Jagan, are you an admirer of Fidel Castro?
Jagan: I have said so, yes.

Luckhoo:	Have you declared him to be the greatest liberator of the 20th century?
Jagan:	Yes.
Luckhoo:	You have. As an admirer do you endeavour to pattern your own Government after his style and fashion?
Jagan:	No, not necessarily....
Luckhoo:	Are there any policies of Fidel Castro to which you do not subscribe?
Jagan:	I am not aware of all the policies.
Luckhoo:	Those that you are aware of?
Jagan:	I am not aware of any....
Luckhoo:	That you oppose?
Jagan:	Yes.
Luckhoo:	Are you an admirer of Nikita Khrushchev?
Jagan:	Yes.
Luckhoo:	And you have publicly proclaimed this?
Jagan:	I have publicly said so, yes....
Luckhoo:	Have you said in unmistakable language that the communist way of life is preferable? Admit it. Yes or no?
Jagan:	Yes. I have said already what I believe communism to be, and I said it is the aim of communism to bring about a society of equality.
Luckhoo:	[Y]ourself, Dr. Jagan — in the Robertson Report [1954] — and Janet Jagan were named by the Commission as being ones who accepted unreservedly the classical communist doctrines of Marx and Lenin. Now, do you accept the classical doctrines of Marx and Lenin?
Jagan:	I believe in Marxism, yes.
Luckhoo:	And Lenin?
Jagan:	Yes.[75]

The Kennedy administration chose Burnham as their man to replace Jagan, but they were still not certain of the mechanics for achieving it. Rusk had apparently suggested that the CIA could help to fix the elections against Jagan (the text is not declassified). However, the President's Special Assistant for National Security Affairs, McGeorge Bundy, had challenged this: 'I think it is unproven that the CIA knows how to manipulate an election in British Guiana without a backfire.'

On July 19, 1962 Schlesinger advised the President, again, that 'the Burnham risk is less than the Jagan risk', but he cautioned him about CIA covert activity in impending elections: such action made him 'nervous' and he wanted the President to verify whether the CIA 'will leave no visible traces which ... [Jagan] can cite before the world, whether he wins or loses'. The President spoke to his trusted friend, Ormsby-Gore, the British Ambassador to Washington, on July 21, with regard to Macmillan's letter of May 30. He repeated his argument that he could not afford another Communist regime in the Hemisphere, and that it was 'unrealistic to hope now that B.G. could be kept on [the] side of the West by a policy of co-operation'. He welcomed new elections in British Guiana, as suggested by the British, noting that these could produce a government of a 'different complexion'.[76]

It is clear that the US government were already planning subversion of any new elections scheduled for the colony, in order to ensure Jagan's defeat. In fact, as Schlesinger reported to the President on September 5, 1962, they were working on an economic plan: should their 'covert programme succeed ... [they wanted] to be in a position to give the successor regime immediate aid'.

It is not possible to document when the US decision to support Burnham in the struggle to defeat Jagan was communicated to him. However, by the time the Constitutional Conference in London finally convened, in late October 1962, he and Peter D'Aguiar were in no doubt that the whole project was designed to oust Jagan. This would have been reinforced by the Cuban missiles crisis of the previous week, which now made it virtually imperative, on the part of both the Americans and the British, that Jagan must, under no circumstances, lead an independent Guyana. By then, too, the United States had, in Duncan Sandys, the new Secretary of State for the Colonies, Churchill's son-in-law and a Churchillian Tory to the bone, a man temperamentally equipped to execute their anti-Jagan scheme. He would brook no such liberal principles as Iain Macleod's, who had sought to minimise Jagan's Marxism and his pro-Castro sentiments since the 1960 Conference.

As predicted, the conference ended in a deadlock: there could be no agreement on the key issues: changing the electoral system to Proportional Representation (PR) — Jagan could not win if this were done; holding of fresh elections before independence; and reducing the voting age from 21 to 18, as advocated by Jagan, to neutralise the potential electoral damage implicit in PR. What is noteworthy is that Duncan Sandys emphasised the necessity for unanimity on these key issues, in adjourning the conference. Ominously, too, he stated that he would have to impose a constitutional settlement if the three fundamental questions could not be resolved. Both the opposition in British Guiana and the US government were now aware that an imposition was very much on the cards: as in 1953, the British could suspend the constitution. The beneficiaries would be Jagan's enemies. However, suspension, even in the aftermath of the Cuban missiles crisis, was fraught with potential political fall-out, especially at the UN. The British government would certainly have liked to have been given the authority to arbitrate by the Guyanese leaders. That would have circumvented some of the ethical and political implications of the suspension of two democratically elected governments of Jagan, while empowering them to impose a constitution amenable to the Americans and the opposition parties. Jagan's interpretation of the implications of the collapse of the conference in October 1962 needs no revision:

> The talks ... broke down principally owing to common interests of the British Government and our Opposition not to transfer residual powers to my government. The intransigence and the insistence of the British government on the principle of unanimity were two sides of the same coin.... On the adjournment of the Conference Sandys declared that if the political parties could not come to an agreement, and if social and economic conditions deteriorated, Her Majesty's Government might have to consider 'imposing a settlement'. This was simply giving the green light to the Opposition for further obstruction and violence, as a result of which he would impose a settlement to his liking. (This is exactly what did follow [in October 1963]). As the Attorney General, Fenton Ramsahoye, aptly put it, the British government, by acceding to the wishes of the Opposition and

insisting on the principle of unanimity, had 'placed a premium on violence, looting, arson and murder'.[77]

The orchestrated violence of early 1962 and the collapse of the conference had taken their toll on Jagan. In December 1962, Governor Grey informed Duncan Sandys that 'Jagan ... is very tired and depressed and I think would prefer to resign and go onto opposition rather than to continue in office and try to put this unhappy country on its feet'.[78] Jagan knew, as Ramsahoye had observed, that Burnham and D'Aguiar now had all the trumps: the final Anglo-American solution was being constructed, and that violence would ensure that the colony was ungovernable, thus preparing the ground for a British imposition of a constitutional settlement. What had wounded Jagan most, however, was the fact that Richard Ishmael, President of the TUC and one of the architects of the violence against him in 1962, was also President of the MPCA, the union recognised by the Sugar Producers' Association as the sole bargaining agent for sugar workers. Yet most would have conceded that the overwhelming majority of those workers, Indians, were solidly behind Jagan. Jagan knew, also, that because it was the largest body of workers in any industry in the colony, a union recognised as their bargaining agent automatically exerted immense influence in the TUC.

This, then, was the context in which Jagan's government introduced the Labour Relations Bill in the House of Assembly on March 25, 1963 in order to secure the right to conduct a poll among workers where there were jurisdictional disputes between rival unions. The proposed legislation read: 'This Bill seeks to ensure the compulsory recognition by employers as bargaining agents on behalf of those unions which, after due inquiry, appear to the Minister of Labour, to be truly representative of the workers in a particular industry, trade or undertaking'. The Minister could then order a ballot; if the union challenging the recognised one secured 65 per cent of the votes, he could then recommend that the employer proceed with its recognition. As in September 1953, when the PPP government had introduced similar legislation, the measure was aimed specifically at ousting the MPCA and gaining recognition for Jagan's GAWU. This time, however, the president of the MPCA, Ishmael, as noted above, was at the heart of the resistance to Jagan.

As president of the TUC, too, Ishmael was seen by Burnham as a key ally: through strikes, the country could be made ungovernable, thus bolstering America's argument and advancing their case for the removal of Jagan. Political instability would ensure, as Sandys had intimated, that the British impose a constitution introducing PR.[79]

Jagan informed Governor Grey that Burnham had told him that the Labour Relations Bill was not the *causa belli* but the *casus belli* — not the cause of the war, rather the occasion for it. The TUC supported Burnham unreservedly, calling a general strike which lasted 80 days. It is noteworthy that the predominantly Indian sugar workers, ostensibly represented by Ishmael's MPCA, did not strike. That was irrefutable evidence that their loyalty was to their political leader, Cheddi Jagan. This did not matter, for the strike wrecked the economy; total collapse was only averted because the Cubans and Russians assisted Jagan with oil and basic food items, thus fuelling further the anti-communist crusade of the opposition. America was deeply involved in what was an exercise in subversion to destroy Jagan: the CIA, in league with the AFL-CIO and the AIFLD, poured about $1 million into the TUC to sustain the strike.[80] The Bill had to be withdrawn towards the end of May 1963, as the PPP was reduced to a minority because several of its members were suspended by the Speaker of the House for unbecoming conduct towards him. The strike, however, continued until early July, as the opposition remorselessly ground the feeble Jagan government into the dust. Throughout this period, racial violence fomented by the opposition and dramatised by the terrorist campaign of the PNC, as manifested in the X-13 Plan, led to virtual civil war between Africans and Indians. This plan, 'a detailed account of a PNC terrorist gang ... suggest[ed] that the Party was more involved in the actual violence than was ever known before. The plan was a detailed document of the PNC line of command in planning and executing violence'.[81] Jagan was mortally wounded, precisely what the Americans desired in their campaign to destroy him. Violence, as in 1962, had bolstered Burnham and D'Aguiar.

The fight of the PNC, UF and TUC could not have been sustained without the concerted effort of the United States, as the PPP contended in June 1963:

Guianese trade unions are being trained in increasing numbers in the US and US trade unionists visit the country one after the other.... It is known that the main purpose of these was organising opposition by trade unionists to the Government. The visitors also conducted courses and seminars at which the ... [focus was] invariably on how to fight communism and ways and means of opposing the Government.... Also apart from interference by trade unions and trade unionists, local [US] consulate officials are working in consort with the TUC to subvert the Government.[82]

Kennedy's unrelenting pressure on the British, to engineer the removal of Jagan, was crucial to the morale of Jagan's local enemies. In March 1963, on the eve of the general strike in British Guiana, the US Consul General in Georgetown, Everett Melby, had advised the State Department on the necessity for urgent action to get the British to commit themselves to a referendum on changing the electoral system to PR, it being 'the most practical device for replacing Premier Cheddi Jagan and the People's Progressive Party (PPP) with a more democratic and reliable government'. He explained:

The longer the delay the more difficult it will be to dislodge Jagan and Jagan's brand of 'socialism' from Government; extended delay presents the possibility of a Cuba-like situation. Since it is definitely not in the best US interests to have either British Guiana or an independent Guyana ruled by Jagan's PPP, the US Government should strive for an immediate referendum on PR .... At appropriate levels, efforts should be intensified to create a greater British awareness that, although it may be temporarily unpleasant and awkward, a PR decision should be quickly implemented. A new PR decision would probably force Jagan from office, lead to some revitalisation of internal economic activity and, speed the date of independence and allow time to correct and eradicate communist influences.[83]

Melby cautioned that as a Labour government would be more inclined to grant independence to Jagan, it was imperative to get an agreement from the present Tory government, which was more likely to be 'receptive to the PR concept'. On April 16, 1963 Jagan wrote to Kennedy, bemoaning that nothing substantial had materialised by way of aid from the US since their talks of October 1961. This, in conjunction with the fact that US-based organisations — the Christian Anti-Communist Crusade through its representatives, Dr Schwartz and Dr Sluis, and the US Government Information Services — had actively campaigned against him, had 'created the impression that your Government is unwilling to assist the presently elected Government of this country and has served to embolden the Opposition to embark on irresponsible courses which are aimed at the forcible overthrow of my Government'. Jagan realised that he was in grave trouble, at home and abroad. Belatedly, he tried to coax some sympathy from Kennedy: 'I share our deep concern not only about the problems of world poverty, but also the growing tendency of the usurpation by reactionary elements of the democratic rights and liberties of free peoples. I am sure you would not want it said that in British Guiana the objectives of your administration were not being realised and fulfilled.'[84] Too little, too late: the President was determined to finish him off. Jagan was crumbling. The despair showed.

By early June 1963 the strikers were still intransigent, although the House was prorogued and the Bill withdrawn. The opposition were implacable. Racial violence escalated. Overwhelmed, Jagan wrote to Governor Grey that the 'instability' in Georgetown was a result of the lack of firmness on the part of the judiciary, the magistracy and the Police. He accused the latter of instances of 'insubordination and cowardice', going further to assert that 'the general public had been given the impression that action amounting to mutiny during a civil disturbance has been condoned by those in charge of administering the Police Force'. Jagan argued that the strike was 'political' not 'industrial', and that the TUC and the opposition were 'being aided by reactionary elements both here and abroad'. He concluded with a clear indictment of the US government in the subversion of his government. It was virtually the end of the road for him; the irrepressible ideological fervour had pitted him against the world's greatest defender of capitalism; he did not have the ammunition for the fight. The impotent rage was eloquent:

[T]he Opposition will use any pretext to ... subvert and destroy my Government. Unfortunately our situation is complicated by the fact that there is outside interference, particularly of the USA, in our affairs .... [O]ur trade unionists are working in close collaboration with the American Institute for Free Labour Development sited in Washington, which is also working in close collaboration with the US State Department and USAID. It is likely that there are CIA agents operating here in devious ways as information officers, trade unionists, etc. The Americans have built up a vast propaganda against my Government. The popular image in the United States is that British Guiana is going to be another Cuba and Jagan another Castro; consequently every means is being used to subvert and destroy my Government .... President Kennedy complained about communist subversion. What about capitalist, imperialist and fascist subversion?[85]

Jagan then questioned the veracity of Kennedy's statement to *Izvestia*, in November 1961, that he had no trouble with his Marxism because he was democratically elected. 'Fine words!', Jagan remarked sarcastically. In fact, the Americans were 'directing the strike behind the scenes', in order to destroy him. Then he asked, portentously: '[I]s it the intention to keep the pot boiling here so that the British Government, goaded by the Americans, can use the "situation" to delay indefinitely the granting of independence to this country as it did last year with the February disturbances to delay the independence talks?' He was correct: the plot was unfolding precisely as he sketched it. In despair, he exclaimed to the Governor: 'This is western democracy in action!'[86]

In March 1963 the American Consul General in Georgetown, in advising the State Department to pressure the British to impose PR, had intimated that he was in communication with 'fairly reliable sources within the PNC'.[87] It is highly likely, therefore, that Burnham was privy to the essence of American thinking on the colony, for his tactical manoeuvres were uncannily congruent with theirs, his nationalist posturing notwithstanding. In April 1963, for instance, on the eve of the general strike, in which American finance was crucial, Burnham observed of Jagan's PPP: 'The governing Party professes to be socialist but by its postures, its statements and the literature it distributes, leads one to the conclusion that its aim is to make Guyana a Soviet satellite.'[88] The PPP's paper, *Mirror*, unrepentantly, was carrying numerous articles critical of America.

One, captioned 'Writing on the Wall for Kennedy', spoke of the 'vast influence' of the Cuban Revolution even on Latin American liberals: '[They] can scorn whatever is identified with communism in the Castro regime, but the fact that Castro has been the first to challenge the authority of the US, refusing to let himself be intimidated despite an economic situation which is extraordinarily difficult as a consequence of the American embargo, places that same Latin American liberal on Castro's side.'[89] *Mirror* would not have helped the Party's case, either, when they carried the comments of their guest, the visiting American communist writer, Scott Nearing, on the Cuban example: '[The Americans] do not wish other Latin American countries to go the Cuban way because it is a threat to their empirical [imperial] expansion .... Mr. Khrushchev's actions in the Cuban crisis last October showed his statesmanship. He prevented a war which America wanted.'[90]

In early July 1963 Burnham had called on Jagan to hold a referendum on PR so that Guyanese could decide on the electoral system for the conduct of fresh elections.[91] It may be recalled that this was precisely what the American Consul General had advocated in his letter of March 14, to the State Department. Little did Burnham know that the fate of his country was already virtually decided in his favour as a result of President Kennedy's personal intervention, during his meeting at Birch Grove, England, with Prime Minister Macmillan, on June 30, 1963. Earlier, on June 21, at a meeting in the White House, at which Helms of the CIA gave a briefing on 'the current situation in British Guiana', the President made it clear that 'British Guiana .... [is] the most important topic he has to discuss with the Prime Minister'. They also spoke of the 'desirability of inviting Duncan Sandys to Birch Grove since he is a significant figure in any decision which HMG may make'.[92] The same day, Dean Rusk informed the US ambassador in London that British Guiana was the 'principal subject' the President intended to raise at the meeting. He then explained forthrightly precisely what they wanted from Macmillan. This was the final solution; it had to be decided before the Constitutional Conference in London, scheduled for October 1963. There was no equivocation:

Our fundamental position is that the UK must not leave behind in the Western Hemisphere a country with a Communist Government in control. Independence of British Guiana with government led by PPP unacceptable to US. *Our objective in London is to get HMG to take effective action to remove Jagan Government prior to independence....* Last Fall Macmillan agreed to this objective but he has now reverted to [the] view [that the] UK should wash its hands of British Guiana by granting early independence, leaving the mess on our doorstep .... I would welcome your thoughts on how best to convince our British friends of deadly seriousness of our concern and our determination that British Guiana shall not become independent with a Communist government [emphasis added].[93]

The decisive meeting between Kennedy and Macmillan took place at Birch Grove on June 30, 1963 with Dean Rusk and Duncan Sandys, Secretary of State for the Colonies in attendance. Sandys proposed four options: (i) 'to muddle on as we are now doing' (he rejected this); (ii) to grant independence (this 'obviously presented grave problems'); (iii) 'to suspend the constitution and institute direct rule'; (iv) 'to establish a Burnham-D'Aguiar government and then grant independence'. Sandys was not certain that a referendum on PR would defeat Jagan, besides it would look too much like a contrivance towards that end, but the implication was that PR was crucial in his removal.[94]

The President then underlined his case for Jagan's removal:

It was obvious that if the UK were to get out of British Guiana now it would become a Communist state. He thought the thing to do was to look for ways to drag the thing out [no immediate independence].... He thought that Latin America was the most dangerous area in the world. The effect of having a Communist state in British Guiana in addition to Cuba in 1964 [the Presidential elections], would be to create irresistible pressures in the United States to strike militarily at Cuba.

In delaying independence Kennedy advised that they should explain that this was necessary to prevent the 'unleashing of racial war', not because of the 'danger of British Guiana becoming

Communist'. The President repeated that Cuba would be the major issue in the elections of 1964: 'adding British Guiana to Cuba could well tip the scales, and someone would be elected who would take military action against Cuba'. He felt that Americans would not tolerate a situation in which the 'Soviet Union had leapfrogged over Cuba to land on the continent on the Western Hemisphere'.[95]

Duncan Sandys then submitted his crucial proposals: that the constitution be changed to introduce a new electoral system, proportional representation, instead of first-past-the-post. This was likely to deprive Jagan of his majority. Sandys thought that 'the best solution was that of a Burnham–D'Aguiar government to which the UK would grant independence'. Rusk replied that if Burnham got in they would 'move rapidly' to provide aid. Kennedy said he was attracted to the idea of PR. Sandys asked him whether the US were prepared to give them public support if the UK were to 'resume direct rule in the colony', as they were worried about the political consequences of the suspension of the constitution a second time. Kennedy assured them: 'It would be a pleasure ... we would go all out to the extent necessary.' The President had finally extracted assurances that Jagan would not be granted independence, as well as the pledge that PR would be imposed to secure his defeat at the next elections. This, though, was not easy for the British: it would require the unpalatable, but inescapable, step of suspending the constitution, the second time in ten years, as a prelude to the imposition of PR.[96]

The mechanics still had to be worked out, but events would move rapidly from here to the reconvened Constitutional Conference in London in October 1963. Central to the larger scheme was the necessity to continue to undermine the morale of Cheddi Jagan, to push him into a position of utter despair. It is interesting that Macmillan had enquired at Birch Grove 'whether it was worthwhile going on with the present strike pressure' — vindication of Anglo-American complicity in the anti-Jagan, politically-inspired strike in British Guiana. On July 17, 1963, after a visit to the colony amidst the continuing racial violence, Sandys told the House of Commons that the constitutional future 'must now be decided without much further delay'. He said that the leaders still disagreed on the issues which had led to the adjournment of the Conference the previous year; but he wished to give them a short period to seek a resolution, before he reconvened it in October. Then, ominously for Jagan, Sandys observed: '[I]f they are able to resolve their differences, that will greatly ease my task. Failing agreement, I think it is now generally accepted that the British Government will have to settle the outstanding issues on its own authority; and that is what we propose to do.'[97]

The imposition of a settlement would enable him to honour the guarantees he had given to Kennedy: it would pave the way for the removal of Jagan. On July 15, 1963 Sandys had stated that 'the Americans were worried about the situation', adding that they favoured suspension of the constitution and the pumping of investments 'until the Indian rural population was gradually weaned from Dr. Jagan's Party'. These pronouncements by Sandys simply aggravated the intransigence of Burnham: he knew he had powerful allies and precisely how politically advantageous the imposition of a solution would be to him. He refused, therefore, to compromise on Jagan's overtures towards the formation of a coalition government; he had no need to — Anglo-American complicity in subverting Jagan was designed to propel him into power, in an independent Guyana.[98]

On the eve of the conference which convened in London on October 22, 1963, the organ of the PPP, *Thunder*, raised doubts about the reconvening of the conference at a time when the PPP and the PNC had agreed that a Commonwealth team should broker a mutually satisfactory settlement. This was, in fact, another demonstration of the machiavellianism of Burnham: he wished for no such solution; he wanted the British imposition but would feign total abhorrence of it, as being fundamentally repugnant to his nationalist instincts — this, to entrap a broken Jagan into misreading a potential Sandys imposition as the last source of his salvation. *Thunder* warned: 'By refusing to allow this team an opportunity to resolve the difficulties, it is mooted that Mr. Sandys has in mind the imposing of a settlement to get the PPP out of office .... Imposition goes against the grain of the PPP'.[99]

Meanwhile the US government was moving in for the kill. On September 19, 1963 Davis Bell, Director of the Agency for International Development, who had attended the crucial meeting with the President at the White House on June 21, announced that Washington had decided against granting any economic aid to the

Jagan government, because they doubted 'whether any useful purpose would be served ... there is no real opportunity that could be helpful'.[100] *The Daily Chronicle*, in a leader entitled, 'Written Off', could see how dire this news was for Jagan on the eve of the London Conference: '[T]he decision of the US has been taken in the long-term interest of democracy.... For it would be a disservice to the US to establish an impenitently Communist government with US money; to give it the respectability which financial aid from the US will give; to give Britain the pretext she needs for handing over the residual power to Dr. Jagan, and to see a second Russian beachhead built up in this hemisphere.'[101]

This final rejection by the US, the 'imperialist vampire', allowed the PPP to expound, without reservation, what their fundamental ideological outlook was for an independent Guyana. In a leader of September 22, 1963, *Mirror* advised Jagan to allow 'history to guide him in the choice of the system he should employ':

> Russia, after the Bolshevik Revolution of 1917, was far behind the USA and the advanced countries of Europe. But she took charge of the economic surplus, socially controlled it, with Government as the sole owner of the means of production deciding just how the surplus was to be invested to achieve the desired result. The sum of this planned exercise is that Russia is one of the world's greatest industrial nations, or in other words, she has accomplished in half a century what the capitalist countries took three centuries to achieve.... It seems to us that the US refusal is a blessing in disguise, for the Premier can go ahead with the socialist system of development, with public ownership of the means of production and centralised planning based on revolutionary change involving the restructuring of society along new lines.[102]

In early September 1963 Jagan had spoken to the US Consul General in Georgetown, expressing concern that the US had adopted a policy of 'Jagan must go'. Belatedly, he sought advice on how relations could be mended, noting that if he were defeated, 'extremists' in the Party would take over, with the possible emergence of a 'Castroite situation'. The State Department rejected his overtures: they seem in contradiction of the attacks in the PPP paper on the US and the President personally. They concluded: 'We wish to avoid creating any impression, or enabling PPP to do so, that [there] exists real possibility of improving relations between PPP and USG.'[103]

The British and the Americans were irrevocably committed to Jagan's removal, but L.F.S. Burnham, too, buoyed by this fact, was rendering his own intriguing spin on proceedings, on the eve of the fateful Constitutional Conference in London in October 1963. As noted above, he set himself the task of feigning total opposition to a Sandys imposition, thereby deviously suggesting to a mortally wounded Cheddi Jagan that there could be a silver lining to an imposition. Towards the end of September 1963, *Mirror* carried an article in which Burnham was quoted as saying that to accept a British imposition 'was a negation of independence and the PNC would oppose any such imposition'. He concluded with a big lie, that the PNC would 'oppose any decision by the British Government to remove the PPP from office'.[104]

Burnham's web of deception on the question of an imposition grew more complex and calculated as the Conference approached:

> [I]t cannot be assumed that any solution that the British Government might have in mind to impose will be a solution acceptable to or in favour of the PNC.... It may well be that the British are not particularly fond of the naïve, incompetent Jagan, who parades throughout the world baring evidence of his attachment to the Soviet Bloc; but, on the other hand, who ever told you that the British are particularly fond of the forthright, nationalist Burnham.[105]

Jagan's communism and Kennedy's implacable fear of it, meant that Burnham could play ball with the Americans and the British while parading his contrived nationalist credentials for regional and Third World consumption.

This was a ruse, for Anglo-American connivance to hand power to Burnham was so blatant that even he would have been embarrassed to be seen as their blue-eyed boy. On September 10, 1963 President Kennedy wrote to Macmillan with regard to the plan which the latter had outlined to him, 'for a series of moves in September or October which would result in the removal of the Jagan Government'. Kennedy added that advance planning was required to help 'to steer

Burnham and D'Aguiar on the right path, creating and launching an alternative East Indian party, and a real economic development program'. He also sought information on the timing of crucial steps, such as the Constitutional Conference, suspension of the Constitution, new elections and the type of PR he envisaged. Kennedy then expressed his gratitude to the Prime Minister for his support on British Guiana:

> I continue to be well aware of the fact that this problem is one in which you have shown a most helpful understanding of my special concern, and I am grateful to you and also to Duncan Sandys for your willingness to take hold of it when there is so little advantage in it for you.[106]

Macmillan responded to Kennedy on September 27, explaining what they planned to do in October to remove Jagan. They were going to invite the three Guyanese leaders to London and inform them that since they had failed to arrive at a constitutional compromise they had to impose a solution. This would include 'a new electoral system designed to counter racialism [PR], and fresh elections when the necessary preparations were made'. He anticipated that Jagan would refuse to cooperate, may resign and ask the Governor to dissolve the Legislature and call new elections; he could even 'sit out and obstruct'. Macmillan said that '[I]n any of these events we shall be forced to suspend the constitution and take over the administration.'[107] It is amusing to note that the Prime Minister felt that Burnham might object to an imposition! Such was the power of Burnham's labyrinthine artifices! One person who would not have been deceived by his machinations was his sister, Jessie Burnham. In a pamphlet written around this time, 'Beware my Brother Forbes', she captured the essence of the man:

> I have watched this brilliant brother use his brain to scheme, to plot to put friend against friend, neighbour against neighbour, and relative against relative. I have watched him use this one and that one, and then quickly discard them when they have served their purpose. I have watched him, with his clever wit and charm, manipulate people like puppets on a string.... Behind that jest, that charm, that easy oratory is a certain dark strain

of cruelty which only surfaces when one of his vital interests is threatened. There are only two Burnhams; the charming and the cruel. I say BEWARE of both. I do not want to see my country become a police state, where a power-hungry man can sacrifice our liberty for his personal gain. Many men are cruel. Many men love power. The world can tolerate such men as individuals. But our beloved country cannot tolerate such men as LEADERS.[108]

As noted earlier, Arthur Schlesinger had concurred with apprehensions of Burnham expressed to him in Guyana in June 1962, but so obsessive was the President's fear of Jagan's communism that neither Schlesinger's nor Jessie's foreboding would have stayed his hand. By the eve of the Constitutional Conference in London in October 1963, the process was inexorable. The British envisaged a period of direct rule, however politically fraught the proposition, in order to maintain stability for the formation of new parties before the next elections under PR. Independence would come after that, presumably when a Burnham–D'Aguiar coalition was installed in government. Then, crucially, Macmillan returned to the thorny question of the suspension of the Constitution: 'It seems likely that we should have to suspend the constitution very shortly after Duncan Sandys has seen the political leaders, though, as I have explained, this will depend on Jagan's reaction. We have sufficient troops in the country.... I am sure we can rely on your support at the United Nations and generally.'[109]

Macmillan was worried, however, that Burnham and Jagan could come to an agreement to form a coalition, or have a UN commission investigate and report on measures towards a rapprochement. This had to be avoided: Burnham must not be so squandered!:

I think that the only thing which could cause our plan to go seriously awry would be if Jagan and Burnham were in the next few weeks to reach some sort of agreement. Burnham has lately shown some signs of supporting Jagan's proposal for an enquiry by a United Nations commission. This could only complicate the position, since it would be bound to recommend early independence, and would be more likely to advise the retention of the present electoral system [first-past-the-post]. *I assume, however, that your people will be doing what they can to discourage*

any joint moves, either for a coalition or for an outside enquiry,
either of which might upset all our plans [emphasis added].[110]

They had to move quickly. The Conference convened in London on October 22, 1963 and, true to the script, Burnham and D'Aguiar refused to compromise with Jagan on the three outstanding issues: (i) the electoral system; (ii) elections before independence; (iii) the voting age. Duncan Sandys then postponed the plenary sessions, while holding separate discussions with each of the three leaders. It was evident that Sandys's threat of an imposition loomed over the deliberations. At the meeting with Jagan, on October 23, Sandys had told him that there were three alternatives: (i) they reached agreement [he did not mean that]; (ii) adjourn without an agreement [and unilateral imposition]; (iii) or the Secretary of State was 'asked to make an arbitral decision [imposition by invitation]'. Jagan responded that he had come 'more or less' to the same conclusion. He therefore decided to make a further effort to reach an agreement with Burnham (this was inherently futile.) — '[f]ailing agreement he was prepared to accept that the Secretary of State would have to impose a decision'.[111]

Sandys then met Burnham the same day, putting the three alternatives to him. Burnham told him that *'in private he accepted that there were only these three possibilities, but he could not accept the third in public* [imposition by invitation] [emphasis added]'. In fact, although he could not be seen to be the poodle of the Americans or the British, he knew that the fuss was about ousting Jagan and slipping him in. Sandys asked what he would like him to do if he and Jagan failed to reach an agreement. He claimed that he could not 'express an opinion unless he knew what sort of an imposed solution' he had in mind. Sandys said he could not divulge that but he was not inclined to impose one unless all parties were in favour of his adjudication. Interestingly, Burnham observed that Jagan 'had already adopted that position'. In short, there was no need for him to seek an agreement with Jagan, as that would have entailed making some concessions, whereas an imposition promised him the whole kingdom. Having affected his nationalist posture, Burnham 'indicated that he would be prepared to accept any imposed solution if it were requested by all three parties, but clearly it would require some manoeuvring to bring such agreement about. He undertook to see Dr. Jagan that afternoon and discuss further with him'.[112] It took no arm-twisting! Burnham, contrary to what he claimed publicly, was always committed to an imposition.

Dr Fenton Ramsahoye, Jagan's Attorney General at the time, told me that they were aware that everything was stacked against them; but in the wake of virtual civil war in 1962 and 1963 they could not contemplate returning home empty-handed, with the daunting prospect of more turmoil. Though unpalatable, they knew that they had to accede to an imposition by Sandys; they even agreed to concede on all three counts — proportional representation, the voting age, even elections before independence — providing they could secure a date for independence. The latter, they assumed, would have inspired a psychological resurgence in their ranks, PR and the elections notwithstanding. This drastic revision of their position, he said, was discussed only among the PPP team, in confidence. Ramsahoye believes, in retrospect, that Lancaster House was bugged, and that Sandys must have known of their change in tactics, involving as it did the fundamental question of setting a date for independence. With the PPP giving ground so substantially, he would, therefore, have been under immense pressure — in a negotiated settlement —

Forbes Burnham: machiavellian

to concede some ground on the PPP's solitary demand: a date for independence. The PPP delegates would have fought to ensure that they got some concession before acceding to an imposition.[113] This would have complicated the prime aim of the British, as promised to Kennedy, the removal of Jagan. Burnham had told Sandys of the necessity for 'some manoeuvring' in order to secure a unanimous request for an imposition. There was, indeed, a great deal of manoeuvring — at the expense of Cheddi Jagan.

Apparently, on the evening of October 24, 1963, Sandys contacted Jagan and requested that they meet the next morning at Lancaster House, but emphasised that he should come alone. Jagan suspecting nothing untoward, did not consult Dr Ramsahoye or any of his other delegates, and went to see Sandys, accompanied only by the secretary of the British Guiana Office in London, Mrs Lee Akbar (the late Lee Samuel, MBE). She has related to me the somewhat bizarre atmosphere at Lancaster House that morning of October 25, 1963. Burnham and D'Aguiar were there, too, but, significantly, they had all their delegates with them, including their legal advisers. She sat alone, behind Dr Jagan. She knew that something was being hatched: she suggested to Cheddi that she should go to the office in Cockspur St. (not far away), and get Dr Ramsahoye and Brindley Benn, two of his delegates, to come. She repeated the offer to him as he sat alone, but he rejected it again. Samuel recalls that a document was passed around which Dr Jagan signed, followed by Burnham and D'Aguiar. Her instincts and the general feel of the place bred a deep foreboding, so much so that as soon as she returned to the office she told Jagan's delegates, who had been waiting unaware of the transactions, that their chief had just given everything away, without realising it.[114]

By indicating to Sandys and Burnham, in advance, that he was in favour of an imposition, Jagan gave himself no space for bargaining. By signing the document which Sandys had prepared, without examining its implications, Jagan had given him a blank cheque to do as he pleased with the future of Guyana. Neither Kennedy, Macmillan nor Burnham could have envisaged so much being given to them on a platter, so easily. There was, as a result, no need for the suspension of the constitution and the unilateral imposition of a solution, of which the British were still apprehensive; no need for horse-trading to secure unanimity for an imposition by invitation; besides the three leaders had agreed, categorically, to abide by Sandys's decisions. The contentious document of October 25, 1963 read thus:

TO THE SECRETARY OF STATE FOR THE COLONIES

At your request we have made further efforts to resolve the differences between us on the constitutional issues which require to be settled before British Guiana secures independence, in particular, the electoral system, the voting age, and the question whether fresh elections should be held before independence.

We regret to have to report to you that we have not succeeded in reaching agreement; and we have reluctantly come to the conclusion that that there is no prospect of an agreed solution. *Another adjournment of the Conference for further discussions between ourselves would therefore serve no useful purpose and would result in further delaying British Guiana's independence and in continued uncertainty in the country.*

In these circumstances we are agreed to ask the British Government to settle on their authority all outstanding constitutional issues, and we undertake to accept these decisions [emphasis added].
Signed:
CHEDDI JAGAN
L.F.S. BURNHAM
P.S. D'AGUIAR[115]

The trick was perpetrated on Jagan, by the inclusion of the sentence in emphasis in the second paragraph above. Read quickly, and bereft of legal scrutiny, it readily lends itself to the interpretation that an imposition would *not* delay independence, nor would the turmoil be prolonged. The suggestion of a possible date for independence (as was agreed by his own delegation at Lancaster House) and peace would certainly have struck a chord in Jagan. However, the fact that the question of whether elections should be held before independence was one of the key issues for adjudication, meant that Sandys was under no compulsion now to fix a date for independence. From what we know of Macmillan's pledges to Kennedy, it is inconceivable how Sandys could have fixed such a date. He had one task — to ensure the removal of Jagan before independence. He therefore decided against him on all counts. He also rationalised the trickery by eschewing any reference whatsoever to fear of Communism, while citing the benefit of PR as an instrument of fostering 'inter-party coalitions and multi-racial groupings', as Kennedy had specifically advised. But Jagan could have made the manoeuvre very awkward for Sandys. If he had made concessions on all three unresolved issues, including elections before independence, Sandys would have had a monumental moral hurdle to scale in rejecting setting a date for independence after fresh elections, as Jagan's delegation had agreed, as a precondition to an imposition by invitation. Jagan's signing of the infamous document made Sandys's task easy beyond his wildest dreams.

The climate of continuous subversion in British Guiana in 1962 and 1963 had placed Jagan in a situation in which he had virtually no allies, apart from the Cubans and Russians, fatal in the circumstances of the Cold War. This had taken its toll: he had virtually no trumps. He was, therefore, predisposed to an imposition and so left himself no room for manoeuvre. The trick played on him on October 25, in isolating him from his advisers, rendered him most vulnerable in dealing with the delicate matter in hand. After they had signed the fatal document, Sandys met the three leaders again, in plenary session, on October 28, ostensibly to discuss the electoral system. This is how the Governor, Sir Ralph Grey, assessed their performances: 'Burnham led off with a quiet and very competent argument against present system and in favour of West German type of Proportional Representation. D'Aguiar bumbled as usual; overstated case against first-past-the-post .... Jagan (who told me afterwards he was so tired he could hardly think) stumbled through a justification of first-past-the-post and his own record.'[116]

Before Sandys announced his decision, Jagan explained why he had taken the initiative to ask for an imposition. (Janet Jagan had said: 'I am surprised they agreed to sign.')[117] *Cheddi said that he was 'assuming that independence was obviously forthcoming'*; he had found the Opposition 'very unreasonable', and faced with the possibility of further fruitless negotiations, he had decided to go for the imposition. He noted that Burnham had initially 'reserved his position but then agreed after D'Aguiar had fallen in with the suggestion'. He obviously had not detected Burnham's ploy. Jagan concluded: 'I have put my confidence in the hands of the British Government and I hope decisions will be taken on the basis of constitutional principles, on British and Commonwealth precedents and conventions...Independence is absolutely necessary... for the country cannot get anywhere without it.'[118]

Jagan was devastated by Sandys's imposition, entirely acceding to the demands of Burnham and D'Aguiar; it evoked a quick response of utter despair — 'the most unprincipled decision in the long history of British colonialism'. Then strangely, he added that he did not feel 'bound' to accept Sandys's decision *because independence was a condition of his imposing a solution* [emphasis added]'. He saw it as 'a betrayal of trust'; he then came to the crux of the matter, something he had known all along: 'It is clear that this decision is in keeping with the wishes of the American Government and is subservient to it.' He concluded: 'The machinations of the Imperialists cannot destroy the PPP. I call upon the people of Guiana to stand firm in this hour of betrayal.' The impotent rage was equal to the defeat.[119]

Burnham pretended that he had nothing to celebrate, playing down the fact that his colonial masters had rescued his political career, again seeking to assert his nationalist credentials. Having won everything through the imposition, he could now affect repugnance at it; he could even pretend to be appalled at the failure to set a date for independence. In fact, he was dancing around Jagan's utter humiliation:

> I am pleased about nothing. A nationalist can never be pleased over the indignity of an imposition. We find no reason for jubilation because B.G. is still without a firm date for Independence.... Perhaps... [Jagan] should rethink his naïve statement in which he expressed great confidence in the British sense of fair-play and justice.... I agree with Dr. Jagan that the people of B.G. should stand firm in this hour of betrayal — of them by him.[120]

Jagan's own Party's newspaper was not charitable either. When he agreed to the imposition, *Mirror* had asked caustically: 'Why this admission of Guianese inferiority, and why the supine and humiliating acceptance of white supremacy, and acknowledgement of a master race?... We ... hope that all is not irretrievably lost. And that out of this ignominious moral capitulation may yet be carved splendid victory.'[121] When the Sandys decision was delivered, the paper sought solace in philosophical reflections, which they commended to an innocent Jagan:

[I]n his hour of travail he must find the balm of consolation in the philosophical sayings and practical maxims which, through the centuries, have served to stimulate man's interest for good.... 'Sweet are the uses of adversity'; 'I am the master of my faith, I am the captain of my soul'; 'A man's reach must exceed his grasp, or what's a heaven for?'; and 'The menace of the years finds, and shall find me unafraid.'[122]

There was a resigned, sarcastic edge to the advice dispensed to their tricked leader.

Futility obtruded as *Mirror* settled down to the reality of the imposition: 'There is hypocrisy. Guianese know British hypocrisy to be the most odious in the whole world and we blush for the decent British citizen who must live among Guianese and justify the perfidy of their Government.'[123] For Jagan, however, this was a minor, tactical set-back in the loftier mission, the glorious fight against Imperialism. The Marxist vision could rationalise these tactical errors in the struggle and energise him for the larger purpose, which leads inexorably to the communist state. In this battle, once again, he would turn to the sugar workers: in 1964, as in 1948 and 1953, they were at the centre of his political mission; no sacrifice was too great to demand of them. They were the unfaltering base which sustained Jagan's communist faith.

It is important to close with a hitherto unrecorded event which took place shortly before the fateful 1963 Conference in London. Lloyd Searwar was not a member of the delegation but he accompanied Jagan to New York and London. His story is revealing for the fount of goodwill many 'capitalists' still had for Cheddi; it also illuminates precisely what Searwar meant when he characterised him as 'closed up', a man with 'hang-ups' who never left the plantation — honest but naïve:

Cheddi went, through New York, to the Constitutional talks at which he was tricked by Duncan Sandys. When we were in New York Mrs. Vijayalakshmi Pandit, India's permanent representative to the U.N., Nehru's sister, asked Cheddi to go and see her. He and I alone went ... to the exquisite Hotel Carlisle, where the Indians were based. He had a chat with Mrs. Pandit....

She said that Lester Pearson, the Canadian Prime Minister, had been on to her. She gathered from him that the British were planning something to get Cheddi out of office, and that he ought to be very careful. She was a tall woman, broad shoulders, with the aristocratic bearing of the Nehrus, but she was warm and she came down to street level to see us off in our taxi. But Cheddi said to me: 'Lloyd, you can't really bother with the Nehrus. They have always been rich, wealthy people', or something to that effect. He wasn't addressing what she had just told him about British machinations. The woman had been almost motherly to him, but he could not see beyond her family's wealth and upper caste. That was Cheddi — very closed up. And, of course, he went on to London and was duly tricked.[124]

In 1990, long after the damage wrought by Anglo-American collusion had rendered Guyana an ungovernable basket-case, its best and brightest in exile in North America, Arthur Schlesinger acknowledged his role in the destruction of Cheddi Jagan:

I felt badly about my role thirty years ago .... There was great feeling after the Bay of Pigs, where the impression arose that Eisenhower had prepared an expedition to get rid of Castro [and] that Kennedy had lacked the resolution to follow through it. It was just politically going to look very bad if the dominoes began to fall in South America.... The fear was that Congress might use aid to British Guiana as a means of attacking the whole aid bill then before it.... Then, of course, what really happened was the CIA got involved, got the bit between its teeth and the covert action people thought [it] was a chance to show their stuff .... I think a great injustice was done to Cheddi Jagan.[125]

Too little, too late!

Endnotes

1. *West India Committee Circular*, December 1958.
2. People's Progressive Party, *Manifesto Programme and Policy* (1957), (mimeo.).
3. CO1031/3907, Copy of a translation of the interview of Dr Cheddi Jagan with the newspaper, *Revolucion* [Havana], September 1960.
4. Ibid.

5.	CO1031/3907, W.F. Dawson (Colonial Office) to R.E. Parsons (American Dept., Foreign Office), confidential, September 7, 1960.

6.	Ibid.

7.	CO1031/3907, W.M. Revell (Colonial Office) to R.E. Parsons (Foreign Office), confidential, September 13, 1960.

8.	CO1031/3907, Ralph Grey to A.M. MacKintosh (Colonial Office), secret, September 2, 1960.

9.	Ibid.

10.	CO1031/3907, Brief [by Foreign Office] for Secretary of State's talk with Mr. Hester (American Embassy), on September 18, 1960, confidential.

11.	Ibid., A.M. MacKintosh (Colonial Office) to Ralph Grey, secret and personal, October 28, 1960.

12.	Ibid., W.F. Dawson (Colonial Office) to M. Johnson (Foreign Office), confidential, November 14, 1960.

13.	Ibid., British Embassy (Washington) to Ralph Grey, November 29, 1960.

14.	Ibid., J.D. Hennings (Colonial Attache, British Embassy, Washington) to A.M. MacKintosh (Colonial Office), secret, January 24, 1961.

15.	Ibid., Extract from a letter, dated February 28, 1961, from Mr Thomas (Foreign Office) to Mr MacKintosh (Colonial Office), secret and personal.

16.	Ibid., Extract from copy of a letter from Ralph Grey to Colonial Attache, Washington [J.D. Hennings], dated February 16, 1961, recording discussion with Mr Foster of US State Department.

17.	T.B. Williamson (Colonial Office) to F.C. Mason (Foreign Office), secret and guard, April 28, 1961.

18.	Ibid.

19.	Nigel Fisher, *Iain Macleod* (London: Andre Deutsch, 1973), 190.

20.	*Chronicle of the West India Committee*, April, May 1960.

21.	Ibid., [Leader], April 1960.

22.	Ibid.

23.	*Chronicle of the West India Committee*, March 1960.

24.	Maurice St. Pierre, *Anatomy of Resistance: Anti-Colonialism in Guyana, 1823-1966* (London: Macmillan, 1999), 166.

25.	CO1031/4177, Grey to Barnes (Colonial Office), August 26, 1961.

26.	Ibid., Grey to A.R. Thomas (Colonial Office), September 26, 1961.

27.	Cheddi Jagan, 'Towards Understanding...', The Text of an Address to the National Press Club, Washington, DC, USA, October 14, 1961.

28.	Thomas J. Spinner, Jr., *A Political and Social History of Guyana, 1945-83* (Boulder, Colorado: Westview Press, 1983), 82-83.

29.	CO1031/4177, Cheddi Jagan on 'Meet the Press' [script of the interview], October 15, 1961.

30.	Ibid.

31.	Lloyd Searwar, interview by the author, Georgetown, August 24, 2000.

32.	See note 24 [p. 167].

33. CO1031/4178, J.H. Hennings (Colonial Attache, British Embassy, Washington) to Ralph Grey, secret and personal, November 19, 1961.

34. Ibid.

35. Arthur M. Schlesinger, Jr., *A Thousand Days: John F. Kennedy in the White House* (London: Andre Deutsch, 1965), 665.

36. Cheddi Jagan, *The West on Trial: My Fight for Guyana's Freedom* (London: Michael Joseph, 1966), 415.

37. Ibid., 415-7.

38. Ibid., 417.

39. See note 31.

40. *New York Times*, October 29, 1961.

41. Ibid., November 29, 1961.

42. See note 35 [p. 668]

43. Ibid., [668-9].

44. *New York Times*, November 4, 1961.

45. CO1031/3714, 'Intelligence Report for the Month of November 1961 [A.J.E. Longden]', secret and personal.

46. Ibid.

47. CO1031/3714, 'Intelligence Report for the Month of October 1961'.

48. *New World Fortnightly*, 'Portraits of the Leaders: Jagan, Burnham, D'Aguiar', no. 3 (November 30, 1964): 27, 31-2.

49. PREM11/3666, Record of a Meeting Held in the State Dept, April 6, 1961.

50. PREM11/3666, Reginald Maudling to the Prime Minister, January 10, 1962.

51. See note 36 [p. 252].

52. *Report of a Commission of Inquiry into Disturbances in British Guiana in February 1962*, Col. No. 354, (Sir Henry Wynn Parry, chairman), (London: HMSO, 1962), 61.

53. Ibid., Chapters III&IV; see also Reynold Burrowes, *The Wild Coast: An Account of Politics in Guyana* (Cambridge, Mass: Schenkman, 1984), 143-61.

54. *Thunder*, July 7, 1962.

55. Ibid.

56. Ibid., July 14, 1962.

57. See note 52 [pp. 51-2].

58. See note 24 [p. 171].

59. PREM11/3666, House of Commons Debates, February 19, 1962.

60. Ibid., Rusk to Home, February 19, 1962.

61. Ibid.

62. See note 24 [p.172].

63. PREM11/3666, Maudling to Macmillan, [PM(62)15], secret, March 2, 1962.

64. Ibid., British Embassy, Washington to Foreign Office, secret, March 8, 1962.

65. US Government Foreign Relations Files on British Guiana, 1961–63 [hereafter cited as USG], Memorandum from the President's Special Assistant (Schlesinger) to the Ambassador to the UK (Bruce), March

1, 1962. (These files were reproduced in *Stabroek News* [Georgetown], December 1996-January 1997, in a series, 'Window on the Sixties'. I am grateful to Mazrul Bacchus for this collection).

66. PREM11/3666, Hugh Fraser to Secretary of State for the Colonies, 'Conversation with the Americans in Washington on British Guiana', secret and guard, [March 1962].

67. Ibid.

68. Ibid.

69. USG, Memorandum from the President's Special Assistant (Schlesinger) to President Kennedy, Washington, March 1962.

70. PREM11/3666, Macmillan to Sir N. Brook, top secret, May 2 1962.

71. USG, Telegram from the Department of State to the Embassy in the UK, June 7, 1962, (encl., letter from Macmillan to Kennedy, dated May 30, 1962).

72. See note 24 [p. 176].

73. USG, Memorandum by the President's Special Assistant (Schlesinger) to President Kennedy, June 21, 1962.

74. USG, Memorandum from Secretary of State (Rusk) to President Kennedy, July 12, 1962.

75. CO887/8, (Commission of Inquiry into the Disturbances in British Guiana in February 1962), Dr C.B. Jagan examined by Lionel Luckhoo, June 22, 1962.

76. USG, Record of Kennedy's discussion with Ormsby-Gore, [Washington], July 21, 1962.

77. See note 36 [p. 269].

78. CO1031/3714, Grey to Sandys, secret and personal, December 8, 1962.

79. See note 36 [p. 302].

80. See Cheddi Jagan, *U.S. Intervention in Guyana*, (PPP Publication, 1966).

81. See note 53 [Burrowes, p. 172].

82. *Mirror*, June 23, 1963. See also leader of the same issue, captioned: 'Big Bad Wolf Howls Again'.

83. USG, Consul General, Georgetown [Melby] to the Dept. of State, March 14, 1963.

84. USG, Letter from Premier Jagan to President Kennedy, Georgetown, April 16, 1963.

85. CO1031/4931, Jagan to Grey, June 12, 1963.

86. Ibid.

87. See note 79.

88. *New Nation*, April 19, 1963.

89. *Mirror*, April 14, 1963.

90. Ibid., April 21, 1963.

91. *New Nation*, July 5, 1963.

92. USG, Memorandum on White House Meeting on British Guiana, June 21, 1963.

93. USG, Telegram from the Department of State to the Embassy in the UK, June 21, 1963.

94. USG, Meeting of Kennedy and Macmillan, Birch Grove, England, June 30, 1963.
95. Ibid.
96. Ibid.; see also Richard Lamb, *The Macmillan Years, 1957–63: The Emerging Truth* (London: John Murray, 1995), 366.
97. *The Times*, July 18, 1963.
98. Ibid., 20, July 22, 1963.
99. *Thunder*, October 1963.
100. *The Daily Chronicle*, September 19, 1963.
101. *The Sunday Chronicle*, [Leader], September 22, 1963.
102. *Mirror*, [Leader], September 22.
103. USG, Telegram from the Dept of State to the Consul General, Georgetown, September 7, 1963.
104. *Mirror*, September 28, 1963.
105. Ibid.
106. CO1031/4402, President Kennedy to Prime Minister Macmillan, top secret, September 10, 1963.
107. CO1031/4402, Macmillan to Kennedy, top secret, September 27, 1963.
108. Jessie Burnham, *Beware My Brother Forbes* [pamphlet, PPP Publication, ca. 1964], quoted in Ashton Chase, *Guyana: A Nation in Transit — Burnham's Role* (Georgetown: self-published, 1994), pp. 2-3.
109. See note 103.
110. Ibid.
111. CO1031/4495, Note of a Meeting Held in the Commonwealth Relations Office, October 23, 1963.
112. Ibid.
113. Dr Fenton Ramsahoye, interview by the author, London, July 25, 1992.
114. Lee Samuel, MBE, interview by the author, June 12, 1997.
115. *British Guiana Constitutional Conference, 1963* , Cmd. 2203, November 1963.
116. CO1031/4495, Grey to Rose (OAG, British Guiana), secret and personal, October 29, 1963.
117. *The Daily Chronicle*, October 26, 1963.
118. Ibid.
119. Ibid., November 1, 1963.
120. Ibid.
121. *Mirror*, October 27, 1963.
122. Ibid., November 3, 1963.
123. *Mirror*, November 17, 1963.
124. See note 31.
125. 'Great Injustice done to Jagan Schlesinger', editorial, *The Nation*, June 4, 1990.

Chapter Thirty-Two

NEITHER REFORM NOR REVOLUTION: JAGAN, CAMPBELL, THE COLD WAR AND THE SUGAR INDUSTRY, 1961–64

In 1960 Lloyd Searwar had remarked that a resilient image of the sugar industry — as the implacable oppressor — was at the core of Indian political sensibility, and that, as in the late 1940s, it tended to be magnified at times of stress. He observed that this could well be the case again if Indian political ascendancy were to be threatened. He had explored the quiescence on the sugar plantations of recent years, the late 1950s, and concluded:

> [I]t has always seemed to me that the peace on the sugar estates of recent years and the freedom from violence owe a great deal to the fact that the Indian sugar estate worker feels that he has power at the centre [Jagan was returned to office in August 1957, after the suspension of the constitution in October 1953]. With the disappearance of such power, political feeling is likely to express itself through the trade unions in much the same way as it first expressed itself.[1]

Indeed, for Cheddi Jagan, as I have argued throughout this book, the trade union was not just an instrument for articulating industrial grievances (he had no such 'bourgeois' conception of unionism); it was the main weapon in the class struggle, what he had described in 1948 as the pursuit of 'scientific socialism'. It was at the heart of his mission, to take control of the 'commanding heights' of the economy, especially sugar, and rid his land of the yoke of imperialism. However admirable were aspects of Campbell's reformism, however sincere was Jock himself, that was too little, too late. Cheddi could not countenance a long-term partnership with Booker, even Campbell's Booker. For tactical reasons, between 1957 and the early 1960s, while he was in office, he would struggle to deflect attention — never successfully — from the fact that nationalisation of sugar was central to his Marxist philosophy.

On December 22, 1994, four days before Jock Campbell died, Dr Fenton Ramsahoye, the Attorney General of British Guiana in the Jagan government of 1961–64, and I spent the day with him at his home in Nettlebed, Oxfordshire, talking about Guyana. I asked them both whether it would have made any difference if Jock had speeded up the reforms in the early 1960s, whether the political evolution might have been less calamitous. Ramsahoye responded:

> I don't think that any attempt to speed up the process of development would have made any difference to the sort of political culture which the political parties were endeavouring to create in Guyana. And the basis of the People's Progressive Party's political culture was, in the end, the nationalisation of the industry and whether the internal processes were speeded up, and the welfare programme speeded up, would in no way have altered that fundamental political philosophy. It would have remained the same whatever the pace of social development within the industry.... [I]t was part of his political theory [Jagan's] that the commanding heights of the economy, which included the sugar and bauxite industries, should be in government's hands.[2]

Campbell endorsed that:

> I thought that the sugar industry would probably be nationalised, so we weren't trying to buy anybody off; we were genuinely trying to behave far better. I said when I first went there everybody hated Booker, and my business was to try and make people if not like Booker — I said it was always easier for a Campbell to go through the eye of a needle than for a big company to be loved — but it could at least be understood and respected. And that was all I was trying to do; I entirely agree with Fenton it wouldn't have made any difference, politically, anything we did at any stage.[3]

This fundamental fact meant that Jagan could see no merits in Campbell's reforms — a crucial potential alliance between 1957 and 1963 was, therefore, squandered. So, too, with Iain Macleod, the Secretary of State for the Colonies, for whom Jock Campbell had considerable respect — he, as noted earlier, had granted internal self-government to Jagan in March 1960, with the assumption that independence would follow in a couple of years — yet Jagan undermined his and Macleod's position (in the Conservative Party), by beginning his relationship with Castro. Yet, even after the anti-Jagan riots in Georgetown in February 1962, Iain Macleod was still prepared to defend him, minimising his communist proclivities to the Americans. On February 27, 1962 he told Arthur Schlesinger, Kennedy's special assistant, that Jagan was not a communist: 'He is a naïve, London School of Economics Marxist filled with charm, personal honesty and juvenile nationalism.' Macleod added that the Kaldor Budget which was the ostensible cause of the riots was 'not a Marxist programme'; it was 'a severely orthodox programme of the "Crippsian" sort [Fabian Socialist]'. He felt that Jagan would win another election if this was held before independence was granted. Like Campbell, Macleod was still unequivocal in his preference for Jagan: 'If I had to make the choice between Jagan and Burnham as head of my country I would choose Jagan any day of the week.'[4]

As Jagan slid fatally into the morass of Cold War politics, Campbell's reforms became increasingly marginal, with the larger politics abroad and virtual civil war at home clouding out issues relating to the local economy. However, between 1961 and 1963, Campbell continued to support Jagan, against the Opposition in British Guiana, although the Booker people in London and in Georgetown often thought otherwise. It had been infinitely easier for Campbell's view of Jagan to prevail in Booker in the 1957-60 period, before the relationship developed between Jagan and Castro, igniting Kennedy's fear of a second communist state in the Hemisphere. In November 1961, for instance, Campbell had responded to the transcript of Jagan's 'Meet the Press' interview in the United States the previous month. He remarked to A.R. Thomas at the Colonial Office: 'He certainly didn't excel himself therein, did he? Indeed, I'm afraid he gave his maddening impression of combined naivete and evasiveness which always emerges when he is under pressure about communism from people like the execrable Mr. Spivak [moderator of the programme].' Yet Campbell could still find something redeeming in Jagan's performance: '[I]t seems generally hopeful that he has expressed his intention of remaining in the Commonwealth, of retaining democratic institutions, that he went to America and Canada first rather than flouncing off to Comrade Khrushchev, and that he does seem genuinely to intend to be politically neutral and economically empirical.' He concluded: 'As I have said before, I am sure that whether Cheddi can remain on his precarious tightrope depends on the goodwill, financial help and investment, and technical assistance that he gets from the West.' [5]

In 1960 Jagan had two very important men on his side; whatever their reservations about his communist creed, Macleod and Campbell considered his main rival, Forbes Burnham, a potentially destructive force in an independent Guyana. By 1962, however, Macleod had left the Colonial Office and Jock Campbell's self-confidence was somewhat shaken after he had had a nervous breakdown in the summer of 1960. He said that the illness resulted in him being away from Booker for nine months, in 1960–61. He told me that the breakdown stemmed from a cancer scare which proved groundless; his 'working frightfully hard'; and his own daughter's breakdown and her attempted suicide. The consequences were quite traumatic. Until 1960 he ran Booker as his own, in total control of everything; he returned in mid-1961 to find that much had changed: many people had carved out areas of autonomy in the company, as expansion was continuing away from Guyana; the character of the place was being transformed. Jock explained how the nervous breakdown affected him on his return to Booker:

> My own fallibility and some loss of confidence .... [were experienced] at this stage.... [O]ne day, as it were, I walked out of Booker absolutely in charge of everything ... and in full flood and not very old, this is 1960 ... 48 years old ... and I come back nine months later with having disclosed my fallibility and my vulnerability ... with less absolute confidence in myself, and with other people having taken over a lot of things ... and I never quite got back my confidence or the hold I had on every nook and

cranny in Booker.... I had been this great patriarch there; I was a hero .... I simply had a depressive nervous breakdown ... it made me feel vulnerable: not that I wasn't infallible; I wasn't invulnerable .... The atmosphere was rather different. Everybody was very kind, but it was patently different .... [I felt] everybody thought I was a bit mad ... [but now] he is a bit more mad than we thought. [6]

Campbell said that it was always a struggle to win the people in Booker to reforms, to the wider responsibilities he felt deep in his bones because of the ancient wrongs inflicted by his own family in the colony since the 1780s. The people who were next in line in Booker, David Powell and George Bishop, harboured no such altruistic sentiments:

[M]y difficulty was ... [that] I had to deal with people on the spot [Follett-Smith, Readwin and Tasker in British Guiana] and I had to deal with a Board in London who didn't take my political views at all. And I don't think ... [they] realised what the real problem of the West Indies was. I mean (not that I'm complaining), but I was a boy scout in the wilderness to some extent and ... in many ways (I say this with all modesty), *I was surprised how much I did get done, considering most of the time I was working alone* [emphasis added].[7]

I have argued that Campbell was totally committed to working with Jagan after his re-election to office in August 1957. Indeed, as early as 1958, he had made an effort to build a partnership with the government, the unions and local investors, so as to reduce Booker's monopoly in British Guiana: 'a state within a state'. Campbell told me of the circumstances of the offer, stating that he had not discussed it with the Board nor with Follett-Smith, the head of Booker Sugar Estates in the colony, when he made it to Cheddi. This was around 1958, before Jock's illness; he was at his peak and had no doubts that he could get the approval of the Board. He recalled:

I did have a long talk with Cheddi (I don't think this is recorded anywhere), but I said to Cheddi: 'Look, suppose I try to work out a scheme whereby the sugar industry of Guyana is owned 51%

by trust in Guyana, in which the Government and the unions are represented and we own the other 49% and we manage it. There ... [would be] a two-tier board as in Germany ... the shareholders' board — there would be shareholders who consist of sugar workers, political parties, the unions, individual Guyanese could have shares — and they would have the controlling interests in the industry and the other Board of Directors would lay down the policy; and then there would be a practical management board on which the top board would be represented as well.' I remember it, in Follett-Smith's office — I turned him out of it — and Cheddi and I talked about two hours. Cheddi said: 'Well, I'll think about it'. But I never heard another word.[8]

In 1991 I asked Cheddi whether he could recall the offer made by Jock. He replied bluntly that he could not remember. Nothing I said could jolt his memory. Some time afterwards I discovered that he had, indeed, under cross-examination by Lionel Luckhoo, revealed to the Wynn Parry Commission in Georgetown, on June 26, 1962 Campbell's offer of joint ownership of the sugar Industry:

Luckhoo:	May I remind you, you wrote a book called *Forbidden Freedom* .... on page 29 it says: 'Nationalising of the sugar industry and, indeed, all industries is the ultimate aim. B.G. is still tied to imperialism. Certain reforms should be undertaken to break the back of imperialism.' Do you still adhere to this?
Jagan:	I still adhere in the main .... There are some persons in the country, immediately on thinking of nationalisation, think of expropriation, think of confiscation without compensation .... As regards sugar, the Chairman of Booker suggested to me — I don't know if it was done in a jocular manner — that the Government should take 50% shares in Booker.
Luckhoo:	Sir Jock [Campbell] said that?
Jagan:	I said I don't know whether this was done jocularly.[9]

In fact, after the conclusion of the Constitutional Conference in London in March 1960, Campbell hosted a reception for Jagan, where he had repeated his offer of government participation in sugar which he said he first made in 1958. Among those present were two of Jagan's ministers: B.H. Benn and Balram Singh Rai. This is how Rai recalls Jock's offer:

> Jagan refused to explore an informal offer made by Sir Jock Campbell, Head of Booker, to make over 49% or 51% of their sugar estates to the Government to be paid out of profits in ensuing years, despite my urging him to do so. This offer was made at a dinner given at the Traveller's Club in London for the British Guiana delegation. [10]

Campbell was an unwavering advocate of decolonisation and the adaptation of expatriate companies to the national aspirations of emerging societies. Conscious of Booker's role in British Guiana, and as if to guide Jagan towards a more moderate but no less radical a stance, this is how he had framed their task in 1959:

> The governments of new nations, in the face of formidable social and economic problems, have no straightforward choice between capitalist and communist systems of economic development .... Strong central planning and control by their governments seem essential to the progress of most of these countries .... It is Western capitalism which must, if it is to survive, adapt itself to, and become part of, the historical processes of these nations. [11]

In October 1964, in explaining why he was voting Labour in the forthcoming elections, Jock explored his belief in the inevitability of radicalism:

> [M]y personal background of the West Indian sugar industry and trading in Africa has taught me that the vast majority of people have not got money, privilege, position and power. Most of the population of the world, and indeed of the Commonwealth, are poor, hungry, insecure and underprivileged. And my experience as a businessman has shown me that the benefits to everybody immeasurably outweigh the disadvantages to a few, of striving to raise general standards and conditions of living .... I support Labour because I am a radical (or at any rate I hope I

am). What do I mean by a radical? It is partly, I suppose, a matter of temperament, a desire to get down to root causes, an inclination to be sceptical about the conventional wisdom which traditionalists take for granted. There is nothing inherently disreputable in being a reformer rather than a conformist, although I don't take any credit for being temperamentally 'agin the established order'. I believe that most progress and nearly all reforms come from radicals. If government was left only to Conservatives we would still be in the Middle Ages: slavery won't have been abolished, women won't have the vote. It is inconceivable that what has been achieved over the last 150 years in this country could have been accomplished by the traditionalists and the conformists.[12]

This radicalism had guided his conception of the role of Booker in post-war Guyana. On February 25, 1965, shortly after Burnham had formed a coalition government with Peter D'Aguiar, following the elections under PR in December 1964, Campbell told the Governor, Sir Richard Luyt, that he would soon meet with Burnham to discuss his call for the 'decolonisation of sugar', adding that it was Booker's intention 'to allow the Government to become a substantial shareholder'. The Governor noted: 'Sir Jock reminded me that he had urged Dr. Jagan to do this some seven years ago [1958] but the British Guiana Government of that time dithered with the idea and ultimately did nothing about it.'[13]

Jagan would have seen Campbell's offer as another manifestation of reformist capitalism, a ploy to divert him from the pure Marxist imperative of nationalisation of 'the commanding heights of the economy'. This attitude was also evident in Jagan's approach to the land question. He ceaselessly indicted the plantations for perpetuating 'land-hunger': 'Large tracts of land are kept idle or are not properly utilised. The sugar planters control directly about 170,000 acres ... and more than 50 per cent of the total land holdings were uncultivated.'[14] However, during the seven years he was in government, 1957 to 1964, he did not provide any freehold land to small farmers to eradicate 'land hunger', although there was a substantial amount of uncultivated state land available on the coastland. Dr Ramsahoye explained the reason for this contradiction:

We did have state lands but Dr. Jagan never believed in freehold tenure; he only believed in leasehold tenure, and the leases which he favoured were for 25 years with the right of renewal — in the business world that type of lease is far too short for a mortgagee or a chargee to take any interest in — so the farmers were in a bit of a difficulty, but the philosophy was then, as it is now [1994], that all land in Guyana should really be owned by the state ... therefore, taking away the land from Booker would not have meant that the Guyanese farmer would have got ... any freehold lands .... [Jagan] would have been willing to concede a lot for housing, he would have been willing to concede a freehold title for that, I believe, but he certainly would not have conceded a grant of 50 or 100 acres to a farmer.[15]

Private ownership of land went against his Marxist grain. That was precisely why, in 1961, the PPP government rejected the Pension Scheme for sugar workers. This, too, would have been read as another strand in the scheme of the sugar producers and their 'company union', the MPCA, to perpetrate another reformist gimmick on the sugar workers. On the eve of the 1961 general elections and the resurrection of the PPP union, the Guiana Sugar Workers' Union (later Guyana Agricultural Workers' Union [GAWU]), accepting the scheme was tantamount to giving credit to their enemies. The sugar workers were seen as the preserve of the PPP: no sacrifice, therefore, was too great to ask of them, in the larger framework of Cheddi Jagan's Marxist mission. For him, politics was not the art of the possible; it was the pursuit of the inevitable communist millennium — there was no room for the individual here; no concession to 'petty bourgeois' capitalist manoeuvrings; no space for a modus vivendi with foreign capitalists, however enlightened.

Yet, as will be seen, Jock Campbell, even through the turbulent times of 1962–63, continued to offer moral support to Cheddi Jagan. In 1962, for instance, he came to the defence of the Kaldor Budget, although the opposition in British Guiana had used it as the pretext to foment violence to delay the independence talks scheduled for May 1962. Campbell interpreted the Budget thus:

It clearly was, in intention, a serious attempt by the Government to get to grips with the formidable economic problems of the country by a hard programme of self-help. *It was a radical budget — what have the people of British Guiana got to be conservative about? — but not confiscatory.* As well as steep increases in import duties, it contained, all in one fell swoop, many new features — a capital gains tax; a tax on net wealth; and compulsory savings, from individuals and companies, for national development. Exchange control was applied, for the first time in British Guiana, to the sterling area. I recognise that the threatening flight of capital from the country made this unavoidable .... I know that many people still question the necessity and desirability of some of the new measures. The burden of the budget on people and business — on the Booker Group and our employees — is unquestionably heavy. There are real problems of administration and enforcement. But our views have been given fair hearing by Ministers. We must now, in keeping with our oft-stated policy to work with and to serve the Government of the day, do all we can to work the new system well.... The Guianese Government's pre-eminent aim — shared I hope by all parties in British Guiana — must now be to restore confidence. In this they can certainly count upon Booker [emphasis added].[16]

He was not inclined to pander to the machinations of Burnham and D'Aguiar in their campaign to delay independence, neither would he support withholding the provision of aid for development, to stifle Jagan. Campbell argued: 'Refusing independence to countries conscious of their new nationhood is politically untenable and morally indefensible. But it is equally indefensible, having imposed our sort of world upon these countries, not to help their development — with money and skills and with resources and trade — in the context of their own societies. What is wanted is a Declaration of Interdependence.'[17]

Booker News endorsed Campbell's policy of cooperation and the necessity for radical change inherent in independence:

The Booker Group is not daunted by change in the economics and societies in which its businesses operate. The Group accepts change, is willing to make adjustments to meet it. In return, it is expected that the new governments, having made the rules, will first explain them then and thereafter stick to them.

> Interdependence is a two-way traffic, not only between nations,
> but between government and the governed.

The paper also commended Campbell's recognition that in the new
nations 'there will be much state control, planning and participation
in industrial enterprise'. They noted, also, his optimism that there
would still be 'plenty of room' for 'profitable investment by private
enterprise'.[18] Indeed, this was the philosophical outlook which had
informed his overtures to Jagan in 1958 and 1960 — to establish a
partnership between government and Booker for the development
of an independent Guyana.

The organ of the PPP, *Thunder*, was impressed with Jock
Campbell's remarks, observing that they were 'bold and realistic ... a
frank and honest appraisal of the problems in British Guiana, as well
as a profound and comprehensive new look at the changing world'.
The paper was equally appreciative of his comments on the budget:
'Sir Jock's analysis of the budget crisis in British Guiana, no doubt,
gave quite a jolt to those who have been shouting themselves hoarse
on the subject, irresponsibly refusing to see the merits of the
austerity budget and the need for a radical budget at this time.' [19]

Earlier, in March 1962, Campbell had called for the government
and the opposition to consolidate the 'unifying forces' rather than
exploit the 'divisive tendencies' in the country. He elaborated: 'For
the Government the situation demands that they explain effectively
to the people why austerity is necessary for their country. For the
Opposition it imposes the obligation when they oppose to do so
constructively and constitutionally.' [20] He was suggesting that the
role of the PNC and UF, in the disturbances of February 1962, was
less than honourable. Always conscious of the interplay between
economic reality and political stability, Jock turned to the question
of world poverty, arguing that the destiny of the poor mattered
'morally, economically and politically' to the rich: 'The trouble .... is
that the rich aren't going to be all right for long with the poor getting
relatively poorer, and more numerous, and more desperate. Our
destinies are inseparable.'[21]

On February 28, 1963, at a press conference in British Guiana,
Campbell was asked specifically about his defence of the controversial
1962 Budget and his attitude to the Jagan government. He replied

that he was 'unrepentant' about his statement and was prepared to repeat it. He had no reasons to revise his assessment that 'Government had made a serious and honourable attempt to get the country going and, in the formidable state of the finances, only a stringent budget, such as that introduced in January 1962, could pull the country out of the rut'. He repeated that there was nothing 'confiscatory' about the budget; indeed, precedents for all the measures introduced existed in the North Atlantic communities. Even the much-maligned compulsory savings levy was 'defensible': 'It was an investment in Government bonds very similar to the post-war credit systems which Britain had used when its economy was threatened.' He was asked whether such stringent budgetary provisions would have been accepted in the UK. He said they would not, but British Guiana was a poor country requiring some austerity in order to move forward. He elaborated, again indicting the opposition for fomenting violence: although he did not like paying heavy taxation, 'he would not try to overthrow the Government because of it'. He continued: 'He would not say that he agreed with the budget, but he understood the reasons for introducing it and, if he had been Premier of British Guiana, he would probably have attempted the same sort of budget.'[22]

Campbell then remarked that there was no room for a right-wing government in Guyana, nor would the people support unbridled capitalism; they were in favour of a mixed economy. He noted: 'Except in the USA and Canada, he had yet to find a country where private enterprise was loved and admired. It was too much to expect voters to choose a government whose stated policy was to pander to private enterprise. People would not vote, for instance, for Booker, and affiliation with Booker would be "the kiss of death" for any political party'. He added that although the Jagan government was 'not particularly stimulating to private enterprise', Booker did not find this 'unduly inhibiting': they could 'do business and exist with a left-wing government'. His support for independence, too, had not waned since 1962: '[C]olonialism was neither politically nor morally desirable, and B.G.'s continuing as an appendage of Great Britain was not practical.'[23] He hoped, however, that the proposed coalition between Jagan's PPP and Burnham's PNC would come to fruition.

In spite of the racial violence in the colony and the orchestrated resistance of the trade unions to the Labour Relations Bill of 1963,

Campbell defended Cheddi Jagan's government, it being the democratically elected authority in the colony. Even when Sandys's imposition of a constitutional plan came down comprehensively and blatantly against Jagan, he defended Cheddi. In November 1963, Dr Rita Hinden, a member of the Waddington Constitutional Commission to British Guiana in 1950-51, had declared in favour of the imposition, contending that it offered the possibility of ending the stalemate. In fact, she was unequivocally opposed to Jagan, thus hardly an impartial judge of the merits of the imposition. She argued from the premise that Jagan's record in office was so discriminatory that it had attracted the odium of non-Indians in Guyana. She therefore opposed independence because it would constitute 'a betrayal' of 'democratic elements' in the colony, including the 'democratic trade unions', which were fighting 'valiantly for their rights and were mainly manned by Guianese of African descent'. Hinden believed that to accede to Jagan meant 'handing over the country to some form of dictatorship'.[24]

A couple days later Jagan explained that when he agreed to the imposed solution, it was 'on the implicit understanding' that Duncan Sandys would 'fix a date for my country's independence'. He felt that the imposition was 'a breach of faith ... [it was] deliberately rigged to prevent my party securing a majority at the next elections'.[25] Campbell, too, soon joined the debate, asking whether Sandys and Hinden had 'forgotten that the Indians were the largest race in British Guiana', a fact that should be recognised as clearly as 'understandable African fears'. He observed that delaying independence was a backward step:

> Dr. Hinden does not mention that independence has yet again been put back. Presumably she approves of this. But so long as it is delayed so long will all sections of the Guianese society lack compelling incentive to assume full responsibility for their destiny. Be it Dr. Hinden in 1951, or Mr. Sandys in 1963, British Guiana has far too long looked outside for solvers — and scapegoats — for its problems. Mr. Sandys had given new life to this basic symptom of colonialism. I am sad to see Dr. Hinden applauding him for it .... I believe that Mr. Sandys should have compelled the leaders and people of British Guiana to face up to early

independence and its stern demands, and that he should have sought to involve the independent members of the Commonwealth in the Western Hemisphere — Canada, Jamaica and Trinidad — in some aspects of this task. Instead, British Guiana continues to drift.[26]

A few days earlier, Jock Campbell had attacked Sandys for having 'contrived a system of political chaos'. He felt that the imposition, 'an experiment in Colonialist anarchy', would 'only exaggerate the existing irresponsibility, impracticality and lack of confidence bred by Colonialism'.[27] The leader of the conservative United Force, Peter D'Aguiar, was incensed by Jock's reaction. Speaking in London, he denounced Booker as a 'colonialist enclave', 'an anachronism', in a country on the threshold of independence. He said that one in five of the local labour force was employed by Booker and, alluding to Campbell, he concluded: 'No matter how much goodwill the leadership of such a company may have, this is too much. And we believe that power corrupts. We stand against the old entrenched order and we seek to change it.'[28]

The Daily Chronicle, too, had challenged Jock's support for independence, and proceeded to submit a number of questions to him for which they sought answers. One of their questions was about the constitutional arrangement which he and Booker favoured. Jock replied:

I would have favoured the setting of a date for independence; a Trinidad-type constitution with a simple first-past-the post electoral system; voting at 21; constituencies drawn as far as possible across racial and urban/rural distinctions; and entrenched clauses, as in Trinidad, requiring large majorities of both houses in bicameral legislature for amendment. Elections to be held immediately after independence, so that electors knew they were really voting for the Government responsible for an independent Guyana.[29]

He was obviously unaware of the strength of Anglo-American machinations to delay independence and their resolve to get rid of Cheddi Jagan — he repeated his contention: 'Like people, nations can only grow up if they are given responsibility, and they will not necessarily be the more fit the longer it is delayed.'[30] His support for Jagan quickly drew opprobrium from Burnham's PNC: shortly after Jock had rejected Sandys's imposition, they demanded that he stop his 'consistent and continuous meddling in the political and constitutional affairs' of Guyana. They denounced his support for the 1962 Budget, as well as his denigration of the Sandys Plan. The PNC concluded: 'It is about time that Sir Jock lets Guyana know where he stands, that he lets it be known once and for all whether he prefers to tie bundle with the incompetent international adventurers [communists] in the PPP or he desires for Guyana and its people a competent government of dedicated nationalists ever seeking, ever striving to improve the lot of the broad masses of Guyanese people [the PNC].'[31]

This, then, was the context in which Cheddi Jagan sought to rescue something from the despair of the imposition. On his return to Guyana in November 1963, he called for 'a hurricane of protests', in order to send a clear signal to the British that they would not accept the imposition. His Party deemed it 'a wickedly cunning innovation ... a diabolical attempt to keep power out of the hands of the PPP for ever'.[32] In early January 1964, Jagan told Indian sugar workers: 'I will talk less and act more.'[33] A few days later, at the West Indian Summit in Jamaica, he deplored the Cold War decisions which had 'raped democracy in British Guiana and blocked independence'.[34] The Jamaican Prime Minister, Alexander Bustamante, when asked whether he would support independence for the colony under Jagan, responded: 'It would depend on his attitude towards the West. We belong to the West in times of war and in times of peace.'[35] It was clear that Jagan's pro-Cuban stance had brought his government to virtual isolation; in the Anglophone Caribbean, as in 1953, he had no support outside of small, inconsequential Marxist groups. Jagan had reflected on this lack of support for him among West Indian leaders:

> It is no use talking brave words like 'the pernicious system of colonialism' and yet when the vital issue of colonialism presents itself in British Guiana no firm stand is taken.... No use saying that differences between the economic and social systems of countries should not prevent developing countries from taking

advantage of expanding markets for trade, and yet not condemn Mr. Sandys for raping democracy in British Guiana. For everyone knows that our political difficulties have arisen because of US antagonism particularly with respect to our trade with Cuba .... B.G. is the acid test. It has expressed the hollowness of Western pronouncements about freedom and democracy. West Indian leadership will stand or fall on its attitude to British Guiana.[36]

The excoriation at home was intense: his own supporters felt let down; the opposition ridiculed him incessantly. Burnham in particular employed his mordant wit in prolonging Jagan's humiliation over his capitulation to Duncan Sandys. In January 1964, for instance, he recalled that Jagan, immediately after the infamous signing, had told the BBC that he had 'great faith in the sense of justice and fair-play of the British'. Burnham then asked: 'If the Premier is this expert on the wicked machinations of the Imperialists, why did he concede this *volte-face*?' With regard to Jagan's allegations of the American Government's instrumentality in the imposition of the constitutional provisions against him, Burnham mocked with mischievous adroitness:

> Let me concede, as a lawyer would, that that proposition is correct and that the US Government was particularly interested in the outcome of the conference and preferred a particular outcome so far as the electoral system is concerned. Is not this naïve of the same Dr. Jagan, who says that the U.S. Government would be interested in a particular outcome, to entrust the political future and the destiny of this country to the greatest friend of the U.S. Government?'[37]

More of this studied ridicule was to emanate from the sagacious brain of this master manipulator. In February 1964 he told a cheering, mammoth crowd in Georgetown of his efforts (spurious, as we have seen) to reach an agreement with Jagan, 'before the fateful document was signed'. He jeered: '[S]ome people have learnt to write ... they had a pen and there was ink!'[38] This was especially galling — provocatively evocative of the barely lettered Indian, the *arriviste* 'coolie' pitted against the African scribe.

After the West Indian Summit in early 1964, Jagan had bemoaned the destruction of the national movement, the PPP of the early 1950s before Burnham had deserted it. He reflected despairingly: 'A decade ago we stood strong and triumphant. We were invincible because we were united. Now the great mass movement of 1953 is split, and we allow ourselves to be led in the paths of fratricidal strife. Violent disagreements and clashes will do our country no good.'[39] Yet, in February 1964, Cheddi Jagan was about to embark on a campaign of violence, to rival that of the PNC and UF in 1962 and 1963 — an aspect of his 'hurricane of protests' strategy — designed to impress the Labour Party (expected to win the 1964 elections in the UK) to repudiate the Sandys plan. The seminal prompting of this futile ploy was that Sandys had rewarded Burnham and D'Aguiar for their violent opposition to his democratically elected government, therefore, violence was justified in his campaign to delay elections scheduled for 1964, under PR. As will be seen later, the sugar workers — Jock Campbell's employees mainly — were the backbone of Jagan's last stand against his 'imperialist' enemies: Booker and the Tory government of Douglas-Home.

This belated resistance to Sandys was stimulated by the specious assumption that the Labour Party, which was opposed to proportional representation in British Guiana, would overturn what Harold Wilson had dubbed 'a fiddled constitutional arrangement'. Labour's spokesman on colonial affairs had also fed the illusion in his reaction to the imposition: 'To change the system to a new one looks far too much like manipulation with the blatant purpose of ousting Dr. Jagan.'[40] Lee Akbar (Samuel), secretary of the BG Government Office in London, had accompanied Jagan many evenings, alone, to meet his left-wing comrades in London, during the fatal talks in 1963. She recalled how frustrated she was to encounter some of these people, such as one of Jagan's confidants, Billy Strachan of the British Communist Party, so-called advisers who could only 'misguide' him; others, too, from the extreme left-wing of the Labour Party. She felt that his modus operandi, eschewing authoritative counsel while indulging the ideological fantasies of his comrades, aggravated his vulnerability to the machinations of Sandys and Burnham.[41] Even after the fatal signing he was energised into a false optimism by the hopes engendered by that great left-winger, his friend, the legendary anti-colonial Labour MP, Fenner Brockway. Writing in *Tribune* in November 1963, Brockway attributed the 'deadly betrayal' of Jagan to British capitulation to America's Cold War objectives. He observed that Douglas–Home's premiership (he had succeeded Macmillan during the Profumo scandal), with Sandys as America's main instrument, had foisted PR on British Guiana in order to remove Jagan; and that another conference would be convened to grant independence to his opponents. Brockway then launched this pie in the sky: 'There is the hope that we may have the opportunity before the last stage of the Sandys betrayal is completed of getting rid of the Government with which he shares the guilt. The immediate repudiation of his plan by Arthur Bottomley, Labour's Colonial spokesman, opens the door to a new start.' This fantasy had seduced the youth arm of the PPP to demand mobilisation of 'the patriotic forces ... to bring about a reversal' of the imposition and the 'retention' of the first-past-the-post electoral system.[42]

Thus was born Jagan's fatal resistance in early 1964 to the imposition which he had, indeed, agreed to abide by. The PPP staged a countrywide march in early February to galvanise their supporters to continue the fight for early independence. Peter D'Aguiar, leader of the United Force, had reacted to this with Burnhamesque mockery:

What can the PPP march achieve? It cannot wipe out Dr. Jagan's signature from the letter (signed for Mr. Sandys). It cannot change the decision of the British Government. If the PPP is dissatisfied with the decision made by the British Government, then they should remonstrate with Dr. Jagan for asking the British Government to decide and agreeing to accept its decision. The march cannot do anything to speed up independence.[43]

The march only served to focus Indian minds on their potential demise. Moreover, it was interpreted by Africans as a show of force by Indians; it won no Africans over. In fact, Burnham, having been awarded the big prize by Sandys, now counselled his people not to be 'provoked' or 'baited' into retaliatory violence by the PPP's campaign of 'civil disruption and hatred'.[44] Violence was a vital instrument in their pursuit of PR and in delaying independence; they had no desire now to disrupt the path to elections (which Jagan could not win) and assured independence. Burnham and D'Aguiar were belated wagers of peace.

At the completion of the march, on February 9, 1964, Jagan addressed his Indian supporters, at the edge of Georgetown. Strangely, he renewed his call for a PPP–PNC coalition in order to defeat the 'fascists', the United Force, and unite Africans and Indians; a new conference to fix a date for independence; and rejection of the Sandys plan. What he said beyond that, however, was designed to foster the cohesion of Indian racial forces to stifle the plan, not to promote racial harmony. The racist tone could not be concealed; it was not a tactful speech in any circumstances; in a volatile environment, it was potentially combustible, a virtual call to arms:

> Let those who think that they can dominate Georgetown, New Amsterdam and Mackenzie [Africans] know that these places are not the whole of British Guiana. Let us tell them that we [Indians] also have strength. We have geographical distribution. There is no doubt that the two main crops of this country are produced by the people in the PPP [Indians]. Take away rice and you will have starvation in this country ... including Georgetown. Take away sugar and what will happen? ... Economically and politically we [Indians] are powerful. Let them [Africans] note that all three elections we have won every time. Let those who preach and practise the psychology of violence and fear [Africans] note these facts, that since 1953 when we [Indians] got into power they [Africans] have tried to make normal government impossible by instigating disturbances and violence and injecting fear in the minds of the people. Those people who do these things must remember that if one side can do it the other side can also do the same. Two sides can play this game .... We [Indians] have been humble and cordial, but it seems that some people [Africans] have taken humility and cordiality for weakness. Instead of respecting these virtues, these people [Africans] have inflicted abuse and beat our comrades [Indians] when they come to Georgetown. Well, comrades, I want to issue a warning to these people [Africans]. We [Indians] have pleaded for calmness for a long time, but it appears that these people [Africans] believe that because we [Indians] are humble and courteous, we are weak. They [Africans] have mistaken humility, courtesy and

our peaceful intention for weakness. Your demonstration today shows that we [Indians] have strength also.[45]

It was as if he had forgotten his Marxist dogma as the racist rhetoric absorbed the pain of despair. But he soon retrieved the tired nostrums when he turned to the old enemy, Booker and King Sugar. Jagan told his followers that there was a distinction between property 'for personal use' and property used 'to exploit the people'. He had no time for those who exploited the masses and took away their resources. There was no room for Booker and other foreign 'exploiters'. He shouted:

> This nonsense must be stopped. What the PPP want is the development of this country and the establishment of more industries. But we want those industries to be controlled by the local people .... Our masters do not want to stop the exploitation of our people .... But the time has come when we have to tell them we are not standing any more of this .... Foreigners bring in a few thousand dollars and took out millions. To hell with them.

The impotent rage showed, as he turned to Duncan Sandys. He said the imposition was 'a gross betrayal of a solemn pledge in 1960 by his predecessor, Mr. Iain Macleod'. He concluded that Sandys wanted to perpetuate colonial rule, but 'we will show ... [him] that the people who are behind me — the people in British Guiana [in fact, Indians] — will not let this nonsense stand.'[46]

The PNC, now on the verge of unseating Cheddi, were more sober in their response: they did not need violence in 1964. After observing that it was the PPP which had helped the United Force to escape electoral annihilation in 1961, they dismissed Jagan's call for unity as 'nothing new'. They advised the Premier that his apprehensions for the future of British Guiana could be removed 'with the country achieving independence with elections under PR'.[47] The PNC had regional and international support; they had no interest in working with a terminally wounded Jagan. They would let him slide into ignominy in his futile campaign to stall PR by his show of force — a strike in the sugar industry, which degenerated into racial violence between February and July 1964. The Sandys imposition remained inviolable.

Towards the end of January the PPP's union, the Guyana Agricultural Workers' Union, resurrected its old claim for recognition by the Sugar Producers' Association. As in the past, they asserted that the recognised union, the Manpower Citizens' Association, was bogus. Coincidental with the claim for recognition, was the initiation of a virtual crusade of violence on the estates, as supporters of Jagan's union burnt canes and sought to disrupt the functioning of the sugar plantations. A strike which had commenced at Leonora (not a Booker estate), over working conditions, and had resulted in the death of a PPP woman worker, Alice [Kowsilla], soon became a national sugar strike for the recognition of GAWU.

In early February the President of GAWU, PPP assemblyman, Harry Lall, said that they would protest to Jock Campbell that the union must be recognised, as it was supported by 90 per cent of sugar workers.[48] It is true that an overwhelming majority of the workers did support Jagan's union over the recognised one, the MPCA, but the collapse of the Labour Relations Bill in 1963, because of opposition from the TUC and the PNC, meant that there was no mechanism to institute a poll. But if the SPA really wanted one they could have agreed to it. The matter had become very politicised and by 1964, with the PPP mortally wounded and Jagan's political fortunes sinking fast, the sugar producers were not inclined to give him ammunition to fight the Sandys plan. By then, too, Campbell's once massive authority in Booker had lessened, as those on the spot, Readwin and Tasker particularly, had acquired the authority to make the major decisions, including the question of recognition. Jock recalls: '[T]hings were getting rather out of my hands.'[49] I asked him if he considered the failure to recognise GAWU a serious error of judgement. He responded: 'No, not a personal error ... because I didn't agree with the policy [of non-recognition]; [but] I am not absolutely sure that if they had recognised it, it would have made much difference. I am not convinced.' I then asked if the potential benefits to Booker of recognition were not exceeded by the damage inflicted through non-recognition. He pondered:

... I see the argument but I don't know the validity of it. I don't know what would have happened. I certainly wanted to recognise them; I thought it was the expedient thing to do. [But] this is the sort of thing after I had been ill [1960–61] .... I couldn't get away with .... but all I am saying is I am not convinced that it would have paid off if they had. It might well have done, but I can't say with confidence what would have happened.[50]

His circumspection was certainly justified, as the recognition issue, by 1964, had became the arena for Jagan's anti-PR campaign. Moreover, as far as Jagan was concerned, it was only a matter of time before he would have nationalised Booker, if he were returned to power in December 1964. Speaking at Vergenoegen, East Bank Essequibo, in February 1964, he said that foreign investors brought little money into the country and took out much more. Jagan added: 'We have got to put an end to this practice. My Government is no longer content with having the profitable sectors of our economy in foreign hands. We want everything to be local for the future development of our country.'[51] The position of the PPP hardened as the strike dragged on: 'We are dealing here with British interests and experience has shown that the British will stoop to any trick to gain an advantage over their opponents in British Guiana.'[52] Notions of the British sense of 'fair play' had evaporated with Sandys's imposition. As Paulette Pierce argues, GAWU had become a key instrument in prosecuting the PPP's political programme, '[w]ith its grip on state power quickly slipping ... [it] sought to strengthen its hand in the labour movement'. She elaborates:

If the party somehow managed to stay in power, having gained recognition for the largest trade union in the country would greatly increase the PPP's control of economic policy and enhance the party's leverage within [the] imperialist dominated T[rade] U[nion] M[ovement]. If, on the other hand, pro-imperialist forces succeeded in overthrowing Jagan's Government, the PPP would be much more powerful as the opposition party. A recognised GAWU would grow in strength and be able to hamstring any Government the imperialists might impose.[53]

Meanwhile the strike for recognition was degenerating into an orgy of arson, bombing and personal attacks on people who refused to strike, as well as those considered scabs. Indeed, the so-called industrial strike, like that by the TUC and the opposition in 1963, could not elude the mutual racial hatred permeating the African and Indian communities. Forbes Burnham had no doubts of the origin of the violence in 1964: '[T]he burning of the canes synchronises and coincides with the campaign of extreme agitation and hatred started by the PPP after the Sandys decision.'[54] He maintained that this was PPP-inspired violence, designed to postpone the elections scheduled to be held in 1964 under PR. In March he was unequivocal that the strike for recognition was political, as was the violence:

> GAWU is the handmaiden of the PPP — being supplied by the PPP with smokeless and noiseless hand grenades, to commit murder, including that of an innocent child [Godfrey Teixeira, son of a Booker employee at Enmore, killed in a school bus bombing]. The strike has little or no industrial significance, but aims at sparking political agitation and intimidation to prevent the holding of fresh elections this year ... under a system of PR.[55]

In early March 1964 Jagan said he had written to Campbell to intervene in the recognition issue, noting: 'You have the weapons in your hand to settle this issue'. Campbell replied that he was sending his deputy, George Bishop, to the colony. Jagan's increasingly uncompromising stance towards Booker, and his fatal political blunders, had undermined Campbell's will and credibility in projecting Jagan as the sole effective politician, to the key people in Booker in London and in Guyana. As in the case of Iain Macleod, Jagan did not appreciate the merits of cultivating alliances: he had squandered another potentially crucial ally in Jock. On March 8, at the funeral of Alice (Kowsilla), the striking worker killed at Leonora, he declared:

> This is a struggle against those who have exploited us for these many years .... [T]he history of B.G. [is] a history of sugar, and the history of sugar [is] a history of blood and tears of suffering sugar workers.... From the days of slavery with the Negroes to

the days of indentured labour with the East Indian and even today, it is the same old story of the blood of the workers being shed in the interest of sugar owners. [I am] against all forms of violence, but so long as the Imperialists continue to exploit the workers, and keep us back from freedom, we shall have to be prepared to die, if necessary, to be free.[56]

For Jagan, it was as if nothing had changed between 1948 and 1964. Campbell's reforms had made no impression on this inveterate fighter of the class war, who felt cleansed by his rooted hostility to Booker, the crusade against the imperialists: there must be no short cut to freedom. 'Bitter Sugar' could not be sweetened. Campbell seemed to have made no special effort to press Jagan's case for the recognition of GAWU, as violence escalated, on and off the plantations. George Bishop did visit Guyana and he met Premier Jagan on March 11. He emphasised 'the urgent need to maintain law and order, to bring about a resumption of work, and to seek an early settlement of the union dispute through the established machinery of the Labour Department'.[57] There was no reference to a poll in the industry.

Jagan observed correctly that if the Labour Relation Bill of 1953 and 1963 had been passed, the mechanism for recognition would have been established. He said that the SPA were not addressing the real issue and that it was not enough that the government should denounce violence and arson: 'We cannot recall the same big business interests of the SPA asking the Leader of the Opposition and the TUC to denounce violence and arson in 1962 and 1963.'[58] The difference, of course, was that the opposition's violence had the sanction of powerful allies, resolved to remove Jagan.

By April 1964 the violence on the estates was becoming an aspect of the Guyanese tragedy, enmeshed in the racial bigotry, with no compensatory reward for the PPP. Jagan therefore returned to his old stalking horse, Booker. Having set the colony's problems so firmly in the context of race, in his speech in Georgetown in February, he tried to defuse aggravated volatile racial passions with a spurious intervention on the class struggle. Speaking to Indians on the West Coast Demerara, where racial atrocities were out of control, he said that African-Indian antipathy was 'an illusion, not a reality'. The real struggle was 'with big forces from outside'. He elaborated: 'The trouble in the country was mixed up with the role of the big companies, such as Booker, interested in having and owning everything and exporting big profits .... This is not a racial question. It is a question of the big shots, like Booker and those Imperialists who want to ride on the backs of the poor people.'[59] This was a cardinal feature of Jagan's politics after 1956: he would preach class struggle, but in *realpolitik*, manipulate and exploit racial symbols while mobilising on the basis of Indian racial proclivity, a guaranteed winner under first-past-the-post. He was at the pinnacle of Indian political endeavour: immovable. He would brook no challenge there, nor would he agonise over this inherent contravention of his Marxist assumptions.

Speaking to Africans on that same coast, Burnham said that the violence was started by the PPP to delay registration and prevent the holding of elections. He repeated his observation of several weeks before, that it commenced after 'the Premier had repudiated his signature to a letter inviting Mr. Duncan Sandys to impose a settlement to the country's constitutional deadlock'. He saw the GAWU strike as 'inspired by the PPP', as part of the strategy to create racial violence to stall the Sandys plan. He added: 'The PPP will try to tell you that Booker is trying to divide you. We agree that the sugar companies do not love us; they would suck us if they can. But were not Jagan and Jock Campbell very close in 1962? Ask Jagan if he did not stay at the home of Sir Jock Campbell.' [60]

Jagan denied ever staying with Campbell or that he was a close associate of him. He observed that Burnham's allegations probably stemmed from the fact that 'Sir Jock' had 'expressed vigorous support' for the controversial 1962 Budget.[61] The violence, meanwhile, had brought the two races to virtual civil war. This was the context in which the Labour Party's spokesman on Colonial Affairs, Arthur Bottomley, stated definitively, towards the end of April 1964, that the violence being perpetrated in British Guiana would not induce them to seek a reversal of the constitutional provisions imposed by the Tories. Another Labour source was more emphatic: 'The reports of violence make me feel that we are dealing with irresponsible leaders .... [T]here is absolutely no chance of the Labour Party committing itself at this time to throwing out PR. Whilst we do not think Sandys has handled matters in the best possible way, we are

certainly not going to make all sorts of promises for the future —
violence or no violence.' [62]

Labour had moved a motion in the Commons to reject PR, but
withdrew it at the conclusion of the debate on the Sandys plan,
because the government had pleaded that such a measure would
exacerbate the situation in the colony if it were pressed to a vote.
Jagan's last hope had folded.[63] Yet the illusion of Labour's will to do
something to rescue the PPP was sustained by Janet Jagan, who was
in London for the debate in the House of Commons on April 27,
1964. She had met Duncan Sandys and told him that his constitutional
imposition on British Guiana was 'a negation of democratic practice,
a betrayal of historical precedents, an oppressive Imperialist design
and a stain on Britain's honour'. Sandys, apparently, was
imperturbable, countering that his formula was conducive to the
flowering of 'every subtle shade of philosophy' in the political arena;
it would blur the lines of racial particularism.[64] Paradoxically, Janet
still argued that all was not lost, that if Labour were elected they
would be 'more sensible' about Guyana. She slid into fantasy:

> I believe that the Labour Party when it comes to power will take
> a very careful look at the whole B.G. problem and not just leap in
> as the Conservatives have done. It is clear that Mr. Sandys hasn't
> produced an answer and it is likely that Labour would be able to
> do better. After all it would be a feather in Labour's cap .... to get
> a proper solution for our country than tamely follow the
> Conservatives.[65]

Clearly, Janet did not understand the bipartisan approach of the
parties on colonial matters. Perhaps the illusion was necessary to
sustain effort in the face of foreboding impending elections under PR
in December 1964.

Booker, though, had no illusion that Labour would countenance
the revocation of the Sandys plan. Even before the escalation of the
violence, in the initial stages of the GAWU claim for recognition,
Martin Carter, the poet and former disciple of Cheddi, now editor of
Booker News, had written a confidential internal paper, underlining
its essentially political foundation. He had predicted the PPP's course
of action, around February 1964:

The forces of the governing party [PPP] are committed to whatever action is considered to prevent the British Government carrying out the plans announced by Mr. Duncan Sandys in October last year. The strike in the sugar industry is mainly one phase of such action. Starting with cane burning as their way of attacking the British Government, anti-personnel violence will now be resorted to. Naïve enough, at first, to believe that the burning of cane ... would exert immediate pressure on the British Government, the forces of the governing party will attempt to practise full-scale terrorism, directed to that section of society which appears to have power in civil, economic and commercial life. The idea being that this section will appeal to the British Government for protection and that the giving of any such protection will lead to so much dislocation of normal life that all plans for constitutional change will be delayed. The forces of the Opposition [PNC and UF] do not want to act in a way that would serve the interests of the governing party. In other words they do not want to retaliate or take serious reprisals for fear that the British Government would be forced to intervene and take such action as might serve to delay elections under Proportional Representation later this year.[66]

On April 7, 1964 Antony Tasker reported to the Booker Board that the PPP tactic was one of 'disruptive agitation', which they thought would pressure the British to revoke PR and delay elections. Moreover, they hoped that the election of a Labour Government in October would give them a 'better deal'. He then explained why Booker was at the centre of the PPP's agitation:

Many Guianese are still extraordinarily naïve in believing that Booker have immeasurably more influence on the Colonial Office and the Governor than Booker in fact have; so they feel that by bringing pressure on Booker they will in turn get Booker to bring pressure on the British authorities. It is easy to equate anti-Booker with anti-British .... [T]he PPP and Dr. Jagan personally are aggravated that Mr. Burnham has his own important union and is influential with organised labour [TUC]; the PPP want to have an important union of their own to divest Mr. Ishmael and the MPCA of their present power. For all these reasons an assault on the sugar industry is particularly attractive.[67]

The Booker Board, on April 13, 1964, had concluded that a Labour government would not pursue 'a significantly different policy'. They noted, perceptively, that it would be 'just as much subject to U.S. pressure as the Conservative Government had been ... [as well] the powerful anti-communist elements in the Labour Party and the TUC would be far from happy to see any danger from communism in B.G.'. Tasker was correct that the PPP wanted to influence the TUC, for the MPCA had been allocated 50 of the 138 votes in the TUC.[68] What neither he nor the Booker Board admitted, however, was that GAWU, the PPP's union, in a free ballot, would have polled an overwhelming majority of the votes of sugar workers. Ishmael's MPCA, therefore, was a bogus union which had used its power in the TUC to subvert Jagan's government in 1962 and 1963. It was as simple as that. Booker, indirectly, had aided the subversion of the democratically elected government.

The Booker Board knew that Jagan's days in government were numbered. They were not inclined to give him a lease on life. Whatever the potential pitfalls of a government under the PNC and UF, by early 1964, Jagan's demise was seen as inevitable. Booker were not prepared to concede a poll to GAWU which they would have won; so they decided to weather the strike, knowing that Jagan had no allies in the TUC: they demanded of the PPP that they repudiate violence before any negotiations could take place. On April 16, 1964, Edgar Readwin, chairman of Booker Sugar Estates in British Guiana, had written to Cheddi airing his concern 'at the extent to which political consideration now appear to dominate the inter-union dispute in the sugar industry'.[69] In early May Campbell wrote to the left-wing paper, *Tribune*, seeking to explain Booker's position on the union dispute:

> The known fact is that over half the sugar workers [58 per cent] still pay union dues [through the check-off] to the union recognised by the employers, the MPCA .... Booker's position in all this, as in 1962 and 1963, is intensely difficult. It is our policy to work with the elected Government of British Guiana. As employers, it is equally our policy to work with established trade unions and to fulfil recognition agreements with them.

And we recognise the right of workers to be represented by the unions of their choice. The problem is how fairly to elicit that choice. When there is conflict between union and union, and between Government and recognised unions, our actions fall between the crossfire of mutually exclusive forces.[70]

This was waffle to rationalise Booker's policy of non-recognition of Jagan's union, which everyone knew would have won a poll convincingly. Besides, there was a successful precedent of a poll having been conducted in the colony a month before, in March 1964, to resolve a jurisdictional dispute between two unions in the timber industry. The old union, the Sawmill and Forest Workers' Union, headed by PPP activist, George Henry, was defeated by the British Guiana Labour Union (BGLU), headed by Forbes Burnham. The Labour Commissioner had intervened in the dispute and this had resulted in the poll.[71] The problem in the sugar industry was that Booker were aware of the awesome power of Burnham and the TUC in Georgetown; aware, too, of the depth of Anglo-American resolve to remove Jagan. Cheddi, on the other hand, did not help his case with his inexhaustible tirades against Booker — implicitly, his potential ally, Jock Campbell — and his praise of communism. In May 1964, for instance, his Minister of Trade and Industry, H.J.M. Hubbard, told an audience in London that big businesses, specifically Booker, were at the 'back of B.G.'s troubles'. He claimed that expatriate big business, in league with the colonial power, were dividing the races in the colony in order to prolong their hegemony. Hubbard declared: 'The people we have to fight are the British imperialists. The sugar producers are still exploiting the country.... We would like to get them out and we are trying very hard to get them out.' Campbell had asked Janet Jagan, over lunch, whether Hubbard's 'violent attack on Booker' was official party policy. She replied, somewhat vaguely: 'There are several levels of conflict with Booker. It is not necessarily the same at the top as it is at the trade union level.' [72] If there was any ambiguity within the PPP with regard to Booker, Cheddi clarified that a few days later. Speaking to his Indian supporters at Annandale, East Coast Demerara, he announced that although they were not sure whether to contest the forthcoming PR elections, they should still register, because 'if the Sandys plan is reversed' the same registration lists would be used.

He concluded: 'The Americans were not worried about Mr. Burnham being Prime Minister because, if that happens, Peter D'Aguiar and Booker would really be ruling British Guiana.'[73] This was the classic Marxist dictum on the evils of capitalism which had alienated Jagan's potential liberal allies, conducing to their minimising or overlooking the discernibly destructive propensity of Burnhamism. Cheddi's intransigence undermined whatever residual influence Campbell might have exerted towards the recognition of GAWU, while bolstering that of his men on the spot against a perceived communist union.

Jagan neither won recognition for his union nor support from the Labour Party for the scuttling of the Sandys plan. As Campbell often remarked: 'Cheddi did not see politics as the art of the possible.' He did not know how to construct alliances; pragmatism would vitiate the Marxist creed, his practice of racial politics notwithstanding. Since 1953, as I have argued, the PPP had blundered abysmally on this question of recognition for its union in the sugar industry. They were so preoccupied with the pure goals of 'scientific socialism', that there was no serious indication, since 1948, that they were interested in the mundane sphere of industrial unionism. Throughout the British West Indies, political parties espousing a form of Fabian socialism were closely aligned to trade unions. The difference with the PPP was its communist orientation, its alignment to the Communist World Federation of Trade Unions (WFTU), and the consequential assumption that Jagan was interested in trade unions only because he saw them as an instrument of communist rule. Yet, in August 1953, as noted earlier, the SPA were prepared to recognise the PPP union, the GIWU, the precursor of GAWU.

It has become a part of the folklore that the GIWU strike in September 1953, which was the final straw which influenced the Governor to recommend suspension of the constitution, was a reaction to the refusal of the SPA to grant them recognition. Sallahuddin, for instance, argues: '[T]he GIWU enjoyed majority support in the sugar industry and had done nothing to move the SPA to proceed in the direction of recognition. To have persuaded the SPA to grant recognition to the GIWU would have been regarded as a victory for the PPP and Whitehall was not prepared to move in that direction.'[74] Ashton Chase, who was the Minister of Labour in the short-lived PPP government from May to October 1953, and very closely involved in the negotiations, tells a truer, but not the whole, story:

> The GIWU came very close to the bull's eye of recognition but there was a slip between cup and lip. As a result of negotiations carried out by the author (as Minister of Labour) with the SPA ... [they] agreed to recognise the GIWU for field workers but to continue recognising the MPCA for the factory workers. This offer was rejected by the GIWU. It wanted unconditional recognition for all field and factory workers previously represented by the MPCA. The SPA's counter proposal included the acceptance by the GIWU of all collective agreements made with the MPCA and the execution by the GIWU of similar agreements .... The GIWU rejected the condition; it reserved the rights to negotiate and settle fresh agreements with the SPA.[75]

In fact, the SPA had given the GIWU an offer which they should have accepted. On July 21, 1953 Ashton Chase had written to the SPA on behalf of the GIWU, requesting recognition as the sole bargaining agent for sugar workers. They wanted to replace the recognised union, MPCA. Chase had noted that the PPP's election manifesto had included enabling legislation for a poll to be conducted so that workers could choose the union of their preference. He added that there would be no necessity for that if the 'situation is approached realistically'. On August 20, the SPA replied to Minister Chase, offering, 'in the first instance, the GIWU would represent the field workers [the overwhelming majority] and the MPCA the factory workers [emphasis added]'. Alternatively, the two unions should merge as the bargaining agent of all sugar workers. They wished that the agreements negotiated with the MPCA would stand, but these were subject to renegotiation, shortly, with effect from January 1, 1954.[76]

The minister said that those terms were communicated to the GIWU but they did not seem inclined to accept some of the conditions. He did not give details but noted that strikes had been called by the union on some estates. The SPA felt that 'the matter had been taken out of his hands'; it was an aspect of the PPP's broader political strategy. On September 2, as the strike engulfed most estates, the

SPA issued a public statement denouncing it as having been 'instigated and fomented by certain political elements which are endeavouring to obtain by force what the SPA have already said they will be willing to consider ... i.e., recognition of the GIWU as a Union representing workers'.[77]

On September 5, 1953 the Union submitted a number of demands to the SPA, but there was no mention whatsoever of the central issue of recognition of GIWU. The demands were all related to wages, prices for farmers' canes, need for pure drinking water, and so forth. The cart was now being put before the horse. On September 8, the SPA met Chase and reminded him that their offer of recognition was still extended to the GIWU when they decided to take strike action; it was not their fault that the question of recognition was not pursued and that the economy was being disrupted. The minister responded: 'Recognition of the MPCA and GIWU on a factory/field basis could ... be examined, but here again because of past hostility he did not think they would get very far with this .... As regards conditional recognition he thought the terms of the SPA letter a fair basis for discussion.'[78] W.A. Macnie of the SPA told the minister that the alternative suggestion of an amalgamation with the MPCA was made on the assumption 'that it might ultimately lead to absorption of the MPCA by the GIWU'. He added that the apparent bone of contention in the GIWU over acceptance of the agreements signed with the MPCA by the GIWU were not insuperable. He thought that the impression should be corrected that these terms were not negotiable. Indeed, the letter of August 20, offering recognition, should be construed thus: 'that the existing agreements with the MPCA should be accepted by the GIWU until new agreements could be negotiated with the latter union and not that they should be accepted indefinitely ... the SPA had contemplated that new agreements with the GIWU would be negotiated and come into force by 1 January 1954'.[79] The SPA were not being unreasonable.

The strike lasted for 25 days, from August 31 to September 24, 1953 when it was announced that a Labour Relations Ordinance to secure a poll for the recognition of the Union would be introduced. The Bill was passed on October 8, 1953; the next day the British government suspended the Constitution and the Bill lapsed. The SPA detected in the whole unsavoury episode the PPP's commitment to a communist programme:

> Although the strike has been called off by its instigators ... there can be little doubt that there are equally, if not more difficult, times ahead. This can be attributed not to uneasiness or any serious discontent among sugar workers, but to the present grave political situation and the apparent determination of the PPP leaders to keep the 'pot boiling' and foment trouble on every possible occasion. The Communist pattern and influence are clear. B.G. extremists will be well represented at the Communist World Federation of Trade Unions [WFTU] Conference at Vienna, commencing on 10 October, by Cheddi Jagan .... It is also interesting to note that Martin Carter, Rory Westmaas and Edwin Ramsarran ... are due to return shortly from attending the Communist-sponsored World Festival of Youth in Romania.[80]

The PPP had never anticipated winning a majority in the elections of April 1953. They expected to win enough seats to be in the opposition, fighting to destroy what they saw as a very restricted constitution. When they got power, however, the PPP government functioned as the opposition, challenging the official element, representatives of imperialism, as they sought to lay the foundation for 'scientific socialism'. Winning control of the trade unions was an integral part of the class struggle, in the battle against capitalism, epitomised by Booker. In 1953 it was not recognition per se that they sought; that was there for the take; the issue provided an arena for fighting the agents of imperialism. Moreover — and of greater significance — as Minister Sydney King [later known as Eusi Kwayana] argued, the party was still bedevilled by the race question: the electoral victory spawned African fear of Indian domination of the PPP government, reflected in the Jagan–Burnham rivalry for leadership of the party; working class unity, therefore, had to be forged in the furnace of the struggle. That was why they would have rejected retention of the representation of factory workers in the hands of the MPCA. These were primarily Africans; the field workers were mainly Indians. Therefore, they would have interpreted the offer of recognition of GIWU for field workers only as another machination by the plantocracy to divide the working class. It had to be rejected. In September 1992 Eusi Kwayana explained to me why he had argued strongly against the SPA's terms of recognition of the PPP's union: 'I opposed it at the Union meeting. I saw it as a direct attempt to split the people along ethnic lines. I moved that the offer be rejected.' So deep-seated were the 'racial insecurities' in British Guiana, especially among Africans, confronted with the Indian leader, Jagan, that Kwayana, the Assistant General Secretary of the PPP, believed that they should guard against the party coming to power prematurely and rupturing the fragile coalition forged since Jagan's election to the Legislative Council in 1947:

> Some people like to ignore reality. I had moved in the PPP Executive *that we should not win a majority*, and my reason was the country was not sufficiently united. I think only Martin Carter and I supported the motion: we should not go for a majority. I knew we could win a majority, but I didn't think the Party was prepared for it because although the racial unity was there — it was a kind of coalition — it was not well grounded; it was tenuous. I told Jagan and Burnham that we would win the elections. They didn't believe it; they thought we would win about eight seats [out of 24]. I said perhaps we should win about eight seats. I moved a motion that we fight about eight seats and try to do, in a multiple of eight, what Jagan alone had done, and really try to unite the country [emphasis added].[81]

This was the context in which the PPP government of 1953 approached their mandate, still very insecure on the race issue (epitomised by the Burnham–Jagan rivalry), indecisive about their role, but trumpeting their anti-imperialism and hatred of Booker as an instrument for cementing the tenuous coalition across the racial divide. As Raymond Smith argues:

> [T]hey did not accept the Waddington Constitution as the proper instrument for the independent government of the country, and therefore never ceased to oppose what they considered the real locus of power. They did not feel themselves to be the government of the country; their aim was complete self-government for British Guiana, and much of the action of the elected members between April and October 1953 must be viewed in the light of

these facts. Such powers as they had were often used to embarrass 'the government', meaning the representatives of the Crown, and to try to further the progress of the party as an instrument uniting Guianese in opposition to outside forces.[82]

This was to be Jagan's dilemma throughout the 1950s to the mid-1960s: a dedicated Marxist with allegiance to Moscow, operating in a multi-racial British colony in the American sphere of influence, he had no patience with having to tread the measured, constitutional path to independence, for he was certain of the superiority of Marxism and enthralled by the supposed advances of the USSR and its satellite states. He believed in the superiority of the Soviet way. That alone would erase even the deep-seated racial insecurities of the African people of perceived Indian ascendancy. Consequently, the 'hinterland of suspicion', in Kwayana's evocative phrase, never did receive the focus from Jagan that this fundamental problem required:

> The two major groups have stereotypes of each other. Africans tended to see Indians as clannish, as having more money, having an interest in land — a lot of them were selling out their lands to Indians when they went broke. Although they were doing it voluntarily, it also alarmed them. Then there was this rumour that someone from India had come and said who owned the land owned the country.... A lot of Africans were unable to go beyond that. They would look at the behaviour of Indians near to them in judging the PPP (the PPP does not understand that until now). If there is an aggressive Indian member of the PPP in their district this is how they see the PPP. Jagan never deals with these things at the subjective level, although he has a lot of rage against Imperialism. That problem was never dealt with; that's one of the reasons why I left the PPP. The psychology of the leader is crucial. We had to fight to get Africans to accept an Indian leader [Jagan]. He didn't have that problem. He never had to accept a leader of another race so he didn't know what it is. He talks about revolution but the personal revolution — nothing. He had a cultural problem. Having rejected colonialism and its intellectual and cultural baggage he had to take something from somewhere else [Russian communism]; he didn't rely on his own personality. If he had Hinduism, it would have made him a different person.[83]

He had no means of comprehending the African–Indian incomprehension. The sugar strike of 1964, initiated primarily to force the British to scuttle the Sandys plan, became the catalyst for racial violence throughout the country. As the Intelligence Report of the period, March to June 1964, stated: 'It is difficult to escape the conclusion that much of the racial violence originated from deliberate provocation, designed to substantiate the PPP arguments .... [V]iolence on the sugar estates continued, directed by strikers at non-strikers and at substitute labour brought in by estate management — largely African.' This ignited racial violence, which the government was unable to control. The Report continued: 'Intimidation became increasingly terrorist and racial in character until, in mid-May, race rather than union membership or willingness to strike became the issue; this caused the extension of disturbances outside the sugar producing areas.'[84] The most atrocious crimes were committed at Wismar and on the Demerara River.

The Wismar atrocities occurred on May 25, 1964 and the Intelligence Report attributed it to the People's National Congress: '[R]esponding ... to events in the coastal strip, the African population at Wismar fell upon the Indian minority; before the disturbances came to an end 160 houses and 17 shops, mainly Indian and some Chinese, had been destroyed, four people lost their lives, and approximately 1,500 Indians were evacuated to Georgetown.'[85] Jagan put these figures a bit higher, adding: 'Women and even children were raped and otherwise savagely maltreated.'[86] There was savage retaliation to this, as about 40 Africans died when the boat plying between Georgetown and the mining town of Mackenzie, near to Wismar, was blasted to bits on the Demerara River in early July. On this Jagan was brief, noting that after an explosion on the 'Sun Chapman', 'more than two dozen persons, mainly Negro workers and their families ... were drowned'.[87] This was believed to have been the work of PPP terrorists. Later in the month Freedom House, the headquarters of the PPP, and Gimpex, its trading arm, were bombed: two died; the three leaders were locked in 'peace talks' at the time![88] This was thought to be the work of PNC terrorists.

Such is the Guyanese futility! 'Wismar' and 'Sun Chapman' became its signature. By the end of May 1964 Jagan knew that he was defeated: the Labour Party had opted for the Sandys plan; the SPA had held out and recognition for GAWU was not going to be achieved; the violence was not likely to delay the elections under PR. The violence of the PNC and UF, in 1962–63, had taken them to the threshold of power. In an address to the nation, on May 30, 1964 Jagan remarked that the opposition had been 'recompensed' by the British: their 'illegal and unconstitutional activities yielded them rich rewards [the Sandys plan]'. He said that all he had fought for 'now hangs in the balance'. In despair he bemoaned:

> [F]actional strife strides the land and our national movement lies divided and weak. For many years, while others spent their time and leisure in the pursuit of wealth or pleasure and frivolity, I trod every nook and cranny of our wide country preaching the gospel of nationalism and freedom and seeking to infuse in our diverse groups a Guyanese consciousness which would transcend the bonds of race and creed.... Today ... my hopes for national unity have been cast into the dust .... I wish to appeal for an end to racial strife. Racial antagonism is not deeply rooted in this country. But it can easily become so if it is not promptly removed.[89]

He insisted that the question of recognition for GAWU had to be resolved, as well as the constitutional issue. The Sandys plan still caused anguish: 'A constitution designed to bring about the defeat of a particular political party and to satisfy the demand of a foreign power cannot provide a framework for peace and orderly development.'[90] So the strike continued. When it was ended in late July 1964, over 160 people were dead; many communities which were once multi-racial had seen the flight of their minorities; new symbols of racial exclusivism scarred the land. GAWU was still not recognised; the Sandys plan was being implemented. Elisabeth Wallace, writing in late 1964, assessed the bitter legacy of the sugar strike:

> The violence it had triggered off ... resulted in over 160 deaths, many more injuries, the destruction of over 1000 houses, financial losses estimated at fourteen million dollars, and racial bitterness of a degree hitherto unknown even in British Guiana. When the strike finally ended, some thirteen thousand Guyanese,

of both Indian and African descent, had fled from their homes and were living as refugees.... The six months' sugar strike which precipitated the sorry chain of events in 1964, was overshadowed, almost from the outset, by the racial strife which it both reflected and accentuated. Indeed, long before it ended the strike had been almost forgotten.[91]

It is ironic — in view of Campbell's support — but understandable, why Cheddi Jagan would choose the sugar industry as the site to resist PR. Apart from the justified outrage at the non-recognition of GAWU, it was the Indian sugar workers, since Enmore, who had sustained his political career. As Janet said of 'the largest group of workers in British Guiana', in 1965: 'It is no secret that the PPP's strength from 1953 to the present has been based on this rock of working class support.'[92] But the strike and the ensuing racial carnage had broken both Jagan and Campbell. Indeed, Jagan's ideological rigidity had not only destroyed him politically, but by 1964, it had rendered Campbell a substantially less effective chairman of Booker, a shadow of his pre-1960 self. Not only were the local people, Readwin and Tasker, totally in charge, but even in England, Campbell's declining authority was evident. On July 23, 1964 Edgar Readwin and George Bishop represented Booker at the Colonial Office; Jock was conspicuously absent. There Readwin had denounced the PPP, arguing that if Jagan won the elections 'the result would be disastrous' for Guyana. He was in favour of a Burnham–D'Aguiar coalition, as they 'could produce a more effective set of ministers than the PPP'. He 'emphasised' that the PPP ministers were 'completely useless' and he had 'no high opinion of Mrs. Jagan as a minister'. Readwin conceded that she was 'probably more efficient' than the others, but thought 'her capabilities were such that she would make a good secretary to a good minister'.[93]

A week later Antony Tasker, too, visited the Colonial Office. He was met by Duncan Sandys's Under-Secretary of State, Nigel Fisher. Tasker remarked that those working for peace wanted the 'Opposition' to agree to a poll in the sugar industry some time after the termination of the strike. He did not say whether he was in favour of that, but proceeded to explain why Jagan called off the strike. The calling in of licensed firearms had left Indians with 'no weapons to protect themselves'. This had led to 'increasing African violence ... and may have tipped the scales'. He thought that the Wismar incidents and the bombing of Freedom House had scared Jagan. Tasker gave the impression that the Premier was mortally wounded, noting what Cheddi had said to him: 'If we win we lose; and if we lose we die.'[94] Campbell was again conspicuously absent. Implicit in Readwin's and Tasker's views was the notion that the recognition of Jagan's union was more an issue for the opposition political parties to decide rather than the sugar industry; since the former were the ascendant force in 1964, it was therefore suicidal for Booker to accede to Jagan.

The Labour Party won the elections in the UK with a very slim majority in October 1964; that changed nothing. In early December Harold Wilson, the new Prime Minister, reportedly assured President Johnson that he had 'no intention of granting independence to strife-torn British Guiana until the contending Negro and East Indian communities have demonstrated an ability to live together in peace'. What he really meant was that a pretext would be found to delay independence if Jagan got 51 per cent of the votes.[95] In the elections held under PR on Monday, December 7, 1964, the PPP failed to get a majority although they polled the highest amount of votes. President Kennedy was dead for more than a year, but the communist who had caused him inordinate worry throughout his thousand days in the White House had been ousted. Burnham and D'Aguiar formed a coalition government. Jagan had polled 45.8 per cent of the votes (24 seats); Burnham 40.5 per cent (22 seats); D'Aguiar 12.4 per cent (7 seats). In November 1965, at a Conference in London boycotted by Jagan, the Labour Party, following the American script, gave independence to the Burnham–D'Aguiar coalition. Unanimity was no longer required for this decisive constitutional advance.

On February 25 and March 20, 1965 Jock Campbell, on his annual tour of British Guiana, saw the Governor, Sir Richard Luyt; he told him that while the new government had started well, he was concerned about the low morale of Indians following the defeat of Jagan. Jock was worried about the implications of this on Booker: 'It was important that East Indians should not take too adverse a view of the firm as they constituted a large proportion of Booker's employees.' He recalled that,

[i]n past years most senior Booker staff had sympathised or even actively supported the PNC or UF. This had been balanced by Booker policy of supporting the Government of the day, and by the fact that .... [he] himself in pursuing this policy had on a number of occasions spoken in favour of Dr. Jagan.... Now the government has changed and Booker's policy of supporting the Government of the day required apparent support for the UF and PNC. There was nothing compensatory in the eyes of East Indians.

Jock also told Governor Luyt that he was still in favour of a modified first-past-the-post electoral system, to reduce the advantages inherent in it for the PPP; he considered it preferable to PR. He observed that Indians 'regarded the [Burnham] Government as almost foreign and certainly not their own'. On the question of independence Campbell expressed considerable reservation for one who had been a consistent supporter of the principle throughout the turbulent years under Jagan. Luyt reported thus:

As regards Independence Sir Jock said that he was still a firm anti-colonialist and believed greatly in the benefits of independence. On the other hand, as far as British Guiana was concerned he was now faced with the dilemma in that he was bound to have anxiety as to whether the present Government would become a right-wing dictatorship in typical South American style. *He was uncertain whether or not to support early independence. He did, however, support an early conference* [emphasis added].[96]

It was certainly clear that Jock was still not enamoured of Burnham, even after he became head of the government. This collided with the modus vivendi which senior Booker people, like Edgar Readwin, Antony Tasker and George Bishop, were determined to pursue with Burnham. An integral part of this policy was the non-recognition of the PPP-backed union, GAWU, which continued to receive overwhelming support from the sugar workers.

The union would not be recognised until 1975, on the eve of the nationalisation of Booker, when it polled 98 per cent of the votes. In return for Jagan's support for nationalisation, Burnham conceded the poll. Booker had been afraid to take that step for fear of antagonising Burnham and the TUC in their stronghold, Georgetown. Paulette Pierce explains the basis of the relationship between Booker and Burnham's PNC since the early 1960s:

> Key PNC leaders were members of Booker local top management. Many of them moved directly from the company into the new Government [in 1964–65].... From the perspective of the PNC leadership Booker was not an alien firm ripping off the country .... [D]ue to the company's programme of Guyanisation, they had become privileged members of the Booker team .... [T]he PNC and Booker shared specific interests in the sugar industry. Both were equally committed to the continued suppression of GAWU. On the one hand, Booker was convinced that GAWU's recognition would mean economic ruin and the company was prepared to forego immediate profits [through strikes for recognition] in order to ensure its survival in the industry. On the other hand, the PNC recognised that GAWU's victory would be a tremendous boon to the PPP. Thereafter, Jagan would attempt to gain control of the ... TUC.[97]

Campbell, however, did not revise his perceptions of Burnham. His chairmanship had limped along through 1966, the year of Guyana's independence, but he resigned in mid-1967, after 15 years as chairman and 27 years with Booker. He was tired. The story of the circumstances of his retirement is fascinating as it reveals the depth of his fundamental distaste for Burnham. He told me:

> I understood that Booker was going to give him [Burnham] a racehorse; and I thought that was the last bloody thing .... I am not prepared to be chairman of a company that does that. They hadn't actually told me they were thinking of it. I discovered it; and I was so shocked .... I think that was probably what made me that particular morning [in mid-1967] decide I had had enough...George Bishop [his deputy] ... a very tough little Lancastrian ... hadn't got the sort of feel that I had for Guyana or anything else ... and he would have told me that you know, we had to keep in with the Government of the day ... that Burnham was a difficult man, but we'd get all sorts of things if we gave him a racehorse, and I wasn't prepared to have that sort of thing ....

I remember now that's what made me say, well, enough is enough.[98]

Jock related to me many times the consuming revulsion he had for Burnham. I asked him why he was so appalled at the gift horse: he paused long, stammered, and concluded:

Oh, it was my business ethics and my recognition that Burnham was a crook and a cheat and a bully and highly racialist...I got on with him; I called him 'Odo' — at his request — [but] he knew I didn't like him...and I knew he didn't like me. He did once say to me the best thing you ever say about me is that I'm a very good speaker. I said: 'Well, I think it's the best thing to say about you.' You see, he was getting tremendous support; I mean, Tasker and the local [Booker] people were playing up to him ... enormously playing up to him, and those people with Booker [in London] were playing up to him, and I don't think he thought I was much danger to him.[99]

Campbell had no illusions about the ferocity of the darker instincts of Burnham. In 1948 Burnham had written from London to his mother about 'the attack I was supposed to have levelled at B.G. Indians'; adding: 'I feel strongly about the Indian attitude but the time has not come yet for me to broadcast those feelings and muddy my water.' In 1964, in the midst of the racial carnage, Burnham gave a London correspondent an insight into those raw feelings — a manifestation of what his sister, Jessie, saw as the 'dark strain of cruelty which only surfaces when one of his vital interests is threatened'.[100] Burnham had warned:

[I]f it came to a showdown, the East Indians must remember that we could do more killing than they could. Everyone knows there are more East Indians than negroes .... But let me say that in an all out race war .... Dr. Jagan's numerical superiority would not be reflected in the results.[101]

Into this cauldron of racism was thrown Jaganite Marxism, a volatile concoction which, as an American scholar argued in early

1965, was bound to redound to the detriment of Jagan's Indian supporters, including Booker's predominantly Indian field workers:

> But although the PPP's appeal is increasingly racist, and its membership, apart from a few Negro and Coloured figureheads, is wholly Indian, the PPP's policy cannot be said to be in the interests of the Indian community. Guiana would already have achieved independence under Indian leadership if only Dr. Jagan had clearly and unequivocally renounced his allegiance to the ideals and policies of world communism. The fact that he had not done so, even though it would have been highly profitable for him, for his party, and for the Indian community, is a clear indication of the strength of his loyalty to the Communist cause.[102]

In the end, both Cheddi Jagan and Jock Campbell were defeated by L.F.S. Burnham, the architect of the destruction of the sugar industry in Guyana after nationalisation in 1976. Burnham was not encumbered by ideological rectitude; his machiavellianism, the eclectic socialism, a contrivance to subvert democratic practices, had no grounding beyond himself — a means of bending all to his will. Jagan's Marxist pontificating, his unflagging admiration for the Soviet Union and his 'critical support', in 1975–76, for a supposedly socialist Burnhamite regime, gave the latter a model and a blank cheque to nationalise 80 per cent of the economy, to continue to rig elections, to establish the 'paramountcy' of his party, to create a dictatorship which impoverished the nation and drove its best and brightest into exile: Africans, Indians and Portuguese (the latter disappeared completely, including an outwitted, demoralised Peter Stanislaus D'Aguiar). Jagan's pro-Moscow communism — 'a kind of homecoming', he called it in 1969 — meant, too, that the Americans, as in the early 1960s, would continue to define Burnham as the less evil of the two, an ally of sorts, however difficult and eclectic: he was therefore beyond restraint. Jagan had become Burnham's best guarantor of continued American support. Jock Campbell's vision of a partnership between Booker and Guyana, therefore, could not take root in this arid environment, poisoned by the perverse experiments, the catastrophic big ideas in Jagan's and Burnham's El Dorado. There was no room for small causes there.

Endnotes

1. Lloyd Searwar, 'Bookers Guiana: A Study in the Development of an Image and the Implications for Independence', (mimeo.), n.d. [1960], p. 9.
2. Jock Campbell and Dr Fenton Ramsahoye, interview by the author, Nettlebed, Oxfordshire, December 22, 1994.
3. Ibid.
4. USG, Memorandum from the President's Special Assistant (Schlesinger) to the Ambassador of the UK, February 27, 1962.
5. CO1031/4178, Jock Campbell to A.R. Thomas (Colonial Office), November 1, 1961.
6. Jock Campbell, interview by the author, Nettlebed, Oxfordshire, February 18, 1994, Tape 10.
7. See note 2.
8. Jock Campbell, interview by the author, Nettlebed, Oxfordshire, July 24, 1992, Tape 5.
9. CO887/8, (Commission of Inquiry into Disturbances in British Guiana in February 1962), Dr C.B. Jagan cross-examined by Lionel Luckhoo, June 26, 1962.
10. I am grateful to Dr Baytoram Ramharack, Rai's biographer, for this reference.
11. The Chairman's Statement, 1959.
12. Jock Campbell, 'Why I am Voting Labour', *The Observer*, October 4, 1964.
13. CO1031/4568, R.E. Luyt to the Colonial Office, February 25, 1965.
14. Cheddi Jagan, *Forbidden Freedom: The Story of British Guiana* (London: Lawrence and Wishart, 1954), 24.
15. See note 2.
16. The Chairman's Statement, 1962.
17. *Booker News*, June 15, 1962.
18. Ibid., [Leader].
19. *Thunder*, June 16, 1963.
20. *The Times*, March 6, 1962.
21. Ibid., July 17, 1962.
22. *Booker News*, March 8, 1963.
23. Ibid.
24. *The Times*, November 7, 1963.
25. Ibid., November 9, 1963.
26. Ibid., November 11, 1963.
27. *The Daily Chronicle*, November 5, 1963.
28. Ibid.
29. Ibid., November 7, 1963.
30. Ibid.
31. *New Nation*, November 8, 1963.
32. *Mirror*, November 10, 1963.
33. *Guiana Graphic*, January 7, 1964.

34. Ibid., January 14, 1964.
35. Ibid., January 17, 1964; February 9, 1964.
36. See note 34.
37. *Guiana Graphic*, February 20, 1964.
38. Ibid., February 9, 1964.
39. Quoted in Cheddi Jagan, *The West On Trial: My Fight for Guyana's Freedom* (London: Michael Joseph, 1966), 372.
40. Lee Samuel, MBE, interview by the author, London, June 12, 1997.
41. *Mirror*, November 17, 1963; *Guiana Graphic*, February 8, 1964.
42. *Mirror*, February 2, 1964.
43. Ibid., February 10, 1964.
44. Ibid.
45. Ibid., February 11, 1964.
46. Ibid.
47. See note 35.
48. See note 6.
49. Jock Campbell, interview by the author, Nettlebed, Oxfordshire, February 18, 1994, Tape 11.
50. Ibid.
51. *Guiana Graphic*, February 17, 1964.
52. *Mirror*, March 22, 1964.
53. Paulette Pierce, *Noncapitalist Development: The Struggle to Nationalize the Guyanese Sugar Industry* (Totowa, NJ: Rowman and Allanheld, 1984), 86.
54. *Guiana Graphic*, February 20, 1963.
55. Ibid., March 26, 1964.
56. Ibid., March 9, 1964.
57. Ibid., March 12, 1964.
58. *Sunday Graphic*, March 15, 1964.
59. *Guiana Graphic*, April 22, 1964.
60. Ibid., April 23, 1964.
61. Ibid., April 26, 1964.
62. Ibid., April 27, 1964.
63. Ibid., April 27, and 28, 1964.
64. See note 60.
65. *Guiana Graphic*, May 1, 1964.
66. Martin Carter, 'Some Implications of the Present Situation', (confidential internal paper, B.S.E., n.d. [1964]), (mimeo).
67. A.G. Tasker to [the Booker Board], 'The Situation in British Guiana', (confidential), April 7, 1964.
68. Ibid.
69. Edgar Readwin to Cheddi Jagan, April 16, 1964 (B.S.E. document).
70. Quoted in *Guiana Graphic*, May 5, 1964.
71. *Guiana Graphic*, March 3, 1964.
72. Ibid., May 6, 1964.
73. Ibid., May 11, 1964.
74. Sallahuddin, *Guyana: The Struggle for Liberation, 1945-92* (Georgetown: self-published, 1994), 127.

75. Ashton Chase, *A History of Trade Unionism in Guyana, 1900 to 1904* (Ruimveldt, Guyana: New Guyana Co, Ltd, n.d., ca. 1964), 208.
76. W.A. Macnie, (Managing Director, SPA), to Ashton Chase, (Minister of Labour, Industry and Commerce), August 20 1953, in Macnie, 'Labour Unrest, Commencing 31 August 1953', (strictly private and confidential), (mimeo.), September 15, 1953, pp. 7-9.
77. Ibid. See Macnie's paper, Chapter IV, 'Action of the SPA after the Strike Started to Spread', pp. 10-12.
78. Ibid., Appendix II; Chapter VI, 'Action by the Minister of Labour....and Correspondence between him and the SPA', pp. 14-16; Appendix III, 'Notes of an Interview with the Minister of Labour....by Representatives of the BGSPA on Tuesday, 8 September 1953'.
79. Ibid., Appendix III.
80. W.A. Macnie, 'Labour Unrest, Commencing 31 August 1953 (Continued)', (strictly private and confidential), (mimeo.), September 28, 1953, p. 17.
81. Eusi Kwayana, interview by the author, Georgetown, September 22, 1992.
82. Raymond T. Smith, *British Guiana* (London: Oxford University Press, 1962), 173.
83. See note 81.
84. CO1031/4758, Intelligence Report for the Period, March 17 - June 22, 1964 (secret and personal).
85. Ibid.
86. See note 39 [p. 358].
87. *Guiana Graphic*, July 8-10, 1964.
88. Ibid., July 18, 1964.
89. *Mirror*, May 31, 1964.
90. Ibid.
91. Elisabeth Wallace, 'British Guiana: Causes of the Present Discontents', *International Journal* XIX, no. 4 (Autumn 1964): 540, 543.
92. Janet Jagan, 'How Left is the New Left?', *New World Fortnightly*, no. 21 (August 20, 1965): 20.
93. CO1031/4567, R.W Piper to R.E. Luyt, secret and personal, July 23, 1964.
94. Ibid.
95. See note 39 [pp. 391-2].
96. CO1031/4568, R.E. Luyt to the Colonial Office, February 25, 1965; March 21, 1965.
97. See note 53 [pp.89-90].
98. Jock Campbell, interview by the author, Nettlebed, Oxfordshire, February 18, 1994, Tape 10.
99. Ibid.
100. Quoted in Ashton Chase, *Guyana: A Nation in Transit — Burnham's Role* (Georgetown: self-published, 1994), 3.
101. *Daily Telegraph*, May 1, 1964.
102. Ernst Halperin, 'Racism and Communism in British Guiana', *Journal of Inter- American Studies* VII, no. 1 (January 1965).

Conclusion

Chapter Thirty-Three

'ON THE ROAD TO NOWHERE': CAMPBELL'S MISSION IN BRITISH GUIANA

Cheddi and I could have worked miracles.

Jock Campbell

In August 1993, nearly a year after Cheddi Jagan was elected President of Guyana after 28 years in the political wilderness, Dr Fenton Ramsahoye, who was his Attorney General between 1961 and 1964, reflected on the legacy which Jagan and Burnham had bequeathed Guyana. After their 40 years of sequential political dominance, this is how he assessed the harvest:

> It is by no means easy to write about Guyana which has become a very complicated society as a result of Cheddi's and Burnham's experiments. One thing is certain and it is that the plight of Guyana and the suffering of the Guyanese people are wholly attributable to them and to their domination of the political scene for the last half of this century. Cheddi is in power presiding over the *damnosa hereditas* (bankrupt legacy), which Burnham left there, but history will not forget that it was Cheddi's position in respect of communism and the Cold War stance he took which caused the British and American Governments to impose Burnham's dictatorship on a fragile people.[1]

On December 22, 1994, four days before Jock Campbell died, Dr Ramsahoye and I met him at his home in Nettlebed, Oxfordshire. He was in good spirits and was delighted to see Fenton after some 25 years. It was obvious that a meal was being prepared for us — it was to be the last supper I had with him. The discussion had the feel, too, of a final statement between two key players in British Guiana, at the end of Empire:

CS: Fenton, what Jock did, was it a case of too little, too late? If the reforms had been speeded up in the 1950s-early 1960s, would it have made any difference to the political evolution of Guyana?

FR: I don't think that any attempt to speed up the process of reforms would have made any difference to the sort of culture which the political parties were endeavouring to create in Guyana. The basis of the People's Progressive Party's political culture, in the end, was the nationalisation of the [sugar] industry, and whether the reforms were speeded up or the welfare programme speeded up, would in no way have altered their fundamental political philosophy. It would have remained the same whatever the pace of social development in the industry.

JC: [W]hen I first went to Guyana [1934–36] I was astonished by how awful everything was, how badly people were treated on the estates, and how low the price of sugar was. We couldn't do anything until we got a better price for sugar. By the time I'd got enough seniority in Booker to start things moving [after the War], I wasn't thinking politically at all: I was always thinking of the unpaid debts and the appalling scars of slavery and indenture .... I thought the sugar industry would probably be nationalised, so we weren't trying to buy anybody off; we were genuinely trying to behave far better ... everybody hated Booker, and my business was to try to make people, if not *like* Booker — I said it was always easier for a Campbell to go through the eye of a needle than for a big company to be loved — but it could at least be understood and respected .... I entirely agree with Fenton, it wouldn't have made any difference, anything we did at any stage.[2]

Sir Michael Caine (1929–99) worked with Campbell for many years, before he became chairman of Booker in 1972. He remembers Jock as a very political animal and a very complicated person. He was no 'softie'; he could be uncompromising in getting rid of someone if he was not up to the job, but he was not mean in awarding compensation for dismissal. He was an 'exceptionally able' man,

The last supper: Jock (seated),
Dr Fenton Ramsahoye (Cheddi's attorney general) and I (standing left),
December 22, 1994, Nettlebed, Oxfordshire.

possessed 'enormous analytical ability', had a clear sense of purpose, endowed with a large social conscience, and motivated by a powerful sense of guilt because of his family's long roots in sugar in British Guiana. Jock admired success, hated boardroom politics, though a good practitioner himself. He was persuasive, could charm or cajole when necessary. He cultivated loyalty to himself. However, people were not afraid to work for him: they were inspired by the power and energy of the man.[3]

Antony Haynes, too, was one of the brilliant young men Campbell attracted to Booker after he became chairman in 1952. Haynes recalls his infectious energy, his 'social purpose' and his ability to 'mesmerise' people:

> You never left Jock's office without feeling excited about something; it might be just that you were going to chair a meeting ... it could be the smallest task but he managed to make it fun. Even when I was in Georgetown [1953–54] a letter would come from Jock, it would be read with great interest, line by line, by everyone. You couldn't be around Jock and not enjoy working for him, and not wanting to do what he wanted you to do.[4]

Sir Peter Parker was another of Jock's young managers from the mid-1950s (he was later chairman of British Rail [1976–83]). He recalls the experience of working for him as a truly exhilarating one, the making of his life:

> Jock's personality had kept Booker in touch with the politics of the business: as a businessman he talked politically and was completely unafraid to do so. When I came to tour abroad I met some of the political leaders and they would speak of him as if he were a friend in the next room. He understood their idealism and was idealist in return; he reckoned that to be idealist was the only realistic thing to do in the circumstances. Idealism and realism had better learn to live together .... [T]here was a humanity in all he did. That did not mean he was easy to work for. He was far better to you when he was winning, not so good when you were down. He drove people hard, himself hardest, but life was exhilarating when he was around, hard, sharp and funny. He had a needling banker's brain (his grandfather had been governor of the Bank of England) and he was amazing with words, delighting in the choice and play of them (Torquemada, the grandest inquisitor among setters of crossword-puzzles, left Jock his papers to edit for the Cambridge University Press).[5]

This was a man who had had control of virtually every facet of Booker's operations, and by advancing a programme of social reform in Guyana, he had bought time for Booker. They could build their hedges to guard against whatever eventuality confronted them in Guyana. The re-investments elsewhere were possible because of their success in reorganising and modernisation there, thus sustaining a good return. In the summer of 1960 Jock, nearly 48, was at the peak of his powers when he got a nervous breakdown. Caine believes that a contributory factor to his illness was the sense that all the efforts at reform in Guyana had not changed the political culture; he was only really interested in sugar and Guyana: 'His romantic hopes for Guyana had not worked out.' He adds that this commitment to Guyana meant that the programme of hedge-building was not pursued as vigorously as possible. But Campbell was resolute that Booker's responsibility to Guyana was inescapable: that was *his* mission.[6]

When he returned to work in mid-1961, Jock felt as if he now had feet of clay. He was always a conservative businessman in terms of loans and overdrafts. He was almost pedestrian in his approach to investment: Michael Caine observes that he would take 'an inordinate amount of time establishing that the value of sugar was larger than borrowings'. This was rooted in his anxiety for success, the need always to win, possibly fostered by the early attack of polio, which meant that he was afraid to make a mistake. This was how he approached all ball games, too, even when playing against his children. Winning, being in control, these were at the core of the man's personality. The breakdown in 1960–61 was a bitter blow to his self-confidence; besides he had recreated Booker since 1950, reshaped it, but the hedge-building in Canada, Africa and the UK meant that it had grown beyond his grasp, almost an alien creature. And the racial violence in Guyana pained him enormously.[7]

His brother, Colin (born 1926), recalls the breakdown but notes that he was still a powerful character, very intelligent, with many contradictions: selfish in emotional matters, not given to touching or an easy expression of affection, but not greedy and motivated by a profoundly deep social conscience. Colin adds that Jock was immensely in love with his second wife, Phyllis, who was intelligent, sophisticated, elegant, well-read. Her background was French and he frequently relied on her counsel; it was a partnership of mutual respect.[8] Yet, as Antony Haynes recalls, when she was dying, in 1983, Jock was obviously very distraught, yet he found it difficult to hold her.[9] Therein lies the paradox of the man: the Presbyterian boyhood inspired in him a strong sense of right and wrong, but it stifled the instinct for ready emotion; spontaneity was suppressed — things would be bottled up, festering. Colin says that the breakdown in 1960–61 was not the first. He had a brief one in 1948, shortly after he had divorced his first wife: the guilt was overpowering; the family had arranged the first marriage to Barbara, a good woman and wonderful mother to his four children, but not intellectually compatible with him.[10]

Colin has doubts about how good a businessman Jock was. He admired his unfaltering social commitment, but feels that at Booker and at the Milton Keynes Development Corporation (he was its chairman responsible for the building of the new town after he left Booker in May 1967), he did not encounter the unrelenting pressure one encounters in most businesses. After 1951 Booker benefited from guaranteed quotas and remunerative prices under the Commonwealth Sugar Agreement. At Milton Keynes the work was administrative, not entrepreneurial. Colin argues:

> I don't think in his hearts of hearts he was really a businessman .... Jock did have it on a plate; it was a family company [Curtis Campbell in the 1930s]. Thank God he did have a social conscience and he abolished the colour bar in Guyana [in Booker]. He had these four-fold responsibilities, too. It wasn't easy; he had to fight. But I never felt that commercially, technically, Booker was a particularly well-run company.

Colin adds that in terms of his social conscience he was unimpeachable, but as a businessman he was not in the top rank; and as Booker got bigger people started to realise this. He could not see Jock as a company chairman today: he did not have the bloody-mindedness and the remorseless pursuit of the bottom line which are indispensable.[11]

Michael Caine observes that Jock was no longer in control of the details after his break-down; he no longer had his fingers on every pulse.[12] George Bishop, who had assumed major responsibilities at Booker during Jock's illness, notes that Jock was not a natural businessman; his four-fold responsibilities were not compatible with the ethos of the city; he was not adept at taking the bold decisions. He would have made a good politician: he had admirable negotiating skills and a daunting command of details, as demonstrated in his versatility in negotiating the Commonwealth Sugar Agreement; and he had a clear idea of the social responsibility of big business.[13]

But after Jock's illness in 1960–61, the size of Booker and the Guyanese futility made him increasingly frustrated; his vision of shaping a new life for Guyanese sugar workers seemed to be slipping away. The pain showed but he hung on until early 1967, by which time Burnham was the unassailable leader of independent Guyana. That was very unpalatable to Jock, but he was tired of Booker too. He had been exhausted by Guyana's slide into virtual racial war. He recalled:

> Booker had got so big and so many decisions were taken with which I didn't agree; it simply became too big to run as I had run it. I was away ill, in 1960–61, and when I got back, inevitably, there had been other forces in Booker. They had got George Bishop into Booker and it wasn't quite the same, and honestly I was getting quite bored with it. I felt I had done all I could do for Guyana to make Booker what I wanted it to be and we had quite a good team, a lot of people whom I had picked: Michael Caine, Antony Haynes, Peter Parker .... I thought I really had done as much as I could do.[14]

But in the City of London as well, the perception that Jock was a socialist did not endear him to many. However tepid his Fabian socialism was to Cheddi Jagan, it created problems in Booker, too, in London and in Georgetown. Campbell elaborated:

> I don't want to make too much of this, but it was a great strain being a socialist and chairman of a public company. Various people we dealt with closed their accounts: they weren't going to deal with that socialist, Jock Campbell. And I got away with it — my annual Chairman's Statements had a lot of socialist content in them; my whole policy in Guyana, my whole policy in the West Indies and the West India Committee was socialist, and a great many people didn't agree with it but I got away with it. But it was a frightful strain. Anybody else in my position would have been on the boards of banks and all those sorts of things, but I never got the invitation because of my political views. It didn't matter much to me because I concentrated on Booker. Come '66 and '67, I had come through a great many years of turbulence in which I tended to be the odd man out. Booker never tried to get rid of me but I suspect when I went in that morning and said I'm going to give it up, they were quite glad.[15]

Campbell never spoke to me of the strain which Jagan's ideological inflexibility inflicted on him. He never bemoaned the fact that Jagan would not meet him half-way, although he offered him 51 per cent of the shares in Booker, drafted a pension scheme and pursued a thorough programme of reform in British Guiana. Yet, as I have argued, in the midst of the Cold War, as Anglo-American rulers, enmeshed in Kennedy's fear of communism, conspired with Jagan's local enemies, in 1962–63, Campbell was unwavering in his defence of Cheddi — the only such voice in Booker. But as Fenton Ramsahoye remarked in December 1994, Jagan was incapable of seeing any merits in Jock's reforms:

> Jagan spent his whole political life believing that capitalism and so-called imperialism would be overthrown by Marxism or communism .... His greatest weakness was his lack of political and economic understanding of how the world goes around, how wealth is created, the sensitivity to money and investment, the need for strong institutions to support investment. These are things which he has not grasped even today .... He thought I was a right-winger, and he always said so within the Party .... I don't agree with his economic theories or his political theories. I think they're wrong.[16]

It is noteworthy that in response to Fenton's observation and my reference to his anti-communist Chairman's Statement of 1954, Jock had reflected on his own path to reform and Cheddi's inherent incapacity for compromise:

> I've always regretted that speech more than I can possibly say .... [At] that time, given the kinds of things we were trying to do [the reforms in British Guiana], I felt that if there was this overt and rather aggressive kind of Marxism, it would become impossible. But I have always regretted that speech. When I talked at the University of the West Indies, somebody asked me: 'Why did you say that'? I said, 'Because I was bloody wrong' .... I was under the most enormous pressure on the Stock Exchange, people refusing to deal with Booker .... because I was socialist .... Funny enough ... when I was at Oxford [in the early 1930s], I was virtually a communist, people my age were: I hoped the great revolution would come. But when I was actually trying to run a business and totally reform it, I realised that the stamp of communism was totally destructive to what we were trying to do.[17]

Campbell has explained why British Guiana did not produce moderate politicians in the mould of Norman Manley, Grantley Adams and Eric Williams:

> I suppose it's true to say that because of the latifundia [large, foreign-owned sugar plantations] and because of the sheer size of Booker in the sugar industry — a state within a state — this meant that there were fewer confident people than there were in Jamaica, Barbados and Trinidad. The whole of the coastland was not only dominated by Booker; it was dominated absolutely physically by Booker, because of the shape of it; and the bauxite company, being up in the bush, too, was a state within a state. And this encouraged, I think, way-out politicians in both directions; and I think it is bad luck that we had a rather naïve but very charismatic communist [Cheddi] and a 'Papa Doc' in Burnham.[18]

The fact that Jock had invested so much on reforms — with a great measure of success — seeking to moderate Jagan's political excesses, but with virtually nothing to show on the political front, undermined his towering stature in Booker, after he returned to work following his breakdown in 1960–61. With the colony now embroiled in the Cold War, following Castro's ascendancy in Cuba and Cheddi's professed admiration for the Cuban Revolution, Jock was unable to take his staff in British Guiana along with him, especially his key players, Edgar Readwin and Anthony Tasker. So that when, in early 1964, Jagan sought to gain recognition from the Sugar Producers' Association for his union and resorted to violence, as Burnham and D'Aguiar had done successfully in 1962–63, to reverse the Sandys imposition, Campbell was impotent to do much. He virtually retired to his bunker, leaving George Bishop to deal with the key issues. I asked him why he did not force Booker's hand towards the recognition of Jagan's union, GAWU, given its overwhelming appeal among sugar workers. His response spoke of his declining influence by 1964, when Jagan's demise seemed inevitable:

> JC: I think it affected Booker badly that we did not recognise it [GAWU]. I was always in favour of it and I was over-ridden by our local people.

CS: Edgar Readwin?

JC: Yes; and, indeed, Tony Tasker .... I was always in favour
        of Independence, of course. I was never trying to buy
        anybody off (it would be folly to think we could); but we
        could behave better .... They [Readwin and Tasker]
        became very political on the spot, which upset me a lot.

CS: Did you feel uncomfortable with the fact that a union
        [MPCA], which everybody knew had very little support
        in the industry, continued to be the bargaining agent
        of the sugar workers?

JC: I thought it was quite wrong but my difficulty was, you
        have to remember, I had to deal with people on the spot
        and I had to deal with a Board in London who didn't
        take my political views at all, and I don't think realised
        what the real problem of the West Indies was .... [T]he
        local plantocracy was definitely anti-Jagan.

CS: Including the Booker people?

JC: Including *most* of the Booker people.

CS: Did the Secretaries of State for the Colonies ever consult
        you about the situation in British Guiana?

JC: Oh, yes.

CS: Duncan Sandys?

JC: Not Sandys; before that.

CS: Iain Macleod, Reginald Maudling?

JC: I talked with successive Secretaries of State: I always
        said we wanted Independence for Guyana and it would
        work — we would be able to work it out. Not Sandys; I
        had no use for him at all.

CS: Why?

JC: Well, because he had made up his mind what he wanted,
        which was to defeat Jagan.[19]

I asked Ian McDonald about Jock's position on the issue of
recognition for GAWU in 1964. He did not discuss the role of the
people on the spot in the failure to recognise, nor did he remark on
their anti-Jagan stance. He did, however, define the context and what
he thought Jock's response might have been, alluding to his
diminishing authority in the vortex of the Guyanese political
maelstrom:

[I]t is a bit sad that Jock doesn't come out of this particular episode looking too good .... One of the most remarkable men in my life-time... the Jock that I knew who was so positive, so imaginative, so much in the lead .... I would have expected him to say at some stage in all this; 'Let's cut out all this nonsense, this is the union that represents the sugar workers who work for my company. The logical and most sensible thing to do, in the end, is to recognise them'. Now that is the Jock that I knew in so many areas — it did not seem that that happened .... [T]his is the sort of action I would have expected, but there is no evidence that he did. My memory of it is that this was never a subject that was thrashed out in a major Booker Sugar Estates board meeting .... [B]ut the background of all the thinking was that you musn't recognise this communist party's trade union arm; it may be that it was one of those set assumptions that you live with all the time. I seem to remember him [Jock] ... being in discussions [possibly in 1963; he did not go there in 1964]: 'My God, this MPCA really does not have the backing of BSE workers, why on earth are we going through this charade?' I'm not saying it was put like that but the feeling came out; but I have to say that no one then took the step and said that we should recognise GAWU.[20]

By 1964, of course, Jagan was virtually dead politically, with the imposition of the Sandys plan in October 1963. The recognition issue, as noted earlier, was now central to his campaign to stall it. This would not have endeared him to Readwin and Tasker. Even if we accept that Campbell did seek to recommend recognition in 1964, given his perceptibly diminishing authority, it is not difficult to see why it would have been rejected in the context of widespread assumptions of Jagan's impending defeat. The previous year, on May 9, 1963, as Jagan battled to save his Labour Relations Bill, to secure a poll for the recognition of GAWU in the sugar industry, he had failed to advance his cause in a meeting he convened with Readwin and other members of the Sugar Producers' Association. In a typically tactless monologue, he reportedly articulated his communist perspective on the future. The SPA reported thus: 'The Premier was obviously in a state of tension and at times very excited and we were treated to a long declamation on the worthlessness of Burnham ... and a long anti-American tirade aimed particularly at the AFL-CIO.'

The context of the meeting was the TUC and PNC-backed general strike, called ostensibly against the Labour Relations Bill but designed to overthrow his government. Booker Sugar Estates had ceased grinding on several estates, confronted with sabotage and threats by the recognised Union, the MPCA. Jagan saw this as demonstrable support by Booker for the PNC and replied,

> that so far as he could see, we were going to have to live with this risk of damage to our assets for the next twenty years, whether he was in power or not; and that we would have to face up to taking the risk or cease to operate at all. If .... he was overthrown by his opponents or thrown out by the British Government, he could and would make just as much trouble for us. Were we going to be held to ransom by the TUC?

Cheddi had also told them that social reform 'could be brought about best by communism — either the peaceful way or by force. .... He himself believed in the peaceful way but, if this proved impossible, then there appeared no alternative but force'.[21]

This would not have helped his case, nor would it have enhanced Campbell's potential to influence the Booker people on the spot or the Booker Board in London, to move towards recognition. The racial violence that the GAWU strike of 1964 unleashed, virtually put the seal on Campbell's role in the matter. It is noteworthy that he cancelled his annual visit to the colony that year. At such a crucial time, he sent the ascendant George Bishop, a tough, pragmatic man with roots in the civil service, a physically brave, pugnacious, little man, an accomplished mountaineer with Himalayan credentials, to tackle the Guyanese tragedy. Defeated by the Guyanese intransigence and sickened by the racial killings, Jock was really admitting that the journey had come to an end. Colin Campbell recalls the time:

> I think that Jock was a very peaceful person, and although he liked playing games, I don't think he was a very physical person in the sense of liking contact sports. [He played no contact sports]. I think he was probably out of his depths once the virtual civil war started in Guyana [1962–64]. As long as the battles he was fighting were emotional ones and political ones, he was all right.

But once the people started hitting each other or worse, I don't think he really had anything to say.[22]

On December 22, 1994 I asked Jock how he would like the people of Guyana to remember him. He replied: 'I don't really know. What they'll remember is the whole business of Booker and so on; they won't remember me, only a few I kept in touch with .... I will be a footnote in books on the history of Guyana — if a footnote.' A few months before I had asked him how he assessed his work in British Guiana; he was more positive on that occasion: 'I'm pleased I had an opportunity to try to do something; obviously what I was able to do fell woefully short of what should and could be done. I am glad that I had the opportunity to try to serve them in some way.... But I will go to my grave with the consciousness of huge debts unpaid.' [23]

He was extremely cautious not to overplay his reforms and the contribution that they made to the improvement of the lives of many sugar workers and their children. And, to the end, he seemed to think that what he did succeed in doing was an obligatory, paltry compensation for huge ancient wrongs committed against the people of Guyana. He was magnanimous, too, to Cheddi Jagan, as the following exchange with him reveals:

CS: Do you feel at times that the Guyanese people have been ungrateful to you?

JC: Not in the least.

CS: And you ended up with Jaganism?

JC: Not in the least.

CS: Can you reconcile some of the rational features of his politics with what you were trying to do in British Guiana?

JC: It was the state of Guyana, the behaviour of British people to Guyanese, the past behaviour of the plantocracy, slavery and indenture, which made it ripe ground for communism, for some attempt to change it. If everybody had been happy and prosperous, Jagan wouldn't have had a look-in, with all his good intentions .... It took great guts of every sort, immensely hard work to get where he did in the Guyana of those times .... I mean, in a way like Mrs. Thatcher with all her

faults, that he had burning will and resolution and
courage and hard work and unself-interestedness, to do
what he did; and it is very difficult, history has shown,
for these people to change their spots .... I think he was
a good man, and he was trying to do his best for the
people of Guyana .... admittedly, he failed partly
because of the Cold War and because of the Russian
communists, but I understand how it happened. [24]

Fenton Ramsahoye, four days before Jock died, had responded
to Jock's statement that he would be only a footnote in Guyanese
history: 'That's not possible anymore. You'll be much more than
that; you've become part of the chapter.... Well, all of the
developments on the sugar plantations which took place in that period
[1950s and early 1960s], right up to the time we lost office in 1964,
would be attributable in great measure to Jock's work, because the
achievements were substantial.'[25]

For Cheddi and Janet Jagan, however, such magnanimity was
impossible — their commitment to the grand cause, the certainty of
the superiority and inevitability of communism, would not permit
it. On the eve of the elections in December 1964, New World, a radical
group of intellectuals in Georgetown, had assessed Cheddi's
contribution and speculated on how he could benefit from the
likelihood of defeat:

[I]t cannot be denied that Cheddi Jagan is the man to whom the
country owes its awakening and the development of political
consciousness. This is a great debt and for this alone he must
play a major role in Guianese history.... Starting from a left-
wing position, nurtured both by his actual experiences and his
acquaintance with Marxist writing, he expressed himself in
dogmatic, anti-colonial terms.... [H]e is still captivated by the
marxist-socialist vision but has been unable to translate it into
concrete terms.... Even if he does not secure a majority at the
elections this is clearly not the end of his political career....
Perhaps this will give Jagan the opportunity to think out his
position more clearly and to get a better idea of what he really
wants to do. *The tired slogans have worn thin and they need new
interpretation and a new inspiration.* The real question is whether

Jagan can learn from his experience and discard irrelevant dogmas and come to grips with the actual problems confronting him. It is this, in the final analysis, that has caused him to fail. It is the necessity to change this that he must recognise [emphasis added].[26]

Jagan was defeated but the 'tired slogans' would not retreat. Indeed, as early as August 1965, Janet Jagan quickly reaffirmed their faith in the ideological fount, the Soviet Union, with a passion befitting true believers. The New World group had deemed both the United States and the USSR imperialist states. This drew a swift, vitriolic response from Janet: their thought was fundamentally flawed, mired in 'a cesspit of lies, inaccuracies and turn-abouts'. The Jagans would henceforth claim sole possession of the true Marxist tenets, unsullied by pragmatism, opportunism and revisionism, the 'new left' virus of New World:

Imperialism is equated to apply to both the USA and Russia, in a remark which exposes the shallowness of thought and the deception of its 'leftism' ... [whereas] Imperialism grows out of capitalism and is the stage of monopoly capitalism. Imperialism is the system by which the resources of poor countries and the labour of peoples are exploited. These countries become the markets for manufactured goods, the sources of raw materials and super profits which are drained abroad. To compare a capitalist state (USA) with a socialist state (USSR) and to declare that they are both imperialist, shows a complete lack of understanding and a deliberate misuse of the propaganda tools of the reactionary, anti-socialist world of opinion. The Soviet Union was the first country to achieve socialism and from its long period of growth, has risen the socialist world. Whatever might be the imperfections of the relations between the USSR and other socialist states, only a non-socialist could equate Russia with the USA and say that the USSR is imperialist.[27]

Jock Campbell's favourite quote was one taken from Boris Pasternak's, *Doctor Zhivago*, and in a brief autobiographical sketch he drafted some years ago, he took a line from Strelnikov — which, amidst the grand ideas of the Russian Revolution, spoke to the small concerns of little people — as if it were the central motif of his life: 'And in order to do good to others he needed, besides the principles that filled his mind, an unprincipled heart — the kind of heart that knows no general causes, but only of particular ones and knows the greatness of small causes.' He added: 'That to me is the very essence of a great man.'[28] Jock did not say whether Cheddi's and Janet's creed had inspired his fear of the grand designs on human kind.

When Campbell died on December 26, 1994, aged 82, Ian McDonald reflected on the fullness of his life and the way it had touched his own:

> In a lifetime, how many men and women do any of us get to know whom we can be sure of ourselves in defining as great? .... For me Jock Campbell was certainly one such man. He had the ideas, the energy, the imagination, the leadership qualities, the enthusiasm and the charisma of a great man. At the height of his powers he exuded a life-force which drove and lifted others to exceed ordinary effort in pursuit of goals which were important in improving the whole community.[29]

McDonald had observed earlier that during Campbell's chairmanship of Booker sugar production in Guyana grew from 170,000 tons to 350,000 tons; estates were consolidated and factories modernised; irrigation and the whole infrastructure of field works revamped; workers' wages 'vastly increased'; the old logies or ranges eliminated and 15,000 new houses in 75 housing areas constructed, with roads and drinking-water supplied; the scourge of malaria eradicated; medical facilities for workers and their children available on the estates; community centres and social welfare established: sports, libraries, girls' and women's clubs, debating and drama societies; an apprentice training centre, a cadets' scheme and scholarships to workers' children to study at home and abroad; and 'Guyanisation' so advanced that when the industry was nationalised in 1976, it was run almost exclusively by Guyanese. He recalls that 'it was an era of tremendous growth and change for the better in the sugar industry'.[30] Booker originally had 250,000 acres of land; at the end they had 160,000 acres, having given the rest to cooperatives for farming and for housing. McDonald recalls: 'Jock would say if you are not using the land, give it to other people who can use it.'[31] Indeed, Campbell's inspiring work — the culture of reform — in the sugar industry, had reverberations at all levels of the society, to the point where people who studied at the University of the West Indies in Jamaica, in the late 1950s and early 1960s, today, still recall the scholarship and intellectual and political maturity of their Guyanese colleagues.

But it is interesting that it is the smaller acts of generosity of the man which spark admiration in McDonald and others who knew him well:

> I will remember him as the man who often reminded me, and others, that it was important to pay attention to one man's grievance as well as to Three-Year Plans. And I vividly remember him as the man who when he retired as Chairman of Booker asked me to keep an eye on six old pensioners who had given him good service in his younger days and made sure every Christmas to send them a card and a gift on his behalf — which I have faithfully done until one by one over the years they have died.[32]

Three of these men were alive in the late 1970s: Fitz Herbert Ashby, Prince Albert Jones and Alfred Sobers. They were African Guyanese who worked for Jock's family firm, Curtis Campbell, and he had met them and befriended them in 1934, on his first sojourn in British Guiana. They respected the honesty and simplicity of the young master. He reciprocated their respect to their last days. On November 23, 1976, 42 years after he had met them, Jock wrote thus to Ian McDonald: 'I am in some difficulty this year about Christmas presents for Fitz Herbert Ashby, Prince Albert Jones and Alfred Sobers. I shall be most grateful if you could send them $25 each on my behalf, allowing me to repay you when next you are in London.' On December 5, 1978 he wrote to Ian again on the same matter:

> I have received (and reciprocated) my usual Christmas cards from Alfred Sobers and Prince Albert Jones .... I should be most grateful if you could give them my usual Christmas present each. I haven't heard from Fitz Herbert Ashby, if the dear man is still in 'the land of the living' — which I expect he is. Anyway, I have sent him a Christmas card and asked him to apply to you. But

please see that these presents are either charged through me; or, that I repay you when you are next over.

On January 5, 1981 Jock wrote to Ian: 'Thanks for arranging for (upped) Christmas presents to Ashby, Jones and Sobers.' On October 20, Ian wrote thus: 'Our old friend, Prince Albert Jones, is very much alive and kicking! Every time we send him a gift with your best wishes, he kicks up a fuss and says that he is sure we have taken part of the proceeds sent by you for ourselves!'[33]

In early May 1976, on the eve of the dictatorial Burnham regime's nationalisation of Booker, a young woman worker from Plantation LBI, Mrs Deosaran Sawh, sent Jock a sympathy card on behalf of her family: 'Sincere sympathy and a prayer that GOD will comfort you and bless you in this dark hour.' Bewildered by this gesture and not seeing it in context, he wrote to Ian McDonald that the card 'must have been sent under a misapprehension': 'I should be most grateful if the right noises could be made tactfully to the family concerned. I don't quite know how to write without embarrassing them.' McDonald responded that though the humour was 'pretty crude', it was not a mistake: the nationalisation of sugar, the woman felt, gave cause for national bereavement; Jock, therefore, must be inconsolable — the card was entirely appropriate in the woman's eyes. Such was the fount of goodwill towards the man, however strong the residual Jaganite passions against Booker and 'bitter sugar'.[34]

On May 18, 1976, a week before the nationalisation of Booker, Campbell responded to McDonald, with the magnanimity of spirit and humility which had characterised his relationship with Guyana since 1934:

> My immediate reaction .... was to wonder whether this card referred to the acquisition of Booker in Guyana .... But I came to the conclusion, after thinking of it, that the balance of probability was that it was not a joke and that I dared not respond for fear of embarrassment. You can imagine how mixed my feelings are: I am convinced that in recent years Booker have done a great deal for Guyana and her people; I believe we could have gone on doing a great deal in partnership with Government — probably with Government as the dominant partner. Despite my political views

and recognition of the political realities, I cannot help feeling miserable that the period when we have been able to do good for Guyana has been so abruptly shortened compared with the generations of slavery and the plantocracy. I really do feel bereaved: but I hope — not very confidently — that the people of Guyana will find a new heaven and a new earth.[35]

The 'mourner' from Plantation LBI was, indeed, prophetic. After nationalisation sugar production declined from over 350,000 tons to 130,000 tons (1990); the infrastructure and husbandry on the plantations, so crucial on this difficult land, had deteriorated to the point where some sugar had to be imported; GAWU was recognised at last, but the workers' standard of living had slumped; the best and the brightest, many trained under Campbell's Guyanisation programme, were fleeing this derelict land for New York and Toronto. This had pained Jock very much in his last years, for over and over he would cite the concluding line from a poem on the West Indies, which his friend, Kenneth Boulding, the economist, had sent out on a Christmas card many years ago: 'And poor Guyana divided against itself on the road to nowhere' — a mantra of the Guyanese futility.

Towards the end of his life, in the early 1990s, Jock had a dutiful housekeeper, Beth Hall, a New Zealander, who served him until the day he died, Monday, December 26, 1994. She told me she had grown so close to him that she felt privileged to be sharing his life: an enriching experience even in his last days. He was still an omnivorous reader, orderly and purposeful in everything he did, punctilious in answering letters and still enjoying the debates in the House of Lords, although he had stopped participating after his stroke. His curiosity was unquenchable, his courtesy and impeccable manners undiminished. Beth recalls: 'He treated me more as a member of his family than as a housekeeper. He was generous with his gifts, his knowledge, very, very generous with his kindness. He was a man who shared his life with so many people, and anybody who met him was enriched ... you would always be thankful for the opportunity to meet him'.[36]

Even in Guyana many still express similar sentiments. In 1973, six years after he had left Booker and three years before nationalisation, Campbell returned to Guyana on a brief visit. It is a measure of the man's legacy that *The Guyana Chronicle*, the paper of the Burnham government, could welcome him as they did:

> [H]is visit is just as significant and welcome as it would have been in the days when old Guiana was 'Booker Guiana' and as head of Booker he wielded untold influence on the life of the people and country as a whole. History will record that Sir Jock did an excellent job. Booker has a low profile in the community these days and is a shining example of how big business should operate in a developing country. Booker has learnt to co-operate with the Government of the day and even in Jagan's day when there were wails about communism in the boardrooms of Water Street, Booker agreed with and co-operated in every suggestion that seemed to promise some improvement in the prosperity and progress of the country. Even though he has spent comparatively few years in Guyana we think of Sir Jock as a Guyanese, or at least a man who has the problems of Guyana at heart.[37]

Jock Campbell loved Guyana and was especially proud on May 24, 1966, two days before independence and 32 years after he first went out to their plantations, to present the title deed for the site of the University of Guyana campus. Curtis Campbell had owned the land at Turkeyen, East Coast Demerara, before it passed to Booker in 1939: where sugar-cane was once grown, the country's premier centre of learning was being established. It is most appropriate that this book leaves us with this image of sugar and books — Jock's consuming passions — and with his learned reflection to the people of Guyana on that auspicious occasion:

> I hope that in its teaching and research this University may be inspired by the principle that men and women are more important than things. That human happiness and well-being should be the true ends of science and technology and must never be sacrificed to them. And that even in this materialist age, truth, beauty and goodness are worth teaching and learning and striving for.[38]

Jock Campbell on the eve of his 80th birthday, 1992.
This picture accompanied an article he wrote for the Observer *(see Appendix V)*

This was the code by which Campbell lived; and he must have been deeply moved by the verdict on his chairmanship of Booker by Guyana's greatest poet. Shortly after Jock resigned in May 1967 Martin Carter wrote:

> For some twenty years Lord Campbell has been, among other things, a leading figure in West Indian affairs, both in the West Indies itself and in Britain. And in the pursuit of this and varied interests, he has combined the judgment of a businessman with the imagination of the intellectual. It is ... this unusual combination of qualities which has so distinguished his career as a businessman, a thinker, and a champion in the cause of the new nations.[39]

Endnotes

1. Personal correspondence from Dr Fenton Ramsahoye (London), August 19, 1993.
2. Jock Campbell and Dr Fenton Ramsahoye, interview by the author, Nettlebed, Oxfordshire, December 22, 1994.
3. Michael Caine, interview by the author, London, July 19, 1995.
4. Antony Haynes, interview by the author, London, November 6, 1996.
5. Sir Peter Parker, *For Starters: The Business of Life* (London: Jonathan Cape, 1989), 109-110.

6. See note 3.
7. Jock Campbell, interview by the author, Nettlebed, Oxfordshire, February 18, 1994, Tape 11.
8. Colin Campbell, interviews by the author, Potters Bar, Hertfordshire, July 20, 1995; November 17, 1998.
9. See note 4.
10. See note 8.
11. Ibid.
12. Michael Caine, interview by the author, London, December 10, 1996.
13. George and Una Bishop, interview by the author, Beaconsfield, Buckinghamshire, February 27, 1997.
14. Jock Campbell, interview by the author, Nettlebed, Oxfordshire, July 24, 1992, Tape 5.
15. Ibid.
16. See note 2.
17. Ibid.
18. Jock Campbell, interview by the author, Nettlebed, Oxfordshire, February 18, 1994, Tape 11.
19. See note 2.
20. Ian McDonald, interview by the author, Georgetown, September 9, 1992.
21. CO1031/4566, Report by the SPA of a Meeting with Cheddi Jagan, Georgetown, May 9, 1963.
22. See note 8.
23. Jock Campbell, interview by the author, Nettlebed, Oxfordshire, February 18, 1994, Tape 12.
24. Ibid., [Tapes 10, 12].
25. See note 2.
26. 'Portraits of the Leaders: Dr. Cheddi Bharat Jagan', *New World Fortnightly*, no. 3 (November 3, 1964): 22-3.
27. Janet Jagan, 'How Left is the New Left', (Appendix to 'Reply to Mrs. Jagan), *New World Fortnightly*, no. 21 (August 20, 1965): 19.
28. See also Ian McDonald, 'Jock Campbell', (Obituary), *Stabroek News*, January 1, 1995.
29. Ibid.
30. Ibid.
31. See note 20.
32. See note 26.
33. I am grateful to Ian McDonald for providing me with photocopies of his correspondence with Jock Campbell on this matter.
34. Ibid.
35. Ibid. (Jock Campbell to Ian McDonald, May 18, 1976).
36. Beth Hall, interview by the author, Ewelme, Oxfordshire, June 8, 1996.
37. Leader, *The Guyana Chronicle*, August 18, 1973.
38. Jock Campbell, 'The University and the Community', *Booker News* (Special Supplement), June 10, 1966.
39. Leader, *Booker News*, March 21, 1967.

Appendix I

MEN OF THE MOMENT: SIXTH GENERATION REFORMER [JOCK CAMPBELL]

Some people think that if there is a Labour Government, Sir Jock Campbell, chairman of the Booker group, will be caught up in it. Sir Jock does not at present share their opinion. He is not a member of the Labour Party, though the party cares about the things he cares about. Apart from that, he says, his chief disqualification is that he is not a party political animal. He has no stomach for the hurly-burly of the hustings and he believes that the mere fact of being connected with a party machine can destroy a man's soul.

Many reluctant men of affairs have said as much before being dragged coyly into service, but Sir Jock's protestations are convincing. The disciplines of party loyalty would irk him because he judges cases on their merits. Liberal and radical though he may be, he is not doctrinaire. The whole pattern of his life has been anti rather than conformist and he has rebelled against the conventions of most of his environments.

The habit started when he was a boy in Southern Ireland [Co. Limerick]. The sixth generation of a family grown rich on the proceeds of sugar plantations, he nevertheless sympathised with the anti-English underprivileged Irish servants. This made him feel odd man out at Eton — an impression heightened by an attack of poliomyelitis. At Oxford it was a relief to escape from the Etonian progression into Exeter College and read for P.P.E., which helped to clarify his radical urges.

In this frame of mind he went dutifully to British Guiana [in 1934], where the [Indian] indenture system that followed slavery had ended ... [only]17 years earlier. The natives were still far from being free agents. According to Sir Jock they were chattels suffering low wages and appalling housing conditions. Mules, because they had to be imported, were treated better. By comparison the Clyde and the Welsh valleys, those British breeding grounds for class bitterness, were lush pastures.

Already different in character and disposition from other young heirs to wealth and commercial power, the young Campbell faced problems which ensured that he would grow still further away from his contemporaries. Even at 22 he started reorganising the firm's set-up in British Guiana [Curtis Campbell]. The war brought him back to England to work part time in the Colonial Office, but before VJ Day he was in British Guiana again. By that time the eighteenth century family firm had been sold to Booker. Campbell was well enough up the ladder to make his presence felt and he determined that the firm would serve local human needs as well as foreign capitalism.

'What was salutary was that faced with the problems of inefficiency, bad labour relations, and political vulnerability I had to decide what the purpose of business was', he said. 'I decided it was to produce wealth, to manufacture goods, and to supply employment. It was responsible to shareholders, employees, and to the community'.

Elsewhere Campbell has said that businesses exist only to fulfil human needs and social responsibilities. In the context of British Guiana, with its legacy of colonialism, slavery and ignorance, that meant more than raising productivity. It meant political activity, dealing with home and local governments. It meant securing the Commonwealth Sugar Agreement of 1950 with its guarantee of security and better wages. Campbell was the chief architect of the agreement and he is still chairman of the Commonwealth Sugar Exporters Group.

Such a man might have a sentimental regard for paternalism, seeing himself as the benevolent supplier of housing, health services, roads, and other amenities. But Campbell hates paternalism as a form of domination or colonialism in a new guise. It may be a necessary transitional phase until a community can stand on its own feet, but as soon as possible the firm must contract out. Thus today the 108 companies under the Booker umbrella are small groups with local boards and local operational responsibility.

'They grow further and further away from Bucklersbury House (the London headquarters), while on the parent board we retain control of hiring and firing directors, sale or purchase of assets, capital expenditure and borrowing powers', Campbell said. 'Anything affecting the broad ethic of the business comes to us. Otherwise responsibility is fairly and squarely on local shoulders'.

What Campbell has done is in line with Britain's transition from colonial rule to Commonwealth partnership. Although originally motivated more by conscience than by business sense he is right for the times — a man of the moment in the fullest sense. Some home-based business barons, still basking in the belief that profitability will be ensured by white supremacy, regard him as an eccentric but they ignore his 30 years' experience. The traditions of Britain's industrial revolution could not be transplanted to his virgin territories. Where private savings did not exist, a belief in public ownership was not necessarily rabid Socialism. Where racial tension occurred the qualifications of a potential manager might be less important than his wife's views on natives. With its wealth of conventional wisdom and state paternalism, British industry was on a totally different wicket. What Campbell perceived — and applauded — was that the new nations would establish their own identity without necessarily copying Soviet communism or Western capitalism. That is why he says that if Western capitalism is to survive it must adapt itself to the process of the new nations.

Climatic conditions and internal strife still bedevil the sugar producing areas and, with its £25 million total net assets, the Booker group is building hedges through diversification. For a century it has dealt in sugar, ships, shops, rum, balata, timber, printing, secondary industries, and at one time even hotels. The range is always widening.

Now 52, Sir Jock has been chairman of the group since 1952 and the average age of the board is 52. At Bucklersbury House his reforming zeal is reflected by the comparative youth of the staff, among whom he inspires great loyalty. Except under the closest scrutiny he is a man of contradictions. He hates power but enjoys influence. His dislike of political machines does nothing to quench an abiding interest in politics. As a member of the Africa Bureau's executive his friends include Trevor Huddleston and Michael Scott, as well as Dr. Hastings Banda and Kenneth Kaunda. Inevitably, Booker is sometimes accused of racial discrimination in reverse.

Campbell sent his sons to Eton and admits to the advantages of his sequestration at Eton and Oxford. He is a member of the Oxford University Appointments Committee and of the Court of Governors of the London School of Economics, but he employs people intuitively without too much regard for their social and economic background. A tense yet kindly man, he drives fast cars very fast and, despite his earlier poliomyelitis, is a good athlete, playing games with a demonic determination to win. Although professing nervousness about making speeches his written work has eloquence, due perhaps to his devotion to 18th and 19th century novelists.

The groundwork for the Commonwealth Sugar Agreement was started when Labour was last in office, which brings this profile back to its starting point. The Labour Party is not rich in businessmen who control 32,000 employees and are closely acquainted with commodities and developing countries. Though Sir Jock is content to keep the Booker group 'on course in its stormy seas' he could also, in the House of Lords, be a valuable navigating aid to a government sailing in perilous Commonwealth waters. There ought still to be jobs of national importance for people without party cards. To get Sir Jock away from Booker it would have to be a big job.

The Times Review of Industry and Technology, (September 1964).

Appendix II

LABOUR'S FIRST YEAR [1964–65]: A REVIEW
RADICAL'S COMMENT ON THE ANNIVERSARY

From **Sir Jock Campbell**

For many Labour supporters it is difficult not to feel *personally* disappointed by the performance of the government, however unfair this might be. Rid of the Tories, there were great expectations of imaginative new priorities, of radical planning for the fairness and quality of life. We had our own hobby-horses: mine were aid to poor countries, and race relations. The White Paper on Immigration is rooted in racial prejudice, and the government have not had the courage to say so. The new tax system makes no distinction between the just and unjust in the field of overseas development...

But the government have, to their everlasting credit, focused attention — in a way in which no previous government has done — on the reality of Britain's economic problems and the need for national planning to surmount them. This had to come first. Now I hope the government will have time to prove that they can establish socialist priorities, and forge their own radical weapons for overcoming *all* the forces of reaction and winning us through to a land looking forward to future national and international hope instead of backwards to past imperial glory.

New Statesman, October 15, 1965.

Appendix III

LORD CAMPBELL ON NORMAN MANLEY (1969)

In Jamaica in 1944 waiting to meet Norman Manley for the first time I remembered an after dinner discussion a couple of years earlier at the Travellers Club in London, about whether illiberal acts could be justified on the grounds that they will prevent greater illiberalism. The two Jamaicans with whom I was arguing — a politician [Alexander Bustamante] and a lawyer [later his Attorney General] — vigorously asserted that an illiberal act could be so justified: citing as their example that if they had their own way Norman Manley would have been shot on the grounds that if he gained power in Jamaica he would set up a Communist police state.

In the event, of course, I met a man who at once impressed me as an exceptionally civilised human being. Norman Manley is often referred to as the Stafford Cripps of the Caribbean. Certainly he had the brilliance and the quality of intellect and all the powers of analysis and exposition of a great advocate. But whereas Cripps (whom I only met two or three times) struck me as almost a disembodied intellect, Norman Manley was far from disembodied. His Military Medal in the First World War, his prowess as an athlete [a Rhodes Scholar at Oxford], his wit and his charm — and indeed his marriage to Edna — were all evidence of the abundance of his humanity. He was an unusually attractive man with an unusually attractive wife — herself the embodiment of civilisation too, deeply concerned with the plight of the people of her country, and a sculptor of international reputation.

There can be, and are, all sorts of criticisms of Norman Manley as a politician: that he was no political tactician: that he was no good at the hurly-burly of political life: above all that he was largely responsible for wrecking the ill-starred West Indies Federation — first by refusing to lead it, and then by allowing Jamaicans to opt out. Perhaps he *was* too civilised, too human, too clever and too logical to be a successful politician. Like all the rest of us he doubtless made plenty of mistakes and errors of judgment. And like all highly logical people he tended to change his position in response to new evidence and new analysis, and was then accused by pragmatists of lacking principles. But the world and the Caribbean desperately need leaders of real human quality as well as political tacticians.

On the sad day of his death [September 2, 1969] I was asked on the Caribbean service of the BBC what I thought Norman Manley's lasting achievements were. I replied that I judged what he *was* much more important than what he *did*. It is not to decry the ardours and the burdens and the indispensability of less radical and more successful political leaders to say that sensibility and integrity, imagination and insight, can bear richer fruits in the long run than ephemeral victories at the hustings. People who mind about the precarious state of mankind and of civilisation, and people who feel deeply about international poverty and racial conflict, all have rich reason to have been grateful to Norman Manley's life, and for grieving his death.

'Obituary', (mimeo.), [September 1969].

Appendix IV

Business Ethics

From **Lord Campbell of Eskan**:

I think I can pride myself on being among the targets of Mr. Peter Morgan's diatribe at the Institute of Directors jamboree: because I believe that there should be values other than money in a civilised society.

I believe that truth, beauty and goodness have a place. Moreover, I believe that if businessmen put money, profit, greed and acquisition among the highest virtues, they cannot be surprised if, for instance, nurses, teachers and ambulance men are inclined to do the same. I am grateful to Mr. Morgan for confirming the misgivings I have always had about the Institute of Directors — even when I was the chairman of a public sector company.

The Independent, March 2, 1990.

Appendix V

A Journey Back To My Roots: Lord Campbell Of Eskan Explains How He Would Vote If He Were Not Barred From Doing So By Being A Peer

In 1964, *The Observer* ran a trio of articles, 'Why I am going to vote Conservative/Labour/Liberal'. I wrote the Labour one [October 4].

As far as I remember, I said, that while I did not necessarily believe that Labour would run the country better than the Tories, they minded more about the things I minded about and disliked what I disliked. Moreover, I thought that a radical party in power even for a time would, as it were, shift the political agenda in the right direction. I quoted my father's response to the local Tory MP who complained that he never held Conservative jamborees in the Kentish village where we lived: 'My dear Charles, everyone in this village votes Conservative — if you make them think about politics, they will vote Labour!'

Perhaps at this point I should explain — not my political credentials, because I have none — but the influences that have made me anti-Conservative since my youth.

After I came down from Oxford in 1933, I went to Demerara (now Guyana), where my family had had sugar estates since the eighteenth century. This had always been romanticised for me by my parents, but what I discovered there was different. The scars of slavery and of the indenture system; the racialism and greed of the plantocracy; the contempt for 'blacks and coolies', who could never expect promotion over or equal to the white 'masters'. I once pointed out to a local director of the company [James Bee, at Albion] that the mules were stabled better than people. 'Mules cost money to replace', he replied.

I did what I could to reform the industry and played a leading part in negotiating the Commonwealth Sugar Agreement. But I came to the irrevocable conclusion that had change been left to the tender mercies of Conservatives, there would have been no end to slavery, or at home, to hanging sheep stealers, child labour and voteless women. I concluded, too, that a mixed economy was best: that business must recognise and balance fourfold responsibilities — to the community, to customers, to the employees and to shareholders — and that reform must be held always in view.

Early in Mrs. Thatcher's reign, I began to wonder whether my father's response was any longer true. Her single-mindedness, courage and resolution to get the country back on its feet, her self-confidence that she always knew best and was always right, her populist policies were persuading many people of the Tory Party's conviction that it is the natural party of government.

As a trustee of Chequers, I was surprised to find how much warmer, more feminine, more personally kind Mrs. Thatcher was than her public image. Although I was never under her political spell, I admired her as a person.

In the event, Thatcherism has shifted the political agenda beyond all reasonable expectation — all on the altar of money and the market. It has derided consensus and exalted confrontational politics. It has destroyed local government; confounded housing, national health and education. The Tories have 'sold off the family silver' by privatising monopolies and, with the proceeds, reduced taxes on the better-off. Their flawed and failed economic policies have so weakened primary industry that we can no longer stand on our own, except as part of the European Community....

Having said all that, can Labour — or any single party — redress the balance? Like it or not, as long as the better-off use private health care and fee-paying schools, the public services are bound to suffer. A flourishing economy is essential to maintain present inadequate levels, let alone improve them. We face again the problem: how to strike the balance between social justice and economic imperatives?

Pleas for social justice trigger hostile reaction. But the poor, the sick and those who cannot fend for themselves are with us in increasing numbers. So, in contrast, are the mega-rich and the lush pastures of the black sheep in the business world, with their gargantuan salaries, expense accounts, company cars and tax fiddles.

Of course, the wealth and employment generated by industry and trade are vital to the nation. But before they can earn our respect and before they, of all people, can talk about our becoming a 'something for nothing society', they must put their house in order. Will a Conservative government, largely financed by them, ensure that they do it? What about escalating violence? It is not difficult to understand the anger of the unemployed and the homeless, and their increasing distrust of the police and the legal system. But how are we to avoid increasing anarchy? The prisons are a disgrace to civilisation. We continue to overfill them, yet refuse to pay for their improvement. What other sanctions are workable?

I don't find that detesting Tory values and inclining towards the values of the Labour Party offers any guarantee that the nation would be much better governed, or more prosperous, or even more socially just than under Labour. The allocation of scarce resources is a problem that would confront Labour just as much as the Conservatives....

Perhaps politics has nothing to do with — and can do nothing about — the evolving behaviour of human beings amid the terrifying pressures of modern life. In short, we are all in real trouble. So how, as almost an octogenarian, would I vote now if, along with lunatics, I were not disfranchised by a life peerage?

In my more cynical moments, I reflect that there may not be all that much to choose between Mr. Major trying to reconcile benign instincts, Treasury disciplines and an unruly part, and Mr. Kinnock trying to reconcile human and civilised values, fiscal disciplines and the centrifugal forces of *his* party.

I then remind myself that under Mr. Kinnock's constructive leadership it is the Labour Party which is now 'behaving well', and the Tories, despite the nice Mr. Major, who have not changed their spots.

If I had the vote, I would cast my ballot for Labour with the hope, rather than the certainty, that they will — or can — get it right. But above all, behind my decision would be the conviction that we *must* get back to consensus government, either through proportional representation and coalition or through a hung Parliament — so that our representatives could at least sometimes put country before party.

The Observer, April 5, 1992 [on the eve of Campbell's 80th birthday].

THE SUGAR PLANTATIONS IN GUYANA TODAY

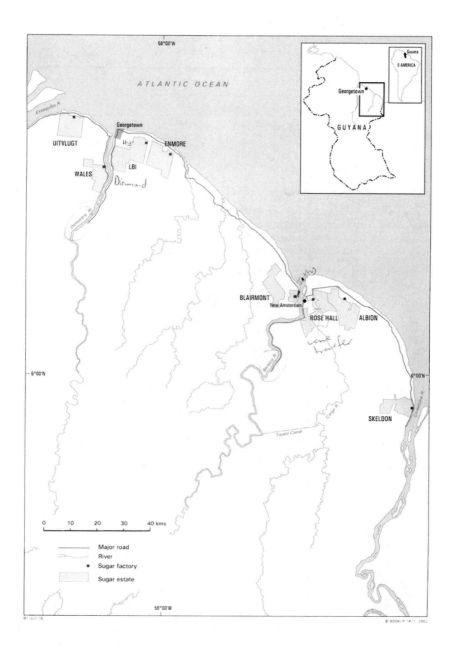

Coastal Villages and Plantations in Demerara and Berbice

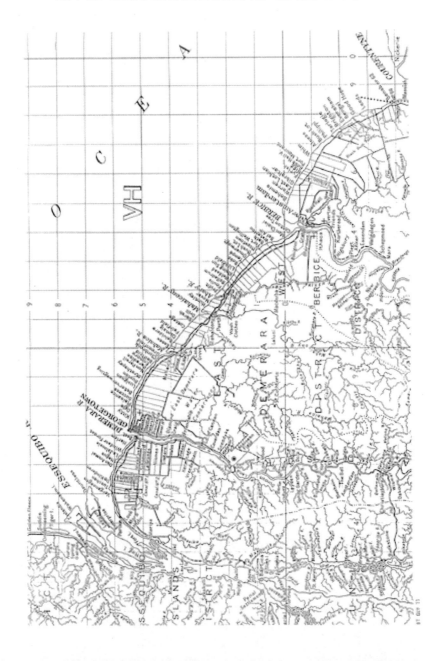

SUGAR PLANTATIONS IN THE EARLY 1950S

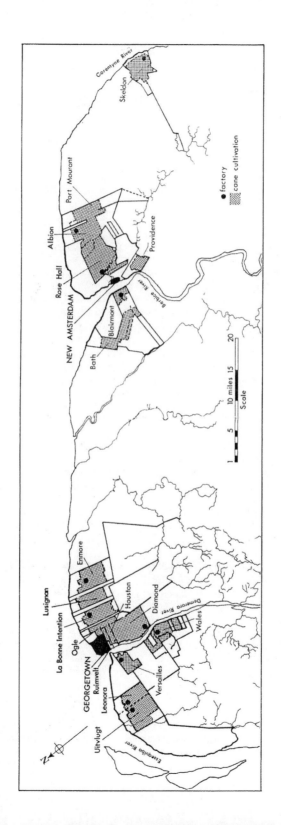

Bibliography

I   PRIMARY SOURCES

A.   Booker Documents [Booker Head Office, London (uncatalogued)]

Booker Brothers, McConnell and Co, Ltd. *Report of the Directors and Statement of Accounts, 1947–66* (incorporating the Chairman's Statements, 1947–66 [written by Jock Campbell]).

Booker Sugar, 1954 (Supplement to the Accounts of Booker Brothers, McConnell and Co, Ltd, 1954).

Booker Sugar Estates (BSE) Files. Chairman's Annual Report of Booker Sugar Estates Ltd and Subsidiary Companies for the Years, 1951-66 (incorporating various annual departmental reports, e.g., Report of the Agricultural Director [Dr Harry Evans]; Report of the Director of Field Operations [Ray Wilkins]; Report of the Director of Social Policy [Roy Close]; Report of the Industrial Relations Officer [E.N. Edwards]).

Booker Sugar Estates (BSE) Files. Minutes of Meetings of the Directors of BSE, 1954-64 (incorporating various correspondence from the Booker Board in London).

Booker Brothers, McConnell and Co, Ltd. Political Files, 1951–54; 1962–64.

British Guiana Sugar Producers' Association (SPA). Industrial Relations Department Files, 1941–47.

British Guiana Sugar Producers' Association. Labour Union Bonuses, 1952–55, [including 'Labour Unrest' Reports of August-September 1953].

British Guiana Sugar Producers' Association. 'Memorandum Regarding Constitutional Reform Presented to the British Guiana Constitution Commission [Sir E.J. Waddington, chairman]', strictly confidential, January 10, 1951.

British Guiana Sugar Producers' Association. 'Memorandum Presented to the British Guiana Constitution Commission [Sir James Robertson, chairman]', strictly private and confidential, January 22, 1954.

British Guiana Sugar Producers' Association. Minutes of Meetings of the Board of Directors, 1948–59.

British Guiana Sugar Producers' Association. Miscellaneous Documents, 1949–64 (including reports of meetings with Governors of British Guiana; the Commissioner of Labour; matters relating to the GIWU-MPCA ongoing union conflict; correspondence from the Demerara Sugar Board, London).

Close, Roy E. 'Notes on Social Policy – 1', Minutes of the Meeting of the Directors of BSE, November 2, 1959, Appendix A, (private and confidential).

The Corentyne Sugar Company Ltd [Curtis Campbell]. Minutes of Meetings of the Directors, 1935–37.

Edwards, E.N. 'Welfare on Sugar Estates: Notes on the Ibberson Report', Managing Director, SPA to the Demerara Sugar Board, London, August 14, 1953, encl.

Evans, Harry Dr 'Water-Relations of Cane During the Current Period [1957]', Minutes of Meeting of the Directors of BSE, December 20, 1957, Appendix B.

_____. 'Toxic Sulphate Soils in Guyana and their Improvement for Sugar-cane Cultivation'. In Report of the Agricultural Director, 1966.

'Mechanisation in the British Guiana Sugar Industry'. Minutes of the Meeting of the Directors of BSE, July 29, 1961, Appendix A.

Scargall, R.B. 'Memorandum on Welfare on the Sugar Estates', (mimeo.), January 3, 1949.

Social Welfare Reports, 1953–64. In SPA, Report of the Proceedings of the Board of Directors, 1953–64.

B   **Campbell Papers (courtesy of the late Lord Campbell)**

1   Chairman's Statements, 1947–66. In *Report of the Directors and Statement of Accounts* for these years. (They were all written by Campbell personally and reflect his style, apart from the Statement for 1960, when he was ill).

2   Articles and unpublished papers and speeches by Jock Campbell

(i)   'Note on the Central Problem of the Economy of British Guiana', (mimeo.), October 14, 1953.

(ii)   'British Guiana' [letter to the editor], *The New Statesman and Nation*, October 24, 1953.

(iii)   'British Capital in the Changing Conditions of the Colony'. Paper delivered at the University of Cambridge, July 12, 1954.

(iv)   'Postscript'. In *Booker Sugar* (Supplement to the Accounts of Booker Bros, McConnell and Co, Ltd, 1954).

(v)   'People are More Important than Ships and Shops and Sugar Estates'. Script of a broadcast given by Mr J.M. Campbell over Radio Demerara, on the British Guiana Government Information Services Programme, 'Sunday-at Noon', on March 4, 1956.

(vi)   'Address by Mr. J.M. Campbell [to the Booker B.G. Group Committee]', [internal] (mimeo.), on March 6, 1956.

(vii)   'Why does man Work?'. Address to the Duke of Edinburgh Study Conference, Oxford, (mimeo.), July 11, 1956.

(viii)   'Safeguarding the Future of Sugar'. *New Commonwealth*, June 24, 1957.

(ix)   'Script of a Broadcast by Mr. J.M. Campbell on the BBC Overseas Service, in the Programme, "Caribbean Commentary"', (mimeo.), June 29, 1957.

(x)   'Paternalism — Good or Bad?'. *Optima*, (June 1958).

(xi)   'Opportunity and Investment in the West Indies'. *West Indian Review*. June 6, 1958.

(xii)   'Alliance Luncheon and Annual General Meeting: Report of Sir Jock Campbell's Speech'. *Cocoa, Chocolate and Confectionery Alliance Journal*, July 10, 1958.

(xiii)   'The Responsibilities of Big Business'. *The Listener*, January 8, 1959.

(xiv)   'What are Directors For?'. *The Director*, (February 1959).

(xv)   'More Sugar from the Commonwealth', *New Commonwealth*, (April 1959).

(xvi)   'Development and Organisation of Booker Bros., McConnell and Co., Ltd.'. Paper delivered at the London School of Economics, (mimeo.), November 24, 1959.

(xvii)   'Industry's Responsibilities Overseas' [A discussion between Sir Jock Campbell and Mr Adrian Liddell Hart, Chief Information Officer of the FBI]. *The F.B.I. Review*, (January 1960).

(xviii)   'What is Booker?'. Text of a Broadcast by Sir Jock Campbell on Radio Demerara, February 21, 1960.

(xix)   Booker Bros, McConnell and Co, Ltd. 'The Group Chairman's Visit to British Guiana and the West Indies, January-March 1960', [confidential], (mimeo.), March 22, 1960.

(xx)   'Bookers: The Transformation of Booker Bros. McConnell and Co.'. *Investors Chronicle*, March 25, 1960.

(xxi)   'Facing up to Facts in the Caribbean'. *The Times*, May 9, 1962.

(xxii)   *The New Africa — Pride and Prejudice: Sense and Sensibility* [The Africa Bureau Anniversary Address, November 29, 1962] (London: The Africa Bureau, 1962).

(xxiii)   'The Role of Big Business in Africa'. *Commonwealth Development*, (January-February, 1963).

(xxiv)   'The West Indies: Can they Stand Alone?'. *International Affairs* 39, no. 3 (July 1963).

(xxv)   'Why I am Voting Labour: Greater Good for the Greater Number'. *The Observer*, October 4, 1964.

(xxvi)   'The Clash of Immigrant Coloured Races in British Guiana'. Text of Address to the Ministry of Education Commonwealth Course, (mimeo.), April 15, 1966.

(xxvii)   'Private Enterprise and Public Morality'. *New Statesman*, May 27, 1966.

(xxviii)   'Text of Speech by Lord Campbell of Eskan to the Chamber of Agriculture in Mauritius', (mimeo.), October 21, 1966

(xxix)   'Men of Note: Lord Campbell of Eskan'. *Jamaica and West Indian Review,* (1966).

(xxx)   'Is the Business of Government the Government of Business?'. *Optima*, (March 1967).

(xxxi)   'Address to Education Conference at Missenden Abbey, Bucks.'. October 4, 1968 [Published in *International Development Review*, (December 1968)].

(xxxii)   'The Sugar Agreements', *Venture*. (March 1969).

(xxxiii)   'One Pair of Eyes: Through the Eye of a Needle' (Script of a film on Lord Campbell of Eskan: tycoon and socialist, undertakes a critical examination of the profit motive). BBC2, April 12, 1969.

(xxxiv) 'Obituary: Norman Manley', (mimeo.), n.d. [September 1969] (Appendix III).

(xxxv) 'Speech by Lord Campbell of Eskan to the Fabian Society, London', (mimeo.), October 22, 1969.

(xxxvi) 'Eulogy for Memorial Service for Guy Eccles', (mimeo.), July 20, 1971.

(xxxvii) 'An Autobiographical Sketch', (mimeo.), n.d, [late 1970s].

(xxxviii) 'A Journey Back to My Roots'. *The Observer*, April 5, 1992 (Appendix V).

(xxxix) 'People are More Important than Ships and Shops and Sugar Estates', [Jock Campbell, interviewed by David deCaires]. *Stabroek News*, July 8, 1989.

(xxxx) 'The 1976 Nationalisation did not Take us by Surprise', [Jock Campbell, interviewed by David deCaires]. *Stabroek News*, July 15, 1989.

C   Jagan   Documents
[Cheddi Jagan Research Centre (Georgetown); Freedom House (Georgetown); National Archives, Guyana; National Library (Georgetown); University of the West Indies Library, (St. Augustine, Trinidad)]

1   Articles, Books and Pamphlets by Cheddi Jagan

(i) 'The Right to Vote'. *The Labour Advocate*, August 6, 1944.

(ii) 'The Need for Consumers' Co-operatives'. *Indian Opinion*, June 2, 1945.

(iii) 'The Co-operative Way'. *Indian Opinion*, Xmas Number, 1945.

(iv) 'Memorandum on the Sugar Industry'. (Submitted to the Venn Commission in 1948), (mimeo.).

(v) *Fight for Freedom: Waddington Constitution Exposed*. Georgetown: self-published, 1952.

(vi) *Bitter Sugar*. Georgetown: self-published, n.d., [1953].

(vii) *Is Imperialism Dead?* Georgetown: self-published, 1953.

(viii) *What Happened in British Guiana*. London: Union of Democratic Control, n.d., [1954].

(ix) *Forbidden Freedom: The Story of British Guiana*. London: Lawrence and Wishart, 1954.

(x) 'Dr Jagan's Open Letter to Mr. D'Aguiar'. *Daily Argosy*, October 15, 1960.

(xi) 'Address by the Honourable Dr Cheddi Jagan, Premier of British Guiana to the Great Neck Forum, [New York]', n.d., [October 1961].

(xii) 'Towards Understanding'. Text of an Address to the National Press Club, Washington, (mimeo.), October 1961.

(xiii) *British Guiana's Future: Peaceful or Violent?* Georgetown: PPP, 1963.

(xiv) 'Guiana Crossroads'. *Labour Monthly*, (September 1963).

(xv)　'Dr the Hon. Cheddi Jagan at the Conference of Heads of Government of the Commonwealth Caribbean Countries held in Jamaica', (mimeo.), January 1964.

(xvi)　'Broadcast to the Nation by the Premier, Dr the Honourable C.B. Jagan on his Return from the Conference of Commonwealth Caribbean Countries held at Kingston, Jamaica, in January 1964', (mimeo.), February 8, 1964.

(xvii)　*Cheddi Jagan Speaks at Freedom Rally, 9 February 1964.* Ruimveldt: New Guyana Co, Ltd, 1964.

(xviii)　'Growing Support for Drastic Reforms in Emergent Nations', Text of a Broadcast ... over Radio Demerara, (mimeo.), April 4, 1964.

(xix)　'The Racialists of Guiana', (mimeo.), April 21, 1964.

(xx)　'Address to the United Nations Committee of Twenty Four', (mimeo.), April 1964.

(xxi)　'Text of Broadcast by the Premier, Dr the Honourable C.B. Jagan', (mimeo.), June 6, 1964.

(xxii)　'The Four Freedoms' (Straight Talk). *Mirror*, September 6, 1964.

(xxiii)　*The Anatomy of Poverty in British Guiana.* Georgetown: PPP, 1964.

(xxiv)　*The West on Trial: My Fight for Guyana's Freedom.* London: Michael Joseph, 1966.

(xxv)　*US Intervention in Guyana.* Georgetown: PPP, 1966.

(xxvi)　'Lenin in Our Time'. *World Marxist Review* 13, no. 4 (April 1970).

(xxvii)　*A West Indian State: Pro-Imperialist or Anti-Imperialist.* [Georgetown]: self-published, 1972.

(xxviii)　[Jagan] and Ramkarran, *Race and Class in Guyana.* Georgetown: PPP, 1974.

(xxix)　'Address to the 18ᵗʰ PPP Congress'. *Thunder*, (October-December 1974).

(xxx)　'Great Injustice Done to Jagan — Schlesinger'. [Editorial], *The Nation*, June 4, 1990.

2　PPP Publications

Manifesto, [April 1953].

Manifesto, Programme and Policy [August 1957].

Independence Now! (1960).

Manifesto, General Election, 1961

Hitler's Force in Guiana (By Moses Bhagwan), n.d., (1962).

Manifesto, General Election, 7 December 1964.

This Too is USA (1965).

Guyana's Road to Socialism; Political Programme of the People's Progressive Party (Adopted by the 20th Congress of the PPP, Annandale, East Coast Demerara, August 6, 1979).

Constitution of the People's Progressive Party (Adopted by the 20th Congress of the PPP, Annandale, August 6, 1979; amended at the 21st Congress, Mon Repos, August 2, 1982).

1983: The Year of Karl Marx — The Greatest Revolutionary of the Epoch!

D   Colonial Office Documents
[Public Record Office, Kew, London]

CAB129/163 — C.(53)261, Memorandum by the Secretary of State for the Colonies [Oliver Lyttelton] to Cabinet, September 30, 1953, top secret [dated September 25, 1953].

CO111/474, (Individuals), [Sir G.W. DesVoeux], November 2, 1894.

CO111/509, (Individuals), [Henry K. Davson to Secretary of State for the Colonies], February 15, 1898.

CO111/509, (Individuals), [W.M. Campbell], August 6, 1898.

CO111/517, Sendall to Chamberlain, no. 53, February 15, 1900.

CO111/518, Sendall to Chamberlain, no. 71, March 15, 1900.

CO111/525, (Individuals), [W.M. Campbell], March 9, 1900.

CO111/525, (Individuals), [H.K. Davson], March 13, 1900.

CO111/527, Sendall to Chamberlain, no. 203, June 6, 1901.

CO111/687/75080 [1930], British Commonwealth Labour Conference, 1930: British Guiana Labour Union, Memoranda.

CO111/689/75141, encl., C.F. Andrews, 'Impressions of British Guiana', (mimeo.), [1930].

CO111/726/60036 [1935], 'Report by County Inspector, J. Nicole, on the Labour Unrest on the Sugar Estates on the West Coast Demerara, during September 1934', (mimeo.).

Ibid., C. Douglas Jones (OAG) to Cunliffe-Lister, no. 29, January 24, 1935.

Ibid., Northcote to MacDonald, no. 238, telegram (confidential), October 17, 1935.

Ibid., Northcote to MacDonald, no. 241, telegram (confidential), October 23, 1935.

Ibid., Northcote to H. Beckles (Colonial Office), December 4, 1935.

Ibid., Beckles to Northcote, January 13, 1936.

CO111/732/60036 [1936], 'Report of the Commission of Inquiry into the 1935 Disturbances', Legislative Council Paper, no. 15 of 1936.

Ibid., Minute, S. Caine, January 22, 1937.

CO111/762/60270 [1939], encl., 'Report of the Leonora Enquiry Commission, 1939'.

Ibid., 'Note of an Interview with F.J. Seaford, O.B.E. (Booker Bros.), Elected Member of the Legislative Council of British Guiana, 20 June 1939'.

CO111/778/60493 [1943], Lethem to Lloyd, September 23, 1943.

Ibid., Lloyd to Lethem, personal, December 20, 1943.

Ibid., 'Notes of a Conversation in Mr. Beckett's Room...Friday, November 5, 1943'.

Ibid., Lethem to Lloyd, February 26, 1944.

CO111/785/60466/13 [1944], Lethem to O.F.G. Stanley, April 17, 1944.

Ibid., F.J. Seaford to Lethem, May 10, 1944.

CO111/796/60270/5, (Ordnance no. 20 of 1947) and B.G. Smallman (CO minute), August 17, 1949.

CO111/797/60270/5/5 [1948], 'Report on a GIWU Meeting Held at Grove, East Bank Demerara, 26 August 1948'.

Ibid., 'Report on a GIWU Meeting Held at Good Intent, West Coast Demerara, 29 August 1948'.

Ibid., W.S. Jones to Woolley, July 15, 1948.

Ibid., Campbell to G.F. Seel (Colonial Office), July 20, 1948.

Ibid., G.F. Seel to Campbell, July 21, 1948.

CO111/813/10, J.M. Campbell to J.A. Venn, personal, December 28, 1949.

Ibid., J.E. Markham [Colonial Office] to Woolley, February 18, 1950.

Ibid., Woolley to J.E. Markham, April 3, 1950.

CO114/237, 'Speech by His Excellency the Governor (Sir Gordon James Lethem), 3 July 1945'.

CO318/421/3, Northcote to J.H. Thomas, no. 66, March 5, 1936, encl.: 'Report on the Sugar Industry of British Guiana' by J. Sydney Dash (February 24, 1936).

CO946/1, Evidence of Sanichari, January 10, 1949.

Ibid., Evidence of Cheddi Jagan, January 14, 1949.

Ibid., Evidence of Lionel Luckhoo, January 17, 1949.

Ibid., Evidence of Baichanie, January 19, 1949.

CO946/3, Jock Campbell to Dr J.A. Venn, April 1, 1949.

Ibid., W.M. Bissell to B.G. Smallman, May 21, 1949; June 8, 1949.

CO950/649, Memorandum of the Sugar Producers' Association (SPA), [1939].

CO950/675, Memorandum of the Manpower Citizens' Association (MPCA), [1939].

CO1031/118, H.L. Steele letter from Georgetown and Campbell's covering note (September 18, 1953).

CO1031/121, Henry Seaford to Jock Campbell, September 8, 1953.

Ibid., Sir Stephen Luke to the Colonial Office, September 12, 1953; Gov. Savage to the Colonial Office, September 13, 1953.

Ibid., CO minute [E.F. for P. Rogers], September 15, 1953.

Ibid., CO minute, [James W. Vernon], September 21, 1953.

Ibid., Ralph Grey to A.M. Mackintosh (Colonial Office), secret, September 2, 1960.

CO1031/3714, 'Intelligence Report for the Month of October 1961', secret and personal.

Ibid., 'Intelligence Report for the Month of November 1961 [A.J.E. Longden]', secret and personal.

Ibid., Grey to Sandys, secret and personal, December 8, 1962.

CO1031/3907, W.F. Dawson (Colonial Office) to R.E. Parsons (American Dept., Foreign Office), confidential, September 7, 1960.

Ibid., W.M. Revell (Colonial Office) to R.E. Parsons (Foreign Office), confidential, September 13, 1960.

Ibid., Copy of a translation of interview of Dr Cheddi Jagan with *Revolucion* [Havana], September 1960.

Ibid., Brief [by Foreign Office] for Secretary of State's talks with Mr Hester (American Embassy, London), on September 18, 1960, confidential.

Ibid., A.M. MacKintosh (Colonial Office) to Ralph Grey, secret and personal, October 28, 1960.

Ibid., W.F. Dawson (Colonial Office) to M. Johnson (Foreign Office), confidential, November 14, 1960.

Ibid., British Embassy (Washington) to Gov Grey, November 29, 1960.

Ibid., J.D. Hennings (Colonial Attache, British Embassy ,Washington) to A.M. Mackintosh (Colonial Office), secret, January 24, 1961.

Ibid., Extract from copy of a letter from Ralph Grey to Colonial Attache, Washington, [Hennings], dated February 16, 1961, recording discussion with Mr Foster of US State Department.

Ibid., Extract from a letter, dated February 28, 1961, from Mr Thomas (Foreign Office) to Mr MacKintosh (Colonial Office), secret and personal.

Ibid., T.B. Williamson (Colonial Office) to F.C. Mason (Foreign Office), secret and guard, April 2, 1961.

CO1031/4178, J.H. Hennings to Ralph Grey, secret and personal, November 19, 1961, encl.

CO1031/4402, President Kennedy to Prime Minister Macmillan, top secret, September 10, 1963.

Ibid., Macmillan to Kennedy, top secret, September 27, 1963.

CO1031/4495, Note of a Meeting held in the Commonwealth Relations Office, October 23, 1963.

Ibid., Grey to David Rose (O.A.G., British Guiana), secret and personal, October 29, 1963.

CO1031/4567, R.W. Piper (Colonial Office) to R.E. Luyt, secret and personal, July 23, 1964, (A brief note of a talk at the Colonial Office between George Bishop and Edgar Readwin [Booker] and Piper and Ian Wallace).

Ibid., Note of a Meeting in Mr Nigel Fisher's Room [Colonial Office], on July 27, 1964, between Antony Tasker [Booker] and Fisher, Sir Hilton Poynton, Ian Wallace and R.W. Piper.

CO1031/4568, R.E. Luyt to Colonial Office, February 25, 1965; March 21, 1965.

CO1031/4758, 'Intelligence Report for the Period, 17 March-22 June 1964'.

CO1031/4931, Jagan to Grey, June 12, 1963.

PREM11/3666, Record of a Meeting in the State Department, April 6, 1961.

Ibid., Reginald Maudling to the Prime Minister, January 10, 1962.

Ibid., Rusk to Home, February 19, 1962.

Ibid., Maudling to Macmillan [PM(62)15], secret, March 2, 1962.

Ibid., Macmillan to Sir N. Brook, top secret, May 2, 1962.

E United States Government Foreign Relations Files on British Guiana, 1961–63 [reproduced in *Stabroek News* (Georgetown), December 1996–January 1997, in a series captioned 'Window on the Sixties'].

USG. 'Prospects for British Guiana', Special National Intelligence Estimate, March 21, 1961.

USG. Message from Foreign Secretary Home to Secretary of State Rusk, London, August 18, 1961.

USG. Telegram from the Dept. of State to the Embassy, UK, August 26, 1961.

USG. Memorandum from the President's Special Assistant (Schlesinger) to the Deputy Under-Secretary of State for Political Affairs (Johnson), September 7, 1961.

USG. Information Airgram from the Dept. of State, 'US Programme for British Guiana', October 4, 1961.

USG. Memorandum of Conversation, 'Call of Premier Jagan of British Guiana on the President', October 25, 1961.

USG. Telegram from the Dept. of State to the Embassy, UK, February 19, 1962.

USG. Memorandum from the President's Special Assistant (Schlesinger) to the Ambassador to the UK (Bruce), March 1, 1962.

USG. Memorandum from the President's Special Assistant (Schlesinger) to President Kennedy, Washington, March 1962.

USG. Telegram from the Dept. of State to the Embassy, UK, June 7, 1962, (encl., Letter from Macmillan to Kennedy, dated May 30, 1962).

USG. Memorandum from the President's Special Assistant (Schlesinger) to President Kennedy, June 21, 1962.

USG. Memorandum from Secretary of State (Rusk) to President Kennedy, July 12, 1962.

USG. Record of Kennedy's discussion with Ormsby-Gore (UK Ambassador, Washington), July 21, 1962.

USG. Consulate General, Georgetown [Melby] to the Dept. of State, March 14 ,1963.

USG. Letter from Premier Jagan to President Kennedy, April 16, 1963.

USG. Memorandum on White House Meeting on British Guiana, June 21,1963.

USG. Telegram from Dept. of State to the Embassy, UK, June 21, 1963.

USG. Meeting of Kennedy and Macmillan, Birch Grove, England, June 30, 1963.

USG. Telegram from the Consulate General (Georgetown) to the Dept. of State, September 5, 1963.

USG. Telegram from the Dept. of State to the Consulate General (Georgetown), September 7, 1963.

F   Reports (in chronological order) [Public Record Office; University of the West Indies Library (St. Augustine, Trinidad)].

Report of the West India Royal Commission (H.W. Norman, chairman). London: Her Majesty's Stationery Office, 1897.

Report of the West Indian Sugar Commission (Lord Olivier, chairman). London: His Majesty's Stationery Office, 1930.

Ibid., Vol. II, Evidence, etc., Relating to British Guiana.

'Report by County Inspector, J. Nicole, on the Labour Unrest on the Sugar Estates on the West Coast Demerara, during September 1934', (mimeo.), [CO111/726/60036 (1935)].

'Report of the Commission of Inquiry into the 1935 Disturbances'. Legislative Council Paper, no. 15 of 1936, [CO111/732/60036 (1936)]

'Report of the Leonora Enquiry Commission', (John Verity, chairman). Legislative Council Paper, no. 10 of 1939 [CO114/230].

The Royal Commission in British Guiana, 1939. Georgetown: The Daily Chronicle Ltd, 1939.

'Report of the British Guiana Franchise Commission, 1941'. Legislative Council Paper, no. 10 of 1944.

'Report by Dr F.C. Benham, Economic Adviser to the Comptroller for Development and Welfare, on the Economic Position of the Sugar Industry'. Legislative Council Paper no. 11 of 1945.

Report of the West India Royal Commission, 1938-9 (Lord Moyne, chairman). Cmd. 6607. London: His Majesty's Stationery Office, 1945.

'Report of the Enmore Enquiry Commission'. Legislative Council Paper, no. 10 of 1948.

Report of a Commission of Inquiry into the Sugar Industry of British Guiana (J.A. Venn, chairman). Col. no. 249. London: His Majesty's Stationery Office, 1949.

British Guiana, Report of the Constitutional Commission, 1950-1 (Sir E.J. Waddington, chairman). Col. no. 280. London: His Majesty's Stationery Office, 1951.

Frank A. Brown, 'Report on Land Settlement Problems in British Guiana with Particular Reference to the Coastal Belt', (mimeo.), dated December 24, 1953.

British Guiana, Suspension of the Constitution. Cmd. 8980. London: Her Majesty's Stationery Office, 1953.

Report of the British Guiana Constitutional Commission, 1954 (Sir James Robertson, chairman). Cmd. 9274. London: Her Majesty's Stationery Office, 1954.

Report on Social Security in British Guiana by J. Henry Richardson. Georgetown: Government of British Guiana, 1954.

Report on Local Government in British Guiana by A.H. Marshall. Georgetown: self-published, 1955.

Report to the Government of British Guiana on Employment, Unemployment and *Underemployment in the Colony in 1956* [compiled by Edward McGale]. Geneva: ILO, 1957.

Report of a Commission of Inquiry into the Causes of a Disturbance which Occurred at *Skeldon on 13 February 1957...* (Kenneth S. Stoby, chairman). Georgetown: Government of British Guiana, 1957.

Report of the British Guiana Constitutional Conference held in London in March 1960. Cmd. 998, (Rt. Hon. Iain Macleod, chairman). London: Her Majesty's Stationery Office, 1960.

Report of a Commission of Inquiry into Disturbances in British Guiana in February 1962. Col. no. 354, (Sir Henry Wynn Parry, chairman). London: Her Majesty's Stationery Office, 1962.

British Guiana Conference, 1962. Cmd. 1870, (Rt. Hon. Duncan Sandys, chairman). London: Her Majesty's Stationery Office, 1962.

British Guiana Conference, 1963. Cmd. 2203, [Prepared by Duncan Sandys]. London: Her Majesty's Stationery Office, November 1963.

'Memorandum by the Government of British Guiana on the Decision by the Secretary of State for the Colonies on the Independence of British Guiana, November 1963'. Sessional Paper, no. 3/1963.

British Guiana, Report by the Commonwealth Team of Observers on the Elections in *December 1964.* Col. no. 359, (Tek Chand, chairman). London: Her Majesty's Stationery Office, 1965.

Report to the Government of British Guiana on Planning Agricultural Development by Rene Dumont. Rome: Food and Agriculture Organisation, 1963.

'Report of a Commission of Inquiry into the Sugar Industry in Guyana' (G.L.B. Persaud, chairman), (mimeo.), September 1968.

G Newspapers [British Library Newspaper Library (Colindale)]; National Archives, [Guyana] and Journals

Booker News (1955–66).
The Daily Argosy (1949–51; 1955–58; 1960).
The Daily Chronicle (1948–53; 1956; 1962–64).
Guiana Graphic (1951–52;1956; 1960–64).
Guiana Review (1938–39).
Indian Opinion (1946).
Indo-Caribbean World (Toronto) (miscellaneous).
The Labour Advocate (1944; 1957–58; 1962–64).
Mirror (1963–66).
The New Daily Chronicle (1930–36).
New Nation (1963–64).
New World Fortnightly [journal] (1964–66).
New York Times (1961–62).
The Old Limerick Journal [special issue on the Barringtons], no. 24, (Winter 1988).
PAC Bulletin (1946–49).
Pepperpot (1946–55).
PPP Thunder [Burnham], (1957).
The Sun (1962–65).
Thunder [1954–63].
The Times (London) (1962–63).
The Tribune (1930-4).
The West India Committee Circular (1951–58); *Chronicle of the West India Committee* [name changed] (1959–64).

H Interviews [on audio tape]

Johnny Appadoo, (retired labourer), Albion, Berbice, September 16, 1992.
Sir George and Una Bishop, (former chairman, Booker), Beaconsfield, Buckinghamshire, February 27, 1997.
Sir Michael Caine, (former chairman, Booker), London, July 19, 1995; December 10, 1996.
John Bart, (administrative manager) and four factory and office workers [Frederick Beera, Harry Dookhie, H.R. Sirjoo, B. Sookhoo], Blairmont Estate, September 17, 1992.
Colin Campbell, (former senior executive, Booker), Potter's Bar, Hertfordshire, July 20, 1995; November 17, 1998.
Jock Campbell [Lord Campbell of Eskan], Nettlebed, Oxfordshire, May 9, 1990, Tape 1; July 23, 1992, Tapes 2-4; July 24, 1992, Tapes 5-7; February 17, 1994, Tapes 8-9; February 18, 1994, Tapes 10-12.
Jock Campbell and Dr Fenton Ramsahoye, Nettlebed, Oxfordshire, December 22, 1994.
Komal Chand, (trade unionist, GAWU), Georgetown, September 11, 1992.
Premchand Das, (trade unionist, GAWU), Georgetown, September 9, 1992.
Joe Dhanna, (former factory worker), Palmyra, Berbice, September 23, 1992.
Habib, (former trade unionist, MPCA), Albion, Berbice, September 18, 1992.

Beth Hall, (Jock Campbell's housekeeper, Nettlebed), Ewelme, Oxfordshire, June 8, 1996.

Antony Haynes, (former senior executive, Booker), London, November 6, 1996.

Yussuph Ishmael, (former medical assistant, Booker), New Amsterdam, Berbice, September 18, 1992.

Dr Cheddi Jagan (1918–97), London, August 8, 1991; Coventry, May 10, 1992; Georgetown, September 8, 1992.

Jainarine, (retired tractor operator), Rose Hall Estate, September 18, 1992.

Patricia Jamieson, (senior executive, Tate and Lyle), London, August 1, 1991.

Kanhai, (retired labourer), Rose Hall Estate, September 18, 1992.

Eusi Kwayana (formerly Sydney King), (politician and writer), Georgetown, September 22, 1992.

Dr Ian McDonald, (former senior executive, Booker), Georgetown, September 9, 1992; September 11, 1992; September 22, 1992; September 11, 1996.

Barry Newton, (former senior executive, Booker), London, May 17, 1995.

Sir Peter Parker, (former senior executive, Booker), [talks to Ray Gosling], 'Charismatics', BBC Radio 4, May 22, 1995.

D.R. Persaud, (former trade unionist, MPCA), New Amsterdam, Berbice, September 15, 1992.

Yesu Persaud, (business executive, born on a plantation), Georgetown, September 1, 1992.

J.B. Raghurai,(administrative manager), Rose Hall Estate, Berbice, September 14, 1992.

Donald Ramotar, (trade unionist, GAWU), Georgetown, September 11, 1992.

Dr Fenton Ramsahoye, (former politician [Attorney General of British Guiana, 1961–64]), London, July 25, 1992; Georgetown, August 8, 1997.

Lee Samuel, MBE, (former secretary, British Guiana Government Office, London), London, June 12, 1997.

Lloyd Searwar, (former government information officer), Georgetown, August 24, 2000.

Edwin Seenauth, (labourer), Palmyra, September 16, 1992.

Jainarine Singh, (former trade unionist [GIWU] and politician), Georgetown, September 10, 1992.

Joe Solomon (former West Indies Test cricketer and sports organiser on the sugar estates), LBI, August 27, 1997.

Deonanan Sukra (Hassa), (former labourer), Palmyra, Berbice, September 20, 1992.

Mrs Tate, (retired labourer), Rose Hall Estate, September 18, 1992.

II   SECONDARY SOURCES

A   Books and pamphlets

Adamson, Alan H. *Sugar without Slaves: The Political Economy of British Guiana, 1838–1904*. New Haven: Yale University Press, 1972.

Barnes, A.C. *The Sugar Cane*. Aylesbury, Bucks: Leonard Hill Books, 1974.

Barnet, Richard J. *Intervention and Revolution: The United States in the Third World*. New York: World Publishing, 1968.

Birbalsingh, Frank and Clem Seecharan. *Indo-West Indian Cricket*. London: Hansib, 1988.

Bolland, O. Nigel. *On the March: Labour Rebellion in the British Caribbean, 1934–39*. Kingston: Ian Randle Publishers, 1995.

Burnham, Jessie. *Beware my Brother Forbes*. Georgetown: self-published, 1964.

Burrowes, Reynold. *The Wild Coast: An Account of Politics in Guyana*. Cambridge, Mass: Schenkman Publishing Co, 1984.

Chase, Ashton. *133 Days Towards Freedom in Guiana*. Georgetown: self-published, n.d. [1954].

_____ . *A History of Trade Unionism in Guyana, 1900 to 1964*. Ruimveldt, Guyana: New Guyana Co, n.d.[1964].

_____ . *Guyana: A Nation in Transit — Burnham's Role*. Georgetown: self-published, 1994.

Dabydeen, David. *Slave Song*. Mundelstrup, Denmark: Dangaroo Press, 1984.

David, Wilfred L. *The Economic Development of Guyana, 1953–1964*. Oxford: Clarendon Press, 1969.

Despres, Leo A. *Cultural Pluralism and Nationalist Politics in British Guiana*. Chicago: Rand McNally and Co, 1967.

Dyett, Harry. *Enigma of Development: Guyana 1900 to 1989 — An Unrealised Potential*. Georgetown: Institute of Development Studies and Faculty of Social Sciences, University of Guyana, 1994.

Edun, Ayube. *London's Heart-Probe and Britain's Destiny*. London: Arthur H. Stockwell, 1935.

Fisher, Nigel, *Iain Macleod*. London: Andre Deutsch, 1973.

Fraser, Cary. *Ambivalent Anti-Colonialism: The United States and the Genesis of West Indian Independence, 1960–64*. Westport, Ct: Greenwood Press, 1994.

Galloway, J.H. *The Sugar Cane: An Historical Geography from its Origins to 1914*. Cambridge: Cambridge University Press, 1989.

Glasgow, Roy A. *Guyana: Race and Politics among Africans and East Indians*. The Hague: Matinus Nijhoff, 1970.

Gopaul, Nanda K. *Resistance and Change: The Struggles of the Guyanese Workers (1964 to 1994), with Emphasis on the Sugar Industry*. New York: Inside News Publications, 1997.

Government Information Services. *Building Confidence: The Story of British Guiana in 1954*. Georgetown: GIS, 1954.

Herbert, Ivor. *The Way to the Top*. London: Robert Maxwell, 1969.

Hogg, Ethel M. *Quintin Hogg*. London: Constable, 1904.

Hubbard, H.J.M. *Race and Guyana: The Anatomy of a Colonial Enterprise*. Georgetown: The Daily Chronicle, 1969.

Jayawardena, Chandra. *Conflict and Solidarity in a Guianese Plantation*. London: The Athlone Press, 1962.

Joseph, Cedric L. *Anglo-American Diplomacy and the Re-opening of the Guyana-Venezuela Border Controversy, 1961-1966*. Georgetown: Free Press, 1998.

Kanhai, Rohan. *Blasting for Runs*. London: Souvenir Press, 1966.

Knowles, William H. *Trade Union Development and Industrial Relations in the British West Indies*. Berkeley: University of California Press, 1959.

Lamb, Richard. *The Macmillan Years, 1957-1963: The Emerging Truth*. London: John Murray, 1995.

Lewis, W.Arthur. *Labour in the West Indies: The Birth of a Workers' Movement* [Fabian Society, Research Series, no. 44]. London: Victor Gollancz, 1939.

Lutchman, Harold A. *From Colonialism to Co-operative Republic: Aspects of Political Development in Guyana*. Rio Piedras, Puerto Rico: Institute of Caribbean Studies, University of Puerto Rico, 1974.

Macmillan, W.M. *Warning from the West Indies: A Tract for the Empire*. Harmondsworth: Penguin, 1938 [1936].

Mandle, Jay R. *The Plantation Economy: Population and Economic Change in Guyana, 1838-1960*. Philadelphia: Temple University Press, 1973.

Mangru, Basdeo. *A History of East Indian Resistance on the Guyana Sugar Estates, 1869-1948*. Lewiston, NY: The Edwin Mellen Press, 1996.

McDonald, Ian. *Sugar in British Guiana: Challenge and Change*. Georgetown: Booker, n.d. [1966].

McTurk, Diane. *The Oldest Industry: Aspects of Sugar in Guyana*. Georgetown: SPA, 1966.

Nath, Dwarka. *A History of Indians in Guyana*. London: self-published, 1970 [1950].

Newman, Peter. *British Guiana: Problems of Cohesion in an Immigrant Society*. London: Oxford University Press, 1964.

Parker, Peter. *For Starters: The Business of Life*. London: Jonathan Cape, 1989.

Pierce, Paulette, *Noncapitalist Development: The Struggle to Nationalize the Guyanese Sugar Industry*. Totowa, NJ: Rowman & Allanheld, 1984.

Premdas, Ralph R. *Ethnic Conflict and Development: The Case of Guyana*. Aldershot: Avebury, 1995.

Reno, Philip. *The Ordeal of British Guiana*. New York: Monthly Review Press, 1964.

Reubens, E.P., and B.G. Reubens. *Labour Displacement in a Labour-Surplus Economy*. Mona, Jamaica: Institute of Social and Economic Research, 1962.

Richardson, Beryl, *Sugar in Guyana*. London: Ginn and Co, Ltd, 1969.

Rohlehr, Gordon. *Kanhai/Gibbs: Tribute to Two Great West Indians*. Port-of-Spain: self-published, 1974.

Schlesinger, Arthur, Jr. *A Thousand Days: John F. Kennedy in the White House*. London: Andre Deutsch, 1965.

Sallahuddin. *Guyana: The Struggle for Liberation, 1945-1992*. Georgetown: self-published, 1994.

Seecharan, Clem. *'Tiger in the Stars': The Anatomy of Indian Achievement in British Guiana, 1919-29*. London: Macmillan, 1997.

_____ .*Bechu: 'Bound Coolie' Radical in British Guiana, 1894-1901*. Mona, Jamaica: University of the West Indies Press, 1999.

____ . *Muscular Learning: Cricket and Education in the Making of the British West Indies, the Late 19th Century*. (Forthcoming).

Shahabuddeen, M. *From Plantocracy to Nationalisation: A Profile of Sugar in Guyana*. Georgetown: University of Guyana, 1983.

Simms, Peter, *Trouble in Guyana*. London: George Allen and Unwin Ltd, 1966.

Singh, Chaitram. *Guyana: Politics in a Plantation Society.* New York: Praeger, 1988.

Singh, Jai Narine. *Guyana: Democracy Betrayed — A Political History, 1948-1993.* Kingston: Kingston Publishers Ltd, 1996.

Smith, Raymond T. *British Guiana.* London: Oxford University Press, 1962.

Southgate, John. *The Commonwealth Sugar Agreement, 1951-1974.* London: C. Czarnikow, Ltd, 1984.

Spinner, Thomas J. *A Political and Social History of Guyana, 1945-1983.* Boulder, Colorado: Westview Press, 1983.

St. Pierre, Maurice. *Anatomy of Resistance: Anti-Colonialism in Guyana, 1823–1966.* London: Macmillan, 1999.

Swan, Michael. *British Guiana: The Land of Six Peoples.* London: Her Majesty's Stationery Office, 1957.

Thomas, Clive Y. *Plantations, Peasants and State: A Study of the Mode of Sugar Production in Guyana.* Los Angeles: Centre for Afro-American Studies, UCLA, 1984.

Vatuk, Ved Prakash. *British Guiana.* New York: Monthly Review Press, 1963.

Walcott, Clyde. *Island Cricketers.* London: Hodder and Stoughton, 1958.

_____ . *Sixty Years on the Back Foot: The Cricketing Life of Sir Clyde Walcott.* London: Orion, 2000.

Williams, Denis. *Giglioli in Guyana, 1922-1972.* Georgetown: National History and Arts Council, n.d.

B Articles, unpublished papers and theses

Antigen [pseud.]. 'Sugar Estates' Drama Festival'. *New World Fortnightly*, no. 3 (November 30, 1964).

Auty, R.M. 'The Structure, Spatial Strategy and Nationalization: Booker McConnell Disinvestment in Guyana', (mimeo.), May 28, 1979.

Bacs, George. 'The Harvesting of Sugar Cane'. *Pepperpot* 3, no. 2 (February 1949).

Drakes, Francis M. [Kimani Nehusi]. 'The Development of Political Organisation and Political Consciousness in Guyana: The *Conscientizacao* of the Middle Class and Masses, 1870- 1964'. PhD thesis, University of London, 1989.

Evans, Harry. 'Field Research in British Guiana: Past, Present and Future'. In *Booker Sugar* (Supplement to the Accounts of Booker Bros, McConnell and Co, Ltd, 1954).

Farley, Rawle. 'Kaldor's Budget: Reason and Unreason in a Developing Area — Reflections on the 1962 Budget in British Guiana'. *Inter-American Economic Affairs* XVI, Pt. 2 (1962).

Fraser, Cary. 'The "New Frontier" of Empire in the Caribbean: The Transfer of Power in British Guiana, 1961-1964'. *The International History Review* XXII, no. 3 (September 2000).

Giglioli, George. 'Malaria in British Guiana, Part I: The Anopheline Mosquitoes of the Colony'. *The Agricultural Journal of British Guiana* IX, no. 2 (June 1938).

_____. 'Malaria in British Guiana, Part II: Which of the Local Anopheline Species is Responsible for the Transmission of the Malaria?'. *The Agricultural Journal of British Guiana* IX, no. 3 (September 1938).

_____. 'Malaria in British Guiana, Part III: Breeding Habits of *A. darlingi*. Natural Factors which Limit the Distribution of this Species and of Malaria'. *The Agricultural Journal of British Guiana* IX, no. 4 (December 1938).

_____. 'Malaria in British Guiana, Part IV: The Distribution of Malaria on the Coastlands. Genesis of Malarial Epidemics'. *The Agricultural Journal of British Guiana* X, no. 1 (March 1939).

_____. 'Malaria and Agriculture in British Guiana'. *Timehri*, no. 27 (fourth series), (1946).

_____ . 'Intermediate and Long-Term Economic Effects Accruing from the Control of Mosquito-Transmitted Disease in British Guiana'. *Timehri*, no. 28 (fourth series), (1948).

_____. 'The Population and Housing Problems on the Sugar Estates of British Guiana'. Legislative Council Paper, no. 11 of 1948.

_____. 'D.D.T. Defeats Malaria in British Guiana'. *The Crown Colonist* 19, no. 211 (1949).

_____. 'Eradication of *Anopheles Darlingi* from the Inhabited Areas of British Guiana by D.D.T. Residual Spraying'. *Journal of the National Malaria Society* 10, no. 2 (June 1951).

_____. 'Reorganisation of Medical Services on the Sugar Estates', (mimeo.), July 19, 1951.

_____. 'Further Developments in the Population and Housing Problems on the Sugar Estates of British Guiana, 1947-1951', (mimeo.), 1952.

_____. 'The Influence of Geological Formation and Soil Characteristics on the Distribution of Malaria and its Mosquito Carrier in British Guiana'. *Timehri*, no. 30 (fourth series), (1951).

_____. 'Maintenance of Malaria Eradication under Continental Conditions, on the Coastlands of British Guiana. Integration of Natural Visible or Invisible Barriers by Limited "Strategic" Use of DDT to Close Possible Reinvasion Routes', (mimeo.), n.d., [1953].

_____. 'Labour Health'. In *Booker Sugar* (Supplement to the Accounts of Booker Bros., McConnell and Co, Ltd, 1954).

_____. 'Medical Services on the Sugar Estates of British Guiana'. *Timehri*, no. 35 (fifth series), (1956).

Giglioli, George and L.J. Charles. 'Reappearance of *Anopheles Darlingi* Root in a Controlled Area of British Guiana's Coastlands'. *American Journal of Tropical Medicine and Hygiene* 3, no. 5 (September 1954).

Halperin, Ernst. 'Racism and Communism in British Guiana'. *Journal of Inter-American Studies* VII, no. 1 (January 1965).

Hares, Leonard. 'Field Routine (A non-technical description of sugar-cane growing in British Guiana)'. In *Booker Sugar* (Supplement to the Accounts of Booker Bros, McConnell and Co, Ltd, 1954).

Hinden, Rita. 'The Case of British Guiana'. *Encounter* II, no. 1 (January 1954).

Hintzen, Percy C. and Ralph R. Premdas. 'Race, Ideology and Power in Guyana'. *The Journal of Commonwealth and Comparative Politics* XXI, no. 2 (July 1983).

Inglis, J.G.H. 'Some Comments on Sugar Cultivation in British Guiana'. *Pepperpot* 1, no. 5 (August 1947).

Jagan, Janet. 'Sugar Estate Housing'. *Indian Opinion*, August 31, 1946.
_____. 'How Left is the New Left?'. *New World Fortnightly*, no. 21 (August 20, 1965).
_____. '30 Years since the P.A.C'. *Thunder*, (January-March, 1977).
Kennard, Gavin. 'Why Cane Farming?'. *New World Fortnightly*, no. 13 (April 30, 1965).
Lewis, Gordon K. '[Review of Jagan's] *The West On Trial: My Fight for Guyana's Freedom*'. *Caribbean Studies* 7, no. 4 (1968).
Litvak, Isaiah A. and Christopher J. Maule. 'Foreign Corporate Social Responsibility in Less Developed Economies'. *Journal of World Trade Law* 9, no. 2 (1975).
Lutchman, Harold A. 'Historical Perspective of Race and the Public Service in Guyana'. *History Gazette*, no. 54 (March 1993).
Mars, Perry. 'The Significance of the Disturbances, 1962-1964'. *History Gazette*, no. 70 (July 1994).
Mcdonald, Ian. 'Arthur Goodland — Obituary'. *Kyk-over-al*, no. 35 (October 1986).
_____. 'Jock Campbell'(Obituary), *Stabroek News*, January 1, 1995.
Meisler, Stanley. 'Meddling in Latin America'. *The Nation*, February 10, 1964.
Menezes, M. Noel. 'The Madeiran Portuguese Woman in Guyanese Society, 1830-1930'. In *The Colonial Caribbean in Transition: Essays on Postemancipation Social and Cultural History*, edited by Bridget Brereton and Kevin A. Yelvington. Kingston: UWI Press, 1999.
Naipaul, V.S. 'A Handful of Dust: Return to Guiana'. *The New York Review of Books*, April 10, 1991.
The Nation. 'Great Injustice done to Jagan — [Arthur] Schlesinger', editorial, June 4, 1990.
New World Fortnightly. 'Portraits of the Leaders [Jagan, Burnham, D'Aguiar]', no. 3 (November 30, 1964).
_____. 'Reply to Mrs. Jagan', no. 21 (August 20, 1965).
Parker, Peter. 'Lord Campbell of Eskan' (Obituary), *The Independent*, January 4, 1995.
Pilgrim, Frank. 'Senior Plays: Sugar Estates' Drama Festival'. *New World Fortnightly*, no. 3 (November 30, 1964).
Potter, Lesley M. 'The Paddy Proletariat and the Dependent Peasantry: East Indian Rice Growers in British Guiana, 1895-1920'. *History Gazette*, no. 47 (August 1992).
Rose, James G. 'British Colonial Policy and the Transfer of Power in British Guiana, 1945–64'. PhD thesis, University of London, 1992.
_____. 'The Enmore Incident of 1948'. *History Gazette*, no. 69 (June 1994).
Rose, James and John Williams. 'International Perceptions of the People's Progressive Party by 1953'. *History Gazette*, no. 72 (September 1994).
Scargall, R.B. 'Welfare on the Sugar Estates'. *Pepperpot* 3, no. 3 (April 1949).
Scott, Brian. 'The Organisational Network: A Strategy Perspective for Development'. PhD thesis, Harvard University, 1979.
Seecharan, Clem. 'Sweetening a Bitter Legacy: Jock Campbell', (Obituary). *The Guardian*, December 30, 1994.
Sheridan, Richard. 'The Role of Scots in the Economy and Society of the West Indies'. *Annals of the New York Academy of Sciences* 292, (1977).

Sukdeo, Fred. 'The Economics of State Control of the Sugar Industry in Guyana', n.d. [1976], (mimeo.).

_____ . 'Economics of Increasing Sugar Production in Guyana', (1977), (mimeo).

'Text of the Commonwealth Sugar Agreement, 1951'. In *Booker Sugar* (Supplement to the Accounts of Booker Bros, McConnell and Co, Ltd, 1954), Appendix 8.

'The Real Challenge of Guiana', [Leader]. *The New Statesman and Nation*, October 24, 1953.

'The Story of British Guiana: Putting the Clock Back in the Colonies'. *The New Statesman and Nation*, October 17, 1953.

'Time when Malaria Wreaked Havoc in Guyana'. *Guyana Graphic* (Independence Souvenir), May 1966.

Thomas, Anthony. 'Men in Command: Sir Jock Campbell'. *The Scotsman*, December 7, 1965.

Thomas, Clive. 'Sugar Economics in a Colonial Situation: A Study of the Guyana Sugar Industry', n.d. [1970], (mimeo.).

_____. 'Sugar and Liberation: An Outline Programme', n.d. [1975], (mimeo.).

Walker-Kilkenny, Roberta. 'The Radicalization of the Women's Movement in British Guiana, 1946-1953'. *Cimarron* 1, no. 3 (1988).

_____ ,'The Leonora Strike of 1939', *History Gazette*, no. 46 (July 1992).

Wallace, Elisabeth. 'British Guiana: Causes of the Present Discontents'. *International Journal* XIX, no. 4 (Autumn 1964).

Williams, J.F. 'An Outline of Sugar Manufacture — Part 2'. *Pepperpot* 1, no. 3 (April 1947).

_____. 'An Outline of Sugar Manufacture — Part 3', *Pepperpot* 1, no. 4 (June 1947).

_____. 'The Development of the Cane Sugar Industry in British Guiana'. *Timehri*, no. 29 (fourth series), (1950).

_____. 'Factory Development'. In *Booker Sugar* (Supplement to the Accounts of Booker Bros, McConnell and Co, Ltd, 1954).

Index